The Reform Spirit in America

in America

A DOCUMENTATION OF THE PATTERN
OF REFORM IN THE AMERICAN REPUBLIC

The
Reform Spirit
in America

A DOCUMENTATION OF THE PATTERN OF
REFORM IN THE AMERICAN REPUBLIC

EDITED WITH INTRODUCTIONS BY
Robert H. Walker

G. P. PUTNAM'S SONS, NEW YORK
CAPRICORN BOOKS, NEW YORK

Library of Congress Cataloging in Publication Data

Main entry under title:

The Reform spirit in America.

Includes index.
1. United States—Social conditions—Sources.
2. Social movements—History—Sources. 3. Social
reformers—United States—Sources. I. Walker,
Robert Harris, 1924-
HN64.R423   1976   309.1′73   75-46558

H N
64
.R423
1976

SBN: 399-11651-6 (CLOTH)

SBN: 399-50364-1 (PAPER)

PRINTED IN THE UNITED STATES OF AMERICA

The words and deeds reflected in this collection dedicate themselves to the continuing work and hope for a better human condition.

The labor of compilation is dedicated to an evolving friend very much in mind as this work was taking shape: to Rachel, a middle child as much an enigma as the process of social change and a gentle reformer in her own lovely way.

Contents

Preface

THIS is not a compilation of the great landmarks in American reform, although many of them are here. It is not a collection of undeservedly overlooked figures and causes, albeit there are some of these too. Nor is it intended—as may sometimes seem the case—as a compendium of facts and artifacts bearing the least likely resemblance to the stereotypes of reform. What this volume most emphatically does *not* pretend is a *coverage* of social and institutional change.

If this is not a comprehensive collection, neither is it a casual gathering. It is something in between. The Introduction attempts to define this book in historical terms. In functional terms it is intended as a framework for organizing and giving a sense of proportion to one's inevitably fractional views of social and institutional change. Beyond its own covers it should be useful whether one is pursuing a topic established in these pages or exploring one barely mentioned. Within its covers it seeks to make a fresh statement about the dominant patterns of reform and to extract from the reform experience the most important consequences for the study of American society as a whole.

The idea for doing this book occurred when I had already been reading and teaching about reform for a number of years. Generalizations that emerge from the interpretive works are not all that complex, I thought. To assemble a group of supportive documents would be the work of but one long hard summer.

Many summers later, having examined pounds of documents, I came to the point of discarding the last of those treasured generalizations gathered from secondary readings. They were simply not supported by the documents. Thus, my old faith cast off, I wandered downcast and lacerated, barefoot on the cinders of chaos. The search for a new and necessary idea of order was surely my own most difficult trial by far; and why not! Reform subsumes such a terrifying lot of the national experience. Almost nothing past is irrelevant. No daily newspaper goes unclipped.

The pattern, once discovered, did not seem as radically revisionary as its search portended, although it does call for important adjustments in some historical categories. It has its own flaws and omissions: it pays relatively little attention, for example, to the kinds of questions asked by sociologists. What marks this pattern is not its astonishing design so much as its fidelity to the nature and circumstances inherent in the documents themselves.

A negative virtue might be found in the refusal to ask: Has reform in America succeeded? If this question could be purged of its amorphousness and wrung of its ambiguities it might still be inappropriate for an effort designed not to measure payoff but to establish patterns. Furthermore, it may be that success in reform, like success in so many other American activities, is wedded to the perpetuation of a process. In one sense, reform succeeds so long as it continues. For just as this nation puts special weight on a "democratic process" or a "process of mass production," so, too, do Americans often seem more concerned with the "process of social change" than with any arbitrary set of results.

ACKNOWLEDGMENTS

MOST of this work was done at the Library of Congress where my debts are mountainous. For help with reference problems I thank Eileen Donahue and Barbara Walsh; with visual materials, Milton Kaplan; with vital logistics Dudley Ball, Herbert Davis, and Edward MacConomy; with copyright questions, Waldo Moore; with typing Viola Bond and Pat Markland. George Washington University helped with a sabbatical; with various grants from the University Research Committee, Arthur E. Burns, Chairman; and with some graduate research assistants among whom Jean Bernard Johnson and Harold Skramstad were truly useful. One paid assistant, Maureen Cole, also did some very good work. At the Smithsonian's Division of Political History, Herbert R. Collins patiently led me to many more telling artifacts than I had space to use.

Toward the end of this project I was priveleged to hold a Fellowship at the Woodrow Wilson International Center for Scholars where an ideal setting had been created by Benjamin Read and his superb staff. I particularly thank Fran Hunter, who oversaw a lot of typing, duplicating, and proofing; Marcella Jones who worked magic to find books that eluded me; and Mildred Pappas who also kindly elicited and produced materials.

One needs to thank one's family not so much for sharing achievement, which is easy, as for abiding frustration, which is not. This labor produced a full crop of barriers and I thank you, Grace, for helping put up with their consequences. A few friends were especially longsuffering during the term of this project: reacting to questions, suggesting sources, and showing an improbable faith. I think particularly of Dan Aaron, Carl Bode, Hennig Cohen, Bill Hutchison, and Bill Ward. It is a pleasure to acknowledge those who generously made available material under their control: R. Buckminster Fuller, the Washington *Post* (through Phil Foisie), James W. Rouse, Budd Schulberg, and Clarence Streit.

Finally, I would like to say in print what I have often said in conversation: namely, that G. P. Putnam's Sons is one publisher with whom it is a pleasure to work. In this project I appreciate the work of Walter Betkowski and his staff, including a sharp-eyed copyeditor named Faith Hanson.

Introduction

AMERICANS have steadily assumed that their society should adjust itself toward a system wherein all citizens share more fully in the good things in life. The reformer begins by discovering this sentiment. He learns to draw on a constant source of energy created by the disjunction between two perceptions: one of society as it ought to be, one as it is. He uses a variety of tools with which to tap and direct this energy—including his own insistent visions of the realizable ideal. He thus becomes a deliberate sculptor of the future and—in a culture extraordinarily marked by change—he becomes disproportionately important.

To represent this important subject accurately within a limited space created a problem of definition and control. This problem began with the word "reform," which tends to lose meaning when separated from a specific subject. Nevertheless, all of its major meanings have been accepted in defining the responsible coverage for this collection with but one conscious exception: namely, the use of reform to indicate advocacy of change that would lead back toward goals or conditions that had existed earlier in the history of the same society. To include this strain of reform would be to cage the cat with the canary; for, next to indifference, the reformer's principal adversary is the advocate of the "good old days." Thus, in order to avoid chronicling "anti-reform" simultaneously with reform, this collection has excluded reformers who would improve public education by bringing back the neighborhood school; those who would minister to the working man by abolishing unions or cure the evils of industrialism by placing every family on a forty-acre farm.

Limiting reform only by ruling out its antithesis leaves a large problem of organization for which the most tempting model could have been constructed by working outward from the monographs and special studies provided by historians. Such a model can be summarized, over-simply, as follows:

> The first reform era took shape in the 1820s and lasted until the attack on Fort Sumter. It arose from no particular crisis and was motivated by a perfectionism inherited from Enlightenment optimism but increasingly colored by such religious influences as millennialism, zionism, and spiritualism. Moral criteria underlay all activities and arguments. The staple subjects of humanitarian reform—labor, education, care for the handicapped, prison reform, temperance, woman's rights—were introduced at this time along with a variety of communitarian experiments. Many leaders, as well as participants, had little formal education and came from working-class backgrounds. Reform activity was notably intense along the Hudson Valley and the Erie Canal; only slightly less so in Southern New England, the new Northwest Territory, and the Middle States—in that order. As this period wore on, the focus of reform narrowed until it centered on the slavery question to the virtual exclusion of other concerns. Although many reform landmarks had been passed in social and humanitarian causes before the Civil War, there was very little permanent legacy from this wave of activity beyond the Emancipation Proclamation.
>
> Until a few years ago, most followers of reform found very little to chronicle in the late nineteenth century and took up their story again with the reveille of a Rough Rider's Progressive bugle. In searching out the roots of Progressivism, however, the scholar has discovered significant reform activity at least by the 1880s: activity which grows constantly, climaxes in the Wilson years, and ends only with American entry into World War I. Although humanitarian crusades arose again, the center of this reform era was its response to the problems of urban industrialization and its technology. A constant concern was inequity in the distribution of wealth whose extremes were dramatically visible in the growing cities. Periods of panic and unemployment exacerbated the problem, as did monopoly, the threat of deflation, labor exploitation, and anti-unionism. The locus of this reform era was in the rural South and Midwest, shifting quickly to the industrialized cities.

Participation and leadership still involved the working class but included growing numbers of middle-class leaders. The issues were economic; the drama lay in the questionable willingness and ability of the political system to solve them.

Consensus is strongly in favor of a picture of the 1920s as a holiday for reformers lasting from World War I to the inauguration of Franklin D. Roosevelt, The new reform era of the 1930s was generated by the problems reflected in the stock market crash and the Great Depression. Aside from the atmosphere of crisis, the issues were identical with those of the earlier period and continued in a direction clearly predictable from a study of Populism and Progressivism. Although the problems were international, Americans looked to Washington for solutions. All classes were involved; but the leadership, considering the pattern of American politics since the Civil War, was remarkably patrician and intellectual. Like the Progressive Era this period can be measured mainly in terms of political and economic achievements. Did the reform momentum of the 1930s end with World War II? Most historians seem to think so, although it is also clear that President Truman—supporting the United Nations and civil rights measures—anticipated the reform issues that were to occupy the nation after 1950: minority rights and world peace. Historians are slow to apply their judgments to the recent past and the years since World War II still lack a clear and dominant interpretation, especially in the subjects that touch closest to reform.

Although every statement in this summary contains considerable truth, it should not be surprising that some major truths are hidden. Very little work has been done on reform as a continuum in American society. Thus the generalizations must be drawn from more limited studies which naturally stress the distinctiveness of their subject while slighting the more prevailing characteristics. For example, the consensus view differentiates between reform activity primarily by period. To accept it one must admit to eras of action punctuated by quiescence. One must find important differences between the various eras. The experience of compiling these documents led to the belief that—whereas there remained a good deal of validity in the consensus view—it was more important to show that reform was a generally continuous activity and that its constants were more important than its variables. The only section offering continuous attention to a single issue (II) reveals a virtually unbroken time sequence. In another section where similar topics are contrasted over a large time lapse (III) the echoes are as loud as the distinctive notes. Hence, although changes seen against a time background are important, they do not necessarily lead to the most important generalizations about reform.

A second problem can be inferred from some of the vocabulary used in the foregoing summary. It should have been possible to arrange documents under the such frequently used and presumably distinctive headings as "moral reform," "humanitarian reform," and "social reform." This rubric too broke down under the weight of exposure. Just how and why this "classic" reform vocabulary expands, shifts, and bows toward rhetorical usage until it loses logical meaning is an interesting story that should be told somewhere. At this point one need only say that the historic terminology failed to provide a logic for the classification of documents. Even when the focus is narrowed to reform *motivations*—as for a long time I thought might provide a basic organizational principle— the categorical terms become more useful for distinguishing one argument from another than for distinguishing one reformer from another. In this discovery, however, is a truth that may easily compensate for the dwindling utility of traditional reform vocabulary. Just as *all* major reform movements are importantly moral, social, and humanitarian, so *all* important reformers argue from the existence of a higher law, toward the health of the body politic, and for the expediency of a practical proposal.

Many alternative ways of reorganizing this subject have occurred to its historians. Most of them were unsuited to the present project because they were directed to a single cause, a place, a period, or a limited group. A method that from my point of view erred in the other direction was that of the sociologists. Whereas social and behavioral scientists have produced more statements of general validity about the process of social and institutional change than have historians, their urge has often been to discover laws of social behavior too general for someone interested in keeping the subject firmly on American grounds and in seeing important differences between varying kinds of reform activity. Thus I have ended with an organizational premise that is not totally logical except in its effort to avoid the inconsequential aspects of the subject. It derives more from the subject matter of reform than from any other primary criterion, but it will not stand on any purely logical consistency. The implicit statement contained in the selection and organization of the present volume can be summarized as follows:

In addition to its obvious function of identifying the main philosophical bases for reform, Part I also suggests that the pursuit of reform in America has been closely allied to the main values, institutions, and objectives around which the culture has defined itself. To trace the history of reform is to record aspects of cultural self-definition and development as important and profound as one can imagine. There are many aspects of reform that are both trivial and ephemeral; but the principal storehouse of reform tradition is inseparable from man's basic understanding of himself, his society, and his maker.

The second section, by its disproportionate size, purposely dominates the collection. It proposes that a principal aspect of American experience has been the extension of political and economic democracy. This impulse was imported with the earliest settlers; the colonial environment encouraged it; the Revolution itself was an episode in the continuing insistence on representative democracy for the sake of economic equity. The documents pick up the expression of this impulse in the early Federal days and trace it through the 1970s. American civilization has found much of its meaning in the evolution of its politico-economic institutions to match a changing set of conditions and objectives. How was this accomplished? There is no single answer that carries more central importance than the one outlined in this section.

If Part II identifies the mainstream, Part III illustrates a fact of reform geography that stresses the essential connection between the mainstream and its tributaries. If each recognizable element in the culture does not flow smoothly into the dominant current, then the total system will flood or evaporate. Thus, in addition to adjusting the nation's large, shared institutions, reformers have devoted a separately considerable effort to drawing once-disadvantaged elements into an equitable relationship with the system as a whole. Of the many movements of this type, none is more interesting and important than the two here presented. The departure from chronology in this section allows for a direct comparison of attitudes and techniques over large time intervals and thus suggests at least a recurring constancy if not a clear continuity in the climate of reform. This section also carries the implication that reform methods and conventions deserve that kind of attention that can even be divorced from subject matter.

Much reform activity is inevitably negative. The reform dynamic typically starts with objections to things as they are. But reformers are also visionaries and contribute to social change in ways that are imaginatively positive as well. Thus Part IV, reflecting a relatively small but very interesting aspect of reform, reveals the development of some American dreams which reformers have proposed in the shape of model social organizations toward which their contemporaries were urged to labor.

The purpose of Part V is not to insist that any single aspect of the American reform experience is unique. Yet it has been assumed that the American reform experience, collectively, has its own character. By selecting some aspects that have reappeared with insistent regularity one may assist in the eventual comparison of these putatively American reform traits with those drawn from patterns of social and institutional change in other cultures or in subcultures within the American national experience.

What is the important meaning of American reform? Most concisely and directly this collection answers that it is the pursuit of economic equity through the extension of political democracy; the quest for full citizenship for all groups outside the dominant culture; and the conceptualization of models for a better society—*in that order.* Other reform activities exist; but, if they are not describable in the above terms, they are not of the first magnitude.

It is also important to learn who are the reformers, how they work, whence they derive their philosophical positions. Is there sometimes a form and rhetoric of reform almost independent of its subject? What has been the role of the major institutions—political, judicial, economic, religious, educational—in social change? These and other questions are answered within the limits of the collection. These answers are most valuable as they add dimensionality to the primary shape of the American reform experience.

It was the study of the documentary history of American reform which gave this collection its design. Thus the first criterion for choosing a document rested on its contribution to an accurate collective representation. A second natural concern was for the prestige of the individual documents. It would have been hard to present a convincing record without some of the celebrated landmarks: Stowe and Dana, Garrison and Debs, George and Bellamy. Yet for every "crucial" landmark included, another score must be omitted.

Thus it soon becomes apparent that this compilation must be *representative* rather than *inclusive* ; when one perceives this fact he acquires a certain kind of freedom. Instead of pursuing the impossible goal of complete coverage, one can choose certain documents so as to represent techniques or modes; one can choose others so as to provoke comparison or contrast. Some documents can be deliberately selected from outside the mainstream of reform so as to show the range and penetration of certain causes. Thus, although many individual documents may be unimportant in their own right, they may collectively represent not only the scope and variety of their subject but also its form and proportions.

BIBLIOGRAPHICAL NOTE

ON each of the many aspects of reform there are biographies, bibliographies monographs, and special studies. I have consulted many and learned from most of them. The ones I used actively I have tried to mention in the headnote most nearly relevant to the point in question. Thus, instead of attempting the impossible task of compiling a bibliography of reform (which would in fact become a bibliography of bibliographies) I have tried to submit the most helpful titles at the point of greatest utility.

There is space here to acknowledge a few works of larger scope which cut across aspects of reform and which might prove especially germane to the user of this collection. The best single bibliography is the Library of Congress, *Guide to the Study of the United States* (Washington, Government Printing Office, 1960). The most current collection of bibliographical essays relating to reform subjects is *American Studies: Topics and Sources* (Westport, Conn., Greenwood, 1976). The most extensive collection of biographical information on reformers is the manuscript card file of the late Lisle A. Rose now at the American Studies Program, George Washington University. Of compendia dealing with reform the most important is still William D. P. Bliss, *Encyclopedia of Social Reform* (New York, Funk & Wagnalls, 1897). Biographical characteristics of Bliss's reformers are analyzed in an unpublished dissertation at the University of Pennsylvania (1963) by Henry J. Silverman entitled "American Social Reformers in the Late Nineteenth and Early Twentieth Century [*sic*]."

Of existing document collections I found two exceptionally applicable: Alpheus T. Mason, *Free Government in the Making* (New York, Oxford, 1956); and John R. Commons, *et al.*, eds., *A Documentary History of American Industrial Society* (New York, Russell & Russell, 1958), 10 vols.

In addition to the many works cited in the headnotes, the following handful of interpretive studies have the value of alerting the student of reform to some broad and important characteristics of the subject: Merle Curti, *The Growth of American Thought*, 3rd edition (New York, Harper & Row, 1964); Ralph H. Gabriel, *The Course of American Democratic Thought*, 2nd edition (New York, Ronald, 1956); Thomas H. Greer, *American Social Reform Movements* (New York, Prentice-Hall, 1949); John Bach McMaster, *The Acquisition of Political and Industrial Rights of Man in America* (Cleveland, Imperial Press, 1903); Charles L. Sanford, *The Quest for Paradise* (Urbana, University of Illinois, 1961); Arthur M. Schlesinger, *The American as Reformer* (Cambridge, Mass., Harvard, 1950). Although I am less qualified to recommend books in sociology, I would like to attest to the usefulness to me of Rudolf Heberle, *Social Movements* (New York, Appleton-Century-Crofts, 1951).

Part I

THE ROOTS OF REFORM

THE roots of American reform go deeper than the colonists. One source is religious and draws from the long range of Judeo-Christian materials and attitudes. Religion has meant, among other things, that morality must enter into social judgments. That most influential of all books in America, the Bible, has moved men and women not so much into isolated contemplation as toward an exercise of conscience intended to improve the individual's relationship with his fellow man.

The Puritan Commonwealth furnished an early example of a particularly tight-knit religious community expressive of a sense of collective moral responsibility readily equatable with social responsibility. The community showed no hesitation in placing religious sanctions against socially unacceptable acts. Leaders, expectant of their own salvation, took reassurance from their power to help individuals who seemed less advanced toward the state of grace. Nor did this community shrink from its role as a model community shaped under God's guiding hand to be an exemplar to the watching world. Many of the targets identified by the Puritans—including slavery and maltreatment of Indians—have lived long in the center of reform interest.

Evangelical Christianity would seem at first glance to be anti-reformist in its stress on the salvation of the individual; and it is true that some of the great revivalists have been markedly conservative in their social attitudes. The main social consequence of evangelism, however, has been a sensitizing of the individual conscience to the point where social crusades demonstrably follow along in the wake of religious crusades.

Outside the mainstream of sectarian revivalism have lain a number of religious groups, like the Shakers and the Rappites, for example, who have contributed to social change through their communitarian experiments.

The force of religion has been consistent in the history of reform. Its impact can be observed from the profound consciousness of a moral law to the very particular presence of church and religious groups in the peace movement and the continuing campaign against slavery and on behalf of civil rights.

A second major source is in that collection of ideas and attitudes called the Enlightenment. This philosophy elevated natural law at the expense of moral law, reason and science at the expense of religion. The attitude toward man was antithetical to the fire-and-brimstone threats that emanated from many a pulpit. Man was seen as inherently good and not basically flawed by his original sin. All men would reveal this essential goodness if they could be freed from handicaps, enslavement, and the accumulated institutional errors of the past.

This set of assumptions carries implications for reform that differ from the moral imperatives of a more religious viewpoint. The appeal for change is made more to reason than to conscience; science and secular education are thought more important tools for reform than appeals to the soul; order and balance infuse the reformer's rhetoric more with restraint than with the evangelist's hell and damnation. But the need for change is just as evident and important. This was a philosophy of progress through reason toward a complete understanding of the visible universe, including the laws that govern both individual and collective human behavior.

Since Enlightenment thought included social laws, it had to accept a philosophical commitment to the essential equality of all human beings; for, if human beings were not equal in their important aspects, how could one discover laws to understand and govern their group behavior? The Enlightenment, then, gave the reformer the important weapon of philosophical equality among men. In postulating the basic goodness of man, it gave the reformer a series of targets which represented ways in which essentially good and equal men and women were being prevented from evincing their goodness: targets such as chattel slavery, alcohol which enslaved the senses, ignorance which enslaved the mind. If the handicaps and restraints could be removed, then American society, free from the historic evils of Europe and close to the unspoiled benignity of a new continent, might have an excellent chance to discover the reasoned laws of harmonious social and institutional life.

A third basis for reform is in an attitude that has deep roots in human nature but that is hard to express in a word or two. It is an attitude that puts a premium on "know-how" as opposed to theory. It is an attitude that accepts pragmatic tests more readily than formal philosophical justification. It has much to do with a world view that stresses growth, change, and "process" as the important laws of the universe. It relates to self-help, to technology, to anti-intellectualism. It is an attitude most succinctly expressed in the motto of that great architect of the possible, Napoleon Bonaparte, "Why not?"

When Franklin stumbled on his way home at night, he did not philosophize, he put in streetlights. When he noted his ballooning book bill he formed a library association. When he got tired of changing eyeglasses he invented bifocals. When he found his great belly warm and his back cold he invented a better stove. Much of the history of American reform has little to do with philosophy or religion. It is more reflective of Franklin's direct response to a need. It makes a New Deal out of a Depression without depending on the philosophical justification of a Maynard Keynes.

Although the roots of American reform antedate the settling of America, it is important to see how they were perceived and expressed in the colonial setting. Thus for general as well as for special reasons this collection opens with a bow toward Cotton Mather, Benjamin Franklin, and Thomas Jefferson.

Document I-1: MATHER ON SOCIAL MORALITY

Many spokesmen could have been chosen to represent the general religious wellsprings for social action in America. They would all identify the will of God as the first cause for the acts and thoughts of man. They would argue the existence of a Higher Law, divinely inspired, which acts through the human conscience to lead toward righteousness. Thus they would see religious reform as a first step in social reform: purification of the church as propaedeutic to reform of the assembly. They would become social activists for religious reasons; and, like

Cotton Mather, many of them would think that Americans had a special duty and mission to perfect their society beyond the common mold.

Member of a great Puritan family and often taken as transitional between the strict theocracy of the seventeenth century and the broader views of the eighteenth, Cotton Mather reflects some very special characteristics in the ancestry of reform. With great prescience he saw that reform would have to focus on the legislatures and the courts. His famous *Bonifacius*, more commonly known by its subtitle, "An Essay Upon the Good" (1710), made that point and expressed a set of attitudes which were influential on Benjamin Franklin and his widely read epigrams and social prescriptions. Like many religious reformers, Mather believed in the "chiliad," a millennial triumph of good over evil. Unlike many Puritans, he professed a belief in religious toleration. Like most American reformers he believed in the primacy of schools and a good education.

Theopolis Americana opens with a dedication to Judge Samuel Sewall, who apparently paid for the printing and with whom Mather shared a strong abhorrence of slavery. It identifies New England as a better place than most, morally speaking, but a place that has a "*Thousand* Reasons" for being "Better than *Other Places*. . . ." (p. 14). If New England can avoid Popish idolators and "Drunken Protestants" (p. 36) and practice honesty and equity, it may be the site of God's establishment of "an HOLY CITY in AMERICA; a *City*, the STREET whereof will be *Pure* GOLD" (p. 42). He not only preaches temperance and better treatment of slaves and Indians, but his argument for honesty in the marketplace may easily remind the reader of a turn-of-the-century consumers' league or a contemporary watchdog like Ralph Nader.

SOURCE: Cotton Mather, *Theopolis Americana, An Essay on the Golden STREET of the Holy City: Publishing a TESTIMONY against the CORRUPTIONS of the Market-Place*. Boston, printed by B. Green, sold by Gerrish, 1710, pp. 12, 18-20, 21-23, abridged.

From *THEOPOLIS AMERICANA*

. . . The STREET must have no *Dirty Ways* of *Dishonesty* in it. . . . Let there be none but *Full* and *Fair* Dealings in the Market-Place. Let all the Actions of the Market-Place be carried on with a *Golden* Equity and Honesty regulating of them. . . .

For men to put off *Adulterated* or *Counterfeited* Wares; or, for men to work up their Wares *Deceitfully*; When the Fish is naught [bad]; the Tar has undue mixtures; there is Dirt & Stone instead of Turpentine; there are thick Laye[r]s of Salt instead of other things that should be there; the Cheese is not made as tis affirm'd to be; the Liquor is not for Quantity or Quality such as was agreed for; the Wood is not of the Dimensions that are promised unto the Purchaser; or perhaps, there was a *Trespass* in the place of Cutting it; the Hay does not hold out Weight by abundance; the Lumber has a false Number upon it; or, the *Bundles* are not as Good *Within* as they are *Without*; *Tis an Abomination!*

For men to *Over-reach* others, because they find them *Ignorant*, or scrue grievously upon them, only because they are Poor and Low, and in great *Necessities*; to keep up the *Necessaries* of Humane Life, (I say, the *Necessaries*, which I always distinguish from the *Superfluities*,) at an *Immoderate Price*, merely because other People want them, when we can more easily spare them; *Tis an Abomination!*

For men to *Employ* others, and not *Reward* them according to *Contract*; [A Crime, not at all the less, because the *Minister* is not seldom the *Sufferer* from it!] Or, to with hold from the *Labourer* his *Wages*, till his *Cry* reach up to Heaven; or break their Faith with their *Creditors*, and keep them out of their Dues! *Tis an Abomination!*

To Rob the *Publick Treasury*, by *False Musters*, or any other Articles of Charge falsely given in; or, to Abett the Robbers, by any Assistence or Connivance at such things in *Auditing* their Accompts; This also is a thing to be *Repented* of, where any have been Guilty of it. . . .

There is one sort of *Trade* also, about which my way of Addressing you, shall be by Reciting the words of the Excellent BAXTER. They are these: [His *Christian Directory*, Part II.Chap. 14.]

"To go as *Pirates*, and Catch up poor *Negroes*, or People of Another Land, that have never forfeited Life, or Liberty, and to make them *Slaves*, and Sell them, is One of the worst kinds of Thievery in the World; and such Persons are to be taken for the common Enemies of Mankind; and they that buy them, and use them as *Beasts*, for their meer Commodity, and betray, or destroy, or neglect their Souls, are fitter to be called *Incarnate Devils*, than *Christians*, tho' they be no *Christians* whom they so Abuse."

I will go on to say; When we have *Slaves* in our Houses, we are to treat
them with *Humanity*; we are so to treat them that their *Slavery* may really
be their *Happiness*; Yea, in our treating of them, there must be nothing
but what the Law of CHRIST will Justify. Above all, we are to do all we
can to *Christianize* them. I will again give you the Words of my Hon-
oured BAXTER.

"So use them, as to preserve Christs Right and Interest in them. Those
that keep their *Negro's* and Slaves, from Hearing of Gods Word, and
from becoming Christians, because, they shall then lose part of their
Service, do openly profess Rebellion against God, and contempt of
Christ the Redeemer of Souls, and a contempt of the Souls of Men, and
indeed, they declare, that their Worldly profit, is their Treasure and their
God."

Fidelity to the cause of *Righteousness*, obliges me to take Notice of
One thing more.

If there be any *English* People, who are concerned with our *Chris-
tianized Indians*, but then take advantage of their *Ignorance*, of their
Indigence, or their unchristian *Love of the Bottel* [*sic*], to decoy them into
their *Debt*; and then use Indirect and Oppressive Wayes, to Exact an
Unreasonable Satisfaction from them, and *Sell* them for Servants, or
Send them out of their own Country; This Trade, will be a Reproach to
our *Christianity*, and I am sure, it will be *Bitterness in the Latter End*.
Certainly, our *Justices* will concern themselves to Rebuke and Prevent
such Doings, lest the Guilt become so *Publick*, as to provoke the Justice
of Heaven to Revenge it, by *Indian* Depredations.

Document I-2: FRANKLIN ON SOCIAL CHANGE

In many respects Benjamin Franklin is an odd choice as a progenitor of
reform attitudes. He was rather cynical concerning human nature and
motives. Often he seemed to "tolerate" democracy in much the same
way he tolerated organized religion: as something flawed but, on the
whole, good for most people. In one of his most careful expositions of
social philosophy, written while in England as an answer to writers who
were agitating the English poor, Franklin outlined a viewpoint that would
have made him welcome in the home of a late-nineteenth-century laissez-
faire, social Darwinist robber baron.

The poor, he wrote, should be grateful for England's laws on their behalf. Such laws were not made by them but for them. Furthermore, it is doubtful that the poor deserve such measures, for

> giving mankind a dependence on any thing for support, in age or sickness, besides industry and frugality during youth and health, tends to flatter our natural indolence, to encourage idleness and prodigality, and thereby to promote and increase poverty, the very evil it was intended to cure. . . . (V, 123 of work cited below)

The other side of that coin is Franklin's well-known advocacy of self-help, which can of course be a cornerstone for reform as well as its opposite. Whether or not Franklin really made a list of thirteen virtues from Temperance through Humility, then charted his breach of them on a daily basis, as he set forth in his *Autobiography*, he at least firmly believed that self-improvement was possible and should begin with the individual. For society to improve it must not only foster individual discipline but must make available the tools for improvement: schools, books, libraries, and laboratories.

His faith in education and experimentation made him a representative citozen of the Age of Reason. But, as Carl Becker has pointed out, Franklin not only reflected but transcended this age. From the reform viewpoint, the most interesting way in which Franklin departed from the Enlightenment was in his acceptance of change and experiment as ends in themselves. In so doing he gave an early voice to the pragmatic set of values and anticipated a social philosophy that would focus much more on processes than on arbitrary values. In the following letter Franklin not only softens the Revolution by calling it the "Change," but at the same time elevates the value of change. Although he seems to accept the social and political experiments of the newly independent colonies as a sop to popular ferment, it is clear that he approved individually as well. Thus Franklin may be cited as an early prototype of that reform attitude which relied heavily on direct action, filtered through reason, applied experimentally, and based fundamentally on the practical exercise of the human will.

SOURCE: Albert H. Smyth, ed., *Writings of Benjamin Franklin*. New York, Macmillan, 1906, vol. IX, pp. 488–491.

LETTER TO JONATHAN SHIPLEY
Philadelphia, Feb. 24th, 1786

DEAR FRIEND, . . .

You seem desirous of knowing what Progress we make here in improving our Governments. We are, I think, in the right Road of Improvement, for we are making Experiments. I do not oppose all that seem wrong, for the Multitude are more effectually set right by Experience, than kept from going wrong by Reasoning with them. And I think we are daily more and more enlightened; so that I have no doubt of our obtaining in a few Years as much public Felicity, as good Government is capable of affording.

Your NewsPapers are fill'd with fictitious accounts of Anarchy, Confusion, Distresses, and Miseries, we are suppos'd to be involv'd in, as Consequences of the Revolution; and the few remaining Friends of the old Government among us take pains to magnify every little Inconvenience a Change in the Course of Commerce may have occasion'd. To obviate the Complaints they endeavour to excite, was written the enclos'd little Piece, from which you may form a truer Idea of our Situation, than your own public Prints would give you. And I can assure you, that the great Body of our Nation find themselves happy in the Change, and have not the smallest Inclination to return to the Domination of Britain. There could not be a stronger Proof of the general Approbation of the Measures, that promoted the Change, and of the Change itself, than has been given by the Assembly and Council of this State, in the nearly unanimous Choice for their Governor, of one who had been so much concern'd in those Measures; the Assembly being themselves the unbrib'd Choice of the people, and therefore may be truly suppos'd of the same Sentiments. I say nearly unanimous, because, of between 70 and 80 Votes, there were only my own and one other in the negative.

As to my Domestic Circumstances, of which you kindly desire to hear something, they are at present as happy as I could wish them. I am surrounded by my Offspring, a Dutiful and Affectionate Daughter in my House, with Six Grandchildren, the eldest of which you have seen, who is now at a College in the next Street, finishing the learned Part of his Education; the others promising, both for Parts and good Dispositions.

What their Conduct may be, when they grow up and enter the important Scenes of Life, I shall not live to *see*, and I cannot *foresee*. I therefore enjoy among them the present Hour, and leave the future to Providence.

He that raises a large Family does, indeed, while he lives to observe them, *stand*, as Watts says, *a broader Mark for Sorrow*; but then he stands a broader Mark for Pleasure too. When we launch our little Fleet of Barques into the Ocean, bound to different Ports, we hope for each a prosperous Voyage; but contrary Winds, hidden Shoals, Storms, and Enemies come in for a Share in the Disposition of Events; and though these occasion a Mixture of Disappointment, yet, considering the Risque where we can make no Insurance, we should think ourselves happy if some return with Success. My Son's Son, Temple Franklin, whom you have also seen, having had a fine Farm of 600 Acres convey'd to him by his Father when we were at Southampton, has drop'd for the present his Views of acting in the political Line, and applies himself ardently to the Study and Practice of Agriculture. This is much more agreable to me, who esteem it the most useful, the most independent, and therefore the noblest of Employments. His Lands are on navigable water, communicating with the Delaware, and but about 16 Miles from this City. He has associated to himself a very skillful English Farmer lately arrived here, who is to instruct him in the Business, and partakes for a Term of the Profits; so that there is a great apparent Probability of their Success.

You will kindly expect a Word or two concerning myself. My Health and Spirits continue, Thanks to God, as when you saw me. The only complaint I then had, does not grow worse, and is tolerable. I still have Enjoyment in the Company of my Friends; and, being easy in my Circumstances, have many Reasons to like Living. But the Course of Nature must soon put a period to my present Mode of Existence. This I shall submit to with less Regret, as, having seen during a long Life a good deal of this World, I feel a growing Curiosity to be acquainted with some other; and can chearfully, with filial Confidence, resign my Spirit to the conduct of that great and good Parent of Mankind, who created it, and who has so graciously protected and prospered me from my Birth to the present Hour. Wherever I am, I hope always to retain the pleasing remembrance of your Friendship, being with sincere and great Esteem, my dear Friend, yours most affectionately,

B. FRANKLIN.

Document I-3: JEFFERSON ON POLITICAL MORALITY

Much of American reform has been based on the presupposition that human beings are basically good. Freed from handicap and error they will behave honorably and responsibly. They can then be governed best by a body which truly represents the collective will of an educated electorate. In the end, this system will produce the highest degree of social justice. The institutions of the aspiring new nation must therefore reflect and protect those assumptions and the process that springs from them.

No single American better represented that point of view than Thomas Jefferson. His principal responsibility for the Declaration of Independence would make him, of itself, a major pillar of American reform. Hardly a cause has existed that did not, at one time or another, adopt phrases from the Declaration for watchwords or, often, paraphrase the entire document. The Declaration has struck a deep chord among crusaders not only because of its eloquent list of unattended grievances but also because of its appeal to the common plight of all human beings and its statement of basic rights without which human dignity cannot be maintained. Accepting philosophical equality, it then presumes that just contracts can be made, through reason and experience, for the collective governance of society.

The two letters that follow, written late in life, reveal this philosophy as they attack questions of special pertinence to reformers. Early in the national history there was a great tendency to revere the Founding Fathers to a degree that made all change sacrilegious. In his letter to Samuel Kercheval, Jefferson attacks this problem head on. Before he has finished his argument against blind worship of the past he has developed a full theory of social change and the need for reform in each generation. In the letter to Thomas Law he addresses himself to the philosophical basis for social action, showing himself to value and defend man's benign social instincts even after years of sometimes bitter political experience. In explaining exceptions to the rule of apparent human goodness he comes again to the reformer's important stress on education.

To look at Mather, Franklin, and Jefferson side by side is to appreciate
the difficulty of generalizing broadly about social attitudes. Jefferson, at
least as skeptical as Franklin about conventional religion, does not
hesitate to support the idea of moral law as a fundamental concept.
Franklin, allegedly as much a child of the Age of Reason as Jefferson,
evinces considerably more cynicism about human motives but can draw
heavily on a social commentary as religiously centered as that of Mather.
Mather, who should have reflected a consistent Calvinistic sense of
predestination, urges men to do good deeds. Franklin and Jefferson, who
should have reflected a relatively static society built on Newtonian and
Descartean models, not only accept but advocate change. With all their
differences they combine to incorporate the basic values and attitudes
underlying the principal features of American reform.

SOURCE: Andrew A. Lipscomb, ed., *Writings of Thomas Jefferson*. Washington,
D.C., Jefferson Memorial Association, 1903, vol. XIV, pp. 138-144; vol. XV, pp.
40-43, abridged.

LETTER TO THOMAS LAW
Poplar Forest, June 13, 1814
    Dear Sir,—The copy of your Second Thoughts on Instinctive
Impulses, with the letter accompanying it, was received just as I was
setting out on a journey to this place, two or three days distant from
Monticello. I brought it with me and read it with great satisfaction, and
with the more as it contained exactly my own creed on the foundation of
morality in man. It is really curious that on a question so fundamental,
such a variety of opinions should have prevailed among men, and those,
too, of the most exemplary virtue and first order of understanding. It
shows how necessary was the care of the Creator in making the moral
principle so much a part of our constitution as that no errors of reasoning
or of speculation might lead us astray from its observance in practice. Of
all the theories on this question, the most whimsical seems to have been
that of Wollaston, who considers *truth* as the foundation of morality. The
thief who steals your guinea does wrong only inasmuch as he acts a lie in
using your guinea as if it were his own. Truth is certainly a branch of
morality, and a very important one to society. But presented as its
foundation, it is as if a tree taken up by the roots, had its stem reversed in

the air, and one of its branches planted in the ground. Some have made the *love of God* the foundation of morality. This, too, is but a branch of our moral duties, which are generally divided into duties to God and duties to man. If we did a good act merely from the love of God and a belief that it is pleasing to Him, whence arises the morality of the Atheist? It is idle to say, as some do, that no such being exists. We have the same evidence of the fact as of most of those we act on, to wit; their own affirmations, and their reasonings in support of them. I have observed, indeed, generally, that while in Protestant countries the defections from the Platonic Christianity of the priests is to Deism, in Catholic countries they are to Atheism. Diderot, D'Alembert, D'Holbach, Condorcet, are known to have been among the most virtuous of men. Their virtue, then, must have had some other foundation than the love of God.

The 𝑇𝑜 𝐾𝑢𝜂𝑜𝜈 of others is founded in a different faculty, that of taste, which is not even a branch of morality. We have indeed an innate sense of what we call beautiful, but that is exercised chiefly on subjects addressed to the fancy, whether through the eye in visible forms, as landscape, animal figure, dress, drapery, architecture, the composition of colors, etc., or to the imagination directly, as imagery, style, or measure in prose or poetry, or whatever else constitutes the domain of criticism or taste, a faculty entirely distinct from the moral one. Self-interest, or rather self-love, or *egoism*, has been more plausibly substituted as the basis of morality. But I consider our relations with others as constituting the boundaries of morality. With ourselves we stand on the ground of identity, not of relation, which last, requiring two subjects, excludes self-love confined to a single one. To ourselves, in strict language, we can owe no duties, obligation requiring also two parties. Self-love, therefore, is no part of morality. Indeed it is exactly its counterpart. It is the sole antagonist of virtue, leading us constantly by our propensities to self-gratification in violation of our moral duties to others. Accordingly, it is against this enemy that are erected the batteries of moralists and religionists, as the only obstacle to the practice of morality. Take from man his selfish propensities, and he can have nothing to seduce him from the practice of virtue. Or subdue those propensities by education, instruction or restraint, and virtue remains without a competitor. Egoism, in a broader sense, has been thus presented as the source of moral action. It has been said that we feed the hungry, clothe the naked, bind up the wounds of the man beaten by thieves, pour oil and wine into him, set him on our own beast and bring him to the inn, because we receive ourselves pleasure from these acts. So Helvetius, one of the best men on earth, and the most ingenious advocate of this principle, after defining "interest" to mean not merely that which is pecuniary, but whatever may procure us pleasure or withdraw us from pain . . . says . . . "the humane man is he to whom the sight of misfortune is insupportable, and who to rescue himself from this spectacle, is forced to succor the unfortunate object." This indeed is true. But it is one step short of the ultimate question. These good acts give us pleasure, but how happens it that they give us pleasure? Because nature hath implanted in our breasts a love of others, a sense of duty to them, a moral instinct, in short, which prompts us irresistibly to feel and to succor their distresses, and protests against the language of Helvetius . . . "what other motive than self-interest could determine a man to generous actions? It is as impossible for him to love what is good for the sake of good, as to love evil for the sake of evil." The Creator would indeed have been a bungling artist, had he intended man for a social animal, without planting in him social dispositions. It is true they are not planted in every man, because there is no rule without exceptions; but it is false reasoning which converts exceptions into the general rule. Some men are born without the organs of sight, or of hearing, or without hands. Yet it would be wrong to say that man is born without these faculties, and sight, hearing, and hands may with truth enter into the general definition of man.

The want or imperfection of the moral sense in some men, like the want or imperfection of the senses of sight and hearing in others, is no proof that it is a general characteristic of the species. When it is wanting, we endeavor to supply the defect by education, by appeals to reason and calculation, by presenting to the being so unhappily conformed, other motives to do good and to eschew evil, such as the love, or the hatred, or rejection of those among whom he lives, and whose society is necessary to his happiness and even existence; demonstrations by sound calculation that honesty promotes interest in the long run; the rewards and penalties established by the laws; and ultimately the prospects of a future state of retribution for the evil as well as the good done while here. These are the correctives which are supplied by education, and which exercise the functions of the moralist, the preacher, and legislator; and they lead into a course of correct action all those whose disparity is not too profound to be eradicated. Some have argued against the existence of a moral sense, by saying that if nature had given us such a sense, impelling us to virtuous actions, and warning us against those which are vicious, then nature would also have designated, by some particular ear-marks, the two sets of actions which are, in themselves, the one virtuous and the other vicious. Whereas, we find, in fact, that the same actions are deemed virtuous in one country and vicious in another. The answer is, that nature has constituted *utility* to man, the standard and test of virtue. Men living in different countries, under different circumstances, different habits and regimens, may have different utilities; the same act, therefore, may be useful, and consequently virtuous in one country which is injurious and vicious in another differently circumstanced. I sincerely, then, believe with you in the general existence of a moral instinct. I think it the brightest gem with which the human character is studded, and the want of it as more degrading than the most hideous of the bodily deformities. I am happy in reviewing the roll of associates in this principle which you present in your second letter, some of which I had not before met with. To these might be added Lord Kaims, one of the ablest of our advocates, who goes so far as to say, in his Principles of Natural Religion, that a man owes no duty to which he is not urged by some impulsive feeling. This is correct, if referred to the standard of general feeling in the given case, and not to the feeling of a single individual. Perhaps I may misquote him, it being fifty years since I read his book.

The leisure and solitude of my situation here has led me to the indiscretion of taxing you with a long letter on a subject whereon nothing new can be offered you. I will indulge myself no farther than to repeat the assurances of my continued esteem and respect.

[Thomas Jefferson]

LETTER TO SAMUEL KERCHEVAL
Monticello, July 12, 1816

. . . Some men look at constitutions with sanctimonious reverence, and deem them like the ark of the covenant, too sacred to be touched. They ascribe to the men of the preceding age a wisdom more than human, and suppose what they did to be beyond amendment. I knew that age well; I belonged to it, and labored with it. It deserved well of its country. It was very like the present; and forty years of experience in government is worth a century of book-reading; and this they would say themselves, were they to rise from the dead. I am certainly not an advocate for frequent and untried changes in laws and constitutions. I think moderate imperfections had better be borne with; because, when once known, we accommodate ourselves to them, and find practical means of correcting their ill effects. But I know also, that laws and institutions must go hand in hand with the progress of the human mind. As that becomes more developed, more enlightened, as new discoveries are made, new truths disclosed, and manners and opinions change with the change of circumstances, institutions must advance also, and keep pace with the times. We might as well require a man to wear still the coat which fitted him when a boy, as civilized society to remain ever under the regimen of their barbarous ancestors. It is this preposterous idea which has lately deluged Europe in blood. Their monarchs, instead of wisely yielding to the gradual change of circumstances, of favoring progressive accommodation to progressive improvement, have clung to old abuses, entrenched themselves behind steady habits, and obliged their subjects to seek through blood and violence rash and ruinous innovations, which, had they been referred to the peaceful deliberations and collected wisdom of the nation, would have been put into acceptable and salutary forms. Let us follow no such examples, nor weakly believe that one generation is not as capable as another of taking care of itself, and of ordering its own affairs. Let us, as our sister States have done, avail ourselves of our reason and experience, to correct the crude essays of our first and unexperienced, although wise, virtuous, and well-meaning councils. And lastly, let us provide in our Constitution for its revision at stated periods. What these periods should be, nature herself indicates. By the European tables of mortality, of the adults living at any one moment of time, a majority will be dead in about nineteen years. At the end of that period then, a new majority is come into place; or, in other words, a new generation. Each generation is as independent of the one preceding, as that was of all which had gone before. It has then, like them, a right to choose for itself the form of government it believes most promotive of its own happiness; consequently, to accommodate to the circumstances in which it finds itself, that received from its predeccessors; and it is for the peace and good of mankind, that a solemn opportunity of doing this every nineteen or twenty years, should be provided by the Constitution; so that it may be handed on, with periodical repairs, from generation to generation, to the end of time, if anything human can so long endure. It is now forty years since the constitution of Virginia was formed. The same tables inform us, that, within that period, two-thirds of the adults then living are now dead. Have then the remaining third, even if they had the wish, the right to hold in obedience to their will, and to laws heretofore made by them, the other two-thirds, who, with themselves, compose the present mass of adults? If they have not, who has? The dead? But the dead have no rights. They are nothing; and nothing cannot own something. Where there is no substance, there can be no accident. This corporeal globe, and everything upon it, belong to its present corporeal inhabitants, during their generation. They alone have a right to direct what is the concern of themselves alone, and to declare the law of that direction; and this declaration can only be made by their majority. That majority, then, has a right to depute representatives to a convention, and to make the Constitution what they think will be the best for themselves. But how collect their voice? This is the real difficulty. If invited by private authority, or county or district meetings, these divisions are so large that few will attend; and their voice will be imperfectly, or falsely, pronounced. Here, then, would be one of the advantages of the ward divisions I have proposed. The mayor of every ward, on a question like the present, would call his ward together, take the simple yea or nay of its members, convey these to the county court, who would hand on those of all its wards to the proper general authority; and the voice of the whole people would thus be fairly, fully, and peaceably expressed, discussed, and decided by the common reason of the society. If this avenue be shut to the call of sufferance, it will make itself heard through that of force, and we shall go on, as other nations are doing, in the endless circle of oppression, rebellion, reformation; and oppression, rebellion, reformation, again; and so on forever. . . .

[Thomas Jefferson]

Part II

POLITICO-ECONOMIC REFORM

This section makes up a disproportionately large part of the documentation of American reform because it represents that part which has been most broad, most continuous, most inclusive, and most truly national. Few citizens from colonial times to the present have escaped the direct impact of the issues here involved. From the earliest efforts of immigrants on American shores to distinguish their society from the European one they had left, there can be traced a strong thread of continuity that comprehends themes and myths central to the culture, as well as the modalities characteristic of reform. Politico-economic reform is also national in that it has involved our largest entities: banks and corporations, labor and government on all levels.

The issues are the ones that have affected great numbers of Americans: the nature and control of money and credit; the regulation of banks and trusts; the process of bargaining for wages, hours, and conditions of labor; the workings of democracy from the conduct of voting places to the methods of assessing their returns; the maintenance of that delicate and shifting balance between property rights and civil rights. The debates on these issues have occupied the center of attention in political platforms, legislative debates, and arguments before the courts. Novels and poems, paintings and lithographs have made their partisan statements. Viewpoints have been etched on snuffboxes, sketched on campaign buttons, lettered on posters, and carried through the streets on banners and transparencies. The momentum of achievement can be seen in photographs and cartoons, newspaper articles and Constitutional amend-

17

ments. The discussion of economic and political issues may be discovered in the smallest crevices of the culture—in personal letters and on small medallions; this discussion is also abundantly present on the most highly visible of the nation's public forums.

Central to this movement have been some of our most familiar symbols and the values they represent: the cap of liberty and the coonskin cap; the bloated belly of the money-vested boss and the stout, bared arm guiding hammer, pitchfork, or plow. The wigs and lace of the Federalists are there, alongside the candidate with a hole in the sole of his shoe. So are the log cabin and the Hoovervilles, the cross of gold and the greenback, the hound dog and the bull moose, the full dinner pail and the empty dinner table. Connecting the more important of these symbols is a rhetorical theme with two clear variations. The negative aspect is a vilification of undeserved privilege and improper power wherever found: monarch or boss, banker or monopolist, dishonest senator or hypocritical influence peddler. The positive aspect is an equivalent glorification of the underprivileged: the poor and the taxpayers, farmers and manual laborers, migrants and settlers, women and minority groups.

Politico-economic issues, symbols, and rhetorical themes constitute one of the most basic meanings of the American polity. A part of the colonial experience—particularly as it led to the revolt against England —was the growing feeling that this New World society should distinguish itself by lessening the social, political, and economic difference that existed between classes in the Old World. Opinions differed widely as to how closely the new society would approach an absolute egalitarianism. A growing consensus insisted that equality of opportunity should be protected from special privilege at the top and from disenabling poverty at the bottom.

This impetus toward economic equity was predicated on the extension of political democracy. Among the many aspects of the reform experience, this one is the most obvious and familiar; yet, curiously, it has seldom been described in terms of a continuing impulse which consistently united political and economic assumptions and goals. Under the heading of political reform a reader can learn to connect the early battles over suffrage with protest politics of the Progressive Era and the New Deal. Under another heading he may readily establish connections between the subtreasury plan, the greenback issue, the question of wages and hours, and the rise of organized labor. The problems of the farmers, the prosecution of monopolies, the creation of consumer pressures—these aspects of the subject may come under still different headings. Or, if the threads are united, the reader may be asked to see periods of intense achievement punctuated by periods of total apathy.

The documents that follow indicate that our tendency to separate history into separate aspects has prevented us from measuring the continuing strength of the impulse toward political and economic democracy. As a concisely phrased slogan for this entire section, one could hardly pick a better phrase than that intensely politico-economic revolutionary battle cry: *"Taxation without representation is tyranny!"* These documents show that this slogan has been applied not only to the king and Parliament of England but—in this precise spirit—to the wielders of political and economic power in the nation. It has been applied in a way that makes it foolhardy to separate political from economic issues. It has been applied with a continuing force that makes periodization risky.

As these documents succeed one another, they reveal a process of increasing access to government through widening the suffrage and through making elected and appointed officials more representative of the people and more responsive to the people in a number of ways. The main interest in this process has never been the achievement of a sterile casebook exercise in representative government. As with the revolutionary watchword, an economic purpose has always underlain the push for more participatory political democracy: the withdrawal of special privilege; the need to regulate some entity operating contrary to the broad public interest; the relief from poverty and exploitation.

The interrelated and continuous process of politico-economic reform goes relentlessly on in spite of obstacles. Its achievements are often more rhetorical than real. Its landmarks sometimes invite new inroads and abuses. Human nature—collective or individual—has been neither repealed nor seriously amended. Yet, when all this is said, there remains no more important central statement of the meaning of the national experience than the one represented by the documentary history of America's politico-economic reforms.

Document II-1: PARTY AND CLASS IN PENNSYLVANIA

Even before the United States had its first president there were clear expressions of the sentiments which were to characterize one aspect of American reform throughout the history of the nation. The issue was the ratification of the Federal Constitution proposed by the convention that ended its labors in September, 1787. As the proposal was circulated each state assembly met to consider ratification and, throughout the winter of 1787-88, a series of debates took place which ended not only in the affirmation of the Constitution but also in the polarization of the new nation into the views which gave birth to the first version of the two-party system. The position backing the Constitution, well known to all through the celebrated ''Federalist Papers,'' sought a more centralized authority to overcome the confusions and perils threatening loosely joined former colonies under the Articles of Confederation.

The Antifederalist position, not nearly so well known, voiced the consistent suspicion that the Constitution was a conspiracy drawn up by men of wealth to protect their property and by men of ambition who sought to join a vested elite. The propagandists against the Constitution showed a confidence that they could arouse opposition by drawing on a majority belief that America should have a system which guaranteed against special privilege for the few and against political power for men of property.

The address that follows makes a useful link between the pre-Revolutionary protests against England and the post-Revolutionary suspicions of class, wealth, and Anglophilia. It carries over a mistrust of a standing army and a strong fear of unjust taxes. Even its style reminds one of the petitions to the English king and Parliament with its carefully enumerated grievances and its rationalistic lists of arguments in point.

To a student of politico-economic reform, this address merits a close look for the remarkable completeness with which it catalogued the central problems of representative government and for the equally remarkable vision which foresaw the ensuing tensions between class and party, state and nation. If the Federalists were mistrustful of the mob, the Antifederalists were equally suspicious of the corrupting influence of political power if held too long, by too few, or at too great a remove from the popular base. Most of the arguments are quite Jeffersonian in their respect for the proper powers of the states and in their assumption that the nation must resist centralization in order to maintain a natural and desirable pluralism of region and class, occupation and faith. Although it may seem strange today to hear so venerated a document so fundamentally criticized, it is true that the Antifederalists objected even to the Constitution's opening "We, the People" on the grounds that it suggested an unwanted single governmental structure in place of the desired retention of state sovereignty.

The address, intended more for publication than for a single hearing, opened with a background statement depicting the process of Constitutional ratification as fraught with procedural traps intended to squelch objections under a blanket of hasty action with the convention membership limited to a simple "take it or leave it" option. The minority dissenters wrote of "gilded chains . . . forging in secret conclave" (p. 1 as cited below) a new enslavement of the population-at-large to the special interests of the few. The paragraphs here quoted give the outline of the argument and some of the justifications. The omitted passages devote most space to concern over abuses of the power to tax and to the possible tyrannization of a large and varied nation by but twenty-seven men (the senate and the president).

SOURCE: *The Pennsylvania Packet and Daily Advertiser.* December 18, 1787, pp. 1-3, abridged.

THE ADDRESS AND REASONS OF DISSENT OF THE MINORITY OF THE CONVENTION OF THE STATE OF PENNSYLVANIA TO THEIR CONSTITUENTS.

. . . The convention met, and the same disposition was soon manifested in considering the proposed constitution, that had been exhibited in every other stage of the business . . . We were prohibited by an express vote of the convention from taking any questions on the separate articles of the plan, and reduced to the necessity of adopting or rejecting *in toto*—'Tis true the majority permitted us to debate on each article, but restrained us from proposing amendments.—They also determined not to permit us to enter on the minutes our reasons of dissent against any of the articles, nor even on the final question our reasons of dissent against the whole. Thus situated we entered on the examination of the proposed system of government, and found it to be such as we could not adopt, without, as we conceived, surrendering up your dearest rights. We offered our objections to the convention, and opposed those parts of the plan which, in our opinion, would be injurious to you, in the best manner we were able; and closed our arguments by offering the following propositions to the convention.

1. The right of conscience shall be held inviolable; and neither the legislative, executive nor judicial powers of the United States shall have authority to alter, abrogate or infringe any part of the constitution of the several states, which provide for the preservation of liberty in matters of religion.

2. That in controversies respecting property, and in suits between man and man, trial by jury shall remain as heretofore as well in the federal courts, as in those of the several states.

3. That in all capital and criminal prosecutions, a man has a right to demand the cause and nature of his accusation, as well in the federal courts as in those of the several states; to be heard by himself and his counsel; to be confronted with the accusers and witnesses; to call for evidence in his favor, and a speedy trial by an impartial jury of his vicinage, without whose unanimous consent he cannot be found guilty, nor can he be compelled to give evidence against himself; and that no man be deprived of his liberty, except by the law of the land or the judgment of his peers.

4. That excessive bail ought not to be required, nor excessive fines imposed, nor cruel nor unusual punishments inflicted.

5. That warrants unsupported by evidence, whereby any officer or messenger may be commanded or required to search suspected places, or to seize any person or persons, his or their property, not particularly described, are grievous and oppressive, and shall not be granted either by the magistrates of the federal government or others.

6. That the people have a right to the freedom of speech, of writing and publishing their sentiments, therefore, the freedom of the press shall not be restrained by any law of the United States.

7. That the people have a right to bear arms for the defence of themselves and their own state, or the United States, or for the purpose of killing game; and no law shall be passed for disarming the people or any

of them, unless for crimes committed, or real danger of public injury from individuals; and as standing armies in the time of peace are dangerous to liberty, they ought not to be kept up; and that the military shall be kept under strict subordination to and be governed by the civil powers.

8. The inhabitants of the several states shall have liberty to fowl and hunt in seasonable times, on the lands they hold, and on all other lands in the United States not inclosed, and in like manner to fish in all navigable waters, and others not private property, without being restrained therein by any laws to be passed by the legislature of the United States.

9. That no law shall be passed to restrain the legislatures of the several states from enacting laws for imposing taxes, except imposts and duties on goods imported or exported, and that no taxes, except imposts and duties upon goods imported and exported, and postage on letters shall be levied by the authority of Congress.

10. That the house of representatives be properly increased in number; that elections shall remain free; that the several states shall have power to regulate the elections for senators and representatives, without being controlled either directly or indirectly by any interference on the part of the Congress; and that the elections of representatives be annual.

11. That the power of organizing, arming and disciplining the militia (the manner of disciplining the militia to be prescribed by Congress) remain with the individual states, and that Congress shall not have authority to call or march any of the militia out of their own state, without the consent of such state, and for such length of time only as such state shall agree.

That the sovereignty, freedom and independency of the several states shall be retained, and every power, jurisdiction and right which is not by this constitution expressly delegated to the United States in Congress assembled.

12. That the legislative, executive and judicial powers be kept separate; and to this end that a constitutional council be appointed, to advise and assist the president, who shall be responsible for the advice they give, hereby the senators would be relieved from almost constant attendance; and also that the judges be made completely independent.

13. That no treaty which shall be directly opposed to the existing laws of the United States in Congress assembled, shall be valid until such laws

shall be repealed or made conformable to such treaty; neither shall any treaties be valid which are in contradiction to the constitution of the United States, or the constitution of the several states.

14. That the judiciary power of the United States shall be confined to cases affecting ambassadors, other public ministers and consuls, to cases of admiralty and maritime jurisdiction; to controversies to which the United States shall be a party; to controversies between two or more states—between a state and citizens of different states—between citizens claiming lands under grants of different states, and between a state or the citizens thereof and foreign states; and in criminal cases to such only as are expressly enumerated in the constitution; and that the United States in Congress assembled shall not have power to enact laws which shall alter the laws of descent and distribution of the effects of deceased persons, the titles of lands or goods, or the regulation of contracts in the individual states.

After reading these propositions, we declared our willingness to agree to the plan, provided it was so amended as to meet those propositions, or something similar to them, and finally moved the convention to adjourn, to give the people of Pennsylvania time to consider the subject, and determine for themselves; but these were all rejected and the final vote taken, when our duty to you induced us to vote against the proposed plan and to decline signing the ratification of the same.

During the discussion we met with many insults, and some personal abuse; we were not even treated with decency, during the sitting of the convention, by the persons in the gallery of the house; however, we flatter ourselves that in contending for the preservation of those invaluable rights you have thought proper to commit to our charge, we acted with a spirit becoming freemen, and being desirous that you might know the principles which actuated our conduct, and being prohibited from inserting our reasons for dissent on the minutes of the convention, we have subjoined them for your consideration, as to you alone we are accountable. It remains with you whether you will think those inestimable privileges, which you have so ably contended for, should be sacrificed at the shrine of despotism, or whether you mean to contend for them with the same spirit that has so often baffled the attempts of an aristocratic faction, to rivet the shackles of slavery on you and your unborn posterity.

Our objections are comprised under three general heads of dissent, viz.

We dissent, first, because it is the opinion of the most celebrated writers on government, and confirmed by uniform experience, that a very extensive territory cannot be governed on the principles of freedom, otherwise than by a confederation of republics, possessing all the powers of internal government; but united in the management of their general and foreign concerns.

If any doubt could have been entertained of the truth of the foregoing principle, it has been fully removed by the concession of *Mr. Wilson*, one of the majority on this question, and who was one of the deputies in the late general convention. In justice to him, we will give his own words; they are as follows, viz. "The extent of country for which the new constitution was required, produced another difficulty in the business of the federal convention. It is the opinion of some celebrated writers, that to a small territory, the democratical; to a middling territory (as Montesquieu has termed it) the monarchical; and to an extensive territory, the despotic form of government is best adapted. Regarding then the wide and almost unbounded jurisdiction of the United States, at first view, the hand of despotism seemed necessary to control, connect, and protect it; and hence the chief embarrassment rose. For, we know that, although our constituents would cheerfully submit to the legislative restraints of a free government, they would spurn at every attempt to shackle them with despotic power."—And again, in another part of his speech, he continues.—"Is it probable that the dissolution of the state governments, and the establishment of one *consolidated empire* would be eligible in its nature, and satisfactory to the people in its administration? I think not, as I have given reasons to show that so extensive a territory could not be governed, connected, and preserved, but by the *supremacy of despotic power*. All the exertions of the most potent emperors of Rome were not capable of keeping that empire together, which in extent was far inferior to the dominion of America."

We dissent, secondly, because the powers vested in Congress by this constitution, must necessarily annihilate and absorb the legislative, executive, and judicial powers of the several states, and produce from their ruins one consolidated government, which from the nature of things will be *an iron handed despotism*, as nothing short of the supremacy of despotic sway could connect and govern these United States under one government.

As the truth of this position is of such decisive importance, it ought to be fully investigated, and if it is found to be clearly ascertained; for, should it be demonstrated, that the powers vested by this constitution in Congress, will have such an effect as necessarily to produce one consolidated government, the question then will be reduced to this short issue, viz. whether satiated with the blessings of liberty, whether repenting of the folly of so recently asserting their unalienable rights against foreign despots at the expense of so much blood and treasure, and such painful abd arduous struggles, the people of America are now willing to resign every privilege of freemen, and submit to the dominion of an absolute government, that will embrace all America in one chain of despotism; or whether they will, with virtuous indignation, spurn at the shackles prepared for them, and confirm their liberties by a conduct becoming freemen.

That the new government will not be a confederacy of states, as it ought, but one consolidated government, founded upon the destruction of the several governments of the states, we shall now show.

The powers of Congress under the new constitution are complete and unlimited over the *purse* and the *sword*, and are perfectly independent of, and supreme over, the state governments, who e intervention in these great points is entirely destroyed. By virtue of their power of taxation, Congress may command the whole, or any part of the property of the people. They may impose what imposts upon commerce; they may impose what land taxes, poll taxes, excises, duties on all written instruments and duties on every other article that they may judge proper; in short, every species of taxation, whether of an external or internal nature is comprised in section the 8th, of article the 1st, viz. "The Congress shall have power to lay and collect taxes, duties, imposts, and excises, to pay the debts, and provide for the common defence and general welfare of the United States."

As there is no one article of taxation reserved to the state governments, the Congress may monopolize every source of revenue, and thus indirectly demolish the state governments, for without funds they could not exist; the taxes, duties and excises imposed by Congress may be so high as to render it impracticable to levy farther sums on the same articles; but whether this should be the case or not, if the state governments should presume to impose taxes, duties or excises, on the same articles with Congress, the latter may abrogate and repeal the laws whereby they are imposed, upon the allegation that they interfere with the due collection of their taxes, duties or excises, by virtue of the following clause, part of section 8th, article 1st, viz. "To make all laws which shall be necessary and proper for carrying into execution the foregoing powers, and all other powers vested by this constitution in the government of the United States, or in any department or officer thereof."

The Congress might gloss over this conduct by construing every purpose for which the state legislatures now lay taxes, to be for the "*general welfare*," and therefore as of their jurisdiction.

And the supremacy of the laws of the United States is established by article 6th, viz. "That this constitution and the laws of the United States, which shall be made in pursuance thereof, and *all treaties* made, or which shall be made under the authority of the United States, shall be the *supreme law* of the *land;* and *the judges in every state shall be bound thereby; anything in the constitution or laws of any State to the contrary notwithstanding.*" It has been alleged that the words "pursuant to the constitution," are a restriction upon the authority of Congress; but when it is considered that by other sections they are invested with every efficient power of government, and which may be exercised to the absolute destruction of the state governments, without any violation of even the forms of the constitution, this seeming restriction, as well as every other restriction on it, appears to us to be nugatory and delusive; and only introduced as a blind upon the real nature of the government. In our opinion, "pursuant to the constitution," will be co-extensive with the *will* and *pleasure* of Congress, which, indeed, will be the only limitation of their powers.

We apprehend that two co-ordinate sovereignties would be a solecism in politics. That, therefore, as there is no line of distinction drawn between the general and state governments, as the sphere of their jurisdiction is undefined, it would be contrary to the nature of things, that both should exist together, one or the other would necessarily triumph in the fulness of dominion. However, the contest could not be for long continuance, as the State governments are divested of every means of defence, and will be obliged by "the supreme law of the land" *to yield at discretion.*

It has been objected to this total destruction of the state governments, that the existence of their legislatures is made essential to the organization of Congress; that they must assemble for the appointment of the senators and president-general of the United States. True, the State legislatures may be continued for some years, as boards of appointment, merely, after they are divested of every other function; but the framers of the constitution, foreseeing that the people will soon become disgusted with this solemn mockery of a government without power and usefulness, have made a provision for relieving them from the imposition, in section 4th, of article 1st, viz. "The times, places, and manner of holding elections for senators and representatives, shall be prescribed in each state by the legislature thereof; *but the Congress may at any time by law make or alter such regulations; except as to the place of choosing senators.*"

As Congress have the control over the time of the appointment of the president-general, of the senators and of the representatives of the United States, they may prolong their existence in office, for life, by postponing the time of their election and appointment, from period to period, under various pretences, such as an apprehension of invasion, the factious disposition of the people, or any other plausible pretence that the occasion may suggest; and having thus obtained life-estates in the government, they may fill up the vacancies themselves by their control over the mode of appointment; with this exception in regard to the senators, that as the place of appointment for them must, by the constitution, be in the particular state, they may depute some body in the respective states, to fill up the vacancies in the senate, occasioned by death, until they can venture to assume it themselves. In this manner, may the only restriction in this clause be evaded. By virtue of the foregoing section, when the spirit of the people shall be gradually broken; when the general government shall be firmly established, and when a numerous standing army shall render opposition vain, the Congress may complete the system of despotism, in renouncing all dependence on the people, by continuing themselves and children in the government.

The celebrated *Montesquieu*, in his Spirit of Laws, vol. I, page 12th, says, "That in a democracy there can be no exercise of sovereignty, but by the suffrages of the people, which are their will; now the sovereign's will is the sovereign himself; the laws, therefore, which establish the right of suffrage, are fundamental to this government. In fact, it is as important to regulate in a republic in what manner, by whom, and concerning what suffrages are to be given, as it is in a monarchy to know who is the prince, and after what manner he ought to govern." The *time, mode* and *place* of the election of representatives, senators and president-general of the United States, ought not to be under the control of Congress, but fundamentally ascertained and established.

The new Constitution, consistently with the plan of consolidation, contains no reservation of the rights and privileges of the state governments, which was made in the confederation of the year 1778, by article the 2nd, viz. "That each state retains its sovereignty, freedom and independence, and every power, jurisdiction and right which is not by this confederation expressly delegated to the United States in Congress assembled."

The legislative power vested in Congress by the foregoing recited sections, is so unlimited in its nature, may be so comprehensive and boundless in its exercise, that this alone would be amply sufficient to annihilate the state governments, and swallow them up in the grand vortex of general empire.

The judicial pngress; powers which do not exist in Pennsylvania, unless , that by legal ingenuity they may be extended to every case, and thus absorb the state judiciaries; and when we consider the decisive influence that a general judiciary would have over the civil polity of the several states, we do not hesitate to pronounce that this power, unaided by the legislative, would effect a consolidation of the States under one government.

The powers of a court of equity, vested by this constitution in the tribunals of Congress; powers which do not exist in Pennsylvania, unless so far as they can be incorporated with jury trial, would, in this state, greatly contribute to this event. The rich and wealthy suitors would eagerly lay hold of the infinite mazes, perplexities and delays, which a court of chancery, with the appellate powers of the supreme court in fact as well as law would furnish him with, and thus the poor man being plunged in the bottomless pit of legal discussion, would drop his demand in despair.

In short, consolidation pervades the whole constitution. It begins with an annunciation that such was the intention. The main pillars of the fabric correspond with it, and the concluding paragraph is a confirmation of it. The preamble begins with the words, "We the people of the United States," which is the style of a compact between individuals entering into a state of society, and not that of a confederation of states. The other features of consolidation we have before noticed.

Thus we have fully established the position, that the powers vested by this constitution in Congress, will effect a consolidation of the states under one government, which even the advocates of this constitution admit, could not be done without the sacrifice of all liberty.

We dissent, thirdly, because if it were practicable to govern so extensive a territory as these United States includes, on the plan of a consolidated government, consistent with the principles of liberty and the happiness of the people, yet the construction of this constitution is not calculated to attain the object; for independent of the nature of the case, it would of itself, necessarily produce a despotism, and that not by the usual gradations, but with the celerity that has hitherto only attended revolutions effected by the sword. . . .

We have not noticed the smaller, nor many of the considerable blemishes, but have confined our objections to the great and essential defects; the main pillars of the constitution; which we have shown to be inconsistent with the liberty and happiness of the people, as its establishment will annihilate the state governments, and produce one consolidated government, that will eventually and speedily issue in the supremacy of despotism.

In this investigation we have not confined our views to the interests or welfare of this state, in preference to the others. We have overlooked all local circumstances—we have considered this subject on the broad scale of the general good: we have asserted the cause of the present and future ages: the cause of liberty and mankind.

Nathaniel Breading	John Ludwig
John Smilie	Abraham Lincoln
Richard Baird	John Bishop
Adam Orth	Joseph Hiester
John A. Hanna	Joseph Powel
John Whitehill	James Martin
John Harris	William Findley
Robert Whitehill	John Baird
John Reynolds	James Edgar
Jonathan Hoge	William Todd
Nicholas Lutz	

The yeas and nays upon the final vote were as follows, viz.

YEAS

George Latimer
Benjamin Rush
Hilary Baker
James Wilson
Thomas M'Kean
William Macpherson
John Hunn
George Gray
Samuel Ashmead
Enoch Edwards
Henry Wynkoop
John Barclay
Thomas Yardley
Abraham Stout
Thomas Bull
Anthony Wayne
William Gibbons
Richard Downing
Thomas Cheyney
John Hannum
Stephen Chambers
Robert Coleman
Sebastian Graff

YEAS

John Hubley
Jasper Yeates
Henry Slagle
Thomas Campbell
Thomas Hartley
David Grier
John Black
Benjamin Pedan
John Arndt
Stephen Balliott
Joseph Horsfield
David Deshler
William Wilson
John Boyd
Thomas Scott
John Nevill
John Allison
Jonathan Roberts
John Richards
F. A. Muhlenberg
James Morris
TImothy Pickering
Benjamin Elliott

NAYS

John Whitehill
John Harris
John Reynolds
Robert Whitehill
Jonathan Hoge
Nicholas Lutz
John Ludwig
Abraham Lincoln
John Bishop
Joseph Hiester
James Martin
Joseph Powell

NAYS

William Findley
John Baird
William Todd
James Marshall
James Edgar
Nathaniel Breading
John Smilie
Richard Baird
William Brown
Adam Orth
John Andre Hannah

Philadelphia Dec. 12, 1787.

Document II-2: FRENEAU ON THE NEW REPUBLIC

Philip Freneau (1752-1832) could easily have claimed the title of America's first protest poet. While still in college he praised in verse America's potential greatness. Following a trail blazed by Tom Paine he baited the British and wrote to encourage the Revolutionary troops. Freneau's revolutionary spirit did not stop with the Peace of Paris. He saw in the Federalist Party a comparable menace to that of the Tories in the 1770s. As a journalist and poet he clung to the cause of popular democracy and, according to Jefferson, did more than anyone else to save a "constitution which was galloping fast into monarchy." (*Writings of Thomas Jefferson*, Paul L. Ford, ed. New York, Putnam's, 1899, vol. I, p. 231.)

He wrote the following poem in 1798, a dark year in many respects. Yellow fever plagued the nation's health and a threat of war with distraught France plagued its peace of mind. President John Adams, assailed by intense criticism from all quarters, reverted to the most narrow and virulent strain of his conservative nature, becoming ever less trustful of the populace and demanding the passage of the notorious Alien and Sedition Laws. Freneau, born in New York of Huguenot ancestry, was convinced that the French thought and experience were pointing toward a desirable future in which the rulers would be less contemptuous of the people. Note how his pro-Jeffersonian political cliché, "It's time for a change," was interlaced with the imagery of revulsion against an incipient American monarchy with its foppish dress and order of the "garter and star." Building on the adversions of 1776, Freneau made a post-revolutionary political cause which fused a mistrust of the rich and well-accoutered with an appeal on behalf of a man of more democratic leanings.

SOURCE: Philip Freneau, *A Collection of Poems, on American Affairs, and a Variety of Other Subjects, Chiefly Moral and Political; Written between the year 1797 and the Present Time.* New York, David Longworth, 1815, pp. 161-162.

REFLECTIONS
On the Mutability of Things—1798

The time is approaching deny it who may,
    The days are not very remote,
When the pageant that glitter'd for many a day,
    On the stream of oblivion will float.

The times are advancing when matters will turn,
    And some, who are now in the shade,
And pelted by malice, or treated with scorn,
    Will pay, in coin that was paid:

The time it will be, when people aroused,
    For better arrangements prepare,
And firm to the cause, that of old they espoused,
    Their steady attachment declare:

When tyrants will shrink from the face of the day,
    Or, if they presume to remain,
To the tune of *peccavi*, a solo will play,
    And lower the royalty strain:

When government favors to flattery's press
    Will halt on their way from afar,
And people will laugh at the comical dress
    Of the knights of the garter and star:

When a *monarch*, new fangled, with lawyer and scribe,
    In junto will cease to convene,
Or take from old England a pitiful bribe,
    To pamper his "highness serene;"

When virtue and merit will have a fair chance
    The loaves and the fishes to share,
And JEFFERSON, you to your station advance,
    The man from the president's chair:

When honesty, honor, experience, approved,
No more in disgrace will retire;
When fops from the places of trust are removed
And the leaders of faction retire.

Document II-3: AMES AND ANTIFEDERALISM

Symbols have been important, both positively and negatively, in the process of social change. Strictly speaking, the first important negative symbol in the history of American reform was the king of England; and, by extension, the trappings and privileges of monarchy. It suited the purposes of the Antifederalists to transfer this negative symbolic value from the British royalty to the wealthy Federalists and, more particularly, to their dress. Thus Parrington could write from his Jeffersonian viewpoint, "Of this testy little world that clung to its smallclothes and tie-wig, refusing to adopt the Jacobin innovation in dress and manners and politics, declining to temper its prejudices to the gusty whims of a leveling age, Fisher Ames was the universal counselor and oracle." (Vernon L. Parrington, *Main Currents in American Thought.* New York, Harcourt, Brace, 1930, vol. II, p. 279.)

Intrinsically, the gentleman's costume of the late eighteenth century demonstrated his exemption from manual labor in its tightly cut smallclothes (knee breeches) that inhibited drastic body movements; in the lace or lawn at neck and sleeves—too white for toil, too tight for freedom; and in the wig or powdered hair which hard work would soon have put awry. These clothes also signaled their wearer's wealth: in the quality of lace, in the rich velvet, silk-lined, long-tailed coat, in the fine leather slippers, and in the softly burnished silver buckles at the knee and ankle.

This portrait of Ames does not exhibit the extremes of foppishness—a frilly jabot at the neck, an elaborate wig, rippling lace protruding from the cuff—that might have produced Freneau's scornful lines in the preceding verse. Yet there is enough. The face looks toward the beholder with an expression quite consistent with his patrician pronouncements: "The chief duty and care of all governments is to protect the rights of property and the tranquility of society. . . ." Although the background for this seated figure was provided by an artist who probably never saw the interior of Ames's well-appointed Boston home, it constitutes a likely collection of objects and furnishings.

This setting, together with its central figure, might suggest an attitude that put property and tranquillity first, popular democracy near the last. The image and words of Fisher Ames help explain Freneau's attempt to win votes for a broadened democracy by poetically clothing his Federalist adversaries in the raiment of English nobility. When Jefferson attempted to turn this symbol around and make a virtue of the plain and even careless dress and grooming he affected at his inauguration, the reaction was mixed at best. The creation of a positive emblem suggestive of the popular will in opposition to wealth and privilege was to be the work of another political generation.

SOURCE: This engraving appeared in Evart A. Duyckinck, *National Portrait Gallery of Eminent Americans*. New York, Johnson, Fry, 1864, vol. I. It was made from a painting by Alonzo Chappel probably based on a Gilbert Stuart portrait, c. 1807. Courtesy of the Library of Congress Prints and Photographs Division.

Portrait of Fisher Ames

Document II-4: BISHOP ON REPUBLICANISM

Between the arguments over the ratification of the Federal Constitution (see II-1) and the various conventions called to revise state constitutions (see II-6), the best vantage point for viewing the march toward increased democracy was the presidential election of 1800. No state was more shaken by this campaign than Connecticut, and no one was more successful at agitating his Connecticut neighbors than Abraham Bishop.

Bishop grew up in an orthodox Congregational family and did well at Yale. A stay in France, however, converted him to religious skepticism and strong advocacy of the natural rights of political man. Connecticut, during his absence, had escaped post-revolutionary turmoil, continuing under the unquestioned leadership of the propertied classes supported by the clergy. Apathy was the reigning mood, with the number of qualified voters shrinking, and the percentage of qualified voters exercising their rights dwindling even more.

In this atmosphere an unsuspecting Yale College invited Bishop to give the 1800 commencement address, expecting something staid and learned, preferably on the natural sciences. His remarks, from which the following are taken, were of course rejected in manuscript by the college; whereupon he engaged a neighboring hall and delivered his talk while the approved speaker enlightened an audience much reduced in number. Bishop's speech, widely distributed, opened the way for an organized party to support Jefferson in Connecticut.

This essay is not especially valuable for its argument on behalf of broadened suffrage, although it does place its main hope on "free and unbiased elections." What makes it unusual is its full and rhetorically mature identification of the factions and forces which the political reformer found inimical. Like Freneau he mistrusted the Anglophiles and excoriated any sign of emerging royalistic pretentions. Like Jefferson he mistrusted organized religion, especially when a powerful church made common cause with the party in office. More prophetic than characteristic of his times was Bishop's vilification of the middle man, the parasitic lawyer, and the "military-industrial alliance," as it would be called in the 1970s.

The reader may find more rhetoric than reason in these remarks. It should be remembered, though, that the only hope for Connecticut Jeffersonians was to arouse a politically dormant state. They had almost nothing to lose. Bishop became a prototype for many who have since argued against established privilege and for an extension of the democratic process.

SOURCE: Abraham Bishop, *Connecticut Republicanism: an Oration on the Extent and Power of Political Delusion. Delivered in New Haven, on the Evening preceding the Public Commencement, September, 1800.* Philadelphia, printed for Mathew Carey, November 13, 1800, pp. 3-7, 8-10, 40, 46-48, 56-58, abridged.

CONNECTICUT REPUBLICANISM

If our government has pursued the course dictated by the spirit of our revolution; if good government requires the subjugation of one half of the community; if republicans have deserved the lashes and contempt which have been most liberally dealt to them in this State for eleven years; or if the spirit of persecution has subsided: then the writer of these pages has been extremely unfortunate in the choice of his subject.

But Intolerance, with its hydra heads, still roams about the state, and no mercy is shewn to those, who doubt the wisdom of the present administration. The efforts of an individual are feeble when opposed to the phalanx which stand prepared to crush, in its infancy, freedom of enquiry and discussion. If these sentiments, claiming no high percentage, should fail of gaining the patronage of *numbers* in the state, they will be unable to endure even through the short period which generally bounds the existence of such ephemeral productions.

These pages present the corner-stone of an AMERICAN PALACE, and the dark vault where are to be entombed, in eternal sleep, the liberties and hopes of this, and future generations. The foundation of a MONARCHY is already laid in 6 per cent. 3 per cent. and deferred stock, in millions of civil list and indirect taxation. The aristocracies already formed, are to be the pillars of this magnificent building. The glory of this latter house is to transcend that of the edifice of freedom, which, erected on the ruins of palaces, lately presented a massy colonnade of human bones. What infant, in his nurse's arms, is to be the progenitor of an illustrious race of AMERICAN MONARCHS, is yet unknown.

Are such suggestions to be lightly regarded when it is now known, that a number of men, who have been our political leaders, were holding their meetings in the year 1787, to contrive ways and means for the establishment of what they termed, *A Confederated Monarchy* ? When we read the speech of General Hamilton, in the Federal Convention, and now find him at the head of our army? When we hear our leading men avow, that this country can never be governed without an *Hereditary Monarch* ? When we see the appropriate plans of *Monarchy* adopted by administration? When we read the federal papers filled with reflections on liberty and republicanism, and with praises of *Monarchical* government? When Fenno, the mouth-piece of the federal party, has just published a scheme of a *Federated, Presidential, Monarchical Aristocracy*?

In the following pages I have endeavored to represent *truly* the tendency of the leading measures of our government; and even if one half of my positions and conclusions be just, *a Monarchy is decidedly before us.* The men now in place have been the contrivers or advocates of these *measures.* If the people approve the *means* and the *end,* they will doubtless continue the instruments in operation; otherwise a new election will open to republicans a new and most desirable prospect.

Our southern brethren wonder that Connecticut, once the garden of liberty, should now appear to be the hot-bed of aristocracy—that Connecticut, internally the most democratic state in the union or in the world—a state, where the opinions of the people have governed for more than a century—where government is less expensive and energetic than in any other state—and where distinction of rank is hardly known, should be attached to expensive, energetic and aristocratic measures, tending to humble the people and to create odious distinctions: But the *people* of Connecticut have not deserved to lose the confidence of republicans: They are radically attached to the principles of 1776, and to the declaration of independence, and are mortal foes to hereditary monarchy; but by certain operations of federal policy . . . *the people* have no opportunity to express their opinions on federal men and measures.

If atheism and modern philosophy prevailed in the state, there might be some fear of the final prevalence of aristocracy; but *there is not an atheist in the state, nor a single modern philosopher among the republican party.* Deism is not prevalent; yet there are deists in both parties, whose infidelity has originated from causes wholly unconnected with politics. It has been suspected that some of the leading clergy wish to combine Church and State; but the body of the clergy, though they have preached Robison and Barruel rather freely, have good intentions, and as fast as they shall discover *the tendency of our measures to be against religion*, they will become good republicans. In the state are some hypocrites, who carry their religion to market, and are willing to take pay for it in public offices and honors; yet the number of these is small and will probably decrease.

For eleven years freedom of the press and of opinion has been restrained; federal measures have been presented to the people, *highly colored and embellished with cuts*; an habitual confidence in the state representation has been extended to the federal representation: After the exertions of the revolutionary war, the people, habitually industrious, retired to their farms and occupations, and the calm, which naturally succeeds the turbulence of war, superinduced by federal opiates, has hitherto preserved them in a state of peaceful submission to the constituted authorities.

But a season has now arrived, when "a little more sleep, a little more slumber, a little more folding of the hands to sleep," and they assuredly wake to a state of *political ruin* more dreadful to freemen than the ruins of empires. Our people are now rapidly declaring themselves on the republican side: The tendency of measures has roused them, and we shall finally prove to the world, that as Connecticut was among the *first to assert*, she will be among the *last to resign*, the blessings of equal government and the inestimable rights of man.

Political Delusion

On the eve of a day set apart for a literary feast of fat things, I have judged that a plain dish would be most acceptable. Indeed had it been assigned to me to speak to you of Greece and Rome; of the inexhaustible treasures of Hebrew, Greek, and Arabic, or to have discussed the height and diameter of the antediluvians, or to have explained the cause why a black man is not a white man, or why an elm-tree does not bear apricots: you must have sat here in silence, and the spirit would never have moved me to address you. Avoiding literary discussion, I have selected as the theme of this occasion, THE EXTENT AND POWER OF POLITICAL DELUSION . . .

The *object* of delusion is, to gain the wealth, honors and favors of men by cheap, false and insidious means.

The *subjects* of delusion are, the laboring and subordinate people throughout the world. Their toil goes to support the splendor, luxury and vices of the deluders, or their blood flows to satiate lawless ambition. Nearly the whole of Africa and a considerable part of Asia, are subject to the delusions of Europe: slaves in immense troops must sweat under a scorching sun to bear or follow the palanquin of a lordly master: slaves by ship-loads must be dragged from their homes to serve imperious tyrants; immense multitudes must be bowing to sticks and stones, or kneeling before images and lighted tapers, to gratify the zeal of imposters.

The *end* of delusion is, the elevation of the deluders to a condition of power, splendor and infallibility, and the reduction of the deluded from knowledge to ignorance, from freedom to slavery, from wealth to want, from present enjoyment to a destitution of all things, and from future hopes to ceaseless doubt. . . .

Having no leisure to make long porches, or to take by house-row, the measures of our government, I shall begin with the COMMERCIAL SYSTEM, which, like a common hall, gives you access to all the rooms of the federal building.

When republicans [The terms "republican and democrat," are used synonomously throughout: because the men who maintain the principles of 1776, are characterised by one or the other of these names in different parts of the country.] complain of a Navy, of diplomatic corps, of Algerine tribute, or British treaty, the uniform reply of the agents of delusion is, "all these things are necessary to commerce, and commerce is the handmaid of industry; abridge our political arrangements, say they, and all your well-earned produce would perish—your ship-timber and ships would be of no value—your seamen would become towns-poor —your rope-walks go to decay, and your merchants become bank-rupt!" . . .

The real object is diametrically opposite to the ostensible one. The agricultural interest, instead of being helped, is vitally attacked. This charming commercial system, so sedulously and artfully addressed to the yeomanry of our country, is a system of indebtedness and eventual bankruptcy. Confining the carrying trade to ourselves, opens an infinite field of credit to the merchant. Millions of property, belonging to the farmers, must constantly be in the hands of the merchants; for if the avails of our produce are to come from all quarters of the globe, there must be an average credit given by the farmers till the returns can be made. This draws on to the water an immense quantity of property, and interests the farmers strongly in the success of the merchants whom they have trusted. This property on the water is within fiscal purview and control. Government has purposes to answer. The merchant is indirectly the collector of a great portion of the revenue. The merchant can lend ships and cargoes to government. The merchant can plan long, circuitous and hazardous voyages apparently at his own risque; but really at the risque of the farmer; for all losses must eventually fall on those who trust. These arrangements lead up great capitals in trade, great bankruptcies and great fortunes. They fill the sea with vessels and sailors,. valuable auxiliaries and reverberators to a naval system. This last being calculated to protect the merchants, secures their perpetual attachment, and they freely advocate the extraordinary expenses of an armament. Their influence is thrown directly in the scale opposed to the farmer, and government has thereby secured a number of capitalists to whom resort may be had in the day when grinding runs low at the treasury.

Before the adoption of this system silver and gold moved according to the laws of industry; but now banks are introduced, giving to paper a forced and unnatural circulation, taking the command of the medium of all business from the agricultural interest,[1] and yielding it wholly to the commercial.

It is no wonder that in the complexity of this policy, the farmer is lost in the midst of paper bills, boundless credit, crouded harbors, princely estates, and made to cry out. O! the depth of the wisdom of administration! little dreaming that he has in fact paid and is paying annually the whole profits of the carrying trade, the whole of the Algerine tribute, the expense of all commercial treaties—of all the consuls abroad—the amount of all the losses by sea—of all bad markets, and of all navy expenses—that the money, which he pays, suffers many sweatings before it gets to the treasury, and that what he does not pay is placed on interest, and that the land from which he raises this produce, which excites such a fatherly care of government, is pledged for the payment of

[1]Money ought to represent industry; the farmer's dollars earned by labor do represent it: bank bills do not. It is hard on the farmer, that the man who earns nothing through the year, should be able with an indorsed note to raise in an hour, double the annual avails of his farm, and to glut the market with money at the very moment when the farmer is ready to bring his dollars to market. Directors of banks can make money scarce or plenty as they please; but though banks are ruinous to the farmers, they are necessary to a forced commerce.

principal and interest, and that his children may always see the date and amount of the mortgage by calling on the surveyors of the revenue. Little short of miracle can redeem men from such masterly strokes of delusion. . . .

For my own part, I am willing to be governed by men greater, wiser and richer than myself: but have no opinion of having men so great that their altitude must be taken by a quadrant and their width by a four rod chain: through excessive indulgence we have, already, a number of men too great for a republic. How comes it that these great men are so very fit to govern? Internal government is designed to control inordinate passions: great men are most proud, avaricious, and tyrannical: will you then select these to curb pride, avarice and tyranny? Republican society is to protect the weak against the strong: but, if the strong are to have all the power the weak will be oppressed. But says one and another, what will become of our great men? My answer is, that they always had address enough to work their own passages. The great host of mankind, the nine-tenths, are those, which a republican government ought to concern itself about; and if this is faithfully attended to, the other tenth will still gain such a portion of power and money as will make them useful instead of dangerous. They are the very men for your purposes whenever you have reduced them to the standard weight and measure of the people.

I am well aware of the great convenience which many of you find in keeping close to these knowing men, in gathering the crumbs which fall from the tables of the rich, and in sailing under the lee of the ecclesiastical convoy ships; but you are taking a bad road: it is a broad road; it is *the* broad road: thousands have paid turnpike toll on it before you were born; and, if you follow it, it may lead you to wealth and honors; it may ruin your country; but will certainly land you where it has landed all your predecessors.

Having little confidence in addressing placemen, court sycophants and those who expect the wages of hirelings, I turn to the last general head of political delusions, which is the subject of ELECTIONS TO OFFICE. . . .

Look at once on the aristocracies, which I have named to you, consider their wealth, their force, their subtlety, the immense interests which they have at stake; remember that these furnish the men, who, in the definition of my subject, were stiled the prime agents of delusion, who know the heart and the avenues to the passions, and who can place before you, with strong impressions, every conceivable motive of hope and fear. Your treasury, supplied with your own money, is to operate against your freedom of election. See the host of your brethren, who depend on that treasury. Tens of thousands of men in our country live on the people: but independent of them and their weight and influence is found mostly in the governing scale. If the first officers lose their election the subordinate ones may lose their offices and emoluments: therefore every new election has exactly all their influence, and generally that of all their connections to balance against an impartial issue, and by all that influence which is incalculably great and increasing those in place have a chance of re-election superior to those not in place. This idea opens to you the inducement which the higher officers have to lead up a funding system, an army, a navy, federal city, valuation tax. All these things lead to new appointments in abundance, to a system of favor,[2] which engages a host of expectants in addition to the successful candidates and whenever these offices amount sufficiently to create a moral certainty of re-election,[3] the government ceases to be republican: you may then call it an oligarchy or a monarchy: to the people it matters not what it is.

But these great men and privileged orders do not oppose to you their single votes; they have about them a host of sycophants or dependants, who must vote according to orders: but not to this false influence alone is Delusion confined. The characters, principles and feelings, of those who are opposed to present men and measures are to be torn in pieces. The election ball is not well opened, till the republicans are bleeding at every pore. The 4th of July occasions,[4] which you imagined yourselves to have earned, have been wrested from you and they have been perverted into days for chastising the enemies of administration by the odious characters of illuminatists, disorganizers and atheists: but as our Indian tribes, when they are torturing a prisoner, suffer him, in the interval of his torments, to sit and smoke or eat with them; so have these federal gentlemen, after a public wounding of you in every part, suffered you to dine with them, to toast men, whom you regard as despoilers of your

[2]Had the constitution vested appointments in a committee to be changed every two years, some evils now experienced would have been avoided: perhaps an amendment on this part would be fully as valuable as an amendment aimed at the person of Albert Gallatin.

[3]Elections would be well guarded if officers of government could be excluded from voting. Their votes and influence cannot be impartial.

[4]These days have been eminently improved to serve the purposes of elections, and to sow the seeds of *federal wrath and animosity.*

rights; and to join them in copious libations to principles and measures, which you hold in abhorrence; and, the penalty for your neglecting or refusing to do and suffer the whole measure of torment has been, to hold you up as a hissing and a bye-word, as jacobins, anarchists, and fit companions for infernal spirits. Such has been part of the system of tyranny, which, even before our own eyes, has been acted repeatedly on the memorable anniversaries of our independence. Happy would it be were this confined to the great cities; but our government has led up a number of little aristocracies no bigger than pea-brush in our small towns—where either priest or lawyer, or federal officers, or modern whigs and their associates, must, like their superiors, be lording it over the poor convicted democrats. . . .

On this subject of elections, delusion always ralies a great cry about the *ins* and *outs*, and it is said by the *ins*, that the *outs* wish to be *in*. This is always said by the same class of men; but how can it be true in the present case; for, according to their own statement, the public officers retire poor and the others could do better at home. Now one or the other side of this proposition must be true. If then theirs be true, that there are constant outgoings of disinterestedness and patriotism, why so unwilling that others should share the burden? Is it because they would not govern as well as you? Suffer me to say you are miserable judges on this point, and your modesty ought to preclude the suggestion. But suppose there are immense advantages attached to the ins; such as the holding as tenants in common all the power in the country; distributing all the money, all the offices; living on the best, keeping the first of company; forming important connections and providing for friends.[5] "If, says the venerable Pelatiah Webster, "the ins do not know how to appreciate such advantages, I pity not them so much as the fools who send them." The six dollars a-day, or four or five or twenty thousand dollars a year, form the smallest item in the account. Will you say, "we have responsibility to balance these extras"? Tell of the responsibility of nine-pins and rattle-boxes! Pray where is your *ability* to respond, if by your mismanagement you take millions of money from the people, or waste thousands of lives in a useless quarrel? Open your purses and see whether you have small change to pay for principles dearly assumed, but idly sacrificed; for expected blessings, thro' your means, turned into curses founded on

---

[5] And speculating in land-warrants.

interminable interest; for rational freedom turned, by your delusive measures, into slavery unchangeable. Will you say that your characters are to pay the bill? alas! while the scrutiny is making they will vanish. This responsibility is all a delusion. The ins have privileges in abundance, and it was once said that in a free government these should be in rotation. Will you say that all mankind are alike, and in similar situations would equally betray?[6] Be it so, when the people let the power go out of their own hands they will always be betrayed. Take away the sovereignty of the people, *which always rests in unbiassed[7] elections*, and all the rest is not worth contending for. Take this away, and it is of no moment to the people who is president or vice-president—who are senators and members, or who are the heads of departments; for when that is gone, all the rest will sooner or later go: but 'tis of infinite moment to the people to know and feel, that if the elected do not conform, they shall not be re-elected. This forms a responsibility, which once established, might preserve a free republic for ever; and this maxim is the corner stone of republicanism. This is the rock founded on which a building would stand strong in the day of the floods and winds. Republicanism may bid defiance to delusion, whenever the people shall have firmness and weight enough to balance president, vice-president, senators, representatives, heads of department, diplomatic corps, army, navy, together with all the subordinate agents which new measures place it in the power of rulers to appoint and support independent of them.

[6]A merchant turns out of employ the man who is ruining him. He never waits to philosophise and say, 'Why all men are knaves. This man has almost ruined me and I may as well become bankrupt through his means as through another's.'

[7]Unbiased by falsehood, clerical influence and terrorism: the bias of truth can do no wrong. Opposition to false bias serves the cause of truth, and produces a reaction, dreadful to political importance.

Document II-5: JEFFERSON ON POLITICAL CHANGE

In the conceptualization of forms and values in the early days of the nation, it is hard to imagine anyone surpassing Thomas Jefferson. Jefferson had special importance to his many contemporaries who were not willing to accept the Revolution and the Constitution as victories so glorious that they made future change unnecessary. These men were the first to fight the idea that tampering with the work of the Founding Fathers was a form of sacrilege.

In the document following this one, David Buel can be seen walking the difficult line between respect for tradition and argument for change. Jefferson took quick advantage of his charter membership among the Founding Fathers to forgive and criticize his own generation simultaneously, thus paving the way for his ideas on extensions of democracy and on the necessity and virtue of change.

Jefferson wrote this letter at the age of seventy-three, finished with officeholding, and free of campaign axes to grind. Never did he express more succinctly the combination of theory and device that made him so essential to any appreciation of American politics. Note how uncompromising was his devotion to direct democracy, right down to ward level, and including the election of judges and juries. Note his confidence, too, in the ability of the rational mind to make democracy work. His connection of a purer democracy with the war on privilege comes through most strongly in the paragraph opening "I have thrown out the loose heads of amendment. . . ."

This letter is appropriate here as a demonstration of the leadership Jefferson provided his contemporaries, even after his presidency, in the continuing improvement of democracy. More generally and lastingly important than any specific relevance, however, is the magnificent manifesto on change which occupies the long paragraph second from the end and which may serve as preamble for the causes of reformers of all persuasions in all ages hence.

SOURCE: Paul L. Ford, ed., *The Writings of Thomas Jefferson.* New York, Putnam's, 1899, vol. X, pp. 37-45.

LETTER TO SAMUEL KERCHEVAL

MONTICELLO, July 12, 1816.

SIR,—I duly received your favor of June the 13th, with the copy of the letters on the calling a convention, on which you are pleased to ask my opinion. I have not been in the habit of mysterious reserve on any subject, nor of buttoning up my opinions within my own doublet. On the contrary, while in public service especially, I thought the public entitled to frankness, and intimately to know whom they employed. But I am now retired: I resign myself, as a passenger, with confidence to those at present at the helm, and ask but for rest, peace and good will. The question you propose, on equal representation, has become a party one, in which I wish to take no public share. Yet, if it be asked for your own satisfaction only, and not to be quoted before the public, I have no motive to withhold it, and the less from you, as it coincides with your own. At the birth of our republic, I committed that opinion to the world, in the draught of a constitution annexed to the "Notes on Virginia," in which a provision was inserted for a representation permanently equal. The infancy of the subject at that moment, and our inexperience of self-government, occasioned gross departures in that draught from genuine republican canons. In truth, the abuses of monarchy had so much filled all the space of political contemplation, that we imagined everything republican which was not monarchy. We had not yet penetrated to the mother principle, that "governments are republican only in proportion as they embody the will of their people, and execute it." Hence, our first constitutions had really no leading principles in them. But experience and reflection have but more and more confirmed me in the particular importance of the equal representation then proposed. On that point, then, I am entirely in sentiment with your letters; and only lament that a copy-right of your pamphlet prevents their appearance in the newspapers, where alone they would be generally read, and produce general effect. The present vacancy, too, of other matter, would give them place in every paper, and bring the question home to every man's conscience.

But inequality of representation in both Houses of our legislature, is not the only republican heresy in this first essay of our revolutionary patriots at forming a constitution. For let it be agreed that a government is republican in proportion as every member composing it has his equal voice in the direction of its concerns (not indeed in person, which would be impracticable beyond the limits of a city, or small township, but) by representatives chosen by himself, and responsible to him at short periods, and let us bring to the test of this canon every branch of our constitution.

In the legislature, the House of Representatives is chosen by less than half the people, and not at all in proportion to those who do choose. The Senate are still more disproportionate, and for long terms of irresponsibility. In the Executive, the Governor is entirely independent of the choice of the people, and of their control; his Council equally so, and at best but a fifth wheel to a wagon. In the Judiciary, the judges of the highest courts are dependent on none but themselves. In England, where judges were named and removable at the will of an hereditary executive, from which branch most misrule was feared, and has flowed, it was a great point gained, by fixing them for life, to make them independent of that executive. But in a government founded on the public will, this principle operates in an opposite direction, and against that will. There, too, they were still removable on a concurrence of the executive and legislative branches. But we have made them independent of the nation itself. They are irremovable, but by their own body, for any depravities of conduct, and even by their own body for the imbecilities of dotage. The justices of the inferior courts are self-chosen, are for life, and perpetuate their own body in succession forever, so that a faction once possessing themselves of the bench of a county, can never be broken up, but hold their county in chains, forever indissoluble. Yet these justices are the real executive as well as judiciary, in all our minor and most ordinary concerns. They tax us at will; fill the office of sheriff, the most important of all the executive officers of the county; name nearly all our military leaders, which leaders, once named, are removable but by themselves. The juries, our judges of all fact, and of law when they choose it, are not selected by the people, nor amenable to them. They are chosen by an officer named by the court and executive. Chosen, did I say? Picked up by the sheriff from the loungings of the court yard, after everything respectable has retired from it. When then is our republicanism to be found? Not in our constitution certainly, but merely in the spirit of our people. That would oblige even a despot to govern us republicanly. Owing to this spirit, and to nothing in the form of our constitution, all things have gone well. But this fact, so triumphantly misquoted by the enemies of reformation, is not the fruit of our constitution, but has prevailed in spite of it. Our functionaries have done well, because generally honest men. If any were not so, they feared to show it.

But it will be said, it is easier to find faults than to amend them. I do not think their amendment so difficult as is pretended. Only lay down true principles, and adhere to them inflexibly. Do not be frightened into their surrender by the alarms of the timid, or the croakings of wealth against the ascendency of the people. If experience be called for, appeal to that of our fifteen or twenty governments for forty years, and show me where the people have done half the mischief in these forty years, that a single despot would have done in a single year; or show half the riots and rebellions, the crimes and the punishments, which have taken place in any single nation, under kingly government, during the same period. The true foundation of republican government is the equal right of every citizen, in his person and property, and in their management. Try by this, as a tally, every provision of our constitution, and see if it hangs directly on the will of the people. Reduce your legislature to a convenient number for full, but orderly discussion. Let every man who fights or pays, exercise his just and equal right in their election. Submit them to approbation or rejection at short intervals. Let the executive be chosen in the same way, and for the same term, by those whose agent he is to be; and leave no screen of a council behind which to skulk for responsibility. It has been thought that the people are not competent electors of judges *learned in the law*. But I do not know that this is true, and, if doubtful, we should follow principle. In this, as in many other elections, they would be guided by reputation, which would not err oftener, perhaps, than the present mode of appointment. In one State of the Union, at least, it has long been tried, and with the most satisfactory success. The judges of Connecticut have been chosen by the people every six months, for nearly two centuries, and I believe there has hardly ever been an instance of change; so powerful is the curb of incessant responsibility. If prejudice, however, derived from a monarchichal institution, is still to prevail against the vital elective principle of our own, and if the existing example among ourselves of periodical election of judges by the people be still mistrusted, let us at least not adopt the evil, and reject the good, of the English precedent; let us retain amovability on the concurrence of the executive and legislative branches, and nomination by the executive alone. Nomination to office is an executive function. To give it to the legislature, as we do, is a violation of the principle of the separation of powers. It swerves the members from correctness, by temptations to intrigue for office themselves, and to a corrupt barter of votes; and destroys responsibility to dividing it among a multitude. By leaving nomination in its proper place, among executive functions, the principle of the distribution of power is preserved, and responsibility weighs with its heaviest force on a single head.

The organization of our county administrations may be thought more difficult. But follow principle, and the knot unties itself. Divide the counties into wards of such size as that every citizen can attend, when called on, and act in person. Ascribe to them the government of their wards in all things relating to themselves exclusively. A justice, chosen by themselves, in each, a constable, a military company, a patrol, a school, the care of their own poor, their own portion of the public roads, the choice of one or more jurors to serve in some court, and the delivery, within their own wards, of their own votes for all elective officers of higher sphere, will relieve the county administration of nearly all its business, will have it better done, and by making every citizen an acting member of the government, and in the offices nearest and most interesting to him, will attach him by his strongest feelings to the independence of his country, and its republican constitution. The justices thus chosen by every ward, would constitute the county court, would do its judiciary business, direct roads and bridges, levy county and poor rates, and administer all the matters of common interest to the whole country. These wards, called townships in New England, are the vital principle of their governments, and have proved themselves the wisest invention ever devised by the wit of man for the perfect exercise of self-government, and for its preservation. We should thus marshal our government into, 1, the general federal republic, for all concerns foreign and federal: 2, that of the State, for what relates to our own citizens exclusively; 3, the county republics, for the duties and concerns of the county; and 4, the ward republics, for the small, and yet numerous and interesting concerns of the neighborhood; and in government, as well as in every other business of life, it is by division and subdivision of duties alone, that all matters, great and small, can be managed to perfection. And the whole is cemented by giving to every citizen, personally, a part in the administration of the public affairs.

The sum of these amendments is, 1. General Suffrage. 2. Equal representation in the legislature. 3. An executive chosen by the people. 4. Judges elective or amovable. 5. Justices, jurors, and sheriffs elective. 6. Ward divisions. and 7. Periodical amendments of the constitution.

I have thrown out these as loose heads of amendment, for consideration and correction; and their object is to secure self-government by the republicanism of our constitution, as well as by the spirit of the people;

and to nourish and perpetuate that spirit. I am not among those who fear the people. They, and not the rich, are our dependence for continued freedom. And to preserve their independence, we must not let our rulers load us with perpetual debt. We must make our election between *economy and liberty,* or *profusion and servitude.* If we run into such debts, as that we must be taxed in our meat and in our drink, in our necessaries and our comforts, in our labors and our amusements, for our callings and our creeds, as the people of England are, our people, like them, must come to labor sixteen hours in the twenty-four, give the earnings of fifteen of these to the government for their debts and daily expenses; and the sixteenth being insufficient to afford us bread, we must live, as they now do, on oatmeal and potatoes; have no time to think, no means of calling the mismanagers to account; but be glad to obtain subsistence by hiring ourselves to rivet their chains on the necks of our fellow-sufferers. Our landholders, too, like theirs, retaining indeed the title and stewardship of estates called theirs, but held really in trust for the treasury, must wander, like theirs, in foreign countries, and be contented with penury, obscurity, exile, and the glory of the nation. This example reads to us the salutary lesson, that private fortunes are destroyed by public as well as by private extravagance. And this is the tendency of all human governments. A departure from principle in one instance becomes a precedent for a second; that second for a third; and so on, till the bulk of the society is reduced to be mere automatons of misery, and to have no sensibilities left but for sinning and suffering. Then begins, indeed, the *bellum omnium in omnia,* which some philosophers observing to be so general in this world, have mistaken it for the natural, instead of the abusive state of man. And the fore horse of this frightful team is public debt. Taxation follows that, and in its train wretchedness and oppression.

Some men look at constitutions with sanctimonious reverence, and deem them like the arc of the covenant, too sacred to be touched. They ascribe to the men of the preceding age a wisdom more than human, and suppose what they did to be beyond amendment. I knew that age well; I belonged to it, and labored with it. It deserved well of its country. It was very like the present, but without the experience of the present; and forty years of experience in government is worth a century of bookreading; and this they would say themselves, were they to rise from the dead. I am certainly not an advocate for frequent and untried changes in laws and constitutions. I think moderate imperfections had better be borne with; because, when once known, we accommodate ourselves to them, and find practical means of correcting their ill effects. But I know also, that laws and institutions must go hand in hand with the progress of the human mind. As that becomes more developed, more enlightened, as new discoveries are made, new truths disclosed, and manners and opinions change with the change of circumstances, institutions must advance also, and keep pace with the times. We might as well require a man to wear still the coat which fitted him when a boy, as civilized society to remain ever under the regimen of their barbarous ancestors. It is this preposterous idea which has lately deluged Europe in blood. Their monarchs, instead of wisely yielding to the gradual change of circumstances, of favoring progressive accommodation to progressive improvement, have clung to old abuses, entrenched themselves behind steady habits, and obliged their subjects to seek through blood and violence rash and ruinous innovations, which, had they been referred to the peaceful deliberations and collected wisdom of the nation, would have been put into acceptable and salutary forms. Let us follow no such examples, nor weakly believe that one generation is not as capable as another of taking care of itself, and of ordering its own affairs. Let us, as our sister States have done, avail ourselves of our reason and experience, to correct the crude essays of our first and unexperienced, although wise, virtuous, and well-meaning councils. And lastly, let us provide in our constitution for its revision at stated periods. What these periods should be, nature herself indicates. By the European tables of mortality, of the adults living at any one moment of time, a majority will be dead in about nineteen years. At the end of that period, then, a new majority is come into place; or, in other words, a new generation. Each generation is as independent as the one preceding, as that was of all which had gone before. It has then, like them, a right to choose for itself the form of government it believes most promotive of its own happiness; consequently, to accommodate to the circumstances in which it finds itself, that received from its predecessors; and it is for the peace and good of mankind, that a solemn opportunity of doing this every nineteen or twenty years, should be provided by the constitution; so that it may be handed on, with periodical repairs, from generation to generation, to the end of time, if anything human can so long endure. It is now forty years since the constitution of Virginia was formed. The same tables inform us, that, within that period, two-thirds of the adults then living are now dead. Have then the remaining third, even if they had the wish, the right to hold in obedience to their will, and to laws heretofore made by them, the other two-thirds, who, with themselves, compose the present mass of adults? If they have not, who has? The dead? But the dead have no rights. They are nothing; and nothing cannot own something. Where there is no substance, there can be no accident. This corporeal globe, and everything upon it, belong to its present corporeal inhabitants, during their generation. They alone have a right to direct what is the concern of themselves alone, and to declare the law of that direction; and this declaration can only be made by their majority. That majority, then, has a right to depute representatives to a convention, and to make the constitution what they think will be the best for themselves. But how collect their voice? This is the real difficulty. If invited by private authority, or county or district meetings, these divisions are so large that few will attend; and their voice will be imperfectly, or falsely pronounced. Here, then, would be one of the advantages of the ward divisions I have proposed. The mayor of every ward, on a question like the present, would call his ward together, take the simple yea or nay of its members, convey these to the county court, who would hand on those of all its wards to the proper general authority; and the voice of the whole people would be thus fairly, fully, and peaceably expressed, discussed, and decided by the common reason of the society. If this avenue be shut to the call of sufferance, it will make itself heard through that of force, and we shall go on, as other nations are doing, in the endless circle of oppression, rebellion, reformation; and oppression, rebellion, reformation, again; and so on forever.

These, Sir, are my opinions of the governments we see among men, and of the principles by which alone we may prevent our own from falling into the same dreadful track. I have given them at greater length than your letter called for. But I cannot say things by halves; and I confide them to your honor, so to use them as to preserve me from the gridiron of the public papers. If you shall approve and enforce them, as you have done that of equal representation, they may do some good. If not, keep them to yourself as the effusions of withered age and useless time. I shall, with not the less truth, assure you of my great respect and consideration.

[Thomas Jefferson]

Document II-6: BUEL ON EXTENSION OF SUFFRAGE

The first document in this section, together with the present one, call attention to a peculiarly American agency for change, the constitutional convention. The popularity of this kind of device may stem from such unrelated national characteristics as gregariousness and respect for the printed word. Yet the fact is that the Articles of Confederation were not allowed, like the English articles of government, to evolve gradually with paste and scissors, like a scrapbook on the polity. Rather, the summer of 1787 gave forth an entire new document which has served with surprisingly few amendments since. The states not only went through a process of establishing their post-colonial governmental structures during the early days of the Revolution but reassembled, after the smoke had cleared and the character of the new nation more clearly expressed itself, to make more careful constitutions.

In spite of their preference for high-sounding, carefully articulated documents, Americans have not regarded their constitutions as cast in bronze. Change can be wrought by electing a new set of officials under an existing constitution, but change can also be brought about by altering the document itself, as has been done with varying periodicity in the several states. The process still goes on.

David Buel, Jr., and his colleagues at the New York Constitutional Convention of 1821 found themselves in a difficult position. The principles they had adopted under the leadership of the Founding Fathers seemed in need of change. Yet most of these patriarchs were still alive; the few who had died were reverently remembered. Thus considerable ingenuity was devoted to walking the reformer's tightrope: promoting change without offending the reputation of the revered forebears.

Buel's remarks have attracted the attention of political scientists because of the careful and extensive treatment of the suffrage question, particularly in response to those who feared that a broadening of the suffrage would endanger private property. Indeed, one should note the range and effect of the arguments against property. But this speech is remarkable for other reasons. Interwoven into many of these appeals were some very persuasive expressions of hope for an open society where upward mobility was to be the pattern. Here was a very early and impressively thoughtful consideration of how social mobility and economic opportunity must be written into the articles of a democratic government.

SOURCE: Nathaniel H. Carter and William L. Stone, reporters; Marcus T. C. Gould, stenographer, *Reports of the Proceedings and Debates of the Convention of 1821, Assembled for the Purpose of Amending the Constitution of the State of New York.* Albany, Hosford, 1821, pp. 239-244, abridged.

NEW YORK CONSTITUTIONAL CONVENTION

MR. BUEL. . . . The question whether it is safe and proper to extend the right of suffrage to other classes of our citizens, besides the landholders, is decided as I think, by the sober sense and deliberate acts of the great American people. To this authority I feel willing to bow. An examination of the constitutions of the different states, will show us that those enlightened bodies of statesmen and patriots who have from time to time been assembled for the grave and important purpose of forming and reforming the constitutions of the states—have sanctioned and established as a maxim, the opinion that there is no danger in confiding the most extensive right of suffrage to the intelligent population of these United States.

Of the twenty four states which compose this union, twelve states require only a certain time of residence as a qualification to vote for all their elective officers—eight require in addition to residence the payment of taxes or the performance of militia duty—four states only *require* a freehold qualification, viz. New-York, North-Carolina, Virginia, and Rhode-Island. The distinction which the amendment of the gentleman from Albany proposes to continue, exists only in the constitution of this state, and in that of North-Carolina.

In some of the states, the possession of a freehold, constitutes one of several qualifications, either of which gives the right of suffrage; but in four only, is the exclusive right of voting for any department of the government confined to Landholders.

The progressive extension of the right of suffrage by the reformations which have taken place in several of the state constitutions, adds to the force of the authority. By the original constitution of Maryland, (made in

1776,) a considerable property qualification was necessary to constitute an elector. By successive alterations in the years 1802, and 1810, the right has been extended to all the white citizens who have a permanent residence in the state. A similar alteration has been made in the constitution of South-Carolina; and by the recent reformations in the constitutions of Connecticut and Massachusetts, property qualifications in the electors have been abolished; the right is extended in the former almost to universal suffrage, and in the latter to all the citizens who pay taxes. It is not in the smaller states only, that these liberal principles respecting suffrage, have been adopted. The constitution of Pennsylvania, adopted in the year 1790, extends the right of suffrage to all the citizens who pay taxes, and to their sons between the age of twenty-one and twenty-two years.

That constitution was formed by men, distinguished for patriotism and talents. At the head of them, we find the name of Judge Wilson, a distinguished statesman, and one of the founders of the constitution of the United States.

The constitution of Pennsylvania was formed on the broad principle of suffrage, which that distinguished man lays down in his writings. "That every citizen whose circumstances do not render him necessarily dependant on the will of another, should possess a vote in electing those, by whose conduct his property, his reputation, his liberty, and his life may be almost materially affected." This is the correct rule, and it has been adopted into the constitution of every state which has been formed since the government of the United States was organized. So universal an admission of the great principle of general suffrage, by the Conventions of discreet and sober minded men, who have been engaged in forming or amending the different constitutions, produces a strong conviction that the principle is safe and salutary.

It is said by those who contend that the right of voting for senators should be confined to the landholders, that the framers of our constitution were wise and practical men, and that they deemed this distinction essential to the security of the landed property; and that we have not encountered any evils from it during the forty years experience which we have had. To this I answer, that if the restriction of the right of suffrage has produced no positive evil, it cannot be shown to have produced any good results.

The qualifications for assembly voters, under the existing constitution, are as liberal as any which will probably be adopted by this Convention. Is it pretended that the assembly, during the forty-three years experience which we have enjoyed under our constitution, has been, in any respect, inferior to the senate? Has the senate, although elected exclusively by freeholders, been composed of men of more talents, or greater probity, than the assembly? Have the rights of property, generally, or of the landed interest in particular, been more vigilantly watched, and more carefully protected by the senate than by the assembly? I might appeal to the journals of the two houses, and to the recollections and information of the members of the committee on this subject; but it is unnecessary, as I understand the gentlemen who support the amendment, distinctly admit, that hitherto the assembly has been as safe a depository of the rights of the landed interest, as the senate. But it is supposed that the framers of our constitution must have had wise and cogent reasons for making such a distinction between the electors of the different branches of the government. May we not, however, without the least derogation from the wisdom and good intentions of the framers of our constitution, ascribe the provision in question to circumstances which then influenced them, but which no longer ought to have weight?

When our constitution was framed, the domain of the state was in the hands of a few. The proprietors of the great manors were almost the only men of great influence; and the landed property was deemed worthy of almost exclusive consideration. Before the revolution, freeholders only were allowed to exercise the right of suffrage. The notions of our ancestors, in regard to real property, were all derived from England. The feudal tenures were universally adopted. The law of primogeniture, by which estates descended to the eldest son, and the rule of descent by which the male branches inherited the paternal estate, to the exclusion of the female, entails, and many other provisions of feudal origin were in force. The tendency of this system, it is well understood, was to keep the lands of the state in few hands. But since that period, by the operation of wiser laws, and by the prevalence of juster principles, an entire revolution has taken place in regard to real property. Our laws for regulating descents, and for converting entailed estates into fee-simple, have gradually increased the number of landholders: Our territory has been rapidly divided and subdivided: And although the landed interest is no longer controlled by the influence of a few great proprietors, its aggregate importance is vastly increased, and almost the whole community have become interested in its protection. In New-England, the inhabitants, from the earliest period, have enjoyed the system which we are progressively attaining to. There, the property of the soil has always been in the hands of the *many*. The great bulk of the population are farmers and freeholders, yet no provision is incorporated in their constitution, excluding those who are not freeholders from a full participation in the right of suffrage. May we not trace the notions of the framers of our constitution respecting the exclusive privilege of the freeholders, to the same source from whence they derived all their ideas of real property? . . .

It is conceded by my honourable friend, that the great landed estates must be cut up by the operation of our laws of descent; that we have already seen those laws effect a great change; and that it is the inevitable tendency of our rules of descent, to divide up our territory into farms of moderate size. The real property, therefore, will be in the hands of the *many*. But in England, and other European kingdoms, it is the policy of the aristocracy to keep the lands in few hands. The laws of primogeniture, the entailments and family settlements, all tend to give a confined direction to the course of descents. Hence we find in Europe, the landed estates possessed by a few rich men; and the great bulk of the population poor, and without that attachment to the government which is found among the owners of the soil. Hence, also, the poor envy and hate the rich, and mobs and insurrections sometimes render property insecure. Did I believe that our population would degenerate into such a state, I should, with the advocates for the amendment, hesitate in extending the right of suffrage; but I confess I have no such fears. I have heretofore had doubts respecting the safety of adopting the principles of a suffrage as extensive as that now contemplated. I have given to the subject the best reflection of which I am capable; and I have satisfied myself, that there is no danger in adopting those liberal principles which are incorporated in almost all the constitutions of these United States.

There are in my judgment, many circumstances which will forever preserve the people of this state from the vices and the degradation of European population, beside those which I have already taken notice of. The provision already made for the establishment of common schools, will, in a very few years, extend the benefit of education to all our citizens. The universal diffusion of information will forever distinguish our population from that of Europe. Virtue and intelligence are the true basis on which every republican government must rest. When these are lost, freedom will no longer exist. The diffusion of education is the only sure means of establishing these pillars of freedom. I rejoice in this view of the subject, that our common school fund will (if the report on the legislative department be adopted,) be consecrated by a constitutional provision; and I feel no apprehension, for myself, or my posterity, in confiding the right of suffrage to the great mass of such a population as I believe ours will always be. . . .

I contend, that by the true principle of our government, property, as such, is not the basis of representation. Our community is an association of persons—of human beings—not a partnership founded on property. The declared object of the people of this state in associating, was, to "establish such a government as they deemed best calculated to secure the rights and liberties of the good people of the state, and most conducive to their happiness and safety." Property, it is admitted, is one of the rights to be protected and secured; and although the protection of life and liberty is the highest object of attention, it is certainly true, that the security of property is a most interesting and important object in every free government. Property is essential to our temporal happiness; and is necessarily one of the most interesting subjects of legislation. The desire of acquiring property is a universal passion. I readily give to property the important place which has been assigned to it by the honourable member from Albany (Chancellor Kent.) To property we are indebted for most of our comforts, and for much of our temporal happiness. The numerous religious, moral, and benevolent institutions which are every where established, owe their existence to wealth; and it is wealth which enables us to make those great internal improvements which we have undertaken. Property is only one of the incidental rights of the person who possesses it; and, as such, it must be made secure; but it does not follow, that it must therefore be represented specifically in any branch of the government. It ought, indeed, to have an influence—and it ever will have, when properly enjoyed. So ought talents to have an influence. It is certainly as important to have men of good talents in your legislature, as to have men of property; but you surely would not set up men of talents as a separate order, and give them exclusive privileges.

The truth is, that both wealth and talents will ever have a great influence; and without the aid of exclusive privileges, you will always find the influence of both wealth and talents predominant in our halls of legislation.

I will present to the committee only one additional consideration. The gentleman, who introduced the amendment, has cited a passage from the writings of the immortal Hamilton, in support of his proposition.

The opinions of that profound statesman, I shall ever regard with the highest reverence. But surely the passage cited from the Federalist, gives no support to the doctrine now contended for; but if I mistake not, the pages of that celebrated work furnish the strongest illustration of the doctrine for which I contend. I will not cite any particular passages to this committee, from a work so familiar as the Federalist must be, to every man who has studied the structure of our government. I will only refer to the general reasoning adopted by the writers of that work, to demonstrate the wisdom of the provisions in our national constitution, in regard to the qualifications of electors and elected. In discussing that important subject, and also the power of taxation confided to the general government, those illustrious statesmen have most satisfactorily shown it to be a prominent feature in the constitution of the United States, and one of its greatest excellencies, that orders and classes of men, would not, and ought not, as such, to be represented; that every citizen, qualified by his talents or his virtues, should be eligible to a seat in either branch of the national legislature, without regard to his occupation or class in society. And it was predicted and expected that men of every class and profession, would find their way to the legislature of the union. That, more safety to the rights of every class, would be found in such an organization; and that although the landed interest would always probably predominate, the rights of all would be more carefully attended to, and more effectually secured, than they would have been, had orders and classes of men been represented as such. The framers of our constitution placed their confidence in the virtue and intelligence of the great mass of the American people. It was their triumphant boast to have formed a government which should "establish justice, ensure domestic tranquility, provide for the common defence, promote the general welfare, and secure the blessings of liberty," without recognizing or creating any odious distinctions, or giving any preference to any particular classes or orders of men. Hence our members of congress are elected by the great body of our citizens. Surely it is as safe to confide to them the election of state senators, as that of national representatives. To congress is confided the high power of declaring war and levying taxes. Their power over property is at least as great as the state legislature possesses. If it is safe to trust the destinies of the nation to men chosen by the same electors who choose our members of assembly, can it be less safe to entrust to that class of electors the right of choosing our state senators? I know that if the right of suffrage is extended; if the distinction between electors for senate and assemblymen is abolished it can never be recalled. I have on that account, attentively reflected on the probable consequence of doing away the distinction, and have satisfied myself that it will be safe, and that it is expedient. The distinction I believe to be useless. The public sentiment in America has pronounced it to be so. The national government is founded on the principle of a diffusive suffrage. Most of the states have adopted the principle; and as our fortunes are embarked with theirs in one common ship, we cannot expect that our government under any regulation of the right of suffrage, will survive the union of the states. If that government is safe without a distinction in the electors founded on property, we need not fear to abolish a distinction which, if retained, will cause much uneasy feeling among the people, and bring an unneccessary odium upon the landed interest. A distinction which will have a tendency to excite combinations unfriendly to the interest of the land holders, and which, but for the distinction in the right of suffrage, will probably never exist.

Document II-7: PRO-LABOR POLITICS

With the steady broadening of the suffrage base the laborer gained a political weapon which he quickly attempted to use. His most widely shared objective was to participate more fully in the expansion and prosperity of the nation as he observed it in the 1820s and early thirties. To achieve this and other objectives the working man multiplied his trade associations, paraded, demonstrated, struck, founded newspapers, and formed political parties and alliances. These activities produced some notable gains for workers: for example, the ten-hour day, which then represented a great step forward. Before the dissension that accompanied the Panic of 1837 diffused the labor movement, politicians had learned to respect the power of labor's vote and employers had learned to expect organized resistance to unfavorable working conditions.

The working man's platform began with opposition to imprisonment for debt and to the lien laws that allowed creditors to attach wages. The laborer's emotional antipathy to banks laid a foundation for the demagogic appeal of President Andrew Jackson's famous veto message in opposition to the rechartering of the Second Bank of the United States. Almost singlehandedly George Henry Evans made the land question a part of labor's agenda. His *The Working Man's Advocate* provided a steady voice throughout this period, eventually absorbing the paper of Robert Dale Owen, patron of New Harmony and eminent Fourierist. (For an excellent summary of the "Workie" position, see the report of "The Committee of Fifty," signed by Owen in the October 31, 1829, issue of Evans's paper, vol. I, number 1, pp. 1-2.)

The Workie movement also included more out-and-out radicals like Thomas Skidmore, whose views were reflected in the *Advocate*'s original motto: "All children are entitled to equal education; all adults, to equal property; and all mankind, to equal privileges." What Skidmore wanted, in brief, was for all property to be turned over to the government, which would in turn then auction it to the full citizenry, each man possessing equal purchasing power. Thus and thus only, thought Skidmore, would the laborer ever get a just return on his labor unencumbered by liens and loans, undistorted by inherited wealth. Skidmore was as irascible as he was radical; yet, for a short time, he did profoundly influence the New York labor movement; whether he actually edited the *Advocate* or not, he did have access to its pages both as a contributor and as a force in shaping the ideas of his colleagues.

This cartoon, like the *Advocate*, promotes the candidates of the Workies' party in their first, and surprisingly successful, New York effort. The cartoon, in its abrupt awkwardness, suggests much of the stark, uncompromising leveling of Skidmore's beliefs. In its proud use of the cap of liberty as a standard, it shows no fear of association with the egalitarianism of the French Revolution. On the left side of the picture, one finds a new villain—the political machine—added to the standard villains of "Monarchy, Aristocracy, Monopolies, Auctions," money, and the devil.

SOURCE: Engraving of 1829 cartoon courtesy of the Kilroe Collection, Columbia University Libraries.

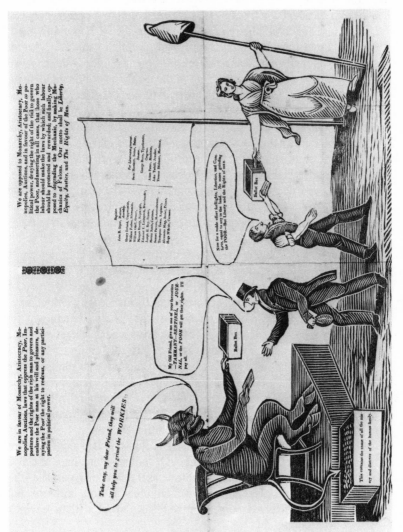

"Workie" cartoon

Document II-8: JACKSON ON THE NATIONAL BANK

Andrew Jackson's message to Congress of July 10, 1832, in which he explained his veto of the bill to recharter the Bank of the United States, has been reproduced as often as any presidential message between Jefferson and Lincoln. The reasons for this are many. Economic historians still argue over the soundness of the decision entailed, whether Jackson postponed or accelerated the imminent panic. Constitutional historians note some important shifts in the legalistic arguments. Historians of politics find many keys to successful demagoguery in the style and content.

Because this document is so readily available, only the opening and closing paragraphs have been reproduced here. Omitted are the detailed constitutional arguments, the defense of the veto on the grounds of preserving states rights, regional interests, and the national defense. The opening and closing passages contain the most powerful rhetoric and explain the central importance of Jackson's message to the kind of politico-economic reformer whose progress this section chronicles.

To review the document already selected would be to heighten one's estimate of President Jackson's shrewdness in choosing a bank for his target. In the constitutional debates, both state and federal, the fear of special favor in the form of bank concessions formed a consistent thread. The early cartoons show money and banks as the principal enemies of the people. The earliest appeals to organized workers made the banker public enemy number one. Jackson, seen against this background, capped a tradition in which popular support had been incited with phrases very much like his own: "exclusive privilege . . . under the authority of the General Government, a monopoly of its favor and support"; "powers, privileges, and favors . . . a gratuity of many millions to the stockholders"; "the richest class"; "a privileged order."

Jackson played more skillfully on more prejudices than any President before or soon after. He aroused emotional responses along lines of class, wealth, and region. He pitted the honest worker against the parasite who gains by speculation. He built on xenophobia in both military and economic ways. Yet as a document in the history of reform, these words constitute a landmark whose constructive value outweighs even its negative ingenuity. In its era, it was the most powerful statement on behalf of the financial interests of the citizenry at large.

SOURCE: James D. Richardson, *A Compilation of the Messages and Papers of the Presidents: 1789-1897.* Washington, D.C., Government Printing Office, 1897, vol. II, pp. 576-78, 589-91, abridged.

JACKSON'S MESSAGE

WASHINGTON, *July 10, 1832*

To the Senate:

The bill "to modify and continue" the act entitled "An act to incorporate the subscribers to the Bank of the United States" was presented to me on the 4th of July instant. Having considered it with that solemn regard to the principles of the Constitution which the day was calculated to inspire, and come to the conclusion that it ought not to become a law, I herewith return it to the Senate, in which it originated, with my objections.

A bank of the United States is in many respects convenient for the Government and useful to the people. Entertaining this opinion, and deeply impressed with the belief that some of the powers and privileges possessed by the existing bank are unauthorized by the Constitution, subversive of the rights of the States, and dangerous to the liberties of the people, I felt it my duty at an early period of my Administration to call the attention of Congress to the practicability of organizing an institution combining all its advantages and obviating these objections. I sincerely regret that in the act before me I can perceive none of those modifications of the bank charter which are necessary, in my opinion, to make it compatible with justice, with sound policy, or with the Constitution of our country.

The present corporate body, denominated the president, directors, and company of the Bank of the United States, will have existed at the time this act is intended to take effect twenty years. It enjoys an exclusive privilege of banking under the authority of the General Government, a monopoly of its favor and support, and, as a necessary consequence, almost a monopoly of the foreign and domestic exchange. The powers, privileges, and favors bestowed upon it in the original charter, by increasing the value of the stock far above its par value, operated as a gratuity of many millions to the stockholders.

An apology may be found for the failure to guard against this result in the consideration that the effect of the original act of incorporation could not be certainly foreseen at the time of its passage. The act before me proposes another gratuity to the holders of the same stock, and in many cases to the same men, of at least seven millions more. This donation finds no apology in any uncertainty as to the effect of the act. On all hands it is conceded that its passage will increase at least 20 or 30 per cent more the market price of the stock, subject to the payment of the annuity of $200,000 per year secured by the act, thus adding in a moment one-fourth to its par value. It is not our own citizens only who are to receive the bounty of our Government. More than eight millions of the stock of this bank are held by foreigners. By this act the American Republic proposes virtually to make them a present of some millions of dollars. For these gratuities to foreigners and to some of our own opulent citizens the act secures no equivalent whatever. They are the certain gains of the present stockholders under the operation of this act, after making full allowance for the payment of the bonus.

Every monopoly and all exclusive privileges are granted at the expense of the public, which ought to receive a fair equivalent. The many millions which this act proposes to bestow on the stockholders of the existing bank must come directly or indirectly out of the earnings of the American people. It is due to them, therefore, if their Government sell monopolies and exclusive privileges, that they should at least exact for them as much as they are worth in open market. The value of the monopoly in this case may be correctly ascertained. The twenty-eight millions of stock would probably be at an advance of 50 per cent, and command in market at least $42,000,000 subject to the payment of the present bonus. The present value of the monopoly, therefore, is $17,000,000 and this the act proposes to sell for three millions, payable in fifteen annual installments of $200,000 each.

It is not conceivable how the present stockholders can have any claim to the special favor of the Government. The present corporation has enjoyed its monopoly during the period stipulated in the original contract. If we must have such a corporation, why should not the Government sell out the whole stock and thus secure to the people the full market value of the privileges granted? Why should not Congress create and sell twenty-eight millions of stock, incorporating the purchasers with all the powers and privileges secured in this act and putting the premium upon the sales into the Treasury?

But this act does not permit competition in the purchase of this monopoly. It seems to be predicated on the erroneous idea that the present stockholders have a prescriptive right not only to the favor but to the bounty of Government. It appears that more than a fourth part of the stock is held by foreigners and the residue is held by a few hundred of our own citizens, chiefly of the richest class. For their benefit does this act exclude the whole American people from competition in the purchase of this monopoly and dispose of it for many millions less than it is worth. This seems the less excusable because some of our citizens not now stockholders petitioned that the door of competition might be opened, and offered to take a charter on terms much more favorable to the Government and country.

But this proposition, although made by men whose aggregate wealth is believed to be equal to all the private stock in the existing bank, has been set aside, and the bounty of our Government is proposed to be again bestowed on the few who have been fortunate enough to secure the stock and at this moment wield the power of the existing institution. I can not perceive the justice or policy of this course. If our Government must sell monopolies, it would seem to be its duty to take nothing less than their full value, and if gratuities must be made once in fifteen or twenty years let them not be bestowed on the subjects of a foreign government nor upon a designated and favored class of men in our own country. It is but justice and good policy, as far as the nature of the case will admit, to confine our favors to our own fellow-citizens, and let each in his turn enjoy an opportunity to profit by our bounty. In the bearings of the act before me upon these points I find ample reasons why it should not become a law.

It has been urged as an argument in favor or rechartering the present bank that the calling in its loans will produce great embarrassment and distress. The time allowed to close its concerns is ample, and if it has been well managed its pressure will be light, and heavy only in the case its management has been bad. If, therefore, it shall produce distress, the fault will be its own, and it would furnish a reason against renewing a power which has been so obviously abused. But will there ever be a time when this reason will be less powerful? To acknowledge its force is to admit that the bank ought to be perpetual, and as a consequence the present stockholders and those inheriting their rights as successors be established a privileged order, clothed both with great political power and enjoying immense pecuniary advantages from their connection with the Government. . . .

Under such circumstances the bank comes forward and asks a renewal of its charter for a term of fifteen years upon conditions which not only operate as a gratuity to the stockholders of many millions of dollars, but will sanction any abuses and legalize any encroachments.

Suspicions are entertained and charges are made of gross abuse and violation of its charter. An investigation unwillingly conceded and so restricted in time as necessarily to make it incomplete and unsatisfactory discloses enough to excite suspicion and alarm. In the practices of the principal bank partially unveiled, in the absence of important witnesses, and in numerous charges confidently made and as yet wholly uninvestigated there was enough to induce a majority of the committee of investigation—a committee which was selected from the most able and honorable members of the House of Representatives—to recommend a suspension of further action upon the bill and a prosecution of the inquiry. As the charter had yet four years to run, and as a renewal now was not necessary to the successful prosecution of its business, it was to have been expected that the bank itself, conscious of its purity and proud of its character, would have withdrawn its application for the present, and demanded the severest scrutiny into all its transactions. In their declining to do so there seems to be an additional reason why the functionaries of the Government should proceed with less haste and more caution in the renewal of their monopoly.

The bank is professedly established as an agent of the executive branch of the Government, and its constitutionality is maintained on that ground. Neither upon the propriety of present action nor upon the provisions of this act was the Executive consulted. It has had no opportunity to say that it neither needs nor wants an agent clothed with such powers and favored by such exemptions. There is nothing in its legitimate functions which makes it necessary or proper. Whatever interest or influence, whether public or private, has given birth to this act, it can not be found either in the wishes or necessities of the executive department, by which present action is deemed premature, and the powers conferred upon its agent not only unneccessary, but dangerous to the Government and country.

It is to be regretted that the rich and powerful too often bend the acts of government to their selfish purposes. Distinctions in society will always exist under every just government. Equality of talents, of education, or of wealth can not be produced by human institutions. In the full enjoyment of the gifts of Heaven and the fruits of superior industry, economy, and virtue, every man is equally entitled to protection by law; but when the laws undertake to add to these natural and just advantages artificial distinctions, to grant titles, gratuities, and exclusive privileges, to make the rich richer and the potent more powerful, the humble members of society—the farmers, mechanics, and laborers—who have neither the time nor the means of securing like favors to themselves, have a right to complain of the injustice of their Government. There are no necessary evils in government. Its evils exist only in its abuses. If it would confine itself to equal protection, and, as Heaven does its rains, shower its favors alike on the high and the low, the rich and the poor, it would be an unqualified blessing. In the act before me there seems to be a wide and unnecessary departure from these just principles.

Nor is our Government to be maintained or our Union preserved by invasions of the rights and powers of the several States. In thus attempting to make our General Government strong we make it weak. Its true strength consists in leaving individuals and States as much as possible to themselves—in making itself felt, not in its power, but in its beneficence; not in its control, but in its protection; not in binding the States more closely to the center, but leaving each to move unobstructed in its proper orbit.

Experience should teach us wisdom. Most of the difficulties our Government now encounters and most of the dangers which impend over our Union have sprung from an abandonment of the legitimate objects of Government by our national legislation, and the adoption of such principles as are embodied in this act. Many of our rich men have not been content with equal protection and equal benefits, but have besought us to make them richer by act of Congress. By attempting to gratify their desires, we have in the results of our legislation arrayed section against section, interest against interest, and man against man, in a fearful commotion which threatens to shake the foundations of our Union. It is time to pause in our career to review our principles, and if possible revive that devoted patriotism and spirit of compromise which distinguished the sages of the Revolution and the fathers of our Union. If we can not at once, in justice to interests vested under improvident legislation, make our Government what it ought to be, we can at least take a stand against all new grants of monopolies and exclusive privileges, against any prostitution of our Government to the advancement of the few at the expense of the many, and in favor of compromise and gradual reform in our code of laws and system of political economy.

I have now done my duty to my country. If sustained by my fellow-citizens, I shall be grateful and happy; if not, I shall find in the motives which impel me ample grounds for contentment and peace. In the difficulties which surround us and the dangers which threaten our institutions there is cause for neither dismay nor alarm. For relief and deliverance let us firmly rely on that kind Providence which I am sure watches with peculiar care over the destinies of our Republic, and on the intelligence and wisdom of our countrymen. Through *His* abundant goodness and *their* patriotic devotion our liberty and Union will be preserved.

Document II-9: GOUGE ON CURRENCY

The attack on banks in general and on the Bank of the United States in particular gradually developed a positive corollary: the "subtreasury" or, as its supporters sometimes preferred, the "independent treasury." This plan opposed bank notes and paper currency of all types on the grounds that such money was unpredictably and harmfully flexible, benefitting only the banker and speculator, and harming the honest merchant and worker alike. It opposed a privately enfranchised national bank since this kind of institution was felt to offer special privilege to the few. It opposed state banks since they were felt likely to add even more unpredictability to the issuance of money and lead very possibly to the attribution of unnatural advantages to any groups involved in currency control.

The subtreasury plan called for a return to specie, gold and silver, as an absolute and inflexible monetary base. The government would issue all money, performing this service through "subtreasuries": that is, subdivisions of the federal treasury. Thus the federal government would be responsible to the voters for maintaining a monetary system which protected the value of the working man's dollar and prevented the speculative profiteering of an influential minority.

The invention, justification, and application of this idea was centered on the career and writings of one man: William M. Gouge. Throughout his life Gouge contributed to financial journals. His research on money and banking was well enough substantiated to impress Europeans as well as Americans. His ideas were enough in tune with Jacksonian Democracy to gain him an appointment in the U. S. Treasury, where he subsequently pushed his policies under both parties.

His most widely circulated work, from which the following excerpt is taken, presented a rationale and an empirical justification for the subtreasury idea. In his system he saw a chance to avoid extremes of both wealth and poverty. Paragraphs 20-23, below, show how he envisaged the impact of his ideas as falling well beyond the economic community, influencing the press, the Congress, and the very fiber of national morality. Because the control of currency, with all its unavoidable technicalities, forms so essential a continuing center of politico-economic reform, it is useful to note some of the details of Gouge's philosophy, particularly his sympathy to silver (paragraph 2) and opposition to flexible currency (paragraphs 8, 11).

In 1837, without the approval of his superiors in the treasury, William Gouge published *An Inquiry into the Expediency of Dispensing with Bank Agency and Bank Paper in the Fiscal Concerns of the United States* (Philadelphia). Together with his earlier work, this argument provided the principal expert testimony on behalf of the subtreasury.

SOURCE: William M. Gouge, *A Short History of Paper-Money and Banking in the United States. Including an Account of Provincial and Continental Paper-Money. To which is Prefixed an Inquiry into the Principles of the System with Considerations of its Effects on Morals and Happiness.* New York, Collins, 1835 (2nd edition), pp. 41-42, abridged.

A SHORT HISTORY OF PAPER-MONEY

SUMMARY.

To place the subject fairly before the reader, we shall bring together the principal propositions that have been supported in this essay, and leave the decision to his candid judgment.

We have maintained:

1.   That real money is that valuable by reference to which the value of other articles is estimated, and by the instrumentality of which they are circulated. It is a *commodity*, done up in a particular form to serve a particular use, and does not differ *essentially* from other items of wealth.

2.   That silver, owing to its different physical properties, the universal and incessant demand for it, and the small proportion the annual supply bears to the stock on hand, is as good a practical standard of value as can reasonably be desired. It has no variations except such as *necessarily* arise from the nature of value.

3.   That real money diffuses itself through different countries, and through different parts of a country, in proportion to the demands of commerce. No prohibitions can prevent its departing from countries where wealth and trade are declining; and no obstacle, except spurious money, can prevent its flowing into countries where wealth and trade are increasing.

4.   That money is the tool of all trades, and is, as such, one of the most useful of productive instruments, and one of the most valuable of labor-saving machines.

5.   That bills of exchange and promissory notes are a *mere commercial medium*, and are, as *auxiliaries* of gold and silver money, very useful: but they differ from metallic money in having no inherent value, and in being evidences of debt. The expressions of value in bills of exchange and promissory notes, are according to the article which law or custom has made the standard; and the failure to pay bills of exchange and promissory notes, does not affect the value of the currency, or the standard by which all contracts are regulated.

6.   That Bank notes are *mere evidences of debt* due by the Banks, and in this respect differ not from the promissory notes of the merchants; but being received in full of all demands, they become to all intents and purposes the money of the country.

7.   That Banks owe their credit to their charters; for if these were taken away, not even their own stockholders would trust them.

8.   That the circulating quality of Bank notes is in part owing to their being receivable in payment of dues to government; in part to the interest

which the debtors to Banks and Bank stockholders have in keeping them in circulation; and in part to the difficulty, when the system is firmly established, of obtaining metallic money.

9.   That so long as specie payments are maintained, there is a limit on Bank issues; but this is not sufficient to prevent successive "expansions" and "contractions," which produce ruinous fluctuations of prices; while the means by which Bank medium is kept "convertible," inflict great evils on the community.

10.   That no restriction which can be imposed on Banks, and no discretion on the part of the directors, can prevent these fluctuations; for Bank credit, as a branch of commercial credit, is affected by all the causes, natural and political, that affect trade, or that affect the confidence man has in man.

11.   That the "flexibility" or "elasticity" of Bank medium is not an excellence, but a defect, and that "expansions" and "contractions" are not made to suit the wants of the community, but from a simple regard to the profits and safety of the Banks.

12.   That the uncertainty of trade produced by these successive "expansions" and "contractions," is but *one* of the evils of the present system. That the Banks cause credit dealings to be carried to an extent that is highly pernicious—that they cause credit to be given to men who are not entitled to it, and deprive others of credit to whom it would be useful.

13.   That the granting of exclusive privileges to companies, or the exempting of companies from liabilities to which individuals are subject, is repugnant to the fundamental principles of American government; and that the Banks, inasmuch as they have exclusive privileges and exemptions, and have the entire control of credit and currency, are the most pernicious of money corporations.

14.   That a *nominal* responsibility may be imposed on such corporations, but that it is impossible to impose on them an effective responsibility. They respect the laws and public opinion so far only as is necessary to promote their own interest.

15.   That on the supposition most favorable to the friends of the Banking System, the whole amount gained by the substitution of Bank medium for gold and silver coin, is equal only to about forty cents per annum for each individual in the country; but that it will be found that

nothing is in reality gained *by the nation*, if due allowance be made for the expense of supporting three of four hundred Banks, and for the fact that Bank medium is a machine which performs its work badly.

16. That some hundreds of thousands of dollars are annually extracted from the people of Pennsylvania, and some millions from the people of the United States, for the support of the Banks, insomuch as through Banking the natural order of things is reversed; and interest paid to the Banks on evidences of debt due by them, instead of interest being paid to those who part with commodities in exchange for Bank notes.

17. That into the formation of the Bank capital of the country very little substantial wealth has ever entered, that capital having been formed principally out of the promissory notes of the original subscribers, or by other means which the operations of the Banks themselves have facilitated. They who have bought the script of the Banks at second-hand, may have honestly paid cent. per cent. for it; but what they have paid has gone to those from whom they bought the script, and does not form any part of the capital of the Banks.

18. That if it was the wish of the legislature to promote usurious dealings, it could not well devise more efficient means than incorporating paper-money Banks. That these Banks, moreover, give rise to many kinds of stock-jobbing, by which the simple-minded are injured and the crafty benefited.

19. That many legislators have in voting for Banks, supposed that they were promoting the welfare of their constituents; but the prevalence of false views in legislative bodies in respect to money corporations and paper-money, is to be attributed chiefly to the desire certain members have to make money for themselves, or to afford their political partisans and personal friends opportunities for speculation.

20. That the banking interest has a pernicious influence on the periodical press, on public elections, and the general course of legislation. This interest is so powerful, that the establishment of a system of sound currency and sound credit is impracticable, except one or other of the political parties into which the nation is divided, makes such an object its primary principle of action.

21. That through the various advantages which the system of incorporated paper-money Banking has given to some men over others, the foundation has been laid of an *artificial* inequality of wealth, which kind

of inequality is, when once laid, increased by all the subsequent operations of society.

22. That this artificial inequality of wealth, adds nothing to the substantial happiness of the rich, and detracts much from the happiness of the rest of the community, that its tendency is to corrupt one portion of society, and debase another.

23. That the sudden dissolution of the Banking System, without suitable preparation, would put an end to the collection of debts, destroy private credit, break up many productive establishments, throw much of the property of the industrious into the hands of speculators, and deprive laboring people of employment.

24. That the system can be got rid of without difficulty, by prohibiting, after a certain day, the issue of small notes, and by proceeding gradually to those of the highest denomination.

25. That the feasibility of getting rid of the system, is further proved by the fact, that the whole amount of Bank notes and Bank credits, is, according to Mr. Gallatin's calculation, only about one hundred and nine million dollars. By paying ten or eleven millions a year, the whole can be liquidated in the term of ten years. If, however, twenty or thirty years should be required for the operation, the longest of these is but a short period in the lifetime of a nation.

26. That it has not been solely through the undervaluation of gold at the mint, that eagles and half-eagles have disappeared. The free use of Bank notes is the chief cause of the disappearance of gold. Nevertheless, a new coinage of pieces containing four and eight, or five and ten dollars' worth of gold is desirable, to save the trouble of calculating fractions. The dollar being the money of contract and account, no possible confusion or injustice can be produced by an adjustment of the gold coinage to the silver standard.

27. That incorporating a paper-money Bank is not "the necessary and proper," or "natural and appropriate" way of managing the fiscal concerns of the Union; but that the "necessary and proper," or "natural and appropriate" way of correcting the evils occasioned by the State Banks, inasmuch as a National Bank, resting on the same principles as the State Banks, must produce similar evils.

29. That "convertible" paper prevents the accumulation of such a stock of the precious metals as will enable the country to bear transitions

from peace to war, and insure the punctual payment of war taxes; and that the "necessary and proper," or "natural and appropriate" way of providing for all public exigencies, is by making the government a *solid money government*, as was intended by the framers of the constitution.

30. That if congress should, from excessive caution, or some less commendable motive, decline passing the acts necessary to insure the gradual withdrawal of Bank notes, they may greatly diminish the evils of the system, by declaring that nothing but gold and silver shall be received in payment of duties, and by making the operations of the government entirely distinct from those of the Banks.

31. That on the abolition of incorporated paper-money Banks, private Bankers will rise up, who will receive money on deposite, and allow interest on the same, discount promissory notes, and buy and sell bills of exchange. Operating on sufficient funds, and being responsible for their engagements in the whole amount of their estates, these private Bankers will not by sudden and great "expansions" and "curtailments" derange the whole train of mercantile operations. In each large city, an office of deposite and transfer, similar to the Bank of Hamburgh, will be established, and we shall thus secure all the good of the present Banking System, and avoid all its evils.

32. That if the present system of Banking and paper-money shall continue, the wealth and population of the country will increase from natural causes, till they shall be equal for each square mile to the wealth and population of Europe. But with every year, the state of society in the United States will more nearly approximate to the state of society in Great Britain. Crime and pauperism will increase. A few men will be inordinately rich, some comfortable, and a multitude in poverty. This condition of things will naturally lead to the adoption of that policy which proceeds on the principle that a legal remedy is to be found for each social evil, and nothing left for the operations of nature. This kind of legislation will increase the evils it is intended to cure.

33. That there is reason to *hope*, that on the downfall of moneyed corporations, and the substitution of gold and silver for Bank medium, sound credit will take the place of unsound, and legitimate enterprise the place of wild speculation. That the moral and intellectual character of the people will be sensibly though gradually raised, and the causes laid open of a variety of evils under which society is now suffering. That the sources of legislation will, to a certain extent, be purified, by taking from

members of legislative bodies inducements to pass laws for the special benefit of themselves, their personal friends and political partisans. That the operation of the natural and just causes of wealth and poverty, will no longer be inverted, but that each cause will operate in its natural and just order, and produce its natural and just effect—wealth becoming the reward of industry, frugality, skill, prudence, and enterprise, and poverty the punishment of few except the indolent and prodigal.

Document II-10: WRIGHT ON THE SUBTREASURY

William Gouge was disappointed to be taken only as a spokesman for Locofocos, levelers, and other "wild-eyed" friends of the downtrodden. Rather, he would point to the number of respectable businessmen who favored the independent treasury as a move toward stable money and bask in Van Buren's estimate of the subtreasury as one idea that had satisfied just about everyone. On Gouge's side, it must be admitted that even among reformers support came for seemingly opposite reasons. Orestes Brownson, for example, supported the Sub-Treasury Bill in the *Boston Quarterly Review* (July, 1838) because of his conviction that it would maintain the status quo.

Yet the loud voices in praise of Gouge did come from popular spellbinders such as Frances Wright (D'Arusmont). Fanny Wright, a handsome, eloquent Scottish woman, became a household symbol for advanced, libertarian thought. Impressed by New Harmony she attempted a communitarian experiment of her own at Nashoba, Tennessee, where she worked toward purchasing freedom for slaves and for easier relations between the sexes. The first woman to command large political audiences in America, Fanny Wright became a "headliner" on behalf of the Working Man's Party in New York. Her freethinking views, mirrored in the attitudes of Thomas Skidmore and Robert Dale Owen (see II-7), gave rise to the "infidel" label which tarred the party in some minds.

The following passage is from a speech she made during her second New York campaign on behalf of labor. In the first part of the address she attempted to arouse sympathy by claiming persecution at the hands of the public hall owners. When she returned to the issue of the independent treasury, she lost none of her sense of outrage. These paragraphs help to explain this issue as one that, although it might logically draw support from many quarters, appealed to the friends of labor as a measure that would commit the federal government to an increased responsibility on behalf of economic equity.

Perhaps the heavy strain of anti-English feelings can be understood in terms of Fanny Wright's Scottish origins, but it is worth noting how successfully she "twists the English lion's tail" for the political purpose of dividing her enemies, the American whigs. A student of reform rhetoric might also wish to note here an early example of the common art of persuasion by labeling the matter under discussion a second Declaration of Independence. A close companion in spirit to this speech is the cartoon reproduced above (II-7).

SOURCE: Frances Wright [Darusomont, or D'Arusmont], *What Is the Matter? A Political Address.* New York, published for the author, 1838, pp. 14-16, abridged.

WHAT IS THE MATTER?

What is the first great national effect of the Independent Treasury bill? I beg you to observe, my friends, that I do not call this vital measure by the name of the Sub-Treasury bill; still less by that of the Sub-Treasury scheme. There is no scheme in the case. A scheme signifies something contrived; something artificial; something got up with ingenuity for purposes difficult to compass. Nothing of all this is in the measure proposed. The scheme was in *the absence* of an Independent Treasury. The scheme was in the substitute contrived for it. The scheme was in a national debt, and in the banking and funding bubble, associated with and based upon the national revenues. The scheme was in the conjurer's trick of a United States Bank, with a secret door leading into the Bank of England. The scheme was in the high tariff, commercial credit, and paper money machinery. Ay! all this was the scheme, my friends; and, in very truth, it was a scheme with a vengeance!

Do you not see how the scheme worked, fellow-citizens? Why, it worked so as to make the people pay high taxes, and to pay them in the worst form of all—that of indirect taxes. It worked so as to throw into the American Branch Bank of England, (called the Bank of the United States,) a surplus revenue for the use of the mother bank in London. It worked so as to make the gold and silver of that surplus revenue serve the double, but most unequal, purpose of supplying what is called *the specie basis of a paper currency* for the United States, and of enabling the Bank of England to supply a *specie currency* to Great Britain. It worked so as to swindle our South of its cotton, our North of its labor, this whole nation of its lands and its treasure. It worked so as to render the State Banks the slaves of the United States Bank, the whole people the slaves of all the banks, the whole banking system the tool of Great Britain, the great American Republic the prey of the Holy Alliance. Ay! all this was the scheme; and such was the working of the scheme, to the prostration of people, country, national honor, wealth, greatness, human liberty, and for the consolidation of the whole land, capital, and labor of this last refuge of freedom, in the hands of the crowned despotisms of Europe.

But the Independent Treasury bill, fellow-citizens, is the reverse of all this. It is not a scheme. It is more even than a measure. It is a principle. It is the national independence realized. It is the effective, definitive annulment of this country's vassalage. It is the first practical, efficient, decisive realization of the Declaration of '76. It is the day-star of constitutional liberty rising upon the earth, with the first cleansing of a national government from the pollutions of financial scheming. It is the first emancipation of a government at once from the odious enthralment, and from the corrupting influences and overwhelming tyranny of the money power. The money power!—that worst—that most deceptive, most corrosive power ever exercised upon earth, and which has been ever until this hour allied—openly or secretly—with administrational authority and executive command.

No, fellow-citizens! I do not call the great decree of the independence of the treasury of the United States by the name of a scheme; nor do I either call it by the paltry name of the Sub-Treasury Bill.

Observe! The name of "Sub-Treasury Bill" is a name descriptive only *of the mode* in which it is judged that a sacred principle may be the most effectually secured, and that a vital measure may be brought to bear. The name of "Independent Treasury Bill" is directly descriptive of the principle itself, and thus consecrates the proposed statute by its very title.

And, say! is there—can there be an American citizen not interested in

the independence of his country's treasury, when that in fact is the
independence of his country itself? Is there—can there be—an American
citizen who conceives of any advantage to himself as likely to accrue
from the young proud eagle of this republic remaining any longer
clutched within the claws of the treacherous leopard of England? Ay! the
leopard. That ancient, true, and faithfully descriptive emblem of English
monarchy! Let the British government keep to that old emblem. It has
nothing of the lion in its nature.

Document II-11: SYMBOLS OF POLITICAL REFORM

The presidential campaign of 1840 produced the first true party platform, drawn up by some of the younger leaders of the National Republican Party (usually called Whigs after their 1834 merger), meeting in
Washington, D.C., in May. The eighth plank carried the resolution
"That the separation of the moneys of the government from banking
institutions, is indispensable for the safety of the funds of the government, and the rights of the people." (Kirk H. Porter and Donald B.
Johnson, *National Party Platforms, 1840-1956.* Urbana, University of
Illinois, 1956, p. 2.) Thus the independent treasury became the public
policy of one of the two major parties. In the last days of the Van Buren
administration an Independent Treasury Act passed after long debate,
only to be repealed by the victorious Whigs. Passed again in 1846, a
similar act became the guide to federal fiscal policy until the Civil War
and, in some respects, until the passage of the Federal Reserve Act.

The campaign of 1840 was interesting not only for the first platform
but also for the first successful positive use of political symbols. The
basic idea seems to have originated in an interview between a Whig who
had supported Clay and a newspaper reporter of Locofoco sympathies.
The reporter advised the disgruntled Whig to offer Harrison a pension
and a barrel of hard cider, whereon he would contentedly sit out his life in
a log cabin. This jibe, picked up by the Whig press across the country,
turned into a national mania. Robert G. Gunderson (in his *Log-Cabin
Campaign*, Lexington, University of Kentucky, 1957, pp. 74, 128-
29) compiled a list of the products and events reflecting this irresistible

fad, including with Tippecanoe Shaving Soap or Log-Cabin Emollient, Tippecanoe Tobacco, Old-Cabin Whiskey, not to mention songs, dances, parades, and parties—all rich in allusions to Tip 'n Ty. A representative rendering of the campaign motif is shown in the accompanying photograph. The ubiquitousness of this symbolism can be suggested by the nature of the object: a snuffbox.

In the long struggle to politicize the economic interests of the voter it is useful to dwell for a moment on this unlikely Whig victory in a campaign that simultaneously featured an independent treasury plank as well as a cluster of surprisingly successful political symbols. The log cabin was well chosen for its associations with the frontier, with ascetic hardihood as opposed to regal luxury, for its supposed uniqueness to American shores. Hard cider was a plain man's drink as opposed to the imported wines and brandies favored by Van Buren. Together with the plow—a third symbol, which is often overlooked but which was nearly always present—the cider represented the fruits of honest agricultural labor. The plow also reverberates with Cincinnatian associations and reminded voters that Harrison had put down his peaceful implements to defend the citizenry against the Indians. Note how the snuffbox design stressed not only the plow but farmyard fowl and the burgeoning apple tree itself.

The pair of medallions (II-11B) reflect both the power of campaign symbolism and the dilemma of temperance Whigs. Many enemies of alcohol, while favoring Harrison, still shuddered at the association of their candidate with the homely intoxicant. In the end they realized the hopelessness of drowning out the hard-cider battle cry; so they joined it. As the medals show, they wedded the log cabin to the virtues of cool well water sipped from the lip of a mossy green bucket.

SOURCE: A: A white metal snuffbox about 2 by 3 inches. B: Two separately struck medallions, brass, about 1 inch in diameter. All items 1840 courtesy of the Ralph E. Becker Collection, Division of Political History, Smithsonian Institution.

A: Campaign snuffbox

B: Medallions

Document II-12: LAND REFORMS AND EVANS

Land reform, in the American antebellum context, had both negative and positive reform aspects. Spokesmen for the masses feared lest land should become the property of the few, as in land-poor Europe, while the working man became the victim of unfair rents and leaseholds. On the positive side, the presence of abundant unoccupied land to the west became a weapon in the worker's arsenal. Rather than endure industrial slavery in the eastern cities, he could claim a plot of his own. George Henry Evans (see II-7), owned not only *The Working Man's Advocate* but also the paper in which the following piece appeared. He may have written this parable pointed at relating the land question to the plight of the city worker.

The People's Rights is itself an interesting reform document. It regularly reproduced two graphic symbols of land reform: the wreathed bust of a figure wearing the familiar cap of liberty associated with the French Revolution, and an appealing diagram of open squares representing a plan for the distribution of free land. Elsewhere a bust of Jefferson accompanied by a long quotation from Andrew Jackson's fourth annual message left no doubt as to the political ancestry of the National Reform Association.

Land reform continued an active issue until the Civil War and was aided by the sympathy of Horace Greeley and his successful *Tribune*. Some success was attained in 1862 with the passage of the Homestead Act and the Morrill Act. The former gave virtually free land to citizens and intended citizens who would live on and improve a quarter section (160 acres). The latter granted land to be used in support of education. There is some doubt as to whether the homesteading experience did move the country toward economic democracy; but the following passages leave no doubt that it was promoted with that end in mind.

SOURCE: *The People's Rights, Organ of the National Reform Association.* New York, vol. I, number 1 (New Series), May 25, 1844, page 1, abridged.

To Cellar Diggers,
And, Incidentally, to Other Working Men.

Who the deuce are the Cellar Diggers? a very natural question this. Well, they are the men that every body sees driving small carts with sand or dirt in them; they are the men that dig out the soil and form the cellars for new buildings. I was passing down the Fifth Avenue a few mornings since, and about the corner of Thirteenth street I saw a crowd of men, and probably sixty horses and carts, all standing still. As I perceived building going on close by, I thought probably an accident had happened to some of the workmen; but, on coming up, I found them all engaged in a very animated and high toned conversation. I soon found that they had *struck* against the *contractors*: not for an advance of wages, but in consequence of an additional hour's labor, daily, being demanded by the contractors. The time which the men had usually worked was from seven in the morning till six in the evening. The contractors demanded that they should commence at *six* and leave off at *six*. The wages received by the cellar diggers are $1.75 per day for a man, his horse and cart. Some said the horses could not stand it, it was too much for them; others, on the contrary, said little, but thought they might better go to work; that some would, whether or not, and that *they* might as well, for if *they* did not do the work others would. Then several were mentioned who were "right in the cellar by six that morning and would be there again by six the next morning." I found a number of carts, which were at work, had been stopped by the men who had struck, consequently they were quarrelling among themselves.

During this, the *contractor* would probably stretch himself out on a block of granite, cover his face with his hat, to keep the sun out of his eyes, take an hour's sleep, and, like the miller in his mill, when the *noise* stopped he would wake up, and find all the men at work and all grumbling.

Now, the question that the Cellar Diggers should ask is this. What is that tremendous *power* that enables one man to lie down and go to sleep, setting a whole host at defiance, well knowing that when he awakes up he shall be the conqueror? This is the question for them to ask, and I shall *answer it.* It is that same *power* which enables the wealthy manufacturer of Manchester, Leeds, Birmingham, and Sheffield to take his luxurious ease, while his thousands of laborers quarrel whether they shall work one hour more or one hour less per day: it is that same *power* which enables him to sleep peacefully and softly in a splendid mansion, while the father, the mother, and the children, who have produced ALL his wealth, starve, sicken and die in the garrets and cellars around him. This *terrible power* is the *power that WEALTH and CAPITAL acquire over labor and life where ALL the surface of the earth is monopolized*, and, consequently, where there is no outlet for the laborer. Where there are thousands on thousands of acres of the richest land in the world lying stretched out in splendid parks, yielding nothing whatever to sustain the human family; there will be thousands on thousands of poverty-stricken laborers who can find no labor. There will be TOO MANY LABORERS to perform the work that is to be done, and the *wealthy capitalist* will command the work of the laborer at any price that will just keep him from starving to death, compelling those whom he employs to labor as many hours as human nature is capable of, that he may support as few of them as possible.

Now, friends, Cellar Diggers, there is one way left, *and only one*, by which you can be relieved from the oppression which you now feel, and which must, unless you adopt it, inevitably increase on you; and not only Cellar Diggers, but every other branch of labor is or will be exactly in the same condition; and the remedy is the same for all. There has been an Association formed, called the "NATIONAL REFORM ASSOCIA-TION." The object of this Association is to prevent any further *sale of the land* belonging to the State and the United States. It is self evident that the lands belonging to the State and the United States belong to the *people.* The land is the gift of God to his people, and the day is fast coming when no man will dare hold up his head and say, that he will do all he can to ROB his fellow man of God's greatest gift and blessing.

The object of the "*National Reform Association*" is to put a stop to the unholy traffic in the soil; to prevent any *farther* monopoly by the *few* of God's gift to ALL. With the lands already in the hands of private individuals, and with all kinds of private property, this Association has nothing to do. Let the man who holds his thousand or ten thousand acres hold it, sell it, will it away, or give it away; *but of the People's Land no more Sale must for ever take place.* This Association proposes that the land shall be laid out by Government in Townships of six miles square, as they now are, divided into Farms of 160 acres each; a mile square in the centre, to be laid out in town and mechanics' Lots of five acres each; and that *any Citizen of the United States*, who is *not possessed of other land,* may enter upon and occupy a farm or lot *free of cost*. This is his *home*, and he is to have a deed of occupancy. If at any time he wishes to leave it, he may sell at auction, or otherwise, all the *improvements* he has made on it, or he may will them to his children, or to any one who is going to occupy the land. The LAND is never to become the *property* of any one; but as soon as one man chooses to leave it, he may transfer his deed of occupancy from the Government to another, provided he hold no other land.

"THE LAND SHALL NOT BE SOLD FOR EVER," says Moses, the great Law Giver of old. And we, of the present day, solemnly declare that it shall not be GIVEN AWAY to any foreign and mercenary aristocracy, who live on the very life's blood of their fellow men, whether for debts contracted or to be contracted. Those who have sculked from their honest debts, under the shadow of a vile bankrupt law, are the readiest to give away the poor man's birthright.

Here is the *only* door that is open to the Cellar Digger, and every other digger; the only mode of escape from the oppressor. The Cellar Digger is the very man to walk straight off to the winds; he has a strong arm, a stout limb, a hard hand, accustomed to the pick axe and spade; his face is already browned with the rays of the sun; he knows the management of the horse and the cart; and there is not one of them, who could not, in two or three years, raise produce enough to support himself and family, and have five hundred dollars worth to exchange for groceries and clothing, and to educate his children. And, if it were necessary, by a little extra exertion, he could raise ten dollars more, which he would willingly do, to pay a tax that would support his government and defend his country. But I should like to see a foreign nation attack a country settled in this manner, where every one had his *own home* to fight for!

Supposing five hundred Cellar Diggers were to leave New York and go on the land, what would be the effect on those who remained behind? Why, the wages of their labor must naturally rise, and if all that were left could not get a *comfortable* living, others would leave and go upon the land, till those left behind *could* get a comfortable living by doing a reasonable day's labor.

Here then is the only *strike* that can ever permanently benefit the laborer and the mechanic, no matter to what branch of business he may belong. Here you do not strike against a *master*, an *employer*, or a *contractor*; you *strike* to do all the poor *good*, and to do none of the rich *harm.* You *strike* for the cause of humanity, justice, and right; you strike for the cause of man and the cause of God: for, in striking down poverty and want, you strike down *crime.*

While you are called upon to consider this great, this all-important cause, that is now presented to you, you are not called upon to relax your efforts in using any other lawful means in your power to better your present condition, by union among yourselves. But you must all well know, from dear bought experience, that all *unions* and all *strikes* are perfectly powerless the moment dull times or a decline in business takes place. And, in many cases, a *strike*, in New York, only has the effect of bringing a great number of hands from all other parts of the country; and the result is, that, in six months from the strike, wages will be lower than before. A strike also frequently causes a great deal of work to be sent from the place where the mechanics strike, to other places where they have not struck, and in this way tends suddenly to reduce the rate of wages where the strike has taken place. On this subject, however, you have your own opinions, and I do not wish to interfere with them. But I do want the whole mass of the laborers and mechanics to reflect seriously on this all-important measure, now brought forward by the *"National Reform Association"* and the papers which advocate its cause. . . .

If every man had his right to land, as proposed by the *National Reform Association,* then would man bless and ASSIST his fellow man, without the fear of bringing himself to want, and, with a full heart, praise his creator for the bounties that surrounded him.

A PRINTER.

Document II-13: KELLOGG ON FINANCE

While William Gouge and his colleagues were nailing down the subtreasury triumph, another politico-economic pamphleteer was beginning to formulate a set of principles, opposite to the subtreasury in many respects, but aimed at helping the same group. Edward Kellogg, who published first under the pseudonym of Goodwell or Gardwell, came out with the "Bible of greenbackism" under his own name in 1849. Although its impact was most directly powerful in the late 1860s and seventies, Kellogg's work is, interestingly, contemporary with that of the European radicals Karl Marx, Pierre Proudhon, and Louis Blanc. "What the socialism of Lassalle and Marx was to Germany, the cooperative anarchism of Proudhon to France, the revolutionary anarchism of Bakunin to Spain, Italy, and Russia, what Fenianism was to Ireland, and land nationalization to England, so was greenbackism to America." (John R. Commons, *et al.*, eds., *A Documentary History of American Industrial Society.* Cleveland, Clark, 1910, vol. IX, p. 33.)

Kellogg subscribed to the labor theory of value and felt that no social system could be justified until it gave the laborer ("producer") just recompense. To bring the American system closer to equity he argued for the central importance of interest rates in determining the ultimate value of labor or property. Then, at a time when working men were still smarting from the unreliability of paper money, he argued against hard currency and sought to convince his readers that money need take no particular shape or form but could function as any government wanted it to. In the climate of the 1840s and 1850s, it is not surprising that Kellogg went unnoticed; however, when events created the need, his theories were apt and ready, designed to persuade not only the laborer but the farmer and manufacturer as well.

The negative aspect of Kellogg's appeal struck a familiar note: opposition to banks in general and to financial speculators ("usurers") in particular. The broad appeal of the work depended on Kellogg's rejection of revolution in favor of the ballot box and legislative act, the preservation of private property, free enterprise, and the rights of contract.

Toward twentieth-century policy, Gouge contributed the idea of regional, federal banks, responsible for the issuance of money. Kellogg added the idea of a flexible, fiat currency controlled by the government and responsive to popular feelings. Also, he introduced the concept of government-controlled interest rates as a function of federal debt as well as public credit. To the small businessman and farmer, Kellogg assured credit at rates he could afford.

SOURCE: Edward Kellogg, *Labor and Other Capital: The Rights of Each Secured and the Wrongs of Both Eradicated. Or, an Exposition of the Cause Why Few Are Wealthy and Many Poor, and the Delineation of a System, Which, Without Infringing the Rights of Property, Will Give to Labor its Just Reward.* New York, published by the author, 1849, pp. xi-xii, 160-163, 270-271, abridged.

LABOR AND OTHER CAPITAL

The laboring classes of all civilized nations have been, and are, as a body, poor. Nearly all wealth is the production of labor; therefore, laborers would have possessed it, had not something intervened to prevent this natural result. Even in our own country, where the reward of labor is greater than in most others, some cause is operating with continual and growing effect to separate production from the producer. The wrong is evident, but neither statesmen nor philanthropists have traced it to its true source; and hence they have not been able to project any plan sufficient for its removal.

The design of the present volume is to show the true cause; and to illustrate its operation so plainly and variously, that any ordinary mind may easily perceive how it has produced and continued this unnatural oppression of laborers. It will also be shown, with equal clearness, that a simple and effectual remedy can be applied to the removal of the evil. A good government must have some system by which it can secure the distribution of property according to the earnings of labor, and at the same time strictly preserve the rights of property: and no government, whether republican or not, that fails in these particulars, can ensure the freedom, and happiness of the people and become permanent. The plan proposed to secure this distribution is obviously safe and certain; and it contemplates no agrarian or other similar distribution of property, nor any interference in contracts between laborers and capitalists, or in the usual course of business. Fulfilling these requirements, it can hardly fail to recommend itself to all thinking men. Therefore, it is confidently believed that when the plan shall become generally known, it will be quickly put into operation, and thus save the producers of this nation from the oppression, degradation and misery which have befallen the laboring classes of all other countries. . . .

It may be said that the reduction of interest on money would cause property to rise in price in proportion to such reduction of interest, and, therefore, the condition of the laborer would not be improved. But whether property rise or fall, or maintain its present price, the reward of labor would be equally increased. To illustrate this position: Suppose H. has a lot that cost him in cash $1,000, and builds a house upon it costing $1,000—together worth $2,000. Interest on money is at six per cent per annum; therefore, to make the property worth the money it cost, H. must let the house for $120 a year, clear of insurance, repairs, and taxes. Labor is then at one dollar per day. Reduce interest on money to one per cent, and, in consequence of this reduction, let the lot and house rise to six times their former price—that is, from $2,000 to $12,000. The interest on $12,000 at one per cent would be $120, the same as when the property would sell for but $2,000. The house could not rise from $2,000 to $12,000, unless labor should rise proportionally—that is, from one dollar a day to six dollars a day. The same amount of labor would as readily build the house at one time as at another. With labor at six dollars per day, the tenant could pay the $120 rent with twenty days' work; whereas, with interest at six per cent, and labor at one dollar per day, it would take one hundred and twenty days' labor to pay the rent, six times more than when interest on money was at one per cent. Now suppose the change in interest to produce no effect upon property, and the house and lot to continue worth only $2,000. The interest on the $2,000 at one per cent would be $20. If property did not rise, labor would not rise, because it would require the same number of days' labor to build the house, and it would take twenty days' labor to pay the rent—the same number of days that it would if the property should rise to $12,000.

A just per centage on money being established, the rise or the fall of property would not affect the relative position of labor and capital. If property should rise in price, the tenant would not be obliged to build another house for the use of one, any sooner than if property should fall in price. He could pay the rent in the one case as easily as in the other, and with the same amount of labor; but a change in the rate of interest would immediately affect him.

The amount of products required as the rent of land would be diminished by reducing the rate of interest. Suppose G. owns a farm of one hundred acres of well improved land worth $100 per acre. H. rents this farm at seven per cent interest on its cost, and consequently must pay to G. $700 a year. If the land produce twenty-five bushels of wheat to the acre, and wheat be worth $1 per bushel, H. must sow, reap, and sell the products of twenty-eight acres, and pay the whole proceeds to G. as the rent of one hundred acres for the year. If interest were at one per cent instead of at seven, the rent of the farm, or of the $10,000 for the year, would be $100, instead of $700; and H. would be obliged to cultivate and sell the products of four acres only to procure one hundred bushels of wheat, or $100 to pay the rent. If he performed the same labor when interest was at one as when it was at seven per cent, he would retain the products of twenty-four acres—i.e., six hundred bushels of wheat as the surplus earnings of his labor, instead of paying them to G. for the use of capital. The reduction of the rate of interest would not lessen the quantity of products, nor decrease their value; it would only give a larger proportion to producers. If G. should cultivate his own farm, he would receive the whole of its products as the earnings of his labor, whether interest were at one, or at seven per cent. But if interest were at one per cent, and H. should rent the second farm, G. could exact but a small proportion of the products of the farm as rent. G. would receive a more just sum for the use of the farm, and H. would likewise receive a more just reward for his labor upon it. . . .

Paper money can be as easily made to exceed coins in value, as coins to exceed paper money, because the value of all money is governed by the per centage interest. Let the Safety Fund loan paper money, and fund it with Safety Fund notes bearing six per cent; let it loan coins, and fund them with Safety Fund notes bearing but four per cent, and the paper money will always be the more valuable, and command a premium in exchange for coins. The paper money will as certainly command a premium above coins, as a ground-rent at six per cent will command more than one at four per cent. If this nation had a sufficient quantity of specie for a currency, it would still be necessary to have an institution similar to the Safety Fund; for interest can only be kept regular by the establishment of an institution to make loans at a uniform rate of interest whenever good security is offered, and to fund the specie whenever it is redundant.

A government may obtain an immense power over the property of the people by furnishing a paper currency at six per cent interest. Suppose our government to establish a Safety Fund, and make its paper money the only tender in payment for debts. Let the Safety Fund lend an amount equal to say $15 to each inhabitant for a population of 20,000,000, that is, $300,000,000, money would become plenty. This sum loaned on double its amount of landed estate, would cover $600,000,000 worth of property. If the government should leave the principal outstanding during the regular payment of the interest, it would receive from the interest, after deducting say $1,000,000 for the expenses of the Safety Fund, an annual revenue of $17,000,000. After a year or two let the

Fund refuse to make further loans, and yearly collect its nett gain of $17,000,000 for ten years, i.e., $170,000,000, and the whole business of the nation must be transacted with the remaining $130,000,000. This would subject the property mortgaged to a great sacrifice, and equally depress the price of other lands and products. In six years more, the government would collect in $102,000,000 additional interest, thereby reducing the currency to $28,000,000. The interest for two years more would amount to $34,000,000, but only $28,000,000 could be paid, because the whole amount of money would be exhausted. By foreclosing its mortgages, the government could buy the $600,000,000 worth of property for the $6,000,000 which would still be due. Hence it is evident that the law has power to make paper money to control property as effectually as gold and silver.

Document II-14: SUFFRAGE FOR BLACKS

This document appears in deliberate interruption of the sequence of testimony which shows how the workers and farmers of America organized, roused an electorate when necessary, and eventually secured a form of representative government more sensitive to their wishes and a general disposition on the part of state and national agencies to intercede in the economy on their behalf. This process began with the struggle for a broadened electoral franchise and the revocation of property qualifications for the vote.

In another section of this collection, considerable space is devoted to the documentary history of the anti-slavery crusade and to efforts on behalf of the rights of Negroes since the Civil War. The Fifteenth Amendment is inserted here to document the time disjunction in the social progress of the races. Just as the predominantly white farm and labor population was organizing nationally, offering presidential candidates, and bargaining with local party bosses, the black worker received for the first time the right to vote. Except for the period of enforced reconstruction policies, this right did not mean much for many, many years.

SOURCE: United States Constitution; Fifteenth Amendment proclaimed March 30, 1870.

UNITED STATES CONSTITUTION

ARTICLE XV

Section 1. The right of citizens of the United States to vote shall not be denied or abridged by the United States or by any State on account of race, color, or previous condition of servitude—

Section 2. The Congress shall have power to enforce this article by appropriate legislation.

Document II-15: LABOR REFORM IN CONVENTION

The ideas of Edward Kellogg, coupled with the greenbacks issued to finance the Civil War, added up to a program for politico-economic action set forth by Alexander Campbell in his long, revealing pamphlet *The True American System of Finance; the Rights of Labor and Capital, and the Common Sense Way of Doing Justice to the Soldiers and their Families. No Banks; Greenbacks the Exclusive Currency* (Chicago, Evening Journal, 1864). The ideas of Kellogg, as applied by Campbell, became an important plank of common interest to both farm and labor leaders as they began their efforts to create a national party for the working man. Campbell proposed using greenbacks to retire the Civil War debt and issuing an additional amount to meet the currency shortage and to make credit available to men of modest means. He built his appeal on the continuing anti-bank sentiment, on the vision of a better financial reward for the producers of wealth, and on the use of the federal influence to keep interest rates moderate. (For a careful discussion of Campbell's role, see Robert P. Sharkey, *Money, Class, and Party: an Economic Study of Civil War and Reconstruction.* Baltimore, Johns Hopkins University, 1959, p. 191ff. Mr. Sharkey proposed that support for the Kellogg-Campbell plan formed an important part of the socio-economic concern not only of farm and labor leaders but also of many Radical Republicans.)

Labor was the first group to give unqualified endorsement to the form of greenbackism indicated in the Kellogg-Campbell publications. The

National Labor Union, organized in 1866, first attempted through local campaigns to achieve the eight-hour working day. Turning toward national politics, they met in Columbus in 1872 as the National Labor and Reform Party, nominated two candidates who deserted the new party after the Liberal Republicans and Democrats had nominated Horace Greeley, and approved the platform which follows. Farmers and middle-class reformers joined this ill-fated effort, but the platform was that of the working man's friend with its opening insistence that all should enjoy the "fruits of their labor," its call for legislation for an eight-hour day and against the contract importation of labor, particularly from China. Planks 1-3 show the acceptance of Kellogg and Campbell; plank 4 nods in the direction of George Henry Evans and land reform. The idea of increasing the responsiveness of the executive to the popular will is housed in plank 12.

In many states the farmers were less avid backers of greenbacks than were the labor party leaders; yet, when a farm-led group produced a national platform in Indianapolis in 1876, it was nearly 100 percent Kellogg-Campbell.

SOURCE: Platform of the National Labor Reform Convention, meeting at Columbus, Ohio, February 21-22, 1872. Edward McPherson, *A Hand-Book of Politics for 1872.* Washington, D.C., Philp & Solomons, 1872, pp. 211-212.

NATIONAL LABOR REFORM PARTY:

THE PLATFORM

We hold that all political power is inherent in the people, and free government founded on their authority and established for their benefit; that all citizens are equal in political rights, entitled to the largest religious and political liberty compatible with the good order of society, as also the use and enjoyment of the fruits of their labor and talents; and no man or set of men is entitled to exclusive separable endowments and privileges, or immunities from the Government, but in consideration of public services; and any laws destructive of these fundamental principles are without moral binding force, and should be repealed. And believing that all the evils resulting from unjust legislation now affecting the industrial classes can be removed by the adoption of the principle contained in the following declaration: Therefore,

Resolved. 1. That it is the duty of the Government to establish a just standard of distribution of capital and labor by providing a purely national circulating medium, based on the faith and resources of the nation, issued directly to the people without the intervention of any system of banking corporations, which money shall be legal tender in the payment of all debts, public and private, and interchangeable at the option of the holder for Government bonds bearing a rate of interest not to exceed 3.65 per cent, subject to future legislation by Congress.

2. That the national debt should be paid in good faith, according to the original contract, at the earliest option of the Government, without mortgaging the property of the people or the future exigencies of labor to enrich a few capitalists at home and abroad.

3. That justice demands that the burdens of Government should be so adjusted as to bear equally on all classes, and that the exemption from taxation of Government bonds bearing extravagant rates of interest is a violation of all just principles of revenue laws.

4. That the public lands of the United States belong to the people and should not be sold to individuals nor granted to corporations, but should be held as a sacred trust for the benefit of the people, and should be granted to landless settlers only, in amounts not exceeding one hundred and sixty acres of land.

5. That Congress should modify the tariff so as to admit free such articles of common use as we can neither produce nor grow, and lay duties for revenue mainly upon articles of luxury and upon such articles of manufacture as will, we having the raw materials, assist in further developing the resources of the country.

6. That the presence in our country of Chinese laborers, imported by capitalists in large numbers for servile use, is an evil, entailing want and its attendant train of misery and crime on all classes of the American people, and should be prohibited by legislation.

7. That we ask for the enactment of a law by which all mechanics and day-laborers employed by or on behalf of the Government, whether directly or indirectly, through persons, firms, or corporations, contracting with the State, shall conform to the reduced standard of eight hours a day, recently adopted by Congress for national employés, and also for an amendment to the acts of incorporation for cities and towns by which all laborers and mechanics employed at their expense shall conform to the same number of hours.

8. That the enlightened spirit of the age demands the abolition of the

system of contract labor in our prisons and other reformatory institutions.

9. That the protection of life, liberty, and property are the three cardinal principles of Government, and the first two are more sacred than the latter; therefore money needed for prosecuting wars should, as it is required, be assessed and collected from the wealthy of the country, and not entailed as a burden on posterity.

10. That it is the duty of the Government to exerise its power over railroads and telegraph corporations, that they shall not in any case be privileged to exact such rates of freight, transportation, or charges, by whatever name, as may bear unduly or unequally upon the producer or consumer.

11. That there should be such a reform in the civil service of the national Government as will remove it beyond all partisan influence, and place it in the charge and under the direction of intelligent and competent business men.

12. That as both history and experience teaches us that power ever seeks to perpetuate itself by every and all means, and that its prolonged possession in the hands of one person is always dangerous to the interests of a free people, and believing that the spirit of our organic laws and the stability and safety of our free institutions are best obeyed on the one hand, and secured on the other, by a regular constitutional change in the chief of the country at each election: therefore, we are in favor of limiting the occupancy of the presidential chair to one term.

13. That we are in favor of granting general amnesty and restoring the Union at once on the basis of equality of rights and privileges to all, the impartial administration of justice being the only true bond of union to bind the States together and restore the Government of the people.

14. That we demand the subjection of the military to the civil authorities, and the confinement of its operation to national purposes alone.

15. That we deem it expedient for Congress to supervise the patent laws, so as to give labor more fully the benefit of its own ideas and inventions.

16. That fitness, and not political or personal considerations, should be the only recommendation to public office, either appointive or elective, and any and all laws looking to the establishment of this principle are heartily approved.

Document II-16: REFORM AND THE RAILROAD

Bankers, along with financiers and speculators, continued to be principal villains in the eyes of those seeking economic equity from before
Jackson until after Roosevelt. Equally feared and vilified, particularly in
the last quarter of the nineteenth century, were the builders and owners of
the railroads. Before the Civil War the term "anti-monopoly" was used
with some frequency; it occasionally referred to a transportation monopoly, almost always it referred to a bank or a banking system. After the
Civil War the target of anti-monopoly sentiment was typically the railroads.

There was good reason for this. The path of the rails, as they were
being laid at an alarming rate (railroad miles increased sevenfold between 1865 and 1900), often spelled the difference between success and
failure for workers and manufacturers, farmers and traders. Before the
age of highways, and particularly in parts of the country where water
transportation was inadequate, the railroad provided the only avenue
toward participation in contemporary life—social as well as commercial.

Resistance against the railroads was expressed in many forms. The
"Great Strike" of 1877 was in essence a railroad strike, and the spectacular Pullman Strike of 1894 was aimed at the manufacturer of railroad
passenger cars. As one of the largest interstate employers, the railroad
became an obvious antagonist for the labor organizers who looked
toward the federal government to set minimum wages and maximum
hours.

The accompanying picture helps make clear how readily the railroads
assumed an additional negative burden associated with special privilege.
Contrast the luxury of this elaborately appointed "varnish" car with the
wagons and coaches on which most people traveled. Contrast the elegant
upholstery and linen-draped tables with the hard benches and rude
jostlings with unwashed neighbors in more typical conveyances. Contrast the rack of wines and the platter of roast pheasant with the ordinary
migrant's lunch box of hard bread and sausage. (A good representation of
more usual rail travel appeared in *Harper's Weekly*, November 13,
1886. It is reproduced in *Everyday Life in the Age of Enterprise* by the
present author [New York, Putnam's, 1967], p. 67.)

SOURCE: This wood engraving, after a drawing by Albert Bingham, appeared in *Frank Leslie's Illustrated Newspaper*, January 15, 1870.

ACROSS THE CONTINENT, ON THE PACIFIC RAILROAD.—DINING SALOON OF THE HOTEL EXPRESS TRAIN. See Page 301.

Hotel-train diner

For those who believed in economic democracy, then, it was easy to resent the list of real and imagined special privileges that came with the railroad: the plush private trains and special cars; the railroad passes awarded influential judges and senators; and the granting of token-priced stock in railroad ventures to well-placed officeholders—as most notably in the infamous Crédit Mobilier scandal of 1872. To organize, to strike, and to vote against this form of exploitation and special privilege occupied considerable reform energy in the Gilded Age.

Document II-17: FARMERS' DECLARATION OF INDEPENDENCE

To the Western farmer, the railroad seemed every bit as oppressive as the distant English government had seemed to the colonists. Carefully, then, he parodied the Declaration of Independence of 1776 and circulated it as his own signal for revolution. This highly emotional and seldom-reproduced document listed effectively the farmer's major grievances. The rhetoric exudes a long-suffering resentment against arbitrary and discriminatory rates, against the large land subsidies awarded the newer roads, and against the failure of routes to serve all the farmers. To the cash-crop farmer, forced to choose between high storage rates and high transportation rates,when both the elevators and the cars were owned by the same company, bitterness was indeed named monopoly and monopoly named railroad.

The farmers' declaration was followed by the Granger cases in which some state responsibility for railroad regulation was established. As these decisions were eroded by the carriers, federal acts were passed in partial response to continued rural pressure: the Interstate Commerce Act of 1887 and the Sherman Anti-Trust Act of 1890. Neither was a perfect solution, but the process of adjudication and legislation had shown that the farmer's vote was a weapon against unfair economic discrimination.

SOURCE: Chicago *Tribune*, June 17, 1873, p. 2.

FARMERS' DECLARATION
Fourth of July, 1873

When in the course of human events it becomes necessary for a class of people suffering from long-continued systems of oppression and abuse, to rouse themselves from an apathetic indifference to their own interests, which has become habitual; to assume among their fellow-citizens that equal station, and demand from the government they support those equal rights, to which the laws of nature and of Nature's God entitles them; as decent respect for the opinions of mankind requires that they should declare the causes that impel them to a course so necessary to their own protection.

We hold these truths to be self-evident; that all men are created equal; that they are endowed by their Creator with certain inalienable rights; that among these are life, liberty, and the pursuit of happiness. That to secure these rights governments are instituted among men, deriving their just powers from the consent of the governed; that whenever the powers of a government become destructive of these ends, either through the injustice or inefficiency of its laws, or through the corruption of its administrators, it is the right of the people to abolish such laws, and to institute such reforms as to them shall seem most likely to effect their safety and happiness. Prudence, indeed, will dictate that laws long established shall not be changed for light and trifling causes, and, accordingly, all experience hath shown that mankind are more disposed to suffer while evils are sufferable, than to right themselves by abolishing the laws to which they are accustomed. But when a long train of abuses and usurpations, pursuing invariably the same object, evinces a desire to reduce a people under the absolute desposition of combinations, that, under the fostering care of Government, and with wealth wrung from the people, have grown to such gigantic proportions as to overshadow all the land, and wield an almost irresistible influence for their own selfish purposes, in all its halls of legislation, it is their right—it is their duty—to throw off such tyranny, and provide new guards for their future security.

Such has been the patient sufferance of the producing classes of these States, and such is now the necessity which compels them to declare that they will use every means, save a resort to arms, to overthrow this despotism of monopoly, and to reduce all men claiming the protection of American laws to an equality before those laws, making the owner of a railroad as amenable thereto as the "veriest beggar that walks the streets, the sun and air his sole inheritance."

The history of the present railway monopoly is a history of repeated injuries and oppressions, all having in direct object the establishment of an absolute tyranny over the people of these States unequaled in any monarchy of the Old World, and having its only parallel in the history of the Medieval ages, when the strong hand was the only law, and the highways of commerce were taxed by the Feudal Barons, who, from their strongholds, surrounded by their armies of vassals, could levy such tribute upon the traveler as their own wills alone should dictate. To prove this, let facts be submitted to a candid world:

They have influenced our executive officers to refuse their assent to laws the most wholesome and necessary for the public good, and when such laws have been passed they have utterly refused to obey them.

They have procured the passage of other laws, for their own benefit alone, by which they have put untold millions into their own coffers, to the injury of the entire commercial and industrial interests of the country.

They have influenced legislation to suit themselves, by bribing venal legislators to betray the true interests of their constituents, while others have been kept quiet by the compliment of free passes.

They have repeatedly prevented the re-election of representatives for opposing with manly firmness their invasions of the people's rights.

They have by false representations and subterfuge induced the people to subscribe funds to build roads, whose rates, when built, are so exorbitant that in many instances transportation by private conveyances is less burdensome.

They have procured charters by which they condemn and appropriate our lands without adequate compensation therefor, and arrogantly claim that by virtue of these charters they are absolutely above the control of legal enactments.

They have procured a law of Congress by which they have dispossessed hundreds of farmers of the homes that by years of toil they have built up; have induced others to mortgage their farms for roads never intended to be built, and after squandering the money thus obtained, they have left their victims to the mercy of courts over which they hold absolute sway.

They have obstructed the administration of justice by injunctions, procured from venal judges by legal quibbles, and appeals, from court to court, with intent to wear out or ruin the prosecutor, openly avowing their determination to make it so terrible for the public to prosecute them that they will not dare to undertake it.

They have virtually made judges dependant on their will alone, and have procured their appointment for the express purpose of reversing a decision of the highest court of the nation, by which millions were gained to them, to the injury of the holders of their bonds and the breaking down of this last safeguard of American freemen.

They have affected to render themselves independent of and superior to the civil power, by ordering large bodies of hirelings to enforce their unlawful exactions, and have protected them from punishment for any injury they might inflict upon peaceful citizens while ejecting them from their conveyances for refusing to pay more than the rate of fare prescribed by law.

They have arrested and summoned from their homes for trial, at distant points, other citizens for the same offence of refusing to pay more than the legal fare, putting them to as great inconvenience as possible, and still further evincing their determination to make it too terrible for the people to dare engage in any legal conflict with them.

They have combined together to destroy competition; contrary to the expressed provisions of our Constitution and the spirit of our laws.

They have virtually cut off our trade with distant parts of the world by their unjust discriminations, and by their exorbitant rates of freight, forcing upon us the alternative of accumulating upon our hands a worthless surplus, or of giving three-fourths of the price customers pay for our products for their transportation.

Under the false and specious pretence of developing the country, they have obtained enormous grants of public land from Congress, and now retard rather than develop its settlement, by the high prices charged for such land.

They have converted the bonds fraudulently obtained from the Government into a great corruption fund, with which they are enabled to bribe and control Legislatures, and subvert every branch of Government to their own base and sordid purposes.

They have increased the already intolerable burden of taxation which the people have to endure (compared with which the tea and stamp-tax, which precipitated the war of the revolution, seem utterly insignificant), by the appropriation of money from the public Treasury, while they have escaped taxation themselves by evading and violating the express provisions of their charters.

In every stage of these oppressions we have petitioned our Legislatures for redress, in the most humble terms. Our repeated petitions have been answered only by silences, or attempts to frame laws that shall seem to meet our wants, but that are, in fact, only a legal snare for courts to disagree upon, and for corporations to disobey.

Nor have we been wanting in attempts to obtain redress through Congress. We have warned them from time to time of these various and repeated encroachments upon our rights; we have reminded them of the circumstances of our emigration and settlement here; we have appealed to them as the administrators of a free and impartial government, to protect us from these encroachments, which, if continued, would inevitably end in the utter destruction of those liberties for which our fathers gave their lives, and the reinstatement of privileged classes and an aristocracy of wealth worse than that from which the War of the Revolution freed us. They, too, have been deaf to the voice of justice and of duty. We must therefore acquiesce in the necessity which compels us to denounce their criminal indifference to our wrongs, and hold them as we hold our Legislatures,—enemies to the producer,—to the monopolists friends.

We, therefore, the producers of this State, in our several counties assembled, on this anniversary of that day that gave birth to a nation of freemen, and to a government of which, despite the corruptions of its officers, we are still so justly proud, appealing to the Supreme Judge of the world for the rectitude of our intentions, do solemnly declare that we will use all lawful and peaceable means to free ourselves from the tyranny of monopoly, and that we will never cease our efforts for reform until every department of our Government gives token that the reign of licentious extravagance is over, and something of the purity, honesty, and frugality with which our father inaugurated it has taken place.

That to this end we declare ourselves absolutely free and independent of all past political connections, and that we shall give our suffrage only to such men for office, from the lowest officer in the State to the President of the United States, as we have good reason to believe will use their best endeavors to the promotion of these ends; and for the support of this declaration, with a firm reliance in Divine Providence, we mutually pledge to each other our lives, our fortunes, and our sacred honor.

THE FARMERS.

Document II-18: THE GRANGE MOVEMENT

Fourth of July for the farmer was typically a time of relaxed sociability (sack races and picnics), patriotic speeches ("'soarin' the eagle"'), and competitive exhibitionism (prize hogs and jams). In 1873, particularly in Illinois and the neighboring states, this holiday took on a more serious note. The accompanying scene reflects this urgent air of purposeful concentration, and the placards carry a message of aggrieved victimization with an implied promise of action. The Grange, like this Grangers' holiday, was about to change its focus from a stress on education and social activity to a concern with political and economic problems.

The air was most frequently filled, on the Farmers' Fourth of July, with the Farmers' Declaration of Independence (see II-17); but the issues went beyond the railroad and the greenbacks. They included a shortage of credit and a resentment against the tariffs which made the farmer pay more for what he bought, yet failed to protect his crops against world competition. Each of these issues was clouded with a tone of victimization.

Often the Grange itself eschewed direct political action; but in many states the farmers formed Independent, Reform, or Anti-Monopoly parties. Sometimes they ran their own candidates. Sometimes they endorsed major-party candidates to gain concessions. They operated most effectively where direct election of judges allowed them to replace "railroad judges" with those more favorable to the farmers. In eleven states the farmers used their power at the ballot box to some effect. (See Solon J. Buck, *The Granger Movement.* Cambridge, Harvard University Press, 1913, Chapter III.)

Somewhat outside the main pattern of politico-economic reform was the farmers' other principal activity of this era: the establishment of producers' and consumers' cooperatives. Although this movement had some important and lasting consequences, it did not provide the hoped-for cure-all. The urge for a more effective democratic expression in order to achieve increased economic equity expressed itself mainly in the fight against the railroads, against the tariff, and in favor of a more responsive system of currency and credit.

SOURCE: Wood engraving after a sketch by Joseph B. Beale captioned "The Farmers' Movement in the West.—Meeting of the Grangers in the Woods Near Winchester, Scott County, Illinois." *Frank Leslie's Illustrated Newspaper*, August 30, 1873.

Farmers' Fourth of July

Document II-19: WHITMAN ON THE LABOR STRIKE

A number of urban parallels to the Farmers' Fourth of July could be cited: the St. Patrick's Day parades, which began in Los Angeles in 1870, and the Labor Day festivities, dating notably from New York City in 1882, provided occasions for exhortations on behalf of the workers. Whereas the public took kindly to speeches and marches, there was considerable reservation about activities that moved more directly in pursuit of the welfare of the working man.

The pattern of public reaction was accurately set in the first national industrial strike, a spontaneous response to drastic wage cuts which eventually stopped all rail traffic east of the Mississippi as well as on some roads to the west. Against the unpopular railroads, the strikers had the early sympathy of the public. But the appearance of violence, notably in Baltimore and Pittsburgh, soon turned the tables. President Hayes reflected a consensus view when he sent federal troops to protect private property and quell the violence. Some years later when Cleveland did the same thing, he was not so free from criticism but still demonstrably within the majority definition of presidential responsibility.

This verse, penned as an immediate reaction to the events, shows some of the problems faced by reformers who worked for economic justice by other than the time-consuming means of petitions and elections. It was written by a self- educated former slave who, one might suspect, would have had a natural sympathy with the oppressed and the impoverished. Yet he reflects a number of attitudes which were probably shared by most Americans outside the small fraternity of labor organizers and third-party agitators.

Is not the sympathy for the workers considerably diluted by the dread of the "commotion" that "chills the circling life of enterprise"? Is there much resistance to the newspapers' headline-style oversimplified linking of labor unrest with "Communism's snaky head"? Although one cannot miss the true sympathy for people who suffer from cold and hunger, is there not also visible a tendency to distinguish between the lewd and lawless poor, on the one hand, and the "deserving poor" on the other hand? And is there not a temptation to seek redress in charity rather than social action?

The author of these lines, an early promoter of Wilberforce College, doubtless considered himself a reformer who urged his readers to work through education and self-cultivation. His attitudes show some of the problems encountered by another style of reformer who sought collective solutions with more immediately visible results.

SOURCE: Albery A. Whitman, *Not a Man and Yet a Man*. Springfield, Ohio, Republic, 1877, pp. 252-253.

The Great Strike

"Strike! Strike! Stop! Stop!" What mean these shouts
    that rise—
This great commotion throughout all the land,
That chills the circling life of enterprise,
While lawlessness stalks forth with torch in hand?

The hands of Industry have to the head
(Aweary grown of swinging to and fro)
Without discretion's sober forethought said:
"We ought to be above, and you below."

Whenever Communism's snaky head
Is raised against the heel of Capital,
I want it crushed 'neath Law's majestic tread,
And yet would heed poor honest labor's call.

The cold long Winter fast is coming on,
His near approach makes sad the leafless year,
And deep snows soon the naked fields upon,
Will hush the voice of Autumn's latest cheer.

The burdened year will soon her treasures yield,
And pile our spacious barns from eaves to floor,
Then vagrant want in lanes and open field,
Can gather scanty sustenance no more.

The howling winds will drive before them then,
This drifting dust of Fortune's feet in clouds;
And higher thither into ditch and den
Mis'ry and crime will rush in babbling crowds.

But while the desp'rate curse, while lewdness cries,
And shiftlessness ought justly to go bare,
Forget it not, full many a Lazarus lies
Before thy gate and *needs* a crumb of care.

While Wealth across his lordly arm will cast
The warmth of scores of God Almighty's poor,
Still houseless want must shiver in the blast,
And childhood's feet go bare from door to door.

While pride upon her easy finger wears
The bread of thousands in a brilliant stone,
The eyes of Wretchedness must stream with tears,
And groaning labor be content to groan.

Let heaven's light upon our nature shine,
Till ev'ry opaque spot with glory beams,
And want no longer at our feet can pine,
But happiness will flow in living streams.

Document II-20: DIRECT PRIMARY ELECTIONS

The following petition rings with the central spirit of political protest as it took shape after the Civil War. It evokes a developing sense of class and attempts to unite the farmers and workers against those who exploited them economically through high interest rates and politically through unfair taxation. The essential grievance was economic. The essential remedy was political and reverted to that characteristic trust in the wisdom of popular will, if accurately expressed. This kind of protest was in part a response to some of the more spectacular postbellum events which eroded public trust in the honesty and efficiency of the contemporary political system.

When the petition alludes to bribery and subsidy, it does so against the immediate background of a rich variety of scandalous headlines. As the Grant administration came to a close in 1877, hardly a day seemed to pass without some fresh news of malfeasance or misappropriation in a series of interlocking "rings" of influence and privilege. The winter of 1876-77, with the capture and return to America of Boss Tweed, brought to light some of the more spectacular episodes in municipal graft. From the presidential cabinet right down to city politics, corruption—the use of political power to produce political spoils—was beginning to seem commonplace. Since the days of Jackson, patronage had always been an important part of the party arsenal; but there is little doubt that it had been abused. The party out of office is always more outraged by spoils revelations; yet, even discounting for the taste of sour grapes, the Democratic platform of 1872 showed in its language a confidence that the public had had enough:

> The civil service of the Government has become a mere instrument of partisan tyranny and personal ambition and an object of selfish greed. It is a scandal and reproach upon free institutions and breeds a demoralization dangerous to the perpetuity of republican government. We therefore regard a thorough reform of the civil service as one of the most pressing necessities of the hour; that honesty, capacity, and fidelity constitute the only valid claim to public employment; that the offices of the Government cease to be a matter of arbitrary favoritism and patronage, and that public station become again a post of honor. To this end it is imperatively required that no President shall be a candidate for reelection.

By 1876 the indictment had become even more elaborate and the call for civil service reform even more uncompromising. An eventual result of this sentiment was the passage in 1883 of the Pendleton Act which helped form the basis for the modern civil service system. It received the necessary bipartisan support, however, only after the assassination of a Republican President by a disappointed office seeker.

The supporters of the following petition saw a remedy for official incompetence in diminishing the power of the parties to name candidates in caucus or convention where an "oligarchy" of the bosses controlled the outcome. The means proposed was the direct primary, a device which was not adopted on a state level until 1902 (Mississippi) and, more sweepingly, in Wisconsin in 1903. By 1917, all but four states had some provisions for direct primaries, mandatory in thirty-two states. This petition represents an early insistence on what eventually became a part of the turn-of-the-century Progressive program. Like the proliferation of third-party movements, it showed a fundamental lack of confidence in the willingness of the two major parties to respond to the real issues of the day.

These petitioners preferred direct primaries and direct election of the President partly because of the dangerous possibility of third-party intrusion on the choice of the true majority. With the disputed election of 1876 fresh in mind, the petitioners offered a complex system of popular elections that would allow the voting public a full role in the nominating process and that would guarantee that the eventual winner would represent a true popular majority. Like most such schemes it had its flaws, but the issues expressed here are basic to understanding the sense of values and tactics held by the politico-economic reformers.

SOURCE: Duncan C. McMillan, *Petition of Nine Millions of Citizens, for the Abolition of the "Political Machine," and the Redress of Other Grievances, to the Congress of the United States*. Kingston, N.Y., by the author, 1878, pp. 1-6, 14-15, abridged. (Note: The only copy of this pamphlet held by the Library of Congress is missing the corner of one page. Thus a few words at the end of the second and the beginning of the third paragraphs have been supplied by the editor.)

To the Senate and the House of Representatives of the United States:

WE, the five millions of citizens of the United States engaged in agricultural occupations, and the four millions of merchants and workingmen engaged in various pursuits connected with manufacturing and mining industries, trade, transportation and personal service, under Article I. of the amendments to the Constitution, respectfully petition to your honorable bodies for a redress of our grievances, and desire to set forth the following facts:—

During the past ten years, in nearly every State in the Union, struggling under onerous taxation which is eating out our substance, we have been vainly trying to better our condition through the exercise of the ballot in the choice of honest and competent public rulers. Our efforts, in the main, have been futile. The mortgages upon our farms have been increasing; the rents to our landlords are high; the value of our crops is being reduced; the wages of our sweat are scarcely sufficient for our subsistence; and a portion of the time the wheels of commerce, which give us employment, have been clogged, and we are forced upon the world, begging from door to door in search of work, subjected to the gibes and insults attendant upon our unfortunate condition.

During this period we have seen Congress voting away subsidies and appropriations to immense corporations already enriched by its favors; large salaries to office-holders, building huge public works for the benefit of architects, contractors, and speculators; increasing the number of public servants; paying an army of marshals to attend elections conducted under State authority—all apparently for the purpose of establishing the influence of individual members with the persons receiving these benefits. Even now strong lobbies are at its doors, and vast schemes of internal improvement for the Southern States are awaiting the sanction of your honorable Congress, while the Scotts, Vanderbilts and Goulds are appealing for additional means for public oppression in asking the increase of the army of the country.

To gain relief from these burdens we have trusted the Democratic and the Republican party; we have demanded change, and our votes have secured it. Yet our debts have not diminished, and our grievances have increased, while our efforts for reform indicate a desperation which is fitly described in the language of thousands of our number who feel that no change can be for the worse.

In California and Oregon we banded ourselves together as Independents and Workingmen; in the New England States as Labor Reformers; in the South as Democratic Independents, and in the West as Grangers; and whether successful or defeated, little has been gained by our efforts. Many of us have joined a new organization called the Nationals, and while we all sympathize with some of the views of that party, we are not unmindful of the obstacles to the formation of a third political force. Our previous experience has shown us that when success is likely to crown our efforts the machinery of our organization is seized by the very elements we desire to exclude, and adroit politicians use our party for the purpose of plundering us more. We are deceived and betrayed when in the majority and when in the minority the temptation to choose the least of two evils impels us to cast our votes for the older political organizations.

Though outnumbering ten to one the few into whose hands our property is passing, and though generally agreed upon the remedies for our grievances, yet there seems to be no means afforded by the ballot through which we can give our voice an effective expression. Although in every community we are able to select hundreds of upright citizens to whom we would willingly confide our public trusts, yet upon the day of election we find ourselves compelled by force of circumstances to make a choice between only *two* men for each office, both of whom by large expenditure of money have purchased the privilege of representing our parties, and have been selected by interested agencies through manipulation, deception, trickery, and bribery. Under such circumstances thousands of us refuse to vote, and many, having little preference between the two candidates, are constrained to yield to the temptations they offer and barter our votes for money. Denied a fair and equal voice in the nominations, no good reason exists why, year after year, we should dance at the beck of politicians and invest their proceedings with a dignity they do not deserve by attending elections in which our voice is negative rather than positive. Seeing little value in the franchise, many are gradually abandoning its use, and all are agreed that the expense attending the exercise of the suffrage might better be saved so long as we are denied an affirmative voice in public affairs, and are limited to the choice of one of the two men, both of whom hope to make as much money as they can out of us and to help their respective friends to do the same thing.

If your honorable bodies feel that we are sufficiently represented in the caucus and convention, a great expense might be saved to us, your constituents, by the repeal of all election laws relating to the election of the President of the United States and the members of Congress. The expense of party machinery is paid by the contractors, lobbyists, officeholders, monopolists, bankers and railroad kings, who manage it in their interests; and action by your body permitting elections to be conducted in the same way would save the people the expense and inconvenience of deciding between the respective claims of these agencies on the day of our so-called election.

To conform the elections to the method of nominations, your honorable Congress might require by legislation that after nominations are made, other delegates should be elected by promiscuous caucus, attended by Democrats, Republicans, aliens, repeaters, minors, convicts, and all passers-by, the law of brute force alone to prevail; such delegates to make the election in accord with their own supreme will. Under such a system of exercising their voice, the people would be relieved of the necessity of attending elections as they now are of attending the caucuses, and the expense of election machinery would be saved to our overtaxed property. As the officers of the Government are nominated in this way, which nomination is the election so far as the party is concerned, no good reason would seem to exist why elections should not be held in precisely the same manner.

If such a proposition be thought absurd for *elections*, the system is no less so for *nominations*; and your petitioners would humbly ask that the exercise of the franchise may be rendered valuable. We would, therefore, respectfully petition:

THAT A SYSTEM OF ELECTIONS FOR CONGRESSMEN AND PRESIDENT BE ADOPTED WHICH WILL GIVE THE PEOPLE THE SAME VOICE IN THE NOMINATION OF PERSONS FOR OFFICE THAT THEY HAVE IN THE ELECTION; THAT THEY MAY BE PROTECTED IN THE CAUCUS BY THE ELECTION LAWS, AND THAT THEIR VOTES CAST DIRECT FOR CANDIDATES MAY BE FAIRLY COUNTED.

The forefathers of your petitioners established the electoral college for the election of President, so that he might be independent of interference by members of Congress. The Constitution said that no member of Congress should be a member of the electoral college; in fact, it excluded all office-holders under the Government. The electors, as your honorable body well knows, were to meet together and pick out, after careful discussion, the very best man for the high office of Chief Magistrate. If the President was so selected, and the electors were honest in their choice, and obeyed the wishes of the people, we would now enjoy the benefits of good government, as far as the Executive patronage is concerned. This patronage is very large, as your petitioners have reason to know, as it extends to every appointment under the United States Government.

Unfortunately for your petitioners, the electoral system miscarried. The electors did not select the candidate at all after the first few elections; and in 1824 the Congressional caucus enjoyed that privilege. The Con-

gressmen excluded from the electoral college performed its duties outside, and thus nullified the Constitution. Dividing itself into two parts,
representing the two parties, Congress selected, or nominated, both
candidates for President, and the people could not vote for a third
candidate without throwing the election into the very Congress which
made the nomination. There was no need of discussion about candidates
in the electoral college, when Congress assumed this authority, and the
electors became an assembly of automata.

The people, though their hands were tied, rebelled; and, to make
matters worse, Congress failing to give them a proper system of nominations, the politicians established one of their own. For the nomination of
President, they instituted the national conventions. The Senators and
Congressmen, to whom the President had formerly owed his nomination
directly, still retained their influence. The monopolists could now enter
into the scheme and manage this new machinery. If they wanted tariff
protection, all they had to do was to combine and use their influence in
the caucus of the leading party in some of the Congressional districts, and
thus they could own the Congressmen. The office-holders, excluded
from the electoral college, now became valuable; for a national convention would not be recognized without their presence. The Congressmen
who wanted a renomination demanded of the President a portion of the
patronage, which insured to him the necessary instrumentalities. His
personal influence with the monopolists he favored enabled him to
enforce his demand. If the President refused, the capitalists could frus-
trate his ambitions and destroy his influence in Congress. The power of
this combination of a hundred thousand office-holders, a thousand
monopolists—greedily grasping for subsidies, for tariffs, for banking
privileges, involving the expenditure or control of hundreds of millions
of dollars—centralized upon small political conventions, composed in
large part of these very office-holders and monopolists—the money-
power of the country—can be but feebly described; and when both
parties have persisted so long in presenting candidates in this manner,
your petitioners feel a sense of congratulation that this great and
domineering oligarchy has permitted them to retain so long the little
possessions they hold.

It is quite needless for your petitioners to describe this machinery, so
open to the designs of the few who have the means to purchase active
effort in their behalf. The convention is a small body. Its members vote

secretly, and are not held accountable for what they do. They may vote for the wisest statesman or for the most dishonest demagogue, and the people would not be the wiser. They may take money for their votes, or, as Benton says, receive the promise of office. All we know is that sometimes they travel a very great way to perform a personal part of which nobody ever hears.

No laws exist excluding Republicans from Democratic, or Democrats from Republican primaries, to say how many times and in how many places they shall vote; aliens have all the privileges of citizens; and even women are afforded a conclusive answer to all their appeals for suffrage, for here the law will not deny them the right.

Your petitioners can do no more than state these facts: that we are peaceable citizens attempting to use the franchise properly; that we desire to attend and participate in the primaries, but owing to the disorders, riots, confusion, false counting, repeating, bribery and other unpleasant surroundings, we find it exceedingly difficult to do so. Nor can we conceive of any useful purpose to be subserved thereby. If our votes are counted, even when only our party votes, we only elect a delegate usually pledged in advance to some person unknown to us, and who may represent the very power we desire to oppose; and we shall never be the wiser, for he will vote in secret.

The vast majority of your petitioners have, therefore, abandoned these assemblies and left them under the control of these purely selfish agencies. When delegates are elected at the primary, who, in turn elect others to an assembly convention, which in turn appoints others to a State convention, there is not one of your petitioners who believes that he has exercised any influence in sending the national delegate to make a nomination for President. Subjected to this process of filtration, no particle of the original substance is permitted to penetrate the convention, and the act of that body becomes the aggregate result of the operation of the individual wills of its delegates, subjected to no restraints, and exposed to the gravest temptations.

Your petitioners have great affection for popular institutions, yet it need not be wondered that in the minds of many of them, monarchical ideas are taking root, for, as moderate men, having abandoned these stormy primary assemblies, they feel it a small matter to be deprived of a franchise whose beneficial exercise they have been compelled to renounce. . . .

. . . The first election would take the place of the primary, and the second would decide between the two persons, of opposite parties. If any person received a majority at the first election, the second would be unnecessary.

Under such a system of elections, your petitioners, intent upon honest government, if in a minority would not refuse to make a choice between political opponents, any of whom if nominated would certainly be elected, rather than to throw away their votes upon their political friends, any one of whom if nominated must be defeated at the subsequent election. Hence honesty and capacity and the real principles of the persons named as candidates would govern the choice of your petitioners, and they would no longer feel compelled to support a candidate, however unworthy, only because he wore the livery of their party. Party contests would be limited to doubtful districts; and in all others the minority would have a genuine representation.

Your petitioners, who are mechanics, merchants, farmers, laborers and tradesmen, have no interest in politics, in parties or in patronage; and seek only the opportunity of giving their votes for HONEST MEN wherever found—men who will represent the true principles of good government. We seek to make our officials responsible to us and not to the agencies now controlling political machinery, without whose assistance political advancement is now impossible.

And we express our confidence that when candidates owe their nominations to us, public advancement will be the reward of honorable performance of public duty; and not as now, due to the activity and number of office-holders and agencies enlisted in the interest of candidates whose influence procures or protects their appointments or privileges. Nor can we see an end to taxation until the present system is destroyed; for through it, each candidate seeking political advancement measures his hopes of success by the number of stipendiaries enlisted in his cause, which number he will aim constantly to increase, and thereby cause a growing demand upon the resources of your petitioners.

The Congressional caucus has been destroyed, but from this evil no relief can be had without the interference of your honorable bodies. We have manifested our disapproval of this system by every means in our power. Driven from our own parties, we have formed immense third organizations; we have always voted as between the two candidates presented for our suffrages, the more honest of the two, the choice of evils; but we realize that though representing a vast majority, our influence in the government is small indeed; and we shall ever be an impotent factor until your honorable body shall grant our petition and give free scope to our will by permitting us to select from the thousands of our fellow-citizens, instead of from only two persons, those most worthy of our free suffrages.

Your petitioners submit that they should not be subjected to the stigma resulting from official mismanagement until they are permitted the fullest latitude in the selection of their agents; and popular government exists in fact as well as in name.

Document II-21: GEORGE ON POVERTY

Progress and Poverty is one of the major documents in the history of American reform. It combined learning and literacy to produce a broad and lasting impact comparable only, in its day, to Edward Bellamy's *Looking Backward* (See IV-9). Both were enormously popular; both stimulated a number of other books in elaboration and response; both had direct political consequences. A distinction between the two might be found in Bellamy's total utopian vision as opposed to Henry George's hard arguments on one major point.

As the following selection makes clear, George's thought was based on the familiar assumption that land is the basic source of wealth and power. Applying this physiocratic principle to the American political situation, George Henry Evans, Horace Greeley, and others had concluded that the public lands, at least, must be treated as though they belonged to the people (see II-12). By 1872 the Democratic Party had been swayed by the land reformers to the extent of nominating Greeley for President and including in its platform the statement: "We are opposed to all further grants of lands to railroads or other corporations. The public domain should be held sacred to actual settlers."

George did not care whether the land was public or private; he demanded that any income or gain whose source could be traced to the land itself, as opposed to the industry of its user, should be taxed so as to return its value fully to the people. Critics argue that the single tax on earned increment in land value was an oversimplified panacea, applicable only to an agricultural age. Others maintain that the George plan is not obsolete and point to the influence it has exercised in discriminatory tax laws in many nations and localities. (The Robert Schalkenbach Foundation today continues to promote George's ideas.)

Progress and Poverty did more than stress that land should be the basic source of economic equity. Representative of his generation was George's emphasis on taxation as a means of righting material imbalance. The history of civilizations showed, he argued, that progress brought with it an increasing maldistribution of wealth. This problem, unless solved, would destroy the very freedom of initiative that has produced the great industrial and commercial empires. Unlike most reformers, George did not find a solution in the extension of suffrage or in any other extension of political democracy. Yet he was very much in tune with his times in his obsession with the injustice of extraordinary wealth existing side by side with abject poverty. He was an important spokesman for a growing number of reformers who sought redress through the introduction of tax systems that would tend to redistribute wealth more evenly. Is there, perhaps, something ironic in the attempts of George and his followers to secure economic reform by the very political means they disparaged?

SOURCE: Henry George, *Progress and Poverty: An Inquiry into the Cause of Industrial Depressions, and of Increase of Want with Increase of Wealth. The Remedy.* New York, Appleton, 1879, pp. 475-478, 295-296, abridged.

PROGRESS AND POVERTY

What has destroyed every previous civilization has been the tendency to the unequal distribution of wealth and power. This same tendency, operating with increasing force, is observable in our civilization to-day, showing itself in every progressive community, and with greater intensity the more progressive the community. Wages and interest tend constantly to fall, rent to rise, the rich to become very much richer, the poor to become more helpless and hopeless, and the middle class to be swept away.

I have traced this tendency to its cause. I have shown by what simple means this cause may be removed. I now wish to point out *how*, if this is not done, progress must turn to decadence, and modern civilization decline to barbarism, as have all previous civilizations. It is worth while to point out *how* this may occur, as many people, being unable to see how progress may pass into retrogression, conceive such a thing impossible. Gibbon, for instance, thought that modern civilization could never be destroyed because there remained no barbarians to overrun it, and it is a common idea that the invention of printing by so multiplying books has prevented the possibility of knowledge ever again being lost.

The conditions of social progress, as we have traced the law, are association and equality. The general tendency of modern development, since the time when we can first discern the gleams of civilization in the darkness which followed the fall of the Western Empire, has been towards political and legal equality—to the abolition of slavery; to the abrogation of status; to the sweeping away of hereditary privileges; to the substitution of parliamentary for arbitrary government; to the right of private judgment in matters of religion; to the more equal security in person and property of high and low, weak and strong; to the greater freedom of movement and occupation, of speech and of the press. The history of modern civilization is the history of advances in this direction—of the struggles and triumphs of personal, political, and religious freedom. And the general law is shown by the fact that just as this tendency has asserted itself civilization has advanced, while just as it has been repressed or forced back civilization has been checked.

This tendency has reached its full expression in the American Republic, where political and legal rights are absolutely equal, and, owing to the system of rotation in office, even the growth of a bureaucracy is prevented; where every religious relief or non-belief stands on the same footing; where every boy may hope to be President, every man has an equal voice in public affairs, and every official is mediately or immediately dependent for the short lease of his place upon a popular vote. This tendency has yet some triumphs to win in England, in extending the suffrage, and sweeping away the vestiges of monarchy, aristocracy, and prelacy; while in such countries as Germany and Russia, where divine right is yet a good deal more than a legal fiction, it has a considerable distance to go. But it is the prevailing tendency, and how soon Europe will be completely republican is only a matter of time, or rather of accident. The United States are therefore, in this respect, the most advanced of all the great nations, in a direction in which all are advancing, and in the United States we see just how much this tendency to personal and political freedom can of itself accomplish.

Now, the first effect of the tendency to political equality was to the more equal distribution of wealth and power; for, while population is comparatively sparse, inequality in the distribution of wealth is principally due to the inequality of personal rights, and it is only as material progress goes on that the tendency to inequality involved in the reduction of land to private ownership strongly appears. But it is now manifest that absolute political equality does not in itself prevent the tendency to inequality involved in the private ownership of land, and it is further evident that political equality, co-existing with an increasing tendency to the unequal distribution of wealth, must ultimately beget either the despotism of organized tyranny or the worse despotism of anarchy.

To turn a republican government into a despotism the basest and most brutal, it is not necessary to formally change its constitution or abandon popular elections. It was centuries after Caesar before the absolute master of the Roman world pretended to rule other than by authority of a Senate that trembled before him.

But forms are nothing when substance has gone, and the forms of popular government are those from which the substance of freedom may most easily go. Extremes meet, and a government of universal suffrage and theoretical equality, may, under conditions which impel the change, most readily become a despotism. For there, despotism advances in the name and with the might of the people. The single source of power once secured, everything is secured. There is no unfranchised class to whom appeal may be made, no privileged orders who in defending their own rights may defend those of all. No bulwark remains to stay the flood, no eminence to rise above it. They were belted barons led by a mitred archbishop who curbed the Plantagenet with Magna Carta; it was the middle classes who broke the pride of the Stuarts; but a mere aristocracy of wealth will never struggle while it can hope to bribe a tyrant.

And when the disparity of condition increases, so does universal suffrage make it easy to seize the source of power, for the greater is the proportion of power in the hands of those who feel no direct interest in the conduct of government; who, tortured by want and embruted by poverty, are ready to sell their votes to the highest bidder or follow the lead of the most blatant demagogue; or who, made bitter by hardships, may even look upon profligate and tyrannous government with the satisfaction we may imagine the proletarians and slaves of Rome to have felt, as they saw a Caligula or Nero raging among the rich patricians. Given a community with republican institutions, in which one class is too rich to be shorn of their luxuries, no matter how public affairs are administered, and another so poor that a few dollars on election day will seem more than any abstract consideration; in which the few roll in wealth and the many seethe with discontent at a condition of things they know not how to remedy, and power must pass into the hands of jobbers who will buy and sell it as the Praetorians sold the Roman purple, or into the hands of demagogues who will seize and wield it for a time, only to be displaced by worse demagogues.

Where there is anything like an equal distribution of wealth—that is to say, where there is general patriotism, virtue, and intelligence—the more democratic the government the better it will be; but where there is gross inequality in the distribution of wealth, the more democratic the government the worse it will be; for, while rotten democracy may not in itself be worse than rotten autocracy, its effects upon national character will be worse. To give the suffrage to tramps, to paupers, to men to whom the chance to labor is a boon, to men who must beg, or steal, or starve, is to invoke destruction. To put political power in the hands of men embittered and degraded by poverty is to tie firebrands to foxes and turn them loose amid the standing corn; it is to put out the eyes of a Samson and to twine his arms around the pillars of national life. . . .

The True Remedy

We have traced the unequal distribution of wealth which is the curse and menace of modern civilization to the institution of private property in land. We have seen that so long as this institution exists no increase in productive power can permanently benefit the masses; but, on the contrary, must tend to still further depress their condition. We have examined all the remedies, short of the abolition of private property in land, which are currently relied on or proposed for the relief of poverty and the better distribution of wealth, and have found them all inefficacious or impracticable.

There is but one way to remove an evil—and that is, to remove its cause. Poverty deepens as wealth increases, and wages are forced down while productive power grows, because land, which is the source of all wealth and the field of all labor, is monopolized. To extirpate poverty, to make wages what justice commands they should be, the full earnings of the laborer, we must therefore substitute for the individual ownership of land a common ownership. Nothing else will go to the cause of the evil—in nothing else is there the slightest hope.

This, then, is the remedy for the unjust and unequal distribution of wealth apparent in modern civilization, and for all the evils which flow from it:

We must make land common property.

We have reached this conclusion by an examination in which every step has been proved and secured. In the chain of reasoning no link is wanting and no link is weak. Deduction and induction have brought us to the same truth—that the unequal ownership of land necessitates the unequal distribution of wealth. And as in the nature of things unequal ownership of land is inseparable from the recognition of individual property in land, it necessarily follows that the only remedy for the unjust distribution of wealth is in making land common property.

But this is a truth which, in the present state of society, will arouse the most bitter antagonism, and must fight its way, inch by inch. It will be necessary, therefore, to meet the objections of those who, even when driven to admit this truth, will declare that it cannot be practically applied.

In doing this we shall bring our previous reasoning to a new and crucial test. Just as we try addition by subtraction and multiplication by division, so may we, by testing the sufficiency of the remedy, prove the correctness of our conclusions as to the cause of the evil.

The laws of the universe are harmonious. And if the remedy to which we have been led is the true one, it must be consistent with justice; it must be practicable of application; it must accord with the tendencies of social development, and must harmonize with other reforms.

All this I propose to show. I propose to meet all practical objections which can be raised, and to show that this simple measure is not only easy of application; but that it is a sufficient remedy for all the evils which, as modern progress goes on, arise from the greater and greater inequality in the distribution of wealth—that it will substitute equality for inequality, plenty for want, justice for injustice, social strength for social weakness, and will open the way to grander and nobler advances of civilization.

I thus propose to show that the laws of the universe do not deny the natural aspirations of the human heart; that the progress of society might be, and, if it is to continue, must be, toward equality, not toward inequality; and that the economic harmonies prove the truth perceived by the Stoic Emperor—

"We are made for co-operation—like feet, like hands, like eyelids, like the rows of the upper and lower teeth."

Document II-22: THE TARIFF QUESTION

In the political theater no economic issue enjoyed a longer run than the great tariff debate. The cast changed periodically but the plot outlines remained recognizable throughout. The political heirs of Jefferson favored a low tariff, for revenue only; whereas the followers of Hamilton approved the protection of "infant" and other industries through a higher tariff aimed primarily at European (later Asian) manufactured goods. Since protection was conceived with the interests of the manufacturer in mind, it found support in the industrial Northeast and high tariff became a Republican watchword. The farmer's produce usually went unprotected against foreign competition while he paid more for the wares he bought than might have been the case in a free-trade economy. Therefore, candidates from rural areas often espoused free trade; those seeking national office usually compromised.

The great tariff debate was typically obscured by the universal political desire to offend no considerable portion of the electorate. Thus it must have been a rare surprise to the Congress of 1887 when Grover Cleveland, about to stand for reelection, called unequivocally for the reduction of a tariff so high it was producing a federal budgetary surplus. The election of 1888, between an incumbent and a relatively unknown challenger, was dominated more than any other by the tariff question and, to an unusual degree, the voters knew where the candidates stood. Cleveland, although no free-trader, wanted to lower the tariff while Harrison wanted it no lower than it was.

124 THE REFORM SPIRIT IN AMERICA

Where, in this great debate, lay the interests of the common man? One side tried to persuade him that the nation as a whole would be better off if worldwide competition were given free reign. Prices in general would be lower and special protection would not contribute to special fortunes and special corruption. To citizens whose livelihood did not depend directly on factory wages, this argument could win votes. Even the labor unions, however, had trouble resisting the kind of statement made by the following poster which asserted (as in the argument over gold) that the worker owed his well-being to his employer and that he had better vote in the direction that would make industry prosper.

If we depend on the 1888 election to answer the tariff riddle, we will be disappointed. Even if we make the rash assumption that the tariff governed the voters' choice, we then must choose between a popular victory for Cleveland of some 100,000 votes and an electoral victory for Harrison of 65 votes. The tariff question, both in limelight and in shadow, remains an important puzzle for the student of politico-economic reform.

SOURCE: 1-by-2-foot broadside, 1888, courtesy of the Ralph E. Becker Collection, Division of Political History, Smithsonian Institution. See also II-26.

Document II-23: POWDERLY ON CURRENCY

A sampling of the thoughts of T[erence]. V. Powderly is a good shortcut to the sentiments of moderate labor leaders in the late nineteenth and early twentieth centuries. He was prominent in the formation of the National Labor Union of 1866, the Industrial Brotherhood of 1874, and the Knights of Labor. The Knights became the largest group of working men up to the American Federation of Labor. Looking backward over thirty ears of activity, Powderly comments on the issues of great continuing import, devoting an entire chapter to "The Circulating Medium."

He fears private or state control of currency as well as usurious practices and special influences. To this point he is consistent with the pleas of the early spokesmen for the subtreasury idea as it was articulated before the Civil War. (See II-9, 10.) In important contradistinction, however, is Powderly's argument not against a runaway inflation that would rob the worker's pay envelope, but against a harmful contraction of the currency that would forestall economic growth and prosperity.

WORKINGMEN!

WHICH DO YOU WANT?

AMERICAN OR EUROPEAN WAGES!

POTTERIES.

	English.	Trenton, N. J.
Plate makers,	$ 7 75	$20 40
Dish makers,	9 67	19 43
Cup makers,	9 97	18 50
Saucer makers,	7 97	18 50
Wash bowl makers,	9 71	25 64
Pressers,	8 18	17 12
Printers,	6 59	13 56
Kilnmen,	6 59	12 00
Saggur makers,	8 50	17 00
Mould makers,	10 29	20 00
Turners,	8 05	18 00
Handlers,	8 43	19 00

WINDOW GLASS.

	Ohio Valley Average, per Week.	Belgium Average, per W'k
Blowers,	$40 09	$20 00
Gatherers,	23 03	6 25
Flatners,	34 45	6 25
Cutters,	27 59	5 00

COAL MINERS AND COKE MAKERS.

TIME, TEN HOURS PER DAY.

Occupation.	W. Va. Wages, per Day.	English Wages, per Day
Blacksmiths,	$2 00	$1 14
Blacksmiths' helpers,	1 25	72
Coal cleaner,	1 25	60
Drivers,	1 60	50
Engineers,	1 75	1 12
Furnacemen,	1 25	72
Laborers,	1 25	72
Miners,	1 40 to 1 87	1 12
Mine boss,	2 50	1 68
Track layer,	1 80	90
Trappers,	50	22
Weighers,	1 80	90

BLAST FURNACES.

	Ohio Valley per Day.	Cumberland, Eng., per Day
Keepers,	$2 25	$1 41
Helpers,	1 65	85
Top fillers,	1 65	1 13
Bottom fillers,	1 65	1 13
Cinder loaders,	1 55	85
Blast engineer,	2 25	1 00
Cindermen,	1 65	1 11
General labor,	1 40	77

The wages of Blast Furnaces here denominated as Ohio Valley wages are the smallest west of the Allegheny Mountains. Those paid in Joliet, Ill., and even in Pittsburgh, are higher than those given here.

ROLLING MILL.

	West of Allegheny M'tn's, per Ton.	England, per Ton.
Puddling,	$5 50	$1 57
Muck rolling,	68¾	24
Bar rolling and catching,	1 13¾	73
Bar heating,	70	34
Hoop rolling and heating 1½" and No. 17,	3 50	1 80
Cotton tie rolling and heating,	4 10	2 37

BESSEMER STEEL WORKS.

	United States, per Day.	England, per Day
Converter men,	$4 35, 12 h'rs.	$1 45
Steel works pit men,	4 00, 8 "	1 15 to 1 25
Steel works ladle men,	3 98, 12 "	1 00 to 1 15
Rail heaters,	5 00, 12 "	1 60
Rail rollers,	7 00, 12 "	2 50
Common laborers,	1 34, 10 "	62
(June, 1888.)		

FLINT GLASS WORKERS.

	WEST VIRGINIA WAGES, PER DAY.	GREAT BRITAIN WAGES, PER DAY
Glass blowers, Pressers and Finishers,	$3 25 to 4 25	$ 96 to 1 20
First-class Castor place Workmen,	4 50 to 6 00	1 25 to 2 40
Punch Tumbler Blowers,	1 50 to 3 75	65 to 96

The hours of work in Europe are longer than in America for the same amount of work.

Tariff Campaign poster

Thus Powderly provides a relatively rare example of coinciding farm and labor views.

The "Mr. Sylvis" he quotes early in this excerpt was the labor theoretician and organizer William H. Sylvis, whom Powderly succeeded as the preeminent spokesman for the worker.

THE CIRCULATING MEDIUM

Those who read the platforms of the National Labor Union and the Industrial Brotherhood will find that the men who attended the conventions of these associations considered the currency question the most important of all that came up for consideration. Mr. Sylvis evidently believed it to be of vital importance. In a document issued by him in 1868 he said:

> We must show them that when a just monetary system has been established there will no longer exist a necessity for trade unions.

When the General Assembly adopted the preamble in 1878 it found the XVIIIth section as follows:

> To prevail upon the government to establish a just standard of distribution between capital and labor by providing a purely national circulating medium based upon the faith and resources of the nation, issued directly to the people, without the intervention of any system of banking corporations, which money shall be a legal tender in the payment of all debts, public or private, and interchangeable at the option of the holder for government bonds, bearing a rate of interest not to exceed three and sixty-five hundredths per cent., subject to future legislation of Congress.

When the convention adjourned the XVth section of the preamble of the Knights of Labor read as follows:

> To prevail upon governments to establish a purely national circulating medium, based upon the faith and resources of the

nation, and issued directly to the people, without the intervention
of any system of banking corporations, which money shall be a
legal tender in payment of all debts, public or private.

. . . No other section of the preamble has attracted less attention than
that, and none other is of more importance to the people. Every Knight of
Labor is in duty bound to labor with what ability he is possessed of to
abolish the system by which so large a supply of the money of the country
is placed under the control of banking institutions. Although the national
bank is a creature of the United States government it affords no greater
safeguard to depositors than any other banking concern. The gains are

NOT SHARED IN BY THE PEOPLE,

and that institution which flourishes beneath the protection of the government of the people is not in any way subordinate to the will of the people.

The fifth paragraph in section VIII, article one, of the constitution of
the United States, says that Congress shall have power ''to coin money,
regulate the value thereof, and of foreign coins, and fix the standard of
weights and measures.'' Instead of issuing money the government permits private institutions to do so. Instead of regulating the value of money
within the boundaries of the United States, banking concerns are practically permitted to do so by controlling the volume. In one part of the
country money is worth two per cent., and in others it is as high as twelve,
and in some places twenty per cent. The value of the money used by the
people is not fixed or regular. It fluctuates at the will of those who have it
to lend, or who are enabled, by reason of their control over a large portion
of it, to withdraw it from circulation at their pleasure.

The right to issue or coin money is a

HIGH SOVEREIGN PREROGATIVE,

which should not be delegated to any lesser creature than the government
itself. The standard of weights and measures is fixed by the government.
It is the same everywhere, but sixteen ounces of sugar can be bought
much cheaper in a State where the rate of interest is but six per cent., than
it can be procured for in one where the rate of interest is twice six per

cent. No State can fix the standard of weights and measures; no State can coin or issue money, but an institution, which is subordinate to no power beyond the extent of its circulation, is permitted to transact business beneath the great name of the national government, and regulate the value of the money it loans according to the necessities of the borrower. The credit of the bank is endorsed by the government, while it demands usury from the citizen.

The fact stands squarely before every man who reads, that those who are engaged in speculation, in banking, in note shaving, in managing corporations and trusts, are growing wealthy with amazing rapidity, while those who use the money, those who do the work of the nation, the laborers of the farm, mine, railway, and workshop, are growing desperately poor each day. . . .

To contract the circulating medium of a nation to an amount which will not allow the full business capacity of its people to be put to the test, is a

GROSS INJUSTICE,

the full extent of which can not be estimated. Such a transaction operates solely in the interest of those who have money to lend. The system which permits it is such as will create a large borrowing class who must of necessity become the slaves of the money changers. So long as national banks exist the volume of money in circulation will not equal the demand for its use.

When money is scarce the borrower will pay a greater price for its use than when it is plenty, and as the chief aim of the banker is to loan money at a high price, it will always be to his interest to keep the volume of currency so low that the wants of the people can not be supplied except through the payment of high rates of interest. The law which permits extortion of that kind is injurious to the welfare of the nation, it is a law which permits one portion of the people, and a mere fraction at that, to take advantage of the necessities of the other, and greater portion. The

CHIEF AIM OF GOVERNMENT,

in a republic, is to do equity to all citizens and residents. In fostering such an institution as a national bank, the congress of a republic shows itself indifferent to the welfare of its people.

The history of the legislation, by the United States Congress, on the currency question since 1862, is one record of partiality to a class that lives on the necessities of others. It is the history of favoritism to Wall Street, New York. Such legislation would not be enacted if industry were consulted as well as that favored class which reaps the greatest reward from its exercise. . . .

Knights of Labor believe that a circulating medium, in sufficient quantity, should be based on the faith and resources of the nation itself, instead of being founded on a gold or silver mine owned and operated by any individual in the United States. They believe, or they ought to believe, that the supply should equal the demand, and if silver dollars to the extent of $4,000,000 may be coined each year, the necessities of the people require that the full sum allowed by law should be coined instead of the minimum of $2,000,000, which has been issued each year since 1879. Congress believes that the country should have a larger circulating medium, but the money power of the country holds a majority of that body too tightly in its grasp to allow the passage of any laws which will relieve the strain upon the industries of the nation.

An attempt was made in January, 1888, to increase the circulation of the national banks ten per cent., but representatives Weaver, of Iowa, Bland, of Missouri, Anderson of Kansas, and Brumm, of Pennsylvania, took so decided a stand against it that the people of the nation heard the discussion which took place at Washington, and the measure was defeated. All legislation enacted in the interest of the banking fraternity has gone

SILENTLY THROUGH CONGRESS.

If a noise is made it is not so likely to go through, and for that reason the existence of such institutions as the order of Knights of Labor, Farmers' Alliance, and kindred organizations, is a necessity. These associations, representing the people, must counteract the pernicious efforts of the Shylock element which rates six per cent. on money invested as of more consequence than the happiness of toiling humanity.

When the Philadelphia session of the General Assembly adjourned in 1884, the XIVth section in the preamble took the place of the XVth on the currency question. On motion of Ralph Beaumont the following was adopted:

> The establishment of a national monetary system, in which a circulating medium in necessary quantity shall issue directly to the people, without the intervention of banks; that all the national issue shall be full legal tender in payment of all debts, public and private; and that the government shall not guarantee or recognize any private banks, or create any banking corporations.

That section speaks for itself. It does not call for any more than enough to do the business of the country. A "necessary quantity" is all that is demanded. It demands that the government of the people shall issue a

PEOPLE'S MONEY DIRECT,

and shall not delegate the authority to do so to any bank or other institution.

Every Knight of Labor, who has studied the principles of the order, realizes that when the transportation facilities of the nation are managed by the chosen agents of the people under governmental control, the land system of the country is properly regulated, and speculation in the earth prohibited, and a national circulating medium established and issued direct to the people without rendering a dividend to the middleman,— banker,—the prosperity of the whole people will be established, and that there will be less of poverty than now exists. Those who will be poor and destitute under such circumstances will be the improvident, intemperate, and those afflicted by nature or accident.

Document II-24: FARMERS' ALLIANCE PROTEST

Reform is often a singing movement. From the Battery to Topeka participants measured the success of their organizational rallies by the volume and beat of the words and music. J. E. Bryan, lecturer for the Farmers' Alliance in Arkansas, collected at the end of his small pamphlet a handful of songs which, coming from this central state, can be taken as typical of the way in which the emotions of many Americans were drawn into politico-economic crusades.

Such collections rarely printed music, only the words. They relied on familiar tunes and, as in this case, mixed true verses with parodies. The hymn "Work, for the Night is Coming" and the anthem "America" were reprinted faithfully. Together with melodies from the hymnal, Civil War airs provided the melodic staples. The musical mood was thus sustained on an evangelical level: exalted, militant, triumphal. Mrs. Florence Olmstead of Douglas, Kansas, was credited for a parody of "Marching Through Georgia" which predicted a victory over politicians through the union of workers from all regions. To the tune "There's a Land That Is Fairer Than Day" the words argue for direct democracy ("By the people our laws must be made") in order to abolish "monopoly's rule." The jute trust is the special target of another parody.

The song quoted below shows some sensitivity to wartime memories evoked by many of the still-popular melodies: in fact, it capitalizes on these memories by producing union of feeling growing out of an initial tension between the Yankee and the boy from Dixie. Typically rousing and nostalgic, this song also attacked the typical reform target: the nation's exploitative financial and industrial powers.

SOURCE: J. E. Bryan, *The Farmers' Alliance: Its Origin, Progress and Purposes.* Fayetteville, Ark., 1891, p. 153.

MEDLEY
From the Alliance Nightingale.
(FOR TWO BOYS.)
FIRST BOY.
Air, first verse—"Yankee Doodle."

Oh, Yankee's got his dander up,
  He's in an awful passion,
He says that things shall not go on
  In such a shameful fashion.
The dudes who shirk shall get to work
  Or starve if it comes handy;
They shan't combine and steal from us
  Says Yankee Doodle Dandy.

SECOND BOY
Air—"Dixie."

And away down South in the land of cotton
Won't we send the "trusts" a trottin'
    Right away, right away, right away from Dixie
    Land.
Hooray! Hooray for Dixie Land! Hooray! Hooray!
    For Dixie Land has taken stand
    To drive away the robber band,
        Right away! right away!
        Away from sunny Dixie.

BOTH BOYS.
Air,—"America."

Our country we shall see
From Mammon's clutches free,
    Free once again.
Thy sons are patriots still,
And by their sovereign will,
O'er every vale and hill
    Justice shall reign.

Document II-25: POPULISTS IN CONVENTION

More than in 1896, when the scene was confused by merger with the Democrats and overlain by the personal rhetoric of William Jennings Bryan, the Populists who met in Omaha in 1892 produced a platform that may be justly taken as a culmination of the politico-economic reform movement of the postbellum era. It opened with a well-rounded list of the many ways in which the nation had hit bottom; it dismissed the meager efforts of both major parties in a few short paragraphs—something the 1896 platform could not convincingly do. Loyal to the long-standing rural causes, it espoused a land reform program and abused the railroads in language of unique intensity. It called, of course, for free coinage of silver but went far beyond that in economic wisdom by endorsing the Macune subtreasury plan.

C. W. Macune is the next name in that series beginning with Gouge, continuing with Kellogg and Campbell (II-9, 13, 15), and culminating in the Federal Reserve System. Macune understood the intensely local problems of the farmer. No one central bank could provide the immediate credit or underwrite crop storage in a way that would save the farmer from the usurer and the speculator. Just as soil and climate vary from region to region, so a system of currency and credit must be made responsive to local needs. In so arguing Macune contributed a concept crucial to the articulation of rural interests. (For Macune's ideas in their political context, see J. E. Bryan, *The Farmers' Alliance: Its Origin, Progress and Purposes.* Fayetteville, Ark., 1891, especially pp. 86-109.)

A further step was the call for a graduated income tax. Pressure in this direction had been sufficient to produce an amendment to the Wilson-Gorman tariff calling for a mild (2 percent on annual incomes over $4,000) levy. Even this, however, was later invalidated in a 1895 Supreme Court decision (*Pollack* v. *The Farmers' Loan and Trust Co.*), where it rested until the Sixteenth Amendment.

Although the Populists never welded an effective political union with the industrial workers, this platform shows evidence of their efforts. Note the support for the eight-hour law, the tirades against scabs and imported labor, and even the particular endorsement of the Knights of Labor in their struggle with the Rochester textile mill owners.

SOURCE: Edward McPherson, *A Hand-Book of Politics for 1892.* Washington, D.C., Chapman, 1892, pp. 269-271.

THE PEOPLE'S PARTY NATIONAL CONVENTION OF 1892

This body met at Omaha, *July 3.*

Mr. EDDINGTON was chosen temporary Chairman, and Mr. H. L. LOUCKS of South Dakota permanent President.

This Platform was adopted:

Assembled upon the one hundred and sixteenth anniversary of the Declaration of Independence, the People's Party of America in their first

National Convention, invoking upon their action the blessing of Almighty God, puts forth, in the name and on behalf of the people of this country, the following preamble and declaration of principles:

The conditions which surround us best justify our cooperation. We meet in the midst of a nation brought to the verge of moral, political and material ruin. Corruption dominates the ballot box, the Legislatures, the Congress, and touches even the ermine of the Bench. The people are demoralized; most of the States have been compelled to isolate the voters at the polling places to prevent universal intimidation or bribery. The newspapers are largely subsidized or muzzled, public opinion silenced, business prostrated, our homes covered with mortgages, labor impoverished, and the land concentrating in the hands of the capitalists. The urban workmen are denied the right of organization for self-protection; imported pauperized labor beats down their wages; a hireling standing army, unrecognized by our laws, is established to shoot them down, and they are rapidly degenerating into European conditions. The fruits of the toil of millions are boldly stolen to build up colossal fortunes for a few, unprecedented in the history of mankind, and the possessors of these in turn despise the Republic and endanger liberty. From the same prolific womb of governmental injustice we breed the two great classes —tramps and millionaires.

The national power to create money is appropriated to enrich bond-holders; a vast public debt, payable in legal tender currency, has been funded into gold-bearing bonds, thereby adding millions to the burdens of the people.

Silver, which has been accepted as coin since the dawn of history, has been demonetized to add to the purchasing power of gold by decreasing the value of all forms of property as well as human labor, and the supply of currency is purposely abridged to fatten usurers, bankrupt enterprise and enslave industry.

A vast conspiracy against mankind has been organized on two continents, and it is rapidly taking possession of the world. If not met and overthrown at once, it forebodes terrible social convulsions, the destruction of civilization, or the establishment of an absolute despotism.

We have witnessed, for more than a quarter of a century, the struggles of the two great political parties for power and plunder, while grievous wrongs have been inflicted upon the suffering people. We charge that the controlling influences dominating both these parties have permitted the existing dreadful conditions to develop without serious effort to prevent or restrain them.

Neither do they now promise us any substantial reform. They have agreed together to ignore, in the coming campaign, every issue but one. They propose to drown the outcries of a plundered people with the uproar of a sham battle over the tariff, so that capitalists, corporations, national banks, rings, trusts, watered stock, the demonetization of silver and the oppressions of the usurers may all be lost sight of. They propose to sacrifice our homes, lives and children, on the altar of mammon; to destroy the multitude in order to secure corruption funds from the millionaires.

Assembled on the anniversary of the birthday of the nation, and filled with the spirit of the grand general and chieftain who established our independence, we seek to restore the Government of the Republic to the hands of the "plain people" with whose class it originated. We assert our purposes to be identical with the purposes of the National Constitution, to form a more perfect Union and establish justice, insure domestic tranquility, provide for the common defense, promote the general welfare and secure the blessings of liberty for ourselves and our posterity.

We declare that this Republic can only endure as a free government while built upon the love of the whole people for each other and for the nation; that it cannot be pinned together by bayonets; that the civil war is over and that every passion and resentment which grew out of it must die with it, and that we must be in fact, as we are in name, one united brotherhood of freedom.

Our country finds itself confronted by conditions for which there is no precedent in the history of the world; our annual agricultural productions amount to billions of dollars in value, which must within a few weeks or months be exchanged for billions of dollars' worth of commodities consumed in their production; the existing currency supply is wholly inadequate to make this exchange; the results are falling prices, the formation of combines and rings, the impoverishment of the producing class. We pledge ourselves that, if given power, we will labor to correct these evils by wise and reasonable legislation, in accordance with the terms of our platform.

We believe that the powers of government—in other words, of the people—should be expanded (as in the case of the postal service) as rapidly and as far as the good sense of an intelligent people and the teachings of experience shall justify, to the end that oppression, injustice and poverty, shall eventually cease in the land.

While our sympathies as a party of reform are naturally upon the side of every proposition which will tend to make men intelligent, virtuous and temperate, we nevertheless regard these questions—important as they are—as secondary to the great issues now pressing for solution, and upon which not only our individual prosperity, but the very existence of free institutions depend; and we ask all men to first help us to determine whether we are to have a Republic to administer, before we differ as to the conditions upon which it is to be administered; believing that the forces of reform this day organized will never cease to move forward, until every wrong is righted, and equal rights and equal privileges securely established for all the men and women of this country. We declare, therefore,

First—That the union of the labor forces of the United States this day consummated shall be permanent and perpetual; may its spirit enter into all hearts for the salvation of the Republic, and the uplifting of mankind.

Second—Wealth belongs to him who creates it, and every dollar taken from industry without an equivalent is robbery. "If any will not work, neither shall he eat." The interests of rural and civic labor are the same; their enemies are identical.

Third—We believe that the time has come when the railroad corporations will either own the people or the people must own the railroads; and should the Government enter upon the work of owning and managing all railroads, we should favor an amendment to the Constitution by which all persons engaged in the Government service shall be placed under a civil service regulation of the most rigid character, so as to prevent the increase of the power of the national administration by the use of such additional Government employes.

1st. We demand a national currency, safe, sound and flexible, issued by the General Government only, a full legal tender for all debts public and private, and that without the use of banking corporations; a just, equitable and efficient means of distribution direct to the people at a tax not to exceed 2 per cent. per annum, to be provided as set forth in the Sub-Treasury plan of the Farmers' Alliance, or a better system, also by payments in discharge of its obligations for public improvements.

(A) We demand free and unlimited coinage of silver and gold at the present legal ratio of 16 to 1.

(B)   We demand that the amount of circulating medium be speedily increased to not less than $50 per capita.

(C)   We demand a graduated income tax.

(D)   We believe that the money of the country should be kept as much as possible in the hands of the people, and hence we demand that all State and National revenues shall be limited to the necessary expenses of the Government, economically and honestly administered.

(E)   We demand that Postal Savings Banks be established by the Government for the safe deposit of the earnings of the people and to facilitate exchange.

2d.   Transportation being a means of exchange and a public necessity, the government should own and operate the railroads in the interest of the people.

The telegraph and telephone, like the post office system, being a necessity for the transmission of news, should be owned and operated by the Government in the interest of the people.

3d.   The land, including all the natural sources of wealth, is the heritage of the people and should not be monopolized for speculative purposes, and alien ownership of land should be prohibited. All land now held by railroads and other corporations in excess of their actual needs, and all lands now owned by aliens, should be reclaimed by the Government and held for actual settlers only.

The following supplementary resolutions, not to be incorporated in the platform, came from the Committee on Resolutions and were adopted, as follows:

Whereas, Other questions having been presented for our consideration, we hereby submit the following, not as a part of the platform of the People's Party, but as resolutions expressive of the sentiment of this Convention:

1.   *Resolved*, That we demand a free ballot and a fair count in all elections, and pledge ourselves to secure it to every legal voter without Federal intervention, through the adoption by the States of the unperverted Australian or secret ballot system.

2.   That the revenue derived from a graduated income tax should be applied to the reduction of the burden of taxation now resting upon the domestic industries of this country.

3.   That we pledge our support to fair and liberal pensions to ex-Union soldiers and sailors.

4. That we condemn the fallacy of protecting American labor under the present system, which opens our ports to the pauper and criminal classes of the world, and crowds out our wage-earners; and we denounce the present ineffective laws against contract labor, and demand the further restriction of undesirable immigration.

5. That we cordially sympathize with the efforts of organized workingmen to shorten the hours of labor, and demand a rigid enforcement of the existing eight-hour law on Government work, and ask that a penalty clause be added to the said law.

6. That we regard the maintenance of a large standing army of mercenaries, known as the Pinkerton system, as a menace to our liberties, and we demand its abolition; and we condemn the recent invasion of the Territory of Wyoming by the hired assassins of plutocracy, assisted by Federal officials.

7. That we commend to the favorable consideration of the people and to the reform press the legislative system known as the initiative and referendum.

8. That we favor a constitutional provision limiting the office of President and Vice-President to one term, and providing for the election of Senators of the United States by a direct vote of the people.

9. That we oppose any subsidy or national aid to any private corporation for any purpose.

10. That this convention sympathizes with the Knights of Labor, and their righteous contest with the tyrannical combine of clothing manufacturers of Rochester, and declare it to be the duty of all who hate tyranny and oppression, to refuse to purchase the goods made by the said manufacturers, or to patronize any merchants who sell such goods.

The following persons were placed in nomination for President:

JAMES B. WEAVER of Iowa.

JAMES H. KYLE of South Dakota.

JAMES G. FIELD of Virginia.

MANN PAGE of Virginia.

The vote, on the morning of the 5th, resulted as follows:

JAMES B. WEAVER, 995.

JAMES H. KYLE, 265.

For Vice-President, JAMES G. FIELD of Virginia was chosen by a vote of 733 to 554 for BEN. TERRELL of Texas. Adjourned.

Document II-26: TARIFF AND INCOME TAX IN CONGRESS

The speaker in the accompanying document indicates in the first sentence of his quoted remarks that taxation is the key to power. Taxation has also been consciously used, as Sidney Ratner pointed out, "for achieving and preserving the economic objectives of democracy . . . placing the weight of taxation on those best able to bear it or on those receiving 'unearned' or 'undeserved' gains." (*American Taxation: Its History as a Social Force in Democracy.* New York, Norton, 1942, p. 14. See also II-21, 25.) One of the more dramatic moments in the history of the use of taxation as a social force in America came on February 1, 1894, as the House of Representatives debated a tariff-reform bill with an income-tax amendment.

Under the vocal review of overflowing galleries Thomas B. Reed, the master Republican orator in the House, enshrined in ringing phrases the basic arguments in favor of protection as outlined in the introduction to II-22. Whatever was good about growing, prospering America in 1894, Reed claimed, was due to the blessings of protection. Charles F. Crisp then stepped down from the chair he occupied as Democratic Speaker of the House and responded to Reed's arguments with an eloquence that won partisan applause from the aroused audience. The true climax of the debate was reached, however, when William L. Wilson, the West Virginia Democrat charged with sponsoring the bill and bringing it through his Ways and Means Committee, took the floor for the last major speech on the subject.

Opening with traditional modesty, he then loosened up his adversaries with a barbed flattery that seemed to turn the famous Reed sarcasm back against the Republican side of the aisle. He then undertook to associate his cause with honor, freedom, and social justice. His enemies, by implication, were the holders of ill-gotten wealth and unjust power, akin to the Stuarts of Cromwellian England and the gaudily dressed British troops that fought against the rude colonials. Taxation, in this speech, became the weapon of democracy indeed. Wilson's oratory triggered a long and boisterous demonstration while he was paraded on the shoulders (happily, he was a man of slight build) of some of his distinguished colleagues.

Almost as an anticlimax, the internal-revenue amendment passed (182-48) and the entire tariff bill as well (204-140).

Although the tariff occupied the center of the stage, the income tax also represented a recurring issue, dating back to early colonial days. If the War of 1812 had lasted a bit longer, speculated Sidney Ratner, an income tax might have been employed at that time in a way that would have avoided later complications over its constitutionality. (Ratner, p. 34.) Taxes on income were accepted only in times of national emergency, as it turned out, and it took the philosophy of the Populists and the Bryan Democrats to bring the subject of a peacetime income tax to the point of congressional enactment.

But even the climate of 1894 and the rhetoric of William L. Wilson were not enough. The idea of a graduated income tax was still an anathema to Americans in power. (Wilson himself had written an article favoring taxes on corporate rather than individual incomes.) Soon the income tax cases were in the courts; and, in one of those cases, ex-Senator George F. Edmunds, who had helped author the Sherman Anti-Trust Act, argued against an act similarly attacking maldistribution of wealth. The Supreme Court eventually declared unconstitutional the Income Tax Law of 1894. Congress finally responded in 1909 with the Sixteenth Amendment (ratified in 1913), which states with succinct finality:

> The Congress shall have the power to lay and collect taxes on incomes, from whatever source derived, without apportionment among the several States, and without regard to any census or enumeration.

The use of this amendment to affect seriously the distribution of wealth awaited the administrations of Franklin D. Roosevelt.

SOURCE: *The Congressional Record* vol. XXVI; the general debate and roll call votes, pp. 1779-1797; Wilson's speech is in the Appendix to vol. XXVI, pp. 203-205, abridged.

CONGRESSIONAL TAX DEBATE: WILLIAM L. WILSON

Mr. Speaker, this is a very old world, but long before human history began to be written the fatal secret was disclosed that there is no easier, no quicker, no more abundant way of gathering wealth and gathering power than by exercising the privilege of taxing the masses of the people. That secret disclosed, and eagerly seized upon before the dawn of human history, is yet the dominant force in all the world. It is but two hundred years since men were willing to fight for the idea that governments are made for the governed and not for the exclusive benefit of those who govern, and not yet in all the world is there a single nation whose government is administered exclusively and evenly in the interest of all the government. That is the goal of perfect freedom. That is the achievement of perfect equality. That is the goal toward which the Democratic party is courageously and honestly moving in this struggle for tariff reform. [Loud applause on the Democratic side.] Whenever that party and whenever the members of it are able to cut loose from local or selfish interest and keep the general welfare alone in their eyes, we shall attain our full freedom and bring to the people of this country blessings that no other people in the world have ever enjoyed. [Applause.]

When Sir Robert Peel was just entering upon his work of tariff reform in England he read to the House of Commons a letter that had been sent him by a canny Scotch fisherman. The writer protested against lowering the duties on herrings, for fear, as he said, that the Norwegian fisherman might undersell him, but he assured Sir Robert, in closing the letter, that in every respect except herrings he was a thoroughgoing freetrader. [Laughter and applause.] I trust that no Democrat to-day will be thinking more about his herrings than the cause of the people. [Applause.] I trust that no man's particular herring will come up to-day and stand between him and the honest, enthusiastic performance of his duty, and his whole duty, to the American people.

I have said, Mr. Speaker, that I do not feel called upon to consider the well-worn arguments which have proceeded from the other side of the House, but if time permitted, I should like to take up two arguments which seem to have found some lodgment among our own friends. The first is that this bill will create a deficit and therefore ought not to pass. In the name of common sense how can you ever pass a tariff-reform bill if you do not reduce the taxation imposed by the law that you seek to reform. [Applause.] And could not protectionists thwart and forever prevent any movement toward tariff reform by extravagant expenditures and other means of keeping down the revenue to the expenses of the Government? Have gentlemen forgotten that there may be a system of high-tariff taxation under which the Government receives little and the protected industries receive much, and that there may be a system of low-tariff taxation under which the Government receives a great deal and the protected industries receive but little? [Applause.] The existing tariff is framed on the first idea, and the present bill is framed on the idea of revenue. [Applause.]

If you will take up the history of the free-trade movement in England you will find that nothing so surprised tariff reformers as the fact that the more they cut down and the more they transferred to the free list the larger revenues accrued to the Government. So that Mr. Gladstone was able to say, when they had finally reduced their schedules from twelve hundred taxed articles to about seven, that the revenue was still as great from the seven as it had been from the twelve hundred. [Loud applause on the Democratic side.]

I have here the report of the Secretary of the Treasury for 1847, which I have no time to read, in which Mr. Walker declared that in the very first year under the operation of the tariff of 1846 the revenues had gone up from $23,500,000 to $31,500,000, an increase of more than one-third in a single year.

Another argument which gentlemen upon this side are using to excuse themselves for hesitating, at least, to vote for this bill is that the income tax has been added to it. I need not say to them that I did not concur in the policy of attaching an income-tax bill to the tariff bill. I have had some doubt as to the expediency of a personal income tax at the present time, but when the committee decided otherwise, I threw in my fortunes earnestly and loyally with them because I had never been hostile to the idea of an income tax. [Loud applause on the Democratic side.] Those were strong words which the gentleman from Georgia quoted in defense of it, from Senator SHERMAN. It has been opposed here as class legislation; it is nothing of the kind, Mr. Speaker; it is simply an effort, an honest first effort, to balance the weight of taxation on the poor consumers of the country who have heretofore borne it all. [Loud applause.] Gentlemen who complain of it as class legislation forget that during the fifty years of its existence in England it has been the strongest force in preventing or allaying those class distinctions that have harassed the other governments of the Old World.

It has also been opposed in this debate as sectional legislation. Gentlemen have gone so far as to declare that it is aimed at New England or New York in no just or friendly spirit by representatives of the South and of the West. Why, sir, when for a generation New England has been sending out from her colleges men imbued with the doctrine that an income tax is a wise and equal system of taxation, when through the text-books of her great economists, her Sumner, and Walker, and Perry, she has taught that doctrine in the colleges of the South and West, she can not justly complain that her own teachings are used as a sectional weapon against her. [Loud applause on the Democratic side.] No, sir, I am in close touch with the men of the North—I am in close touch with the men of the West—I am bone of the bone of the men of the South. [Loud applause.] And to-day I can affirm that in all my conferences with them I have heard no man suggest as the motive for this scheme of taxation, that he supported it in any sectional spirit or with any feeling of resentment or hostility to any part of the country. [Loud applause.]

And now, Mr. Speaker, I see that I have but a moment or two left. Gentlemen (addressing the Republican side of the House), I doubt not the sincerity, I doubt not the love of your fellow-men that impels you to champion your side of this question any more than I doubt the high and patriotic motives of my own associates. I agree with the gentleman from Maine that the question of the wages and welfare of the American workingman is the vital point in this controversy. We are trying in this country the experiment whether, under God's favor, with the blessings of religion and education and free government and unbounded resources, we can have a country where every man will be born to the possibility that he can rise to a life of culture and not be condemned from his birth to a life of unending mechanical toil or hopeless drudgery for the mere comforts and necessities of existence. [Applause.] That is the meaning of tariff reform. That is the feeling which animates those who, through victory and defeat, have stood loyally by its cause. We want to make this a country where no man shall be taxed for the private benefit of another man, but where all the blessing of free government, all the influences of church and school, all our resources, with the skill and science and invention applied to their development, shall be the common untaxed heritage of all the people, adding to the comforts of all, adding to the culture of all, adding to the happiness of all. [Loud applause.]

And now, but one word more: We are about to vote upon this bill. If I knew that when the roll is called every Democratic name would respond in the spirit of that larger patriotism which I have tried to suggest, I should be proud and light-hearted today. Let me say to my brethren who are doubting as to what they shall do, that this roll call will be entered, not only upon the Journals of this House, it will be written in the history of this country, it will be entered in the annals of freedom throughout all time. [Applause.]

This is not a battle over percentages, over this or that tariff schedule— it is a battle for human freedom. [Applause.] As Mr. Burke truly said, every great battle for human freedom is waged around the question of taxation. You may think to-day that some peculiar feeling or view of your own will excuse you for not supporting this great movement: you may think to-day that some excuse which seems to cover you as a garment will be sufficient in the future; that some reason which seems strong and satisfactory to you, some desire to oblige a great interest behind you, may justify a negative vote when the roll is called, but the scorching gaze of a liberty-loving posterity will shrivel them away from you forever. [Applause.] The men who had the opportunity to sign the Declaration of Independence and refused or neglected because there was something in it which they did not like—thank God there were none such; but if there had been, what would be their standing in history to-day? If men on the battlefield at Lexington or at Bunker Hill, from some ground of personal or local dissatisfaction, had thrown away their weapons, what think you would have been their feelings in all the remaining years of their lives when the Liberty Bell rang out on every recurring anniversary of American independence? [Applause.] This is a roll of honor. This is a roll of freedom, and in the name of honor and in the name of freedom, I summon every Democratic member of this House to inscribe his name upon it. [Loud and prolonged applause.]

Document II-27: BRYAN AS REFORMER

The development of political symbols has been an inevitable part of this section (see II-3, 7, 11). Although the invention of negative symbols with which to vilify one's adversaries has been fairly common, the creation of effective positive symbols has been rare indeed: the log cabin and hard cider of 1840; the rail splitter of 1860; and William Jennings Bryan's "cross of gold," which cleverly combined positive and negative responses. The man who composed the poster here reproduced did not choose to dramatize, visually, that striking Christian metaphor. Instead he assembled a veritable catalogue of political symbols representing the miscellany of causes and crusades which Bryan headed in 1896 as the candidate for both Populist and Democratic parties.

Familiar to students of the Harrison campaign are the plow and fowl, evocative of rural associations. Across the blade of the plow is laid the working man's sledgehammer, thus pictorially unifying farm and labor. All the dependable national symbols are there: the flag, the Declaration, liberty, justice, and a liberty bell ringing now against imperialism. A more recent pejorative symbol, the octopus, is depicted with vipers' heads at the ends of its tentacles. This enemy of farmer, worker, and honest businessman is specified as the steel, tobacco, biscuit, and oil trusts, along with that ever-present rural adversary, the railroad. Following the octopus's startled eyes, one finds him confronted by a hatchet-wielding lady who strongly suggests, in her posture and arsenal, the contemporary depictions of the largely female war on alcohol. No doubt there is an appeal here to the emancipated woman as an appropriate force behind democracy's sharp-edged weapon of reform. The tableau in the lower right-hand corner represents Bryan's stand against the annexation of territories freed from Spain in the hostilities of 1898. (Page 146)

SOURCE: Campaign poster lithographed by Strobridge, copyright Neville Williams, Columbus, Ohio, 1900. Courtesy of the Prints and Photographs Division, Library of Congress. See also II-29.

Document II-28: DAVENPORT ON TRUSTBUSTING

When William Randolph Hearst decided to make the New York *Journal* into a muckraking dreadnaught, he imported for his front turret a relatively unremembered cartoonist, Homer Davenport. Davenport not only fired graphic salvos against the Spaniards in Cuba, he also created one of the most damning caricatures of "Dollar Mark" Hanna, the Ohio political boss who supported McKinley.

His third great pictorial campaign was directed against the monopolies, or "trusts," as they were beginning to be more commonly called. To represent the primitive power of the trusts Davenport created a

Bryan campaign poster

Cro-Magnon colossus, ten times human scale with a bearded bullet-head and a loincloth adorned with human skulls. The birth of the trust was depicted as a genielike emergence from a bottle while a baffled wisher, Uncle Sam, wonders how to get his monstrous creation back inside the jar. The answer to this dilemma is given by means of a Swiftian metaphor as Lilliputian citizens are shown ensnaring the monster in the web of their votes. In the visual language of Homer Davenport, the anti-trust campaign became a prime example of economic inequities that would respond only to political remedies. Nowhere were these inequities depicted more melodramatically than in the sketch here reproduced.

A student of politico-economic agitation will recognize in the anti-trust campaign of the 1890s a direct descendant of the war on the rechartering of the Second Bank of the United States, a private monopoly enjoying special federal concessions. For the intermediate generation special grievances were directed mainly at railroad monopolies. What was new in the nineties was the number of productive areas in which

"Two ends of the national table . . ."

monopolies or oligopolies were becoming dominant—sugar, oil, coal, steel, to name but the more notorious—and the incredibly high percentage of the national wealth they could be shown to control. For some reformers the war on the trusts was just one battle in a larger campaign aimed at public ownership of all productive facilities. For all reformers the trust issue was a major one for twenty-five years. It produced two landmark pieces of federal legislation (the Sherman Anti-Trust Act of 1890 and the Clayton Act of 1913; see II-34) and it forced each of the prime political figures of the era to take a stand.

SOURCE: Pen and ink drawing by Homer Davenport, courtesy of the Prints and Photographs Division, Library of Congress. This particular cartoon appeared in the New York *Journal*, April 25, 1902, with the caption: "Two ends of the national table. The strange thing is the heartlessness of the brute on the left."

Document II-29: GOLD V. SILVER: REFORM SYMBOLS

Bryan's "cross of gold" speech was only part of a battle of symbols between the partisans of gold and silver (see II-27). The case for silver was parallel to the general argument for currency reform as represented by the various subtreasury schemes. Farmers, debtors, and some spokesmen for the working man felt that general prosperity was being restricted by the failure of the national currency to expand with the country and its population. This group advocated a retention of the greenbacks, the creation of new fiat money, and the free and unlimited coinage of silver at a ratio (to gold) of 16-to-1. Thus the "silver question" became the great politico-economic debate of the nineties and persisted through the campaign of 1900.

Those opposed to silver included many of the business and financial leaders of the country who feared inflation, instability, and international complications following a unilateral abandonment of monometallism. To make their appeal political they had at their disposal all the familiar connotations of gold: the sun, the wedding ring, grandfather's watch, and all that is sound and dependable. To this arsenal they added the epithet "goldbug," which they depicted as a scarab, that beetle revered by the ancient Egyptians and connotative of jeweled wealth, power, and benign magic.

To this cluster of associations Bryan's main retort was the symbolic suggestion that gold was crucifying the common man. His colleagues drew also on the respect for the Founding Fathers by reminding voters that the Constitution had named both gold and silver as authorized currency and that the first dollar unit was silver. Thus the Bryan poster (II-27) not only showed a silver dollar sixteen times the size of the gold one (to suggest the desired expansionary ratio) but labeled the silver coin the "dollar of the daddies," in a somewhat flippant allusion to the Founding Fathers.

Reproduced below is a photograph of a bronze-plated cast-iron pin. Just below the neck the legend "Prosperity 1900" suggests that the pin must originally have carried a picture of William McKinley (instead of Theodore Roosevelt) and been used in the campaign of 1900. Once a shiny gold, the pin photographs darkly and, with its outstretched legs and feelers, weirdly suggests the octopus symbol it was designed to combat.

SOURCE: Ralph E. Becker collection, Division of Political History, Smithsonian Institution.

Gold bug

Document II-30: DEBS AND SOCIALISM

Socialism in America has meant a number of things: a philosophy; a force in the labor movement; a communitarian vision; a program for politican action; a cry for revolution. Those socialists who held a concept of a new and different society, articulate in all its inner relations, have been represented in another part of this collection along with other reformers who worked with a total model in mind.

The kind of socialism that has appealed to most Americans belongs here, alongside other movements that had for their primary goal a more direct political democracy and a more complete economic democracy. The outstanding spokesman for this kind of socialism, Eugene V. Debs, was a Midwestern American, like so many Populists and Progressives, who began his public life by working hard for the working man within the structure of the Democratic Party. He was converted to socialism by reading and by witnessing the failure of the Pullman Strike and the defeat of Bryan. In socialism he saw not so much an imported ideology as a culmination of native goals; he saw no widespread violence but an orderly electoral process.

Socialists suffered from several stigmata. They proposed an alternative to the two-party system; they were associated with alien radicalism and with the lunatic fringe that sometimes appeared in third-party guise. In a 1900 article Debs complained of these irrational handicaps (see "The Outlook for Socialism in the United States" as reprinted on pp. 86-92 in the volume cited below). As great a problem was the complex factionalism of the socialists themselves. Debs was not able to overcome prejudice and internal confusions but his leadership provided a considerable force toward unity.

By 1912 the Socialist Party had reached a kind of predictable maturity. The platform for that year opened with the class rhetoric that was employed internationally. When the party got down to domestic issues it reflected—except for the important emphasis on collective ownership of industry—the same progressive attitudes that had come to characterize the major parties at this time. Although they made their best showing in 1912, the Socialists probably showed their special zeal and flavor more noticeably in earlier campaigns. Reproduced below is Debs's opening speech of the 1904 presidential campaign delivered in Indianapolis.

SOURCE: Bruce Rogers, ed., *Debs: His Life, Writing, and Speeches.* Girard, Kans., The Appeal to Reason, 1908, pp. 357-373, abridged.

DEBS' CAMPAIGN SPEECH

Mr. Chairman, Citizens, and Comrades:

There has never been a free people, a civilized nation, a real republic on this earth. Human society has always consisted of masters and slaves, and the slaves have always been and are today, the foundation stones of the social fabric.

Wage-labor is but a name; wage-slavery is the fact.

The twenty-five millions of wage-workers in the United States are twenty-five millions of twentieth century slaves.

This is the plain meaning of what is known as

THE LABOR MARKET

And the labor market follows the capitalist flag.

The most barbarous fact in all christendom is the labor market. The mere term sufficiently expresses the animalism of commercial civilization.

They who buy and they who sell in the labor market are alike dehumanized by the inhuman traffic in the brains and blood and bones of human beings.

The labor market is the foundation of so-called civilized society. Without these shambles, without this commerce in human life, this sacrifice of manhood and womanhood, this barter of babes, this sale of souls, the capitalist civilizations of all lands and all climes would crumble to ruin and perish from the earth.

Twenty-five millions of wage-slaves are bought and sold daily at prevailing prices in the American Labor Market.

This is the

PARAMOUNT ISSUE

in the present national campaign.

Let me say at the very threshold of this discussion that the workers have but the one issue in this campaign, the overthrow of the capitalist system and the emancipation of the working class from wage-slavery.

The capitalists may have the tariff, finance, imperialism, and other dust-covered and moth-eaten issues entirely to themselves.

The rattle of these relics no longer deceives workingmen whose heads are on their own shoulders.

They know by experience and observation that the gold standard, free silver, fiat money, protective tariff, free trade, imperialism and anti-imperialism all mean capitalist rule and wage-slavery.

Their eyes are open and they can see; their brains are in operation and they can think.

The very moment a workingman begins to do his own thinking he understands the paramount issue, parts company with the capitalist politician and falls in line with his own class on the political battle-field.

The political solidarity of the working class means the death of despotism, the birth of freedom, the sunrise of civilization. . . .

The capitalist system is no longer adapted to the needs of modern society. It is outgrown and fetters the forces of progress. Industrial and commercial competition are largely of the past. The handwriting blazes on the wall. Centralization and combination are the modern forces in industrial and commercial life. Competition is breaking down and cooperation is supplanting it. . . .

The hand tools of early times are used no more. Mammoth machines have taken their places. A few thousand capitalists own them and many millions of workingmen use them.

All the wealth the vast army of labor produces above its subsistence is taken by the machine owning capitalists, who also own the land and the mills, the factories, railroads and mines, the forests and fields and all other means of production and transportation.

Hence wealth and poverty, millionaires and beggars, castles and caves, luxury and squalor, painted parasites on the boulevard and painted poverty among the red lights.

Hence strikes, boycotts, riots, murder, suicide, insanity, prostitution on a fearful and increasing scale. . . .

The capitalist parties can do nothing. They are a part, an iniquitous part, of the foul and decaying system. . . .

CLOSING WORDS

These are stirring days for living men. The day of crisis is drawing near and Socialists are exerting all their power to prepare the people for it.

The old order of society can survive but little longer. Socialism is next in order. The swelling minority sounds warning of the impending change. Soon that minority will be the majority and then will come the co-operative commonwealth. . . .

The overthrow of capitalism is the object of the Socialist party. It will not fuse with any other party and it would rather die than compromise.

The Socialist party comprehends the magnitude of its task and has the patience of preliminary defeat and the faith of ultimate victory.

The working class must be emancipated by the working class.

Woman must be given her true place in society by the working class.

Child labor must be abolishee by the working class.

Society must be reconstructed by the working class.

The working class must be employed by the working class.

The fruits of labor must be enjoyed by the working class.

War, bloody war, must be ended by the working class.

These are the principles and objects of the Socialist party and we fearlessly proclaim them to our fellowmen.

We know our cause is just and that it must prevail.

With faith and hope and courage we hold our heads erect and with dauntless spirit marshal the working class for the march from Capitalism to Socialism, from Slavery to Freedom, from Barbarism to Civilization.

Document II-31: PROGRESSIVISM: STEFFENS ON U'REN

One of the most famous muckraking journalists of the turn of the century was Lincoln Steffens, most noted for his exposures of city and state governments. Some of the reasons for his impact can be seen in the following example of his lively, colloquial style, his love of ironies and contrasts, and his power to evoke quick understanding and sincere appreciation. In this frank, sometimes shocking, account of the questionable ways and means of the successful reformer, Steffens and his subject remind one of other cynical idealists like John Jay Chapman (see V-5).

William S. U'Ren, the subject of this sketch, became associated with a package of "tools," as this blacksmith would have called them, which were meant to make governments truly responsive to the needs of the people at large rather than static, captive agencies subservient to the power centers and enraptured of the status quo. The package included the initiative, referendum, recall of judges, careful registration of voters, secret and simplified ballots, corrupt practices acts, direct election of Senators, proportional representation, direct primaries, and lobbies in the public interest. These measures were aimed at wiping out easy bribery and callous use of private funds; at eliminating the middlemen (party bosses, special-interest lobbies, overly powerful legislative committees and appointed officials); and at putting the government as much as possible into the hands of the people themselves. (For a view of this agenda as of 1897 see V-2.)

These passages, to be sure, raise a number of questions. How close were men like U'Ren to arguing that the means justified the ends? All of the means at U'Ren's disposal produced only another set of means: that is, tools for change rather than changes themselves. Was it realistic of him to believe that "Reform begins in 1910"?

SOURCE: Lincoln Steffens, *The Upbuilders*. New York, Doubleday, Page, 1909, pp. 285-323, abridged.

W. S. U'REN, THE LAWGIVER

OREGON has more fundamental legislation than any other state in the Union excepting only Oklahoma, and Oklahoma is new. Oregon is not new; it is and it long has been corrupt, yet it has enacted laws which enable its people to govern themselves when they want to. How did this happen? How did this state of graft get all her tools for democracy? And, since it has them, why don't her people use them more? The answer to these questions lies buried deep in the character and in the story of W. S. U'Ren (accent the last syllable), the lawgiver.

They call this man the Father of the Initiative and Referendum in Oregon, but that title isn't big enough. U'Ren has fathered other Oregon laws, and his own state isn't the limit of his influence. The Dakotas have some similar legislation. Meeting on a Western train one day a politician who seemed to know all about things there, I inquired into the origin of the Dakota laws.

"There's a fellow over in Oregon," he answered—"funny name—he tipped us off and steered us; sent drafts of bills and pamphlets containing arguments. I can't recall his name."

"U'Ren?"

"That's it; that's the man."

They are getting good laws in the State of Washington, also. I asked in Seattle where they came from. Very few knew, but those that did said: "U'Ren of Oregon."

The first time I heard this name was in Rhode Island. Ex-Governor Garvin, the advocate of democratic legislation for that law-bound state, knew about U'Ren. After that I used to come upon his influence in many states and cities where men were tinkering with the sacred constitutional machinery that won't let democracy go. But my last encounter with the mysterious ubiquity of this singular man's influence was amusing. Spreckels, Heney, and the other fighters for San Francisco thought of going to the people on a certain proposition and, seeing thus the uses of the referendum, wanted it. I suggested writing to U'Ren. They never had heard of him, but they wrote, and he came. And he heard them out on their need of the referendum.

"But I think," said U'Ren, "that you have it in your city charter." Everybody looked incredulous. "Where is the book?" U'Ren asked. "I think I can find it. I certainly had some correspondence with the makers of that charter; I think I drafted a section—yes, here it is. [He read it to himself.] It isn't mine—not very clear—but [handing back the book] good enough for your purpose, you see."

William Simon U'Ren, the lawgiver, was born January 10, 1859, at Lancaster, Wisconsin. His father is a blacksmith, and his father's seven brothers were blacksmiths; their father was a blacksmith, and their father's father, and his father, and his. As far as the family can trace from Cornwall, England, back into Holland, they see an unbroken line of blacksmiths. And preachers. Five of U'Ren's seven uncles preached and, among their ancestors, other blacksmiths preached. And William U'Ren himself is both a blacksmith and a preacher in a way; in a very essential way.

"Blacksmithing is my trade," he says. "And it has always given colour to my view of things. For example, when I was very young, I saw some of the evils in the conditions of life, and I wanted to fix them. I couldn't. There were no tools. We had tools to do almost anything with in the shop, beautiful tools, wonderful. And so in other trades, arts and professions; in everything but government. In government, the common trade of all men and the basis of all social life, men worked still with old tools, with old laws, with constitutions and charters which hindered more than they helped. Men suffered from this. There were lawyers enough; many of our ablest men were lawyers. Why didn't some of them invent legislative implements to help the people govern themselves? Why had we no tool makers for democracy?". . .

Politics comes first with U'Ren. He makes his living with his left hand; his right is for the state. And that such citizenship can be effective is demonstrated by this remarkable fact: The Father of the Initiative and Referendum, the first legislator of Oregon, has held office but once in his career. He has done what he has done as a citizen in politics.

His first experience of the game was in Denver when he was a law student. The Presidential campaign of 1880 was on and U'Ren had just come of age. The Republican Party needed the help of all good men and true, and first-voters were invited to work. U'Ren volunteered. He offered his services with the enthusiasm of youth and the fervour of that secret inspiration of Moses. And the leaders welcomed the boy. They put him to work. They directed him to aid in colonizing voters in a doubtful ward!

U'Ren was stunned. He did not know such things were done. He was horrified, but fascinated. He said nothing; he didn't do the work, but he hung about watching it done. The dreamer was allowed to see the inside. There were anti-Chinese riots in the town. The mob marched through the streets crying "The Chinese must go!" and threatening to kill them. U'Ren became excited. Here was oppression of the weak. At his request, he was appointed a deputy to "protect the poor Chinamen," and he served in all earnestness till an insider explained to him that the mob was organized and the riots were faked—to get the good citizens out to the polls to vote for "law and order and the Republican party."

The elders forget how young people feel when they first discover that the world isn't what schools and grown-ups have taught them. It would be better to teach the truth; then the new citizens would be prepared for the fray. As it is, the sudden shock carries away not only the "illusions," but more often the character of youth. Not so with U'Ren, however. His dream of Congress vanished, but his hope of inventing laws to make such evils less easy and profitable—that stayed. Indeed, this was the time when the dominant idea of his life took its first definite form.

"As I watched this fraud, and saw that it was the means by which the other evils were maintained, I felt clearly that a modicum of the thought and ingenuity which had been devoted to machinery, if given to government, would make this a pleasant world to live in. That men were all right at bottom, I was convinced, for I noticed that we young men were honest and capable of some unselfish service. It was the older men that were 'bad.' ". . .

U'Ren went to the people. They were ready for him. The year was 1893. Discontent was widespread. Agitation had taken the form of a demand that the Legislature to be elected in 1894 should call a constitutional convention to rectify all evils, and U'Ren was one of the many workers who went about pledging candidates. But he and the Luellings concentrated on the "I. & R.," as they called the initiative and referendum. As secretary of the Direct Legislation League he got up a folder stating simply the democratic principle underlying the initiative and referendum and the results to be expected from it. Direct legislation was an acknowledgment of the right of the people to govern themselves and a device to enable them to do so. The "I. & R." would put it in the power of the voters to start or stop any legislation, just like a boss. In other words, it would make the people boss; the legislators would have to represent the voters who elected them, not railroads and not any other "interest." Nobody could object (openly) to this; at least, nobody would out there in that Western state where the failures of democracy were ascribed, not as in the East, to the people, but to the business and political interests that actually are to blame.

Everybody worked. The women sewed the folders; two-thirds of the houses in Milwaukee were thus engaged that winter (1893-94); they prepared 50,000 folders in English and 18,000 in German; and the alliances and labour unions saw that the voters got and read them. The effect was such that when the politicians pleaded ignorance of the initiative and referendum, U'Ren could answer: "The people know about them." And that was true. After the election, these same workers, men and women, circulated a petition which, with 14,000 signatures, was presented to the Legislature.

Now, that is as far as a reform movement usually goes. U'Ren went further. Knowing that the representatives elected by the people are organized in the Legislature to represent somebody else, U'Ren went to Salem as a lobbyist, a lobbyist for the people, and he talked to every member of that Legislature. He saw the chicanery, fraud, and the politics of it all, but he wrung from a clear majority promises to keep their pledge.

"And we lost," he told me quietly. "We lost by one vote in the House and in the Senate also—by one vote."

"Fooled?" I asked.

"Fooled," said U'Ren. "It was done in the Senate by a wink, a wink from Joe Simon" (president of the Senate and boss of Portland).

"You understood. How did you feel?"

"We were angry," U'Ren answered. "I completely lost my self-control and I said and did things that were wrong. And when I saw my mistake, I remembered what my father used to say about self-control, and I tied a string on my finger to remind me. That device of the children worked with me. I think I never afterward completely lost my temper."

The act which U'Ren calls his mistake was to go out from that Legislature to punish the members who had broken their pledges; and that is what I can't help believing must be done. But U'Ren is one of those very, very few men that believe, after these 2,000 years, in the Christian spirit as a *practical* force. . . .

The answer is, as before, "W. S. U'Ren." He knows the "I. & R." is nothing but a tool; that it is worth while only as it can be used to change the "conditions that make men do bad things"; and he means to use it. Indeed, he proposed, when he got it, to proceed at once to economic reforms. But wiser heads counselled that, until the new instrument had been tempered by custom, it would be better to use the

"I. & R." only to get other new tools. So the Direct Legislation League gave way to a Direct Primary League, and W. S. U'Ren, secretary, drew a bill for the people to initiate that should enable them to make their own nominations for office and thus knock out the party machines. While this was doing, a railroad planned a referendum to delay a state road which the Chamber of Commerce wanted, and the Chamber, in alarm, threatened an initiative for a maximum rate bill. That settled the railroad, pleased the business men and showed *them* the use of the new tool. And when, in July, 1903, a circuit court declared the "I. & R." unconstitutional, there was backing for the tool. U'Ren was able to get Senator Mitchell, Brownell, and eight other political and influential corporation attorneys to appear before the Supreme Court, to defend the "I. & R.", which was sweepingly upheld.

The Direct Primary Bill was passed by the people in July, 1904, 56,000 to 16,000. A local option liquor bill was passed by initiative at the same time, and in November several counties and many precincts went "dry." U'Ren had nothing to do with this last, but he did have very much to do with another important enactment—the choice of United States Senators by direct vote of the people.

This radical reform was achieved without secrecy, but yet without much public discussion. It was a bomb planted deep in the Direct Primary Bill, and U'Ren planted it—with the help of Mitchell, Brownell, Bourne and two or three editors of newspapers. The idea occurred to U'Ren to write into the Primary bill a clause: that candidates for nomination for the Legislature *"may"* pledge themselves to vote for or against the people's choice for United States Senators, "regardless of personal or party preference." Mitchell helped to draw the clause, now famous as Statement No. 1, which legislators might sign, and he expected to be and, if Heney hadn't caught him grafting, he would have been elected on it without having to bribe legislators. U'Ren would have helped him. As it happened, Mulkey (for a short term of six weeks) and Bourne were the first Senators elected under the amazing law which hardly anybody but U'Ren realized beforehand the full effect of.

That Jonathan Bourne, Jr., should have been the first product of the popular election of Senators has been used to disparage this whole Oregon movement, but Bourne had backed all these reforms with work and money, and U'Ren says he is sincerely for them. But U'Ren tried to get another man to run, and turned to Bourne only when he was convinced that, to establish Statement No. 1 as a custom in Oregon, the first candidate must be a man rich enough to fight fire with fire if the legislators should be bribed to go back on their pledges. So, you see, U'Ren was still thinking only of the tool, and he won again. For the knowledge of Bourne's resources and character (and, also, a warning from the back country that the men with guns would come to Salem if their Legislature broke its pledge) did have its effect. The Legislature confirmed Bourne without bribery and with only four votes against him.

The direct Primary Law settled, a People's Power League was organized (W. S. U'Ren, secretary) to use the people's power, but U'Ren still stuck to tool making. Other reformers used the "I. & R." for particular reforms. The Anti-Saloon League passed a local option bill; the State Grange enacted two franchise tax acts, which the Legislature had failed on; and U'Ren's league put through a constitutional amendment to cut out the state printer's graft. On the other hand, a graft bill to sell the state a toll road, another for woman's suffrage, and a liquor dealers' amendment to the local option bill were all beaten by referendum. But U'Ren and the League worked hardest for and passed, by initiative, bills extending the "I. & R." to cities and towns, and giving municipalities complete home rule— more tools. And so—next year, initiative bills were passed to let the people discharge any public officer of the state and choose his successor by a special election (this is the famous "recall"); a corrupt practice act; to make the people's choice of United States Senators mandatory; and, deepest reaching of all, proportional representation. All tools. There were referendum petitions out, also; two against appropriations, one to make passes for public officials compulsory, another to beat a sheriff's graft. But U'Ren was still after the tools.

But will this tool-making never be over? "Yes," said U'Ren; and he added very definitely, "Reform begins in 1910." And one proposition in the list for 1908 showed what we may expect. This was a bill "to exempt from taxation factory buildings and machinery; homes and home improvements, but not the lots nor the farms." Quietly worded though this was, the reform involved is economic, and economic reforms are, as we have seen, what U'Ren is after. And he will get them, he and the people of Oregon. I believe that that state will appear before long as the leader of reform in the United States, and if it is, W. S. U'Ren will rank in history as the greatest lawgiver of his day and country. . . .

Document II-32: INITIATIVE AND REFERENDUM

The Progressive movement formed an important chapter in the history of American reform and had particular application to the subject entertained in this section. It grew out of the labor and farm movements of the late nineteenth century, taking from them an appeal to the exploited, both farmers and laborers; an antipathy to monopoly and parasitic wealth; and a determination to pursue economic democracy by purifying political democracy (see II-20). By bringing to this task intelligence and a sense of political realism, the Progressives hoped for success at all levels of government where naive crusaders had failed. William S. U'Ren, whose career was sketched by Lincoln Steffens, typified many of the Progressive attitudes; his package of electoral reforms was close to the heart of Progressivism.

The following document centers on the argument for direct legislation in a way that reveals, albeit hyperbolically, the faith and value structure of the Progressives. Good legislative reforms would bring good men into government. Good men and good laws would wipe out inequity and ensure justice. Furthermore, as part of this process, all voters would become literate, enlightened citizens; their nation would shine out to the world as a beacon light of participatory democracy victorious over the dark shadows of corruption and special interests.

The first section explains initiative, referendum, and recall, taking a line of sight on that popular Progressive model, the New England town meeting. Self-government is then expounded in terms that make the virtues of direct democracy inescapable. Parallels in world history— ancient Greece, the Swiss cantons—are cited as precedents. The list of advantages of direct democracy, of which but a part has been here reproduced, include the development of manners and morals, the education of the press and the people, the achievement of economy and social stability. Whereas W. S. U'Ren had made important use of the agrarian Populists in his campaigns in Oregon, this document made a more special appeal to the interests of the laboring man; thus, combining this argument with the preceding sketch, one gets something like a true composite picture of Progressive origins and connections.

At the end of this pamphlet were printed recent amendments to state constitutions authorizing initiative and referendum. This list was not complete, for it might have gone back as far as the first state constitution of Georgia in 1777. However, that provision, as well as those of South Dakota (1898) and Utah (1900), had features which prevented their true utilization. Therefore, most historians of this subject credit Oregon with the first modern, workable provision for direct democracy at the state level. It is here reproduced from this same contemporary source.

SOURCE: Frank E. Parsons, as edited by Milton T. U'Ren, *Direct Legislation.* Washington, D.C., Government Printing Office, 1914 (Document #360 of the 63rd Congress, 2nd Session), pp. 3-64, abridged.

DIRECT LEGISLATION

In early days the legislative function was exercised by the whole body of enfranchised citizens assembled for the purpose. The laws of the Commonwealth were made by the voters directly, in substantially the same way that the laws of a New England town are made to-day. But after a time the body of freemen became too large to meet in this way and a system of lawmaking by delegates was adopted. Towns and districts elected men to represent them in legislative council, and government by representatives took the place of government by the people except in respect to the local affairs of towns that possess the town-meeting system.

The change from legislation by the people to legislation by final vote of a body of representatives chosen for a specified term was a transformation fraught with the most momentous consequences. Under the former system the people had complete control of legislation. No laws were passed that the people did not want and all laws were passed that the people did want. But under the delegate or representative-final-vote system this is not true. The representatives can and do make and put in force many laws the people do not desire and they neglect or refuse to make some laws the people do desire. The people can not command or veto their action during their term of office. The representatives are the real masters of the situation for the time being. Between elections the sovereign power of controlling legislation is not in the hands of the people, but in the hands of a small body of men called representatives. It appears, therefore, that the change from legislation by the voters in person to legislation by delegates was a change from a real democracy to an elective aristocracy, from a continuous and effective popular sovereignty to an intermittent, spasmodic, and largely ineffective popular sovereignty; from a government of the people, by the people, and for the people to a government of the people, by a few for—the people? Yes, sometimes, but too often for the legislators, and the lobbies, bosses, rings, monopolies, and party leaders who control them. It was a change in which self-government was fettered and the soul of liberty was lost.

What, then, shall be done? Shall we give up the representative principle? Clearly not. Division of labor and expert service are as essential in lawmaking as in any other business. It is not representation, but misrepresentation that is wrong—not the representative system per se, but the unguarded and imperfect form of it in use at present. What we want is not a body of legislators beyond the reach of the people for one, two, four or six years, as the case may be, but a body of legislators subject at all times to the people's direction and control. It is good to have powerful horses to draw your load, but it is well to have a bit and rein and whip if they are frisky or likely to shy or balk. It is good to choose strong men to manage municipal and State affairs, but it is well too to provide the means to hold them in check or make them move at the people's will.

The problem is to keep the advantages of the representative system— its compactness, legal wisdom, experience, power of work, etc., and eliminate its evils, haste, complexity, corruption, error, over legislation and under legislation—departure from the people's will by omission or commission.

The solution lies in a representative system guarded by constitutional provisions for popular initiative, adoption, veto, and recall. Elect your councilmen and legislators and let them pass laws exactly as they do now, except that no act but such as may be necessary for the immediate preservation of the public peace, health, or safety shall go into effect until

30 days after its passage in case of a city ordinance or 90 days in case of a State law. If within the said time a certain percentage of the voters of a city or State (say 5 or 10 per cent) sign a petition asking that the law or ordinance be submitted to the people at the polls, let it be so submitted at the next regular election, or at a special election if 15 or 20 per cent of the voters so petition. If the majority of those voting on the measure favor it, it becomes a law; if the majority are against it, it is vetoed by the people.

Let it be further provided that if the council or legislature neglect or refuse to take any such action by ordinance, law, contract, franchise, etc., as the people desire, the matter may be brought forward for prompt decision by a petition signed by a reasonable percentage (say 5 or 10 per cent) of the voters of a city or State. The petition may simply state the general purpose and scope of the desired measure, leaving the council or legislature to frame a bill to be submitted to the voters; or it may embody a bill or ordinance, whereupon the petition, with the bill or ordinance, will go to the council or legislature, which may adopt it, reject it, pass an amendment or substitute, or do nothing—in any case the proposed measure (together with the action of the council or legislature upon it, if any) will go to the polls for final decision at the next election, or earlier, if a sufficient number (say 15 or 20 per cent) of the voters so petition. Or the petition may require that the proposed law be placed directly before the people, without reference to the legislative body, for their adoption or rejection.

These methods of law-making by the people are called direct legislation, which includes two main processes known as the initiative and the referendum. . . .

DIRECT LEGISLATION IN USE IN AMERICA

It is already a fundamental fact in American government and a settled principle in our legislative system.

The suggested improvement of our representative system to make it harmonize with the law of self-government does not require the adoption of any new principle or method. Both the initiative and the referendum have been in constant use in America ever since the *Mayflower* crossed the sea. All that is needed is an extension of established principles and methods to cases quite as much within their reason, purpose, and power as those to which they are now applied.

In many New England towns we have the ideal of democracy in respect to local affairs. They are controlled by the people directly. Any 10 men, by petition to the selectmen, may secure the insertion of an item in the warrant for a town meeting, and so bring the matter before the town. Anyone may make a motion or enter the discussion, and all may vote. The town-meeting plan is the initiative and referendum applied to town business.

Direct legislation is also used by all our States except Delaware in making and amending their constitutions, from which it would seem that our citizens are already convinced that it is the best possible plan of legislation, since it is the one they adopt in respect to their highest and most important law. . . .

REASONS FOR THE REFERENDUM.

THE DOORWAY OF REFORM.

1.   It is the key to progress. It will open the door to all other reforms. It is not the people who defeat reform. The people want honest government, civil-service reform, and just taxation. They vote overwhelmingly against monopoly rule, and for public ownership of street franchises and public utilities almost every time they have the opportunity. It is the power of money and corporate influence and official interest that checkmates progress. Miles of petitions have gone in to Congress for a postal telegraph. By the million our people have expressed the wish for such an institution, and Hon. John Wanamaker says in his very able argument on the subject that the Western Union is the only visible opponent of the movement.

Hundreds of instances might be named in which councils, legislatures, and Congresses have persistently defeated the well-known will of the people. It is not sufficient now to educate the people to a new idea, or even to elect representatives on the promise to carry it into execution; you have also to fight the power of money and corruption in your legislature that will steal away or put to sleep the ardor of your legislators.

How important it is that progress should rest with the people free of hindrance from their rulers is clearly brought out in this fine passage from the great historian, Buckle:

No great political improvement, no great reform, either legislative or executive, has ever been originated in any country by its rulers. The first suggesters of such steps have invariably been bold and able thinkers, who discern the abuse and denounce it and point out how it is to be remedied. But long after this is done, even the most enlightened governments continue to uphold the abuse and reject the remedy.

Wendell Phillips said:

No reform, moral or intellectual, ever came from the upper classes of society. Each and all came from the protest of the martyr and the victim. The emancipation of the working people must be achieved by the working people themselves.

The referendum is the key that will unlock the door to every onward movement. It will give us new reforms as fast as the people want them, without the necessity of waiting till the millionaires and politicians are ready for the curtain to go up. In this great fact lies the tremendous and immediate importance of the referendum, although it is by no means the only irresistible reason for favoring the movement.

Direct legislation will give the people the power of voluntary movement; it will bring the public mind into connection with the motor muscles of the body politic; it will gear the power of public sentiment directly and effectively to the machinery of legislation, with no slipping belts, switched-off currents, or broken circuits.

At present the pocket nerve and the corporation ganglion are frequently able to paralyze the progressive muscles and the civic conscience and control the body politic, and the party ganglia compel it to remain inactive, or else go to enormous labor and perform a large number of actions that are against its wish in order to accomplish a few things it desires—as though a man were obliged to lift a 50 or 100 pound spoon to his lips with each sip of soup and endure the pricks of several pins and needles or sit down on a tack with each mouthful of bread or fragment of beef, the bill of fare being written with those conditions, to be accepted or rejected as a whole, like the conglomerate platforms of our parties.

The separation of measures accompanying direct legislation is another thing that makes it par excellence the friend of progress. Each reform will receive as a rule the full support of all who believe in it without suffering from the alienation and subtraction of the votes of citizens who favor it but oppose some other measure with which it may be linked in the platform, or object to the party in whose platform the reform is suggested, or dislike the candidate whose name is tied to the movement and whose election is the only means of securing its success.

PURE GOVERNMENT.

2. Direct legislation will tend to the purification of politics and the elevation of government. It is not the people who put up jobs on themselves, but corrupt influences in our legislative bodies; the referendum will kill the corrupt lobby and close the doors against fraudulent legislation. It will no longer pay to buy a franchise from the aldermen, because the aldermen can not settle the matter; the people have the final decision, and they are so many that it might cost more to buy their votes for the franchise than the privilege is worth. It is comparatively easy for a wealthy briber to put his bids high enough to overcome the conscience or other resistance of a dozen councilmen. It is quite a different matter to overcome the consciences or other resistance of 10,000 or 100,000 citizens. Legislative bribery derives its power from the concentration of temptation resulting from the power of a few legislators to take final action.

It will not do to leave the referendum option with the legislators. They submit questions that are immaterial to them or in respect to which they wish to act honestly; but they never submit a franchise steal to the people. When they are acting from honest motives, they often find the referendum very helpful in coming to a wise and just conclusion; but when they are acting from corrupt and selfish motives they have no use for the referendum.

The reader will remember that in examining the facts relating to the use of the referendum in the United States we found that the people have voted down all propositions that were suspected of being accessory to any job, and the strenuous opposition of the corruptionists to the extension of the referendum shows that they appreciate its power for purity. They know very well that corporation frauds could not go on, and that valuable gas, electric light, and street-railway franchises could no longer be given to lobbying corporations if we had the referendum.

A legislator may be subjected to successful pressure by street railways, gas and electric light companies, the railroads, the oil trust, or the coal combine, but the citizens are too numerous, too much interested in their own pocketbooks, and too wide awake to their welfare to be wheedled or bribed or threatened into giving away their property or endowing big corporations with privileges and powers to be used to the disadvantage and oppression of the donors. As Prof. Bryce says: "The legislators can be 'got at'; the people can not."

Prof. Bemis tells of a corporation voting $100,000 to buy the Chicago council as calmly as it would vote to buy a new building, and says that, according to a reliable attorney, such a proceeding was an ordinary thing. Under the referendum such proceedings would not take place, because they would be of no use. The referendum destroys the power of legislators to legislate for personal ends.

The referendum will be the death of the lobby. It will be impracticable to lobby the people because of their number. And it will be useless to lobby the legislators, for they can not deliver the goods.

No doubt persuasion will still be used with legislators as the first and easiest method of initiating legislation, but the lack of finality in the action of legislative bodies will take away its commercial value, and the lobby or "third house" as it exists to-day will dissolve. Log-rolling and minority obstruction will also lose their power, and dishonest men will be much less likely to buy legislative positions and other offices, because they can not make them pay.

Blackmailing will be destroyed as well as the corrupting power of the lobby. The referendum works both ways; it keeps the corporations from using the legislature for their private gain, and it also keeps the legislators from blackmailing the corporations by introducing bills injurious to them, so that they will offer large sums to have the bills quashed—a shameful practice prevailing to a large extent in some of our legislative bodies.

The unguarded representative system or delegation of uncontrolled law-making power to a small body of legislators has utterly failed to check class legislation or the growth of monopoly and corruption. On the contrary, these evils have increased in city and State where the delegate system has control, whereas in town affairs and constitution making, and city business so far as referred to and controlled by the people, the said evils are comparatively unknown. This contrast vividly illustrates the power for purity that direct legislation possesses.

As we shall see below, the force of partisanship will diminish by the referendum. Party success will no longer mean power to mold the laws of a city or State for one or more years. And the intensity of party feeling will diminish as the value of the prize to be won is lessened. The weakening of partisanship will react on the executive department, and the spoils system will have less hold on the Government, even before civil-service regulations are thoroughly formed and enforced.

As we have seen, the obligatory referendum would be most effective in checking corruption; but even the optional referendum will make corrupt legislation a dangerous and unprofitable thing. The mere fact that the right of appeal to the people exists within the reach of a reasonable percentage of voters will purify legislation at its source.

3. Demagoguery and the influence of employers over the votes of their employees will be diminished factors in elections. When the question is voting an office to A or to B, one as good as the other for all the voter knows, a $2 bill or the wish of his employer may seem to the voter to be worth more than the problematical difference between the two candidates, for whatever their platforms and promises there is little possibility of telling what they will do when elected. But when the question comes directly home to the self-interest of the voter on a bill to give away public property, or franchises, or make an extravagant contract, etc., the voter will use the protection of the secret ballot and record his opinion, regardless of $2 bills or the wishes of employers.

Even the ignorant voter will be rescued by the referendum to some extent. The demagogue and politician will lose a large part of their power to prejudice and confuse when the issue is a single clear-cut question of money, property, or public policy, instead of the present entanglement of measures and men tossed together in a confused heap for the express purpose, one might think, of affording demagogues their golden opportunity to prejudice men against the whole "heap" by centering attention upon some objectionable feature of it and ignoring the good features or lying about them, or to prejudice men in favor of the whole by reversing the process of deception.

4. The power of rings and bosses will be greatly reduced by the referendum; directly so far as concerns the large portion of their power, which depends on controlling legislation; indirectly so far as concerns their administrative power. Nothing will do more than the referendum for the cause of civil-service reform, and the awakening of a strong interest

in politics and the ballot on the part of our best people, and these things will quickly abolish the boss and the ring. . . .

9.   The referendum will elevate politics as a profession and bring the best men again into political life. Government is intrinsically the noblest of all professions, for it includes and controls all others, as the captain of a ship holds the destiny of all on board. But when power is prostituted to evil ends it becomes despicable. The people no longer regard membership in a city council or a legislature as a badge of honor, but rather as a mark of suspicion. He is most probably in league with the powers of darkness or he would not have been elected. Honest men have little weight in the councils of many of our cities; they find the atmosphere uncongenial, and retire in disgust, or if they persist in their duty they are soon hounded out by the ring, which finds them inconvenient. Many of our wisest and purest men look on politics as too dirty to touch. They will not descend to the meanness and cunning usually necessary to secure office, nor subject themselves to the cruel suspicions and slanders that often accompany public life. Mud slinging and the winning power of chicanery too often discourage the wise and good and leave the field to the most callous and unscrupulous.

With the referendum all this will change. Attention will be directed from men to measures. The power for evil of our office holders will shrink to a small fraction of its present bulk. Bad men will be discouraged from entering or continuing in politics because they will no longer be able to accomplish their evil purposes. With these changes the suspicions and mud flinging now so prevalent will decrease, because their causes will subside. As discussion of specific measures takes the place of partisan abuse, men of probity and wisdom will feel their influence with the people increase, and will delight to exercise their powers of mind and conscience in the direction of public affairs when they can do so without stain or ignominy. The increasing weight of goodness and the returning purity of political life will induce our best men once more to take a leading part in it and stand for office in council, legislature, and Congress as they used to do in the patriotic days of the Revolution. . . .

OREGON.

Section I of Article IV of the constitution of the State of Oregon shall be, and hereby is, amended to read as follows:

"SECTION 1. The legislative authority of the State shall be vested in a legislative assembly, consisting of a senate and house of representatives, but the people reserve to themselves power to propose laws and amendments to the constitution, and to enact or reject the same at the polls, independent of the legislative assembly, and also reserve power at their own option to approve or reject at the polls any act of the legislative assembly. The first power reserved by the people is the initiative, and not more than 8 per cent of the legal voters shall be required to propose any measure by such petition, and every such petition shall include the full text of the measure so proposed. Initiative petitions shall be filed with the secretary of state not less than four months before the election at which they are to be voted upon. The second power is the referendum, and it may be ordered (except as to laws necessary for the immediate preservation of the public peace, health, or safety), either by petition, signed by 5 per cent of the legal voters or by the legislative assembly, as other bills are enacted. Referendum petitions shall be filed with the secretary of state not more than 90 days after the final adjournment of the session of the legislative assembly which passed the bill on which the referendum is demanded. The veto power of the governor shall not extend to measures referred to the people. All elections on measures referred to the people of the state shall be had at the biennial regular general elections, except when the legislative assembly shall order a special election. Any measure referred to the people shall take effect and become the law when it is approved by a majority of the votes cast thereon, and not otherwise. The style of all bills shall be: 'Be it enacted by the people of the State of Oregon.' This section shall not be construed to deprive any member of the legislative assembly of the right to introduce any measure. The whole number of votes cast for justice of the supreme court at the regular election last preceding the filing of any petition for the initiative or for the referendum shall be the basis on which the number of legal voters necessary to sign such petition shall be counted. Petitions and orders for the initiative and for the referendum shall be filed with the secretary of state, and in submitting the same to the people he and all other officers shall be guided by the general laws and the act submitting this amendment until legislation shall be especially provided therefor."

Adopted, June 2, 1902.

Document II-33: FEDERAL RESERVE IN CONGRESS

The Federal Reserve Act of 1913 must stand as one of the principal points of climax in the history of American politico-economic reform. In its several provisions it represents a response to more varied tones in the collective voice of protest than any other single piece of federal legislation. The Antifederalists who cried out against economic privilege; the opponents of the Bank of the United States in Jacksonian days and the Populists who made archvillains of the New York bankers; the heirs of Jefferson who wanted decentralized authority; the authors of the various subtreasury plans who sought regional fiscal autonomy and— eventually—a flexible currency; the greenbackers and free-silver advocates; the farm and labor leaders and currency reformers—all these groups and many others would have found some answer to their pleas in this act.

The act as passed was by no means perfect; considerable experience and courage were to be required before it could be used effectively. Its importance lay in its recognition that the federal government had a continuing responsibility to regulate the economy in a way that responded to the changing tides of economic well-being and that allowed for variation from region to region. Policy decisions were taken out of the hands of private banks and relegated to boards whose membership represented the affected elements in the population. By issuing currency (Federal Reserve Notes), by authorizing credit, and by influencing interest rates, the Federal Reserve System could react appropriately to an economy that was either under- or overstimulated. In these decisions the role of private profit, special privilege, and irresponsible speculation was notably decreased.

The legislative mood in 1913 favored the passage of a measure such as this. The mandate of the electorate in 1912 had been clearly in the direction of Progressivism, so much so that the provisions of the Federal Reserve Act could be construed as a fulfillment not only of Wilson's promises, but those of Roosevelt, Taft, or Debs as well. But Wilson had spoken with particular vindictiveness against the sinister monopoly on money and credit enjoyed and abused by the private bankers and speculators of the East; and the Pujo Committee, early in 1913, had amassed a considerable case against these abuses.

Thus Senator Claude A. Swanson, a Democrat from Virginia, opened his December 8, 1913, arguments by calling this legislation a nonpartisan fulfillment of a Democratic election promise. In the spirit of the Pujo Committee, and with overt references to its report, he made a wicked example of the bankers of New York for their unresponsiveness to the problems created by the Panic of 1907. Stressing a need for governmental protection against an oligarchy of privilege, Swanson then turned to the constructive features of the measure: its provision for economic justice on a regional basis, for an elastic currency and credit to respond to the nation's needs; its supervision by representative, disinterested parties; and the security of its deposits system. His peroration rhetorically links Jackson and Wilson and identifies the farming and laboring masses with their legislative protectors.

(Like all such sweeping devices, the Federal Reserve has created its own problems. For a recent negative appraisal see Gary Allen, *The Bankers and The Federal Reserve*. Belmont, Mass., American Opinion, 1970.)

SOURCE: *The Congressional Record*, vol LI, pp. 428-30, 435, abridged.

SPEECH OF SENATOR CLAUDE A. SWANSON

The banks in New York are dominated by the large financiers and speculators of this country, and these reserves have been used for their enrichment and not for public good. By this great concentration of reserves here the few financiers who control these banks in New York have been able to precipitate panics and produce depression and financial disturbance whenever their selfish interest dictated. The panic of 1907 has taught this Nation a lesson which it will never forget. It proved beyond dispute that the banks and financiers of New York felt no public responsibility for the bank reserves under their control. The panic of 1907 was precipitated by wild stock speculations in the city of New York, engineered by the financiers there who control the great banks. This is clearly shown by an article written by Prof. Sprague for the National Monetary Commission and printed with its publications. Everything was adroitly and spectacularly arranged for a great rise and boom in stocks in order to unload and sell them to the public. Previous to this panic the dividend upon the Union Pacific stock was increased from 6 to 10 per cent. The Southern Pacific stock was placed upon a 5 per cent dividend basis. Dividend upon United States Steel common stock was resumed. The national bank note circulation was increased more than $100,000,000, and $54,000,000 worth of gold was imported from Europe. The Government of the United States was induced to deposit in the banks $23,000,000 of Treasury money. All of this occurred within the year preceding the panic, and everything was done to make the skies look bright and everything appear propitious and prosperous. Not a cloud appeared to portend the coming disastrous storm. Money was readily obtained from the banks on stocks as collateral security. The prices of stocks advanced rapidly, and the public, excited and wild, made immense purchases. Thus the first act in the well-planned drama was most successful. The intended tragedy soon followed.

In the autumn of 1907, when the banks outside of New York desired to withdraw the reserves and money they had deposited in these banks to be used for the purpose of moving the crops of cotton, wheat, corn, and oats, they were unable to obtain their money. The report of the Comptroller of the Currency on the 38 New York banks of August 22, 1907, just preceding the panic, shows that from the banks of New York there was due to national banks $250,300,000; was due from national banks $45,500,000; was due to other banks $206,100,000, and from other banks $9,700,000, making an aggregate due to other banks a balance of about $410,000,000. On October 31, 1907 the banks of New York telegraphed their correspondents that they would no longer honor their drafts for money and actually suspended payments. This suspension continued until the 1st of January. These banks in New York suspended payment with $224,000,000 in their vaults, as shown by their statement on November 2. On November 23, nearly three weeks afterwards, their statement shows that this reserve had only been reduced $9,000,000. What a contrast does this action of the New York banks present to the condition of the Banks of England at that time, which also practically held the reserves of all the banks of England. The reserve of the Bank of England which was only $120,000,000—in two weeks of this crisis was reduced to $85,000,000, and yet the Bank of England did not suspend payments. The lowest reserve that the banks of New York had during the entire suspension was $215,000,000. Thus the lowest reserve of the banks of New York was more than double that of the Bank of England, and yet they suspended payment and refused to make payments to banks outside of the city of New York. What is still more remarkable, in regard to these banks of the city of New York, was that while they refused to make payments to the interior banks they actually increased their loans during that time. In the three weeks preceding November 9 the New York banks increased their loans to the extent of $110,000,000. They could not pay their depositors, but they could accommodate their favored customers. The report made to the Comptroller of the Currency on December 3, 1907, by the banks shows that between August 22, 1907, and December 3, 1907, the loans of the entire country were contracted $85,000,000, while in New York they were increased $63,000000 of which $54,000,000 was on call-collateral loans and $4,000,000 on time-collateral loans, thus showing that while these banks would not pay the interior banks the money due them on deposits they were making loans to their customers for stock speculation.

The banks of New York have claimed credit that during the panic from time to time they would ship currency out to interior banks. This is true, but the currency they shipped to interior banks was less than the Government and other deposits made to the banks of New York. During this panic the Government deposited in the banks of New York $36,700,000, most of it coming from outside sources, more than $30,000,000 of it in the six leading banks, which mostly make loans for stock speculations. The New York banks assert that they improved the situation by importing $96,000,000 in gold, for which they claim much praise. They had nothing to do with the importation of this gold except as agents through whom the importation was made. The gold was imported in exchange for the commodities of the West and South which were exported to Europe, the payment for which passed through New York. The $96,000,000 of gold did not belong to New York; the bills of exchange simply passed through New York, as is usually done. This $96,000,000 belonged to the West and South. During the panic New York sent to the interior $106,000,000. It received in gold which belonged to the West and South $96,000,000 and from Government deposits $36,000,000, aggregating $132,000,000 that it received during the panic which did not belong to it, and only sent out $106,000,000, thus really gaining during the panic $26,000,000. The suspension of payments in New York practically compelled the rest of the country to suspend. The banks of only 53 cities in the United States were able to continue payments. Two of these cities were located in Virginia—Richmond and Norfolk. No one can estimate the disaster that was brought to this country by the action of the banks in New York during this emergency.

Business was suspended, commerce paralyzed, factories made idle, the stocks and securities unloaded on the public reduced one-half in value, and fortunes swept away. The disastrous effect of this panic is perceptibly felt to-day. All this disaster was produced because the banks of New York holding the deposits of and a large part of the reserves of interior banks stubbornly refused to surrender them. These funds were used by these banks and their customers to repurchase the stocks and securities, which they had previously sold at high prices, at the greatly reduced prices. This panic has convinced the country of the necessity of making some changes in our banking system. It has conclusively shown the necessity of not congesting and concentrating our reserves in banks with no public responsibility and controlled for individual purposes. In addition, this great concentration has had a tendency to create in this country, to a large extent, a "money trust," in which a few large financiers and their associates are enabled practically to dominate the money supply and the bank credits of this country. This state of affairs was disclosed in a remarkable degree by the Pujo investigation committee of last year. The report of this committee shows that a small group of financiers, usually acting in accord, control bank and trust companies, insurance companies, express companies, railroads, industrial and public-utility companies aggregating resources of more than $23,000,000,000. This group of financiers are enabled, as their interests or caprices may dictate, to produce good times or bad times. They can frequently contract credit and produce money stringency whenever their interest or caprices may dictate. They largely control the construction of new lines of railways. Large industrial and manufacturing enterprises feel their dependency upon them.

Until the Interstate Commerce Commission was created which regulates the charges made by railroads for transportation, they completely dominated the transportation of the country, and thus made and unmade communities, cities, sections, and almost States. Heretofore their power has been so great that frequently Federal administrations were elected or overthrown as they might desire. Language can hardly overestimate the vast control exercised by these groups of financiers upon the industrial and financial life of this Nation. Their domination is so tyrannical and complete that even men of large wealth, influence, and courage are afraid to antagonize them, and become subservient and submissive. The pathways of their power are marked by wrecked fortunes and ruined enterprises. Men of independent spirit, of great business genius and activity, are their most prized victims. These are conditions which exist and menace the industrial freedom and the future welfare of this people. Many of these evils will have to be corrected by legislation other than what is contained in this banking and currency bill. The Interstate Commerce Commission has been created to regulate the railroads, to see that all communities, sections, and individuals are treated with justice and fairness. Legislation is necessary upon the trust question to eliminate industrial monopoly and bring back again competition and free and fair opportunity. This bill reforming our currency and banking system proposes, as far as possible, to create a system of banking, and to provide for the issuance of currency which shall save the Nation from the domination of small groups of financiers and give to each individual, every business, every lawful corporation an opportunity to obtain all proper and legitimate needs for bank credit and currency. This is accomplished in the bill by providing that 6 per cent of the capital and surplus of all national banks shall be assessed to form a fund which shall be used for the creation of Federal reserve banks, the banks thus created to be not less than 8 and not more than 12, the country to be divided into as many sections, and 1 of the Federal reserve banks to be located in each. All banks that shall continue as national banks must become members of the Federal reserve bank of the section in which they are located.

The bill contains liberal provisions for State banks and trust companies, without losing their present identity and useful functions, becoming members of these Federal reserve banks. The member banks are required finally to deposit all the reserves required by law within their own vaults or in these Federal reserve banks. Each of these reserve banks is controlled by a board of directors consisting of nine members, six to be elected by the banks and three to be elected by a Federal reserve board, which has general supervision over these Federal reserve banks, the members of the Federal reserve board consisting of seven members, six appointed by the President and confirmed by the Senate, and the other being the Secretary of the Treasury. Three of the six members selected by the banks must be selected to represent the general public interests of the reserve district by the stockholding banks. The Federal reserve board, constituted as above, which shall have general supervision of all these reserve banks, is given authority to remove these three directors if they find that they do not fairly represent the general public interests. Thus without taking away the control of these banks from the member banks, who furnish the capital and money, assurance is given that these banks will be run for the general public interest, and also the advantage and profit of the member banks. These banks will have, as previously stated, a capital of about $105,000,000 and deposits of $531,000,000, provided all the national banks enter the system, which I am satisfied they will do. This capital and deposits will be increased to the extent that the State banks and trust companies enter the system. There can be no question that many of these will enter the system and thus greatly add to the capital and deposits of these reserve banks. Thus there will be created banking resources of more than $600,000,000, to be used for the general public good in developing the commercial, manufacturing, and agricultural interests of this country.

There are many who oppose this system of regional banks and prefer a great central bank with branches such as exists in other countries. After careful thought and investigation, I am satisfied that this system of regional banks is far preferable to a great central bank. I would prefer not less than 12 banks, and these to be increased as investigation and experience may prove beneficial. The advantages of the regional system over the one central bank are many. It prevents the danger of monopoly and concentration of money and credits in the hands of a few people. I would view with great apprehension a law which would compel the 25,000 banks of this country to contribute capital and deposits to one bank, which would become supreme in finance in this Nation. Those who should control this one central bank would control the industrial, commercial, and agricultural life of this nation. It is too vast a power to be put in the hands of a few men. The Democratic Party has clearly and positively declared against a central bank. Such a bank when once created would be dominant alike in the financial and political history of this country. If this bank were entirely under governmental control it would offer but a large prize for the small group of financiers of this country to grasp and control government and through it this bank. This system of regional banks requires the capital and resources of a regional bank to be held in and used for the accommodation of those interests existing in that section or region. It does not take the resources and capital of one section and transfer it to another. These resources are continued in the section from which they are furnished. In case of emergency or business distress these regional banks are expected to use their resources primarily for the sections in which they exist. Besides, it has been wisely thought that there is such a diversity in the various industrial, agricultural, and commercial conditions of our Nation that a system of regional banks with one for each section or region could be more successfully and profitably conducted for the benefit of that section than one great central bank. The success of our various State governments has clearly proven that this diversity renders necessary separate governments to take care of peculiar local conditions.

Our wonderful banking development under our system of individual banks, each suited to do the business of its locality, has also shown the wisdom of permitting this diversity. The more one examines into the matter the more one must be convinced that the system of regional banks is far preferable to one central bank. Of course those who are benefited by monopoly, whether in industry or in banking credits, will naturally prefer the central bank. But monopoly is one of the evils against which we are contending and which the regional banks will be instrumental in destroying. There are some who contend that a central bank offers superior advantages for relief in times of emergency. There is some truth in this. The reserves of a central bank being more concentrated and mobilized can be more readily and promptly used. But this advantage is far offset by the other evils and disadvantages which would inevitably come from a central bank, however created and however controlled. This bill has a wise provision which obtains all the advantages that can accrue from a central bank without its evils and disadvantages. A Federal reserve board is created, as previously stated, which will have general supervision of these regional banks, seeing that they are honestly administered and fulfill the purposes of their creation. This Federal reserve board is also empowered to require one Federal reserve bank to rediscount the discounted paper of another Federal reserve bank. This provision practically gives all the advantages that could accrue from a central bank. It permits the entire reserves and resources of all the regional banks to be used where most needed in time of financial distress or emergency. A central bank could do no more than this. What is most remarkable is that those who most favor a central bank are most opposed to this provision which, when needed, practically unifies the resources and reserves of all the banks. Thus by this method the only advantage which comes from a central bank is obtained without its accruing evils.

The benefits which will accrue from these regional, or, as named in the bill, Federal reserve banks are great and many. The reserves of the Nation, which are needed in times of financial distress and stringency, will be held by those who have a public responsibility for their just and proper use, and not as now, by those who have no such responsibility and no purpose of public benefit in their use. The member banks, being satisfied that their reserves and deposits are held where they will always be forthcoming when needed and are held to take care of these banks and the public in times of emergencies, will be relieved of daily apprehension of trouble and distress. These Federal reserve banks will become to all the banks of this country like the Bank of England is to the English banks, the Bank of France is to the French banks, and the Reichsbank of Germany is to the German banks—places of refuge and hope in time of financial trouble. The banks of this country removed from this apprehension can accommodate their customers and the legitimate demands of business without continual trepidation. These reserve banks, practically under Government control and supervision, having a broad vision of financial matters, can be used to prevent dangerous inflation or ruinous depression. They will have a steadying influence on the finances of the country and produce that stability which is the most propitious for the growth and development of the Nation. This bill provides that the rediscounts that these reserve banks shall make for their member banks shall be for paper arising out of actual commercial transactions and for agricultural, industrial, and commercial purposes. This prohibits the resources of these reserve banks being used for the purposes of stock speculation. It provides that $636,000,000 shall be set aside and dedicated for the development of our commerce, our agriculture, and our manufactures. It gives preference to legitimate business over stock speculations. It makes impossible another panic in this country, with its distress and disaster, precipitated by Wall Street speculation with the reserves and deposits of interior banks.

When this bill becomes law the farmers of this country can sow and plant with the confidence that money will be available for the profitable marketing of their crops. The manufacturer can enlarge his operations with the assurance that from these reserve banks funds will be forthcoming to successfully finance his undertakings. The merchants can liberally buy and sell, knowing that currency and bank credits can be obtained for all prudent and legitimate purposes. Genuine business and enterprise will be stimulated and only stock speculation lessened. If this bill accomplish no other purpose than setting aside and devoting this vast sum of money to legitimate business interests, it would produce inestimable benefits and is deserving of support. This bill, by the creation of these reserve banks, will create in this country, which has long been needed, a discount market where commercial paper can be readily discounted. This will enable all the banks of this country to extend to their customers all prudent and legitimate accommodation. This will be to the alike benefit of the banks and their patrons. It removes the perils of a money trust and brings relief to all American industries.

Mr. President, the next great purpose sought to be accomplished by this bill is the creation of an elastic currency. It is universally admitted that there is a great necessity in this country for such a currency. Our present currency is rigid. It does not ebb and flow according to the needs and demands of commerce and business. At times it becomes redundant and encourages reckless speculation with the consequent reaction and depression. At other times our currency becomes so stringent that the rates of interest become exorbitant and business of all kinds is practically paralyzed. We need a currency that can increase and decrease according to the legitimate demands of business and commerce. All nations who have a modern financial system have provided for such a currency. Every year during the three autumn months there is a great demand for currency in order to move our great agricultural crops. During these three months we market and move our great cotton crop, which practically clothes the world, our great oats, corn, and wheat crops, which fill the granaries of the world, and our great crops of tobacco, which are distributed in all the markets of the world.

We must have the currency to pay cash for these during these few months of marketing and moving. The cash thus expended in the purchase of these vast crops in this short time can only be returned when these vast crops are sold and distributed in the world's markets. It takes nearly a year for this to be completely accomplished. It is estimated that it takes more than $200,000,000 each autumn to market and move these crops. Heretofore we have been enabled to accomplish this by drawing drafts and getting accommodations in London, Berlin, and Paris. When we can get these accommodations upon what is known as financial bills our crops are marketed and moved without much financial disturbance. But if the financial conditions of Europe are such as to prevent us from getting these loan accommodations, then during these months we have acute financial stringency which brings depression and distress. For years everyone has recognized the necessity of making provision for this yearly recurring currency demand. Yet from year to year relief has been delayed and denied, resulting in immense losses to our merchants and farmers which it is impossible to estimate. This bill provides for the creation of such a currency which will give prompt and efficient relief. It provides that the Federal reserve board may, in its discretion, issue to the Federal reserve banks on application currency in amount equal to collateral presented and indorsed by this Federal reserve bank and member banks deposited with it as security for such currency issues, the collateral thus deposited being notes, drafts, or bills of exchange arising out of actual commercial transactions or being issued or drawn for agricultural, commercial, or industrial purposes, or the proceeds of which have been used or are to be used for such purposes, having a maturity not exceeding 90 days. The currency is issued by the United States Government, is its obligation, and is redeemed by the United States Government or any Federal reserve bank to which it is presented for redemption.

The Federal reserve bank is required to keep a reserve of 35 per cent either in gold or lawful money for the redemption of these notes. Such portion of this redemption fund as is necessary may be required to be deposited in the Treasury of the United States in order to facilitate the redemption of this currency. This currency is perfectly safe. First there is deposited as collateral security for its issuance notes and bonds indorsed by a member bank with the additional indorsement of the Federal reserve bank. The Federal reserve board may require at any time it thinks necessary the deposit of additional collateral security. There is kept a reserve fund of 35 per cent to provide for prompt redemption and in addition this currency is a first lien upon all the assets of the Federal reserve bank. I can not conceive how greater security could be provided. . . .

The President, during the months he has exercised his great office, has displayed in a preeminent degree capacity and courage, the two great elements of statesmanship. In this conflict he has without hesitation and without fear stood by the masses of the people, and determined, as far as he was able, to give the country a banking and currency system promotive of all the interests of all the people and with a view to save the country from the paralyzing influence of monopoly of money and bank credits. He has refused to either compromise or capitulate to a few strong and powerful financiers or banking interests who slowly surrender the privilege hitherto enjoyed of despoiling the many for their enrichment. In this conflict he has been sustained by the Democratic Members of the House and Senate. The day of his and our triumph is fast approaching. The time for the passage of this bill may be delayed, but not defeated. Before many weeks have passed this country will have witnessed the passage of this measure with all its great reforms and benefits. The country will receive with acclaim a Democratic President and a Democratic House of Representatives and a Democratic Senate who have the courage and the constancy to fulfill their promises and to enact this measure, and thus enable the agricultural, commercial, manufacturing, and legitimate banking interests of this country to be freed from selfish and sinister domination, and thus permit this mighty Republic to advance rapidly and continuously along the pathways of progress, prosperity, and equal opportunity.

Document II-34: ANTI-TRUST IN CONGRESS

At least since the controversy over the rechartering of the Bank of the United States, the attack on monopoly had been a consistent aspect of politico-economic reform. In this tradition monopoly was equated with an alliance between wealth and political power that meant unfair privilege and inequitable distribution of wealth. Even in the very earliest days of the Republic the Antifederalists had attempted to arouse public support by pointing to the dangers of perpetuating in power a group of wealthy men with strong allegiance to English, Episcopalian ways. As farm and labor interests emerged in the nineteenth century, they consistently centered their attacks on industrial and commercial monopolies, especially railroads and utilities.

The Sherman Anti-Trust Act of 1890 represented a symbolic victory for those who advocated a broadening of federal responsibilities in the regulation of large business combinations. The consequences of this act were disappointing to those who saw in it a means of attacking the concentration of power and of broadening the distribution of wealth. The law had loopholes which made successful prosecution of business trusts difficult at best, and the act was in fact used with considerable effect against organized labor.

The Clayton Act was offered, as a part of Woodrow Wilson's New Nationalism, in order to close some of the loopholes of the Sherman Act, to exempt organized labor explicitly from anti-trust prosecution, and to express Wilson's faith that the future of America lay with a healthy competition among smaller businesses. During the House debate on this measure, M. Clyde Kelly, a Republican Congressman and newspaper publisher from Western Pennsylvania, took the floor on May 22, 1914, to argue more for the spirit of monopoly regulation than for the bill itself. Surprisingly, considering that he was a Republican from the land of the steel trust, Kelly not only pleaded for open competition but inveighed against the "invisible government" which replaced popular sovereignty with the "trickery" and "debauchery" of improper influence.

With the Progressives and Wilsonians, he feared that a bill already weakened by too many compromises would be further vitiated by amendment until it came to reflect the negative features of the Sherman Act. His fears were well grounded. The Clayton Act fell far short of the explicit provisions that would have been needed to prevent the stock manipulations of the 1920s and the business abuses that have continued throughout the century. Yet Kelly's remarks serve to summarize the anti-monopoly spirit as it continued into the Progressive Era. His rhetoric recalls with clarity the appeal of the Populists, the vilification of Morgan and Hanna, and the conviction that the machinery of political democracy must somehow be used to eradicate the principal abuses of economic democracy. For the reformers in this tradition there was no "golden mean," as Kelly concluded, "between the people's rights and monopoly."

SOURCE: *The Congressional Record*, vol. LI, pp. 9085-87.

SPEECH OF M. CLYDE KELLY

Mr. Chairman, the gentleman from Illionois [Mr. MADDEN] has just stated that the demand for antitrust legislation at this time comes from disgruntled agitators. He completely mistakes the temper and the will of the American people. The trusts and monopolies of this country are themselves responsible for the demand for remedial action, and their disregard of justice and every fundamental principle of this Republic has made the solution indispensable. Enterprises with great capital have deliberately sought not only industrial domination but political supremacy as well. They have entered the realm of government with insolent bearing and have attempted to name officials from the highest to the lowest.

Organized money, rioting ruthlessly in savage impulses, has forced this question upon us. We must decide whether wealth is to rule or manhood, whether this Nation is to be one of equal rights to all or special privileges to a few, whether honor and ability is to weigh in the selection of officials or cringing submission to corporate capital.

The conscience of the American people demands that action be taken, and any delay now will be a betrayal of their will. Great combinations of capital for many years have flaunted their power in the face of the citizenship, they have forced their corrupt way into politics and government, they have dictated the making of laws or scorned the laws they did not like, they have prevented the free and just administration of law. In doing this they have become a menace to free institutions, and must be dealt with in patriotic spirit, without fear or favor.

It is a common practice for standpatters to decry every forward step by denunciation of agitators. It would be well to pay some little attention to the fawning followers of crooked big business in the press, on the platform and in public office. They sell themselves for price and place, and it would be well if they were dissected and their treason examined, while men are cataloguing the enemies of the Nation.

Mr. Chairman, I am in complete accord with the purpose and aim of this legislation, but I fear that its terms are such that if enacted into law it will only add more jests to the long list which has marked the antitrust legislation of America in the past. Trusts have been ordered dissolved in the past, and the only change effected was one in the methods of bookkeeping. It is time for straightforward action and an honest effort to protect the people from the powers that prey upon them.

GROWTH OF TRUST DOMINATION.

For 35 years combinations of capital have sought to form monopolies and profit from the community through the private taxing power which goes with the ability to control prices. In 1879 the Standard Alliance, composed of oil refiners, led the way, through a pooling system, and in a short time controlled 95 per cent of the refining business of the country. The Western Exporters' Association, made up of whisky distillers, followed, and it soon was in absolute control of the business. Others followed in the same path, and this pooling system flourished for a time.

But it did not give the complete control desired. It did not concern itself with the management of individual plants, but simply apportioned out the pro rata share of production. Each member of the pool could withdraw without notice, and thus the agreement had no stability. In their anxiety for quick and large profits the producers broke the market by their very greediness. The Whisky Trust and the Wire-Nail Trust Association went so far as to raise prices 200 per cent in the midst of falling prices. Jealousy caused trouble also, and the Lackawanna Iron & Steel Co. once broke the steel-rail pool because it was allowed only 17 per cent of the production.

Such defects in the control of prices stirred the producers to find other schemes to secure their aim, that of throttling the public and forcing the highest possible prices for products.

The next plan was the trust agreement, through which trustees were assigned the majority stock in constituent refineries. They controlled the boards of directors and collected all dividends on stock and distributed them to the holders of trust certificates. It was a better plan than the pool, for the pool was an outlaw in the courts, while in the trust agreement the trustees had the law on their side and could enforce their contracts.

The injustices which followed such control of prices, however, stirred lawmaking bodies to action. In 1890 many State legislatures passed antitrust laws, and in the same year the Sherman antitrust law was enacted for the purpose of dealing with combinations doing an interstate business.

So, another plan was necessary, and legal sharps were set to work to discover some juggling trick which would enable great combinations to wring millions for helpless consumers. While they sought for this ideal plan, the producers, having tasted the sweets of despotic control, carried on their nefarious plans through a system known as "community of interest." By the knowledge gained through close association, officials of different companies were able to act together and to prevent competition even without any formal agreement.

This plan was still weak, for disagreements and misunderstandings meant a return to competition at any time, and that was what the different companies were striving to prevent.

Then came the discovery of the ideal scheme—the "holding corporation." It provided for a corporation to own the stock of competing companies, and it was proved in a short time to be a method in which to legally violate both law and justice. It excelled other plans, because it was not necessary to purchase the companies outright. Buying up a majority of the stock of the companies served every purpose. It escaped the troubles of the trust agreement, which was declared illegal because it was a conspiracy of several individuals, and this plan meant having one person, in the form of a corporation, control all the individual companies.

The Sugar Trust was the first to put this plan into operation, but others followed thick and fast. In 1897 there were 63 "holding companies" in existence, and in 1898-99 there were formed 183 such companies with a capitalization of $4,000,000,000, representing one-twentieth of the entire wealth of the country and twice the amount of money in circulation.

From that time trusts have flourished until to-day a trust controls almost every commodity of daily life. This has been done in spite of all efforts to prevent restraint of trade. Suits have been entered against these vast combinations, but in most instances they have failed, and the victory won in the others was but a shadow victory. The decisions of the Supreme Court have involved legal somersaults and twistings and turnings, but the old issue still remains. It is to-day a muddle of 24 years' stirring, and the time for clearing is certainly here.

In clearing that muddle straightforward measures are necessary. It is not necessary to specifically describe every unfair trade practice, but it is necessary that some tribunal have the power to deal with every unfair trade practice which leads to monopoly. This measure mentions a few—and only a few—of these practices; and, even if they could be thus rooted out, others are sure to take their place, to remedy which other legislation will be needed.

Such an interstate trade commission as that proposed in the Progressive bill before this body would prevent confusion, delay, and injustice. It would prevent the evils mentioned in this measure, price discriminations, "tying" contracts, and so forth, and would be empowered to deal with every evasion as it might arise. Time will prove that only through a tribunal with proper powers can these unfair practices be prevented.

EXEMPTION OF LABOR UNIONS.

Section 7 of this measure, with the change necessary to clearly prevent application of antitrust laws to fraternal, labor and other voluntary organizations, is a great step in advance. The section reads:

> That nothing contained in the antitrust laws shall be construed to forbid the existence and operation of fraternal, labor, consumers, agricultural, or horticultural organizations, orders, or associations instituted for the purpose of mutual help and not having capital stock or conducted for profit, or to forbid or restrain individual members of such organizations, orders, or associations from carrying out the legitimate objects thereof.

This section, properly amended, will help to write the gospel of humanity into law. It is a recognition of a fundamental difference between human labor and the products of labor. Legislation dealing with trusts which control the products of labor can not be justly applied to the association of workers for their own betterment and improvement. One deals with materials, the other with men; one with mines, the other with miners; one with machines, the other with machinists; one with farms, the other with farmers; one with buildings, the other with builders; one with factories, the other with factory workers; one with tools, the other with toilers; one with property, the other with persons. You can not classify them together for they are essentially different.

The free workers of America own themselves and their labor power. They may sell their labor power to others or they may withhold it. They may act together for the protection of their rights and interests, and it is a sham and a fraud to say that they may organize without the power to use means necessary to make organization a vital force in demanding and securing justice.

I stand for the right of labor to organize for its own advancement and to work for that purpose without being outlawed for it. This measure is right in purpose, and I hope it will be amended so that there shall be no shadow of doubt as to the right of the workers of this country to organize and exert themselves in legitimate activities without the danger of being prosecuted under antitrust laws. It is not a case of class legislation nor a demand for special privileges. It is simply a demand of humanity for freedom from restrictions and shackles that deny common justice.

The Sherman antitrust law has been made a potent force against organized labor, even while it proved unable to restrain marauding combinations of capital. In 1892 it was brought into action when some union men in New Orleans went on strike. Teamsters and workmen in many lines were concerned. Judge Billings, of the United States district court, declared that the strike was in restraint of interstate commerce and granted an injunction. The United States court of appeals agreed in his decision.

Two years later the point was again reached in the Pullman strike in Chicago. Injunctions against the strikers were granted by the courts under the Sherman Act and a number of the strikers were jailed for several months for disobeying the injunction.

Several years later another labor phase came into evidence. In Danbury, Conn., a small firm of hat manufacturers operated an open shop and was boycotted by labor unions. The court decided that the unions were acting as a combination in restraint of trade under the meaning of the Sherman antitrust law.

Many other instances might be cited to show that the antitrust laws have been used as a club over voluntary organizations, which were never intended to come within their scope. When the Sherman antitrust law was passed in the Senate it was clearly and unequivocally stated that its provisions would not cover such organizations. But history shows that the victories won under it have been the suits against labor organizations, while great trusts and monopolies have grown and flourished. It is to remedy such a flagrant injustice that this provision is included in this measure; and after it is amended to clearly accomplish its purpose of exemption, it should have the support of every Member of this House.

INJUNCTIONS AND JURY TRIAL.

The provisions in this measure for the regulation of injunctions and the procedure in contempt cases, while somewhat beyond the scope of antitrust legislation, are reforms long demanded by the American people. The expression "government by injunction" has become current because in almost every labor controversy in recent years the courts have been used by powerful corporations in the carrying out of their plans to subjugate employees and to prevent the exercise of lawful rights. The abuse of the right of injunction in the past 10 years has been sufficient to arouse the public, and this legislation is demanded by every right-thinking American citizen to-day.

Similar to that demand is the determination that the constitutional provision that "no person shall be deprived of life, liberty, or property without due process of law and the judgment of his peers" shall be maintained. Freemen since the days of King John and Runnymede have demanded jury trial. It is a fundamental American doctrine. If jurors are competent to judge the law and the fact in criminal cases, why are they not competent in matters of injunction and contempt? The judge is not more competent to judge of a litigant's rights when his life is not at stake than when it is, and the individual or corporation that is afraid to submit his case to a jury for trial has no right to dictate laws for the administration of justice.

THE INVISIBLE GOVERNMENT.

Mr. Chairman, the invisible government which has controlled the visible Government in this Nation for many years has been unscrupulous big business. We have been tracing some of its insidious, slimy ways in our lobby investigations of recent date. We have seen its arts of trickery and debauchery. It manipulations and its conspiracies. The time for forbearance is over and the time to strike has come. If this Nation is to be a government of the people by crooked big business, the doom of our free institutions is assured. I believe that firm and decisive action now will be for the best interest not only of the Nation at large but of business itself. Brazen defiance of the spirit of laws made to protect the public and cunning jugglery to evade them is in the final analysis the worst thing possible for business. Business protects itself against fires by vast expenditures for fire insurance, but there are other dangers worse than fires. One is the danger that the masses of the people will forget their patient endurance of injustice and longsuffering submission to wrong on the part of exploiting combinations and start a conflagration against which fire insurance will offer no protection.

Good business depends on the permanence of law and order. This Nation can not stand much more of fraud and plunder, savage inpulses left unchecked, a controlled press, and misrepresentation of the truth and continue to have good business.

The real defenders of property to-day are not those who attempt to forestall every attempt at reform by denunciation and who put the blame for unrest not on those who pummel the people but on those who call attention to the black and blue spots. The real defenders of property are not the standpatters, who cry out against any change and shout, "let well enough alone," when the very worst thing that could happen would be to have things remain exactly as they are, no better and no worse.

No; the real defenders of property are the upholders of the rights of humanity, the Progressives, who believe that "new occasions teach new duties. Time makes ancient good uncouth. They must upward still and onward who would keep abreast of truth."

To-day, as always, there are men like Demetrius of Ephesus, who, when he saw that the preaching of Paul the apostle was harming his business of making silver idols, gathered his fellows together and raised a great hue and cry, shouting "Great is Diana of the Ephesians." Their fervid devotion to Diana was as false as that of monopolists and their defenders to-day who shout "Great is property," when the public conscience demands that justice be done.

The greatest security to property comes from the security of human rights, and the sooner business realizes that fact the better it will be for all concerned.

THE PERIL OF COMPROMISE.

Mr. Chairman, the American people have a right to expect a better measure than this weak, halting, halfway attempt at remedy of intolerable conditions. It does not go to the root of the evils which have brought concentration of wealth and diffusion of poverty. I sincerely hope that it may be amended so that its expressed purposes may be accomplished, for there is a deadly peril in compromise with the forces that prey. There is no golden mean between right and wrong, between courage and cowardice, between honor and dishonor, between patriotism and treason, between the people's rights and monopoly. I believe in industrial and commercial peace, but not the peace that is purchased at the expense of justice and human liberty. There can be no peace in America except with the destruction of the sordid social wrongs and the putrid political methods which have attended the growth of the great combinations and monopolies of this country. This is an irrepressible conflict and there is no middle ground. The Nation looks to its Congress to strike a fair and square blow at hoary wrongs, and thus better the living conditions of the people of America. Lawmakers can concern themselves with nothing greater than that, and it is the duty as well as privilege of every representative of the people to make that his chief end and aim in his decision upon every measure before this Congress. [Applause.]

Document II-35: INHERITANCE TAX IN THE SENATE

One function of the accompanying commission report is a continuation of the effort to identify the "Progressive spirit" (see II-31, 32). The concept of a governmental commission was itself typically Progressive. Before action was proposed, the facts should be gathered carefully and impartially. In introducing the report, Frank P. Walsh, chairman of the commission, offered it "as a model of efficiency and scientific treatment" in which "none but undisputed facts" had been submitted (p. 9 of the source cited below). The work had been done, he continued, "in a spirit of social justice"; and he underlined the competence and impartiality of the group by listing them according to their special interests and viewpoints.

Basil M. Manly, the commission's research director who authored its principal part, opened by asserting that to the citizen, industrial organization was at least as important as political organization. Ending the introduction was a quotation from Thomas Carlyle on behalf of the forgotten masses, a note of emotional concern for the economically underprivileged that was sustained through the report. Obviously, these Progressives were not so objectively scientific as they imagined; but they did spare few pains in the thoroughness of their labors, crossing bureaucratic lines whenever logic so indicated. They displayed a palpable commitment to the idea that political and economic affairs were insepar-

able and that the government was responsible for improving the distribution of wealth.

It was not surprising that a commission so composed would place so
much collective stress on the idea of an inheritance tax. Indeed, with
equal opportunity as his constantly expressed goal, the American democrat came later than might have been expected to this device for insuring
citizens a more nearly equal start in the economic race. One recalls the
early restrictions of the English system of primogeniture and entail, and
one may also note that during the Progressive Era the number of states
having inheritance taxes rose from twenty-six to forty-two. Yet except
for wartime emergencies, the federal government had never made use of
inheritance taxes.

Manly recommended a tax that would limit any estate to one million
dollars. In spite of much dismay at extremes of wealth and poverty
resulting in an outpouring of books and magazine articles on the subject,
the public was apparently not ready for this much economic democracy.
John R. Commons, a member of Walsh's commission, submitted a more
modest recommendation which became the basis for the 1916 Revenue
Act, America's first permanent federal inheritance tax. Under this act,
taxes began at 1 percent of estates over $50,000 net, and increased to
only 10 percent of estates over $5 million. As with many Progressive
precedents, it remained for the New Deal to make more drastic use of it
(e.g., by 1935 the maximum rate had increased from 10 percent to 70
percent). Professor Commons provided a more acceptable proposal; but
Basil Manly provided the rhetorical as well as some of the factual basis
for bringing into play this long-neglected weapon in the arsenal of those
who believe in using federal powers to redistribute wealth.

(For a discussion of this subject, and for useful citations and tables, see
Sidney Ratner, *American Taxation.* New York, Norton, 1942, pp.
354-58; Appendix.)

SOURCE: "Final Report and Testimony Submitted to Congress by the Commission on
Industrial Relations," (1st of 10 vols.), *Senate Documents.* Washington, D.C.,
Government Printing Office, 1916, vol. XIX, pp. 29-35, abridged.

CAUSES OF INDUSTRIAL UNREST

It is presumed that Congress had in mind, in directing the commission
to inquire into the "causes of dissatisfaction in the industrial situation,"

something far different from that "dissatisfaction with the present which is the hope of the future," that desire for better things which drives men forever forward. Such dissatisfaction is the mainspring of all progress and is to be desired in every nation in all walks of life.

It is believed that Congress intended the inquiry to be directed to that unrest and dissatisfaction which grows out of the existence of intolerable industrial conditions and which, if unrelieved, will in the natural course of events rise into active revolt or, if forcibly suppressed, sink into sullen hatred.

Of the existence of such unrest ample evidence has been found. It is the basis of the establishment and growth of the I. W. W., whose card-carrying members number only a few thousands, but which as "a spirit and a vocabulary" permeates to a large extent enormous masses of workers, particularly among the unskilled and migratory laborers. But entirely apart from those who accept its philosophy and creed, there are numberless thousands of workers, skilled and unskilled, organized and unorganized, who feel bitterly that they and their fellows are being denied justice, economically, politically, and legally. Just how wide-spread this feeling is or whether there is imminent danger of a quickening into active, nation-wide revolt, none can say. But no one who reads the papers from which the workers get their ideas and inspiration; no one who has studied with care the history of such strikes as those at Lawrence and Paterson, in West Virginia and Colorado, and has understood the temper of the strikers; no one who has associated with large numbers of workers in any part of the country, can fail to be impressed by the gravity of the situation.

This sense of tension and impending danger has been expressed by numerous witnesses before the commission, but by none more forcibly than by Mr. Daniel Guggenheim, a capitalist whose interests in mines and industrial plants extend to every part of the country.

    Chairman WALSH. What do you think has been accomplished by the philanthropic activities of the country in reducing suffering and want among the people?

    Mr. GUGGENHEIM. There has a great deal been done. If it were not for what has been done and what is being done, we would have a revolution in this country.

The sources from which this unrest springs are, when stated in full detail, almost numberless. But upon careful analysis of their real character they will be found to group themselves almost without exception under four main sources which include all the others. The four are:

1. Unjust distribution of wealth and income.
2. Unemployment and denial of an opportunity to earn a living.
3. Denial of justice in the creation, in the adjudication, and in the administration of law.
4. Denial of the right and opportunity to form effective organizations.

1. UNJUST DISTRIBUTION OF WEALTH AND INCOME.

The conviction that the wealth of the country and the income which is produced through the toil of the workers is distributed without regard to any standard of justice is as widespread as it is deep-seated. It is found among all classes of workers and takes every form from the dumb resentment of the day laborer, who, at the end of a week's back-breaking toil finds that he has less than enough to feed his family while others who have done nothing live in ease, to the elaborate philosophy of the "soap-box orator," who can quote statistics unendingly to demonstrate his contentions. At bottom, though, there is the one fundamental, controlling idea that income should be received for service and for service only, whereas, in fact, it bears no such relation, and he who serves least, or not at all, may receive most.

This idea has never been expressed more clearly than in the testimony of Mr. John H. Walker, president of the Illinois State Federation of Labor:

> A workingman is not supposed to ask anything more than a fair day's wage for a fair day's work; he is supposed to work until he is pretty fairly tuckered out, say eight hours, and when he does a fair day's work he is not supposed to ask for any more wages than enough to support his family; while with the business man the amount of labor furnishes no criterion for the amount they receive. People accept it as all right if they do not do any work at all, and are given credit for getting the greatest amount of money with the

least amount of work; and those things that are being accepted by
the other side as the things that govern in every-day life, and as
being right, have brought about this condition, this being in my
judgment absolutely unfair; that is, on the merits of the proposition in dealing with the workers.

The workers feel this, some unconsciously and some consciously, but all of them feel it, and it makes for unrest, in my
judgment, and there can be no peace while that condition obtains.

In the highest paid occupations among wage earners, such as railroad
engineers and conductors, glass blowers, certain steel-mill employees,
and a few of the building trades, the incomes will range from $1,500 to
$2,000 at best, ignoring a few exceptional men who are paid for personal
qualities. Such an income means, under present-day conditions, a fair
living for a family of moderate size, education of the children through
high school, a small insurance policy, a bit put by for a rainy day—and
nothing more. With unusual responsibilities or misfortunes, it is too
little, and the pinch of necessity is keenly felt. To attain such wages,
moreover, means that the worker must be far above the average, either in
skill, physical strength, or reliability. He must also have served an
apprenticeship equal in length to a professional course. Finally, and most
important, he or his predecessors in the trade must have waged a long,
aggressive fight for better wages, for there are other occupations whose
demand for skill, strength, and reliability are almost as great as those
mentioned, where the wages are much less.

These occupations, however, include but a handful compared to the
mass of the workers. What do the millions get for their toil, for their skill,
for the risk of life and limb? That is the question to be faced in an
industrial nation, for these millions are the backbone and sinew of the
State, in peace or in war.

First, with regard to the adult workmen, the fathers and potential
fathers, from whose earnings, according to the "American standard,"
the support of the family is supposed to be derived.

Between one-fourth and one-third of the male workers 18 years of age
and over, in factories and mines, earn less than $10 per week; from
two-thirds to three-fourths earn less than $15, and only about one-tenth
earn more than $20 a week. This does not take into consideration lost
working time for any cause.

Next are the women, the most portentously growing factor in the labor force, whose wages are important, not only for their own support or as the supplement of the meager earnings of their fathers and husbands, but because, through the force of competition in a rapidly extending field, they threaten the whole basis of the wage scale. From two-thirds to three-fourths of the women workers in factories, stores and laundries, and in industrial occupations generally, work at wages of less than $8 a week. Approximately one-fifth earn less than $4 and nearly one-half earn less than $6 a week.

Six dollars a week—what does it mean to many? Three theater tickets, gasoline for the week, or the price of a dinner for two; a pair of shoes, three pairs of gloves, or the cost of an evening at bridge. To the girl it means that every penny must be counted, every normal desire stifled, and each basic necessity of life barely satisfied by the sacrifice of some other necessity. If more food must be had than is given with 15-cent dinners, it must be bought with what should go for clothes; if there is need for a new waist to replace the old one at which the forewoman has glanced reproachfully or at which the girls have giggled, there can be no lunches for a week and dinners must cost 5 cents less each day. Always too the room must be paid for, and back of it lies the certainty that with slack seasons will come lay-offs and discharges. If the breaking point has come, and she must have some amusement, where can it come from? Surely not out of $6 a week.

Last of all are the children, for whose petty addition to the stream of production the Nation is paying a heavy toll in ignorance, deformity of body or mind, and premature old age. After all, does it matter much what they are paid? For all experience has shown that in the end the father's wages are reduced by about the amount that the children earn. This is the so-called "family wage," and examination of the wages in different industries corroborates the theory that in those industries, such as textiles, where women and children can be largely utilized, the wages of men are extremely low.

The competitive effect of the employment of women and children upon the wages of men, can scarcely be overestimated. Surely it is hard enough to be forced to put children to work, without having to see the wages of men held down by their employment.

This is the condition at one end of the social scale. What is at the other?

Massed in millions, at the other end of the social scale, are fortunes of a size never before dreamed of, whose very owners do not know the extent nor, without the aid of an intelligent clerk, even the sources of their incomes. Incapable of being spent in any legitimate manner, these fortunes are burdens, which can only be squandered, hoarded, put into so-called "benefactions" which, for the most part, constitute a menace to the State, or put back into the industrial machine to pile up ever-increasing mountains if gold.

In many cases, no doubt, these huge fortunes have come, in whole or in part, as the rich reward of exceptional service. None would deny or envy him who has performed such service the richest of rewards, although one may question the ideals of a Nation which rewards exceptional service only by burdensome fortunes. But such reward can be claimed as a right only by those who have performed service, not by those who through relationship or mere parasitism chance to be designated as heirs. Legal right, of course, they have by virtue of the law of inheritance, which, however, runs counter to the whole theory of American society, and which was adopted, with important variations, from the English law, without any conception of its ultimate results and apparently with the idea that it would prevent exactly the condition which has arisen. In effect the American law of inheritance is as efficient for the establishment and maintenance of families as is the English law, which has bulwarked the British aristocracy through the centuries. Every year, indeed, sees this tendency increase, as the creation of "estates in trust" secures the ends which might be more simply reached if there were no prohibition of "entail." According to the income-tax returns for 10 months of 1914, there are in the United States 1,598 fortunes yielding an income of $100,000 or more per year. Practically all of these fortunes are so invested and hedged about with restrictions upon expenditure that they are, to all intents and purposes, perpetuities.

An analysis of 50 of the largest American fortunes shows that nearly one-half have already passed to the control of heirs or to trustees (their vice regents) and that the remainder will pass to the control of heirs within 20 years, upon the deaths of the "founders." Already, indeed, these founders have almost without exception retired from active service, leaving the management ostensibly to their heirs but actually to executive officials upon salary.

We have, according to the income-tax returns, 44 families with incomes of $1,000,000 or more, whose members perform little or no useful service, but whose aggregate incomes, totaling at the very least $50,000,000 per year, are equivalent to the earnings of 100,000 wage earners at the average rate of $500.

The ownership of wealth in the United States has become concentrated to a degree which is difficult to grasp. The recently published researches of a statistician of conservative views [Prof. Willard I. King] have shown that as nearly as can be estimated the distribution of wealth in the United States is as follows:

The "rich," 2 per cent of the people, own 60 per cent of the wealth.

The "middle class," 33 per cent of the people, own 35 per cent of the wealth.

The "poor," 65 per cent of the people, own 5 per cent of the wealth.

This means in brief that a little less than 2,000,000 people, who would make up a city smaller than Chicago, own 20 per cent more of the Nation's wealth than all the other 90,000,000.

The figures also show that with a reasonably equitable division of wealth, the entire population should occupy the position of comfort and security which we characterize as middle class.

The actual concentration has, however, been carried very much further than these figures indicate. The largest private fortune in the United States, estimated at $1,000,000,000, is equivalent to the aggregate wealth of 2,500,000 of those who are classed as "poor," who are shown in the studies cited to own on the average about $400 each.

Between the two extremes of superfluity and poverty is the large middle class—farmers, manufacturers, merchants, professional men, skilled artisans, and salaried officials—whose incomes are more or less adequate for their legitimate needs and desires, and who are rewarded more or less exactly in proportion to service. They have problems to meet in adjusting expenses to income, but the pinch of want and hunger is not felt, nor is there the deadening, devitalizing effect of superfluous, unearned wealth.

From top to bottom of society, however, in all grades of incomes, are innumerable number of parasites of every conceivable type. They perform no useful service, but drain off from the income of the producers a sum whose total can not be estimated.

This whole situation has never been more accurately described than by Hon. David Lloyd-George in an address on "Social waste":

I have recently had to pay some attention to the affairs of the Sudan, in connection with some projects that have been mooted for irrigation and development in that wonderful country. I will tell you what the problem is—you may know it already. Here you have a great, broad, rich river upon which both the Sudan and Egypt depend for their fertility. There is enough water in it to fertilize every part of both countries; but if, for some reason or other, the water is wasted in the upper regions, the whole land suffers sterility and famine. There is a large region in the upper Sudan where the water has been absorbed by one tract of country, which, by this process, has been converted into a morass, breeding nothing but pestilence. Properly and fairly husbanded, distributed, and used, there is enough to fertilize the most barren valley and make the whole wilderness blossom like the rose.

That represents the problem of civilization, not merely in this country but in all lands. Some men get their fair share of wealth in a land and no more—sometimes even the streams of wealth overflow to waste over some favored regions, often producing a morass, which poisons the social atmosphere. Many have to depend on a little trickling runlet, which quickly evaporates with every commercial or industrial drought; sometimes you have masses of men and women whom the flood at its height barely reaches, and then you witness parched specimens of humanity, withered, hardened in misery, living in a desert where even the well of tears has long ago run dry.

Besides the economic significance of these great inequalities of wealth and income, there is a social aspect which equally merits the attention of Congress. It has been shown that the great fortunes of those who have profited by the enormous expansion of American industry have already passed, or will pass in a few years, by right of inheritance to the control of heirs or to trustees who act as their "vice regents." They are frequently styled by our newspapers "monarchs of industry," and indeed occupy within our Republic a position almost exactly analogous to that of feudal lords.

These heirs, owners only by virtue of the accident of birth, control the livelihood and have the power to dictate the happiness of more human beings than populated England in the Middle Ages. Their principalities, it is true, are scattered and, through the medium of stock ownership, shared in part with others; but they are none the less real. In fact, such scattered invisible industrial principalities are a greater menace to the welfare of the Nation than would be equal power consolidated into numerous petty kingdoms in different parts of the country. They might then be visualized and guarded against; now their influence invisibly permeates and controls every phase of life and industry.

"The king can do no wrong," not only because he is above the law but because every function is performed or responsibility assumed by his ministers and agents. Similarly our Rockefellers, Morgans, Fricks, Vanderbilts, and Astors can do no industrial wrong, because all effective action and direct responsibility is shifted from them to the executive officials who manage American industry. As a basis for this conclusion we have the testimony of many, among which, however, the following statements stand out most clearly:

Mr. John D. Rockefeller, Jr. [Before congressional investigating committee.]:

> Those of us who are in charge there elect the ablest and most upright and competent men whom we can find, in so far as our interests give us the opportunity to select, to have the responsibility for the conduct of the business in which we are interested as investors. We can not pretend to follow the business ourselves.

Mr. J. Pierpont Morgan:

> Chairman WALSH. In your opinion, to what extent are the directors of corporations responsible for the labor conditions existing in the industries in which they are the directing power?
> Mr. MORGAN. Not at all I should say.

The similitude, indeed, runs even to mental attitude and phrase. Compare these two statements:
Mr. John D. Rockefeller, Jr.:

> My appreciation of the conditions surrounding wage earners and my sympathy with every endeavor to better these conditions are as strong as those of any man.

Louis XVI:

> There is none but you and me that has the people's interest at heart. ("Il n'y a que vous et moi *aimions* [sic] le peuple.")

The families of these industrial princes are already well established and are knit together not only by commercial alliances but by a network of intermarriages which assures harmonious action whenever their common interest is threatened.

Effective action by Congress is required, therefore, not only to readjust on a basis of compensation approximating the service actually performed, the existing inequalities in the distribution of wealth and income, but to check the growth of an hereditary aristocracy, which is foreign to every conception of American Government and menacing to the welfare of the people and the existence of the Nation as a democracy.

The objects to be attained in making this readjustment are: To reduce the swollen, unearned fortunes of those who have a superfluity; to raise the underpaid masses to a level of decent and comfortable living; and at the same time to accomplish this on a basis which will, in some measure, approximate the just standard of income proportional to service.

The discussion of how this can best be accomplished forms the greater part of the remainder of this report, but at this point it seems proper to indicate one of the most immediate steps which need to be taken.

It is suggested that the commission recommend to Congress the enactment of an inheritance tax, so graded that, while making generous provision for the support of dependents and the education of minor children, it shall leave no large accumulation of wealth to pass into hands which had no share in its production. The revenue from this tax, which we are informed would be very great, should be reserved by the Federal Government for three principal purposes:

1.   The extension of education.

2.   The development of other important social services which should properly be performed by the Nation, which are discussed in detail elsewhere.

3.   The development, in cooperation with States and municipalities, of great constructive works, such as road building, irrigation, and reforestation, which would materially increase the efficiency and welfare of the entire Nation.

We are informed by counsel not only that such a tax is clearly within the power of Congress, but that upon two occasions, namely, during the Civil War and in 1898, such graded inheritance taxes were enacted with scarcely any opposition and were sustained by the Supreme Court, which held that the inheritance tax was not a direct tax within the meaning of the Constitution. We are aware that similar taxes are levied in the various States, but the conflict with such State taxes seems to have presented little difficulty during the period in which the tax of 1898 was in effect. Under any circumstances this need cause no great complication, as the matter could be readily adjusted by having the Federal Government collect the entire tax and refund a part to the States on an equitable basis.

There is no legislation which could be passed by Congress the immediate and ultimate efforts of which would be more salutary or would more greatly assist in tempering the existing spirit of unrest.

Document II-36: LABOR LEGISLATION IN CONGRESS

The labor movement has represented a continuing force toward economic democracy, and a student of reform should be fully aware of its intricate history. (See II-7, 10, 15, 19, 23.) It may be worthwhile to make some distinction between those activities of labor that have been direct manifestations of self-interest and those that have placed the concerns of the working man in a broader context of social reform. Both kinds of activity have been present from the earliest days to the present; in any era it is possible to find issues as immediate as the length of the working day alongside issues as general as the level of free and compulsory education. Yet a notable shift of emphasis did take place in the late nineteenth and early twentieth centuries. The Adamson Act was a result.

During those years labor moved away from a position represented by the Knights of Labor, resisted the various socialistic programs, and settled for a position fairly represented by Samuel Gompers and the American Federation of Labor. This shift had several consequences. It meant that, for the time being at least, there was even less chance of common cause between agricultural and industrial workers (see II—25). It meant that labor had less interest in legislative programs requiring broad popular endorsement, such as a takeover by the government of the utilities, railroads, or—more sweepingly—the means of production. Slightly more special programs, such as taxation and currency reform, also receded in priority.

In their place came a more pragmatic interest in wages, hours, and working conditions. The primary means for achieving these ends was collective bargaining buttressed by stricter union organization and the use of such weapons as strikes and boycotts. As Samuel Gompers wrote, after recalling one of his early efforts to work through legislation, "Our labor movement in its rational program to improve working conditions through legislation met with little assistance from the general public. I have found it easy enough to find critics, but there were few to help constructively." (*Seventy Years of Life and Labor.* New York, Dutton, 1925, p. 198.)

Union statements continued to call for certain types of legislation: against the importation of foreign labor, against unsafe working conditions. For a while it was felt, however, that even wages and hours should be the subject of legislation only in the case of women and children. Adult males, it was assumed, would do better through direct bargaining than through governmental intervention. Partly due to the proddings of Eugene V. Debs, pressure again mounted for legislative action, albeit different in nature from the programs of the now-defunct Knights of Labor (see II-30.) There were calls for better anti-trust legislation that would not be used against unions as had the Sherman Anti-Trust Act of 1890 (see II-34); there was some anticipation of the New Deal's Wagner Act in the sentiment that the government might be needed as a referee in collective bargaining (see II-41); and there was a willingness to support federal legislation for wages and hours in interstate commerce beyond the protection of women and children.

The Adamson Act was introduced to prevent a threatened railway strike and its inevitable repercussions on all aspects of the nation's life. In some ways the crisis situation makes this an untypical piece of reform legislation, yet there are so many instances of national emergencies leading to social and economic reforms that one might also make the opposite argument. The debate shows that, crisis or no, Congress had no fear of proposing federal intervention in the "free workings of the economy." Not only was the prevention of a damaging strike presumed to be well within the legislative purview, but many of the speakers also assume a congressional obligation to protect the bargaining rights of labor and to make stipulations on wages and hours as a part of that protective process. President Wilson had only recently come to a similar position; whereas the Supreme Court, in its veto of the Keating-Owen Act of 1916, remained unconvinced of the rights of federal intervention to protect (child) labor.

The following debate, which took place on September 1, 1916, led to the passage and signing of the Adamson Act. It demonstrates a broad shift in public attitudes as well as a new realism about the need for explicit strictures and enforcement provisions. The document includes a reading of the complete bill under discussion. The principal speakers in the debate were the following Congressmen: William C. Adamson (Georgia); William P. Borland (Missouri); Charles P. Caldwell (New York); John C. Cooper (Ohio).

SOURCE: *The Congressional Record*, vol. LIII, pp. 13582-83.

ADAMSON ACT DEBATE

Mr. COOPER of Ohio. Mr. Speaker and gentlemen of the House, I rise to say a word in defense of the railroad men who belong to railroad organizations in this country.

The gentleman from New York [Mr. BENNET] left the impression that the railroad organizations were trying to hold up this Congress at the point of a gun. The railroad organizations did not bring the question to Congress. They were having a negotiation with the employers in New York City, and when these negotiations were broken off the President of the United States asked the railroad organizations to come to Washington. The President used his best influence to try and settle the controversy between the employers and the employees, and when he could not settle it the President of the United States came to Congress and appealed to this body to pass this legislation. The railroad men have not asked Congress to pass this piece of legislation that we are considering to-day.

Mr. MOORE of Pennsylvania. Did they ask the President to interfere?

Mr. COOPER of Ohio. I have not time to yield—but they did say that if this House would pass this bill to-day and the Senate would pass it to-morrow, so that it would become a law, they would have the power to call this strike off. Mr. Speaker, I know of no body of workingmen in the United States to-day who are a better, more law-abiding class of citizens, honest, and industrious, than the railroad men of this country. [Applause.] They have been conservative in asking for better conditions, and I do not believe that the railroad men of the country have had a strike since 1894, and I rise at this time in defense of the railroad organizations and say again that it was not the railroad men who brought this question to Congress, and they should not be accused here on the floor of this House of coming to Congress and trying to hold us up at the point of a gun. [Applause.]

Mr. HARRISON. Mr. Speaker, I yield two minutes to the gentleman from New York [Mr. CALDWELL].

Mr. CALDWELL. Mr. Speaker, I for one am glad that the responsible Democratic Party of these United States has accepted the responsibility for this wise legislation. Since I can remember, the issue between the people of the United States has been whether the Democracy really recognized the interests of the workingman, and to-day we have a demonstration here on the floor of this House as to whether a Republican stands by his organized-labor friends or whether the Republicans will stand by them and the people of these United States and coerce those people who are trying to keep in their own pockets the great prosperity that the Democracy has brought to our Nation. [Applause on the Democratic side.] And the proof is they do not. I believe that the man who works with his hands is entitled to a fair return for his toil, and when the country is prosperous he is entitled to an increase in his wage. I believe that eight hours are long enough for any man to work at a skilled trade. When the clock goes round in its circle it should be divided into three periods, as was provided by the King of France in ancient times. It is for that principle that the workingman of America has been fighting, and I am proud that the Democracy of the United States has taken this great step toward the establishment of that principle, which is recognized in the mind of every free-thinking American as just and proper. [Applause on the Democratic side.]

Mr. HARRISON. Mr. Speaker. I yield two minutes to the gentleman from Missouri [Mr. BORLAND].

Mr. BORLAND. Mr. Speaker, I am heartily for this bill to provide an eight-hour day for men in the train service on interstate railroads, and I want to say that I would be glad to support it if there were no strike impending. It is not a piece of temporary legislation, but is, as the President of the United States has pointed out, a very much needed addition to our code of laws, brought on, of course, by the exigencies of the occasion, but not confined to the particular crisis in which we are now involved. I believe that the people of the United States generally recognize the great social principle of an eight-hour day for labor. I think that Congress in responding to that demand is voicing the appeal of the laboring people, the producers, and the great masses of the United States of America. I do not believe that the expense of putting in force an eight-hour day will equal what the railroads have claimed. I was in the railroad business myself years ago, but that was before the day when legislation, enacted by Congress, had guaranteed to the railroads a fixed income upon their property. To-day the railroads are the only class of business in the United States that is absolutely guaranteed a profit upon its business. The men who work for them are not guaranteed a living wage, the men who ship over them are not guaranteed a profit, the farmer who raises the produce which constitutes the commerce of the railroads is not guaranteed a profit, but the one business institution in the United States that is guaranteed a fixed return upon its investment isothe railroad itself. [Applause on the Democratic side.]. . . .

Mr. ADAMSON. Mr. Speaker . . . I will not say with the apostle that I am neither for Paul nor Apollos. I will say that I am against neither party in this case. I am for both of them. They occupy the position of two parties who are conducting an affray in the streets to the terror of the king's subjects. I represent the people. All of these carrier officials and employees are our servants. If they do not realize it, they will have to come to the realization that they are as much servants of the public as you and I. A condition presents itself and not a theory. There may be ten thousand different opinions as to what ought to be done to adjust relations between our two classes of servants when we have time and opportunity to give deliberate consideration to those questions.

This is inaptly described as temporary legislation. It is hasty legislation, I admit, to meet an emergency. There is but one substantial thing in it, and that is the eight-hour law. We have been committed to the hours-of-service law for years and years. We have a 16-hour law and a 9-hour law, and gentlemen who can read the provision of the Constitution declaring that Congress can regulate commerce between States and then cavil about the constitutionality of Congress doing anything to regulate commerce reads the Constitution with different kind of glasses to mine. We now put in the eight-hour law and provide to preserve the status quo until a commission can investigate the dispute between these two classes of our servants. Afterwards, we will make complete and adequate regulation, taking care of the interests of both classes of our servants and doing justice to the people, to whom all service belongs. [Applause.]. . .

The Clerk read as follows:

Be it enacted, etc., That beginning December 1, 1916, eight hours shall, in contracts for labor and service, be deemed a day's work and the measure or standard of a day's work for the purpose of reckoning the compensation for services of all employees who are now or may hereafter be employed by any common carrier by railroad which is subject to the provisions of the act of February 1, 1887, entitled "An act to regulate commerce," as amended, and who are now or may hereafter be actually engaged in any capacity in the operation of trains used for the transportation of persons or property on railroads, from any State or Territory of the United States or the District of Columbia to any other State or Territory of the United States or the District of Columbia, or from one place in a Territory to another place in the same Territory, or from any place in the United States to an adjacent foreign country, or from any place in the United States through a foreign country to any other place in the United States.

SEC. 2.   That the President shall appoint a commission of three, which shall observe the operation and effects of the institution of the eight-hour standard workday as above defined and the facts and conditions affecting the relations between such common carriers and employees during a period of not less than 6 months nor more than 9 months, in the discretion of the commission, and within 30 days thereafter such commission shall report its findings to the President and Congress; that each member of the commission created under the provisions of this act shall receive a compensation as may be fixed by the President. That the sum of $25,000, or so much thereof as may be necessary, be, and hereby is appropriated, out of any money in the United States Treasury not otherwise appropriated, for the necessary and proper expenses incurred in connection with the work of such commission, including salaries, per diem, traveling expenses of members and employers, and rent, furniture, office fixtures and supplies, books, salaries, and other necessary expenses, the same to be approved by the chairman of said commission and audited by the proper accounting officers of the Treasury.

SEC. 3. That pending the report of the commission herein provided for and for a period of 30 days thereafter the compensation of railway employees subject to this act for a standard eight-hour workday shall not be reduced below the present standard day's wage, and for all necessary time in excess of eight hours such employees shall be paid at a rate not less than the pro rata rate for such standard eight-hour workday.

SEC. 4. That any person violating any provision of this act shall be guilty of a misdemeanor and upon conviction shall be fined not less than $100 and not more than $1,000, or imprisoned not to exceed one year, or both.

Document II-37: SUFFRAGE FOR WOMEN

As World War I came to a close the Progressive movement climaxed in two Constitutional amendments that made many reformers at least temporarily jubilant. Both were related to the emergence of women as agents of direct political action. Before the Civil War, the Margaret Fullers and Fanny Wrights were rare, and it took the high intensity of the anti-slavery debate to bring to the platform such capable, politically inclined women as the Grimké sisters. After 1865, many women went to work educating and otherwise assisting the freedmen. By the end of the nineteenth century, however, most reform-minded women had attached themselves to one or both of the closely related campaigns for temperance and women's rights. Thus it was no mere coincidence that the Eighteenth and Nineteenth amendments came into being in two consecutive years (1919 and 1920).

Between the end of Reconstruction and the passage of the Nineteenth Amendment, organizations dominated by women showed that they had mastered all kinds of political techniques—from direct action to abstract moralizing. Most effective, however, were the careful assaults on the educational process associated with Frances Willard's Women's Christian Temperance Union, and the pressure lobbying associated with the Anti-Saloon League. Both these techniques were useful against alcohol as well as for the vote.

Many localities had, long before 1920, allowed women to vote in local elections, especially for school-board members. Gradually the franchise was extended to women on a statewide basis, beginning with Wyoming in 1890 and including all Far Western states plus Kansas, New York, South Dakota, Oklahoma, and Michigan by 1918. Still, the Nineteenth Amendment represents more quantitative progress in extending democracy than any other single act in the nation's history. It will never be possible to demonstrate whether or not the suffrage, thus broadened, has accelerated the thrust toward economic and social democracy; nonetheless, there is no more important milestone in the history of American political reform than the one reproduced below.

SOURCE: United States Constitution; Nineteenth Amendment ratified August 18, 1920.

ARTICLE XIX

The right of citizens of the United States to vote shall not be denied or abridged by the United States or by any State on account of sex.

Congress shall have the power to enforce this article by appropriate legislation.

Document II-38: RADICALISM IN REFORM

This drawing represents two familiar protest themes that grew increasingly important in the United States through the 1920s and 30s: the sense of outrage at the continuing cheek-by-jowl existence of extremes of wealth and poverty; and the chilling yet somehow glamorous prospect of violent revolution.

Revolution was something remote from the experience of all but a handful of twentieth-century Americans. To a segment of the intellectual and artistic left, it stood for a retribution, rising from the earth, sanctioned by Marx and nature, against the parasitic lords of unearned power and wealth. The Mexican and Russian revolutions were foremost in mind; and it is worth noting that these struggles occurred far away from New York City, in primarily agricultural countries whose workers were easy to render as picturesque and appealing in costume, song, and attitude. Up until the disillusioning experiences of the Spanish Civil War and the Russian pact with Hitler's Germany, a sizable number of articulate Americans—provoked by such injustices as the conviction of Sacco and Vanzetti—seriously advocated revolution as the answer to the ills of their own country.

Writers and artists were central to radicalism. Edmund Wilson openly invited his creative colleagues to join with a working-class revolution on the Russian model. Max Eastman, Floyd Dell, Joseph Freeman, Mike Gold, Randolph Bourne, V. F. Calverton, and many others responded. Even so politically unconcerned a writer as F. Scott Fitzgerald turned out a complex 1920 short story whose deliberately ominous title, "May Day," covered a juxtaposition of scenes very sharply suggestive of the one depicted below. Two proletarian soldiers, recently discharged, wait in the mop closet of New York's posh Delmonico's for a waiter to procure them whiskey from a beautifully appointed all-night revel of Gamma Psis from Yale; simultaneously touching the two groups, a gang of drifters and soldiers wander about town hunting and baiting the "Reds."

Cartoons were a prominent mode for expressing the discontent with maldistribution of wealth and suggesting a violent, revolutionary alternative. Some of them were reminiscent of the drawings of Homer Davenport at the turn of the century (see II-28), or of the several IWW cartoonists who published in *Solidarity* and the *Industrial Worker*. The twenties and thirties produced a generation of radical cartoonists for the left-wing periodicals: George Luks, Robert Minor, Boardman Robinson, John Sloan, and Art Young. The picture reproduced below was done as an illustration for a novel embracing a kind of halfway socialism. It was reproduced in Upton Sinclair's compendium of revolutionary art and literature, *Cry for Justice* (Philadelphia, Winston, 1915). It represents, at least as well as any of the cartoons of the 20s and 30s, the revolutionary sentiments of the left.

American radicalism, complex and factional, was well described by C. Hartley Grattan in "Red Opinion in the United States" (*Scribner's Magazine*, vol. XCVI [November, 1934], pp. 299-305) which, together with a good sampling of representative views, is conveniently reproduced in Daniel Aaron and Robert Bendiner, eds., *The Strenuous Decade: A Social and Intellectual Record of the 1930s* (New York,

SOURCE: Illustration by William Balfour Ker from John A. Mitchell, *The Silent War.* New York, Life, 1906, facing p. 200.

"From the depths"

Doubleday-Anchor, 1970). Most of these radical spokesmen placed themselves outside the mainstream of reform by advocating the sudden and possibly violent overthrow of democratic capitalism. Yet radicalism was important because of the weight it provided in moving the center of public opinion leftward. Franklin D. Roosevelt made visible use of the popular fear of violent revolution in gaining acceptance for a politico-economic program which many Americans might otherwise have regarded as itself unacceptably radical. In the speech reproduced below (see II-40) he can be observed to take the issue of radicalism by frontal assault, cloak it in the respectability of religion, and make it a part of his presidential campaign appeal.

Document II-39: DEPRESSION ISSUES VIA LANGE

The New Deal was willing and able to go as far as it did toward the redistribution of American wealth not just because of the fear of drastic change; a more basic motivation lay in the severity of the Great Depression itself. There are many ways to document the kind of despair produced by the prolonged slump in the economy signaled by the crash of 1929 and reaching its full negative dimensions in the unemployment and poverty of the thirties. The statistics themselves are appalling. There were breadlines, wasted landscape, deteriorating dwellings, boarded factories, and enforced idleness of many kinds. But the most impressive document to one human being is probably the face of another human being.

This kind of documentation of the Depression years is available in quality and in abundance thanks in large degree to a remarkable group of photographers brought to work for the Farm Security Administration and encouraged to point their cameras straight into the faces of impoverished America: Jack Delano, Carl Mydans, Ben Shahn, Walker Evans, Arthur Rothstein, John Vachon, and others. One of the well-recognized members of this group, Dorothea Lange, took a series of photographs of one family of peapickers in California. The subjects of this photograph, migrants from the dust bowl, help focus attention on rural poverty in general, and on the consequences of soil exhaustion and migrant labor in particular. The despair reflected in the attitudes of the children juxtaposed with the handsome, lean, suffering, yet determined face of the mother made this a classic Depression photograph. One version is

reproduced in the upper left-hand corner of the accompanying poster.
The row of abandoned, boarded-over dwellings in the upper right
makes an urban parallel with the photograph of the "migrant mother."
Together they visualize the dimensions of national despair. The other
parts of this information panel, prepared for use by the Resettlement
Administration in 1936, indicate some of the New Deal responses. In
addition to emergency relief and employment measures, the Roosevelt
administration, through agencies like the Farm Security Administration,
the Home Owners Loan Corporation, the Reconstruction Finance Corporation, and the Agricultural Adjustment Agency, offered low-cost housing, employment assistance, non-interest and low-interest loans. As
much of the legacy from the Great Depression reminds us, these measures did not promptly or totally erase the long flat months of unemployment and the acid taste of poverty. Artists like John Steinbeck and
Dorothea Lange helped the nation to understand this experience and
helped force new thoughts about the responsibilities of the body politic.

SOURCE: Photograph in the files of the Farm Security Administration—Office of War
Information, Prints and Photographs Division, Library of Congress.

Document II-40: FDR AND SOCIAL JUSTICE

The era of Franklin D. Roosevelt and the New Deal was not particularly notable for putting the government more directly in the hands of the
people. It is true that the legislature, theoretically more representative of
popular will than the other two branches of government, won an eventual
victory over several Supreme Court vetoes of New Deal enactments and
over the Constitution in allowing a popular President to serve for more
than two terms. A more obvious political consequence of this era was the
enormous growth in the powers of the federal government, and particularly of the executive. It is true that these powers were built on the
foundation of an overwhelmingly popular mandate, but the interest here
lies not so much in the source of this power as in the way it was used.
   Roosevelt worked toward an economic policy by identifying what he
opposed. In the speech reproduced below he attacked laissez-faire
economics and the "trickle" theory of restoring prosperity by putting
money into the system at the top. He attacked poverty, finding intolerable a condition that had rendered "one-third of a Nation ill-nourished,
ill-clad, ill-housed." He attacked unproductive wealth, speaking of

FOR BADLY HOUSED CITY
WORKERS & FARMERS
THE RESETTLEMENT
ADMINISTRATION IS

BUILDING
20,785
HOMES

RURAL   SUBURBAN

700 000
RELIEF FAMILIES
AIDED

BY LOANS & GRANTS FROM THE
RESETTLEMENT ADMINISTRATION

FOR LIVESTOCK

FOR FARM
EQUIPMENT

FOR HOME
REPAIRS—

New Deal poster

"economic royalists" and decrying those who selfishly husbanded their own resources while great numbers suffered. He opposed radicalism by depicting himself as the conservator of the liberal tradition and by gathering some of the radical discontent into his own rhetorical appeal.

His constructive answer was popularly known as "pump-priming": that is, stimulating the economy by putting money in the hands of the consumers. To do this he made full use of the powers of the government to tax and to regulate. Through surtaxes, corporation taxes, inheritance taxes, and the graduated income tax he extracted large amounts of capital from wealthy corporations and individuals. Most of this money went to the poor and unemployed through emergency relief, through work projects, and through an astounding increase in the employment rolls of the government itself. As the nation worked its way out of the Depression, the government established itself in countless new ways as an agent for guarding against inequities in the distribution of wealth.

In working out his position, Roosevelt was attempting to provide an alternative not only to violent revolution. Communism, and the other "imported" political ideologies, had never been as popular in America as a group of native remedies, some of which appealed very powerfully to particular groups: Father Divine to the poor, especially Blacks in Eastern cities; Francis Townsend to the aged, especially Midwestern farmers; Father Coughlin to working-class city dwellers, especially Roman Catholics; Upton Sinclair in California; Huey Long in Louisiana and the South. (A good, condensed representation and analysis of these views is in the collection by Aaron and Bendiner cited in II-38, pp. 137-212.) Technocracy, propounded by Harold Scott, appealed to a broad stripe in the national character by arguing that the country should become more—rather than less—productive and at the same time more efficient. Thus more people would work shorter hours. All of these schemes involved tampering in some way with private property and/or laissez-faire economics; yet each leader clearly thought that he was extending the American dream rather than countervailing it.

It is interesting to note that "social justice" was a prominent phrase in the rhetorical armament of these men and movements, both separately and in coalitions. In the context of the thirties, "social justice" probably meant nothing more than a better break economically, just as "social security" has only meant a little money for people over sixty-five. Roosevelt, as a campaigner, showed himself in the following speech as adept at stealing the rhetorical thunder from homegrown reformers as from foreign radicals. Thus his second paragraph expresses a faith in "social justice, through social action" and the last paragraph commits "Americans everywhere" to the "path of social justice." In Roosevelt's New Deal, then, one sees a program that accepted the complaints of the radicals and the domestic innovators, that faced squarely the enormous crisis that was the Depression, that picked a careful path between alternative solutions outside the recognized direction of politico-economic change. The New Deal offers the student of reform no innovations in philosophy or general method. It merits most serious attention, however, for the sheer magnitude of its impact on politico-economic relations and of the extension of government into the lives of the citizens.

SOURCE: This is a stenographic text provided by the Franklin D. Roosevelt Library, Hyde Park, N.Y. and reproduced courtesy of the Library.

ADDRESS OF GOVERNOR FRANKLIN D. ROOSEVELT
NAVAL ARMORY, BELLE ISLE BRIDGE, DETROIT, MICHIGAN, OCTOBER 2, 1932

My old friend Mayor Murphy, my old friend Governor Comstock, (applause) and you—many of you—my old friends of Detroit and of Michigan: (Applause)

I have had a wonderful reception today, and I am awfully glad to be back in Detroit, and I am especially glad to be once more the guest of the Navy. (Applause) There is only one fly in the ointment, and I might just as well be perfectly frank with you—I would much rather be cruising the Great Lakes on the U.S.S. DeBuque. (Laughter, applause)

You know today is Sunday, and I am afraid that some of you people today in Detroit have been talking politics. (Laughter) Well, I am not going to. I want to talk to you about Government. Well, that is a very different thing. (Laughter, applause) And I am not going to refer to Parties at all. I am going to refer to some of the fundamentals that antedate parties, and antedate republics and empires, fundamentals that are as old as mankind itself. They are fundamentals that have been expressed in philosophies for I don't know how many thousands of years in every part of the world. And today, in our boasted modern civilization, we are facing just exactly the same problem, just exactly the same conflict between two schools of philosophy that they faced in the earliest days of America, and indeed of the world. One of them—one of these old philosophies—the philosophy of those who would "let things alone", and the other, the philosophy that strives for something new—something that the human race has never attained yet; but something which I believe the human race can attain, and will attain—social justice, through social action. (Prolonged applause)

The philosophy of "letting things alone" has resulted in the days of the cave man, and in the days of the automobile—has resulted in the jungle law of the survival of the so-called fittest. But this philosophy of social action results in the protection of humanity and the fitting of as many human beings as possible into the scheme of surviving. And in that first philosophy of "letting things alone", I am sorry to say that there are a lot of people in my community back home—which is a little village—and in the farming districts of the Nation and in the great cities of the country, such as yours—we can fit in a great many splendid people who keep saying, not only to themselves and to their friends, but to the community as a whole, "Why shouldn't we 'let things alone'? In the first place they are not as bad as they are painted, and in the second place they will cure themselves. Time is a great healer." An easy philosophy! The kind of philosophy, my friends, that was expressed the other day by a Cabinet officer of the United States of America, when he is reported to have said, "Our children are apt to profit rather than suffer from what is going on." (Applause)

While he was saying that, another branch of your Government, and mine, the United States Public Health Service, which believes in my kind of philosophy, I think—telling the truth—said this: "Over six million of our public school children haven't enough to eat. Many of them are fainting at their desks. They are a prey to disease. Their future health is menaced." (Applause)

What school do you believe in?

And in the same way, there are two theories of prosperity and of well-being: First, the theory that if we make the rich richer, somehow they will let a part of their prosperity trickle through to the rest of us. (Applause)

And the second theory—and I suppose this goes back to the days of Noah—I won't say Adam and Eve, because they had a less complicated situation (laughter, applause)—but, at least, to the days of the flood—

there was that second theory that if we make the average of mankind comfortable and secure, their prosperity will rise upward, just as yeast rises up, through the ranks. (Applause)

Now, my friends, the philosophy of social justice that I am going to talk about this Sabbath day, the philosophy of social justice through social action, calls definitely, plainly for the reduction of poverty. And what do we mean when we talk about the reduction of poverty? We mean the reduction of the causes of poverty. And when we have an epidemic of disease in this land, in these modern days, what do we do? We turn to find out in the first instance the sources from which the disease has come, and when we have found those sources, those causes, we turn the energy of our attack upon them.

We have got beyond the point in modern civilization of merely trying to fight an epidemic of disease by taking care of the victims after they are stricken. We do that, but we do more. We seek to prevent it, and the attack on poverty is not very unlike the attack on disease. We are seeking the causes and when we have found them, we turn our attack upon them. What are the causes? What are the causes that destroy human beings, driving millions of them to destruction? Well, there are a good many of them, and there are a good many of us who are alive today who have seen tremendous steps taken towards the eradication of those causes.

For instance, ill health: You and I know what has been accomplished by community effort, State effort, the effort and the association of individual men and women towards the bettering of the health of humanity.

We have spent vast sums upon research. We have established a wholly new science, the science of public health, and we are carrying what we call today "instruction in health" into the most remote corners of our cities and our country districts. Well, the result is what? It is two-fold: First, an economic saving. It has been money which has been returned to the community a thousand times over because you and I know that a sick person—a man, woman or child, who has to be taken care of—not only takes the individual who is sick out of active participation and useful citizenship, but takes somebody else, too, and so, from the purely dollars and cents point of view that we Americans are so fond of thinking about, public health has paid for itself.

And what have we done along other lines for the prevention of some of the causes of poverty?

I go back twenty-two years to a day when in my State of New York we had tried to pass in the Legislature what we called a Workmen's Compensation Act, knowing, as we did, that there were thousands of men and women who every year were seriously injured in industrial accidents of one kind or another, who became a burden on their community, who were unable to work, unable to get adequate medical care—and a lot of us youngsters in the Legislature in those days were called radicals. We were called Socialists—they didn't know the word Bolshevik in those days, but if they had known that, we would have been called that, too. (Applause) And we put through a Workmen's Compensation Act, and the courts, as some courts do, thinking in terms of the Seventeenth Century, declared it to be unconstitutional, so we had to go about amending the Constitution, and the following year we got a Workmen's Compensation Act.

What has it done? We were not the first state to have it. One of the earliest states, by the way, was New Jersey, which, the year before the action in the State of New York, passed a Workmen's Compensation Act at the bidding of that great humanitarian governor, Woodrow Wilson. (Prolonged applause)

But the result has been that almost every state of the Union has eliminated that cause of poverty among the masses of the people.

And take another form of poverty in the old days. Not so long ago, you and I know, there were families in attics—in every part of the Nation—in country districts and in city districts—there were thousands and hundreds of crippled children. Crippled children who could get no adequate care. Crippled children who were lost to the community and who were a burden on the community, and so we have in this past twenty or thirty years gradually provided means for restoring crippled children to useful citizenship, and it has all been a factor in going after and solving one of the causes of poverty and disease.

And then in these later years, we have been wondering about old people, and we have come to the conclusion in this modern civilization that the theory and the idea of carting old people off to the county poorhouse is not perhaps the best thing after all. (Applause)

I will tell you what sold me on old age insurance—old age pension. Not so long ago—about ten years—I received a great shock. I had been away from my home town of Hyde Park during the winter time and when

I came back I found that a tragedy had occurred. One of my farm neighbors, who had been a splendid old fellow—Supervisor of his town, Highway Commissioner of his town—one of the best of our citizens. And before I left, around Christmas time, I had seen the old man, who was eighty-nine, and I had seen his old brother, who was eighty-seven, and I had seen his other brother, who was eight-five, and I had seen his kid sister, who was eighty-three. (Applause)

And they were living on a farm; I knew it was mortaged. I knew it was mortgaged to the hilt, but I assumed that everything was all right, for they still had a couple of cows and a few chickens. But when I came back in the spring, I found that in the heavy winter that followed there had been a heavy fall of snow and one of the old brothers had fallen down on his way out to the barn to milk the cow, and had perished in the snow drift, and the town authorities had come along and they had taken the two old men and they had put them into the county poorhouse and they had taken the old lady and had sent her down, for want of a better place, to the Insane Asylum, although she was not insane, she was just old.

That sold me on the idea of trying to keep homes intact for old people.

And then in another respect modern science has been good to us. It is not so very long ago that a young person, or an old person, who had anything the trouble with their mentality—they were put into what was called an asylum and not long before that they used to call it a "madhouse". Even when I was a boy, the states of the Nation used to provide asylums and when anybody wasn't entirely complete mentally— anyone was a mental defective, as we call them today, in any shape, manner or form, they used to be carted off to the asylum and they would always stay there until they came out to go to the graveyards.

Today that is not true, and medical science today is doing two things; first, that the young people, the young people who are not mentally deficient but who require special mental training, and when schools allow them to remain in most cases in the bosom of their own families, we are applying special treatment and special education to them so that, instead of becoming a burden when they grow up, they are going to be useful citizens. (Applause)

And then, on the other side of it, there are the older people, the people who do have to go to hospitals for mental troubles—and the other day, just before I left Albany, I got a report from my State Department that showed that instead of the old-fashioned system by which the rule was observed of ''once in, always in'', this past year in the State of New York we had sent back to their families 23% of all those in our hospitals for mental cases, sent them back cured to their families. (Applause)

Now, those are the causes, the causes that have destroyed in past ages thousands, countless thousands of our fellow human beings. They are the causes that we must attack if we are to make the future safer for humanity. We can go on taking care of the handicapped and the crippled and the sick and the feeble-minded and the unemployed, but common sense, like humanity, calls on us to turn our back definitely on these destroyers. Poverty resulting from these destroyers is largely preventable, but, my friends, poverty, if it is to be prevented, requires a broad program of social justice. (Applause)

We cannot go back, we cannot go back to the old prisons, the old systems of mere punishment under which when a man came out of prison he was not fitted to live in our community alongside of us. We cannot go back to the old system of asylums. We cannot go back to the old lack of hospitals, the lack of public health. We cannot go back to the sweatshops of America. We cannot go back to children working in factories— (applause) those days are gone. (Applause)

And there are a lot of new steps to take. It is not a question of just not going back. It is a question also of not standing still. (Applause)

For instance, the problem in the long run, and I am not talking about the emergency of this year, but the problem of unemployment in the long run can be and shall be solved by the human race. (Applause) Some leaders have wisely declared for a system of unemployment insurance throughout this broad land of ours, and we are going to come to it. (Applause)

But I do not believe the Secretary of the Interior would be for it. (Laughter, applause) He would say that great good is coming to this country because of the present situation. (Laughter) Yes, the followers of the philosophy of let alone—the people have been decrying all of these measures of social welfare. What do they call them? They call them ''paternalistic''. All right, if they are paternalistic, I am a father. (Laughter, applause)

They maintain that these laws interfere with individualism, forgetful of the fact that the causes of poverty in the main are beyond the control of any one individual, any czar, either a czar of politics or a czar of industry. (Applause) And the followers of the philosophy of social action for the prevention of poverty maintain that if we set up a system of justice we shall have small need for the exercise of mere philanthropy. Justice, after all, first is the goal we seek. Believing that when justice has been done, individualism will have a greater security to devote the best that individualism itself can give. In other words, my friends, our long range objective is not a dole, but a job. (Applause)

At the same time, we have in this Nation—and I know you have in Detroit, because Frank Murphy has talked to me of it many times in the past year or two—all of us in the city and country alike have got to do everything we can to tide over. All agree that the first responsibility for the prevention of poverty and the alleviation of distress and the care of its victims rests upon the locality, the individuals, the organizations and the Government. First of all, perhaps, upon the private agencies of philanthropy, just as far as we can drag it out of them, and secondly, the other social organizations, and last, but not least, the Church. And yet all agree that to leave to the locality the entire burden would result in placing the heaviest proportion of the burden in most cases upon those who are the least able to bear it. In other words, the communities that have the most difficult problem, like Detroit, would be the communities that would have to bear the heaviest of the burdens.

And so the State steps in to equalize the burdens by providing for a large portion of the care of the victims of the poverty and by providing assistance and guidance for local communities, and above and beyond that the National Government has a responsibility. (Applause)

I would like to enlarge on that a lot, but that would be politics, and I cannot. (Applause) My friends, the ideal of social justice of which I have spoken—an ideal that years ago might have been thought overly advanced, is now accepted by the moral leadership of all of the great religious groups of the country. Radical? Yes, and I will show you how radical it is. I am going to cite three examples of what the churches say, the radical churches of America—Protestant, Catholic and Jewish. (Applause)

And first I will read to you from the Sunday Sermon, the Labor Sermon sent out this year by the Federal Council of Churches of Christ in

America, representing a very large proportion of the Protestants in our country.

Hear how radical they are: They say:

"The thing that matters in any industrial system is what it does actually to human beings. . . .

"It is not denied that many persons of wealth are rendering great service to society. It is only suggested that the wealthy are overpaid in sharp contrast with the underpaid masses of the people. The concentration of wealth carries with it a dangerous concentration of power. It leads to conflict and violence. To suppress the symptoms of this inherent conflict while leaving the fundamental causes of it untouched is neither sound statesmanship nor Christian good will.

"It is becoming more and more clear that the principles of our religion and the findings of social sciences point in the same direction. Economists now call attention to the fact that the present distribution of wealth and income, which is so unbrotherly in the light of Christian ethics, is also unscientific in that it does not furnish purchasing power to the masses to balance consumption and production in our machine age." (Applause)

And now I am going to read you another great declaration and I wonder how many people will call it radical. It is just as radical as I am— (applause) a declaration from one of the greatest forces of conservatism in the world, the Catholic Church, and it is a quotation, my friends, from the scholarly encyclical letter issued last year by the Pope, one of the greatest documents of modern times, and the letter says this:

"It is patent in our days that not alone is wealth accumulated, but immense power and despotic economic domination are concentrated in the hands of a few, and that those few are frequently not the owners but only the trustees and directors of invested funds which they administer at their good pleasure. . . .

"This accumulation of power, the characteristic note of the modern economic order, is a natural result of limitless free competition, which permits the survival of those only who are the strongest, which often means those who fight most relentlessly, who pay least heed to the dictates of conscience. (Applause)

"This concentration of power has led to a three-fold struggle for domination: First, there is the struggle for dictatorship in the economic sphere itself; then the fierce battle to acquire control of the Government, so that its resources and authority may be abused in the economic struggle, and, finally, the clash between the governments themselves.''

And finally, I would read to you from another great statement, a statement from Rabbi Edward L. Israel, Chairman of the Social Justice Commission of the Central Conference of American Rabbis, (applause) and here is what he says:

"We talk of the stabilization of business. What we need is the stabilization of human justice and happiness and the permanent employment of economic policies which will enable us to preserve the essential human values of life amid all the changing aspects of the economic order. We must have a revamping of the entire method of approach to these problems of the economic order. We need a new type of social conscience that will give us courage to act. . . .

"We so easily forget. Once the cry of so-called prosperity is heard in the land we all become so stampeded by the spirit of the god Mammon, that we cannot serve the dictates of social conscience. . . . We are here to serve notice that the economic order is the invention of man; and that it cannot dominate certain eternal principles of justice and of God.'' (Applause)

And so, my friends, I feel a little as if I had been preaching a sermon. I feel a little as if I had been talking too much of some of the fundamentals, and yet those fundamentals enter into your life and my life every day. More, perhaps, than we can realize. If we realized that far more, it would result throughout this country in a greater activity, a great interest on the part of the individual men and women who make up our Nation, in some of the problems which cannot be solved in the long run without the help of everybody.

We need leadership, of course. We need leadership of people who are honest in their thinking and honest in their doing. We need leadership if it is straight thinking—that is, unselfish; but in the last analysis we have got to have the help of the men and women all the way from the top to the bottom, expecially of the men and women who believe in the school of philosophy which is not content to leave things as they are.

And so, in these days of difficulty, we Americans everywhere must and shall choose the path of social justice—the only path that will lead us to a permanent bettering of our civilization, the path that our children must tread, the path of faith, the path of hope and the path of love towards our fellow men. (Prolonged applause)

Document II-41: NEW DEAL IN THE SENATE

The incredibly high level of unemployment and the drastic condition of the laborers during the first years of the Depression had doubtless tipped the scales of public sympathy away from the heroes of economic entrepreneurship. From the reformer's point of view, there had always been an imbalance between the rights of the employer and the rights of the employee. Strikes and boycotts, once an anathema to most Americans, were coming to be viewed more sympathetically as legitimate weapons through which the working man achieved something like the wages, hours, and working conditions he deserved.

The Progressives (see II-36) and the New Dealers were willing, in certain cases, to project the federal government into an active role as referee in the contest between employer and worker. The first move of the New Deal Congress in this direction was the National Recovery Act, which offered only mild assurances for collective bargaining and which was further vitiated by the Supreme Court's decision that federal prosecution of local abuses under the NRA was unconstitutional.

Incensed by the court decision, President Roosevelt swung his weight behind congressional leaders like Robert F. Wagner, Senator from New York, who had already built up considerable support for a new piece of legislation which would create a powerful National Labor Relations Board. This board would maintain a constant vigilance on the labor front, preventing management from undermining the cause of organized labor through the formation of company unions, through discriminatory hirings, recriminatory firings, and other devices that had inhibited the effective organization of labor on a national basis.

As Robert Wagner took the floor on May 15, 1935, he began by citing the long history of decisions against labor to conclude that—in a technological age—it was a clear duty of the government to enforce the rights of labor to fair collective bargaining. Collective bargaining, he insisted, was not un-American. He found a counter-thread of more ''moral'' court decisions on behalf of working men's associations dating from an 1842 verdict of Chief Justice Shaw in *Commonwealth of Massachusetts* v. *Hunt.* (In a radio speech of April 21, 1935, read into the *Congressional Record* [LXXIX, 6183-84], he pursued a similar line, deprecating strikes as loudly as lockouts, appealing for the support of small businessmen and traditionally anti-labor property owners.) In the section of his Senate speech that follows, Wagner shows most clearly that he regards this legislation as a necessary application of political democracy in order to further the cause of economic equity.

Senator Wagner and his supporters carried the argument as well as the President's signature. The resulting Wagner Act (National Labor Relations Act) became a landmark in the history of the federal government's assumption of responsibility toward working men in an industrial age.

SOURCE: *The Congressional Record*, vol. LXXIX, pp. 7567-68, abridged.

ROBERT WAGNER'S SENATE SPEECH

ECONOMIC BACKGROUND: INDUSTRIAL CONCENTRATION AND THE DEPRESSION

These cases which I have cited are not mere records of mock trials in moot courts. They are the external evidence of sweeping political and economic developments completely out of line with our professed desires to make opportunity equally available to all.

The fragile resistance of the antitrust laws did nothing to prevent the compounding of business into larger and larger units. In 1909 there was one small enterprise or manufacturing establishment for every 250 people in the Nation: by 1929 there was only one for every 900 people. In 1904, over 50 percent of the manufacturers in the United States were small enterprisers, each producing less than $20,000 worth of goods per year. By 1929, these small enterprisers had shrunk in number to 32 percent of the total. During the same span of time, producers of goods valued at $100,000 or more per year rose from 16.9 percent of the total to 31.5 percent. And while only one-quarter of the workers in America were employed by million-dollar-a-year concerns in 1904, about three-fifths of the workers were employed by such concerns in 1929.

These technological changes doubled the productive capacity of the average worker between 1919 and 1933. In manufacturing alone, they increased his hourly product by 71 percent. They opened up new vistas of comfort and security to the average man. But despite reassuring discourse about profit sharing and employee participation in industry, the increasing size of business brought concentration of wealth in geometric ratio. By 1929, 200 huge corporations owned one-half of our total corporate wealth. Two years later, 100 general industrial corporations out of a total of 300,000 controlled one-third of the general industrial wealth of the Nation. As a natural corollary, the wage earners' share in the product created by manufacturing has declined steadily for nearly a century. Standing at 51 percent in 1849, it fell to 42 percent in 1919 and to 36 percent in 1933. The isolation of the individual worker has been reflected glaringly in the distribution of the Nation's goods.

The tremendous disparity between the few and the many became most pronounced in that glittering era which we regarded as the zenith of American prosperity. Between 1922 and 1929 the real wages of employees increased by slightly less than 10 percent. But during the same period industrial profits rose by 86 percent, while in the shorter span from 1926 to 1929 dividend payments mounted by 104 percent.

If we had succeeded in providing the minimum requirements of health and decency for every deserving person in the United States, we might have said that the maldistribution of income was a fair price to pay for our industrial efficiency. But we know that we suffered from the prevalence of poverty in a land of plenty. In 1929, 6,000,000 families, or more than 21 percent of our total population, had incomes of less than $1,000 per year. About 12,000,000 families, or more than 42 percent of the total, earned less than $1,500 yearly. Sixteen million families, or 60 percent of the people, had annual incomes below the $2,000 per year necessary for the basic requirements of health and decency. And nearly 20,000,000 families, constituting 71 percent of all America, received less than $2,500 a year. At the same time, in the highest income bracket, one-tenth of 1 percent of the families in the United States were earning as much as the 42 percent at the bottom. It is not surprising that in *America's Capacity to Consume*, the most complete study of family income ever presented to the general reader in this country, the statement is made without equivocation that during the past decade "inequality in the distribution of income has been accentuated."

Not only the preachments of moralists but also the teachings of economists have proved that this injustice wrought its hardships upon those who were temporarily favored as well as those who had been permanently neglected. The low level of income prevented the vast majority of consumers from draining the market of its flood of goods. This was particularly serious in an age of mass production, which had built 21,000,000 automobiles and over 20,000,000 radio sets. At the same time, the extraordinary concentration of income placed excessive savings in the hands of a few. While 60 percent of the families in America contributed only 1.6 percent to the total savings of the country, 2.3 percent of all families contributed 66 2/3 percent to all savings, and 60,000 families at the top of the economic ladder saved almost as much as 25,000,000 families on the lower rungs. Corporate surpluses rose from $8,500,000,000 in 1923 to $16,000,000,000 in 1929. These accumulations of the few sought outlet through investments in plant facilities. Contrasted with the 10-percent rise in wages between 1922 and 1929, the production of machinery increased 91 percent and of capital equipment 70 percent. Production mounted beyond any possibilities of market absorption.

For a short while we staved off inevitable disaster by the pipe dream of installment selling and by lending Europe money with which to buy our own products. But when the domestic market finally closed to further investment, and foreign trade collapsed because our own people had no money with which to buy European goods, the crash came.

This thesis, which places the failure of purchasing power at the center of all explanations of depression, has long received recognition. It has been further substantiated this year in a stimulating book entitled *The Formation of Capital*, by Dr. H. G. Moulton. This volume states:

> The base of the economic pyramid is the production of con-
> sumption goods. The demand for plant and equipment is derived
> from the demand for consumption goods . . . A slight shrinkage at
> the base of the pyramid very nearly eliminates the top . . . The
> primary need is a larger flow of funds through consumptive
> channels.

During 4 long years after the depression came we clung to the same policies which had brought the calamity and which were prolonging its ravages. While the level of wages dropped 60 percent between 1929 and 1932, property income fell only 29 percent. The remarkable report of the Research and Planning Division of the National Recovery Administration shows that while wages stood at 44 percent of the 1926 level in 1932, and the national income at only 62 percent of that level, dividend payments remained as high as 142 percent of that level. And day by day the downward spiral gained in momentum.

POLICY OF THE RECOVERY PROGRAM AND SECTION 7(A) OF THE N. I. R. A.

It was only when over 15,000,000 people were unemployed, when banks were closed, when business was uprooted, and when our whole economic system hung perilously on the precipice, that we embarked upon a new program. This new program was projected in terms of recovery and reform. It was designated not merely to set the forces of revival in motion, but, above all, to eradicate permanently the evils that had done so much harm in the past.

The first hypothesis was that the interpenetration of all industries throughout the country, the nonconformity of economic organization to State lines, and the deep-seated and wide-spread character of the national calamity, made Nationwide action essential. For the purpose of rationalizing production, outlawing cutthroat competition, and bringing order into the distribution of goods, not only were the antitrust laws in part suspended but the Government itself embarked upon the diametrically opposed policy of stimulating coast-to-coast cooperation among business men. It was thought that in this manner a permanent equilibrium of the various factors in industry might be maintained.

In addition, there was a second phase of the program which struck at the very core of the depression. Congress determined to fix wages and hours at a level that might, by reemployment and higher pay, spread adequate purchasing power among the masses of consumers and thus prime the pump of business. Equally in the foreground was the intent to insure a decent measure of security and comfort to those who worked, while protecting the fair-minded employer from the cutthroat tactics of the exploiting few.

But the Government never for a moment proposed to set up a benevolent despotism, or to extend its arm into every nook and cranny of private business. It did not contemplate regulation of every scale of wages or supervision of every schedule of hours. Acting in an emergency, it desired only to create a solid foundation upon which might be built the mutual efforts of a revived industry and a rehabilitated labor. And if industry and labor were to act in unison, it was clear that they would need equal opportunities for intelligent and effective action. Just as industry was organized, so labor was to be allowed to organize. It was for this purpose that section 7 (a) was written into the National Industrial Recovery Act and reinforced last June by Public Resolution No. 44, providing for the election of representatives for the purpose of collective bargaining.

I think it may be safely said that whatever controversy now rages as to the wisdom of many phases of the recovery program, and of the National Industrial Recovery Act in particular, there is practically unanimous agreement in Congress that section 7 (a) was sound in inception, and that the right of employees to organize and bargain collectively through representatives of their own choosing should be safeguarded at all times. If Congress recognized that right for decades, Congress must shoulder the responsibility to protect it now that employers are more united than ever before in trade associations blanketing the entire country. The developments of the past two years have not given employees any guaranties to which they were not entitled. But the events of the past two years have intensified the social necessity of protecting these guaranties against repudiation.

Document II-42: POLITICAL SYMBOLS: STEVENSON

The effective use of positive symbols—either deliberately or fortuitously—has been rare in twentieth-century America. The towering exception to this statement was Theodore Roosevelt, already shown ornamenting a goldbug (see II-29), who gave cartoonists the choice of a Rough Rider, a teddy bear, a night-time figure of caped glamour (reminiscent of his days as New York City police commissioner), or a grinning diplomat holding behind him a large club. So many symbols attached themselves to "Teddy," however, that one is forced to conclude that these representations show more about the power of his personality than of his political ideas. On the negative side, the early thirties saw one of the most cruelly effective uses of symbols in our history: the ascription of the name "hooverville" to every propped-up conglomeration of packing-crate shelters as refuge for the displaced, unhoused, and unemployed.

The campaign of 1956, although not a close or exciting one, provided the most recent interesting use of symbols. The incumbent, Republican President Dwight D. Eisenhower, needed no symbols. He was the popular, magnetic, and able organizer of the Allied invasion of France in

1945, and as such stood for the kind of calm efficiency which Americans courted in those nervous days of nuclear uncertainties, bipolar international politics, and troublesome Koreas. The flaming sword, worn as a shoulder patch by the men of General "Ike" in the Supreme Headquarters, Allied Expeditionary Forces, Europe, summarized what voters most respected in this man. It was eventually transformed into a monument just south of the White House.

On the Democratic side, for Vice President, was a man who had been nominated in one of the few instances when a presidential candidate has refused to name a running mate and thrown open the choice to the national party convention. The convention chose Estes Kefauver, a Tennessean best known for his relentless and conscientious efforts to end abuses in drug manufacture. He chose as his symbol the coonskin cap, reviving a symbol first used by Benjamin Franklin in his disingenuous effort to appear in the salons of Paris as an unsophisticated frontiersman. Kefauver's choice coincided with a revival of interest in frontier associations and particularly with a nostalgic vogue for Davey Crockett, supposedly "born on a mountaintop in Tennessee." As a political figure, Kefauver had earned the right to associate himself with the frontier qualities of courage, self-reliance, and independence of action.

The presidential candidate, running against Eisenhower for the second time, was the grandson of a former Vice President, Adlai E. Stevenson, a lawyer, New Deal administrator, and successful reform governor of Illinois. Only Woodrow Wilson rivaled Stevenson in twentieth-century politics for appeal to the nation's intellectuals; what he revealed in his urbanity, however, he lacked in that essential common touch. It therefore appeared as something of a godsend when a photographer caught the candidate, sitting with legs crossed on a platform waiting to speak, with a quite visible, jagged hole in the middle of his shoe sole. The picture was widely reproduced and the shoe itself became a symbol broadcast in many forms.

Like Stevenson, the symbol was complex and understated. To some it meant that the candidate, even as you and I, forgot to have his shoes repaired. To some it symbolized the miles he had trod bringing his message to the people. To some it personified an unpretentious public personality who was not ashamed to be caught with his worst foot exposed. It may even have reminded some historically informed voters of the plain, nearly shabby costume worn by Jefferson to his 1800 inauguration. These connotations were seen by Stevenson supporters in contrast to sleek, efficient, impersonal Republicans. The "party of the people," as the Democrats like to style themselves, is the party with holes in its shoes. Somehow there was even a hint of an appeal to the underdog, a supposedly American trait that made supporters of "Champ" Clark in 1912 ready to associate him with a folksong that opened, "Everytime I come to town, Folks keep kickin' my dog aroun'. . . ." Doubtless there was a deliberate attempt to remind voters of the last surprising Democratic triumph, when another folksy underdog from Missouri (Harry S. Truman) had defeated a polished New Yorker to whom nearly everyone had conceded victory.

Stevenson and Kefauver presented themselves as perpetuators of the New Deal position: increased federal watchfulness on behalf of the ordinary citizen; graduated taxation and hence redistribution of wealth; alertness against the creation of special privilege. Toward these familiar reform objectives, the coonskin cap and the worn shoe sole were appro-

Stevenson campaign button

priate symbols. They helped attract over 26 million votes. The flaming sword of the rescuers of France, in the hands of Ike and a young California Senator famous for prosecuting Communists, drew 37.5 million.

SOURCE: Drawing reproduced on a campaign button, approximately 3 1/2 inches in diameter. Courtesy of the Ralph E. Becker Collection, Division of Political History, Smithsonian Institution.

Document II-43: MINORITY VOTING RIGHTS

One of the earliest efforts in political reform is also one of the most current: the extension of the suffrage. An obvious and recent case in point produced 25 million new voters for the presidential election of 1972. Some of these new voters had not been twenty-one years of age in 1968, but most of them would be voting because of the Twenty-sixth Amendment to the Constitution for which ratification was completed on June 30, 1971. The amendment reads:

> 1.   The right of citizens of the United States, who are 18 years of age or older, to vote shall not be denied or abridged by the United States or any state on account of age.
> 2.   The Congress shall have the power to enforce this article by appropriate legislation.

Constitutional guarantees of voting rights have not always been sufficient to make them a reality, however. The Fifteenth Amendment (see II-14), for example, has been one of the most difficult to enforce, even though a mountain of debate, committee reports, court hearings, and legislation has been accumulated on the subject. Voting rights legislation itself has provided enough material for courses and texts. One complication stemmed from the tendency of each new piece of legislation, usually a section in a civil rights act, to appear in the form of an amendment to a prior act.

The Voting Rights Act of 1965 was an attempt to simplify this problem by beginning again from the beginning. It is reproduced at length for several reasons. In the first place, the act shows how detailed and specific the legislation must be to close the loopholes that had allowed for the discouragement of qualified voters. Voting rights had been denied not only because prior legislation had been overly general but also because the enforcement mechanism was neither practical nor detailed; the 1965 Act attempts at length to overcome that fault. Note that Section 10 (c) keeps enforcement proceedings from becoming bogged down in local courts by explicitly routing appeals through district courts to the Supreme Court when necessary.

This act goes beyond the question of Negro voting rights in at least two important respects. Section 4 (e) bears on the question of voters for whom English is not a first language and has particular relevance to another large minority that has tended to be underrepresented at the polls: Spanish-speaking Americans. The poll tax, although used with special effect against Southern Blacks, transcends the race question and harks back to a much older issue: property qualifications for voting. In acting against the poll tax in Section 10 (a and b), this measure recognizes once again that economic and political issues continue to be interrelated and that the modern definition of participatory democracy in America does not include a restriction of the vote to only those who have money to pay a poll tax, however small the actual amount.

SOURCE: *United States Statutes-at-Large*, vol. LXXIX, pp. 437-444, abridged.

PUBLIC LAW 89-110
89TH CONGRESS, S. 1564
AUGUST 6, 1965

An Act

TO ENFORCE THE FIFTEENTH AMENDMENT TO THE CONSTITUTION OF THE
UNITED STATES,
AND FOR OTHER PURPOSES

Be it enacted by the Senate and House of Representatives of the United States of America in Congress assembled, That this Act shall be known as the "Voting Rights Act of 1965".

SEC. 2.   No voting qualification or prerequisite to voting, or standard, practice, or procedure shall be imposed or applied by any State or political subdivision to deny or abridge the right of any citizen of the United States to vote on account of race or color.

SEC. 3.   (a)   Whenever the Attorney General institutes a proceeding under any statute to enforce the guarantees of the fifteenth amendment in any State or political subdivision the court shall authorize the appointment of Federal examiners by the United States Civil Service Commission in accordance with section 6 to serve for such period of time and for such political subdivisions as the court shall determine is appropriate to enforce the guarantees of the fifteenth amendment (1) as part of any interlocutory order if the court determines that the appointment of such examiners is necessary to enforce such guarantees or (2) as part of any final judgment if the court finds that violations of the fifteenth amendment justifying equitable relief have occurred in such State or subdivision: *Provided*, That the court need not authorize the appointment of examiners if any incidents of denial or abridgement of the right to vote on account of race or color (1) have been few in number and have been promptly and effectively corrected by State or local action, (2) the continuing effect of such incidents has been eliminated, and (3) there is no reasonable probability of their recurrence in the future.

(b)   If in a proceeding instituted by the Attorney General under any statute to enforce the guarantees of the fifteenth amendment in any State or political subdivision the court finds that a test or device has been used for the purpose or with the effect of denying or abridging the right of any citizen of the United States to vote on account of race or color, it shall suspend the use of tests and devices in such State or political subdivisions as the court shall determine is appropriate and for such period as it deems necessary. . . .

SEC. 4.   (a)   To assure that the right of citizens of the United States to vote is not denied or abridged on account of race or color, no citizen shall be denied the right to vote in any Federal, State, or local election because of his failure to comply with any test or device in any State with respect to which the determinations have been made. . . .

(e)(1)   Congress hereby declares that to secure the rights under the fourteenth amendment of persons educated in American-flag schools in which the predominant classroom language was other than English, it is necessary to prohibit the States from conditioning the right to vote of such persons on ability to read, write, understand, or interpret any matter in the English language.

(2)   No person who demonstrates that he has successfully completed the sixth primary grade in a public school in, or a private school accredited by, any State or territory, the District of Columbia, or the Commonwealth of Puerto Rico in which the predominant classroom language was other than English, shall be denied the right to vote in any Federal, State, or local election because of his inability to read, write, understand, or interpret any matter in the English language, except that in States in which State law provides that a different level of education is presumptive of literacy, he shall demonstrate that he has successfully completed an equivalent level of education in a public school in, or a private school accredited by, any State or territory, the District of Columbia, or the Commonwealth of Puerto Rico in which the predominant classroom language was other than English. . . .

SEC. 7.   (a)   The examiners for each political subdivision shall, at such places as the Civil Service Commission shall by regulation designate, examine applicants concerning their qualifications for voting. An application to an examiner shall be in such form as the Commission may require and shall contain allegations that the applicant is not otherwise registered to vote.

(b)   Any person whom the examiner finds, in accordance with instructions received under section 9 (b), to have the qualifications prescribed by State law not inconsistent with the Constitution and laws of the United States shall promptly be placed on a list of eligible voters. A challenge to such listing may be made in accordance with section 9 (a) and shall not be the basis for a prosecution under section 12 of this Act. The examiner shall certify and transmit such list, and any supplements as appropriate, at least once a month, to the offices of the appropriate election officials, with copies to the Attorney General and the attorney general of the State, and any such lists and supplements thereto transmitted during the month shall be available for public inspection on the last business day of the month and in any event not later than the forty-fifth day prior to any election. The appropriate State or local election official shall place such names on the official voting list. Any person whose name appears on the examiner's list shall be entitled and allowed to vote in the election district of his residence unless and until the appropriate election officials shall have been notified that such person has been removed from such list in accordance with subsection (d): *Provided*, That no person shall be entitled to vote in any election by virtue of this Act unless his name shall have been certified and transmitted on such a list to the offices of the appropriate election officials at least forty-five days prior to such election.

(c)   The examiner shall issue to each person whose name appears on such a list a certificate evidencing his eligibility to vote.

(d)   A person whose name appears on such a list shall be removed therefrom by any examiner if (1) such person has been successfully challenged in accordance with the procedure prescribed in section 9, or (2) he has been determined by an examiner to have lost his eligibility to vote under State law not inconsistent with the Constitution and the laws of the United States.

SEC. 8.   Whenever an examiner is serving under this Act in any political subdivision, the Civil Service Commission may assign, at the request of the Attorney General, one or more persons, who may be officers of the United States, (1) to enter and attend at any place for holding an election in such subdivision for the purpose of observing whether persons who are entitled to vote are being permitted to vote, and (2) to enter and attend at any place for tabulating the votes cast at any election held in such subdivision for the purpose of observing whether votes cast by persons entitled to vote are being properly tabulated. Such persons so assigned shall report to an examiner appointed for such political subdivision, to the Attorney General, and if the appointment of examiners has been authorized pursuant to section 3 (a), to the court. . . .

SEC. 10.   (a)   The Congress finds that the requirement of the payment of a poll tax as a precondition to voting (i) precludes persons of limited means from voting or imposes unreasonable financial hardship upon such persons as a precondition to their exercise of the franchise, (ii) does not bear a reasonable relationship to any legitimate State interest in the conduct of elections, and (iii) in some areas has the purpose or effect of denying persons the right to vote because of race or color. Upon the basis of these findings, Congress declares that the constitutional right of citizens to vote is denied or abridged in some areas by the requirement of the payment of a poll tax as a precondition to voting.

(b)   In the exercise of the powers of Congress under section 5 of the fourteenth amendment and section 2 of the fifteenth amendment, the

Attorney General is authorized and directed to institute forthwith in the name of the United States such actions, including actions against States or political subdivisions, for declaratory judgment or injunctive relief against the enforcement of any requirement of the payment of a poll tax as a precondition to voting, or substitute therefor enacted after November 1, 1964, as will be necessary to implement the declaration of subsection (a) and the purposes of this section.

(c)   The district courts of the United States shall have jurisdiction of such actions which shall be heard and determined by a court of three judges in accordance with the provisions of section 2284 of title 28 of the United States Code and any appeal shall lie to the Supreme Court. It shall be the duty of the judges designated to hear the case to assign the case for hearing at the earliest practicable date, to participate in the hearing and determination thereof, and to cause the case to be in every way expedited.

(d)   During the pendency of such actions, and thereafter if the courts, notwithstanding this action by the Congress, should declare the requirement of the payment of a poll tax to be constitutional, no citizen of the United States who is a resident of a State or political subdivision with respect to which determinations have been made under subsection 4 (b) and a declaratory judgment has not been entered under subsection 4 (a), during the first year he becomes otherwise entitled to vote by reason of registration by State or local officials or listing by an examiner, shall be denied the right to vote for failure to pay a poll tax if he tenders payment of such tax for the current year to an examiner or to the appropriate State or local official at least forty-five days prior to election, whether or not such tender would be timely or adequate under State law. An examiner shall have authority to accept such payment from any person authorized by this Act to make an application for listing, and shall issue a receipt for such payment. The examiner shall transmit promptly any such poll tax payment to the office of the State or local official authorized to receive such payment under State Law, together with the name and address of the applicant.

SEC. 11.   (a)   No person acting under color of law shall fail or refuse to permit any person to vote who is entitled to vote under any provision of this Act or is otherwise qualified to vote, or willfully fail or refuse to tabulate, count, and report such person's vote.

(b)   No person, whether acting under color of law or otherwise, shall intimidate, threaten, or coerce, or attempt to intimidate, threaten, or coerce any person for voting or attempting to vote, or intimidate, threaten, or coerce, or attempt to intimidate, threaten, or coerce any person for urging or aiding any person to vote or attempt to vote, or intimidate, threaten, or coerce any person for exercising any powers or duties under section 3 (a), 6, 8, 9, 10, or 12 (e).

(c)   Whoever knowingly or willfully gives false information as to his name, address, or period of residence in the voting district for the purpose of establishing his eligibility to register to vote, or conspires with another individual for the purpose of encouraging his false registration to vote or illegal voting, or pays or offers to pay or attempts payment either for registration to vote or for voting shall be fined not more than $10,000 or imprisoned not more than five years, or both: *Provided, however,* That this provision shall be applicable only to general, special, or primary elections held solely or in part for the purpose of selecting or electing any candidate for the office of President, Vice President, presidential elector, Member of the United States Senate, Member of the United States House of Representatives, or Delegates or Commissioners from the territories or possessions, or Resident Commissioner of the Commonwealth of Puerto Rico.

(d)   Whoever, in any matter within the jurisdiction of an examiner or hearing officer knowingly and willfully falsifies or conceals a material fact, or makes any false, fictitious or fraudulent statements or representations, or makes or uses any false writing or document knowing the same to contain any false, fictitious, or fraudulent statement or entry, shall be fined not more than $10,000 or imprisoned not more than five years, or both.

SEC. 12.   (a)   Whoever shall deprive or attempt to deprive any person of any right secured by section 2, 3, 4, 5, 7, or 10 or shall violate section 11 (a) or (b), shall be fined not more than $5,000, or imprisoned not more than five years, or both.

(b)   Whoever, within a year following an election in a political subdivision in which an examiner has been appointed (1) destroys, defaces, mutilates, or otherwise alters the marking of a paper ballot which has been cast in such election, or (2)   alters any official record of voting in such election tabulated from a voting machine or otherwise, shall be fined not more than $5,000, or imprisoned not more than five years, or both.

(c) Whoever conspires to violate the provisions of subsection (a) or (b) of this section, or interferes with any right secured by section 2, 3, 4, 5, 7, 10, or 11 (a) or (b) shall be fined not more than $5,000, or imprisoned not more than five years, or both.

(d) Whenever any person has engaged or there are reasonable grounds to believe that any person is about to engage in any act or practice prohibited by section 2, 3, 4, 5, 7, 10, 11, or subsection (b) of this section, the Attorney General may institute for the United States, or in the name of the United States, an action for preventive relief, including an application for a temporary or permanent injunction, restraining order, or other order, and including an order directed to the State and State or local election officials to require them (1) to permit persons listed under this Act to vote and (2) to count such votes. . . .

Document II-44: BLACK POLITICS IN CONVENTION

Political reformers had long been aware that full participation in the democratic process would not arrive even with perfectly free, untaxed, and uncoerced access to the polls. Behind and beyond the polls lay the political parties, whose methods have only faintly reflected the ideal of broad representation. One way to give the public a greater voice in the party was identified in the direct primary (see II-20). Another, more complex, but perhaps more realistic effort has involved a long struggle within the party to represent fairly all groups to which the party hopes to appeal.

Suggestive in its aims of a voting system called "proportional representation," which has had some success in bringing about fair minority representation in local elections, the Democratic Party began a series of internal reforms first apparent at the 1972 national convention. Adopting guidelines prepared under the sponsorship of Senator George S. McGovern and Congressman Donald M. Fraser, the Party's credentials committee held each state to an open process of delegate selection and to an equitable representation of women, adults under thirty, and ethnic minorities. The result was a convention population which contrasted markedly with the familiar party regulars of former quadrennia. Eighty percent of the faces were new; and issues that had been raised violently outside the party's 1968 Chicago convention were often discussed heatedly but nonviolently within the convention itself. The Republican Party, in the process of adopting similar new rules, may experience a parallel change when it convenes in 1976. On the other hand, George McGovern, following his defeat in the presidential campaign of 1972 and apparently in the interest of restoring harmony in the defeated party, withdrew his support for two of the reform guidelines which had led to increased participation by women and young people and to the exclusion of some of the entrenched local machines. (See the Washington *Post*, April 11, 1973, pp. A-1, 6.) The road to reform has never been straight.

For the last hundred years, more consistent attention has been directed toward the political recognition of black Americans than toward any other minority. The two platforms reproduced below were engendered by associations of Negro voters at an interval of almost exactly one hundred years. The earlier document, coming only seven years after the ending of the Civil War, reveals an understandable loyalty to the party which had freed the slaves and saved the Union. In spite of the grievous tone of the sections that enumerate the black man's mistreatment, there is a pathetically frank admission that activities outside the GOP would be pointless. Instead of the threat of independent power, there is but a hope that party loyalty, if honored by the Negro voter, will be rewarded with party-sponsored redress for his civil wounds.

The more recent document falls into a tradition reminiscent of the Populists, Progressives, and other elements that had despaired of help from either major party. That independent action could be contemplated in 1972 was due to many changes: to the enforcement of voting and civil rights legislation, to social and economic advances, and to the demographic shifts that made the Negro an element of the national—as opposed to predominantly regional—population. The "Gary Manifesto," as this document was called, fell on attentive ears in both major parties; Democrats and Republicans were more avid than ever in their pursuit of the black vote. Nor was the publication of this manifesto and the reforms in the selection of major-party delegates in the same year a mere coincidence.

SOURCE: A: Edward McPherson, *A Hand-Book of Politics for 1872.* Washington, Philp & Solomons, 1872, pp. 212-13. B: The preamble to the National Black Political Convention as printed in the Washington *Post*, March 19, 1972, p. B3. Courtesy of the Washington *Post.*

A: NATIONAL COLORED CONVENTION.

New Orleans, April 10-14, 1872

[Met under call of the "southern States convention of colored men," issued from Columbia, South Carolina, October 18, 1871.]

THE PLATFORM

Regretting the necessity which has called into existence a colored convention, and deeply sensible of the responsibilities which have been intrusted to our consideration, we hereby acknowledge our gratitude for past triumphs in behalf of equal rights, and respectfully submit our peculiar grievances to the immediate attention of the American people in the following platform and resolutions:

1. We thank God, the friends of universal liberty in this and other lands, the bravery of colored soldiers, and the loyalty of the colored people for our emancipation, our citizenship, and our enfranchisement.

2. Owing our political emancipation in this country to Republican legislation, to which all other parties and political shades of opinion were unjustly and bitterly opposed, we would be blind to our prospects and false to our best interests did we identify ourselves with any other organization; and as all roads out of the Republican party lead into the Democratic camp, we pledge our unswerving devotion to support the nominees of the Philadelphia convention.

3. We sincerely and gratefully indorse the administration of President U. S. Grant in maintaining our liberties, in protecting us in our privileges, in punishing our enemies; in the dawn of recognition of the claims of men without regard to color, by appointing us to important official positions at home and abroad; in the assurances that he has given to defend our rights, and that while we in our gratefulness acknowledge and appreciate his efforts in behalf of equal rights, we are not unmindful of his glory as a soldier and his exalted virtues as a statesman.

4. Our thanks are due and are hereby tendered to President Grant for overriding the precedents of prejudice in the better recognition of the services of men without regard to color in some parts of the country, and we earnestly pray that colored Republicans of States where there are no

Federal positions given to colored men may no longer be ignored, but that they may be stimulated by some recognition of Federal patronage.

5.   It would be an ingratitude, loathed by men and abhorred by God, did we not acknowledge our overwhelming indebtedness to the services of the Hon. Charles Sumner, who stood for a long time alone in the Senate of the United States the Gibraltar of our cause and the north star of our hopes; who forfeited caste in the estimation of a large portion of his countrymen by his unswerving devotion to equal rights; who has been maligned for his fidelity to principles; who has been stricken down by an assassin for advocating liberty throughout all the land and unto all the inhabitants thereof, and in whose giant body, rising as it were almost out of the grave to marshal the hosts of impartial justice with his mighty ideas, going to the farthest part of the land, and finding a responsive echo in the triumph of liberty over slavery, we have an assurance of this good, great, and beloved patriot that he will be as faithful to the Republican party in the future as he has been unfaltering in the past.

6.   Having been by solemn legislation of the American Congress raised to the dignity of citizenship, we appeal to law-abiding people of the States, and especially to those who in the days of the fugitive slave law exhorted obedience to statutes however offensive, to protect and defend us in the enjoyment of our just rights and privileges upon all conveyances which are common carriers, at all resorts of public amusements, where tastes are cultivated and manhood is quickened, and in all places of public character or corporate associations which owe their existence to the legislation of the nation or States; against the spirit of slavery, which attempts to degrade our standard of intelligence and virtue by forcing our refined ladies and gentlemen into smoking-cars amid obscenity and vulgarity; which humiliates our pride by denying us first-class accommodations on steamboats, and compelling us to eat and sleep with servants, for which we are charged the same as those who have the best accommodations; and which closes the doors of hotels against famishing colored persons, however wealthy, intelligent, or respectable they may be, while all such public places and conveyances welcome and entertain all white persons, whatever may be their character, who may apply. Now, in view of this disgraceful inconsistency, this affectation or prejudice, this rebellion against the laws of God, humanity, and the nation, we appeal to the justice of the American people to protect us in our Civil rights in public places and upon public conveyances, which are

readily accorded, and very justly, to the most degraded specimens of our white fellow citizens.

7.   That wherever Republicans have betrayed color constituencies, we recommend that better men be elected to succeed them, and especially do we pledge ourselves to elect successors in Congress, wherever we have the power, to every Republican who voted against or dodged the supplementary civil rights bill recently introduced into the United States Senate by Hon. Charles Sumner; and also successors to those who shall not show a satisfactory record on the civil rights bill now in the United States House of Representatives.

8.   That while men professing strong radical sentiments, and elected to Congress by overwhelming majorities of colored voters, were found voting against the supplementary civil rights bill in the Senate of the United States, we honor that manly exhibition of devotion to the principles of the Republican party which influenced the Hon. Schyler Colfax, Vice President of the United States, to honor the cause of justice by recording his casting vote as President of the Senate in favor of equality before the law as indicated in the supplementary civil rights bill as it passed the Senate by virtue of the aforesaid casting vote.

9.   That we, in the name of the colored men of the United States, repudiate any sympathy or connection whatever with the late Labor Reform convention, lately held at Columbus, Ohio, and also the convention of Liberal Republicans called for the 1st of May, 1872, at Cincinnati.

FOLLOWING IS THE PREAMBLE ADOPTED BY THE NATIONAL BLACK POLITICAL CONVENTION HELD AT GARY, IND., ON MARCH 11 [1972].

We come to Gary in an hour of great crisis and tremendous promise for black America. While the white nation hovers on the brink of chaos, while its politicians offer no hope of real change, we stand on the edge of history and are faced with an amazing and frightening choice: We may choose in 1972 to slip back into the decadent white politics of American life, or we may press forward, moving relentlessly from Gary to the creation of our own black life. The choice is large, but the time is very short.

Let there be no mistake. We come to Gary in a time of unrelieved crisis for our people. From every rural community in Alabama to the high-rise compounds of Chicago, we bring to this convention the agonies of the masses of our people. From the sprawling black cities of Watts and Nairobi in the West to the decay of Harlem and Roxbury in the East, the testimony we bear is the same. We are witnesses to social disaster.

Our cities are crime-haunted, dying grounds. Huge sectors of our youth—and countless others—face permanent unemployment. Those of us who work find our paychecks able to purchase less and less. Neither the courts nor the prisons contribute to anything resembling justice or reformation. The schools are unable—or unwilling—to educate our children for the real world of our struggles. Meanwhile, the officially approved epidemic of drugs threatens to wipe out the minds and strength of our best young warriors.

Economic, cultural, and spiritual depression stalk black America, and the price for survival often appears to be more than we are able to pay. On every side, in every area of our lives, the American institutions in which we have placed our trust are unable to cope with the crises they have created by their single-minded dedication to profits for some and white supremacy above all.

And beyond these shores there is more of the same. For while we are pressed down under all the dying weight of a bloated, inwardly decaying white civilization, many of our brothers in Africa and the rest of the Third World have fallen prey to the same powers of exploitation and deceit. Wherever America faces the unorganized, politically powerless forces of the non-white world, its goal is domination by any means necessary—as if to hide from itself the crumbling of its own systems of life and work.

But Americans cannot hide. They can run to China and the moon and to the edges of consciousness, but they cannot hide. The crises we face as black people are the crises of the entire society. They go deep, to the very bones and marrow, to the essential nature of America's economic, political, and cultural systems. They are the natural end-product of a society built on the twin foundations of white racism and white capitalism.

So, let it be clear to us now: The desperation of our people, the agonies of our cities, the desolation of our countryside, the pollution of the air and the water—these things will not be significantly affected by new faces in the old places in Washington, D.C. This is the truth we must face here in Gary if we are to join our people everywhere in the movement forward toward liberation.

A black political convention, indeed all truly black politics must begin from this truth: The American system does not work for the masses of our people, and it cannot be made to work without radical fundamental change. (Indeed, this system does not really work in favor of the humanity of anyone in America.)

In the light of such realities, we come to Gary and are confronted with a choice. Will we believe the truth that history presses into our face—or will we, too, try to hide. Will the small favors some of us have received blind us to the larger sufferings of our people, or open our eyes to the testimony of our history in America?

For more than a century we have followed the path of political dependence on white men and their systems. From the Liberty Party in the decades before the Civil War, to the Republican Party of Abraham Lincoln, we trusted in white men and white politics as our deliverers. Sixty years ago, W. E. B. DuBois said he would give Woodrow Wilson and the Democrats their "last chance" to prove their sincere commitment to equality for black people—and he was given white riots and official segregation in peace and in war.

Nevertheless, some 20 years later, we became Democrats in the name of Franklin Roosevelt, then supported his successor Harry Truman, and even tried a "non-partisan" Republican General of the Army named Eisenhower. We were wooed like many others by the superficial liberalism of John F. Kennedy and the make-believe populism of Lyndon Johnson. Let there be no more of that.

Here at Gary, let us never forget that while the times and the names and the parties have continually changed, one truth has faced us insistently, never changing: Both parties have betrayed us whenever their interests conflicted with ours (which was most of the time), and whenever our forces were unorganized and dependent, quiescent and compliant. Nor should this be surprising, for by now we must know that the American political system, like all other white institutions in America, was designed to operate for the benefit of the white race: It was never meant to do anything else.

That is the truth that we must face at Gary. If white "liberalism" could have solved our problems, then Lincoln and Roosevelt and Kennedy would have done so. But they did not solve ours nor the rest of the nation's. If America's problems could have been solved by forceful, politically skilled and aggressive individuals, then Lyndon Johnson would have retained the Presidency. If the true "American Way" of unbridled monopoly capitalism, combined with a ruthless military imperialism could do it, then Nixon would not be running in panic around the world, or making speeches comparing his nation's decadence to that of Greece and Rome.

If we have never faced it before, let us face it at Gary: The profound crisis of black people and the disaster of America are not simply caused by men, nor will they be solved by men alone. These crises are the crises of basically flawed economics and politics, and of cultural degradation. None of the Democratic candidates and none of the Republican candidates—regardless of their vague promises to us or to their white constituencies—can solve our problems or the problems of this country without radically changing the systems by which it operates.

So we come to Gary confronted with a choice. But it is not the old convention question of which candidate shall we support, the pointless question of who is to preside over a decaying and unsalvageable system. No, if we come to Gary out of the realities of the black communities of this land, then the only real choice for us is whether or not we will live by the truth we know, whether we will move to struggle for fundamental transformation, for the creation of new directions, toward a concern for the life and the meaning of man. Social transformation or social destruction, those are our only real choices.

If we have come to Gary on behalf of our people in America, in the rest of this hemisphere, and in the Homeland—if we have come for our own best ambitions—then a new black politics must come to birth. If we are serious, the black politics of Gary must accept major responsibility for creating both the atmosphere and the program for fundamental, far-ranging change in America. Such responsibility is ours because it is our people who are most deeply hurt and ravaged by the present systems of society. That responsibility for leading the change is ours because we live in a society where few other men really believe in the responsibility of a truly humane society for anyone anywhere.

The challenge is thrown to us here in Gary. It is the challenge to consolidate and organize our own black role as the vanguard in the struggle for a new society. To accept that challenge is to move to independent black politics. There can be no equivocation on that issue. History leaves us no other choice. White politics has not and cannot bring the changes we need.

We come to Gary and are faced with a challenge. The challenge is to transform ourselves from favor-seeking vassals and loud-talking, "militant" pawns, and to take up the role that the unorganized masses of our people have attempted to play ever since we came to these shores: that of harbingers of true justice and humanity, leaders in the struggle for liberation.

A major part of the challenge we must accept is that of redefining the functions and operations of all levels of American government, for the existing governing structures—from Washington to the smallest county—are obsolescent. That is part of the reason why nothing works and why corruption rages throughout public life. For white politics seeks not to serve but to dominate and manipulate.

We will have joined the true movement of history if at Gary we grasp the opportunity to press man forward as the first consideration of politics. Here at Gary we are faithful to the best hopes of our fathers and our people if we move for nothing less than a politics which places community before individualism, love before sexual exploitation, a living environment before profits, peace before war, justice before unjust "order," and morality before expediency.

This is the society we need, but we delude ourselves here at Gary if we think that change can be achieved without organizing the power, the determined national black power, which is necessary to insist upon such change, to create such change, to seize change.

So when we turn to a black agenda for the seventies, we move in the truth of history, in the reality of the moment. We move recognizing that no one else is going to represent our interests but ourselves. The society we seek cannot come unless black people organize to advance its coming. We lift up a black agenda recognizing that white America moves toward the abyss created by its own racist arrogance, misplaced priorities, rampant materialism, and ethical bankruptcy. Therefore, we are certain that the agenda we now press for in Gary is not only for the future of black humanity, but is probably the only way the rest of America can save itself from the harvest of its criminal past.

So, brothers and sisters of our developing black nation, we now stand at Gary as a people whose time has come. From every corner of black America, from all liberation movements of the Third World, from the graves of our fathers and the coming world of our children, we are faced with a challenge and a call. Though the moment is perilous we must not despair. We must seize the time, for the time is ours.

We begin here and now in Gary. We begin with an independent black political movement, an independent black political agenda, an independent black spirit. Nothing less will do. We must build for our people. We must build for our world. We stand on the edge of history. We cannot turn back.

Document II-45: DIRECT ELECTION OF THE PRESIDENT

Efforts to perfect the machinery of American democracy, to allow it to represent the population more accurately and to increase the level of popular participation, continue to the present moment and possess a momentum that will propel them into the near future, at least. Three examples of causes-in-progress will represent the situation.

For the last several years the visitor to the national capital may have wondered at the bumper stickers with the legend "D.C. The Last Colony." The reference is to the fact that residents of the District of Columbia have had no vote in either local or national elections throughout most of the history of this community. Pressure to end that condition has gradually but steadily mounted over the years. Grudgingly, concessions have been made. As of 1972, a resident of the District may vote for party committee persons, school-board members, presidential primary and electoral candidates, and for a member of the House of Representatives who has no vote. The city has a mayor and a council; these appointive offices became elective only in 1974. The right to elect voting members of Congress awaits the future. If the history of political change in this country has any meaning, however, home rule for the District of Columbia will be granted; the question is only how soon.

A second example could be made of the pressures applied by party reformers and the courts to force the states to redefine political units in terms that accurately reflect shifts in population. To adjust voting districts in defiance of logic and geography is an art as old as voting. One thinks of England's "rotton boroughs" and the early Massachusetts resourcefulness that produced the famous "gerrymander." Yet, in a country of growth and change, inaccurate representation can occur as much by neglect as by connivance. It was therefore important that the courts recognized their responsibility to enforce periodic reapportionment of voting districts. To be sure, redistricting can still be made to serve partisan ends, but the general direction of this change has been toward accurate representation. (See Richard Claude, *The Supreme Court and the Electoral Process.* Baltimore, Johns Hopkins University, 1970.)

A more long-standing (see II-20) and more truly national issue is represented in the following document. The proposed amendment would abolish the electoral college and put the selection of a President directly in the hands of voters (the term "elector" in the proposal is used as synonymous with "voter"). The principal sponsor of this proposal, Senator Birch Bayh, has pointed to both the injustices of the past and the dangers of the present—particularly when more than two candidates appear on the ballot. In defending this reform he has declared that any system should guarantee that the recipient of the most popular votes be elected and that each voter have an equal voice in the electoral process. "Only direct popular elections meet these tests." (Press Release dated February, 1970.)

Senator Bayh cited an opinion poll that placed 81 percent of the population behind his reform and added the endorsement of then-President Richard Nixon. However, when Senator Bayh's report came from committee to the Senate, it contained a lengthy minority report against the direct election of the President signed by six of his colleagues who nearly outweighed the majority in terms of seniority. In spite of the obvious dangers and inequities present in the electoral college, its abolition may not be near at hand.

SOURCE: "Direct Popular Election of the President," issued as U. S. Senate Report #1123, Ninety-first Congress, second session. August 14, 1970. Abridged.

SENATE REPORT

The Committee on the Judiciary, to which was referred the resolution (S.J. Res. 1) proposing an amendment to the Constitution of the United States relating to the election of the President and the Vice President, having considered the same, reports favorably thereon, with an amendment in the nature of a substitute, and recommends that the resolution, as amended, do pass.

The text of Senate Joint Resolution 1, as amended, is as follows:

AN AMENDMENT IN THE NATURE OF A SUBSTITUTE

That the following article is proposed as an amendment to the Constitution of the United States, which shall be valid to all intents and purposes as part of the Constitution when ratified by the legislatures of three-fourths of the several States within 7 years from the date of its submission by the Congress:

ARTICLE —

SECTION 1.   The people of the several States and the District constituting the seat of government of the United States shall elect the President and Vice President. Each elector shall cast a single vote for two persons who shall have consented to the joining of their names as candidates for the offices of President and Vice President. No candidate shall consent to the joinder of his name with that of more than one other person.

SEC. 2.   The electors of President and Vice President in each State shall have the qualifications requisite for electors of the most numerous branch of the State legislature, except that for electors of President and Vice President, the legislature of any State may prescribe less restrictive residence qualifications and for electors of President and Vice President the Congress may establish uniform residence qualifications.

SEC. 3.   The pair of persons having the greatest number of votes for President and Vice President shall be elected, if such number be at least 40 per centum of the whole number of votes cast for such offices. If no pair of persons has such number, a runoff election shall be held in which the choice of President and Vice President shall be made from the two pairs of persons who received the highest number of votes.

SEC. 4.   The times, places, and manner of holding such elections and entitlement to inclusion on the ballot shall be prescribed in each State by the legislature thereof; but the Congress may at any time by law make or alter such regulations. The days for such elections shall be determined by Congress and shall be uniform throughout the United States. The Congress shall prescribe by law the time, place, and manner in which the results of such elections shall be ascertained and declared.

SEC. 5.   The Congress may by law provide for the case of the death, inability, or withdrawal of any candidate for President or Vice President before a President and Vice President have been elected, and for the case of the death of both the President-elect and Vice-President-Elect.

SEC. 6.   The Congress shall have power to enforce this article by appropriate legislation.

SEC. 7.   This article shall take effect 1 year after the 15th day of April following ratification.

PURPOSE OF THE PROPOSED CONSTITUTIONAL AMENDMENT

Senate Joint Resolution 1 proposes an amendment to the Constitution of the United States to abolish the antiquated electoral college and undemocratic "unit vote" system and substitute direct popular election of the President and Vice President. The proposed amendment provides, further, that in the unlikely event no candidate receives at least 40 percent of the total popular vote, a runoff election shall be held between the top two candidates. . . .

Document II-46: ANTI-MONOPOLY IN THE SENATE

A tradition that can be traced back to attacks on the state and federal banks also goes on. It opens with accusations against the centers of wealth and nonelective power. Special privilege is alleged: government subsidy, absence of necessary regulation, tax loopholes. The wealth is said to be based on something other than productive work and fair return on investment. Government is therefore asked to withdraw the special privilege and—expanding its powers if necessary—provide the kind of regulation in the public interest that will ensure economic equity.

The document offered below is a classic example of the pattern described above. It shows itself a product of 1971 in the stress it places on environmental pollution and racial discrimination. More traditional is the insistence that the proposal will alleviate poverty and that it will enhance—rather than destroy—competitive enterprise. The student of reform rhetoric will also be reassured to note that even a figure on the contemporary political left will conclude his peroration by insisting that his proposal takes its ultimate validity from the manner in which it would fulfill that highest goal of all: the realization of the intentions of the Founding Fathers.

Another interesting aspect of this proposal is the way in which it stresses the viewpoint of the consumer. Not since the turn of the century with its consumer leagues and consumer cooperatives has the nation seen so much interest in the consumer, or so many appeals to his power. Ralph Nader, to whom Senator Harris alludes in a section not quoted, has received most of the headlines on this front, first by alerting automobile owners to dangerous defects in mass-produced cars. The point was well enough made so that manufacturers have come to recall large numbers of cars rather than face damaging consumer rebukes, and Presidents have come to have advisers on consumer affairs.

Senator Fred R. Harris of Oklahoma has been interesting to a student of reform for more reasons than are suggested by this anti-monopoly bill. He has been largely responsible, during 1971-72, for the revived currency of the term "populism"—for a while seeking the Democratic presidential nomination and for a while offering to be a "populist" candidate. In common with the Populists of the late nineteenth century is his interest in attacking not only the manufacturing monopolies singled out below, but also the phenomenon now called "agribusiness," meaning heavily capitalized industries owning large tracts of land, and practicing monopolistic combinations of farming, extractive industry, manufacturing, distribution, and sales. Like the older Populists he has sought to represent the small farmer and has despaired of significant help in the major parties. Unlike the Populists he has not singled out the railroads and the Eastern bankers as prime villains; he has not asked for currency inflation; he has shown no strains of nativism in the Populistic sense; and he has to date remained within the Democratic Party.

SOURCE: *The Congressional Record*, vol. CXVII, pp. 15442-3, 15446, abridged. September 30, 1971. Senator Harris drew the data for this report from a number of sources, but principally from William G. Shepherd, *Market Power and Economic Welfare*. New York, Random House, 1970.

CONCENTRATED INDUSTRIES ACT

Mr. HARRIS. Mr. President, today I am introducing a bill which attacks the fundamental source of inordinate concentration of economic power in this country—the monopoly power of big corporations.

I believe we can be faithful to America's free enterprise tradition and make it work. We can meet the challenge of growing foreign competition. We can cut consumer prices significantly. We can speed technological innovation.

The American consumer loses a minimum of $50 to $60 billion because of shared monopolies. If our Government moves aggressively against these shared monopolies, prices will fall by as much as 20 percent. Our economy will move toward full employment and stable prices without inordinate Government controls.

Concentrated economic power often becomes concentrated political power as well.

As President Nixon indicated in August of this year, the old remedies to control inflation do not work any more. They will not work until we cut down the power of the big corporations to raise prices without regard to market pressures.

We must return to real competition in our economy. We must make the free enterprise system work.

Now is the time for the Congress to challenge the myth that big is always best, that what is good for the big corporations like GM is good for the American people. We must face up to the mountain of evidence to the contrary.

I hope this legislation will focus the attention of the Congress and the country on the heavy burden the average American carries because of monopolies.

It is time for fundamental reform.

Mr. President, I appreciate that it has been the fashion in our country to dismiss those who believe industrial reform in America is an urgent matter. On the one hand, we have been told that there is no such thing as monopoly in America. The "trusts" of the late 19th century were, one learns in high school civics classes, all broken up, or at least broken up as much as the country thought desirable, by Teddy Roosevelt in the first decade of this century. But when evidence is presented that this view of the matter is not entirely accurate—that industrial monopolies are still very much with us—we are taught by some that these monopolies of the "new industrial state" are performing well and hence should be tolerated and even encouraged. Several questions are thus presented:

First. Do we actually have a significant amount of monopoly in America?

Second. If so, is it increasing or decreasing?

Third. If there are monopolies in America, are their net economic and social effects, from the standpoint of the general public, good, bad, or indifferent?

I have concluded that we do indeed have a serious monopoly problem in this country; that it is getting larger, not smaller; and that it is imposing a very large social cost on our citizens. . . .

I think it is a fair summary of the economic evidence on monopoly in America to say, Mr. President, that a reduction in concentration in our important industries could reasonably be expected to have at least the following effects:

First. A lowering of prices across the board to the consumer by perhaps 20 percent or more, thus immediately increasing consumer purchasing power or real standard of living by that amount.

Second. A staunching of the gigantic flow of unearned monopoly profits that America's monopolists and oligopolists are currently "redistributing" from consumers to themselves each year.

Third. A dispersal of the great masses of economic power that are currently causing, by this private "redistribution" of income away from others and to themselves and their stockholders—and their use of that power to influence our legal and political processes—so much social unrest in the country.

Fourth. A significant reduction in the incidence of poverty in the country and the social illnesses—particularly crime—that poverty inevitably spawns, by effecting a fairer, more equitable distribution of income.

Fifth. A further reduction of poverty and unjustified income inequality by permanently eliminating the inflation-unemployment dilemma, the black box of despair we've gotten ourselves into that requires us to keep 5 million of our citizens out of work, and 27 percent of our plant capacity idle—at a cost of $70 billion in real wealth down the drain each year—in order to contain an inflation created by a few dozen corporate executives.

Sixth. A restoration of our strength in international markets by this increase in the competitiveness of our industries and the resulting lowering of their prices.

Seventh. A stimulation of the inventive and innovative capacity of our industries by eliminating the high concentration that leads them, at present, to conspire among themselves to suppress rather than promote innovations that would have improved the health, safety, and general welfare of our citizens.

Eighth. Last but hardly least, a lessening, by removing the monopoly profits that make such uneconomic practices possible, of the racial discrimination in employment that so tragically gives the lie to the promise of equal opportunity in America.

Mr. President, a distinguished panel of economic and legal experts appointed by President Johnson to study this problem of monopoly in America, the "White House Task Force on Antitrust Policy," issued a detailed report of its findings, conclusions, and recommendations in 1968. Finding that the antitrust agencies, the Federal Trade Commission and the Antitrust Division of the Department of Justice, have refused over the years to use the existing antitrust laws to deconcentrate our major monopolies and oligopolies, this group recommended the passage of a new statute, a "Concentrated Industries Act," one that would make it the affirmative duty of those two agencies to bring deconcentration suits against all major "oligopoly industries" a term defined in the proposed statute as an industry first, having sales of $500 million or more and second, in which the four largest firms had accounted for 70 percent or more of the industry's sales for a designated period of years. A special antitrust court is proposed to hear these deconcentration cases. And a "scale-economies" defense is provided: Deconcentration would not be ordered if, in order to reduce the firms in the industry to the prescribed level—no firm with more than 12 percent of the industry's total sales—it could be shown that inefficiencies would be created and consumer prices thus increased.

This proposed statute is, on the whole, a sound if perhaps unduly conservative one. Its "cut-off point" between legal and illegal concentration, for example, four-firm shares of 70 percent or more, is clearly on the high side. A voluminous body of economic data goes to the point that, whereas collusion—price fixing—may not even be necessary in order for a group of firms to impose monopoly prices when four of them control 70 percent or more of the market, such collusion is rampant in the intermediate concentration ranges of tight oligopoly, those between four-firm shares of 50 percent and 70 percent. This statute would, however, according to Dr. Shepherd's figures on current concentration, reach approximately one-third of all U.S. manufacturing even in its present form. That is to say, in making four-firm shares of 70 percent or more unlawful, it would reach industries that currently account for, by Dr. Shepherd's data, 34 percent of all manufacturing output.

With these considerations in mind, Mr. President, I am introducing the Concentrated Industries Act drafted by the President's Task Force on Antitrust Policy in 1968, but with the view of proposing, if further study confirms my present feeling that it should be strengthened in one or more particulars, appropriate amendments.

It is, even in its present form, Mr. President, a landmark bill, one that would go, I believe, a long way indeed toward restoring economic justice in America.

One further point should be emphasized here, Mr. President. All of the evils I have described here are, in my view—and in that of a number of distinguished scholars in this area—already illegal under existing antitrust law. Section 2 of the Sherman Act of 1890, for example, declares it unlawful to "monopolize" any part of the trade or commerce of the United States. And violations of that statute are, by long-standing judicial interpretation, also violations of section 5 of the Federal Trade Commission Act of 1914. The officials charged with the enforcement of these two statutes have, however, resolutely refused for more than half a century to bring deconcentration lawsuits, contenting themselves with an occasional action against isolated examples of price-fixing and coercive acts of one businessman against another. These officials insist that, absent a showing of actual collusion on price, there is nothing wrong with four firms gathering 50 percent or 70 percent of an industry's sales volume into their hands and then exercising that monopoly power by overcharging the consuming public by the billions of dollars I have called to your attention here today.

I have concluded, therefore, that, despite the apparent adequacy of the existing law to deal with monopoly in America, there is no way to get it enforced in its present permissive form. Given the well-known power of the monopolies to influence the regulatory agencies in Washington, there is no way to get relief for the public from the looting involved here other than to define the evil in question in sharp numerical terms and then make it mandatory for the officials involved to carry out the deconcentration ordered by the statute.

Monopolies have ostensibly been illegal in America since 1890, Mr. President. For these past 80 years, however, the antitrust laws have been just one more of the long list of our broken promises to our people. Eight decades of failure to honor the key promise of economic democracy in America are enough. If the people of this country, and the peoples of the other countries of the world, are to take our boasts of economic justice seriously, it is time for us to take them seriously ourselves. I would lift this scourge of monopoly and the corruption it brings from the backs of the American people and make our country the real economic democracy the Founding Fathers intended it to be.

Document II-47: JOHNSON ON POVERTY

It is fitting to conclude this section with a look at the question of poverty, since the distribution of wealth is, in the most literal sense, a test of the success or failure of the whole history of political and economic reform. Has the American system—broadening the electorate, honing the implements of participatory government—been able to reduce the extremes of wealth and poverty and produce, after two hundred years, something approaching economic equity?

A generation ago, the answer to this question seemed rather smugly affirmative. The Depression and World War II had indeed redistributed income to some extent. The wealthy paid more taxes and the poor had found wartime jobs. A postwar boom prolonged the feeling that things were getting better for everyone. (See Frederick L. Allen, *The Big Change.* New York, Harper, 1952.) For most middle- and upper-class Americans this euphoria lasted until the disturbances in Watts and other ghettoes dramatized the depths of urban poverty or until they were slapped in the face with Michael Harrington's *The Other America: Poverty in the United States* (New York, Macmillan, 1962) or some comparable shock. Contemporary concern with poverty dated from the early sixties. It was marked by a return to the kind of photojournalism that had made Louis Hine and Jacob Riis famous (see also II-39). It engendered poor people's armies, marches, and coalitions. Another symptom was the concern of President Kennedy, who had begun to work toward the program eventually set forth by President Johnson in the accompanying message to Congress.

Today's answer to the question of wealth distribution is confused.

Most econometrists agree that, over the long haul, the share of America's economic pie has remained fairly constant in its apportionment between rich and poor. There have been periods when differences were exaggerated; there have been eras when the trends shifted one way or another. But the basic triumph of the American economy was in creating an ever-expanding pie so that the poor, even with no better percentage of wealth, could be better off in absolute terms. Since the data base for these conclusions is neither perfect nor complete, there are those (fewer in number) who come to other conclusions: who insist that America is constantly leveling its wealth-distribution curve or that the meaning emerges only when compared with the experience of other industrial societies.

Likewise, the nature and extent of poverty is actively argued. Some scholars (Daniel P. Moynihan) find conditions that would tend to keep certain groups permanently at the low end of the scale, while others (Stephan Thernstrom) point out the absence of any body of evidence defining a permanent core of indigent. Special groups have been singled out for help in local, state, and federal programs: migrant workers, ghetto dwellers, residents of Appalachia and the Ouachita Valley. The results of these programs would prove neither case conclusively.

Poverty is not just a matter of food, dollars, and demography; it is also a state of mind. In a culture concerned with growth and material abundance, it is not surprising that the level of poor people's desires should also be rising. For example, as recently as 1968 the accepted minimum annual income for a family of four was $3,200. By 1972 a Poor People's Coalition had mustered considerable pressure for a federal program supporting this same family of four at the more-than-doubled minimum of $6,500. Clearly, one can have a great deal more income today (even discounting inflation) and still be considered poor. Still outweighing the welfare pressure groups, however, is the familiar work ethic which conditions the views of most Americans of all classes. Hence programs that guarantee income are still less popular than those that seek to guarantee work.

However the data are interpreted, the President's message strongly suggests that Americans still accept the challenge of impoving economic democracy. At the moment, the method of meeting this challenge is under considerable debate. The federal programs enacted under Lyndon

Johnson did not meet with great success, nor have the programs of his successors. There is increasing talk of a negative income tax, of tax reforms involving flat federal payments to the poor, of work or income guarantees. (A convenient place to consult a number of viewpoints on poverty, income distribution, and proposed solutions is Kenneth S. Davis, ed., *The Paradox of Poverty in America*. New York, Wilson, 1969.) Despite the disagreement over means, it is evident that the reformer in this politico-economic tradition will not rest until the last voter has registered and the last poor person has been provided with economic citizenship.

SOURCE: President Lyndon B. Johnson's message to Congress of March 16, 1964, as reproduced in *Public Papers of the Presidents of the United States: Lyndon B. Johnson*. Washington, D.C., Government Printing Office, 1965, vol. I, pp. 375-380, abridged.

PRESIDENTIAL MESSAGE

To the Congress of the United States:

We are citizens of the richest and most fortunate Nation in the history of the world.

One hundred and eighty years ago we were a small country struggling for survival on the margin of a hostile land.

Today we have established a civilization of free men which spans an entire continent.

With the growth of our country has come opportunity for our people—opportunity to educate our children, to use our energies in productive work, to increase our leisure—opportunity for almost every American to hope that through work and talent he could create a better life for himself and his family.

The path forward has not been an easy one.

But we have never lost sight of our goal: an America in which every citizen shares all the opportunities of his society, in which every man has a chance to advance his welfare to the limit of his capabilities.

We have come a long way toward this goal.

We still have a long way to go.

The distance which remains is the measure of the great unfinished work of our society.

To finish that work I have called for a national war on poverty. Our objective: total victory.

There are millions of Americans—one fifth of our people—who have not shared in the abundance which has been granted to most of us, and on whom the gates of opportunity have been closed.

What does this poverty mean to those who endure it?

It means a daily struggle to secure the necessities for even a meager existence. It means that the abundance, the comforts, the opportunities they see all around them are beyond their grasp.

Worst of all, it means hopelessness for the young.

The young man or woman who grows up without a decent education, in a broken home, in a hostile and squalid environment, in ill health or in the face of racial injustice—that young man or woman is often trapped in a life of poverty.

He does not have the skills demanded by a complex society. He does not know how to acquire those skills. He faces a mounting sense of despair which drains initiative and ambition and energy.

Our tax cut will create millions of new jobs—new exits from poverty.

But we must also strike down all the barriers which keep many from using those exits.

The war on poverty is not a struggle simply to support people, to make them dependent on the generosity of others.

It is a struggle to give people a chance.

It is an effort to allow them to develop and use their capacities, as we have been allowed to develop and use ours, so that they can share, as others share, in the promise of this Nation.

We do this, first of all, because it is right that we should.

From the establishment of public education and land grant colleges through agricultural extension and encouragement to industry, we have pursued the goal of a Nation with full and increasing opportunities for all its citizens.

The war on poverty is a further step in that pursuit.

We do it also because helping some will increase the prosperity of all.

Our fight against poverty will be an investment in the most valuable of our resources—the skills and strength of our people.

And in the future, as in the past, this investment will return its cost manyfold to our entire economy.

If we can raise the annual earnings of 10 million among the poor by only $1000 we will have added $14 billion a year to our national output. In addition, we can make important reductions in public assistance payments which now cost us $4 billion a year, and in the large costs of fighting crime and delinquency, disease and hunger.

This is only part of the story.

Our history has proved that each time we broaden the base of abundance, giving more people the chance to produce and consume, we create new industry, higher production, increased earnings and better income for all.

Giving new opportunity to those who have little will enrich the lives of all the rest.

Because it is right, because it is wise, and because, for the first time in our history, it is possible to conquer poverty, I submit for the consideration of the Congress and the country, the Economic Opportunity Act of 1964.

The Act does not merely expand old programs or improve what is already being done.

It charts a new course.

It strikes at the causes, not just the consequences of poverty.

It can be a milestone in our 180-year search for a better life for our people.

This Act provides five basic opportunities.

It will give almost half a million underprivileged young Americans the opportunity to develop skills, continue education, and find useful work.

It will give every American community the opportunity to develop a comprehensive plan to fight its own poverty—and help them to carry out their plans.

It will give dedicated Americans the opportunity to enlist as volunteers in the war against poverty.

It will give many workers and farmers the opportunity to break through particular barriers which bar their escape from poverty.

It will give the entire Nation the opportunity for a concerted attack on poverty through the establishment, under my direction, of the Office of Economic Opportunity, a national headquarters for the war against poverty. . . .

Through this program, we offer new incentives and new opportunities for cooperation, so that all the energy of our Nation, not merely the efforts of government, can be brought to bear on our common enemy.

Today, for the first time in our history, we have the power to strike away the barriers to full participation in our society. Having the power, we have the duty.

The Congress is charged by the Constitution to "provide . . . for the general welfare of the United States." Our present abundance is a measure of its success in fulfilling that duty. Now Congress is being asked to extend that welfare to all our people.

The President of the United States is President of all the people in every section of the country. But this office also holds a special responsibility to the distressed and disinherited, the hungry and the hopeless of this abundant Nation.

It is in pursuit of that special responsibility that I submit this message to you today.

The new program I propose is within our means. Its cost of $970 million is 1 per cent of our national budget—and every dollar I am requesting for this program is already included in the budget I sent to Congress in January.

But we cannot measure its importance by its cost.

For it charts an entirely new course of hope for our people.

We are fully aware that this program will not eliminate all the poverty in America in a few months or a few years. Poverty is deeply rooted and its causes are many.

But this program will show the way to new opportunities for millions of our fellow citizens.

It will provide a lever with which we can begin to open the door to our prosperity for those who have been kept inside.

It will also give us the chance to test our weapons, to try our energy and ideas and imagination for the many battles yet to come. As conditions change, and as experience illuminates our difficulties, we will be prepared to modify our strategy.

And this program is much more than a beginning.

Rather, it is a commitment. It is a total commitment by this President, and this Congress, and this Nation, to pursue victory over the most ancient of mankind's enemies.

On many historic occasions the President has requested from Congress the authority to move against forces which were endangering the well-being of our country.

This is such an occasion.

On similar occasions in the past we have often been called upon to wage war against foreign enemies which threatened our freedom. Today we are asked to declare war on a domestic enemy which threatens the strength of our Nation and the welfare of our people.

If we now move forward against this enemy—if we can bring to the challenges of peace the same determination and strength which has brought us victory in war—then this day and this Congress will have won a secure and honorable place in the history of the Nation, and the enduring gratitude of generations of Americans yet to come.

Part III

SOCIAL JUSTICE FOR ALL

IF all Americans were equal the pattern of reform could be adequately represented by Part II. They are not. Many readily identifiable groups have not been equipped or allowed to compete without handicap for economic equity by means of political democracy. Reform movements by and for these disadvantaged groups made up an aspect of the reform experience second only to the politico-economic record, if that. In fact, to make somewhat less of a partially arbitrary distinction, it is useful to perceive of these crusades on behalf of special groups as methods of introducing neglected portions of the population into the mainstream. Thus the documents that follow may be considered as a logical extension of Part II.

Reform on behalf of special groups includes movements:

on behalf of the deaf, dumb, blind, insane, or otherwise physically or mentally handicapped;

to provide full social participation for Indians, Negroes, religious and ethnic minorities;

to assist those who have been victimized by excessive use of alcohol, tobacco, and other drugs/narcotics and to move toward temperance/prohibition legislation;

to protect and sustain the young (child labor, education) and the aged;

to provide a more full and fair participation in society for women;

to improve police practices, courtroom procedures, prison life;

to moderate excessive punishments; and to offer more effective rehabilitative programs;

to assist groups that can be defined by place (e.g., ghetto dwellers, residents of Appalachia) or by occupation (e.g., miners, seamen, prostitutes).

The list could be extended. There is almost no identifiable group which has failed to attract some efforts to prevent its exploitation or to improve its relative status, although groups as large as the "poor" or the "working man" suggest less the special flavor that characterizes this section and more the general thrust toward economic democracy represented in the foregoing section.

If there is a special rationale behind the reforms proposed on behalf of special groups, it probably has more to do with the Enlightenment origins of American society. People are imagined as naturally good—if only they were not handicapped, enslaved, or disenabled. Thus a good society can be achieved by freeing its members of their disabilities. From the slave—whether he be a bondsman or a slave to alcohol—this kind of reformer would remove the chains. For the handicapped, he would overcome those disabilities that prevent full participation in society. For those whose main burden has been oppression, he would remove the hand of the oppressor. Thus would he restore the equality presumed in the Declaration and provide the full participation guaranteed in the Bill of Rights.

The Enlightenment philosophers tended to appeal to natural law; but the advocates of many of these movements on behalf of special groups drew their primary inspiration from religion. Considerable evangelistic zeal went into some of the movements to "save" the drunkard, the prostitute, and the criminal. "Heaven will protect the working girl," but only if the mission house or the Salvation Army is close at hand. Thus the churches themselves, through their domestic missions or through church-related enterprises like the Young Men's or Women's Christian or Hebrew associations, have offered charity, training, and religiously based education to various disadvantaged groups.

Among these causes may also be located most of what is generally meant by "humanitarian reform," and much of the charity in America's generous society of givers has found its way to the special groups identified in the above list. Talented leaders like Dorothea Dix or Jane Addams have been able to draw attention to special needs like asylums and slums. But even when no particular fashions dominate the reform agenda, there are always those twin streams of continuing reform activity on behalf of special groups: temperance/prohibition (whether the target is whiskey or heroin) and women's rights (whether the target is the franchise or the right to abortion). These constant items on the reform docket, together with the many others that appear and recede, combine to make up an unstated philosophy of social change which devotes itself to strengthening the social body by ministering to those parts which have been neglected.

It being impossible to document even one of the topics subsumed under this section, the burden of compilation shifts to the selection of documents representing not only the more centrally important movements but also the most useful insights into the American reform experience. With this purpose in mind the choice becomes obvious: (a) antislavery and civil rights and (b) woman's rights and woman's liberation. The latter will be discussed beginning with Document III-10.

Reform movements addressed to the situation of Afro-Americans existed well before the Revolution; they have far from ended. At the center of the movement is the largest, most readily identifiable minority with a drastic and visible history of victimization. The debate concerning this minority has involved our greatest public figures from Thomas Jefferson to Martin Luther King, Jr., and has produced an incomparable literature including no lesser talents than Henry David Thoreau, Frederick Douglass, W. E. B. DuBois, and John Steinbeck. In magnitude, duration, and intensity this movement is unique.

For these reasons, the anti-slavery-civil rights movement can be used to represent—at a high level of importance and quality—the reform experience in general. Documents from its rich history can be chosen so as to point out the dominant motivations, appeals, and methods of reform and reformers in America. For example, a number of documents have been chosen to illustrate how certain reformers attempt to make of a social issue a moral question, and thence come to expect the involvement of the churches. For others, reform is more a matter of a higher law reflected in the individual's conscience and thus superior to the institutions of society (III-7). The key to many is collective human reason; one can show an important segment of the reform effort to have been engaged in explaining a social problem and in persuading contemporaries— through data and logic—to a particular course of action (III-8). In still other reformers, the basic position stems from a pragmatic grasp of what will work best. Thus, although there may have been no superior logical or moral position that dictated a civil rights campaign in the courts, there was a pragmatic feeling that it might work best to interest judges in the problem of law school admission (III-8).

It has also been possible to suggest the enormous variety of shapes and forms assumed by reform activity: from legends on children's savings boxes to Biblical exegesis. Several good specimens are here offered of that typical reform beginning, the exposé. Thence one can move on to the elaboration of a theme of protest in art and fiction, in personal drama and in photographs. To convince one's neighbors one may resort to parades, demonstrations, oratory, or violence. One may attempt to move the mind through logical petitions, or the emotions through poetry. The cause goes forth in symbols; it cries out in the magic of oratorical rhetoric; it reaches a climax in flames and martyrdom. Meanwhile, often in the background, its progress may be marked in court decisions and legislative acts.

As Lord Bryce observed, there is in America a distinctive way of changing society through the expression of public opinion. This opinion is channeled and focused by voluntary organizations and spread by the press. To Bryce's observation might be added the importance of the role of the artist in dramatizing social problems and thus in arousing the public. Fortunate is the crusade that has at its disposal the imaginative eloquence of Stowe, Whittier, King, and Steinbeck. Then there are the drawings and cartoons, the songs and song covers, and the evocative symbols in words or stone. The crusading use of the press and other media seems to present an example of the reform dynamic wherever it is found in societies open to change; whereas the intimate involvement of literature and the arts may be more distinctive of the American way. Bryce justifiably stressed the importance of voluntaristic groups made up of men and women who have no personal stake in the cause they carry forth. In agreement with this proposition come those final documents in this section which suggest that—when the haunting rhetoric has ceased to echo and the massed bodies have deserted the demonstration sites—the momentum of reform is most truly sustained by organizations like the Anti-Slavery Society and the National Association for the Advancement of Colored People.

Even though the narrative histories of the anti-slavery crusade and the civil rights movement have been set down in many places from a number of viewpoints, still the chronological approach is given up with some reluctance. The principal reason for substituting a more analytical approach is to learn from this great subject something about what is permanent and what is temporary in the appeals and tactics of the reformers. But it should also be pointed out that comparison is invited not among trivia but from documents taken mainly from both the anti-slavery and civil rights movements at their high points: the 1830s and 1840s; the 1950s and 1960s. The echoes across this 120-year chasm produce both startling harmonies and puzzling discords.

In the 1830s and 1840s there was a *Liberator* and an *Emancipator*, so in the 1950s and 1960s there is a *Messenger* and a *Crisis*. If there was a Lane Revolt then, there is a Southern Christian Leadership Conference now. If there was a John Brown then, a Malcom X now; a *Slavery As It Is* then, a Moynihan Report now; an *Uncle Tom's Cabin* then, a *Manchild in the Promised Land* now. Some of the parallels contain reversals or ironies; as in the difference between the American Colonization Society and modern-day black separatism. David Walker urged opportunistic violence against slave holders; there is a question as to whether his approach is reflected today in the arsenals of the Panthers. Similarly, the petition campaign in Congress merely aimed to open the question of slavery to legislative enactment; whereas the civil rights acts and court decisions of the past generation have led to palpable guarantees with enforcement provisions built in.

Although there is never space in which to document all the essential truths of a subject, it should at least be admitted that the reform movements centering around black and female Americans are distinctive in their complexity and as such may be ultimately unrepresentative. There is nothing like gender and race to evoke confusion, irrationality, complexity, and genuine bewilderment among usually rational and self-perceptive individuals. To savor the tangled nuances of this condition—succinctly and memorably—one would do well to consult two contemporary writers of fiction not usually associated with race and reform: John Steinbeck and John Updike.

Toward the end of *Travels with Charley in Search of America* (New York, Viking, 1962) Steinbeck describes his shocked attendance at a performance of the "Cheerleaders," those white mothers of New Orleans who protested integration by lining the streets and verbally pelting the black children with passionately delivered gutter epithets. Concern and sensitivities aroused, the author sets down a number of random subsequent contacts in which he elicited views on the race question from Southerners of different views and hues. Agreeing with the enlightened Southerner that integration constitutes the only acceptable goal, Steinbeck also joins him in puzzling over "the dreadful uncertainty of the means" (p. 242).

John Updike's comment is much less explicit but serves to illuminate a parallel confusion and to predict the transformation of Boston from a hub of liberalism in the 1960s into a racial sorespot in regard to school busing in the mid-'70s. Through the sensibilities of a young father, plagued with a cold in the head and blisters on the feet, Updike describes a civil rights protest march through the streets of a damp and indifferent Boston. At the story's end the young Yankee liberal, feverish and fatigued, lapses into a Southern planter drawl, inviting the well-loved slaves up to the big house for a holiday feast. ("Marching through Boston," *The New Yorker* vol. XLI [January 22, 1966], pp. 34-38.) Perhaps only the creative imagination can do justice to the emotion-fraught self-contradictions involved in questions of race and gender, exacerbated as they are by histories of place, juxtapositions in time, and a thread of perverseness that seems to lie close to the center of the human condition.

Document III-1: SYMBOLS OF OPPRESSION

Appreciation of reform on behalf of a special group begins with the understanding of how members of that group perceive themselves. It is possible to discuss slavery as a kind of labor contract. It is doubtless true that many slaves were better off than many free persons. But to understand the situation at all is to realize that the condition of servitude— however benign—involves a fundamental degradation of the human condition. A dramatic shortcut to the central outrage of slavery and racial prejudice lay in the comparison of slave and beast.

The *Liberator* masthead showed slaves being auctioned, in the shadow of the U.S. Capitol, from a block which advertised cattle auctions as well. Nicholas Brimblecomb, the pseudonymous author of an ironic rebuttal to Mrs. Stowe's critics (*Uncle Tom's Cabin in Ruins!* Boston, Waite, 1853), based his bitter logic on the equation between horse and slave. After all, the term "chattel," as in chattel slavery, derives from the same word as cattle. In her original subtitle for *Uncle Tom's Cabin*, "The Man That Was a Thing," Mrs. Stowe succinctly stressed the inhuman aspects of slavery; and, in a particularly dramatic moment, she had the slave girl Cassy complain that even the swamp creatures had better homes than the persecuted slaves. "Down in the darkest swamps, their dogs will hunt us out, and find us. Everybody and everything is against us; even the very beasts side against us—and where shall we go?" (Page 346 of the 1852 London edition.)

The hounds, trained not only to track but to attack and kill runaway slaves, were a memorable part of the horror created by Mrs. Stowe. It is not surprising that illustrators consistently focused on scenes featuring the hunting dogs. In the first illustrated edition of the novel the rendering was faithful to the author's sense of proportion. It depicted a vulgar and frightening scene, men and beasts equally involved (A).

After the Civil War when *Uncle Tom* took to the road, the drama took two forms: the "Tom Show," a melodrama often played on riverboats, which was climaxed by the death of Little Eva and her ascent into the company of angels, or whoever inhabits the upper flies of riverboats. The "Tom Tent Show," on the other hand, featured the use of real mastiffs who were paraded beforehand and purportedly drew customers in proportion to their viciousness. In these shows, the high point was the chase of the fleeing Eliza across the frozen Ohio by the (leashed, one hopes) hounds. In neither Mrs. Stowe's novel nor her play were any hounds involved in Eliza's escape or Haley's pursuit; however, the theatrical poster represents a high point in the sheer melodrama of helpless human versus ferocious beast (B).

It is interesting to follow the illustrated editions of *Uncle Tom* as they continue to reflect the reform temper of their day. James Daugherty's chiaroscuros (Coward, McCann, 1929) suggest an elevation of style over social concern; whereas the mighty pictorial testimonials of Miguel Covarrubias (Heritage, 1938) stress the human oppressors of the proletariat. The recent sequel to the ironies of *Uncle Tom* is not in any drawing but in the use of cattle prods to control crowds of men descended from chattel slaves and in the continuing reenactment of scenes similar to the one photographed below (C). This particular photograph was taken at a labor disturbance where black workers were protesting "segregation wages." Similar scenes occurred at demonstrations during the sixties relating to segregated transportation, education, and voting. The caption reported that "Six men were injured, four of them hospitalized, as officers with three dogs cleared railroad tracks of prostrate strikers. . . ."

SOURCES: A: Harriet B. Stowe, *Uncle Tom's Cabin.* Boston, Jewett, 1853, p. 510. B: Lithograph by W. J. Morgan & Co., Cleveland, 1881. C: Clip from United Press International Newsfilm, Suffolk, Virginia, May 6, 1964.

A: *Uncle Tom* illustrated

B: "Tom Tent Show"

Document III-2: MUCKRAKING DOCUMENTARIES

Once the condition of the oppressed or disadvantaged group has been perceived the reformer then attempts to arouse the public. A typical first step is the publication of an exposé. Although candidly one-sided in its selection of detail, the exposé does not usually offer a remedy for the problem it describes. Rather, it builds toward a sense of outrage through

C: Strike photo, 1964

the compilation of authentic detail—explicit and often statistical. Theodore Roosevelt saw the compilers of such exposures as so preoccupied with the sordid aspects of their subjects that he compared them—enduringly and unflatteringly—with the character in *Pilgrim's Progress* who never raised his eyes from the muck he was doomed perpetually to rake. Thus "muckracking," originally applied to a group of journalists concerned with politico-economic abuses of the Progressive Era, has come to designate that uncompromising literature of exposure so vital to any reform movement.

The great muckraking work of the anti-slavery movement was Theodore Dwight Weld's *American Slavery As It Is.* First published in 1839 by the Anti-Slavery Society, it both alarmed the North and shattered Southern confidence. Its sales, spectacular for their day, helped fill the society's coffers. Its evidence—much of it taken from Southern newspapers—revealed countless episodes of violence and injustice. No treatment of the protest against slavery, however selective, can fail to mention this work or its author. Weld, who allowed the work to be published anonymously, often preferred to work behind the scenes and may therefore have contributed to a common failure among historians to recognize his eminence as organizer, proselytizer, and moral leader. His work in Washington alone, were the full story known, would earn him a firm place in the history of reform as the founder of the first successful social-action congressional lobby.

For special reasons, however, the muckraking work excerpted below is not Weld's but another largely influenced by it. When Harriet Beecher Stowe became inspired to make her statement on slavery in the form of a sentimental novel, she had already begun to collect evidence for a Weld-like documentation. Later, when her famous novel was accused of being inaccurate and unrepresentative, she went back to her abundant collection of clippings and correspondence, organized it so as to parallel the events of the novel as closely as possible, and published her "key" to the credibility of her fiction. Whereas Weld had preferred a large number of relatively short accounts, Stowe's creative imagination suggested the greater effect of somewhat longer and more dramatic sections. The episode reproduced below allows for comparison both with her fiction and with the document that immediately follows.

Were one to search out the most precise modern parallel to *American Slavery As It Is* he might well select the widely publicized report prepared by Daniel P. Moynihan for the Department of Labor in the early 1960s. Although never formally published, this extensive demographic study of hopelessly repetitive patterns of futility in black ghettos influenced federal programs to a degree reminiscent of Weld's bombshell. On the other hand, "The Trial of T" is offered more in the spirit of Mrs. Stowe's "State v. Castleman": a spirit that draws the reader to his own heartbreaking conclusions.

That the experience of "T" is available to us is due to circumstances surrounding the riots in Watts district of Los Angeles in August, 1965. Before the smoke of this conflagration had finally lifted, Budd Schulberg, the well-known author who is a native of that city, set up a writers' workshop in the Westminster settlement house referred to in the narrative. Feeling that Watts was part of his city too, Schulberg sought a constructive way to direct those energies so spectacularly expressed in molotov cocktails and handgunfire. He offered his prime professional competence: the teaching of writing. His presence there has led to the formation of the now famous Writers' Workshop and an impressive if unsuspected discovery of serious talent and competence.

SOURCE: A: Harriet Beecher Stowe, *A Key to Uncle Tom's Cabin; Presenting the Original Facts and Documents upon which the Story is Founded. Together with Corroborative Statements Verifying the Truth of the Work.* Boston, Jewett, 1853, p. 100-104. (For reasons of editorial convenience these pages have been reproduced from the undated London printing published by Clarke, Beeton; pp. 193-200.) B: Watts Writers' Workshop, *From the Ashes: Voices of Watts.* Edited with an introduction by Budd Schulberg. New York, New American Library, 1967, pp. 261-275.

A: Stowe's *KEY TO UNCLE TOM'S CABIN*

MODERATE CORRECTION AND ACCIDENTAL DEATH— STATE *V.* CASTLEMAN.

The author remarks that the record of the following trial was read by her a little time before writing the account of the death of Uncle Tom. The shocking particulars haunted her mind and were in her thoughts when the following sentence was written:—

What man has nerve to do, man has not nerve to hear. What brother man and brother Christian must suffer, cannot be told us, even in our secret chamber, it so harrows up the soul. And yet, O my country, these things are done under the shadow of thy laws! O Christ, thy Church sees them almost in silence!

It is given precisely as prepared by Dr. G. Bailey, the very liberal and fair-minded editor of the *National Era.*

From the "National Era," Washington, November 6, 1851.

HOMICIDE CASE IN CLARKE COUNTY, VIRGINIA.

Some time since, the newspapers of Virginia contained an account of a horrible tragedy, enacted in Clarke County, of that State. A slave of Colonel James Castleman, it was stated, had been chained by the neck, and whipped to death by his master, on the charge of stealing. The whole neighborhood in which the transaction occurred was incensed; the Virginia papers abounded in denunciations of the cruel act; and the people of the North were called upon to bear witness to the justice which would surely be meted in a slave State to the master of a slave. We did not publish the account. The case was horrible; it was, we were confident, exceptional; it should not be taken as evidence of the general treatment of slaves; we chose to delay any notice of it till the courts should pronounce their judgment, and we could announce at once the crime and its punishment, so that the State might stand acquitted of the foul deed.

Those who were so shocked at the transaction will be surprised and mortified to hear that the actors in it have been tried and acquitted; and when they read the following account of the trial and verdict published at the instance of the friends of the accused, their mortification will deepen into bitter indignation.

From the "Spirit of Jefferson."

"COLONEL JAMES CASTLEMAN.—The following statement, understood to have been drawn up by counsel, since the trial, has been placed by the friends of this gentleman in our hands for publication.

"At the Circuit Superior Court of Clarke County, commencing on the 13th of October, Judge Samuels presiding, James Castleman and his son Stephen D. Castleman were indicted jointly for the murder of negro Lewis, property of the latter. By advice of their counsel, the parties elected to be tried separately, and the attorney for the commonwealth directed that James Castleman should be tried first.

"It was proved on this trial, that for many months previous to the occurrence the money drawer of the tavern kept by Stephen D. Castleman, and the liquors kept in large quantities in his cellar, had been pillaged from time to time, until the thefts had attained to a considerable amount. Suspicion had, from various causes, been directed to Lewis, and another negro, named Reuben (a blacksmith), the property of James Castleman; but by the aid of two of the house-servants they had eluded the most vigilant watch.

"On the 20th of August last, in the afternoon, S. D. Castleman accidentally discovered a clue, by means of which, and through one of the house-servants implicated, he was enabled fully to detect the depredators, and to ascertain the manner in which the theft had been committed. He immediately sent for his father, living near him, and after communicating what he had discovered, it was determined that the offenders should be punished at once, and before they should know of the discovery that had been made.

"Lewis was punished first; and in a manner, as was fully shown, to preclude all risk of injury to his person, by stripes with a broad leathern strap. He was punished severely, but to an extent by no means disproportionate to his offence; nor was it pretended in any quarter that this punishment implicated either his life or health. He confessed the offence, and admitted that it had been effected by false keys furnished by the blacksmith Reuben.

"The latter servant was punished immediately afterwards. It was believed that he was the principal offender, and he was found to be more obdurate and contumacious than Lewis had been in reference to the offence. Thus it was proved, both by the prosecution and the defence, that he was punished with greater severity than his accomplice. It resulted in a like confession on his part, and he produced the false key, one fashioned by himself, by which the theft had been effected.

"It was further shown, on the trial, that Lewis was whipped in the upper room of a warehouse, connected with Stephen Castleman's store, and near the public road, where he was at work at the time; that after he had been flogged, to secure his person, whilst they went after Reuben, he was confined by a chain around his neck, which was attached to a joist above his head. The length of this chain, the breadth and thickness of the joist, its height from the floor, and the circlet of chain on the neck. were accurately measured; and it was thus shown that the chain unoccupied by the circlet and the joist was a foot and a half longer than the space between the shoulders of the man and the joist above, or to that extent the chain hung loose above him; that the circlet (which was fastened so as to prevent its contraction) rested on the shoulders and breast, the chain being sufficiently drawn only to prevent being slipped over his head, and that there was no other place in the room to which he could be fastened, except to one of the joists above. His hands were tied in front; a white man who had been at work with Lewis during the day was left with him by the Messrs. Castleman, the better to insure his detention, whilst they were absent after Reuben. It was proved by this man (who was a witness for the prosecution) that Lewis asked for a box to stand on, or for something that he could jump off from; that after the Castlemans had left him he expressed a fear that when they came back he would be whipped again; and said, if he had a knife, and could get one hand loose, he would cut his throat. The witness stated that the negro 'stood firm on his feet,' that he could turn freely in whatever direction he wished, and that he made no complaint of the mode of his confinement. This man stated that he remained with Lewis about half an hour, and then left there to go home.

"After punishing Reuben, the Castlemans returned to the warehouse, bringing him with them; their object being to confront the two men, in the hope that by further examination of them jointly, all their accomplices might be detected.

"They were not absent more than half an hour. When they entered the room above, Lewis was found hanging by the neck, his feet thrown behind him, his knees a few inches from the floor, and his head thrown forward—the body warm and supple (or relaxed), but life was extinct.

"It was proved by the surgeons who made a post-mortem examination before the coroner's inquest, that the death was caused by strangulation by hanging, and other eminent surgeons were examined to show, from the appearance of the brain and its blood-vessels after death (as exhibited at the post-mortem examination), that the subject could not have fainted before strangulation.

"After the evidence was finished on both sides, the jury from their box and of their own motion, without a word from counsel on either side, informed the Court that they had agreed upon their verdict. The counsel assented to its being thus received, and a verdict of 'Not Guilty' was immediately rendered. The attorney for the commonwealth then informed the Court that all the evidence for the prosecution had been laid before the jury; and as no new evidence could be offered on the trial of Stephen D. Castleman, he submitted to the Court the propriety of entering a *nolle prosequi*. The judge replied that the case had been fully and fairly laid before the jury upon the evidence; that the Court was not only satisfied with the verdict, but, if any other had been rendered, it must have been set aside; and that if no further evidence was to be adduced on the trial of Stephen, the attorney for the commonwealth would exercise a proper discretion in entering a *nolle prosequi* as to him, and the Court would approve of its being done. A *nolle prosequi* was entered accordingly, and both gentlemen discharged.

"It may be added that two days were consumed in exhibiting the evidence, and that the trial was by a jury of Clarke County. Both the parties had been on bail from the time of their arrest, and were continued on bail whilst the trial was depending."

Let us admit that the evidence does not prove the legal crime of homicide: what candid man can doubt, after reading this *ex parte* version of it, that the slave died in consequence of the punishment inflicted upon him?

In criminal prosecutions the federal constitution guarantees to the accused the right to a public trial by an impartial jury; the right to be informed of the nature and cause of the accusation; to be confronted with the witnesses against him; to have compulsory process for obtaining witness in his favour; and to have the assistance of counsel; guarantees necessary to secure innocence against hasty or vindictive judgment—absolutely necessary to prevent injustice. Grant that they were not intended for slaves; every master of a slave must feel that they are still morally binding upon him. He is the sole judge; he alone determines the offence, the proof requisite to establish it, and the amount of the punishment. The slave, then, has a peculiar claim upon him for justice.

When charged with a crime, common humanity requires that he
should be informed ot it—that he should be confronted with the
witnesses against him—that he should be permitted to show evidence in favour of his innocence.

But how was poor Lewis treated? The son of Castleman said he
had discovered who stole the money; and it was forthwith "determined that the offenders should be punished at once, and before
they should know of the discovery that had been made." Punished
without a hearing! Punished on the testimony of a house-servant,
the nature of which does not appear to have been inquired into by
the Court! Not a word is said which authorises the belief that any
careful examination was made as it respects their guilt. Lewis and
Reuben were assumed, on loose evidence, without deliberate
investigation, to be guilty; and then, without allowing them to
attempt to show their evidence, they were whipped until a confession of guilt was extorted by bodily pain.

Is this Virginia justice?

Lewis was punished with "a broad leathern strap;" he was
"punished severely:" this we do not need to be told. A "broad
leathern strap" is well adapted to severity of punishment. "Nor
was it pretended," the account says, "in any quarter that this
punishment implicated either his life or his health." This is false;
it was expressly stated in the newspaper accounts at the time, and
such was the general impression in the neighborhood, that the
punishment did very severely implicate his life. But more of this
anon.

Lewis was left. A chain was fastened around his neck, so as not
to choke him, and secured to the joist above, leaving a slack of
about a foot and a half. Remaining in an upright position, he was
secure against strangulation, but he could neither sit nor kneel;
and should he faint he would be choked to death. The account says
that they fastened him thus for the purpose of securing him. If this
had been the sole object, it could have been accomplished by safer
and less cruel methods, as every reader must know. This mode of
securing him was intended probably to intimidate him, and, at the
same time, afforded some gratification to the vindictive feeling
which controlled the actors in this foul transaction. The man
whom they left to watch Lewis said that, after remaining there
about half an hour, he went home; and Lewis was then alive. The
Castlemans say that, after punishing Reuben, they returned, having been absent not more than half an hour, and they found him

hanging by the neck, dead. We direct attention to this part of the testimony to show how loose the statements were which went to make up the evidence.

Why was Lewis chained at all, and a man left to watch him? "To secure him," say the Castlemans. Is it customary to chain slaves in this manner, and set a watch over them, after severe punishment, to prevent their running away? If the punishment of Lewis had not been unusual, and if he had not been threatened with another infliction on their return, there would have been no necessity for chaining him.

The testimony of the man left to watch represents him as desperate, apparently with pain and fright. "Lewis asked for a box to stand on." Why? Was he not suffering from pain and exhaustion, and did he not wish to rest himself without danger of slow strangulation? Again: he asked for "something he could jump off from." "After the Castlemans left, he expressed a fear when they came back that he would be whipped again; and said, if he had a knife, and could get one hand loose, he would cut his throat."

The punishment that could drive him to such desperation must have been horrible.

How long they were absent we know not, for the testimony on this point is contradictory. They found him hanging by the neck, dead, "his feet thrown behind him, his knees a few inches from the floor, and his head thrown forward," just the position he would naturally fall into had he sunk from exhaustion. They wish it to appear that he hung himself. Could this be proved (we need hardly say that it is not) it would relieve but slightly the dark picture of their guilt. The probability is that he sank, exhausted by suffering, fatigue, and fear. As to the testimony of "surgeons," founded upon a post-mortem examination of the brain and blood-vessels, "that the subject could not have fainted before strangulation," it is not worthy of consideration. We know something of the fallacies and fool cries of such examinations.

From all we can learn, the only evidence relied on by the prosecution was that white man employed by the Castlemans. He was dependent upon them for work. Other evidence might have been obtained; why it was not is for the prosecuting attorney to explain. To prove what we say, and to show that justice has not been done in this horrible affair, we publish the following communication from an old and highly-respectable citizen of this place, and who is very far from being an Abolitionist. The slaveholders whom he mentions are well known here, and would have promptly appeared in the case had the prosecution, which was aware of their readiness, summoned them.

"To the Editor of the Era.

"I see that Castleman, who lately had a trial for whipping a slave to death, in Virginia, was 'triumphantly acquitted'—as many expected. There are three persons in this city, with whom I am acquainted, who stayed at Castleman's the same night in which this awful tragedy was enacted. They heard the dreadful lashing and the heart-rending screams and entreaties of the sufferer. They implored the only white man they could find on the premises, not engaged in the bloody work, to interpose; but for a long time he refused, on the ground that he was a dependant, and was afraid to give offence; and that, moreover, they had been drinking, and he was in fear for his own life, should he say a word that would be displeasing to them. He did, however, venture, and returned and reported the cruel manner in which the slaves were chained, and lashed, and secured in a blacksmith's vice. In the morning, when they ascertained that one of the slaves was dead, they were so shocked and indignant that they refused to eat in the house, and reproached Castleman with his cruelty. He expressed his regret that the slave had died, and especially as he had ascertained that he was innocent of the accusation for which he had suffered. The idea was that he had fainted from exhaustion; and, the chain being round his neck, he was strangled. The persons I refer to are themselves slaveholders—but their feelings were so harrowed and lacerated that they could not sleep (two of them are ladies); and for many nights afterwards their rest was disturbed, and their dreams made frightful, by the appalling recollection.

"These persons would have been material witnesses, and would have willingly attended on the part of the prosecution. The knowledge they had of the case was communicated to the proper authorities, yet their attendance was not required. The only witness was that dependant who considered his own life in danger.

"Yours, S&c., "J. F."

The account, as published by the friends of the accused parties, shows a case of extreme cruelty. The statements made by our correspondent prove that the truth has not been fully revealed, and that justice has been baffled. The result of the trial shows how irresponsible is the power of a master over his slave; and that, whatever security the latter has, is to be sought in the humanity of the former, not in the guarantees of law. Against the cruelty of an inhuman master he has really no safeguard.

Our conduct in relation to this case, deferring all notice of it in our columns till a legal investigation could be had, shows that we are not disposed to be captious towards our slaveholding countrymen. In no unkind spirit have we examined this lamentable case; but we must expose the utter repugnance of the slave system to the proper administration of justice. The newspapers of Virginia generally publish the account from the "Spirit of Jefferson," without comment. They are evidently not satisfied that justice was done; they, doubtless, will deny that the accused were guilty of homicide, legally; but they will not deny that they were guilty of an atrocity which should brand them for ever in a Christian country. . . .

PRINCIPLES ESTABLISHED—STATE *V*. LEGREE; A CASE NOT IN THE BOOKS.

From a review of all the legal cases which have hitherto been presented, and of the principles established in the judicial decisions upon them, the following facts must be apparent to the reader:—

First. That masters do, now and then, kill slaves by the torture.

Second. That the fact of so killing a slave is not of itself held presumption of murder in slave jurisprudence.

Third. That the slave in the act of resistance to his master may always be killed.

From these things it will be seen to follow that, if the facts of the death of Tom had been fully proved by two white witnesses in open court, Legree could not have been held by any *consistent* interpreter of slave-law to be a murderer, for Tom was in the act of resistance to the will of his master. His master had laid a command on him in the presence of other slaves. Tom had deliberately refused to obey the command. The master commenced chastisement, to reduce him to obedience. And it is evident, at the first glance, to every one, that if the law does not sustain him in enforcing obedience in such a case, there is an end of the whole slave power. No Southern Court would dare to decide that Legree did wrong to continue the punishment as long as Tom continued the insubordination. Legree stood by him every moment of the time, pressing him to yield, and offering to let him go as soon as he did yield. Tom's resistance was *insurrection.* It was an example which could not be allowed for a moment on any Southern plantation. By the express words of the constitution of Georgia, and by the understanding and usage of all slave-law, the power of life and death is always left in the hands of the master, in exigencies like this. This is not a case like that of Souther *v.* the Commonwealth. The victim of Souther was not in a state of resistance or insurrection. The punishment, in his case, was a simple vengeance for a past offence, and not an attempt to reduce him to subordination.

There is no principle of slave jurisprudence by which a man could be pronounced a murderer, for acting as Legree did, in his circumstances. Everybody must see that such an admission would strike at the foundations of the slave system. To be sure, Tom was in a state of insurrection for conscience' sake. But the law does not, and cannot, contemplate that the negro shall have a conscience independent of his master's. To allow that the negro may refuse to obey his master whenever he thinks that obedience would be wrong, would be to produce universal anarchy. If Tom had been allowed to disobey his master in this case, for conscience' sake, the next day Sambo would have had a case of conscience, and Quimbo the next. Several of them might very justly have thought that it was a sin to work as they did. The mulatto woman would have remembered that the command of God forbade her to take another husband. Mothers might have considered that it was more their duty to stay at home and take care of their children, when they were young and feeble, than to work for Mr. Legree in the cotton-field. There would be no end to the havoc made upon cotton-growing operations, were the negro allowed the right of maintaining his own conscience on moral subjects. If the slave system is a right system, and ought to be maintained, Mr. Legree ought not to be blamed for his conduct in this case; for he did only what was absolutely essential to maintain the system; and Tom died in fanatical and foolhardy resistance to "the powers that be, which are ordained of God." He followed a sentimental impulse of his desperately depraved heart, and neglected those "solid teachings of the written word," which, as recently elucidated, have proved so refreshing to eminent political men.

B: "THE TRIAL OF T."
Part I: Statement from T.

Leaving school one day, going southeast to Compton, I boarded a bus on
Central Avenue at 103rd Street. I was going to take care of some legal
business pertaining to the Selective Service System. As the door closed I
saw my sister. "Hey, Marsha," I called, and waved my hand. I could
hear her voice calling back to me as the bus took off.

While I was saying to myself, I'll go over there to visit her as soon as I
get back, I was looking at all the old places that I had seen so many times
before. It was familiar to me—I'd lived there seventeen years. The only
sight out of the ordinary—a group of girls whose looks were so sweet that
they sparked my eyes.

Buzz-zz. I had pulled the cord, to let the bus driver know I wanted to
get off, at Rosecrans and Central. I snapped my finger, saying to myself,
Goddam, Ring, Stop. It was too late. The bus continued. Oh, well, I said
to myself, I'll get off at the next stop. I did and started walking until I got
to Compton Boulevard.

Turning left to proceed east, I heard a familiar high-frequency sound.
Yes, it was a siren about four hundred feet away. I quickened my steps to
see what was going on. When I arrived, I saw a man being stopped for a
ticket. Since I was working in the civil rights movement, I decided to
stick around and watch the procedure.

Standing next to a nice-looking lady, later known to me as defendant
R.'s wife, I said, "What is happening?" I was concerned. She said the
police were stopping him for a ticket. "What for? Speeding?" "No, for
not signing the ticket," she told me.

Mr. R. and the arresting officers began to get a little on the loud side,
so I made sure I was out of the way: a good ten feet away. Defendant R.
said, "I'm not going to sign that ticket." Some people stopped. The
police called more policemen.

While R. was talking to the ticketing officer, another officer came
from behind and grabbed R.'s arm and neck, choking and squeezing him.
I asked for his badge number. Because, as I said, "That's the way riots
get started." The officers pushed and shoved R., who was not resisting. I
said, "We shall overcome this." I watched them brutally shove R. into
the police car. R. was saying, "If you stop hurting me, I'll sign the

ticket.'' The policemen said, ''It's too late, goddammit,'' and pushed him onto the seat.

Suddenly, someone said to me, ''Move, you dirty punk!'' I looked up, saw it was a police officer, and asked myself, Is he crazy . . .? I said to the officer, ''No, this is public sidewalk.'' He said, ''Move, you black punk,'' again. I wondered, Is this man out of his mind? I replied the second time, in a very polite way, ''No, it's a public sidewalk, and I'm going to stay here if I want to.'' He called another officer over to us. I was standing there quietly and he said, ''I told this dirty punk to move nicely , and he wouldn't move. Will you witness for me?'' Then he said again, ''Move, you dirty black punk.''

I had gotten angry and was ready to fight, but I thought, The law is backing them. So I just stood there looking him angrily in the eyes. Because this time I said to myself, I've just got to go to jail. My mind was reacting very rapidly. I had already said, ''I'll fight to the federal court if I have to.''

I put my hands behind my back and let them arrest me. The officer pushed me into the car, slammed the door, and said, ''Let's get the hell out of here.'' He got in the other side of the car, and the second officer got in the front and they headed for the Compton Police Department. They were later known to me as Officers J. and O.

Officer J. said, ''You motherfucker, you think you are smart, don't you?'' I felt a swift, fast, and hard chop to my intestines. ''Answer me, you dirty punk,'' he insisted, striking me again. I still said nothing. He got very angry and said, ''You motherfucking punk-ass bastard, you answer me!'' He struck me a few more times. I was thinking, Should I laugh, or let the baby have his fun? ''What's your name?'' he asked, grabbing me by the neck. I finally gave in. I realized these bruises weren't doing me any good. ''T.,'' I said. One of them said to me, ''You wait until you get down to the station. We're going to kick your black ass. We're going to see how tough you are.''

We drove up to the police station. They dragged me out of the car and started pushing me. I was pushed into a jail cell. ''After you eat your dinner, I'm going to beat your ass.'' ''I can't wait to see this!'' said another police officer.

The booking procedure was not long for that particular station. He fingerprinted me on three sets of large filing cards. ''Write your ABC's and your numbers one to nine.'' After completing that part of the procedure, I took my first mug shot, turning to the side and looking at the X on the wall. He then pointed to the west wall of the room. "Sign on the three lines that are marked with an X."

After signing my name, I was put under security. I looked around the small cell, and I saw an old dirty mattress, which was mine. I dreaded to lie on it. . . . It would have been easier to lie on the floor balled up like a squirrel. I woke up next morning with my chest all congested, my nose running, and my eyes watering. I was kept in the same cell for three days.

When I got out I called Mr. Schulberg, whose writing class I had been attending. I told him what had happened and asked if he would come to the court with me on the day I was to appear.

Part II: Statement from Budd Schulberg

Nineteen-year-old T., then enrolled in Westminister's Youth Training Program, was one of the early members of our Writers' Workshop. He called to say he had missed our last class session because he had been arrested. He was upset because he had had no previous police record, which in itself is something of a record for a young man growing up in the streets of Watts. He asked me if I would accompany him to the court in Compton.

We agreed to reach the court an hour before he was to plead so that there would be time to discuss the case with the public defender. We were both concerned that he might be railroaded because his case balanced on his word against the word of four police officers. We could not find the public defender until just before the case was to be called. He was a white man who seemed completely uninterested in T.'s problem. I told him I was interrupting my own work and devoting this entire day to T.'s case because I felt he was making a serious effort to advance his education at Westminster and in my class, and a conviction on this kind of a charge would seriously disrupt his young life. The public defender did not seem at all impressed by my intervention in the case. He obviously regarded me as one extra nuisance with which to cope. "Before you get too involved, take a look at what this boy had done!" he told me. He showed me the detailed police complaint. It accused T. of shouting the most extreme obscenities at the police and exhorting the crowd that had gathered to "get those white motherfucking cops—let's start the revolution now!"

"That is not necessarily what he did," I said. "That is only what the police *say* he did. Just because they're policemen doesn't make them any more reliable as witnesses than T. is. He swears he never said these things. He says the police built up that case to cover up their own unfair arrest and their beating him in the police car. I came with him because I wanted to see that he gets a proper defense."

The public defender shrugged and said, "I better get you somebody else."

He called over a Negro public defender in his middle thirties, Mr. P.D. He took us to a small office, studied the charges, and asked T. to tell him his version. He said he knew of my work as a writer and had heard of the Watts Writers' Workshop, and he thought it would be helpful to T.'s side of the case if I testified for him. But he said that even while he believed T.'s story, it was his duty to warn him that he saw little chance of getting an acquittal when there were four police officers lined up against him. He felt the wisest thing might be to have T. plead guilty to a lesser charge and then he would talk to the judge about suspending the sentence due to T.'s youth and efforts to improve himself despite having dropped out of high school.

"But it isn't fair," T. said. "I don't want to plead guilty, even to a lesser charge. I will swear I am innocent. I was just walking along and saw the police using what I thought was excessive force to make an arrest, and I asked the man for his badge number. After all I'm a citizen of this country. Don't I have the right to ask him for his badge number?"

"Theoretically, you do," our Public Defender said. "But sometimes you have to be practical in this world. I can't tell you how to plead. I can only advise you. Faced with this line-up of witnesses it's my duty to warn you that I think we'll lose the case if we plead not guilty."

It was at this sticky moment that a new element entered the case. The attorney for R., the other defendant, had located a witness, a white house-painter who had been working outside the radio store and standing close to T. at the time of his alleged "inciting to riot" and "obstructing arrest" and "resisting arrest," etc. This unexpected witness was in his mid-sixties, still wearing his paint-daubed overalls. And to improve matters, he was a retired deputy sheriff.

"Well, now I think maybe we've got a case," our P.D. said. "I'm still not sure we can win it against the police department. But there's a fighting chance."

The next decision was whether to let the judge hear the case himself, or to try it with a jury. Mr. R. preferred the judge because he was anxious to get back to his job as manager of a restaurant. But T. and I talked it over and decided to take our chances with a jury.

The case proceeded with all the solemnity and attention to detail of a major trial. It took half a day to fill the jury box. I was the first witness for T.'s defense. Under our P.D.'s questioning, I described T.'s faithful attendance at the writing class. I also tried to place his questioning of the police badge number in some perspective. T. was on the student council at Westminster and he had discussed in the writing class his plan to make a report on the police behavior in Watts that he felt provoked gathering crowds and incited the kind of spontaneous combustion that had set off the week-long uprising of August, 1965. He was also engaged in helping to form a Watts teen-age group called Youth Organization for Progress that would help to improve conditions for his peers in Watts. He and his associates believed that police brutality, one of the most pressing problems of Watts, could be lessened if the police were made to feel they were themselves under watchful and thoughtful observation. I said that although T.'s actions may seem provocative to an outsider, it might be understood if seen within the context of T.'s ideas and activities.

The cross-examination from the district attorney was unexpectedly severe. My credentials as a character witness were questioned on the grounds that I saw the defendant only at my class for a few hours once a week. I answered that our Workshop often went on for three or four hours and that writing is such a personal activity that one exposes himself far more through writing and discussing his work than one would in a math or science class. It seemed a strange platform from which to be discussing the Writers' Workshop but in Watts one becomes accustomed to the long arm of the police reaching through most unexpected windows.

Our P.D. felt that this testimony had strengthened T.'s case, especially when it was followed by that of the white house-painter, who insisted that he was within hearing distance of T. and had not heard any of the inflammatory statements T. was alleged to have hurled at the police in an effort to incite the crowd and prevent the arrest.

The three uniformed policemen and one plainclothes detective all repeated their charges against T. But Lieutenant J. did not seem to help his case when he testified that he had not struck the defendant in the police car or called him "Nigger," but that he had said, "You dirty little punk, where's your big mouth now?" and "It's dirty punks like you that give the rest of them a bad name." He and his fellow officers seemed to have no awareness of the fact that no matter what they thought, T. was innocent until proven guilty and they had no right to pass judgment on him in the police car or challenge or insult him.

The trial began on a Monday morning and was not concluded until Friday evening. Mrs. Schulberg and I attended every day of the trial and our secretary, Miss Sally Bowman, took down the entire courtroom proceedings in shorthand. The full text is too lengthy to include here but the entire cross-examination of T. is reproduced and the summation of the Public Defender. It should be noted that taking the case on the spur of the moment, Mr. P.D. provided a conscientious, shrewd, and finally eloquent defense of T. And throughout the week-long, hard-fought trial, The Honorable H.S. proved himself a judge of deep understanding and concern for fair play. Aside from the unheralded verdict rendered in this case, which will be found at the end of the transcript that follows, there was also an unexpected bonus as a result of this trial. It might literally be called "poetic justice." Judge S. found himself so interested in the Watts Writers' Workshop at Douglass House that he came to attend Workshop sessions and later became a member of our Board of Directors. As such he has been active in advising our writers as to their legal rights, helping them extricate themselves from pressing legal problems, and in one vital case using his good offices to recommend to fellow judges that some young men be paroled to Douglass House, where they could work and develop, rather than stagnate in the county jail.

Part III: In the Courtroom

Public Defender made opening statement: "Our case is very simple . . .

Defendant intends to show by his evidence that he came upon the scene, saw what appeared to be an unlawful arrest, asked for a badge number, when it was refused, retired from the scene. When the emergency came to end, was then asked to remove himself from the sidewalk in a derogatory manner. He refused to do so, as he had a legal right to be there. He would have removed himself though if he had been asked in a prudent manner.

   T. sworn in.

Public Defender.

Q: What is your business occupation?

A: I am in school—Westminster—and high school at night.

Q: In connection with those duties do you counsel?

A: Yes, in my own age group.

Q: At approximately 8 P.M. in reference to events in this case, can you tell us what transpired.

A: . . . went to see what was going on, heard loud voices. I stood aside and one of the policemen seemed to be very belligerent.

Judge: You approached the scene, you heard loud voices. Tell us, tell the jury what the officer was doing, what Mr. and Mrs. R. were doing. You cannot say he was not acting right, or come to a conclusion.

Public Defender.

Q: After hearing loud voices, you approached the officer?

A: Yes, I did.

Q: Did you say anything to him?

A: I asked for his badge number. I saw one of the officers grab Mr. R. I said, "See, that's what makes these riots get started."

Q: Did you say it in the voice you are using now?

A: No (and he raised his voice to indicate how he said it).

Q: Where were you standing?

A: About twelve feet from the scene.

Q: Had persons gathered?

A: If they had gathered I didn't know because I was not facing them.

Q: After you made that statement, did you say anything else to the officer?

A: Yes, I said we shall overcome this. Someone was telling me I was some kind of nationalist—one of the officers said this to me.

Q: Prior to your making this statement, had Mr. R. been handcuffed?

A: No. The officer still had him around his neck and . . .

Q: Anything unusual in the face of Mr. R.?

A: Yes, he looked as though he was about to choke.

Q: Why did you say this is how riots started?

A: Something I had seen in August seemed like a similar occasion.

Q: Who were you addressing this remark to?

A: To one of the officers.

Q: Did you say this to influence the crowd?
A: No, I was trying to get the officer to stop doing what might arouse a crowd into a negative attitude towards the police.
Q: In other words, you tried to get something across to the officer to avoid anything further happening. Had a crowd gathered?
A: A few high school students . . .
Q: Did you at any time turn your face in the direction of the crowd and admonish them from doing anything in reference to the officers?
A: No.
Q: Did you notice how many persons were in the crowd?
A: Approximately twenty to twenty-five.
Q: Teen-agers?
A: Yes, some, and some business people from establishments nearby.
Q: Was the crowd noisy?
A: No, it was not.
Q: Did you hear any profanity in the crowd?
A: No.
Q: Did you use any profanity?
A: No.
Q: Now you heard testimony of the officers, and you heard certain statements attributed to you. Did you make any of these statements?
A: No.
Q: Where were you standing when these police officers came to the scene?
A: When police officers [names] came to the scene I was standing approximately five feet from the police car and Officer J. said . . .
Q: Were you standing near anyone when Officer J. made these remarks?
A: No.
Q: What was the first thing Officer J. did when he came out of the car?
A: He came towards another officer and said something to him.
Q: Did you hear him order the crowd to disburse?
A: No. Not Officer J.
Q: Did you hear him say the crowd was an unlawful assembly?
A: No.
Q: Did he say anything to you?
A: Yes. "Move, you dirty punk."
Q: Did he ask anyone else to move?
A: No.
Q: When he said, "Move, dirty punk," where was Mr. R.?
A: He was already handcuffed and in the car.
Q: How many patrol cars were there?
A: Two, and four or five others arrived on the scene.

Q: In what kind of voice did Officer J. speak to you? Loud, moderate, or soft?

A: In a loud voice, "Move, you dirty punk." I said, "I am not moving."

Q: Was it any louder than that?

A: No. When he told me, "Move, you dirty punk!" I said, "I am not moving, this is a public sidewalk." Then he called another officer and said if I didn't move, I would be under arrest.

Q: Did you at any time walk between the officers and Mr. and Mrs. R.?

A: No.

Q: How far was the closest person to you when you were under arrest?

A: Four or five feet.

Q: Did Officer J. come over and ask you to move after you attempted to get his badge number?

A: Yes.

Q: Did he give it to you?

A: No, he didn't.

Q: What was the first thing that happened after you were under arrest?

A: He put me in the car. When we were driving Officer J. started hitting me.

Q: What were you doing?

A: Nothing.

Q: Were you handcuffed?

A: Yes.

Q: Where were you sitting?

A: In the back of the car.

Q: Was it a light blow?

A: No, it wasn't exactly light.

Q: Did you have any discussion in the car?

A: He said I was the type that was bad for . . .

Q: I am asking this question because . . . I don't want you to misquote the officer and use your own words. Do you recall the specific words?

A: I don't recall specific words, couldn't quote exactly.

Q: From what you recall, what were his words?

Objection . . .

Q: As best you can recall, what did the officer say?

A: . . . your kind of Nigger that makes it bad for the good Negroes.

Q: He used Nigger and Negro?

A: Yes.

Q: Did you state anything prior to his making this remark?

A: No, I did not.

Q: What did you hope to accomplish by asking the officer for his badge number?

A: It goes back to more than that particular time . . . I had been doing quite a bit of research . . . I asked for his badge number because I thought it might put some fear in him.

Q: Did you have it in mind that in some way it could avoid an explosive occurrence?

A: Yes, I did.

District Attorney.

Q: Where were you coming from when you arrived on the scene?

A: From school.

Q: Where is school?

A: In Watts.

Q: Where is that?

A: . . . Westminster Neighborhood Association.

Q: Did you take a bus?

A: Yes.

Q: Where did you get off?

A: Rosecrans and Central.

Q: You walked, how many blocks?

A: I am not sure.

Q: As you were walking, did you meet any friends?

A: No, I didn't.

Q: How wide is the sidewalk at the radio shop?

A: I wasn't standing there.

Q: Well, where were you standing?

A: . . . six to eight feet.

Q: Did you notice that that sidewalk is unusually narrow?

A: No, they all seem the same to me.

Q: Could you tell the court and jury what you first noticed when you arrived in this place?

A: When I arrived . . . they were talking very loud . . . R. and the police officer.

Q: Will you describe the instance which preceded your asking for the police badge number?

A: Actually it was the way he was acting with the defendant.

Q: How long had you been standing there before you asked for his badge number?

A: Not very long.

Q: What did he do?

A: He was shouting.

Q: . . . outrageous?

A: I didn't say outrageous—I never heard a policeman talk in that loud a voice.

Q: How loud—shouting?

A: Yes—louder.

Q: Did you know the nature of the transaction between R. and police officer?

A: By that time, yes.

Q: So before the officer started to place arms around his neck, you were watching this scene so closely you didn't notice a crowd gathering?

A: I would have had to turn around to see, and I was watching R. and the officer.

Q: You testified at some time you saw twenty or twenty-five p ople. At what point?

A: About twenty seconds after the officer had placed his arms around defendant's neck.

Q: Is that when you made your statements?

A: I said, "We shall overcome this."

Q: And you were unaware of other pedestrians?

A: Yes, of those behind me.

Q: Did the crowd get larger than twenty to twenty-five?

A: Yes, forty or forty-five.

Q: Did you make any statements to the officers after Mr. R. was hand-cuffed?

A: No.

Q: You didn't hear any announcement for the crowd to disburse?

A: No, I wasn't interested in the crowd.

Q: Did you ever turn around and make any statements to the crowd?

A: No. I directed my statements to the officer that his actions were what started riots.

Q: In the meantime an officer stepped out of his vehicle and went directly to you?

A: Yes.

Q: And just the two of you there until Officer———came? How many times did he tell you to move?

A: Three times.

Q: Then when he returned with another officer, how many times?

A: Once.

Q: And did you move?

A: No, I didn't.

Q: Are you concerned about rioting?

A: Yes.

Q: At this time you were going to demand your rights to stand on the sidewalk. Didn't you think this might influence the situation?

A: No, I didn't, it was just between me and the officer.

Q: And you weren't concerned about your arrest?

A: Yes, I would think twice before doing this again, but he came to me and talked to me like I was a junkie or something, and I had to stand my ground.

Part IV: Public Defender's Summation

I will try to make my remarks as brief as possible. You've heard two sides. Instead of arguing, I would like to reason. I believe firmly that our system is the greatest in the world . . . I believe that the law as it stands is color-blind. It always has been . . . in reams of evidence we can lose sight of the essential issue . . . not so much who said it, but what was said. It is not a case of T. against the police, or the police against T.—it may be a Madison Avenue expression, but there is a credibility gap here . . . if we believe everything we have heard here . . . does this mean that one or the other must be a liar? I don't think so . . . sometimes we fill in . . . and we think something happened that didn't happen . . . by the time it gets to the other end of the table it is completely emasculated. This is a principle of the human mind . . . the power of suggestion.

Officers came upon the scene . . . there was an arrest . . . persons gathered. From evidence it was a rather quiet crowd. Neither one of the officers admitted they were threatened by the crowd, but there must have been excitement. Someone comes along this scene, carrying books . . . hears sound of loud voices, observes out of curiosity . . . voices loud. Something in the officer made T. pause, observe the scene, then ask the officer for his badge number. You did recall officer said he was engaged in a struggle with R., but was still able to watch the mouth of T. verbalizing. There is reasonable doubt that he could do this. There must have been some sound. The rest he filled in with his imagination, remembering what happened last August . . . and this youngster had the audacity to ask him for his badge number. There are indications of his not being sure of himself and he might have been afraid when he was asked for his badge number. T. did not approach the cars . . . simply asked for his badge number . . . he was a youngster. Why didn't the officer arrest him for disturbing the peace? He didn't. He ordered him to move. He was simply standing there. When officer said, "Move, you punk," he refused to move. He was then arrested. The witness, a house painter standing beside him, heard no profanity. T. submitted to arrest. The officer in the car initiated a conversation with, "Where is your big mouth now?" Officer J. admitted that the crowd did disburse when he asked them to. The defendant was standing alone on the sidewalk. Inspector ———————— said he was trying to inflame the crowd. Would you ask a man to join the crowd he was trying to inflame? He is nineteen years old, in many ways immature, attempting to play the role of a good Samaritan, now being accused of disturbing the peace. He was asked many times to move. Why would you ask him many times? Defendant refused because of the manner in which he was requested. I believe he had a legal right to stand his ground . . . dignity and right of the individual . . . an officer as an agent of the state is not free to implant the idea of crime in the mind of an individual . . . but to prevent it. If he was disturbing the peace, he should have been arrested.

How can he obstruct the arrest? It implies that by not leaving, public interest was threatened. A similar argument was made before the Supreme Court in 1956 arising out of the incident in Little Rock. School officials had to deprive Negro litigants' right to attend a school. In order to keep the peace, they deprived them of their rights. R. and his wife were already in the car, the crowd had dispersed, where was T. to go? It is clear the officers were angry, defendants were angry, and there was poor judgment on the part of all concerned.

We had some character reference from Mr. Schulberg. Young T. was known to be peaceful, honest. One thing came out in his testimony, T. has taken an interest in counsel with others, very interested in averting occurrences in the street. That is why he asked officer for his badge number. In T.'s testimony, he was asked why he asked for the officer's badge number. He said because of certain things he had heard. He was asked why he didn't say something to Mr. R.? On the basis of his experience in working with a group, he knew he shouldn't talk to a defendant in the matter, but to the officer. I would expect the officer to act in a more mature fashion than the defendant . . . I don't think there is any proof that the defendant violated this statute.

Some of you may have come to the conclusion that T. was morally guilty, that it was not an error of his heart, but his intellect. You are not being asked to find him morally guilty, but legally guilty of resisting arrest . . .

This case has much to do with the way T. said, "This is the way riots start." There was nothing wrong with that when he saw R. being choked. A reasonable amount of force could have been used to make this arrest. At least say, "You are under arrest, put up your hands" . . . and this was not said. T.'s saying, "This is the way riots start," was reasonable. I hope you will render a decision we could be proud of as Americans . . . There is a poem of Walt Whitman's . . . "If there is a reasonable doubt, do justice and you too will look at the sign of the stars as truth and justice."

Part V: Judge H.'s Concluding Instructions to the Jury

. . . weigh the evidence and apply the law and reach a just verdict. This verdict on each of the charges must express the opinion of each of you. The attorneys for the defense are entitled to the opinion of each of you. When you reach a judgment, you must not change it merely to bring about a unanimous verdict. Render your verdict according to your final decision. Do not speculate to be true any insinuations—questions are not evidence. Defendant in a criminal action is considered innocent until proven guilty beyond a reasonable doubt . . . evidence of . . . character involved is regarded by the law as evidence . . . evidence of the character of the witness should be considered for the purpose of determining credibility . . . every witness is presumed to speak the truth . . . a witness wilfully false in one . . . is to be distrusted in all . . . you may treat all of their evidence on suspicion . . . however, discrepancies do not mean a witness should be discredited. Each witness may see the same thing differently . . . the rise or fall of my voice should not be considered to influence . . . you. Go now, and bring back a just decision.

Part VI: Budd Schulberg's Epilogue

The jury was out all afternoon and into the evening before rendering their verdict. On three counts: two against defendant R.; one against T. As we sat there waiting we could hear loud discussion crackling into anger. We felt like an audience that somehow had passed through the proscenium arch of "Twelve Angry Men." At last they returned. They stood 12 to 0 for the acquittal of T.

It was a long, long trail from that opening morning when the first, bored public defender had shown us the police charges against T with "Don't you see here what this boy has done?" Between that conviction without trial and our Negro Public Defender's appeal to Walt Whitman and American justice to which both Judge and the jury responded, there spread the whole spectrum from the frequent miscarriage of justice for the black man in America to the occasional and hopeful twelve-strike for justice.

This trial went unnoticed in the local papers of Los Angeles. To the local press it may have seemed just another traffic case, involving an unknown and insignificant teen-ager, one of thousands of invisible men in the dark ghetto. Actually the incident leading to young T.'s arrest was almost identical with the one involving the Frye brothers and their mother which sparked the furious fires of '65. That was the true significance of the T. case. In the eyes of T., the police in their rough handling of a traffic violator, were inviting another riot. In the eyes of the police it was T. who was guilty of setting the fuse. Although unreported it was a trial of profound significance for Los Angeles, both as to content and verdict. It was, in its small way, a microcosm of the tensions that pulse on in Los Angeles. When it came to the attention of a columnist for the *New York Post*, Pete Hamill, he devoted his entire space to it. He saw it for what it was, an obscure, yet monumental trial. It may not be literature but we thought it deserved to be included in this book because it is the stuff of literature. For out of the T.'s and their trials both literal and figurative are stories waiting to be told.

Document III-3: PROTEST NARRATIVES

One of the more notable characteristics of reform in America has been the involvement of the creative artist. Part II included in its documentation of politico-economic reform the contributions of cartoonists and photographers, of imaginative journalists, essayists, orators, and versifiers. Much of the literature devoted explicitly to social questions tends to suffer aesthetically; but such is not always the case. There is in fact a tradition of meritorious protest fiction that might begin with Richard Henry Dana's *Two Years Before the Mast* in 1840, with its exposé of the brutalization of merchant seamen, and which would reach an apogee in works like Upton Sinclair's *The Jungle* and John Steinbeck's *Grapes of Wrath*. Very seldom do works of literature produce immediate tangible results in the way that Sinclair's book led directly to a pure food and drug act; on the other hand, every major reform campaign has benefited importantly from the contributions of creative artists.

Uncle Tom's Cabin occupies an exalted place among protest novels because of its substance and style, because of the immediacy of its impact and the duration of its influence. Through the late nineteenth century it survived as melodrama on showboats and in carnivals. The twentieth century has seen an upward revision of its intellectual and literary worth: Edmund Wilson finding it important for its modification of Calvinism and Kenneth Lynn finding it a pioneering work in literary realism. Still, its historic importance is as that book which Abraham Lincoln is supposed to have said—surely in oversimplification but by no means in jest—caused the Civil War.

The book deserves to be read; and only a complete reading can show why it aroused the nation far beyond books like *American Slavery As It Is*, beyond a comparable exposure to William Lloyd Garrison's firebrand journalism, and perhaps as much as the martyrdom of John Brown. What will strike the modern reader most forcefully is the failure of the central character to live up to the stereotype created for him through the derogatory epithet "Uncle Tom." It is true that this character speaks softly and uses the deferential language of servitude, but in no other way is he a toady to the white man's whims. His meaning in the story is just the opposite: a man who defies to the death the will of the white man when this will conflicts with moral principles. Tom may not be a believable character in this flawed world, but he is presented as a consistent practicing Christian, a man of great physical courage and endurance, and a vivid prototype for active, nonviolent resistance.

The first passage was chosen to show that Mrs. Stowe had no narrow, doctrinaire view about the problem of slavery and its solution. In the dialogue between Ophelia and St. Clare, she allows herself a measure of despair as the full dimensions of the race problem are confronted. St. Clare understands the Southern white but does not forgive him. Ophelia understands the Northern reformer but does not expect too much of him.

The balanced nature of this conversation shows that one strength of the book was its depiction of all varieties of people: slaveowners who were cruel and kind; Negroes who were silly, brutal, and noble. This same passage also offers a glimpse of what Edmund Wilson meant by the religious importance of the novel. The other passages allow the reader to observe Tom at the time of his major testing. They also include some of the recurrent equations between slaves and animals (see III-1). The characters, in addition to Tom and the infamous slavemaster Legree, are Sambo and Quimbo, two brutal slaves who serve as Legree's sergeants-at-arms in administering discipline.

As the example of *Uncle Tom's Cabin* made clear, people can be more profoundly moved by works of the imagination, based on fact, than by the facts themselves however carefully selected and evocatively reported. People have come emotionally to understand the black view-point through the creations of Richard Wright, Langston Hughes, Claude Brown, and others, where statistics on unemployment, crime, addiction, and infant mortality have moved them only intellectually. Thus a complete history of the efforts to move Americans toward concepts of full justice for black citizens would include not only lawyers and legislators, but also a long list of artists—some of whom are just now beginning to receive their deserved acclaim—who have depicted the plight of this large and visible minority in paintings and photographs, plays and cinemas, poems and narratives.

The second document, like III-2B above, appeared in the Watts collection. It shows, along with Mrs. Stowe's fiction, how the creative imagination can transport a subject from a reportorial frame of reference into a completely different emotional range. It also signals another truth. Just as fiction and verse have tended to supplement the journalistic exposés of other social problem areas, so the plight of black Americans has been particularly illuminated by the autobiography, from Frederick Douglass to Malcolm X. If the autobiography of Harry Dolan is less celebrated than those of Eldridge Cleaver and Claude Brown, it is perhaps even more representative.

SOURCE: A: Harriet Beecher Stowe, *Uncle Tom's Cabin.* London, Cassell, 1852, pp. 270-72, 308-10, 341-43, abridged. (The novel was first published in serial form in *The National Era,* 1851-52; in 1852 there appeared both English and American editions.) B: *From the Ashes: Voices of Watts,* (see III-2B), pp. 27-33.

A: *UNCLE TOM'S CABIN*

"What a sublime conception is that of the last judgment!" said he.*
"A righting of all the wrongs of ages!—a solving of all moral problems,
by an unanswerable wisdom! It is, indeed, a wonderful image."

"It is a fearful one to us," said Miss Ophelia.

"It ought to be to me, I suppose," said St. Clare, stopping thoughtfully. "I was reading to Tom this afternoon that chapter in Matthew that
gives an account of it, and I have been quite struck with it. One should
have expected some terrible enormities charged to those who are
excluded from Heaven, as the reason; but no, they are condemned for *not*
doing positive good, as if that included every possible harm."

"Perhaps," said Miss Ophelia, "it is impossible for a person who
does no good not to do harm."

"And what," said St. Clare, speaking abstractedly, but with deep
feeling, "what shall be said of one whose own heart, whose education,
and the wants of society, have called in vain to some noble purpose; who
has floated on, a dreamy, neutral spectator of the struggles, agonies, and
wrongs of man, when he should have been a worker?"

"I should say," said Miss Ophelia, "that he ought to repent, and
begin now."

"Always practical and to the point!" said St. Clare, his face breaking
out into a smile. "You never leave me any time for general reflections,
cousin; you always bring me short up against the actual present; you have
a kind of eternal *now*, always in your mind."

"*Now* is all the time I have anything to do with," said Miss Ophelia.

"Dear little Eva—poor child!" said St. Clare, "she had set her little
simple soul on a good work for me."

It was the first time since Eva's death that he had ever said as many
words as these of her, and he spoke now evidently repressing very strong
feeling.

"My view of Christianity is such," he added, "that I think no man can
consistently profess it without throwing the whole weight of his being
against this monstrous system of injustice that lies at the foundation of all
our society; and if need be, sacrificing himself in the battle. That is, I
mean that *I* could not be a Christian otherwise, though I have certainly

*Mozart's *Requiem*.

had intercourse with a great many enlightened and Christian people
who did no such thing; and I confess that the apathy of religious people
on this subject, their want of perception of wrongs that filled me
with horror, have engendered in me more scepticism than any other
thing.''

"If you knew all this," said Miss Ophelia, "why didn't you do it?''

"Oh, because I have had only that kind of benevolence which consists
in lying on a sofa, and cursing the church and clergy for not being martyrs
and confessors. One can see, you know, very easily, how others ought to
be martyrs.''

"Well, are you going to do differently now?" said Miss Ophelia.

"God only knows the future," said St. Clare. "I am braver than I was,
because I have lost all; and he who has nothing to lose can afford all
risks.''

"And what are you going to do?''

"My duty, I hope, to the poor and lowly, as fast as I find it out," said
St. Clare, "beginning with my own servants, for whom I have yet done
nothing; and perhaps at some future day, it may appear that I can do
something for a whole class; something to save my country from the
disgrace of that false position in which she now stands before all civilised
nations.''

"Do you suppose it possible that a nation ever will voluntarily emancipate?'' said Miss Ophelia.

"I don't know," said St. Clare. "This is a day of great deeds. Heroism
and disinterestedness are rising up, here and there, in the earth. The
Hungarian nobles set free millions of serfs, at an immense pecuniary
loss; and, perhaps, among us may be found generous spirits, who do not
estimate honour and justice by dollars and cents.''

"I hardly think so," said Miss Ophelia.

"But suppose we should rise up to-morrow and emancipate, who
would educate these millions, and teach them how to use their freedom?
They never would rise to do much among us. The fact is, we are too lazy
and unpractical ourselves ever to give them much of an idea of that
industry and energy which is necessary to form them into men. They will
have to go north, where labour is the fashion—the universal custom; and
tell me, now, is there enough Christian philanthropy among your northern states to bear with the process of their education and elevation? You
send thousands of dollars to foreign missions; but could you endure to

have the heathen sent into your towns and villages, and give your time, and thoughts, and money, to raise them to the Christian standard? That's what I want to know. If we emancipate, are you willing to educate? How many families in your town would take in a negro man and woman, teach them, bear with them, and seek to make them Christians? How many merchants would take Adolph, if I wanted to make him a clerk; or mechanics, if I wanted him taught a trade? If I wanted to put Jane and Rosa to a school, how many schools are there in the northern states that would take them in? how many families that would board them? and yet they are as white as many a woman, north or south. You see, cousin, I want justice done us. We are in a bad position. We are the more *obvious* oppressors of the negro; but the unchristian prejudice of the north is an oppressor almost equally severe.''

"Well, cousin, I know it is so," said Miss Ophelia. "I know it was so with me, till I saw that it was my duty to overcome it; but I trust I have overcome it, and I know there are many good people at the north who in this matter need only to be *taught* what their duty is to do it. It would certainly be a greater self-denial to receive heathen among us than to send missionaries to them; but I think we would do it.''

"*You* would, I know," said St. Clare. "I'd like to see anything you wouldn't do, if you thought it your duty!''

"Well, I'm not uncommonly good," said Miss Ophelia. "Others would, if they saw things as I do. I intend to take Topsy home, when I go. I suppose our folks will wonder, at first; but I think they will be brought to see as I do. Besides, I know there are many people at the north who do exactly what you said.''

"Yes, but they are a minority; and, if we should begin to emancipate to any extent, we should soon hear from you. . . .''

Slowly the weary, dispirited creatures wound their way into the room, and, with crouching reluctance, presented their baskets to be weighed.

Legree noted on a slate, on the side of which was pasted a list of names, the amount.

Tom's basket was weighed and approved; and he looked with an anxious glance for the success of the woman he had befriended.

Tottering with weakness, she came forward, and delivered her basket. It was full weight, as Legree well perceived; but, affecting anger, he said—

"What, you lazy beast! short again! Stand aside, you'll catch it, pretty soon!"

The woman gave a groan of utter despair, and sat down on a board.

The person who had been called Misse Cassy now came forward, and, with a haughty, negligent air, delivered her basket. As she delivered it, Legree looked in her eyes with a sneering yet inquiring glance.

She fixed her black eyes steadily on him, her lips moved slightly, and she said something in French. What it was no one knew; but Legree's face became perfectly demoniacal in its expression as she spoke; he half raised his hand, as if to strike—a gesture which she regarded with fierce disdain, as she turned and walked away.

"And now," said Legree, "come here, you Tom. You see, I telled ye I didn't buy ye jest for the common work. I mean to promote ye, and make a driver of ye; and to-night ye may jest as well begin to get yer hand in. Now, ye jest take this yer gal and flog her; ye've seen enough on't to know how."

"I beg mas'r's pardon," said Tom; "hopes mas'r won't set me at that. It's what I ain't used to—never did—and can't do, no way possible."

"Ye'll larn a pretty smart chance of things ye never did know, before I've done with ye!" said Legree, taking up a cow-hide, and striking Tom a heavy blow across the cheek, and following up the infliction by a shower of blows.

"There!" he said, as he stopped to rest; "now will ye tell me ye can't do it?"

"Yes, mas'r," said Tom, putting up his hand, to wipe the blood that trickled down his face. "I'm willin' to work, night and day, and work while there's life and breath in me; but this yer thing I can't feel it right to do; and, mas'r, I *never* shall do it—*never*."

Tom had a remarkably smooth, soft voice, and an habitually respectful manner, that had given Legree an idea that he would be cowardly, and easily subdued. When he spoke these last words, a thrill of amazement went through every one; the poor woman clasped her hands, and said, "O Lord!" and every one involuntarily looked at each other and drew in their breath, as if to prepare for the storm that was about to burst.

Legree looked stupefied and confounded; but at last burst forth.

"What! ye blasted black beast! tell *me* ye don't think it *right* to do what I tell ye! What have any of you cussed cattle to do with thinking what's right? I'll put a stop to it? Why, what do ye think ye are? May be ye think ye'r a gentlemen, master Tom, to be a telling your master what's right, and what ain't! So you pretend it's wrong to flog the gal?''

"I think so, mas'r," said Tom. "The poor crittur's sick and feeble; 'twould be downright cruel, and it's what I never will do, nor begin to. Mas'r, if you mean to kill me, kill me; but, as to my raising my hand agin any one here, I never shall—I'll die first!''

Tom spoke in a mild voice, but with a decision that could not be mistaken. Legree shook with anger; his greenish eyes glared fiercely, and his very whiskers seemed to curl with passion; but, like some ferocious beast, that plays with its victim before he devours it, he kept back his strong impulse to proceed to immediate violence, and broke out into bitter raillery.

"Well, here's a pious dog, at last, let down among us sinners!—a saint, a gentleman, and no less, to talk to us sinners about our sins! Powerful holy critter, he must be! Here, you rascal, you make believe to be so pious—didn't you never hear, out of yer Bible, 'Servants, obey your masters?' An't I your master? Didn't I pay down twelve hundred dollars, cash, for all there is in yer old cussed black shell? An't yer mine, now, body and soul?'' he said, giving Tom a violent kick with his heavy boot! "Tell me!''

In the very depth of physical suffering, bowed by brutal oppression, this question shot a gleam of joy and triumph through Tom's soul. He suddenly stretched himself up, and, looking earnestly to heaven, while the tears and blood that flowed down his face mingled, he exclaimed—

"No, no, no! my soul ain't yours, mas'r! You haven't bought it—ye can't buy it! It's been bought and paid for by one that's able to keep it! no matter, no matter, you can't harm me!''

"I can't!'' said Legree, with a sneer; "we'll see! Here, Sambo! Quimbo! give this dog such a breakin' in as he won't get over this month!''

The two gigantic negroes that now laid hold of Tom, with fiendish exultation in their faces, might have formed no unapt personification of powers of darkness. The poor woman screamed with apprehension, and all rose, as by a general impulse, while they dragged him unresisting from the place. . . .

"What the devil's got into Tom?'' Legree said to Sambo. "A while ago he was all down in the mouth, and now he's peart as a cricket.''

"Dunno, mas'r; gwine to run off, mebbe."

"Like to see him try that," said Legree, with a savage grin, "wouldn't we, Sambo?"

"Guess we would! haw! ho!" said the sooty gnome, laughing obsequiously. "Lord, de fun! To see him sticken' in the mud, chasin' and tarin' through de bushes, dogs a-holdin' on to him! Lord, I laughed fit to split, dat ar' time we cotched Molly. I thought they'd had her all stripped up afore I could get 'em off. She car's de marks o' dat ar' spree yet."

"I reckon she will to her grave," said Legree. "But now, Sambo, you look sharp! If the nigger's got anything of this sort going, trip him up."

"Mas'r, let me 'lone for dat!" said Sambo. "I'll tree de coon! Ho, ho, ho!"

This was spoken as Legree was getting on his horse to go to the neighbouring town. That night, as he was returning, he thought he would turn his horse and ride round the quarters, and see if all was safe.

It was a superb moonlight night, and the shadows of the graceful china-trees lay minutely pencilled on the turf below, and there was that transparent stillness in the air which it seems almost unholy to disturb. Legree was at a little distance from the quarters when he heard the voice of some one singing. It was not a usual sound there, and he paused to listen. A musical tenor voice sang—

> "When I can read my title clear
>   To mansions in the skies,
> I'll bid farewell to every fear,
>   And wipe my weeping eyes.
>
> "Should earth against my soul engage,
>   And hellish darts be buried,
> Then I can smile at Satan's rage,
>   And face a frowning world.
>
> "Let cares like a wild deluge come,
>   And storms of sorrow fall,
> May I but safely reach my home,
>   My God, my heaven, my all."

"So ho!" said Legree to himself, "he thinks so, does he? How I hate these cursed Methodist hymns! Here, you nigger!" said he, coming suddenly out upon Tom, and raising his riding-whip, "how dare you be gettin' up this yer row, when you ought to be in bed? Shut your old black gash, and get along in with you!"

"Yes, mas'r" said Tom, with ready cheerfulness, as he rose to go in.

Legree was provoked beyond measure by Tom's evident happiness; and, riding up to him, belaboured him over his head and shoulders.

"There, you dog," he said, "see if you feel so confortable after that!"

But the blows fell now only on the outer man, and not, as before, on the heart. Tom stood perfectly submissive; and yet Legree could not hide from himself that his power over his bond-thrall was somehow gone. And, as Tom disappeared in his cabin, and he wheeled his horse suddenly round, there passed through his mind one of those vivid flashes that often send the lightning of conscience across the dark and wicked soul. He understood full well that it was God who was standing between him and his victim, and he blasphemed him. That submissive and silent man, whom taunts, nor threats, nor stripes, nor cruelties could disturb, roused a voice within him, such as of old his Master roused in the demoniac soul, saying, "What have we to do with thee, thou Jesus of Nazareth? Art thou come to torment us before the time?"

"I REMEMBER PAPA"
by Harry Dolan

The other night after attending a gratifying function which had been initiated to help the black man, specifically to help build a nursery for children of working mothers, and after seeing and hearing white people make speeches professing their understanding and desire to go to any length to help, I found myself suddenly cornered and forced to defend the fabled laziness of the black man.

What was especially surprising was the fact that I assumed this white acquaintance—since he had paid thirty dollars to attend this dinner held for the purpose of helping the black man—did, at least in part, have some sympathy with what his, the white people, had tried to accomplish.

As I stood there watching his eyes I became suspect of my own sincerity, for I stood attentively nodding my head and smiling. I lit a cigarette, raised an eyebrow, performed all of the white man's laws of etiquette, and all the while I knew if it had been others of my black brothers, they would have cursed him for his smugness and invited him outside to test his theory of black man's courage and laziness. Of course I did none of these things. I grinned as he indicated in no uncertain terms that as soon as the black man got off his lazy butt and took advantage of all the blessings that had been offered him for the last two hundred years, then he, the white man, would indeed be willing to help.

I could have answered him—and was tempted to, for he was obviously sincere. Instead, I found an excuse to slip away and let a white man fight my battle, a friend, even a close friend. I went to a far corner and blindly played a game of pool by myself as the voices of this man and my friend dissected me. I stacked the pool balls, leaned over the table, and remembered a black man I had known.

It was said of him later in his life that he had let his family down. He'd been lazy, no-account, a troublemaker. Maybe so, maybe so, but I can't help remembering nights of his pacing the squeaking floor muttering to himself, coming back across the floor, sitting down, his legs trembling as he listened to the woman plead for him not to do anything bad.

"I'll go to hell first before I'll let you and the children starve." God, how many times had I heard him say that! How many other men standing bunched in helpless stagnation have I heard vow to take a gun and get some food for their children! Yes, they were planning to commit a crime; yes, they were potential criminals. Then. They are usually black too—another crime, it seems.

I remember that man, but more I remember his woman, my mother. Curiously though, I never remember her dancing, running, playing; always lying down, the smell of disinfectant strong, the deep continuous coughing, the brown paper bag filled with the toilet paper red with bubbly spit and blood, lying half concealed under the bed.

I never remember her eating food such as bread, meat, potatoes; only apples and only Delicious apples. In those days five cents apiece. She was a small woman, barely five foot.

"Junior," she would say softly. She never spoke above a whisper. "Go to the store and get me an apple." The thin trembling hand would reverse itself and slide up and under the covers and under the pillow and then return as though of its own volition, the weight almost too much, and as I'd start out the door, she would always smile and say, "Hurry, Junior."

I'd nod, and always, always there seemed to be a need to hurry. Those trips were always made with a feeling of breathless fear. I didn't know why then, only that for some reason I must always come back as soon as possible.

I was returning with an especially large apple, walking along, tempted to bite just a tiny piece, when I turned the corner and saw the black police ambulance standing in front of my door. Suddenly I had to go to the bathroom so bad I couldn't move. I stood watching as two uniformed men came out with the stretcher, and then the sound of my mother's shrill voice hit me.

"Mama, Mama," she was screaming. I could see her twisting and swinging at the lady next door as she was held back. I stood there feeling the hot piss run down my trembling legs, feeling cold chills spatter through my body, causing frozen limbs to spasmodically begin to move. I forced myself toward the police wagon as the men opened the doors and slid the stretcher along the bare metal. I saw my mother's head bounce on the floor.

"Wait," I moaned, "don't hurt her." Then I was running, screaming. "Please don't hurt her."

I looked down at her pain-filled face, and she smiled, even then she smiled. I showed her the apple. The effort to nod seemed a terrible effort but she did, her eyes so very bright, so very shiny.

"You eat it, Junior, you and sis."

"What's wrong, Mama?" I asked softly. "You really, really sick now?"

She nodded.

"Your father will be home soon. Tell him I'm at the General Hospital. Tell him to—to hurry."

"I'll tell him, Mama," I promised. "I'll tell him to hurry, Mama." She nodded sadly and puckered her lips as she always did since we weren't allowed to kiss her.

That was the last time I saw my mother except at the grave. My father came to the funeral with two white men who stood on each side of him all the time. There were people crying all around us. My grandmother kept squeezing me and moaning. I saw my father try to cover his face but one of the men said something and he stood up stiffly after that. I didn't cry, because my mother seemed to look happier, more rested than I had ever seen her. For some reason, I was glad she was dead. I think maybe, except for us, she was too.

I was nine, my sister five. It was not until ten years later that I saw my father again.

We sat on opposite sides of a screen and talked into telephones. I had come there to tell him that in spite of my beginning, I had made it. I was nineteen, and a radioman in the U. S. Coast Guard, ready to fight and die for my country. There had been something mysterious about his smile.

"I'm proud of you, boy," he said. "You're a real man. You know I volunteered for the front lines too, but they turned me down."

We don't want you, I thought, we're not criminals, we're honest, strong. Then I looked again at this thief, this "Loaf-of-bread gunman" as the papers had tagged him. He had taken five loaves of bread, along with twelve dollars. Suddenly I could not stay there condemning this man, my father. It seemed such a waste, this magnificently strong man sitting there, his tremendous chest barely moving, hands resting quietly. He seemed to have accepted his fate and yet I felt as though he were talking to me, his whole being showering torrents of words about me.

"Be careful, boy, there are so many ways to fail, the pitfall sometimes seems to be the easiest way out. Beware of my future, for you must continue, you must live. You must, for in you are all the dreams of my nights, all the ambitions of my days."

A bell rang and we stood up and a man pointed me toward a heavy door. I looked back, and saw him standing easy, hands at his side, so very calm, yet my mind filled to overflowing with the many things he had not said. It was to be ten years before he walked again as a free man, that is, as a physically free man.

I remember an earlier time, an earlier chapter of my growing up. I remember the first time my mother said we were taking lunch to my father's job. We had been down to the welfare line and I had stood with her, our feet burning against the hot pavement, and slowly moved forward in the sun. Years later I stood in chow lines over half of the world, but no desert, no burning deck was as hot as that day.

At last we reached the man sitting at the desk and my mother handed him the book of stamps. She smiled, a weak almost timid smile, as he checked her name and thumbed her to the food line.

As we headed home, my wagon was loaded with cans of corned beef, powdered milk, powdered eggs, and white margarine that she would later color yellow to look like butter.

At home we made sandwiches and off we went to my father's job, to take him his lunch. I pulled my sister along in my wagon, a Red Flyer.

It was to be a picnic, a celebration really, my father's new job.

I remember the wagon did not have a tongue or handle but only a rope with which I pulled it wobbling along. We were excited, my sister and I, as we left our district of dirt streets and unpaved sidewalks and began to make our way along roads called boulevards and malls we had never had occasion to travel. The streets themselves were fascinating, so different. They were twice as wide, and there were exotic trees along the sidewalks and lo and behold trees down the center of the street as far as I could see and then we turned the corner and before us stretched an overwhelming sight. An overhead highway was being built. Columns rose to staggering heights, bulldozers thrust what seemed to me mountains of dirt before them, and hundreds, no thousands of men seemed to be crawling like ants hurrying from one point to another. Cranes lifted nets of steel and laid them in rows on the crushed rock.

I stared in awe at important-looking white men in metal hats, carrying rolls of papers which they intermittently studied, then pointing into space at what to me seemed only emptiness.

And then I saw my father. He sat among fifty other black men, all surrounded by great boulders marked with red paint. They all held steel chisels with which they cut along the marked lines. They would strike a certain point and the boulder would split into smaller pieces and as we approached there was a silence around them except for the pinging of the hammer against the chisel. In all the noise it was a lonely sound, futile, lost, oppressive. My father seemed to be concentrating, his tremendous arm whipping the air. He was stripped to the waist, black muscles popping sweat, goggled eyes for the metal and stone only. We stood there, the three of us, my mother, my sister, and I, and watched my father work for us, and as he conquered the huge boulder my chest filled with pride. Each stroke shouted for all the world to hear: This is my family and I love them! No one can tell me this was the act of a lazy man.

Suddenly a white man walked up and blew a whistle and the black men all looked up and stopped working. My father glanced over at me, grinned and winked. He was glistening with sweat, the smell strong and powerful. He dropped his big hand on my shoulder and guided me to a large boulder.

"Hey, boy, you see me beat that thing to bits? This one's next," he said, indicating the one that shaded us from the sun. "I'll pound it to gravel by nightfall." It was a challenge he expected, he welcomed. That was my lazy, shiftless father.

And then one day they brought him home, his thumb, index, and middle finger gone from his left hand. They sat him in the kitchen chair and mumbled something about carelessness. He sat there for two hours before he answered our pleadings.

"Chain broke, I—I was guiding boulder. I couldn't, I just couldn't get my hand out from under in time—I, goddam it, Jean, they took my fingers off. I layed right there, my hand under the rock, and they nipped them like butchering a hog. Look at my goddam hand."

My mother held him in her arms and talked to him. She spoke softly, so softly my sister and I, standing in the corner, couldn't hear the words, only the soothing softness of her voice.

"Joe, Joe, we can." And then he began to cry like—like I sometimes did when I was hurt deep inside and couldn't do anything about it.

After that there was a change in him. My father had been a fighter. He had feared no man white or black. I remember the time we were sitting on a streetcar and a woman had forgotten her fare—or maybe she never had any in the first place. Anyway, the driver slammed the doors on her and held her squeezed between them.

My father jumped up, snatched the driver out of the seat, and let the woman out. He and the driver had words that led to battle and Pop knocked the driver down just as a patrolman arrived. The patrolman didn't listen to any of the people that tried to explain what had happened. He just began to swing his night stick at my father's head. It was a mistake. My father hit him once and even today I can see all the people laughing at the funny look on the policeman's face as he staggered back all the way across the street and up against a building, slowly sagging down.

The police wagon arrived with four other policemen and one told him they were going to beat his brains in when they got him downtown.

My pop had laughed then and backed against the building.

"I guess ain't no sense me going peaceable then."

They knocked out all his upper front teeth that day, but as he said later, "Them four white boys will think of me every time they shave."

They finally overpowered him and dragged him, still struggling, to the wagon. One of them kept muttering, "He's one fighting son of a black bitch, he's a fighting son of a bitch."

All the time I hadn't said a word or cried or yelled as they stomped and kicked him. I had shut my eyes and held my lips tightly pressed together and I had done just as he'd always told me.

"You stay out of it, boy, stay real quiet, and when that wagon leaves, you run behind and keep it in sight. If they lose you, you ask someone where the closest police station is—that's where I'll be. You go home and tell your mother."

That's the way he had been before losing his left hand. Afterwards, well, it took a lot from him. He told me one day, laughing and shaking the nub as he called it, "If I'd only had the thumb, just the lousy thumb, I'd have it made."

Gradually he lost the ability to see humor in the nub. I think the whole thing came to a head the night I killed the kitten.

We hadn't had meat or potatoes for over two weeks. Even the grease drippings were gone and my mother was too sick to raise her head from the pillow. So I had gotten the skillet and put it in the open grate. We had two cups of flour so I mixed water with it and poured it into the greasy skillet. I can still recall the coldness of the room on my back and the warmth from the grate on my face as my sister and I knelt and hungrily watched the flour brown.

You know, today my wife marvels at how, no matter what she puts before me, I eat with relish. My children say that I eat very fast. I pray to God they never have to experience the causes of my obsession. But back to the story—the flour finally hardened and I broke a piece for my sister and a piece for my mother and left mine in the skillet on the table.

I took my mother's piece over to the bed and put it in her hand. She didn't move so I raised her hand to her mouth and she began to suck on it. Then I heard my sister scream, "Topsy is eating your food, Junior, Topsy's eating your food!" I turned around to see the cat tearing at my tiny piece of hard dough. I went wild. I leaped across the room and grabbed the kitten by the tail and began slamming her against the wall.

"That's my food," I kept yelling, "my food!" At last I heard my sister screaming, "She's bleeding, you're killing Topsy. Here, here, eat my bread. Please don't kill her."

I stopped, horrified, staring at the limp nothing I now held. It was two weeks later that they got me to speak and that same night my father left the house for the last time. I don't say that what he did was right. No, it most assuredly was wrong. But what I do ask is, what else could he have done? I need an answer quickly, now, today, for I tell you this, my children will not starve, not here, not in this time of millions to foreign countries and fountains to throw tons of water upward to the sky, and nothing to the hungry, thirsty multitudes a stone's throw away.

Document III-4: PROTEST IN WORDS AND MUSIC

Songs have been associated with many reform movements. Most of them have been ephemeral. Only archivists can produce the words and music to the "campaign songsters" that have appeared each quadrennium. Except for the ballad "Joe Hill" even the colorful and sometimes original songs of the Industrial Workers of the World have passed from currency. Perhaps because their roots were close to folk and spiritual music, however, the songs associated with the anti-slavery and civil rights movements have remained nearer the surface of public memory.

One example of this is the song "We Shall Overcome," which music critic Irving Lowens appropriately called "the Marseillaise of the civil rights movement." According to Lowens (*Washington Star*, July 11, 1965, p. E8; see also Robert Shelton in the *New York Times*, July 23, 1963, p. 21), the words are traceable to a song copyrighted in 1901 and the tune to gospel singing in Chicago in the 1940s. Coming together in the late forties, words and music were sung at strikes and workshops, prisons and rallies. Pete Seeger made some important revisions and sang it wherever he went. Both the above newspaper articles quoted at length from a statement by the Reverend Wyatt Tee Walker, a close associate of Martin Luther King, concerning the impact of this song among blacks and civil rights workers throughout the South. The published version, copyrighted by Seeger along with Frank Hamilton, Guy Carawan, and Zilphia Horton, contained an announcement that royalty proceeds would be used in support of the "freedom movement."

A suggestion of longer continuity is provided by the two pieces of music that follow. The first is a song expressing the slaves' determination to be free. According to Thomas W. Higginson, it grew out of the Civil War conflict and was first sung by slaves conscripted to build forts at Hilton Head and Bay Point under General Beauregard. John Lovel indicated that it may have been among those songs used as signals along the underground railway. (*Black Song: the Forge and the Flame.* New York, Macmillan, 1972, pp. 333-34). It has the measured pace of a work song; in fact, its slow stateliness might lead one to suspect its use as accompaniment for one of slavery's favorite forms of passive sabotage: the work slowdown.

The second song was second only to "We Shall Overcome" as a rallying point for civil rights gatherings in the 1960s and early 1970s. Every socially active group singer had it in the front of his repertoire and, according to a Library of Congress routine search in 1966, there were at least seventy-five recordings of it available.

Comparing these two numbers, one can see the large degree of continuity that pervades the singing protests of the 1860s and 1960s. The songs are both expressive of the same mood: long-suffering patience near its end. In spite of composer Bob Dylan's notation in favor of a "bright, spirited" rendition, both songs are usually sung with measured dignity. Leaving out the refrains, the melodic lines mirror each other with very little variation. Comparing Dylan's song with the most accessible modern version of "Many Thousan' Gone" (*Fireside Book of Folksongs,* edited by Margaret Bradford Boni, arranged by Norman Lloyd. New York, Simon and Schuster, 1947, p. 187), one finds them both in the same key with the same chord sequence.

Whether or not Bob Dylan created "Blowin' in the Wind" from "Many Thousan' Gone" (and it would be very hard to prove), it is interesting that the two songs resemble each other so strongly—that the American Negroes and their sympathizers could be similarly moved by songs so much alike in mood and melody even though the two songs emerged at an interval of one hundred years.

SOURCE: A: "Many Thousan' Gone" is also known as "Many Thousand Go," "No more auction block for me," "No more driver's lash for me," and so forth, depending on which first line was locally first sung. The "pint o' salt" and the "peck o' corn" referred to in some versions was a typical slave ration. This version is from

MANY THOUSAND GO.

1. No more peck o' corn for me, No more, no more;

No more peck o' corn for me, Man-y tousand go.

2 No more driver's lash for me.

3 No more pint o' salt for me.

4 No more hundred lash for me.

5 No more mistress' call for me.

A: "Many Thousand Go"

B: "Blowin' in the Wind"

Slave Songs of the United States, William F. Allen, Charles P. Ware, and Lucy McKim Garrison, eds. New York, Simpson, 1867, p. 48. B: "Blowin' in the Wind," words and music by Bob Dylan. New York, M. Witmark, 1962.

Document III-5: MILITANT PRESS

The history of the periodical press in America is rich with examples of social crusades, each one different in setting and detail, but each with its own colorful personalities and issues. The republic was hardly born before Jefferson and the Federalists were warring through the press, as every textbook reader knows. Document II-7 recorded the establishment of a working man's press in New York City in the 1820s with many branches and varieties to come. The famous Hearst-Pulitzer newspaper war two generations later aroused feelings not only against Spain but also against the trusts (see II-28). The flurries, the debates in words and pictures, the causes and crusades go on. "The inkstand," Garrison said, "is the greatest stand for civilization." (Ralph Korngold, *Two Friends of Man.* Boston, Little, Brown, 1950, p. 383.)

The following pair of documents is intended primarily to illustrate the role and value of the press. Neither selection is meant to be representative: rather, each allows for the examination of what has been generally perceived as an extreme and incendiary position. The spokesmen behind these papers—William Lloyd Garrison and Elijah Muhammad—are both strong and predictable, but by no means simple. They and their words need to be seen against the background of some complex issues.

The *Liberator* was born with Garrison's conversion from gradualism to the vision of slavery as sin. As a moral absolutist he could not compromise with sin. Thus his paper persisted, unswervingly, until emancipation had been achieved . . . and persisted not one moment longer.

The paper itself was not so narrow as one might suppose. It gave space to the discussion of several reform causes other than slavery: temperance and woman's rights, for example. It was even complimented on its willingness to entertain a variety of views on the slavery question, as was indeed Garrison's rule at the meetings over which he presided (see III-6). Yet there was no mistaking the heavy, black, block letters that announced the title of the unadorned early numbers of the *Liberator*. The typography perfectly matched the iron words of the editor's opening address to his public, inimitable in their fierce rigidity. In the later excerpt one sees a veteran reformer put down his composing stick, not greatly mellowed, but buoyed by a sense of sure achievement.

In between these first and last issues the *Liberator* served as a landmark in the history of social agitation. No publication was so consistently despised for so long a time on a single issue. No editor, covering such a complex and changing question, remained so singlemindedly unflinching, bending the issues to his arguments rather than vice versa. The *Liberator* never made any money. Its circulation was never very large. It was not a handsome or gracious publication. It simply represents the greatest sustained effort in reform journalism.

Whether or not *Muhammad Speaks* can be viewed as a contemporary equivalent to Garrisonian journalism depends on whether one insists on exact or relative parallels. Certainly Islam has been much less horrified by violence than was Garrison. The verses quoted from each paper force one to realize even more basic differences in attitudes—e.g., which race is in a position to liberate the other? Crucial to comparing the two movements and their eras is the question of black separatism. Separatism as proposed by whites (in the form of colonization) was of course the form of gradualism that Garrison had found most pernicious.

Separatism as proposed by blacks has operated from the high intellectual level of a W. E. B. DuBois and his pan-African movement, to the electric, controversial Jamaican Marcus Garvey and his ''Back to Africa'' scheme. During the last decade, the separatist impulse has appeared most clearly in the Black Muslims. Their leader, Elijah Muhammad, who was once a member of Marcus Garvey's splendidly uniformed corps, has chosen a religious rather than a military form of organization. Like Garvey, however, he had always made closer identification with Africa a major part of his appeal to American blacks. Malcolm X, apparently finding the leader's views vague and his patience too abiding, had formed, before his assassination, a splinter group called the Organization for Afro-American Unity. Other separatists have followed the lead of Robert S. Browne, who has called for the establishment of a wholly black new nation within the present boundaries of the United States.

There is little evidence to suggest many American blacks wish either to emigrate to Africa or to establish a separate North American community. It is clear, however, that black leaders have always offered two distinct paths toward social justice and that the division between these two paths is at least as plainly marked as ever. One path leads directly toward integration. It accepts the values of the dominant culture (including Christianity) and it makes use of white participation. It does not seek to change American society in a revolutionary way; it wants for blacks a fair and integrated place in that society. It can be represented by organizations like the National Association for the Advancement of Colored People (see III-9B), by leaders like Martin Luther King, Jr. (see III-7B), and by events like the March on Washington (see III-6B).

The second path begins with black identity (as separate from white) and black pride. The ability of blacks—past and present—to achieve important goals in a nonwhite context is an important message. Thus the Muslims, building on African and Southern lore, have constructed a web of custom, language, and diet designed to set off the black population and to give it pride in its distinctiveness. Giving up their "slave names" of European origin, they accept names of Muslim significance. (See E. U. Essien-Udom, *Black Nationalism.* Chicago, University of Chicago, 1962.) Finding in the term Negro a heritage of white condescension (as did David Walker) they write and speak of the "so-called Negro" and accept "black" as a preferable term. As the following article by the leader makes clear, the Muslims have taken upon themselves the awkward task of transferring the normal Christian allegiance of black Americans to a new framework. It is also clear that at this stage the Bible still serves as the principal useful fount of authority.

SOURCE: A: the *Liberator*, vol. I, no. 1 (January 1, 1831), p. 1; vol. XXV, no. 52 (December 29, 1865), p. 206. Garrison reprinted his "To the Public" of the opening issue in the closing number, titling it "Salutatory" and following it with his "Valedictory." He did not reprint the verse called "The Salutation," which is understandable; harder to understand is his omission of the original italics in the reprinting of his prose. B: *Muhammad Speaks*, vol. II, no. 17 (May 13, 1963), pp. 1, 13.

A: The *Liberator*

THE SALUTATION.

To date my being from the opening year,
I come, a stranger in this busy sphere,
Where some I meet perchance may pause and ask,
What is my name, my purpose, or my task?

My name is 'LIBERATOR'! I propose
To hurl my shafts at freedom's deadliest foes!
My task is hard—for I am charged to save
Man from his brother!—to redeem the slave!

Ye who may hear, and yet condemn my cause,
Say, shall the best of Nature's holy laws
Be trodden down and shall her open veins
Flow but for cement to her offspring's chains?

Art thou a parent? shall thy children be
Rent from thy breast, like branches from the tree,
And doom'd to servitude, in helplessness,
On other shores, and thou ask no redress?

Thou, in whose bosom glows the sacred flame
Of filial love, say, if the tyrant came,
To force thy parent shrieking from thy sight,
Would thy heart bleed—*because thy face is white?*

Art thou a brother? shall thy sister twine
Her feeble arm in agony on thine,
And thou not lift the heel, nor aim the blow
At him who bears her off to life-long woe?

Art thou a sister? will no desp'rate cry
Awake thy sleeping brother, while thine eye
Beholds the fetters locking on the limb
Stretched out in rest, which hence, must end,
    for him?

Art thou a lover?—no! naught e'er was found
In lover's breast, save cords of love, that bound
Man to his kind! then, thy professions save!
Forswear affection, or release thy slave!

Thou who art kneeling at thy Maker's shrine,
Ask if Heaven takes such offerings as thine!
If in thy bonds the son of Afric sighs,
Far higher than thy prayer his groan will rise!

God is a God of mercy, and would see
The prison doors unbarr'd—the bondmen free!
He is a God of truth, with purer eyes
Than to behold the oppressor's sacrifice!

Avarice, thy cry and thine insatiate thirst
Make man consent to see his brother cursed!
Tears, sweat and blood thou drink'st, but in
    their turn,
They shall cry 'more!' while vengeance bids
    thee burn.

The Lord hath said it!—who shall him gainsay?
He says, 'the wicked, they shall go away'—
Who are the wicked?—Contradict who can,
They are the oppressors of their fellow man!

Aid me, NEW ENGLAND! 'tis my hope in you
Which gives me strength my purpose to pursue!
Do you not hear your sister States resound
With Afric's cries to have her sons unbound?

TO THE PUBLIC

In the month of August, I issued proposals for publishing 'THE LIBERATOR' in Washington city; but the enterprise, though hailed in different sections of the country, was palsied by public indifference. Since that time, the removal of the Genius of Universal Emancipation to the Seat of Government has rendered less imperious the establishment of a similar periodical in that quarter.

During my recent tour for the purpose of exciting the minds of the people by a series of discourses on the subject of slavery, every place that I visited gave fresh evidence of the fact, that a greater revolution in public sentiment was to be effected in the free states—*and particularly in New England*—than at the south. I found contempt more bitter, opposition more active, detraction more relentless, prejudice more stubborn, and apathy more frozen, than among slave owners themselves. Of course, there were individual exceptions to the contrary. This state of things afflicted, but did not dishearten me. I determined, at every hazard, to lift up the standard of emancipation in the eyes of the nation, *within sight of Bunker Hill and in the birth place of liberty.* That standard is now unfurled; and long may it float, unhurt by the spoiliations of time or the missiles of a desperate foe—yea, till every chain be broken, and every bondman set free! Let southern oppressors tremble—let their secret abettors tremble—let their northern apologists tremble—let all the enemies of the persecuted blacks tremble.

I deem the publication of my original Prospectus unnecessary, as it has obtained a wide circulation. The principles therein inculcated will be steadily pursued in this paper, excepting that I shall not array myself as the political partisan of any man. In defending the great cause of human rights, I wish to derive the assistance of all religions and of all parties.

Assenting to the 'self-evident truth' maintained in the American Declaration of Independence, 'that all men are created equal, and endowed by their Creator with certain inalienable rights—among which are life, liberty and the pursuit of happiness,' I shall strenuously contend for the immediate enfranchisement of our slave population. In Park-street Church, on the Fourth of July, 1829, in an address on slavery, I unreflectingly assented to the popular but pernicious doctrine of *gradual* abolition. I seize this opportunity to make a full and unequivocal recantation, and thus publicly to ask pardon of my God, of my country, and of my brethren the poor slaves, for having uttered a sentiment so full of timidity, injustice and absurdity. A similar recantation, from my pen, was published in the Genius of Universal Emancipation at Baltimore, in September, 1829. My conscience is now satisfied.

I am aware, that many object to the severity of my language; but is there not cause for severity? I *will be* as harsh as truth, and as uncompromising as justice. On this subject, I do not wish to think, or speak, or write, with moderation. No! no! Tell a man whose house is on fire, to give a moderate alarm; tell him to moderately rescue his wife from the hands of the ravisher; tell the mother to gradually extricate her babe from the fire into which it has fallen;—but urge me not to use moderation in a cause like the present. I am in earnest—I will not equivocate—I will not excuse—I will not retreat a single inch—AND I WILL BE HEARD. The apathy of the people is enough to make every statue leap from its pedestal, and to hasten the resurrection of the dead.

It is pretended, that I am retarding the cause of emancipation by the coarseness of my invective, and the precipitancy of my measures. *The charge is not true.* On this question my influence,—humble as it is,—is felt at this moment to a considerable extent, and shall be felt in coming years—not perniciously, but beneficially—not as a curse, but as a blessing; and posterity will bear testimony that I was right. I desire to thank God, that he enables me to disregard 'the fear of man which bringeth a snare,' and to speak his truth in its simplicity and power. And here I close with this fresh dedication:

> 'Oppression! I have seen thee, face to face,
> And met thy cruel eye and cloudy brow;
> But thy soul-withering glance I fear not now—
> For dread to prouder feelings doth give place
> Of deep abhorrence! Scorning the disgrace
> Of slavish knees that at thy footstool bow,

I also kneel—but with far other vow
Do hail thee and thy herd of hirelings base:—
I swear, while life-blood warms my throbbing veins,
Still to oppose and thwart, with heart and hand,
Thy brutalising sway—till Afric's chains
Are burst, and Freedom rules the rescued land,—
Trampling Oppression and his iron rod:
Such is the vow I take—SO HELP ME GOD!'

—William Lloyd Garrison

Boston, January 1, 1831

VALEDICTORY.

THE LAST NUMBER OF THE LIBERATOR.

"The last! the last! the last!
O, by that little word
How many thoughts are stirred—
That sister of THE PAST!"

The present number of the *Liberator* is the completion of its thirty-fifth volume, and the termination of its existence.

Commencing my editorial career when only twenty years of age, I have followed it continuously till I have attained my sixtieth year—first, in connection with *The Free Press*, in Newburyport; in the spring of 1826; next, with *The National Philanthropist*, in Boston, in 1827; next, with *The Journal of the Times*, in Bennington, Vt., in 1828-9; next, with *The Genius of Universal Emancipation*, in Baltimore, in 1829-30; and, finally, with the *Liberator*, in Boston, from the 1st of January, 1831, to the 1st of January, 1866;—at the start, probably the youngest member of the editorial fraternity in the land, now, perhaps, the oldest, not in years, but in continuous service,—unless Mr. Bryant, of the New York *Evening Post*, be an exception.

Whether I shall again be connected with the press, in a similar capacity, is quite problematical; but, at my period of life, I feel no prompting to start a new journal at my own risk, and with the certainty of struggling against wind and tide, as I have done in the past.

I began the publication of the *Liberator* without a subscriber, and I end it—it gives me unalloyed satisfaction to say—without a farthing as the pecuniary result of the patronage extended to it during thirty-five years of unremitted labors.

From the immense change wrought in the national feeling and sentiment on the subject of slavery, the *Liberator* derived no advantage at any time in regard to its circulation. The original "disturber of the peace," nothing was left undone at the beginning, and up to the hour of the late rebellion, by Southern slaveholding villainy on the one hand, and Northern pro-slavery malice on the other, to represent it as too vile a sheet to be countenanced by any claiming to be Christian or patriotic; and it always required rare moral courage or singular personal independence to be among its patrons. Never had a journal to look such opposition in the face—never was one so constantly belied and caricatured. If it had advocated all the crimes forbidden by the moral law of God and the statutes of the State, instead of vindicating the sacred claims of oppressed and bleeding humanity, it could not have been more vehemently denounced or more indignantly repudiated. To this day—such is the force of prejudice—there are multitudes who cannot be induced to read a single number of it, even on the score of curiosity, though their views on the slavery question are now precisely those which it has uniformly advocated. Yet no journal has been conducted with such fairness and impartiality; none has granted such freedom in its columns to its opponents; none has so scrupulously and uniformly presented all sides of every question discussed in its pages; none has so readily and exhaustively published, without note or comment, what its enemies have said to its disparagement, and the villification of its editor; none has vindicated primitive Christianity, in its spirit and purpose—"the higher law," in its supremacy over nations and governments as well as individual conscience—the Golden Rule, in its binding obligation upon all classes—the Declaration of Independence, with its self-evident truths—the rights of human nature, without distinction of race, complexion or sex—more earnestly or more uncompromisingly; none has exerted a higher moral or more broadly reformatory influence upon those who have given it a careful perusal; and none has gone beyond it in asserting the Fatherhood of God and the brotherhood of man. All this may be claimed for it without egotism or presumption. It has ever been "a terror to evil-doers, and a praise to them that do well." It has excited the fierce hostility of all that is vile and demoniacal in the land, and won the affection and regard of the purest and noblest of the age. To me it has been unspeakably cheering, and the richest compensation for whatever of peril, suffering and defamation I have been called to encounter; that one uniform testimony has been borne, by those who have had its weekly perusal, as to the elevating and quickening influence of the *Liberator* upon their character and lives; and the deep grief they are expressing in view of its discontinuance is overwhelmingly affecting to my feelings. Many of these date their subscription from the commencement of the paper, and they have allowed nothing in its columns to pass without a rigid scrutiny. They speak, therefore, experimentally, and "testify of that which they have seen and do know." Let them be assured that my regret in the separation which is to take place between us, in consequence of the discontinuance of the *Liberator*, is at least as poignant as their own; and let them feel, as I do, comforted by the thought that it relates only to the weekly method of communicating with each other, and not to the principles we have espoused in the past, or the hopes and aims we cherish as to the future.

Although the *Liberator* was designed to be, and has ever been, mainly devoted to the abolition of slavery, yet it has been instrumental in aiding the cause of reform in many of its most important aspects.

I have never consulted either the subscription list of the paper or public sentiment in printing, or omitting to print, any article touching any matter whatever. Personally, I have never asked any one to become a subscriber, nor any one to contribute to its support, nor presented its claims for a better circulation in any lecture or speech, or at any one of the multitudinous anti-slavery gatherings in the land. Had I done so, no doubt its subscription list might have been much enlarged.

In this connection, I must be permitted to express my surprise that I am gravely informed, in various quarters, that this is no time to retire from public labor; that though the chains of the captive have been broken, he is yet to be vindicated in regard to the full possession of equal civil and political rights; that the freed men in every part of the South are subjected to many insults and outrages; that the old slaveholding spirit is showing itself in every available form; that there is imminent danger that, in the hurry of reconstruction and readmission to the Union, the late rebel States will be left free to work any amount of mischief; that there is manifestly a severe struggle yet to come with thenSouthern "powers of

darkness,'' which will require the utmost vigilance and the most determined efforts on the part of the friends of impartial liberty—&c., &c.,
&c. Surely, it is not meant by all this that I am therefore bound to
continue the publication of the *Liberator*; for that is a matter for me to
determine, and no one else. As I commenced its publication without
asking leave of any one, so I claim to be competent to decide when it may
fitly close its career.

Again—it cannot be meant, by this presentation of the existing state of
things at the South, either to impeach my intelligence, or to impute to me
a lack of interest in behalf of that race, for the liberation and elevation of
which I have labored so many years! If, when they had no friends, and no
hope of earthly redemption, I did not hesitate to make their cause my
own, is it to be supposed that, with their yokes broken, and their friends
and advocates mutiplied indefinitely, I can be any the less disposed to
stand by them to the last—to insist on the full measure of justice and
equity being meted out to them—to retain in my breast a lively and
permanent interest in all that relates to their present condition and future
welfare!

I shalt sound no trumpet and make no parade as to what I shall do for
the future. After having gone through with such a struggle as has never
been paralleled in duration in the life of any reformer, and for nearly forty
years been the target at which all poisonous and deadly missiles have
been hurled, and having seen our great national iniquity blotted out, and
freedom ''proclaimed throughout all the land to all the inhabitants
thereof,'' and a thousand presses and pulpits supporting the claims of the
colored population to fair treatment where not one could be found to do
this in the early days of the anti-slavery conflict, I might—it seems to
me—be permitted to take a little repose in my advanced years, if I desired
to do so. But, as yet, I have neither asked nor wished to be relieved of any
burdens or labors connected with the good old cause. I see a mighty work
of enlightenment and regeneration yet to be accomplished at the South,
and many cruel wrongs done to the freedmen which are yet to be
redressed; and I neither counsel others to turn away from the field of
conflict, under the delusion that no more remains to be done, nor
contemplate such a course in my own case.

The object for which the *Liberator* was commenced—the extermina-
tion of chattel slavery—having been gloriously consummated, it seems
to me specially appropriate to let its existence cover the historic period of

the great struggle; leaving what remains to be done to complete the work
of emancipation to other instrumentalities, (of which I hope to avail
myself,) under new auspices, with more abundant means, and with
millions instead of hundreds for allies.

Most happy am I to be no longer in conflict with the mass of my
fellow-countrymen on the subject of slavery. For no man of any refinement or sensibility can be indifferent to the approbation of his fellow-
men, if it be rightly earned. But to obtain it by going with the multitude to
do evil—by pandering to despotic power or a corrupt public sentiment—
is self-degradation and personal dishonor:

> "For more true joy Marcellus exiled feels,
> Than Caesar with a senate at his heels"

Better to be always in a minority of one with God—branded as madman,
incendiary, fanatic, heretic, infidel—frowned upon by "the powers that
be," and mobbed by the populace—or consigned ignominiously to the
gallows, like him whose "soul is marching on," though his "body lies
mouldering in the grave," or burnt to ashes at the stake like Wickliffe, or
nailed to the cross like him who "gave himself for the world,"—in
defence of the RIGHT, than like Herod, having the shouts of a multitude,
crying, "It is the voice of a god, and not of a man!"

Farewell, tried and faithful patrons! Farewell, generous benefactors,
without whose voluntary but essential pecuniary contributions the
Liberator must have long since been discontinued! Farewell, noble men
and women who have wrought so long and so successfully, under God, to
break every yoke! Hail, ye ransomed millions! Hail, year of jubilee!
With a grateful heart and a fresh baptism of the soul, my last invocation
shall be—

> "Spirit of Freedom! on—
>   Oh! pause not in thy flight
>   Till every clime is won
>   To worship in thy light:
>   Speed on thy glorious way,
>   And wake the sleeping lands!
>   Millions are watching for the ray,
>   And lift to thee their hands.

Still Onward!' be thy cry—
  Thy banner on the blast;
And, like a tempest, as thou rushest by,
  Despots shall shrink aghast.
On! till thy name is known
  Throughout the peopled earth;
On! till thou reign'st alone,
  Man's heritage by birth;
On! till from every vale, and where the mountains rise,
The beacon lights of Liberty shall kindle to the skies!''

—*Wm. Lloyd Garrison.*

Boston, December 29, 1865.

B: *Muhammad Speaks*

KILLERS TO JUDGE?
By ELIJAH MUHAMMAD

Can we expect justice? Day after day, the Defense Attorneys for the Muslims seek a panel of jurymen from among the very brothers of our killers. Will they judge according to justice? History shows that our enemies will not judge according to the law of justice. From the day (1555) that our fathers were brought to the Western Hemisphere by our enemy (John Hawkins) we have not received justice.

On that fatal and memorable day of April 27, 1962, in Los Angeles, California, seventy-five heavily armed Los Angeles Policemen raided our meeting place (Mosque No. 27) in such a savage and beastlike manner that most civilized people were unable to conceive. They shot down six (6) innocent, unarmed brother Muslims in cold blood without warning, killing one, Ronald T. X. Stokes, instantly.

Another was shot in the back; consequently, paralyzing him for life. They lined others against the wall of the Mosque. The savage policemen threatened to kill all of the men, women and children of the Muslims who showed the least resistance. They cursed and called us filthy, indecent names.

This wholesale killing of my followers cannot be forgotten nor forgiven! The killing of one of my followers means the death for ten to ten times ten of the infidels besides the great loss of their property. Believe it or not, but calculate on your ever increasing loss of lives and property on the land, air and sea.

As it is written: (Matt. 18:6) "Whosoever shall offend one of these little ones (The so-called Negro Muslims) which believe in me, it were better for him that a millstone were hanged about his neck, and that he were drowned in the depth of the sea." This is now being fulfilled—not two thousand years ago!

The devils killed not only Jesus' least ones, but they killed Jesus, himself, and all of his disciples but one (John). The Christians have suffered many losses as a result of the death of Jesus to the death of Muhammad in the seventh century. And she (America) is suffering universal rejection, even by her own people. And she will suffer finally total destruction by fire from Almighty Allah (God) to Whom be praised forever.

The devils' attack upon us (The Muslims) was made mainly because Allah (God) has revealed to us the truth of them being the real devils, and the time for their doom. Surely we the black people have suffered injustices at the hands of our slave masters and their children. But the time is near and has arrived that our God, Allah, will make our enemies to suffer. But how can the Scriptures be fulfilled (Isa. 59:14 "Justice Standeth afar off") if we the righteous (The Muslims) do not suffer?

There is no justice in this people for us (The "Black Muslims" and so-called Negroes). This people is the real enemy of Allah (God) and His Prophets and all members of the Black Nation. They are charged with being the murderers of the Prophets and the righteous, Matt. 23:27. You and I have experienced such inhuman treatment at their hands for the past 400 years that we have been here in America.

Our enemies do not like that the so-called Negroes know the truth of them being the real devils and that their religion called Christianity is not the true religion of Allah (God). Their religion, Christianity, is an organized religion by those who oppose the true religion, Islam, of Allah which means entire submission to the will of Allah (God).

After the death of Jesus, they organized the religion called Christianity and called it the teachings of Jesus while they know that Jesus was a Prophet of the religion of Islam as Moses and all the Prophets before him were of the religion of Islam.

By my Allah you are just not going to get away with killing my followers (the Black Muslims as we are called, and it is a very honorable name). Why should not we have fifty Muslims and fifty Christians to make up the Jury panel? By excluding the Muslims as jurymen is the first step towards injustice. What kind of justice can we expect from the very brothers of the killers?

HURRY AND JOIN ONTO YOUR OWN KIND! THE TIME OF THIS WORLD IS AT HAND!

MUHAMMAD'S MOSQUE
No. 2
5335 S. Greenwood Ave.
Chicago 15, Illinois.

HOME AGAIN

Hello Africa! I am your kidnaped brother
Greed intoxicated Crowned Heads tore me from
your virgin shores to build empires upon
stolen land. If I am a stranger, it is not
to the curse of slavery.

Calloused hands have humanized a nation by
the rocking of the cradle.
We reset our destiny with the plough and hoe.
We conquered barbarians with a patient smile.
Our pathos projected justice in a new dimension.

We are the soul of America.

Shallow graves in southern cottonfields did
not hold our hope.

Our ancestral image sustained us from
the Bleached Cross
Black jungles
Spangled animals
Dusty people
Proud people

> Which were left at home until we were free.
> Let the reaching Ethiopian hand
> Return them to me.

—Waldo Phillips

Document III-6: PUBLIC DYNAMICS

There is no denying the presence or importance of violence in the history of reform especially in relation to movements complicated by racial tensions. Generalizations on this subject must begin with the recognition of two distinct levels of violence. One is more or less controlled, is directed at property more than people, and often takes the form of resistance to unwelcome authority. Many groups in this century—from the English agitators for women's votes to American resisters to the war in Southeast Asia—have initiated this kind of violence with the aim of dramatizing their causes. Civil rights demonstrators in the South illustrated the use of this technique by provoking their own submission and arrest, thus showing themselves to be more the victims of violent restraint than destroyers of the rights of others.

The incitement to riot and rebellion constitutes another level of violence altogether, and reform causes have been associated with this level of violence from the days of *Walker's Appeal* and John Brown's raid on Harper's Ferry through the riots of the 1960s and the candid militancy of the Black Panthers. Violence is not, however, the way of the reformer; in fact, reform causes have been enhanced much more by acts of victimization than by acts of aggression. David Walker contributed some incendiary prose, but he assumed stature in the movement against slavery not as an armed rebel but as an individual benefactor to escaping slaves, as an advocate of black achievement through education, and as a possible martyr himself at the hands of a putative pro-slavery poisoner when he died at the early age of thirty-four. Similarly, Union soldiers sang of John Brown's hanging and not of the raid that led to it. Panthers became usable reform symbols not with gun in hand but as victims of police and the courts. An awareness of the value of martyrs pervades Elijah Muhammad's article (III-5B).

The cause of reform is best served when violence is avoided, as in the two instances documented below. Both accounts describe gatherings where the power of oratory was conspicuously superior to the threat of violence. Both assemblages carry something of the flavor of a revival meeting, albeit Garrison at times seemed more to be chairman of a debating society.

High among the skills of William Lloyd Garrison was the manipulation of meetings whether the occasion called for packing an assemblage in advance or taking spontaneous advantage of circumstances. In this role Garrison was much admired by that "practical agitator" John Jay Chapman (see V-5), who put together the following account in a way that shows a reverence across three generations of reform. Note Chapman's stress on the superior courage required of the nonviolent, on the value of open debate, and on the central importance of the conversion experience. There is room to speculate as to whether this kind of personal dynamic can persist in an age of large population and mass communications.

In a megalopolitan age, the March on Washington may be taken as a rough equivalent of the kind of anti-slavery rally visited by the Rynders Mob. The equivalent violence occurred not in the appearance of militant bands but in the anticipation of gross disorder. In spite of careful planning by responsible organizations (Council on Racial Equality, Southern Christian Leadership Conference, National Association for the Advancement of Colored People) the city retired fearful on the night of August 27, 1963. Normal traffic was blocked from the area long before the scheduled convocation. Uniforms were abundantly in evidence. In spite of negative anticipation, a small miracle took place. Some 200,000 people came together in 83-degree weather in a limited area, gave vent to their deepest feelings on an extremely emotional subject, dispersed and went home. Nearly two thousand were treated for heat prostration and minor complaints; violence was absent. Relief mingled with quiet purposefulness in the collective response to this occasion so difficult to describe and so impossible to forget.

Amid the prayer and the singing there was an atypical amount of good old-fashioned oratory. Some were stirred by A. Philip Randolph (Brotherhood of Sleeping Car Porters); some by Walter Reuther (United Auto Workers). In retrospect, however, the note most clearly remembered came from Martin Luther King, Jr. "I have a dream," he said, paused, and described a portion of it. Again: "I have a dream. . . ." "I have a dream that one day on the red hills of Georgia the sons of former slaves and the sons of former slaveowners will sit down at the table of brotherhood.''

Newspapers the next day tried to estimate the impact of this demonstration on Congress—then considering civil rights legislation. There is, of course, no sure way to make such calculations, and deliberative bodies do not like to admit to being moved by crowds. Yet social reform has surely generated momentum through torchlit parades and rallies, and the singing fellowship of group action. It is hard to resist the notion that, particularly in the long run, demonstrations of harmony and controlled nonviolence advance the cause of social change more effectively than any number of killings and explosions.

SOURCE: A: John Jay Chapman, *William Lloyd Garrison*. New York, Moffat, Yard, 1913, pp. 199-218. B: Page-one feature in the Washington *Post* of August 29, 1963.

A: THE RYNDERS MOB

The Anti-slavery meeting at the Broadway Tabernacle on May 7, 1851, which goes by the name of the Rynders Mob, has an interest quite beyond the boundaries of its epoch. It gives an example of how any disturbance that arises in a public meeting ought to be handled by the managers of the meeting. It has a lesson for all agitators and popular speakers. It gives, indeed, a picture of humanity during a turbulent crisis, a picture that is Athenian, Roman, Mediaeval. modern,—a scene of democratic life, flung to us from the ages. I shall copy the account of this meeting almost verbatim from the large Life of Garrison. No comment can add to the power of it.

We have to remember that Webster had made his famous Compromise speech just two months before this meeting; and that the phalanxes of all conservative people, from George Ticknor, in Boston, to the rowdies on the Bowery in New York, were being marshalled to repress Abolition as they had not been marshalled since 1835. It must be noted also that this attempt succeeded on the whole. In spite of the triumph which the Abolitionists scored at this particular meeting, it became impossible for them to hold meetings in great cities for some time afterwards. The complicity of the Churches with Slavery is now almost forgotten. Among the Abolitionists during the critical epoch there was to be found no

Episcopal clergyman (save the Rev. E. P. Wells, of Boston, who early withdrew from the Cause) and no Catholic priest. The Abolition leaders were, nevertheless, drawn largely from the clerical ranks; but they were Unitarians, Methodists, Congregationalists, Baptists, etc., and were generally driven from their own pulpits in consequence of their opinions about Slavery. The Ecclesiastical Apologists for Slavery founded their case upon the New Testament. A literature of exegesis was in existence of which the ''View of Slavery'' by John Henry Hopkins, D.D., L.L.D., Episcopal Bishop of the Diocese of Vermont, is a late example. At this time Zachary Taylor, a slaveholder and a devout Episcopalian, was president of the United States.

The situation was a difficult one for the Evangelical, anti-sectarian mind to deal with. What was the use of quoting the New Testament to slaveholders, who were already fortified out of that very volume? The effect of the situation on Garrison's temperament may be seen in the meeting at the Tabernacle. There is a demonic element in what he says: his utterance is forced out of him: it is not calculated. You could not reproduce the spirit of this utterance except at the cost of two centuries of human passion. There is a demonic element also in Garrison's courage. He displays, on this occasion, at least two kinds of genius, the genius of satire,—Voltaire might have uttered the scathing slashes about ''Christ in the presidential chair,''—and the all but antipodal genius of infinite sweetness of temperament.—

The *New York Herald* in advance of the meeting denounced Garrison for many days in succession, and advised the breaking up of the meeting by violence. According to the *Herald*, ''Garrison boldly urges the utter overthrow of the churches, the Sabbath, and the Bible. Nothing has been sacred with him but the ideal intellect of the negro race. To elevate this chimera, he has urged the necessity of an immediate overthrow of the Government, a total disrespect for the Constitution, actual disruption and annihilation of the Union, and a cessation of all order, legal or divine, which does not square with his narrow views of what constitutes human liberty. Never, in the time of the French Revolution and blasphemous atheism, was there more malevolence and unblushing wickedness avowed than by this same Garrison. Indeed, he surpasses Robespierre and his associates, for he has no design of building up. His only object is to destroy. . . In Boston, a few months ago, a convention was held, the object of which was the overthrow of Sunday worship. Thus it appears that nothing divine or secular is respected by these fanatics. . . . When free discussion does not promote the public good, it has no more right to exist than a bad government that is dangerous and oppressive to the common weal. It should be overthrown. On the question of usefulness to the public of the packed, organized meetings of these Abolitionists, socialists, Sabbath-breakers, and anarchists, there can be but one result arrived at by prudence and patriotism. They are dangerous assemblies— calculated for mischief, and treasonable in their character and purposes. Though the law cannot reach them, public opinion can; and, as in England, a peaceful dissent from such doctrines as these fellows would promulgate—a strong expression of hisses and by counter statements and expositions, so here in New York we may anticipate that there are those who will enter the arena of discussion, and send out the true opinion of the public. . . .''

The meeting of May 7, at the Tabernacle, was a vast assembly which contained many respectable people, intermingled with whom was an organized element of impending mob. The leader of the mob was a well-known ruffian called Isaiah Rynders, ''a native American, of mixed German and Irish lineage, now some forty-six years of age. He began life as a boatman on the Hudson River, and, passing easily into the sporting class, went to seek his fortunes as a professional gambler in the paradise of the Southwest. In this region he became familiar with all forms of violence, including the institution of slavery. After many personal hazards and vicissitudes, he returned to New York city, where he proved to be admirably qualified for local political leadership in connection with Tammany Hall. A sporting-house which he opened became a Democratic rendezvous and the headquarters of the Empire Club, an organization of roughs and desperadoes who acknowledged his 'captaincy.' His campaigning in behalf of Polk and Dallas in 1844 secured him the friendly patronage of the successful candidate for Vice-President, and he took office as Weigher in the Custom-house of the metropolis. He found time, while thus employed, to engineer the Astor Place riot on behalf of the actor Forrest against his English rival Macready, on May 10, 1849, and the year 1850 opened with his trial for this atrocity and his successful defense by John Van Buren. On February 16 he and his Club broke up an anti-Wilmot Proviso meeting in New York—a seeming inconsistency, but it was charged against Rynders that he had offered to 'give the State of New York to Clay' in the election of 1844 for $30,000, and had met with reluctant refusal. In March he was arrested for a brutal assault on a gentleman in a hotel, but the victim and the witnesses found it prudent not to appear against a ruffian who did not hesitate to threaten the district-attorney in open court. Meanwhile, the new Whig Administration quite justifiably discharged Rynders from the Custom-house, leaving him free to pose as a savior of the Union against traitors—a savior of society against blasphemers and infidels wherever encountered. . . .''

When the meeting was brought to order Mr. Garrison, as an opening exercise, read certain passages of the Bible, chosen with reference to their bearing upon the slave trade: ''The Lord standeth up to plead, and standeth to judge the people. . . . What mean ye that ye beat my people to pieces, and grind the faces of the poor? saith the Lord God of Hosts. . . . Associate yourselves, O ye people, and ye shall be broken in pieces; gird yourselves, and ye shall be broken in pieces. . . . They all lie in wait for blood; they hunt every man his brother with a net. . . . Hide the outcasts, betray not him that wandereth; let mine outcasts dwell with thee; be thou a covert to them from the face of the spoiler.''

''To Dr. Furness, who sat beside Mr. Garrison, these selections (in full, not in our abstract) seemed 'most admirably adapted to the existing state of our country. His reading, however, was not remarkably effective. It was like the ordinary reading of the pulpit,'—and hence not calculated to stir the wrath of the ungodly.

''The reading of the Treasurer's report followed, and then Mr. Garrison, resigning the chair to Francis Jackson, proceeded to make the first speech of the day.

''He began,'' says Dr. Furness, ''with stating that they, the members of the Anti-slavery Society, regarded the Anti-slavery cause as emphatically *the* Christian movement of the day. Nothing could be more explicit than his recognition of the truth and divine authority of the Christianity of the New Testament. He went on to examine the popular tests of religion, and to show their defectiveness. In so doing, his manner was grave and dignified. There was no bitterness, no levity. His manner of speaking was simple, clerical, and Christian. His subject was, substantially, that we have, over and over again, in all the pulpits of the land—the inconsistency of our profession and practice—although not with the same application. . . . Mr. Garrison said great importance was attached to a belief in Jesus. We were told that we must believe in Jesus. And yet this faith in Jesus had no vitality, no practical bearing on conduct and character. He had previously, however, passed in rapid review the chief religious denominations, showing that they uttered no protest against the sins of the nation. He spoke first in this connection of the Roman Catholic Church, stating that its priests and members held slaves without incurring the rebuke of the Church.''

Up to this time the only symptoms of opposition had been some ill-timed and senseless applause—or what seemed such. And as it came from one little portion of the audience, Dr. Furness asked Wendell Phillips at his side what it meant. 'It means,' he said, 'that there is to be a row.' The reference to the Catholic Church gave the first opening to the leader of the gang.''

The following is from the *New York Herald*'s account of the meeting: ''Captain Rynders (who occupied a position in the background, at one side of the organloft, and commanding a bird's eye view of the whole scene beneath) here said: Will you allow me to ask you a question? (Excitement and confusion.)

''Mr. Garrison—Yes, sir.

''Captain Rynders—The question I would ask is, whether there are no other churches as well as the Catholic Church, whose clergy and lay members hold slaves?

''Mr. Garrison—Will the friend wait for a moment, and I will answer him in reference to other churches.'' (Cheers.)

(Dr. Furness says that Mr. Garrison expressed no surprise at the interruption. There was not the slightest change in his manner or his voice. He simply said: ''My friend, if you will wait a moment, your question shall be answered,'' or something to that effect. There instantly arose a loud clapping around the stranger in the gallery, and from the outskirts of the audience, at different points.)

Captain Rynders then resumed his seat. Mr. Garrison thus proceeded: ''Shall we look to the Episcopal Church for hope? It was the boast of John C. Calhoun, shortly before his death, that that church was impregnable to Anti-slavery. That vaunt was founded on truth, for the Episcopal clergy and laity are buyers and sellers of human flesh. We cannot, therefore, look to them. Shall we look to the Presbyterian Church? The whole weight of it is on the side of oppression. Ministers and people buy and sell slaves, apparently without any compunctious visitings of conscience. We cannot, therefore, look to them, nor to the Baptists, nor the Methodists; for they, too, are against the slave, and all the sects are

combined to prevent that jubilee which it is the will of God should
come. . . .

"Be not startled when I say that a belief in Jesus is no evidence of
goodness (hisses); no, friends.

"Voice—Yes it is.

"Mr. Garrison—Our friend says 'yes'; my position is 'no.' It is
worthless as a test, for the reason I have already assigned in reference to
the other tests. His praises are sung in Louisiana, Alabama, and the other
Southern States just as well as in Massachusetts.

"Captain Rynders—Are you aware that the slaves in the South have
their prayer-meetings in honor of Christ?

"Mr. Garrison—Not a slaveholding or a slave-breeding Jesus. (Sensation.) The slaves believe in a Jesus that strikes off chains. In this
country, Jesus has become obsolete. A profession in him is no longer a
test. Who objects to his course in Judaea? The old Pharisees are extinct,
and may safely be denounced. Jesus is the most respectable person in the
United States. (Great sensation, and murmurs of disapprobation.) Jesus
sits in the President's chair of the United States. (A thrill of horror here
seemed to run through the assembly.) Zachary Taylor sits there, which is
the same thing, for he believes in Jesus. He believes in war, and the Jesus
'that gave the Mexicans hell.' (Sensation, uproar, and confusion.)

"The name of Zachary Taylor had scarcely passed Mr. Garrison's lips
when Captain Rynders, with something like a howl, forsaking his
strategic position on the border-line of the gallery and the platform,
dashed headlong down towards the speaker's desk, followed, with shouting and imprecations and a terrifying noise, by the mass of his backers.
The audience, despite a natural agitation, gave way to no panic. The
Abolitionist leaders upon the platform remained imperturbable. 'I was
not aware,' writes Dr. Furness, 'of being under any apprehension of
personal violence. We were all like General Jackson's cotton-bales at
New Orleans. Our demeanor made it impossible for the rioters to use any
physical force against us.' Rynders found himself in the midst of Francis
and Edmund Jackson, of Wendell Phillips, of Edmund Quincy, of
Charles F. Hovey, of William H. Furness, of Samuel May, Jr., of
Sydney Howard Gay, of Isaac T. Hopper, of Henry C. Wright, of Abbey
Kelley Foster, of Frederick Douglass, of Mr. Garrison—against whom
his menaces were specially directed. Never was a human being more out
of his element."

The following, according to the *Herald*, was what greeted Mr. Garrison's ear:

"Captain Rynders (clenching his fist)—I will not allow you to assail the President of the United States. You shan't do it (shaking his fist at Mr. Garrison).

"Many voices—Turn him out, turn him out!

"Captain Rynders—If a million of you were there, I would not allow the President of the United States to be insulted. As long as you confined yourself to your subject, I did not interfere; but I will not permit you or any other man to misrepresent the President."

Mr. Garrison, as the Rev. Samuel May testifies, "calmly replied that he had simply quoted some recent words of General Taylor, and appealed to the audience if he had said aught in disrespect of him." "You ought not to interrupt us," he continued to Rynders—in the quietest manner conceivable, as Dr. Furness relates. "We go upon the principle of hearing everybody. If you wish to speak, I will keep order, and you shall be heard." The din, however, increased. "The Hutchinsons," continues Dr. Furness, "who were wont to sing at the Anti-slavery meetings, were in the gallery, and they attempted to raise a song, to soothe the savages with music. But it was of no avail. Rynders drowned their fine voices with noise and shouting." Still, a knockdown argument with a live combatant would have suited him better than mere Bedlamitish disturbance. He was almost gratified by young Thomas L. Kane, son of Judge Kane of Philadelphia, who, seeing the rush of the mob upon the platform, had himself leaped there, to protect his townsman, Dr. Furness. "They shall not touch a hair of your head," he said in a tone of great excitement; and, as the strain became more intense, he rushed up to Rynders and shook his fist in his face. He said to me (Dr. Furness) with the deepest emphasis: "If he touches Mr. Garrison I'll *kill* him." But Mr. Garrison's composure was more than a coat of mail.

The knot was cut by Francis Jackson's formal offer of the floor to Rynders as soon as Mr. Garrison had finished his remarks; with an invitation meanwhile to take a seat on the platform. This, says Mr. May, he scoutingly refused; but, seeing the manifest fairness of the president's offer, drew back a little, and stood, with folded arms, waiting for Mr. Garrison to conclude, which soon he did,—offering a resolution in these terms:

"Resolved, That the Anti-slavery movement, instead of being

'infidel,' in an evil sense (as is falsely alleged), is truly Christian, in the primitive meaning of that term, and the special embodiment in this country of whatever is loyal to God and benevolent to man; and that, in view of the palpable enormity of slavery—of the religious and political professions of the people—of the age in which we live, blazing with the concentrated light of many centuries—indifference or hostility to this movement indicates a state of mind more culpable than was manifested by the Jewish nation in rejecting Jesus as the Messiah, eighteen hundred years ago.''

With these words the speaker retired, to resume the presidency of the meeting.

''The close of Mr. Garrison's address,'' says Dr. Furness, ''brought down Rynders again, who vociferated and harangued, at one time on the platform, and then pushing down into the aisles, like a madman followed by his keepers. Through the whole, nothing could be more patient and serene than the bearing of Mr. Garrison. I have always revered Mr. Garrison for his devoted, uncompromising fidelity to his great cause. To-day I was touched to the heart by his calm and gentle manners. There was no agitation, no scorn, no heat, but the quietness of a man engaged in simple duties.''

After some parleying, it appeared that Rynders had a spokesman who preferred to speak after Dr. Furness.

''Accordingly,'' says the latter, ''I spoke my little, anxiously prepared word. I never recall that hour without blessing myself that I was called to speak precisely at that moment. At any other stage of the proceedings, it would have been wretchedly out of place. As it was, my speech fitted in almost as well as if it had been impromptu, although a sharp eye might easily have discovered that I was speaking *memoriter*. Rynders interrupted me again and again, exclaiming that I lied, that I was personal; but he ended with applauding me!''

No greater contrast to what was to follow could possibly be imagined than the genial manner, firm tones, and self-possession, the refined discourse, of this Unitarian clergyman, who was felt to have turned the current of the meeting. There uprose, as per agreement, one ''Professor'' Grant, a seedy-looking personage, having one hand tied round with a dirty cotton cloth. Mr. Garrison recognized him as a former pressman in the *Liberator* office. His thesis was that the blacks were not men, but belonged to the monkey tribe. His speech proved dull and tiresome, and was made sport of by his own set, whom Mr. Garrison had to call to order. There were now loud cries for Frederick Douglass, who came forward to where Rynders stood in the conspicuous position he had taken when he thought the meeting was his, and who remained in it, too mortified even to creep away, when he found it was somebody else's. "Now you can speak," said he to Douglass; "but mind what I say: if you speak disrespectfully (of the South, or Washington, or Patrick Henry) I'll knock you off the stage." Nothing daunted, the ex-fugitive from greater terrors began:

"The gentleman who has just spoken has undertaken to prove that the blacks are not human beings. He has examined our whole conformation, from top to toe. I cannot follow him in his argument. I will assist him in it, however. I offer myself for your examination. Am I a man?"

The audience responded with a thunderous affirmative, which Captain Rynders sought to break by exclaiming: " *You* are not a black man; you are only half a nigger." "Then," replied Mr. Douglass, turning upon him with the blandest of smiles and an almost affectionate obeisance, "I am half-brother to Captain Rynders!" He would not deny that he was the son of a slaveholder, born of Southern "amalgamation"; a fugitive, too, like Kossuth—"another half-brother of mine" (to Rynders). He spoke of the difficulties thrown in the way of industrious colored people at the North, as he had himself experienced—this by way of answer to Horace Greeley, who had recently complained of their inefficiency and dependence. Criticism of the editor of the *Tribune* being grateful to Rynders, a political adversary, "he added a word to Douglass's against Greeley. 'I am happy,' said Douglass, '*to have the assent of my half-brother here,*' pointing to Rynders, and convulsing the audience with laughter. After this, Rynders, finding how he was played with, took care to hold his peace; but someone of Rynders' company in the gallery undertook to interrupt the speaker. 'It's of no use,' said Mr. Douglass, '*I've Captain Rynders here to back me.*' " "We were born here," he said finally, "we are not dying out, and we mean to stay here. We made the clothes you have on, the sugar you put into your tea. We would do more if allowed." "Yes," said a voice in the crowd, "you would cut our throats for us." "No," was the quick response, "but we would cut your hair for you."

Douglass concluded his triumphant remarks by calling upon the Rev. Samuel R. Ward, editor of the *Impartial Citizen*, to succeed him. "All eyes," says Dr. Furness, "were instantly turned to the back of the platform, or stage rather, so dramatic was the scene; and there, amidst a group, stood a large man, so black that, as Wendell Phillips said, when he shut his eyes you could not see him. As he approached, Rynders exclaimed: 'Well, this is the original nigger.' 'I've heard of the magnanimity of Captain Rynders,' said Ward, 'but the half has not been told me!' And then he went on with a noble voice and his speech was such a strain of eloquence as I never heard excelled before or since.'' The mob had to applaud him, too, and it is the highest praise to record that his unpremeditated utterance maintained the level of Douglass's, and ended the meeting with a sense of climax—demonstrating alike the humanity and the capacity of the full-blooded negro.

"When he ceased speaking, the time had expired for which the Tabernacle was engaged, and we had to adjourn. Never,'' continues Dr. Furness, ''was there a grander triumph of intelligence, of mind, over brute force. Two colored men, whose claim to be considered human was denied, had, by mere force of intellect, overwhelmed their maligners with confusion. As the audience was thinning out, I went down on the floor to see some friends there. Rynders came by. I could not help saying to him: 'How shall I thank you for what you have done for us to-day?' 'Well,' said he, 'I do not like to hear my country abused, but that last thing that you said, that's the truth.' That last thing was, I believe, a simple assertion of the right of the people to think and speak freely.''

B: *No Tension, Only a Quiet Sense of Purpose*

A MOUNTING TIDE . . .

TOWARD LINCOLN'S TEMPLE . . .

By Marya Mannes

Critic, essayist and author of several books, Miss Mannes is a well-known commentator on the American scene.

At ten o'clock the city was so empty that it looked as if a plague had struck it, or—the streets stretching silently out in the sun, the cops and guardsmen at every corner waiting, as in ''High Noon''—as if ambush was prepared for an enemy. Shops were closed and the people who normally inhabit Washington presumably fled. Echoes from friends further north assailed the ears: "Wouldn't be there for a million bucks." "Bound to cause harm." "Potentially dangerous."

On the green slopes at the Washington Monument, only a sprinkling of people had gathered. There was an air of bustle and expectancy, but the only drama by 10:30 was that a child had been found and that his name was Roosevelt Johnson.

What happened then happened slowly but mightily, and by 11:30 a mounting tide of people, placards aloft or handbags hanging, were walking down Constitution Avenue towards Lincoln's temple.

"Americans don't know how to march," said a walking reporter, and then added: "Thank God."

There was, indeed, no attempt at lines, at rhythm, at any formation whatsoever. They did not even stick together except in the loosest way, by groups or states, or organizations, or bus-loads. They just walked—mostly black, but partly white—like people who know where they are going but are not making a show of it.

By noon two great rivers flowed along either side of the Reflecting Pool until both verges and all the approaches to the Memorial of the man who thought he had freed them were solid with people.

What people? No enemy, no plague. A people serious but relaxed; almost festive. Among the neatly suited men, who did not even in the sun take off their coats and ties, were many handsome and stalwart young Negroes, many middle-aged ones of substance and gravity. Many of the young women were beautiful, many of the older ones distinguished. To one of them, by the banks of the pool, under the trees, I said, "I think Lincoln is moved by this: he must know what is happening." She glanced suddenly and said, "The dead know much more than we think they do. I am so proud of my people!"

And the whites? Many of the men were clergymen, or looked like teachers. They had thin, serious faces that seemed unsoftened by money. There were many young men who held placards that said Unitarian Universalists, or Religious Liberals, Students, or CORE: and comparatively few beatniks. These, wet-lipped, sparse-bearded, with hair long on the nape, usually walked with their inevitable counterparts, the girls whose dank straight hair escapes from pins and ribbons, whose toes are dirty. The older white women—and there were many—looked, again, like teachers, or the wives of teachers; more concerned with others than with themselves.

Whoever they were, wherever they sat, there was no tension, only a sort of quiet sense of purpose. They spoke little, they laughed rarely, although they smiled often; they ate their picnics, they listened to their transistors, they clapped their speakers.

Brown legs and white legs hung down into the pool, a Negro youth gave a final shove to a white boy struggling up the limb of a tree, and no matter who jostled or stepped over whom, there was always the low "excuse me . . ." "excuse me, please."

Great amplified voices sang "Oh Freedom—Oh Freedom" . . . "before I'll be a slave, I'll be buried in my grave . . ." and they clapped to that and to "the whole world in my hands" and listened quietly to "How many times must a man look up before he can see the sky?"

The loudest sounds from their throats came in response to the words of Walter Reuther, but only one woman really shouted like a revivalist. She was walking back from the March with a transistor to her ear, and with a voice like a bronchial crow she screeched "Yes!" and "Right!" right into it.

It was a wonderful and immensely important thing that happened here. And the only pity of it was that the people who fled it, the people who deplored it, the people who resented it, missed one of the great democratic expressions of this century: a people claiming, with immense control and dignity, the American rights long denied them.

The March had to happen. Nietzsche said "Great problems are in the street." This one, certainly, can never be under the rug again.

Document III-7: ARGUING FROM THE "HIGHER LAW"

Not only were the churches excoriated when they failed to respond to their imputed social duty by exerting their organized force against slavery, but they were also transcended by having their language, their laws, and their very spiritual logic applied outside the pulpit. Stating that "Great reforms on moral subjects do not occur except under the influence of religious principle," Albert H. Barnes brought religion directly to bear on a social question in his *An Inquiry into the Scriptural*

Views of Slavery (Philadelphia, Parry & McMillan, 1857, p. 25; first published in 1846). The ubiquitous Theodore Dwight Weld had already entered the lists with the contentiously titled *The Bible Against Slavery* (New York, American Anti-Slavery Society, 1837); while, from the Southern viewpoint, no less a contender than John C. Calhoun, deviating from his favorite metaphor of a Greek democracy, employed Biblical arguments in favor of slaveholding. The complexity of this debate can be evidenced even in the cumbersome titles, as for example J. Holmes Agnew's *Reply to Professor Tayler [sic] Lewis' Review of Rev. Henry J. Van Dyke's Sermon on Biblical Slavery* (New York, Appleton, 1861). This title also confirms that by 1861 this social debate had opened the church doors.

Nor were the religious aspects of the slavery debate confined to seminary arguments and scriptural exegesis. When Parker Pillsbury, himself famous in the abolition movement, wrote its history he deliberately called it *The Acts of the Anti-Slavery Apostles* (Boston, Cupples, Upham, 1884). To him the anti-slavery crusade became a great Christian mission, directly parallel to the ministry of Jesus' apostles. Garrison, he wrote, had been granted the anointed vision to penetrate the *spiritual* heart of earthly wickedness (see pp. 9, 18). In song, as well as in word and deed, the movement had a spiritual cast; most of the songs against oppression carried a moral message and were set to hymns, as titles of these collections readily indicate: *The Christian Lyre, The Anti-Slavery Harp, Anti-Slavery Hymns.*

Above the earthly church, perhaps above the songs and scriptures transcribed by man, and surely above the Constitution—as William H. Seward had publicly averred in arguing against the Compromise of 1850—was a "higher law." It was the duty to this higher law that had sent Henry David Thoreau to jail in protest against pro-slavery taxes and which produced his famous essay "On Civil Disobedience." Although Thoreau's deeds and words have appealed with great force to twentieth-century protestors, invocations of the higher law which moved the antebellum public are more fairly represented by the documents reproduced below.

The idea that a man must not be coerced by the laws of the state to violate the urgings of his moral sense is not special to any place, time, or cause. In derivation as well as application, however, a fifty-four-page anonymous pamphlet appearing soon after the Compromise of 1850 best represented the contemporary American feeling. It invoked, in a succinct appendix, the authority not only of the Bible, but of classical and renaissance worlds and of the English jurists. A law of society could be disobeyed, the pamphlet argued, if it violated the law of nature, the law of common sense, the law of self-preservation, or any of the freedoms guaranteed in the Bill of Rights. In thus combining reason with authority, natural with moral law, and adding the sanctions of pragmatism and democracy, this statement firmly identified itself with a time and place.

The author was promptly identified as a Cincinnati bookseller who, fittingly enough, eventually became Librarian of Congress. There is evidence, thanks to a recent discovery, of the direct influence of this pamphlet on Ralph Waldo Emerson, then one of the nations most popular lecturers, who was speaking out forcefully against the Fugitive Slave Law and committing, as he wrote, "unblushing plagiarisms" against pamphleteer Spofford. (See John C. Broderick, "Emerson and Moorfield Storey: a Lost Journal Found," *American Literature*, vol. XXXVIII [May, 1966], pp. 182-83.) If Spofford's logic directly underlay the passionate lectures of Emerson, it also indirectly underlay that masterpiece of poetic political assassination, "Ichabod!," in which Whittier wrote of Webster, "All else is gone; from those great eyes—The soul has fled. . . ."

In contemporary America there is abundant evidence of the continuity of those forms for precipitating change represented by Thoreau and Spofford: passive resistance, civil disobedience, the appeal to a higher law. They exist not only in the civil rights movement but in the anti-war crusade, in student revolts, in citizens' protests against environmental and urban problems, and in draft resistance. Within the context of the civil rights movement, however, no single figure carries so much representative importance as the late Martin Luther King, Jr.

As an ordained minister he reflected the religious orientation of much civil rights activity and, with many others, came to leadership in the black community through the church. He led the Southern Christian Leadership Conference which helped organize direct action in the South and contributed importantly to the March on Washington, where the Reverend Dr. King furnished a crucially powerful piece of oratory (see III-6).

The document reproduced below is particularly appropriate, also for a number of reasons. Written from jail, it reminds one of Thoreau's act and essay. Being a statement from one clergyman to others, it parallels the famous Lane debate and other schisms caused by the slavery question in antebellum churches. With Spofford, King points out the many ways in which man can recognize a higher law that leaves him no alternative but to disobey certain man-made statutes and accept the consequences.

The consequences of King's imprisonment, and of the very widespread and effective direct action on behalf of civil rights in the South throughout the 1950s and 1960s, were major indeed. Anthony Lewis called the resulting breakdown of segregation in schools, stores, and buses a "second American revolution." There may be some exaggeration in this phrase, but it would be hard to exaggerate the general effectiveness of King and his colleagues as they put to work techniques consciously borrowed from Thoreau and Gandhi. The direct action forced negotiation, concession, legislation. The nonviolence robbed the aggressor of his principal excuse. As King himself paraphrased, there is nothing so powerful as the right idea in the right place at the right time.

SOURCE: A: [Ainsworth R. Spofford], *The Higher Law Tried by Reason and Authority*. New York, S. W. Benedict, 1851, pp. 11-21. B: Martin Luther King, Jr., "Letter from Birmingham Jail," as published in *Why We Can't Wait*. New York, Harper & Row, 1964, pp. 177-200.

A: Spofford's *HIGHER LAW*

Thus we might go on, citing instance after instance to prove, that there are some laws which are ridiculous, and fall to the ground by the Higher Law of common sense;—some laws which are obsolete, and are defeated by the Higher Law of human progress;—some laws which are inconvenient and are overruled by the Higher Law of necessity;—some laws which are unnatural, and are null by the Higher Law of instinct and of nature; and some laws which are *unjust*, and are void by the Higher Law of conscience and of God.

But it may be argued, that in saying that many laws are not obeyed, we have not said all, and that the mere fact that they *cannot* be executed, is no evidence that they *should not* be.

If they cannot be executed, because defeated by public opinion, one would say that there is at least no remedy,—since we have already shown that the sole foundation of law is public opinion.

But the true answer to the question lies deeper, and brings us to state the ultimate fact in this matter, viz.:—that *as the actual foundation of all law is public opinion, so* ITS SOLE SANCTION IS ITS REASON AND JUSTICE. And here lies the real question between the opponents and the advocates of the Higher Law doctrine; the former assert the binding obligation of all laws, just or unjust,—the latter deny the obligation of all unjust enactments.

The ground of this denial may be thus stated. Justice is the Supreme Law of the universe. It is synonymous with the Law of Nature, and means the same thing as the Will of God. All men are bound, by the very fact of their existence in the constitution of nature, to obey its laws in preference to all others. It is each man's primary duty to do what is right, and to avoid what is wrong. There is such a thing as Natural Right; there is a distinction between right and wrong anterior to Human Law. To prove this, it is only necessary to say, that were there no justice, there could be no law; were there no natural and necessary distinction between right and wrong, the law which recognizes the distinction would never be made. No law can create right, or make wrong. Its function is merely declaratory of the right and wrong which previously exist. The law is not the foundation of justice; justice is the foundation of the law. He who asserts the contrary, turns the universe upside down, puts the cause for the effect, and the effect for the cause.

If what has been said is true, then Justice is higher than the law; and if Justice is higher than the law, then no *unjust* law has any sanction whatever, and obedience to it is wrong. Now it is well known that many unjust laws do get enacted; some by hasty legislation,—some by violations of the constitution,—some by the legislators personally misrepresenting the people,—and a few,—(though these are among the rarest),—by a public opinion which is itself wrong.

Here, then, we have an unjust law enacted, and it calls on us for obedience. Now one of two things must be done; either we must yield implicit obedience to the law, because it is law, thus violating the duty we owe to reason and justice, to conscience and to God,—or else we must disobey the unjust law, and take the consequences. Our action in this dilemma will depend very much on the circumstances of each case as it occurs.

If the law in question be one of the absurd or obsolete kind, then the injustice of it is grounded on its unreasonableness, and the chances are that it will not be pushed to extremity, and no one will be reduced to the alternative of disobedience. However men may theorize, it will be found in practice, that some sentiment of justice is natural to man; and public opinion will much sooner violate its own law, than push to the extremity the unreasonable or supererogatory enactments which are found on the statue book. I know it is often said that "the law is the perfection of reason;" but most lawyers, and some who are not, know that a more absurd falsehood was never uttered. If the converse of the maxim were true, and the perfection of reason were always law, there might be some rational hope of always getting justice done. The law books are not wanting in cases of this kind, where laws have proved in practice wholly inoperative, because not founded in reason or necessity. And this fact alone is a sufficient confutation of the notion of the *sacred supremacy* of the law. Law, no more than government, has any Divine right, or any inherent authority. It is always amendable to the reason and public opinion that made it. A senseless statute is no very sacred thing, and to say that all laws are sacred and supreme, because they are laws, is a kind of logic which it is charitable criticism to call absurd. Law is at the best, a temporary expedient,—reason is a perpetual force: law is artificial,—common sense is natural. That our fathers stultified themselves, is no reason why we should,—and the Egyptian law, requiring men to eat garlic in worship of the cats, though both "sacred" and "supreme," was not very rigidly observed by their posterity.

Again, if the law in question be simply inconvenient, or if it deprive one of no natural right, or violate no man's conscience, though subjecting him to pecuniary or other disadvantage, it is generally best to obey it,—that is, provided public opinion insists on its enforcement. Of this class are many laws regulating pecuniary matters, and those actions which are in themselves indifferent, *i.e.*, neither right nor wrong. But even in this case there may be a stern and overruling necessity which renders obedience impracticable,—as in the case of a business pressure, where a breach of the laws regulating interest may be absolutely necessary to save hundreds of men from ruin.

Again, the law regulating the sacredness of human life may be overruled by the higher necessity of self-defence. A spontaneous instinct in every man tells him that self-preservation is the Higher Law, and if he take the life of his antagonist to preserve his own, most juries will suspend the law of manslaughter in his favor.

But in the last place, the law in question may be so plain a violation of natural right, so direct an outrage upon justice, or humanity, or both, as to take away all its obligation from the start, and in fact to oblige us to its disobedience.

Let us look at a few instances.—Nobody will pretend that a law commanding murder would be binding for a moment,—and the reason is plain, that such a law is a subversion of all the plainest dictates of nature and morality.

Nearly all legal writers are agreed that all *immoral* laws are *ipso facto* void. Any law against chastity, of whatever nature, so far from binding a man to obey it, makes it his duty to break it at every hazard,—since man's virtue is his very self, and each one has a natural right to protect the morality of him and his against whatever power.

Any law restraining the freedom of speech or of the press is void. The human mind knows its rights, and sooner or later it will have them,—if not by law, then in spite of law. It is needless to quote arguments in proof of so plain a thing. Every man feels his right to say what he thinks, and the government which cannot stand againt the most perfect liberty of speech, must be either very wicked or very weak.—So also, the laws prohibiting profane swearing, however moral in their tendency, are yet contrary to natural right, as the universal disregard of them sufficiently shows.

Any law restricting men from one kind of religious worship, or compelling them to another, is void. God allows no human statute to come between him and his creatures. Under whatever government a man may live, all experience and reason prove that the rights of conscience are reserved, and no law can for any length of time put fetters on the free will of man, or make him believe what in his soul he feels to be false.

So any law suspending the sanctions of human brotherhood is void. No enactment can prevent me from helping or sheltering, feeding or clothing a fellow-man who has not forfeited his claims by committing a crime. Any attempt to enforce laws against kindness and hospitality is as vain as it is wicked. Talk of prohibiting humanity by statute, of putting fines on charity, and penalties on pity! Such laws may be made, but they will never be obeyed, until common humanity is obliterated from the heart, and human nature itself abolished.

So, also, any law compelling me to aid in enslaving or re-enslaving a man, is void. No law can possibly bind me to do that to another, while innocent of crime, which would be unjust and cruel, if done to myself. I cannot be bound to aid in robbing another of a natural and inalienable right. I cannot be made to commit injustice and cruelty by statute. There is no just distinction between the obligation of such a law, and that of a law commanding murder, which all will agree is void. My neighbor's right to liberty is as inalienable as his right to life. It is just as sacred, just an inviolable, just as precious; it is equally a natural right with the other, and until he forfeit it, by interfering with another's liberty, nothing can take it from him. To take his life is not a higher crime than to take his liberty, since he may rather choose to die than be made a slave. Patrick Henry's sentiment, "Give me liberty, or give me death," is at once seen to be fatal to the obligation of a law which compels me to aid in taking the right to liberty away.

It is no answer to this to say that our fathers contracted for us that we would do this, and that the contract is binding. Suppose our fathers had contracted for us that we would stone every Catholic who came amongst us, or return in irons every fugitive escaped from the Algerines, *that* contract would be binding, would it? Some one may answer that there is no analogy between the cases, since one-half the nation made a bargain with the other half, and founded the Constitution upon the bargain, and exchanged considerations, and we have received our *quid pro quo*. But we have *not* received it, in point of fact; it has been denied us over and over again; Charleston and Mobile put our citizens in dungeons in open defiance of the Constitution and the "bargain;" and if *they* do not keep the compact where it is just, why should we where it is unjust and inhuman too? But if you say that one breach of it cannot justify another, and that the Constitution does positively promise that these fugitives shall be re-enslaved, and the Union is founded upon it, and will go to pieces if it isn't done, then we answer, Be it so,—grant that the Constitution promises to re-enslave them, it does *not* promise that you and I shall make scoundrels of ourselves to do it. We will give no more than is nominated in the bond. If the southern Shylocks must have their pound of flesh, and no considerations can move them to be merciful, then they must be content with "only justice and the bond." The bond does not require the freemen of the north to turn slave catchers; they may preserve their manhood and still keep the bond; *that* crowning infamy was reserved for the law of Congress of the year of grace 1850. The law of Congress makes it the duty of "all good citizens" to aid the *posse*, if called upon by the Marshal, in binding and delivering back the fugitive;

but the Constitution gives Congress no power to compel the citizens to do anything of the kind. Let the law of Congress execute itself by the proper officers, and not call on the people to do its dirty work. Because the Constitution says that fugitives shall be re-delivered, it does not follow that you and I must re-deliver them. Because the law says this man must be hung, it does not follow that you or I must be made to hang him, let him deserve it never so richly. The law of Congress may perhaps find *some* northern men willing to be "disinterested villains;" but "all good citizens" will keep on their way, and leave the Marshal and the *posse*, and the Shylocks, to their own peculiar calling.

'Tis curious to consider how plainly this law of Congress contradicts another, passed when the nation had fewer men, but larger souls than now. It is not difficult, on the Statute Book of the United States itself, to find a Higher Law than this passed last year. By the law of Congress, of March 2, 1807, it is piracy and murder—crimes punishable by death,— to enslave a man on the coast of Africa; yet here is another law of Congress compelling you and me to *re*-enslave every man we find on any coast of America! Strange anomaly that right and wrong should be reversed by longitudinal degrees, that crime should depend on climate, that what is illegal piracy and murder in Africa, should be legal duty and obligation in the United States! Tell us not that to send a man back to slavery is by no means so bad as to *make* him a slave at first;—by every standard of reason and right it is infinitely worse. In the one case, there may seem some small excuse,—and, no matter how flimsy, it is better than none at all;—that he is willing, or that it will better his condition; in the other—there is no single shadow of a plea for sending him to a condition he has fled from—a bondage he has escaped. In the one case—it may not be a man, but an idiot, or a fool—in the other, it is crushing down the manhood of as complete a man as ever God fashioned in his image. In the one case, it may be he knows not the value of freedom, and cares not much for liberty; in the other, he has conquered his freedom and holds on to it,—he has achieved his liberty and asserted his right to be a man. Yes, it is a far deeper crime to re-enslave a man than to enslave him at the first; he who does the latter treads upon a law of nature—he who dares do the former, tramples upon human nature itself.

From all that has now been said, the conclusion is plain, that nothing can sanction or legalize injustice; in other words, that no law subversive of natural right has any binding obligation. All the laws we have just enumerated under this head seem to come clearly within the category of unjust laws; and to every man so believing, disobedience to them is a duty.

B: "LETTER FROM BIRMINGHAM JAIL" *
April 16, 1963

MY DEAR FELLOW CLERGYMEN:

While confined here in the Birmingham city jail, I came across your recent statement calling my present activities "unwise and untimely." Seldom do I pause to answer criticism of my work and ideas. If I sought to answer all the criticisms that cross my desk, my secretaries would have little time for anything other than such correspondence in the course of the day, and I would have no time for constructive work. But since I feel that you are men of genuine good will and that your criticisms are sincerely set forth, I want to try to answer your statement in what I hope will be patient and reasonable terms.

I think I should indicate why I am here in Birmingham, since you have been influenced by the view which argues against "outsiders coming in." I have the honor of serving as president of the Southern Christian Leadership Conference, an organization operating in every southern state, with headquarters in Atlanta, Georgia. We have some eighty-five affiliated organizations across the South, and one of them is the Alabama Christian Movement for Human Rights. Frequently we share staff, educational and financial resources with our affiliates. Several months ago the affiliate here in Birmingham asked us to be on call to engage in a nonviolent direct-action program if such were deemed necessary. We readily consented, and when the hour came we lived up to our promise.

---

*AUTHOR'S NOTE: This response to a published statement by eight fellow clergymen from Alabama (Bishop C. C. J. Carpenter, Bishop Joseph A. Durick, Rabbi Hilton L. Grafman, Bishop Paul Hardin, Bishop Holan B. Harmon, the Reverend George M. Murray, the Reverend Edward V. Ramage and the Reverend Earl Stallings) was composed under somewhat constricting circumstances. Begun on the margins of the newspaper in which the statement appeared while I was in jail, the letter was continued on scraps of writing paper supplied by a friendly Negro trusty, and concluded on a pad my attorneys were eventually permitted to leave me. Although the text remains in substance unaltered, I have indulged in the author's prerogative of polishing it for publication.

So I, along with several members of my staff, am here because I was invited here. I am here because I have organizational ties here.

But more basically, I am in Birmingham because injustice is here. Just as the prophets of the eighth century B.C. left their villages and carried their "thus saith the Lord" far beyond the boundaries of their home towns, and just as the Apostle Paul left his village of Tarsus and carried the gospel of Jesus Christ to the far corners of the Greco-Roman world, so am I compelled to carry the gospel of freedom beyond my own home town. Like Paul, I must constantly respond to the Macedonian call for aid.

Moreover, I am cognizant of the interrelatedness of all communities and states. I cannot sit idly by in Atlanta and not be concerned about what happens in Birmingham. Injustice anywhere is a threat to justice everywhere. We are caught in an inescapable network of mutuality, tied in a single garment of destiny. Whatever affects one directly, affects all indirectly. Never again can we afford to live with the narrow, provincial "outside agitator" idea. Anyone who lives inside the United States can never be considered an outsider anywhere within its bounds.

You deplore the demonstrations taking place in Birmingham. But your statement, I am sorry to say, fails to express a similar concern for the conditions that brought about the demonstrations. I am sure that none of you would want to rest content with the superficial kind of social analysis that deals merely with effects and does not grapple with underlying causes. It is unfortunate that demonstrations are taking place in Birmingham, but it is even more unfortunate that the city's white power structure left the Negro community with no alternative.

In any nonviolent campaign there are four basic steps: collection of the facts to determine whether injustices exist; negotiation; self-purification; and direct action. We have gone through all these steps in Birmingham. There can be no gainsaying the fact that racial injustice engulfs this community. Birmingham is probably the most thoroughly segregated city in the United States. Its ugly record of brutality is widely known. Negroes have experienced grossly unjust treatment in the courts. There have been more unsolved bombings of Negro homes and churches in Birmingham than in any other city in the nation. These are the hard, brutal facts of the case. On the basis of these conditions, Negro leaders sought to negotiate with the city fathers. But the latter consistently refused to engage in good-faith negotiation.

Then, last September, came the opportunity to talk with leaders of Birmingham's economic community. In the course of the negotiations, certain promises were made by the merchants—for example, to remove the stores' humiliating racial signs. On the basis of these promises, the Reverend Fred Shuttlesworth and the leaders of the Alabama Christian Movement for Human Rights agreed to a moratorium on all demonstrations. As the weeks and months went by, we realized that we were the victims of a broken promise. A few signs, briefly removed, returned; the others remained.

As in so many past experiences, our hopes had been blasted, and the shadow of deep disappointment settled upon us. We had no alternative except to prepare for direct action, whereby we would present our very bodies as a means of laying our case before the conscience of the local and the national community. Mindful of the difficulties involved, we decided to undertake a process of self-purification. We began a series of workshops on nonviolence, and we repeatedly asked ourselves: "Are you able to accept blows without retaliating?" "Are you able to endure the ordeal of jail?" We decided to schedule our direct-action program for the Easter season, realizing that except for Christmas, this is the main shopping period of the year. Knowing that a strong economic-withdrawal program would be the by-product of direct action, we felt that this would be the best time to bring pressure to bear on the merchants for the needed change.

Then it occurred to us that Birmingham's mayoral election was coming up in March, and we speedily decided to postpone action until after election day. When we discovered that the Commissioner of Public Safety, Eugene "Bull" Connor, had piled up enough votes to be in the run-off, we decided again to postpone action until the day after the run-off so that the demonstrations could not be used to cloud the issues. Like many others, we waited to see Mr. Connor defeated, and to this end we endured postponement after postponement. Having aided in this community need, we felt that our direct-action program could be delayed no longer.

You may well ask: "Why direct action? Why sit-ins, marches and so forth? Isn't negotiation a better path?" You are quite right in calling for negotiation. Indeed, this is the very purpose of direct action. Nonviolent direct action seeks to create such a crisis and foster such a tension that a community which has constantly refused to negotiate is forced to confront the issue. It seeks so to dramatize the issue that it can no longer be ignored. My citing the creation of tension as part of the work of the nonviolent-resister may sound rather shocking. But I must confess that I am not afraid of the word "tension." I have earnestly opposed violent tension, but there is a type of constructive, non-violent tension which is necessary for growth. Just as Socrates felt that it was necessary to create a tension in the mind so that individuals could rise from the bondage of myths and half-truths to the unfettered realm of creative analysis and objective appraisal, so must we see the need for nonviolent gadflies to create the kind of tension in society that will help men rise from the dark depths of prejudice and racism to the majestic heights of understanding and brotherhood.

The purpose of our direct-action program is to create a situation so crisis-packed that it will inevitably open the door to negotiation. I therefore concur with you in your call for negotiation. Too long has our beloved Southland been bogged down in a tragic effort to live in monologue rather than dialogue.

One of the basic points in your statement is that the action that I and my associates have taken in Birmingham is untimely. Some have asked: "Why didn't you give the new city administration time to act?" The only answer that I can give to this query is that the new Birmingham administration must be prodded about as much as the outgoing one, before it will act. We are sadly mistaken if we feel that the election of Albert Boutwell as mayor will bring the millennium to Birmingham. While Mr. Boutwell is a much more gentle person that Mr. Connor, they are both segregationists, dedicated to maintenance of the status quo. I have hope that Mr. Boutwell will be reasonable enough to see the futility of massive resistance to desegregation. But he will not see this without pressure from devotees of civil rights. My friends, I must say to you that we have not made a single gain in civil rights without determined legal and nonviolent pressure. Lamentably, it is an historical fact that privileged groups seldom give up their privileges voluntarily. Individuals may see the moral light and voluntarily give up their unjust posture; but, as Reinhold Niebuhr has reminded us, groups tend to be more immoral than individuals.

We know through painful experience that freedom is never voluntarily given by the oppressor; it must be demanded by the oppressed. Frankly, I have yet to engage in a direct-action campaign that was "well timed" in the view of those who have not suffered unduly from the disease of segregation. For years now I have heard the word "Wait!" It rings in the ear of every Negro with piercing familiarity. This "Wait" has almost always meant "Never." We must come to see, with one of our distinguished jurists, that "justice too long delayed is justice denied."

We have waited for more than 340 years for our constitutional and God-given rights. The nations of Asia and Africa are moving with jetlike speed toward gaining political independence, but we still creep at horse-and-buggy pace toward gaining a cup of coffee at a lunch counter. Perhaps it is easy for those who have never felt the stinging darts of segregation to say, "Wait." But when you have seen vicious mobs lynch your mothers and fathers at will and drown your sisters and brothers at whim; when you have seen hate-filled policemen curse, kick and even kill your black brothers and sisters; when you see the vast majority of your twenty million Negro brothers smothering in an airtight cage of poverty in the midst of an affluent society; when you suddenly find your tongue twisted and your speech stammering as you seek to explain to your six-year-old daughter why she can't go to the public amusement park that has just been advertised on television, and see tears welling up in her eyes when she is told that Funtown is closed to colored children, and see ominous clouds of inferiority beginning to form in her little mental sky, and see her beginning to distort her personality by developing an unconscious bitterness toward white people; when you have to concoct an answer for a five-year-old son who is asking: "Daddy, why do white people treat colored people so mean?"; when you take a cross-country drive and find it necessary to sleep night after night in the uncomfortable corners of your automobile because no motel will accept you; when you are humiliated day in and day out by nagging signs reading "white" and "colored"; when your first name becomes "nigger," your middle name becomes "boy" (however old you are) and your last name becomes "John," and your wife and mother are never given the respected title "Mrs."; when you are harried by day and haunted by night by the fact that you are a Negro, living constantly at tiptoe stance, never quite knowing what to expect next, and are plagued with inner fears and outer resentments; when you are forever fighting a degenerating sense of "nobodiness'—then you will understand why we find it difficult to wait. There comes a time when the cup of endurance runs over, and men are no longer willing to be plunged into the abyss of despair. I hope, sirs, you can understand our legitimate and unavoidable impatience.

You express a great deal of anxiety over our willingness to break laws. This is certainly a legitimate concern. Since we so diligently urge people to obey the Supreme Court's decision of 1954 outlawing segregation in the public schools, at first glance it may seem rather paradoxical for us consciously to break laws. One may well ask: "How can you advocate breaking some laws and obeying others?" The answer lies in the fact that there are two types of laws: just and unjust. I would be the first to advocate obeying just laws. One has not only a legal but a moral responsibility to obey just laws. Conversely, one has a moral responsibility to disobey unjust laws. I would agree with St. Augustine that "an unjust law is no law at all."

Now, what is the difference between the two? How does one determine whether a law is just or unjust? A just law is a man-made code that squares with the moral law or the law of God. An unjust law is a code that is out of harmony with the moral law. To put it in the terms of St. Thomas Aquinas: An unjust law is a human law that is not rooted in eternal law and natural law. Any law that uplifts human personality is just. Any law that degrades human personality is unjust. All segregation statutes are unjust because segregation distorts the soul and damages the personality. It gives the segregator a false sense of superiority and the segregated a false sense of inferiority. Segregation, to use the terminology of the Jewish philosopher Martin Buber, substitutes an "I-it" relationship for an "I-thou" relationship and ends up relegating persons to the status of things. Hence segregation is not only politically, economically and sociologically unsound, it is morally wrong and sinful. Paul Tillich has said that sin is separation. Is not segregation an existential expression of man's tragic separation, his awful estrangement, his terrible sinfulness? Thus it is that I can urge men to obey the 1954 decision of the Supreme Court, for it is morally right; and I can urge them to disobey segregation ordinances, for they are morally wrong.

Let us consider a more concrete example of just and unjust laws. An unjust law is a code that a numerical or power majority group compels a minority group to obey but does not make binding on itself. This is *difference* made legal. By the same token, a just law is a code that a majority compels a minority to follow and that it is willing to follow itself. This is *sameness* made legal.

Let me give another explanation. A law is unjust if it is inflicted on a minority that, as a result of being denied the right to vote, had no part in enacting or devising the law. Who can say that the legislature of Alabama which set up that state's segregation laws was democratically elected? Throughout Alabama all sorts of devious methods are used to prevent Negroes from becoming registered voters, and there are some counties in which, even though Negroes constitute a majority of the population, not a single Negro is registered. Can any law enacted under such circumstances be considered democratically structured?

Sometimes a law is just on its face and unjust in its application. For instance, I have been arrested on a charge of parading without a permit. Now, there is nothing wrong in having an ordinance which requires a permit for a parade. But such an ordinance becomes unjust when it is used to maintain segregation and to deny citizens the First-Amendment privilege of peaceful assembly and protest.

I hope you are able to see the distinction I am trying to point out. In no sense do I advocate evading or defying the law, as would the rabid segregationist. That would lead to anarchy. One who breaks an unjust law must do so openly, lovingly, and with a willingness to accept the penalty. I submit that an individual who breaks a law that conscience tells him is unjust, and who willingly accepts the penalty of imprisonment in order to arouse the conscience of the community over its unjustice, is in reality expressing the highest respect for law.

Of course, there is nothing new about this kind of civil disobedience. It was evidenced sublimely in the refusal of Shadrach, Meshach and Abednego to obey the laws of Nebuchadnezzar, on the ground that a higher moral law was at stake. It was practiced superbly by the early Christians, who were willing to face hungry lions and the excruciating pain of chopping blocks rather than submit to certain unjust laws of the Roman Empire. To a degree, academic freedom is a reality today because Socrates practiced civil disobedience. In our own nation, the Boston Tea Party represented a massive act of civil disobedience.

We should never forget that everything Adolf Hitler did in Germany was "legal" and everything the Hungarian freedom fighters did in Hungary was "illegal." It was "illegal" to aid and comfort a Jew in Hitler's Germany. Even so, I am sure that, had I lived in Germany at the time, I would have aided and comforted my Jewish brothers. If today I lived in a Communist country where certain principles dear to the

Christian faith are suppressed, I would openly advocate disobeying that country's antireligious laws.

I must make two honest confessions to you, my Christian and Jewish brothers. First, I must confess that over the past few years I have been gravely disappointed with the white moderate. I have almost reached the regrettable conclusion that the Negro's great stumbling block in his stride toward freedom is not the White Citizen's Counciler or the Ku Klux Klanner, but the white moderate, who is more devoted to "order" than to justice; who prefers a negative peace which is the absence of tension to a positive peace which is the presence of justice; who constantly says: "I agree with you in the goal you seek, but I cannot agree with your methods of direct action"; who paternalistically believes he can set the timetable for another man's freedom; who lives by a mythical concept of time and who constantly advises the Negro to wait for a "more convenient season." Shallow understanding from people of good will is more frustrating than absolute misunderstanding from people of ill will. Lukewarm acceptance is much more bewildering than outright rejection.

I had hoped that the white moderate would understand that law and order exist for the purpose of establishing justice and that when they fail in this purpose they become the dangerously structured dams that block the flow of social progress. I had hoped that the white moderate would understand that the present tension in the South is a necessary phase of the transition from an obnoxious negative peace, in which the Negro passively accepted his unjust plight, to a substantive and positive peace, in which all men will respect the dignity and worth of human personality. Actually, we who engage in nonviolent direct action are not the creators of tension. We merely bring to the surface the hidden tension that is already alive. We bring it out in the open, where it can be seen and dealt with. Like a boil that can never be cured so long as it is covered up but must be opened with all its ugliness to the natural medicines of air and light, injustice must be exposed, with all the tension its exposure creates, to the light of human conscience and the air of national opinion before it can be cured.

In your statement you assert that our actions, even though peaceful, must be condemned because they precipitate violence. But is this a logical assertion? Isn't this like condemning a robbed man because his possession of money precipitated the evil act of robbery? Isn't this like condemning Socrates because his unswerving commitment to truth and his philosophical inquiries precipitated the act by the misguided populace in which they made him drink hemlock? Isn't this like condemning Jesus because his unique God-consciousness and never-ceasing devotion to God's will precipitated the evil act of crucifixion? We must come to see that, as the federal courts have consistently affirmed, it is wrong to urge an individual to cease his efforts to gain his basic constitutional rights because the quest may precipitate violence. Society must protect the robbed and punish the robber.

I had also hoped that the white moderate would reject the myth concerning time in relation to the struggle for freedom. I have just received a letter from a white brother in Texas. He writes: "All Christians know that the colored people will receive equal rights eventually, but it is possible that you are in too great a religious hurry. It has taken Christianity almost two thousand years to accomplish what it has. The teachings of Christ take time to come to earth." Such an attitude stems from a tragic misconception of time, from the strangely irrational notion that there is something in the very flow of time that will inevitably cure all ills. Actually, time itself is neutral; it can be used either destructively or constructively. More and more I feel that the people of ill will have used time much more effectively than have the people of good will. We will have to repent in this generation not merely for the hateful words and actions of the bad people but for the appalling silence of the good people. Human progress never rolls in on wheels of inevitability; it comes through the tireless efforts of men willing to be co-workers with God, and without this hard work, time itself becomes an ally of the forces of social stagnation. We must use time creatively, in the knowledge that the time is always ripe to do right. Now is the time to make real the promise of democracy and transform our pending national elegy into a creative psalm of brotherhood. Now is the time to lift our national policy from the quicksand of racial injustice to the solid rock of human dignity.

You speak of our activity in Birmingham as extreme. At first I was rather disappointed that fellow clergymen would see my nonviolent efforts as those of an extremist. I began thinking about the fact that I stand in the middle of two opposing forces in the Negro community. One is a force of complacency, made up in part of Negroes who, as a result of long years of oppression are so drained of self-respect and a sense of "somebodiness" that they have adjusted to segregation; and in part of a few middle-class Negroes who, because of a degree of academic and economic security and because in some ways they profit by segregation, have become insensitive to the problems of the masses. The other force is one of bitterness and hatred, and it comes perilously close to advocating violence. It is expressed in the various black nationalist groups that are springing up across the nation, the largest and best-known being Elijah Muhammad's Muslim movement. Nourished by the Negro's frustration over the continued existence of racial discrimination, this movement is made up of people who have lost faith in America, who have absolutely repudiated Christianity, and who have concluded that the white man is an incorrigible "devil."

I have tried to stand between these two forces, saying that we need emulate neither the "do-nothingism" of the complacent nor the hatred and despair of the black nationalist. For there is the more excellent way of love and nonviolent protest. I am grateful to God that, through the influence of the Negro church, the way of nonviolence became an integral part of our struggle.

If this philosophy had not emerged, by now many streets of the South would, I am convinced, be flowing with blood. And I am further convinced that if our white brothers dismiss as "rabble-rousers" and "outside agitators" those of us who employ nonviolent direct action, and if they refuse to support our nonviolent efforts, millions of Negroes will, out of frustration and despair, seek solace and security in black-nationalist ideologies—a development that would inevitably lead to a frightening racial nightmare.

Oppressed people cannot remain oppressed forever. The yearning for freedom eventually manifests itself, and that is what has happened to the American Negro. Something within has reminded him of his birthright of freedom, and something without has reminded him that it can be gained. Consciously or unconsciously, he has been caught up by the *Zeitgeist*, and with his black brothers of Africa and his brown and yellow brothers of Asia, South America and the Caribbean, the United States Negro is moving with a sense of great urgency toward the promised land of racial justice. If one recognizes this vital urge that has engulfed the Negro community, one should readily understand why public demonstrations are taking place. The Negro has many pent-up resentments and latent frustrations, and he must release them. So let him march; let him make prayer pilgrimages to the city hall; let him go on freedom rides—and try to understand why he must do so. If his repressed emotions are not released in nonviolent ways, they will seek expression through violence; this is not a threat but a fact of history. So I have not said to my people: "Get rid of your discontent." Rather, I have tried to say that this normal and healthy discontent can be channeled into the creative outlet of nonviolent direct action. And now this approach is being termed extremist.

But though I was initially disappointed at being categorized as an extremist, as I continued to think about the matter I gradually gained a measure of satisfaction from the label. Was not Jesus an extremist for love: "Love your enemies, bless them that curse you, do good to them that hate you, and pray for them which despitefully use you, and persecute you." Was not Amos an extremist for justice: "Let justice roll down like waters and righteousness like an ever-flowing stream." Was not Paul an extremist for the Christian gospel: "I bear in my body the marks of the Lord Jesus." Was not Martin Luther an extremist: "Here I stand; I cannot do otherwise, so help me God." And John Bunyan: "I will stay in jail to the end of my days before I make a butchery of my conscience." And Abraham Lincoln: "This nation cannot survive half slave and half free." And Thomas Jefferson: "We hold these truths to be self-evident, that all men are created equal . . ." So the question is not whether we will be extremists, but what kind of extremists we will be. Will we be extremists for hate or for love? Will we be extremists for the preservation of injustice or for the extension of justice? In that dramatic scene on Calvary's hill three men were crucified. We must never forget that all three were crucified for the same crime—the crime of extremism. Two were extremists for immorality, and thus fell below their environment. The other, Jesus Christ, was an extremist for love, truth and goodness, and thereby rose above his environment. Perhaps the South, the nation and the world are in dire need of creative extremists.

I had hoped that the white moderate would see this need. Perhaps I was too optimistic; perhaps I expected too much. I suppose I should have realized that few members of the oppressor race can understand the deep groans and passionate yearnings of the oppressed race, and still fewer have the vision to see that injustice must be rooted out by strong, persistent and determined action. I am thankful, however, that some of our white brothers in the South have grasped the meaning of this social revolution and committed themselves to it. They are still all too few in quantity, but they are big in quality. Some—such as Ralph McGill,

Lillian Smith, Harry Golden, James McBride Dabbs, Ann Braden and Sarah Patton Boyle—have written about our struggle in eloquent and prophetic terms. Others have marched with us down nameless streets of the South. They have languished in filthy, roach-infested jails, suffering the abuse and brutality of policemen who view them as "dirty nigger-lovers." Unlike so many of their moderate brothers and sisters, they have recognized the urgency of the moment and sensed the need for powerful "action" antidotes to combat the disease of segregation.

Let me take note of my other major disappointment. I have been so greatly disappointed with the white church and its leadership. Of course, there are some notable exceptions. I am not unmindful of the fact that each of you has taken some significant stands on this issue. I commend you, Reverend Stallings, for your Christian stand on this past Sunday, in welcoming Negroes to your worship service on a nonsegregated basis. I commend the Catholic leaders of this state for integrating Spring Hill College several years ago.

But despite these notable exceptions, I must honestly reiterate that I have been disappointed with the church. I do not say this as one of those negative critics who can always find something wrong with the church. I say this as a minister of the gospel, who loves the church; who was nurtured in its bosom; who has been sustained by its spiritual blessings and who will remain true to it as long as the cord of life shall lengthen.

When I was suddenly catapulted into the leadership of the bus protest in Montgomery, Alabama, a few years ago, I felt we would be supported by the white church. I felt that the white ministers, priests and rabbis of the South would be among our strongest allies. Instead, some have been outright opponents, refusing to understand the freedom movement and misrepresenting its leaders; all too many others have been more cautious than courageous and have remained silent behind the anesthetizing security of stained-glass windows.

In spite of my shattered dreams, I came to Birmingham with the hope that the white religious leadership of this community would see the justice of our cause and, with deep moral concern, would serve as the channel through which our just grievances could reach the power structure. I had hoped that each of you would understand. But again I have been disappointed.

I have heard numerous southern religious leaders admonish their worshipers to comply with a desegregation decision because it is the law, but I have longed to hear white ministers declare: "Follow this decree because integration is morally right and because the Negro is your brother." In the midst of blatant injustices inflicted upon the Negro, I have watched white churchmen stand on the sideline and mouth pious irrelevancies and sanctimonious trivialities. In the midst of a mighty struggle to rid our nation of racial and economic injustice, I have heard many ministers say: "Those are social issues, with which the gospel has no real concern." And I have watched many churches commit themselves to a completely otherworldly religion which makes a strange, un-Biblical distinction between body and soul, between the sacred and the secular.

I have traveled the length and breadth of Alabama, Mississippi and all the other southern states. On sweltering summer days and crisp autumn mornings I have looked at the South's beautiful churches with their lofty spires pointing heavenward. I have beheld the impressive outlines of her massive religious-education buildings. Over and over I have found myself asking: "What kind of people worship here? Who is their God? Where were their voices when the lips of Governor Barnett dripped with words of interposition and nullification? Where were they when Governor Wallace gave a clarion call for defiance and hatred? Where were their voices of support when bruised and weary Negro men and women decided to rise from the dark dungeons of complacency to the bright hills of creative protest?"

Yes, these questions are still in my mind. In deep disappointment I have wept over the laxity of the church. But be assured that my tears have been tears of love. There can be no deep disappointment where there is not deep love. Yes, I love the church. How could I do otherwise? I am in the rather unique position of being the son, the grandson and the great-grandson of preachers. Yes, I see the church as the body of Christ. But, oh! How we have blemished and scarred that body through social neglect and through fear of being nonconformists.

There was a time when the church was very powerful—in the time when the early Christians rejoiced at being deemed worthy to suffer for what they believed. In those days the church was not merely a thermometer that recorded the ideas and principles of popular opinion; it was a thermostat that transformed the mores of society. Whenever the early Christians entered a town, the people in power became disturbed and immediately sought to convict the Christians for being "disturbers of the peace'' and "outside agitators.'' But the Christians pressed on, in the conviction that they were "a colony of heaven,'' called to obey God rather than man. Small in number, they were big in commitment. They were too God-intoxicated to be "astronomically intimidated.'' By their effort and example they brought an end to such ancient evils as infanticide and gladiatorial contests.

Things are different now. So often the contemporary church is a weak, ineffectual voice with an uncertain sound. So often it is an archdefender of the status quo. Far from being disturbed by the presence of the church, the power structure of the average community is consoled by the church's silent—and often even vocal—sanction of things as they are.

But the judgment of God is upon the church as never before. If today's church does not recapture the sacrificial spirit of the early church, it will lose its authenticity, forfeit the loyalty of millions, and be dismissed as an irrelevant social club with no meaning for the twentieth century. Every day I meet young people whose disappointment with the church has turned into outright disgust.

Perhaps I have once again been too optimistic. Is organized religion too inextricably bound to the status quo to save our nation and the world? Perhaps I must turn my faith to the inner spiritual church, the church within the church, as the true *ekklesia* and the hope of the world. But again I am thankful to God that some noble souls from the ranks of organized religion have broken loose from the paralyzing chains of conformity and joined us as active partners in the struggle for freedom. They have left their secure congregations and walked the streets of Albany, Georgia, with us. They have gone down the highways of the South on tortuous rides for freedom. Yes, they have gone to jail with us. Some have been dismissed from their churches, have lost the support of their bishops and fellow ministers. But they have acted in the faith that right defeated is stronger than evil triumphant. Their witness has been the spiritual salt that has preserved the true meaning of the gospel in these troubled times. They have carved a tunnel of hope through the dark mountain of disappointment.

I hope the church as a whole will meet the challenge of this decisive hour. But even if the church does not come to the aid of justice, I have no despair about the future. I have no fear about the outcome of our struggle in Birmingham, even if our motives are at present misunderstood. We will reach the goal of freedom in Birmingham and all over the nation, because the goal of America is freedom. Abused and scorned though we may be, our destiny is tied up with America's destiny. Before the pilgrims landed at Plymouth, we were here. Before the pen of Jefferson etched the majestic words of the Declaration of Independence across the pages of history, we were here. For more than two centuries our forebears labored in this country without wages; they made cotton king; they built the homes of their masters while suffering gross injustice and shameful humiliation—and yet out of a bottomless vitality they continued to thrive and develop. If the inexpressible cruelties of slavery could not stop us, the opposition we now face will surely fail. We will win our freedom because the sacred heritage of our nation and the eternal will of God are embodied in our echoing demands.

Before closing I feel impelled to mention one other point in your statement that has troubled me profoundly. You warmly commended the Birmingham police force for keeping "order" and "preventing violence." I doubt that you would have so warmly commended the police force if you had seen its dogs sinking their teeth into unarmed, nonviolent Negroes. I doubt that you would so quickly commend the policemen if you were to observe their ugly and inhumane treatment of Negroes here in the city jail; if you were to watch them push and curse old Negro women and young Negro girls; if you were to see them slap and kick old Negro men and young boys; if you were to observe them, as they did on two occasions, refuse to give us food because we wanted to sing our grace together. I cannot join you in your praise of the Birmingham police department.

It is true that the police have exercised a degree of discipline in handling the demonstrators. In this sense they have conducted themselves rather "nonviolently" in public. But for what purpose? To preserve the evil system of segregation. Over the past few years I have consistently preached that nonviolence demands that the means we use must be as pure as the ends we seek. I have tried to make clear that it is wrong to use immoral means to attain moral ends. But now I must affirm that it is just as wrong, or perhaps even more so, to use moral means to preserve immoral ends. Perhaps Mr. Connor and his policemen have been rather nonviolent in public, as was Chief Pritchett in Albany, Georgia, but they have used the moral means of nonviolence to maintain the immoral end of racial injustice. As T. S. Eliot has said: "The last temptation is the greatest treason: To do the right deed for the wrong reason."

I wish you had commended the Negro sit-inners and demonstrators of Birmingham for their sublime courage, their willingness to suffer and their amazing discipline in the midst of great provocation. One day the South will recognize its real heroes. They will be the James Merediths, with the noble sense of purpose that enables them to face jeering and hostile mobs, and with the agonizing loneliness that characterizes the life of the pioneer. They will be old, oppressed, battered Negro women, symbolized in a seventy-two-year-old woman in Montgomery, Alabama, who rose up with a sense of dignity and with her people decided not to ride segregated buses, and who responded with ungrammatical profundity to one who inquired about her weariness: "My feets is tired, but my soul is at rest." They will be the young high school and college students, the young ministers of the gospel and a host of their elders, courageously and nonviolently sitting in at lunch counters and willingly going to jail for conscience' sake. One day the South will know that when these disinherited children of God sat down at lunch counters, they were in reality standing up for what is best in the American dream and for the most sacred values in our Judaeo-Christian heritage, thereby bringing our nation back to those great wells of democracy which were dug deep by the founding fathers in their formulation of the Constitution and the Declaration of Independence.

Never before have I written so long a letter. I'm afraid it is much too long to take your precious time. I can assure you that it would have been much shorter if I had been writing from a comfortable desk, but what else can one do when he is alone in a narrow jail cell, other than write long letters, think long thoughts and pray long prayers?

If I have said anything in this letter that overstates the truth and indicates an unreasonable impatience, I beg you to forgive me. If I have said anything that understates the truth and indicates my having a patience that allows me to settle for anything less than brotherhood, I beg God to forgive me.

I hope this letter finds you strong in the faith. I also hope that circumstances will soon make it possible for me to meet each of you, not as an integrationist or a civil-rights leader but as a fellow clergyman and a Christian brother. Let us all hope that the dark clouds of racial prejudice will soon pass away and the deep fog of misunderstanding will be lifted from our fear-drenched communities, and in some not too distant tomorrow the radiant stars of love and brotherhood will shine over our great nation with all their scintillating beauty.

Yours for the cause of Peace and Brotherhood,
MARTIN LUTHER KING, JR.

Document III-8: REASON AND LEGALISMS

The preceding documents have been intended to demonstrate the religious and moral elements in reform as distinguished from the political, economic, and legalistic aspects. It is tempting to contrast the exalted emotionalism and angry rhetoric of the moralistic arguments with the dry, meticulous logic of the courtroom and countinghouse. It will soon become apparent that these distinctions—like so many others in the area of reform—are far from pure. Economic arguments are shot through with moral judgments; political points are capped with flaming exhortations, and categorical dividing lines are traceable only in invisible ink.

Still, there is a difference between the reformer who sees violence as a ready weapon or freely risks martyrdom for his cause, and the more patient advocate of change who feels that logic, spiced with rhetoric, can alter peacefully the course of human events. The following documents represent the latter persuasion as it has manifested itself in a wide range of experiences from abolitionist editorials through civil rights court cases.

In comparing the anti-slavery movement with the civil rights movement one discovers an earlier America that seems to have been considerably more susceptible to reasoned argument than has been the case in recent years. Witness the evident impact of Weld's *American Slavery As It Is* (as discussed in III-2). Witness the widespread interest in James G. Birney's prose (see III-9). Additionally there were Joshua Leavitt's two long pieces in *The Emancipator* attacking first "The Political Power of Slavery" and then "The Financial Power of Slavery" (see the October 15 and 22 issues of 1840). Addressed to the farmers and small businessmen of the North, these arguments attacked slavery as a monopoly and "demonstrated" that capital "drained" from the North by slavery had to be replaced with the tax dollars of non-slaveholders. In another widely influential work Lewis Tappan tried to arouse the Southern petit bourgeoisie by convincing them that the large slaveholders were their worst economic enemies (*Address to the Non-Slaveholders of the South on the Social and Political Evils of Slavery.* New York, Anti-Slavery Society, 1843). A modern equivalent might be found in the argument, voiced by William Faulkner and others, that the South was permanently mortgaging its future by the unusual expense needed to support two separate school systems under the practice of segregation.

Persuasion cannot be disembodied; it needs to be attached to a device for producing political action. For Birney and many others the answer lay in a third party: the device that ultimately brought the argument to a head and led to its solution by trial-at-arms. Weld and his friends moved toward Congress as the most likely source of peaceful political action.

The first document reproduced below gives insight into the congressional campaign against slavery as led by that brilliant former President, John Quincy Adams, returned to Washington as a member of the House. The document opens with the tail end of a public listing of some 840 anti-slavery petitions addressed to Adams alone. The sheer number of these petitions, together with their careful registry and classification, is meant to suggest the unrelenting and persistent volume of anti-slavery concern.

Acknowledging the petitioners, Adams then turns to an analysis of the issues and particularly of the pro-slavery arguments that had persuaded Congress to adopt its notorious "gag rule" forbidding the discussion of slavery. His discussion breathes the emotional logic of religion, of scripture, of history, of political science, of the Constitution and the Declaration and all that these documents evoked. Like Tappan, Adams hoped for the end of slavery from within the South. Like Leavitt, Birney, and Weld, he relied on rational suasion to move existing institutions toward nonviolent change. (Adams continued this discussion in a further letter to the *Daily National Intelligencer* of May 28, 1839, pp. 2, 3.) Victory over the gag rule, achieved in 1844, made possible some further compromises on the slavery question.

The most obvious modern parallel to the petition campaign of the 1830s and 1840s has been the congressional legislation of the 1950s and 1960s: the Civil Rights Acts of 1957, 1960, 1964, and 1968; the Voting

Rights Act of 1965 (see II-43). The enactment of this legislation required enormous patience and ingenuity as well as the judicious application of considerable pressure. The seniority and committee systems had to be challenged; and such parliamentary devices as riders, quorum calls, and filibusters had to be overcome.

A less obvious yet more precise parallel to the petition campaign, however, may be found in the series of court cases which generously preceded the above-mentioned legislation and which established a momentum in recognition of social change without which Congress could not have found support for its actions. The prosecution of a series of court cases on behalf of Negro petitioners represented a sustained act of patience and courage, as well as calculated tactics and attention to detail. The lawyers who argued these cases mirrored the attributes of Weld and Adams, while in the background the National Association for the Advancement of Colored People (and later the American Civil Liberties Union) played a role similar to that of the American Anti-Slavery Society, soliciting personal and financial support, gathering crucial data, and conducting a long public relations campaign through house organs and the daily press.

By the time of the formation of the NAACP it had become obvious to many people interested in minority rights that much of the battle for social justice would have to be fought in the courts. The Supreme Court was importantly responsible for establishing a nadir in the history of blacks in America with the *Dred Scott* v. *Sanford* decision in 1857. Almost fifty years later, the court had decided that the Fourteenth Amendment could be satisfied by separate-but-equal facilities for blacks (*Plessy* v. *Ferguson*, 1896). Thus, if segregation of the races was to be peacefully vanquished, the battle must be fought in the courts, where segregation had been legally identified and successfully protected.

Although circumstances dictated some of the actions, it is also clear that civil rights leaders made some strategic decisions quite deliberately. It was decided that the most damaging consequences of segregation arose from separate educational systems. These consequences were sometimes more readily discernible at a high professional level where, for example, a career depended on a state license (as in law or medicine) and where in-state education was virtually necessary in order to pass the licensing examination. Furthermore, the minority group would soon need a large number of well-trained lawyers in all states. Judges, who themselves were lawyers, could be expected to take special interest in cases involving law schools.

The pressure against segregation was developed, therefore, in a series of court cases involving the admission of black students to the law schools of state universities. Reproduced below are excerpts from several of these cases through which the outlines of this campaign are clearly visible. The first case, *University* v. *Murray*, was heard in Maryland in 1935. It grew out of a situation in which the state had provided no legal education for blacks; the decision has been reproduced in some detail since it contains most of the major arguments on the subject and has been regularly cited since as making an important precedent. The court here refused to excuse the state from its obligations either because there were few black applicants, because there were elements of private control, or because the state needed more time.

In many states black applicants to law schools had been served through scholarships allowing them to attend black or integrated schools outside their home state. *Missouri ex rel. Gaines* v. *Canada* attacked this practice by establishing that equal facilities must be provided *within* the state. In *Sweatt* v. *Painter* the issue was altered by the establishment of a state-supported law school for Negroes; and in this instance the court—although unwilling to reopen the basic issues of separate-but-equal—took a hard, fair look at the meaning of "equal." This case might appear as the most thorough justification of the NAACP tactics in the detailed realism with which the Justices regarded legal education, clearly a subject close to their hearts and consciences.

The court's definition of equality progressed one step further in *McLaurin* v. *Oklahoma*. The black student here had been permitted use of the white facilities but on a segregated basis. But the court, pointing out the need for developing black leadership in education, found the remnants of segregation a disability to true equality. With this succession of cases in mind, then, the justifiably famous *Brown* v. *Board of Education* can be seen as the inevitable culmination of an evolving attitude rather than a sudden thunderclap from the clear blue sky of social stasis. Even the famous phrase, "with all deliberate speed," as applied to ending racial discrimination in education, had been foreshadowed by one of the arguments in *University* v. *Murray*.

Brown v. *Board of Education* actually covers Supreme Court rulings on four separate cases appealed from four separate states: Kansas, South Carolina, Virginia, and Delaware. It was a crucial decision for many reasons. It dealt with a problem that was not simply regional but nationwide. It dealt with a problem growing directly out of the Civil War and Reconstruction and it did so self-consciously by attempting to look into the motives surrounding the passage of the Fourteenth Amendment and by admitting as evidence the findings of child psychologists and historians of education. It followed a series of cases wherein a confrontation with *Plessy* v. *Ferguson* was explicitly avoided, and concluded that this ruling had no applicability in the area of education. Finally, in response to the April 11-14, 1955, rearguments, the court took considerable pains to insure court-supervised enforcement of the conclusions reached in the decision.

These cases constitute not only a technical history of the movement toward civil rights but also a sensitive index to cultural change evident as often in what was unsaid as in what was said. The earliest of these cases is hardly ancient history; yet a remarkable change has accompanied the shift in attitudes that can be symbolized by the simple orthographic change from "negro" to "Negro." Out of this composite document the courts emerge as instruments which provide abundant technicalities behind which the opponents of change can barricade themselves with seeming impregnability. Yet when the tide of battle begins to shift, the courts are fully capable of becoming as powerful a force for change as once they were defenders against it.

(The editor takes pleasure in acknowledging the enlightenment he received on this question from his acquaintance with Franklin H. Williams, who served as Assistant Special Counsel to the national office of the NAACP from 1945-50 and who participated in arguing two of the cases cited above.)

SOURCE: A: The Daily *National Intelligencer.* April 23, 1839, pp. 2, 3. B: *University of Maryland* v. *Donald G. Murray,* 169 Maryland, 478-9, 480, 483-5, 486-8, 489, abridged; *Missouri ex rel. Gaines* v. *Canada, Registrar of the University of Missouri,* 305 US 337, 342-6, 348-52, abridged; *Sweatt* v. *Painter,* 339 US 632-6, abridged; *McLaurin* v. *Oklahoma State Regents for Higher Education,* 332 US 640-2, abridged; *Brown* v. *Board of Education of Topeka,* 347 US 490-6, abridged; and 349 US 298-301, abridged.

A: ANTI-SLAVERY IN CONGRESS

LIST OF PETITIONS, & c.*
Presented to the House of Representatives at the Third
Session of the Twenty-fifth Congress.
BY Mr. JOHN QUINCY ADAMS, of Massachusetts.
CONCLUDED.

1. For the abolition of slavery in the District of Columbia.
2. Abolition of slavery in the Territories.
3. Prohibition of the internal slave-trade.
4. Against the admission of any new slave State.
5. Against the annexation of Texas to the United States.
6. For a select committee, & to be heard in person or by counsel.
7. For the recognition of the Republic of Hayti.
8. To rescind the resolutions of 12th December, 1838.
9. Miscellaneous.

NAME OF FIRST SIGNER	PLACE	PRAYER	NO.
Ezra Carler & Hannah Kimball—47-27	Leyden, N.Y.	1 2 3 6	74
Same 46, and same 27	do	4 5 6	73
Solomon E. Moore	Alton, & c., Ill.	1 2 3 4	144
Virgil Noble	Otter Creek, do	2 3	20
Same	do	4	20
John Pitts & Susan D. Hurlbut—21 11	Hornellsville, N.Y.	1 2 3 6	32
Same 22, and same 11	do	4 5 6	33
Same 22, and same 11	do	7	33
James Hathaway	Berkley, Mass.	8	34
Cynthia R. Daggett	Pawtucket, do	1 2 3	169
Rachel C. Bliss	Rehoboth, do	1 2 3	50
Same	do	3	51
Sarah Anne Rogers	Clermont, Ohio	1 3	70
Same	do	4 5	65
Jacob Latting	Lattingtown, N.Y.	*	
Elias Babcock	Adams, do	1 2 3	44
Same	do	4 5	43
Arabella Harwood	Ware Village, Ma.	1 2 3	64
Lucy Gilbert	do	5	70
Isaac Cross, Jr.	Cherry Valley, N.Y.	1 2 3	19
Same	do	4 5	18
William Voorhees, Jr.	Sharon, do	1 2 3	8
Benjamin J. Sammons	do	4 5	8
D. W. Le Roy	Canajoharie, do	1 2 3	7
Same	do	4 5	7
Napoleon B. & Louisa A. Buell—35 20	Batavia, do	1	55
Same 35, and same 20	do	3	55
Same 41, and same 21	do	4	62
Same 32, and same 23	do	5	55

*Symbols in Prayer column indicate special forms of anti-slavery petitions.

NAME OF FIRST SIGNER	PLACE	PRAYER	NO.
Esek Wilbur	Macedon, do	1 2 3 6	29
Same	do	4 5 6	32
Abby Sandford	E. Bridgewater, Ma.	8	37
John Elmore & Amency Eastman—62 52	Nelson, N.Y.	1 2 3 6	114
Same 65, and same 50	do	4 5 6	115
William & Deborah Sims—15 16	Cazenovia, do	1 2 3 6	31
Same 15, and same 16	do	4 5 6	31
Thomas Austin	Poughkeepsie, do	8	73
John Amen	Highland, Ohio	1 3	18
Same	do	3	19
Same	do	4 5	20
Same	do	8	17
J. W. Ward	Abington, Mass.	†	51
Jeremiah Fowler	Lubec, Maine	‡	79
Lydia Faxou	do	‡	101
John Jay	New York, N.Y.	§	43
Samuel Thompson	Poughkeepsie, do	1 2 3	141
Isaac Requa	do	4 5	167
Edward Wilbur & Abigail Camp—24 17	Pittsford, do	1 2 3 6	41
Same 21, and same 16	do	4 5	37
Same 23, and same 17	do	1 2 3 6	41
Joshua Maynard	Senaca, Ohio	1 3	32
Same	do	3	34
Same	do	4	42
Same	do	5	38
Mary Maynard	do	1 3	44
Same	do	3	42
Same	do	4	44
Same	do	5	44
Henry & Rebecca Archibald—20 12	Bow, N.H.	1 2 3 4 5 6	32
James W. Willis	Delavan, & c. Ill.	1 2 3 6	22
D. B. Waterman & L. M. Hopkins—26 18	Annsville, N.Y.	1 2 3	44
H. W. Thorne & Lydia M. Hopkins—28 16	do	4 5	46
Jonathan Woodworth	Hartford, Ohio	Slavery	1
Ira A. Van Duger	Franklin, Vt.	π	72
Asa, Jr. & Martha Turner—53 45	Denmark, &d. Iowa	1 2 3 6	98
Same 55, and same 44	Des Moines, & c. do	4 5 6	99
J. F. Mure	Point Coupee, La.	π	1
Jesse Phillips & Leah Moore	_ _ _ _, Indiana	Slavery	432
Same	do	5	137
Ellis Davis	_ _ _ _, do	Slavery	137
Same	_ _ _ _, do	5	165
Timothy Abbot	Wilton, N.H.	1 2 3 4 6	49
Phoebe Abbot	do	4 5	53

The following petitions were received after the close of the session:

NAME OF FIRST SIGNER	PLACE	PRAYER	NO.
Asa Meacham	Oswego, N.Y.	†	
W. R. Williams & W. Branch—63 40	VanBuren, & c, Mn.	5	102
James C. Fuller & M. C. Edwards—54 16	Skaneateles, N.Y.	1 2 3 6	70
Same 55, and same 16	do	4 5 6	71
Elizabeth Spear	Friendship, do	1 2 3 6	48
Same	do	4 5 6	44
J. C. Tibbets	Jefferson, & c.	8	20
Gordon & Phebe Henry—48 51	Farmersville, N.Y.	1 2 3 6	99
Same 50, and same 52	do	4 5 6	102
Maria S. Medbery	Mercer, Ohio	1	45
Abigail Thomas	Duxbury, Mass.	1 2 3 6	79
Same	do	4 5 6	76
Same	do	7	78
Orin Bradford & Caroline Rollin—113 74	Crown Point, N.Y.	1 2 3 6	188
Same 117, and same 73	do	4 5 6	190
Same 114, and same 72	do	7	186

To the Citizens of the United States, whose Petitions, Memorials, and Remonstrances have been entrusted to me, to be presented to the House of Representatives of the U. States at the Third Session of the 25th Congress.

Washington, April, 1839.

FELLOW-CITIZENS: In the National Intelligencers of 24th December, 1838, 11th and 23rd January, 14th March, and of this day, lists are contained of all the petitions presented by me to the House of Representatives of the United States, at the session of Congress recently concluded. The names, male and female, of the first signer of each petition, the place and State whence they came, the object prayed for, and the number of petitioners, are all included in the lists. The number of petitions amounting to 825, besides 16, received by me since the close of the session of Congress.

I received with many of the petitions letters from the persons by whom they were forwarded to me, expressing much anxiety to be informed whether they were duly received by me; whether they had been presented to the House and what destiny attended them there. The impossibility of answering all or any considerable portion of those letters has been my principal motive for making out those lists and causing them to be published.

With regard to the fate of the petitions, I deem it proper to say that they received very little attention from the House. By a general resolution of the 12th of December, all those relating in any manner to slavery were laid on the table, without being read, printed or referred. This resolution, adopted at the last four successive sessions of Congress, has introduced an habitual disregard or neglect of all petitions, which has extended to the resolutions of the State Legislatures.

The right of petition for any object not agreeable to the ruling majority in the House must be considered as suspended; and should the resolutions to lay on the table motions to receive petitions, (the form of rejection adopted by the Senate,) or to receive and lay them on the table without reading or considering them, be adopted as standing orders of the two Houses, it is manifest that the right of petition itself will be more effectively *abridged* than it possibly could be by any law of Congress, and that the first article amendatory to the Constitution of the United States would be, so far as regards the right, as completely nullified as it could be by law, were the power to enact such law not expressly interdicted to Congress.

The right of petition is one of those granted by the laws of Nature and of Nature's God to man, and the exercise of which has never, under the most despotic Governments upon earth, been formally forbidden. Of all free government it has ever been considered a vital part, and the last and heaviest charge in the Declaration of Independence against the King of Great Britain was, that the repeated *petitions* of the people of the colonies for redress had been answered only by repeated injuries.

The resolutions to lay all anti-slavery petitions on the table, without reading, printing, or debating, have usually been concerted out of the House, introduced by suspension of the rules, preceded by a speech from the introducer, closing with a motion for the *Previous Question*, which precludes not only all debate, but even all answer to the speech itself. This mode of proceeding annihilates, to the extent of its operation, not only the right of petition, but the freedom of speech in the House, and by direct consequence the freedom of the press.

At the recent session of Congress, the resolution to suppress all consideration of anti-slavery petitions was preceded by several others, containing a sort of syllogism in Baroco—beginning with a major proposition which it seems to have been supposed that no one would dare deny—''that this Government is a Government of limited powers; ''AND that, by the Constitution of the United States, Congress has no jurisdiction whatever over the institution of slavery in the several States of the Confederacy''—a compound proposition—the first part of which was a truism, without bearing at all upon the anti-slavery petitions; and the second a mere nullity, since it is not competent for the House of Representatives, by any resolution, to determine what is, or is not, within the jurisdiction of Congress. A proposition, too, perfectly nugatory, inasmuch as not one of the anti-slavery petitions had asked Congress to exercise jurisdiction over the institution of slavery in any of the States.

The second of these propositions was, ''That petitions for the abolition of slavery in the District of Columbia and the Territories of the United States, and against the removal of slaves from one State to another, are a part of a plan of operations set on foot to affect the institution of slavery in the several States, and thus indirectly to destroy that institution within their limits.''

There is, in this proposition, a remarkable slide from logic into rhetoric—what the writers upon the Belles Lettres call a euphemism—a soft name for a harsh thing. It speaks of petitions ''*against the removal of slaves from one State to another.*'' There never has been such a petition presented to either House of Congress. The petitions are against the SLAVE-TRADE between the States. It is not the *removal,* but the trade—the purchase and sale of the human chattel—between the States against which the petitions are pointed. And wherefore this glaring misrepresentation of the purport of the petitions? Why is it that petitions against the SLAVE-TRADE between the States are denominated petitions against *the removal of slaves from one State to another?* Why this slander upon the petitioners? Was it the burning blush of shame which dared not call the practice by its true name; or was it a magnanimous device to make the petitioners odious by representing them as petitioning against the removal of slaves from one State to another, when in fact the petitions were against nothing but the SLAVE TRADE?

With regard to the averment that these petitions are a part of a plan of operations set on foot to affect, and thus indirectly to destroy, the institution of slavery, to test its validity, suppose that, instead of abolition petitions, you say that the Declaration of Independence, or the Act of Congress making the *African* slave-trade *piracy,* is a part of a plan of operations set on foot to affect the institution of slavery in the several States, and thus indirectly to destroy that institution within their limits. It would certainly be as true of the Declaration of Independence or the

Slave-Trade Piracy Act as it can be of abolition petitions. The tenth article of our last treaty of peace with Great Britain is in these words: "Whereas *the traffic in slaves* is irreconcileable with the principles of humanity and justice; and whereas both his Majesty and the United States are desirous of continuing their efforts to promote its *entire abolition*, it is hereby agreed that both the contracting parties shall use their best endeavors to accomplish so desirable an object."

The TRAFFIC IN SLAVES—not the African slave-trade. This article is a part of the supreme law of the land. It pledges the United States to use their best endeavors to promote its *entire* abolition. If *petitions* for its abolition between the States are part of a plan of operations set on foot to affect, and thus indirectly destroy, the institution of slavery within the limits of the several States, what is this article?

The next of these syllogistic resolutions is another curious compound, the first part of which is, "That Congress has no right to do that *indirectly* which it cannot do *directly*"; a position too absurd for serious refutation. The second part of it is, "And that the *agitation* of the subject of slavery in the District of Columbia or the Territories, as a means and with the view of disturbing or overthrowing that institution in the several States, is against the true spirit and meaning of the Constitution, an infringement of the rights of the States affected, and a breach of the public faith on which they entered into this Confederacy."

The obvious purport of this resolution is to do that indirectly which its framers could not do directly. The direct proposition would have been that Congress have, by the Constitution, no right to abolish slavery in the District of Columbia or the Territories. But the Northern men with Southern principles were not yet quite prepared for that; and so, by laying down as an axiom that Congress has no right to do that indirectly which it cannot do directly, and coupling with it an averment that "the *agitation* of the subject of slavery in the District of Columbia or the Territories, as a means and with the view of disturbing or overthrowing that institution in the several States, is against the true spirit and meaning of the Constitution, an infringement of the rights of the States affected, and a breach of the public faith," the strainers at the gnat were brought to swallow the camel.

This resolution is, by its internal evidence, a Southern composition, to relieve the Northern men who were to vote for it from their scruples of conscience, straining at a direct averment that Congress have no right to abolish slavery in the District of Columbia or the Territories. But in its wary generalities, its looseness of phraseology, and its total want of precision, it brought them to an assertion far more comprehensively false than would have been th *direct* denial of the constitutional right of Congress to abolish slavery in the District or the Territories.

If the first part of the resolution were true, the logical conclusion from it would be that Congress has not, and, *a fortiori*, that neither House of Congress has, the right to refuse to read or consider any petition which they have received; because that is indirectly to *abridge* the right of petition, which the first article of the amendments to the Constitution expressly forbids them to do *directly*. But if Congress has the constitutional right to abolish slavery in the District or the Territories, how is it possible that the *agitation* of the subject of slavery, with whatever purposes or designs, or as means to whatever end, can be unconstitutional? Not does the resolution even affirm it to be unconstitutional. The *agitation*—by whom? by petitions? by Congress? by the press? You are left at a loss to conjecture. The *agitation*—of what? of the *subject* of slavery in the District or the Territories? of the *subject*, not of abolition, but of slavery—as a certain *means* and with a certain *view*—all this the resolution pronounces unconstitutional? No! but against the true spirit and meaning of the Constitution, &c. a breach of faith, &c. Why all this world of windy circumlocution but to evade the denial of the right of Congress to abolish slavery in the District of Columbia and the Territories, and yet affirm that the *agitation* of the subject as means and with a view to something else, is *not* unconstitutional, but against the true spirit and meaning of the Constitution?

The fourth resolution is another pillar of the composite order, in two parts:

First. "That the Constitution rests on the broad principle of equality among the members of this Confederacy." Equality of what? The Constitution provides that no State, without its consent, shall be deprived of its equal suffrage in the Senate; but Delaware, as a member of the Confederacy, has one member in the House of Representatives, and New York, as a member of the Confederacy, has forty. Is this upon the broad principle of equality? In the election of President of the United States, Michigan, as a member of the Confederacy, has three votes, and Pennsylvania has thirty. What sort of an equality is that? The Constitution rests on the broad principle of equality among men, as members of this Union; but if the framers of this resolution were to inquire, equality of what? they might be puzzled to find an answer in the "institutions of one portion of the States."

Secondly. "And that Congress, in the exercise of its acknowledged powers, has no right to discriminate between the institutions of one portion of the States and another, with a view of abolishing the one and promoting the other."

There are in the Constitution of the United States many things which all the States are expressly interdicted from doing; some in an unqualified manner, others without the consent of Congress. Suppose one State or one portion of the States should have, or in the exercise of their sovereign powers should adopt, *institutions* directly in the face of these prohibitions; would Congress. in the exercise of its acknowledged powers, have no right to discriminate between these unconstitutional *institutions* and the *constitutional* institutions of the other States, with a view to abolish the one and to promote the other?

I put no imaginary case. The second section of the fourth article of the Constitution declares that "the citizens of each State shall be entitled to all privileges and immunities of citizens of the several States." Among the petitions presented by me and by others at the recent session of Congress, which were *received*, but, under the general order, neither read, printed, debated, nor considered, there were several from petitioners complaining that, by the operation of the peculiar institutions of one portion of the States, they had been not only deprived of this constitutional right, but abused, insulted, and compelled to fly for their lives to escape from the peculiar institutions. Has Congress, in the exercise of its acknowledged powers, no right to discriminate between these institutions and those of other States, which *secure* to every citizen of the Union the enjoyment of this great constitutional right? This resolution is obviously another *indirect* attempt to deny the right of Congress to abolish slavery in the District of Columbia and the Territories, without denying it in form.

The fifth and crowning resolution of this suit, also in two parts, was:

1. "*Resolved, therefore*, That all attempts on the part of Congress to abolish slavery in the District of Columbia or the Territories, or to prohibit the removal of slaves from State to State, or to discriminate between the institutions of one portion of the Confederacy and another, with the views aforesaid, ARE in violation of the Constitution, destructive

of the fundamental principle on which the union of these States rests, and beyond the jurisdiction of Congress.''

The looseness and inaccuracy of expression noticed in the former resolutions is equally remarkable in this, which is the conclusion of the syllogism, the Q.E.D. of the demonstration—*Resolved, therefore*—an ergo as lucidly deduced from the premises as the argal of the grave-digger's crowner's quest law in Hamlet. *Se offendendo.*

For the real violation of the Constitution was the presumption of the House in declaring, by resolution, attempts which it supposes to be actually made on the part of *Congress,* violations of the Constitution. It is clear that if the House had any constitutional right to pass this resolution, their successors will have the same right to pass a resolution directly the reverse, affirming what these resolutions deny, and denying what they affirm.

All attempts on the part of Congress to do such and such things "*are* in violation of the Constitution,'' necessarily implying that on the part of Congress such attempts *are* actually made, and assuming to declare, by resolution of one branch of the Legislature, attempts imputed to the whole Congress, unconstitutional.

2. And (the cream of all) "that every petition, memorial, resolution, proposition, or paper, touching or relating, in any way or to any extent whatever, to slavery as aforesaid, or the abolition thereof, shall, on the presentation thereof, without any further action thereon, be laid upon the table, without being debated, printed, or referred.''

This last half of the 5th resolution is the practical result of oppression and abridgment of the right of petition, of the freedom of speech in the House of their Representatives, and of the press throughout the Union. All the rest being merely a winding staircase of preamble to argufy Congress out of the right to abolish slavery in the District and Territories without denying it.

These resolutions were introduced by a motion to suspend the rules of the House, which could be carried only by a majority of two-thirds of the members present. I invite your attention to the fact that this majority was obtained, and that without it the resolutions could not have been offered. The vote to suspend the rules was 137 to 66; three votes more on the negative would have prevented the introduction of the resolutions.

They were introduced, preceded by a speech of about half an hour from the introducer, who closed it with a motion for the previous question. Not one word of discussion was allowed upon any one of the resolutions. The last three resolutions were divided, and separate questions taken upon the two members of each of them. They were all adopted; the practical or second member of the last resolution by a vote of 128 to 78, considerably short of two-thirds; and of those who voted against the resolution, seven had voted for the suspension of the rules.

There runs through all the resolutions a vein of State right and Nullification doctrines, utterly unconstitutional, and betraying their Southern origin. The Government of the Union is, throughout, considered as if it were exclusively a confederacy; and the averment that the Constitution rests on the broad principle of equality among the members of this Confederacy, is just as true as if the House of Representatives should resolve that vegetation upon earth rests on the broad principle that the light of day is an emanation from the moon.

The only part of the resolutions to which I could have given my assent was to the averment in the first member of the first resolution, "That this Government is a Government of limited powers." That is true; and, if true of the whole Government, must be true of all its parts, and of course of the House of Representatives. Now, among the limited powers of the House, that of defining or declaring by resolution what are and what are not the powers of the Government is not included, and the resolution is a suicide. It destroys itself. The second member of the same resolution contains a misrepresentation injurious to the non-slaveholding States, and an averment altogether unfounded. It says that by the Constitution Congress has no jurisdiction whatever over the institution of slavery in *the several States*—an expression which implies that the institution exists in *all* the States—a gross misrepresentation. The averment that Congress has no jurisdiction over the institution of slavery, in the States where it exists, is equally unfounded. Congress has a jurisdiction of *protection* over the institution of slavery in the slaveholding States. The institution of slavery is protected by the slave-representation in the House of Representatives, by the article in the Constitution which binds the United States to protect each State, on application of the Legislature, or of the Executive when the Legislature cannot be convened, against *domestic violence*; by the article which stipulates for the delivery up of all fugitive persons held to labor; by the act of Congress of the 12th February, 1793, respecting fugitives from justice, and persons escaping from the service of their masters; by all the negotiations with Great Britain for indemnity to the owners of slaves carried away during and at the close of the late war; and even now by negotiations with Great Britain for indemnity to the slave-traders of the Comet, Encomium, and Enterprize. What is it but a jurisdiction over the institution of slavery in the States where it exists, that authorizes a claim of indemnity to slave-traders for the liberation of their slaves, from a Government with which the United States are bound by treaty to use their best endeavors to promote so desirable an object as the total abolition of the traffic in slaves, because it is irreconcileable with the principles of humanity and justice?

I voted against this resolution with only five other members of the House; one hundred and ninety-eight members of the House voted for it. Had five minutes of discussion upon it been allowed, it is impossible that it should have been adopted.

The previous question is a weapon always in the power of a majority to use as an expedient for smothering debate. It is justifiable, after a proposition has been thoroughly debated, and the minority manifest a disposition to prevent the decision, by speaking against time; but the application of it to a new unconsidered proposition is a total suppression of the freedom of speech, and takes from the assembly where it is practiced, all pretension of being a deliberative body.

All the resolutions were voted for by many members who, if discussion had been allowed, would have voted against them. I voted against them all, and, immediately after the last of them had passed, asked leave to offer, as my justification, the following resolution: "Resolved, That the powers of Congress being conferred by the Constitution of the United States, no resolution of this House can add to or deduct from them." But the House adjourned without receiving my resolution. The next morning I asked a suspension of the rules for leave to offer the same resolution, which was refused by a vote of 75 to 124. But on the 14th of January, a day set apart for the reception of resolutions, when I needed not a suspension of the rules to enable me to offer the resolution, I did offer it, and it was adopted without a word of opposition from any quarter; and there it stands on the journal of the House, a recorded demonstration of the futility of all the preambulatory resolutions of the 12th of December.

All the members of the House from the slaveholding States, with two or three exceptions, voted for the gag resolution—and those exceptions were of members who were for refusing to receive all abolition or anti-slavery petitions. The members from the slaveholding States would have voted unanimously against *receiving* any such petitions—but the Northern confederates could not be brought to "toe the mark" at that stage. Their distinction was, that the constitutional and sacred duty of the House was to *receive* the petitions, but that the House was under no sort of obligation to *read* or *consider* them. The acuteness of this distinction affords a good measure, both moral and intellectual, of the *principle* which associated with it a resolution that Congress has no right to do indirectly that which it cannot do directly.

The resolution that all petitions, memorials, resolutions, or papers relating in any manner to slavery or its abolition, shall be laid on the table without being read, printed, debated, or acted upon by the House, has been adopted at four successive sessions of Congress. It has during that time *indirectly* abridged the right of petition, and *suppressed* the freedom of speech in the House, and the freedom of the press throughout the Union, upon all subjects relating to slavery or its abolition. This resolution has always been adopted without deliberation, by the application of the previous question; no argument has ever been allowed against it; no reason has ever been given for it, unless the syllogistic preambular resolutions of the 12th of December are to be considered as reasons. No discussion of them was then allowed, and that is my principal reason for thus freely commenting upon them in this letter to you.

But the right of petition, thus unceremoniously though indirectly *abridged* by the House of Representatives of the United States, has also become a subject of discussion in some of the State Legislatures, and occasionally at popular meetings. Its extent and its limitations have thus become controverted points. The gag resolutions have been pointedly condemned in resolutions of more than one State Legislature, and of many popular meetings. Multitudes of petitions to the House to rescind them have been presented to the House and laid on the table; many of them are among those which you have entrusted to me, and will be found on the lists in the National Intelligencer, to which I now refer you. In some instances efforts have been made to justify the gag, and reasons have been given elsewhere for the measure, which it has never been thought worth while to assign in the House itself: among these it has been said that in this republican democracy the People have the right to *command,* and therefore have no occasion to *petition.* The reply to this is, that the power to command is in the whole People or a majority of them, and can be exercised only in forms recognised or prescribed by law;

while the right of petition is an individual right, intended to ʋɐ secured to every portion of the People in their capacity as *subjects* to the law. That this right is not only needed, but indispensable, in the estimation of the People, is signally proved by the fact, that the Constitution of the United States reported by the Convention of 1787 having omitted an express recognition of this right, it became one of the most formidable objections against the adoption of that instrument, and the very first amendment to it, which was adopted, supplied that omission.

It has been also said that the Constitution only prohibits Congress from enacting a *law* to abridge the right of the People to assemble and petition for a redress of grievances; that its object is only to secure the enjoyment and free exercise of an individual right; but that when that right has been exercised, and the petition has been presented, the right of the petitioner ceases; and, that the Constitution having given to each House of Congress the power to determine the rules of its proceedings, it may, by virtue of that power, receive or reject all petitions at its pleasure.

The ingenuity of this argument cannot disguise the revolting features of its character. Its vital principle is, that although the Constitution has most anxiously guarded the right of the People to petition against violation by *law*, requiring the concurrent action of both Houses of Congress, and the qualified assent of the President of the United States, yet each House of Congress by its mere rules of proceedings has the arbitrary power, at its pleasure, to reduce this right of petition to a dead letter, by refusing even to receive it.

Now, it is an universal maxim, not only of reason and common sense, but of law, that the existence of a *right* carries necessarily with it every thing indispensable to its exercise and enjoyment. The right of petition would be a cruel and insulting mockery, if it did not carry with it the right of being heard, and the duty of the petitioned party to hear and consider— which is denied by the refusal to receive.

The author of the argument to which I now refer, appears conscious of its weakness; for, while he insists that the right of the petitioner ceases from the moment that his petition is presented, and that the House may refuse even to receive it, he explicitly admits that a right to *ask* necessarily implies a duty in the House to *hear*. The argument seems to suppose that the hearing precedes the reception, which doubtless may be but that is not the practice of the House; the House receives the petition, but refuses to *hear* it. And this it has a right to do, if the argument be sound that the right of the petitioner ceases from the moment when the petition is presented. In conceding that it is the duty of the House to *hear*, the author has surrendered at once his own argument and the justification of the gag resolutions.

There is in the same argument a resort to another principle of frequent application in judicial courts, but not altogether suitable to the question of right and wrong in the conduct of a legislative assembly. In admitting that the House may *abuse* its power in refusing to *receive* petitions, the argument avers that this abuse of power is a *political* and not a *legal* injury. That a petitioner has no action at law against a member of the House who votes against receiving his petition, and that his only remedy is the ballot box. This is a lawyer's argument, founded upon a maxim of English law, that the King can do no wrong. And this, the English lawyers tell you, is founded upon another maxim, that where there is no remedy there is no right. If a King of England commits murder, by this maxim he does no wrong, and violates no right. It is an abuse of power—a political and not a legal wrong.

As a set-off, to justify this abuse of power in the House, which is a political and not a legal injury, and for which the sufferer has no remedy but the ballot box, the author of the argument affirms that it is an abuse and a fraudulent abuse of the power to petition to obtain the names of hundreds of children under ten years of age, and to let them pass as persons whose opinions are entitled to weight. That the *opinions* of children under ten years of age are or are not entitled to weight, depends upon the subject to which the opinions relate. The right of petition, as the argument observes, is a mere right to *ask*, which children are quite as competent to exercise as the hoary head. This objection to the signing of petitions by children belongs to the same school with that which holds it unbecoming in *women*. It is not much in the spirit of Him who said, Suffer little children to come unto me, and forbid them not. As for letting the names of children pass as of persons whose opinions are entitled to weight, if there has been any misrepresentation of the names of children as being the names of adults, it might deserve the charge of being fraudulent; but the right of petition depends in no sort whatever on the weight of the opinions of the petitioners. The right to ask, as the argument concedes, necessarily implies the duty to *hear*, and not only to hear, but to *consider*. In that consideration, the weight of opinions to which the petitioners are entitled, the *age*, the *sex*, the *condition*, the *moral charac-*

ter, and the *numbers* of the petitioners, may be all-important to the proper final disposal of the petition by the House; but the duty of the House to *consider* is as binding upon the House as the duty to hear, and as necessarily implied in the right of petition. The right of the House to reject the prayer of the petition has never been contested, nor have I ever denied that the exercise of that right is discretionary; but it is not arbitrary. The refusal to *receive* a petition is an arbitrary abridgment of the petitioner's right. A refusal to grant the prayer of a petition is the exercise of a discretionary and strictly constitutional power.

On the petitions which I have presented to the House there are the names of many children from 10 and 11 to 21 years of age; in some of them whole columns of minors, male and female, with the age of each individual at the side of the name. I consider the right of children of age to sign their names to petition as perfect as that of their fathers, even legal voters; nor should I deem it fraudulent if, among the tens and hundreds of thousands of names subscribed to the petitions which I have presented, there should be many hundreds of children under ten years of age, without notice of the fact.

There is, no doubt, among some of the ardent abolitionists, an excessive zeal to increase the number of signers to their petitions, and that it has occasionally prompted expedients unwarrantable in themselves, and which would forfeit even the right of having their petitions considered or presented. I have received several petitions which I have not thought it my duty to present. I have presented many without knowing who the petitioners were, or whence they came. The refusal of the House to consider any of them has relieved me from the necessity of authenticating the signatures, or of discriminating between those which it was the duty of the House to consider, and those which it might reject. I did present one which the House refused to *receive*, on the ground that it was disrespectful to the House; and although I voted for its reception because I did not think it intentionally disrespectful, I admitted explicitly the right of the House to refuse to receive a petition upon that ground.

The greatest fallacy of the argument to which I now refer is, the inference from the right of the House to *reject* a petition for good and special reasons, that it has an arbitrary right of refusal to *receive* any petition—and very naturally it proceeds from the maxim of the English law, that the King can do no wrong, or, in other words, that where there is no remedy there is no right—to the authority of *precedents* in the British House of Commons.

It cannot but strike any person acquainted with the history of the American Revolution as strange, that precedents in the British House of Commons should be adduced as authority for an arbitrary power of refusal to receive petitions in *American legislature assemblies.* It is no doubt a standing order of the British House of Commons to receive no petition *against the imposing of duties*; and the author of the argument might have added that this was the main cause of the American Revolution. Every one of the precedents cited by him as authorities for the refusal by the British House of Commons to receive petitions was upon bills *for imposing duties.* There was a precedent much more to the point of this controversy than all these, which the author of the argument has not thought proper to cite, but to which I now call your attention to show what is the worth of authority of precedents in the British House of Commons, to justify a refusal to *receive* petitions by an American legislative assembly.

In the Journal of the House of Commons of Thursday, 26th January, 1775, is found the following entry:

"Sir George Saville offered to present a petition of William Bollan, Benjamin Franklin, and Arthur Lee, Esqs. stating themselves to have been authorized by the persons who signed one of the papers presented to the House by the Lord North, upon Thursday last, by his Majesty's command, intituled '*Petition of sundry persons on behalf of themselves and the inhabitants of several of his Majesty's Colonies in America,*' to procure the said papers to be presented to his Majesty, and praying that they may be heard at the bar of this House in support thereof.

"And the question being put that the said petition be brought up,

"The House divided—yeas 68, noes 218.

"So it passed in the negative."

The paper intituled Petition of sundry persons, &c. was the petition of the first Congress of 26th October, 1774, to the King—and which by his command Lord North had presented to the House of Commons.

Here is a precedent far more instructive than the whole cluster of those from April, 1694, to 1732, so shortly after the famous Declaration of Rights of 1688 to prove the practice of the British House of Commons of refusing to receive petitions.

Here was a *refusal* by a British House of Commons, by a majority of 218 to 68, to *receive* a petition from the agents of the American colonies, praying to be heard at the bar of the House in support of the petition from the American Congress to the King, which he had referred to the House.

Nothing can be more decisive to substantiate the practice of the British House of Commons. But is this an authority to be held up as an example to be followed by an American legislative assembly? On the question of the reception of this petition a violent debate arose. It was insisted by the Ministry that the Congress was an illegal body, and that petitions from the colonies could only be received through the colonial governments. What was the answer?

"That this Congress, however illegal to other purposes, was sufficiently legal for presenting a petition. It was signed by the names of all the persons who composed it, and might be received as from individuals; that it was the business of the House rather to find every plausible reason for receiving petitions than to invent pretenses for rejecting them; that the rejection of petitions was one principal cause, if not the most powerful cause of the present troubles; that this mode of constantly rejecting their petitions, and refusing to hear their agents, would infallibly end in universal rebellion; and not unnaturally, as those seem to give up the right of government who refuse to hear the complaints of the subject."— [American Archives, vol. I, p. 1532]

But the author of the argument, apparently distrusting the authority of his precedents from the journal of the British House of Commons, has endeavored to strengthen them by a recent decision in the Senate of the United States still more unfortunate for him, if possible than those drawn from beyond the seas.

The Senate of the United States, it seems, on the 17th of March, 1834, on the motion of Mr. Clay, refused to receive what the argument calls a petition or remonstrance of the citizens of York, Pennsylvania, approving the act of the President in removing the deposites, presented by the presiding officer of that body. The yeas and nays were called by Mr. PRESTON, and the reception of the paper was refused by a vote of 24 to 20.

But this refusal to receive rested upon several grounds, none of which abridged in the slightest degree the right of petition; but all of which, on the contrary, marked the highest respect for it. The paper was not a petition, though it may properly be termed a remonstrance. It was a series of resolutions approving the removal of the deposites, and protesting against a recharter of the Bank of the United States, certified to have been adopted at a meeting of citizens of York Pennsylvania. It was presented by the Vice President in a mutilated condition; one of the resolutions, grossly insulting to a member of the Senate, having been previously struck out by authority of the Senators from Pennsylvania. Another of the resolutions, imputing corruption to the majority of the Senate, had not been struck out; but one of the Senators from Pennsylvania said that it ought to have been, and would have been, if he had noticed it before the presentation.

Mr. PRESTON, who called for the yeas and nays on the question of reception, said that the memorial, in its mutilated state, was not that which has been transmitted from the meeting, and could not be received as their voice. Mr. WEBSTER read a protest against the paper, signed by 53 persons who had been present at the meeting, and a letter stating that the pretended resolutions had not been adopted at the meeting, but rejected by a majority of at least three to one.

The following are some of the observations of Mr. CLAY, on making the motion *not to receive* the paper:

"He agreed with the honorable member from South Carolina that the paper had lost its identity. That it is *not* a memorial coming from any portion of the people of York county; that it was not such a paper as they had transmitted for the purpose of being transmitted to the Senate; and therefore that it could not be received, unless it was admitted that while a paper was in *transitu*, nay, what was worse, whilst in the hands of the officers of this House, a paper might be changed in its character, and made a new and altered instrument altogether. From the conclusion to which the honorable Senator from South Carolina had come, it was perfectly evident that if they who had made it had a right to make an erasure, they had also the right of insertion. *Now, if they could do either of these things, then, he would ask, what had become of the right of petition—a sacred and inviolable right, and one that ought to be preserved and maintained inviolate, as it had been in all times heretofore?"*

Again: "He would move the Senate that the petition be not received, and he made the motion on all the grounds which had been stated. He made it, in the first place, because the memorial had lost its identity; because it was not a genuine document; because it had been altered; because it was not the same paper that was transmitted to the Senate. And he made it also on the same ground that had been taken by the gentleman from Mississippi—that it was couched in language which ought not to be addressed to that body, and was unbecoming those who employed it, and ought not to be received.''

And thus this precedent, instead of countenancing the doctrine of an arbitrary right of refusal by the Senate to receive petitions, is the most conclusive of authorities to the contrary. For here the vote on both sides was in favor of the *right of petition*; both agreeing that disrespectful language was a sufficient reason for refusing to receive; but one side, from reverence for the right of petition, being of opinion that the presiding officer of the Senate might authorize the striking out from a petition the offensive part, and the Senate would be bound to receive the rest; while the other side, from the same reverence, held that there was no power in the Senate or its President to alter a petition or memorial; but that it must be received as it came from those who sent it, or not at all. It is needless to add, that in all the recent questions in the Senate upon the reception of the abolition petitions, Mr. CLAY's opinion has always been for *receiving* them.

There is one point of view in which this recurrence to precedents in the British House of Commons as authority for refusal by either House of Congress to receive petitions is so important that it calls not only for your profound attention, but for that of the whole People of the Union.

It appears from these precedents that there is *one* subject of great and general interest, upon which it is the habitual though not universal practice of the House of Commons to refuse to *receive* petitions—and that subject is *taxation*.

It appears, also, that this standing order of the House of Commons, repeatedly resorted to by the refusal to receive the petitions of the colonies against the acts for taxing them, was one of the principal causes of the American Revolution.

But it appears further, that even in the House of Commons this practice is confined to the single subject of taxation, and to that only upon tax bills in the process of enactment. The remarks of Hatsell upon the practice, after citing all the precedents concerning it, are full of admonition to us.

''We learn (says he) from an examination of all these instances, that this practice has been confined, as it ought to be most strictly, to the refusing to receive such petitions only as object against a tax which is imposing for the current service of the year; and has not been applied to petitions which have been presented in a subsequent session, desiring a repeal or reconsideration of the taxes imposed in a former. Indeed, the House ought to be particularly cautious not to be over rigid in extending this rule beyond what the practice of their ancestors, in former times, can justify them in. To *receive*, and *hear*, and *consider* the petitions of their fellow-subjects, when presented decently, and containing no matter intentionally offensive to the House, is a duty incumbent upon them antecedent to all rules and orders that may have been instituted for their own convenience; justice and the laws of their country demand it of them.'' Hatsell 3, 174.

Now if the precedents of the House of Commons are to be cited as authority for the practice of an American legislative assembly, especially for a purpose so odious as that of restricting the right of petition, the acknowledged limitations upon the rules of the British House must be still more authoritative in the land or republican freedom.

If the British precedents are of any authority whatever in this country, they only show that either House of Congress may refuse to receive petitions against tax bills, or bills for raising revenue. What would the People of this Union say if the precedents should be resorted to for *that* purpose? Let them seriously think of it. For if the British precedents are of any authority, it is to that point alone; and if the refusal of the British House of Commons to receive petitions against the stamp act and the tea tax are authorities to either House of Congress for refusing to receive petitions for the abolition of slavery and the slave-trade, they are much more authoritative to warrant the refusal to receive petitions against any tax bill which may at any time hereafter be introduced into Congress. Neither House of the British Parliament ever refused to receive petitions for the abolition of slavery or the slave-trade; *nor could* they refuse to receive them without flying in the face of those principles so explicitly and so emphatically laid down in the above passage from Hatsell. They received them by thousands, and after many and many a year of persevering resistance against their prayer, they finally granted it to the full extent of their power, made the slave-trade piracy, and emancipated their slaves by millions.

Reflect upon the solemn caution in this passage of Hatsell to the British House of Commons against *extending* their rule for refusing to receive petitions. This is the fatal and inevitable consequence of adopting any rule for refusing to *receive*, or to *hear*, or to *consider* petitions upon any one subject of great public interest. It is that which I have most earnestly pressed whenever I have been permitted, even incidentally, to remark in the House upon these proscriptive exclusions of abolition petitions. By this recurrence to the practice of the British House of Commons in refusing to receive petitions against tax bills as authority for refusing to receive petitions for the abolition of slavery, the rule is, in effect, extended to petitions upon every subject whatever. The rule in the House of Commons itself is restricted to the single subject of tax bills before the House. It is adduced as authority here, without any limitation.

Of the encroaching character of the rule we have already had melancholy experience. The rule being once settled, of refusing to *hear* a class of petitions, forming the major part of all those presented to the House, the members of the majority in the House extended the practice by separate motions to lay on the table every petition which they were pleased to consider as affecting the same interests. During the time when the acquisition of Texas was a darling project of the Administration, hundreds and hundreds of petitions against that measure were thus laid on the table without allowing a word of discussion upon them. At the recent session of Congress all the petitions against it were laid on the table, because the formal application of that Republic to be annexed to the United States had been withdrawn, but still more because the ruling party in the House, still panting for that illegitimate union, were unwilling to have the fact of their disappointment appear on the journals or documents of the House. All the petitions and resolutions of the State Legislatures, condemning the gag resolutions, and demanding that they should be rescinded, were disposed of in the same manner.

In the order of business originally prescribed by the rules of the House of Representatives, the first business of the House every morning, after the reading of the journal, was the call by the Speaker on the members from all the States and Territories in succession for PETITIONS; and this may serve to show that, in the primitive constitution and practice of the House, the first duty of the House, in the transaction of business was the consideration of petitions. For the first thirty days of the session, it was the business of every day; and, after that, the special business of the first day of the House's sitting in every week. Shortly after the introduction of these rules for laying on the table, unheard and unread, all anti-slavery petitions, a new rule was established, by which every alternate Monday was devoted to the presentation of resolutions by members of the House, and thus the days for the reception of petitions were reduced to two in every month; and, at the recent session, even those days were so reduced, by special motions to suspend the rules for the reception of petitions, that of the first thirty days, upon every one of which, by the standing rules of the House, the States should have been called for petitions, there was but one single day upon which they were called, and that was Thursday, the 20th of December, when I presented seventy-three petitions, the list of which was published in the National Intelligencer of the 24th of that month. That the only days in the month of January when petitions were received were Monday, the 7th, when I presented ninety-four, and Monday, the 21st, when I presented one hundred and seventy six. The lists of these are published in the National Intelligencer of the 11th and 23d of January. That the only day after this upon which petitions were called for was the 4th of February when I had two hundred on hand to present, but the call of the States did not reach Massachusetts, and I was put off to the 18th of February, the next semi-monthly day; and when that came, the role of the House requiring the Speaker to call the States for petitions was suspended, and an order was passed authorizing the members to hand in their petitions at the Clerk's table, but of course no order of the House was taken upon any of them. On that day I did deliver at the Clerk's table 413 petitions, several of which were upon subjects having no relation whatever with slavery or the slave-trade. The list of them is in the National Intelligencer of the 14th of March; and on the last day of the session I delivered 78 more, which, with 16 received after the close of the session, are in the Intelligencer of this day. The result is that of upwards of eight hundred and thirty petitions which I received in the course of the session, there were only three days upon which I was permitted to present any one of them.

Another recent innovation upon the rules of the House, apparently founded upon the broad principle of equality among the members of this Confederacy, produced at this session a result directly the reverse. The original rule of the House was in these words:

"As soon as the Journal is read, the Speaker shall call for petitions from the members of each State, *beginning with Maine*; and if on any day the whole of the States and Territories shall not be called, the Speaker shall begin on the next day where he left off the previous day: Provided that, after the first thirty days of the session, petitions shall not be received, except on the first day of the meeting of the House in each week."

The alteration was by adding to the words "beginning with Maine" the words *"and the Territory of Wisconsin alternately."* This was apparently fair and impartial between the States; but what was the result? The 4th of February was the alternate day upon which the Speaker commenced the call with the *Territory of Wisconsin*; and he proceeded till he came to the State of Vermont, and then the House adjourned. Four of the New England States were thus deprived of the right of having any of the petitions of their people presented, while those of all the rest of the Union were presented and received. They were put off for another fortnight, and then, by a suspension of the rule, cut off from the right of having any of their petitions considered by the House, with a paltering permission to have them handed in at the Clerk's table, and entered upon the journals of the House. Nearly five hundred of *your* petitions, committed to my care, were thus disposed of, whether relating to slavery and the slave-trade, or to any other subject. At least five times that number, in the hands of members from the four excluded New England States, shared the same fate.

Those are not the only consequences subversive of the right of petition which have flowed from the exclusion of slavery and the abolition of slavery from the consideration of the House. Besides the expedient of laying on the table by separate motions, all petitions having such indirect reference to those subjects as not to bring them within the rule of general exclusion, another practice has arisen, of referring petitions which could not be excluded either by the general rule or by separate motions to committees which never report upon them. And in this practice it was openly avowed by one of the size-tray committees appointed by the late Speaker, that they did not hold themselves bound to look into and had not looked into one of many hundred petitions, including resolutions of State Legislatures referred to them by the House.

And thus, I. By the gag resolution to lay on the table, without *reading*, (as the rule has been construed by the Speaker,) debating, printing, or any other action of the House, all petitions, memorials, resolutions, propositions, or papers, touching or relating to slavery or the abolition thereof; 2. By the practice of laying on the table in the same way, without reading or hearing, by separate motions of majority members, all petitions and papers which, though having no relation to those topics, may yet, in the opinion of the majority have an indirect bearing upon them; 3. By the other practice of referring petitions still more remote in their bearing upon slavery (such, for example, as the recognition of the Republic of Hayti) to committees which will not report upon them, nor even look into them; and 4. By the systematic diminution of the days upon which petitions *can* be presented, which, at the recent session, was reduced down to *three* in the whole session, your right of petition to the House of Representatives of the United States, and that of the whole People of this Union, may be considered as all but annihilated.

I incline rather to consider it, to use an expression familiar to the lawyers, as *in abeyance.* I cannot bring myself to believe that the People of this Union will long endure the *abridgment* of this right, and to be told that though Congress cannot do it by law, yet the House can do it by its rules of proceeding; or that their right is not abridged, because their petitions, though neither read, heard, nor considered, are yet RECEIVED. I must believe that a House of Representatives more observant of the Constitution which its members are sworn to support, more true to that sacred right of the People which ought never to be infringed, will not only receive, but *read, hear,* and *consider* their petitions, whether relating to slavery, the abolition of slavery, or any other subject of great interest to the community, or to the individual praying for relief. I believe it, because, in my judgment, the inevitable alternative is that the days of this Union and of this nation, as a free People, are numbered, and will soon pass away like a scroll.

But, fellow-citizens, you will not understand me as affirming that this *duty* of the House to receive, hear, and consider your respectful petitions involves necessarily that of complying with their demands. A sincere and earnest desire to grant your requests is a duty from the representative to the constituent; but to that which you desire, others, equally his fellow-citizens, may be equally or more intensely adverse; and the duty of the legislator is to hold the scales of justice in even balance between you, and consulting the wishes of all, when they are irreconcileable together, to grant or deny your prayer, as justice, the Constitution, and prudence may require.

It is known to most of you that at the late session of Congress I repeated a declaration which I had frequently made before, that I was myself not prepared to vote for the immediate abolition of slavery in the District of Columbia, nor in the Territory of Florida; nor for the refusal to admit that Territory, as a slaveholding State, into the Union. These were all prayers of multitudes of your petitions which I had presented. My opinion upon

them had never varied since I first took my seat in the House of Representatives; but from the zeal which I had uniformly manifested in support of
the right of petition, and from the perseverance with which I persisted in
presenting abolition petitions, inferences had been drawn in both divisions of the Union, not only that I was a confirmed abolitionist, but that I
was affecting to place myself at the head of the abolition movement
throughout the land. Having no such ambition, and wishing to avoid all
appearance of tampering between the parties, I made the above-
mentioned declaration; but had neither then, nor at any other time, a
suitable opportunity of assigning my reasons for the opinions which I
entertain upon these subjects. This I propose to do in another letter to
you; and in the mean time remain, with grateful and respectful attachment, your friend and fellow-citizen,

—John Quincy Adams.

B: CIVIL RIGHTS IN THE COURTS

UNIVERSITY OF MARYLAND *v.* DONALD G. MURRAY

[No. 53, October Term, 1935.]

*State University—Law School—Admission of Negro—Equal Protec-
tion of Laws.*

The Law School of the University of Maryland is a state agency, or a
part of one, although the greater part of its support comes from tuition
fees, it having been, by Acts 1920, ch. 480, consolidated with the
Maryland State College of Agriculture, a state institution, under one and
the same board of trustees, appointed and controlled by the State.

The Law School of the University of Maryland being a state agency, or
a part of one, is subject to the equal protection clause of the Fourteenth
Amendment to the United States Constitution, and is consequently
required to furnish equal facilities for legal training to white and colored
students, unless such facilities are otherwise furnished by the State.

By the Fourteenth Amendment a state is required to extend to its
citizens of the two races substantially equal treatment in the facilities
which it provides from the public funds, and this requirement involves

equal treatment in respect to any one facility or opportunity furnished to citizens, though not necessarily the provision of privileges to the members of the two races in the same place.

There being no separate law school provided for colored students, the right of the University of Maryland to exclude negroes from its law school depends on whether the State furnishes negroes equality of treatment with white persons, as regards legal training, by means of scholarships enabling them to study law outside the state, and this is not effected by the creation of scholarships of $200 each, to defray tuition fees of negroes attending colleges outside the state. pp. 485-487.

It appearing that the State of Maryland can furnish equal facilities for the legal training of white persons and negroes only by the admission of negroes to the Law School of the University of Maryland, a negro, complying with the requirements for admission, was entitled to the writ of mandamus to compel his admission.

There being in Maryland no officers or body of officers authorized to establish a separate law school for negroes, and no legislative declaration of a purpose to establish one, the court cannot, on a mandamus proceeding to compel the admission of a negro to the Law School of the University of Maryland, undertake to remedy the inequality of treatment accorded the two races as regards legal training, by ordering the establishment of a law achool for negroes.

As the officers and regents of the University of Maryland are agents of the State entrusted with the conduct of the law school of the university, a writ of mandamus requiring the admission of a negro to the law school was properly directed to them.

Decided January 15th, 1936.

Bond, C. J., delivered the opinion of the Court.

The officers and governing board of the University of Maryland appeal from an order for the issue of the writ of mandamus, commanding them to admit a young negro, the appellee, as a student in the law school of the university. The appellee and petitioner, Murray, graduated as a bachelor of arts from Amherst College in 1934, and met the standards for admission to the law school in all other respects, but was denied admission on the sole ground of his color. He is twenty-two years of age, and is now, and has been during all his life, a resident of Baltimore City, where the law school is situated. He contests his exclusion as unauthorized by the laws of the State, or, so far as it might be considered authorized, then as a denial of equal rights because of his color, contrary to the requirement of the Fourteenth Amendment of the Constitution of the United States. The appellants reply, first, that by reason of its character and organization the law school is not a governmental agency, required by the amendment to give equal rights to students of both races. Or, if it is held that it is a state agency, it is replied that the admission of negro students is not required because the amendment permits segregation of the races for education, and it is the declared policy and the practice of the State to segregate them in schools, and that, although the law school of the university is maintained for white students only, and there is no separate law school maintained for colored students, equal treatment has at the same time been accorded the negroes by statutory provisions for scholarships or aids to enable them to attend law schools outside the state. A further argument in defense is that, if equal treatment has not been provided, the remedy must be found in the opening of a school for negroes, and not in their admission to this particular school attended by the whites. . . .

As a result of the adoption of the Fourteenth Amendment to the United States Constitution, a state is required to extend to its citizens of the two races substantially equal treatment in the facilities it provides from the public funds. ''It is justly held by the authorities that 'to single out a certain portion of the people by the arbitrary standard of color, and say that these shall not have rights which are possessed by others, denies them the equal protection of the laws.' * * * Such a course would be manifestly in violation of the fourteenth amendment, because it would deprive a class of persons of a right which the constitution of the state had declared that they should possess.'' *Clark* v. *Maryland Institute*, 87 Md. 643, 661, 41 A 126, 129. Remarks quoted in argument from opinions of courts of other jurisdictions, that the educational policy of a state and its system of education are distinctly state affairs, have ordinarily been answers to demands on behalf of non-residents, and have never been meant to assert for a state freedom from the requirement of equal treatment to children of colored races. ''It is distinctly a state affair. * * * But the denial to children whose parents, as well as themselves, are citizens of the United States and of this state, admittance to the common schools solely because of color or racial differences without having made provision for the education equal in all respects to that afforded persons of any other race or color, is a violation of the provisions of the Fourteenth Amendment of the Constitution of the United States." *Piper v. Big Pine School Dist.*, 193 Cal. 664, 226 P. 926, 928; *Board of Education v. Foster*, 116 Ky. 484, 76 S.W. 354; *Ward v. Flood*, 48 Cal. 36.

The requirement of equal treatment would seem to be clearly enough one of equal treatment in respect to any one facility or opportunity furnished to citizens, rather than of a balance in state bounty to be struck from the expenditures and provisions for each race generally. We take it to be clear, for instance, that a state could not be rendered free to maintain a law school exclusively for whites by maintaining at equal cost a school exclusively for whites by maintaining at equal cost a school of technology for colored students. Expenditures of this State for the education of the latter in schools and colleges have been extensive, but, however they may compare with provisions for the whites, they would not justify the exclusion of colored citizens alone from enjoyment of any one facility furnished by the State. The courts, in all the decisions on application of this constitutional requirement, find exclusion from any one privilege condemned. *State v. Duffy*, 7 Nev. 342; *Tape v. Hurley*, 66 Cal. 473, 6 P. 129; *Marion v. Territory*, 1 Okl. 210, 32 P. 116; *State v. Board of Trustees*, 126 Ohio St. 290, 185 N.E. 196; *State v. McCann*, 21 Ohio St. 198; *People v. Gallagher*, 93 N.Y. 438; *Wong Him v. Callahan*, (C.C.) 119 Fed. 381; *Puitt v. Gaston County Commissioners*, 94 N.C. 709; *Bonitz v. Board of Trustees*, 154 N.C. 375, 70 S.E. 735. See notes, reviewing decisions, 32 *Law Notes*, 147, 149. *Ann. Cas.* 1915C, 482. Equality of treatment does not require that privileges be provided members of the two races in the same place. The State may choose the method by which equality is maintained. "In the circumstances that the races are separated in the public schools, there is certainly to be found no violation of the constitutional rights of the one race more than of the other, and we see none of either, for each, though separated from the other, is to be educated upon equal terms with that other, and both at the common public expense." *Ward v. Flood*, 48 Cal. 36, 51; *Gong Lum v. Rice*, 275 U.S. 78, 48 S.Ct. 91, 72 L.Ed. 172; *State v. McCann*, 21 Ohio St. 198; *People v. Gallagher*, 93 N.Y. 438; *Roberts v. Boston*, 5 Cush. (Mass.) 198.

Separation of the races must nevertheless furnish equal treatment. The constitutional requirement cannot be dispensed with in order to maintain a school or schools for whites exclusively. That requirement comes first. See review of decisions in note 13 *Ann. Cas* 342. And as no separate law school is provided by this State for colored students, the main question in the case is whether the separation can be maintained, and negroes excluded from the present school, by reason of equality of treatment furnished the latter in scholarships for studying outside the state, where law schools are open to negroes. . . .

The court is clear that this rather slender chance for any one applicant at an opportunity to attend an outside law school, at increased expense, falls short of providing for students of the colored race facilities substantially equal to those furnished to the whites in the law school maintained in Baltimore. The number of colored students affected by the discrimination may be comparatively small, but it cannot be said to be negligible in Baltimore City, and moreover the number seems excluded as a factor in the problem. In a case on discrimination required by a state between the races in railroad travel, the Supreme Court of the United States has said: "This argument with respect to volume of traffic seems to us to be without merit. It makes the constitutional right depend upon the number of persons who may be discriminated against, whereas the essence of the constitutional right is that it is a personal one. * * * It is the individual who is entitled to the equal protection of the laws, and if he is denied by a common carrier, acting in the matter under the authority of a state law, a facility or convenience in the course of his journey which, under substantially the same circumstances, is furnished to another traveler, he may properly complain that his constitutional privilege has been invaded." *McCabe v. Atchison, T. & S. F. R. Co.*, 235 U. S. 151, 160, 35 S. Ct. 69, 71, 59 L. Ed. 169. Whether with aid in any amount it is sufficient to send the negroes outside the state for like education is a question never passed on by the Supreme Court, and we need not discuss it now.

As has been stated, the method of furnishing the equal facilities required is at the choice of the State, now or at any future time. At present it is maintaining only the one law school, and in the legislative provisions for the scholarships that one school has in effect been declared appropriated to the whites exclusively. The officers and members of the board appear to us to have had a policy declared for them, as they thought. No separate school for colored students has been decided upon and only an inadequate substitute has been provided. Compliance with the Constitution cannot be deferred at the will of the State. Whatever system it adopts for legal education now must furnish equality of treatment now. "It would, therefore, not be competent to the Legislature, while providing a system of education for the youth of the State, to exclude the petitioner and those of her race from its benefits, merely because of their African descent, and to have so excluded her would have been to deny her the equal protection of the laws within the intent and meaning of the Constitution." *Ward v. Flood*, 48 Cal. 36, 51. And as in Maryland now the equal treatment can be furnished only in the one existing law school, the petitioner, in our opinion, must be admitted there. . . .

The case, as we find it, then, is that the State has undertaken the function of education in the law, but has omitted students of one race from the only adequate provision made for it, and omitted them solely because of their color. If those students are to be offered equal treatment in the performance of the function, they must, at present, be admitted to the one school provided. And as the officers and regents are the agents of the State entrusted with the conduct of that one school, it follows that they must admit, and that the writ of mandamus requiring it would be properly directed to them. There is identity in principals and agents for the application of the constitutional requirement. *Ex parte Virginia*, 100 U.S. 339, 346, 25 L. Ed. 676.

Order affirmed.

MISSOURI ex rel. GAINES *v.* CANADA, REGISTRAR OF THE UNIVERSITY OF MISSOURI, et al.

CERTIORARI TO THE SUPREME COURT OF MISSOURI.

No. 57. Argued November 9, 1938.—Decided December 12, 1938.

Mr. Chief Justice Hughes delivered the opinion of the Court.

Petitioner Lloyd Gaines, a negro, was refused admission to the School of Law at the State University of Missouri. Asserting that this refusal constituted a denial by the State of the equal protection of the laws in violation of the Fourteenth Amendment of the Federal Constitution, petitioner brought this action for mandamus to compel the curators of the University to admit him. On final hearing, an alternative writ was quashed and a peremptory writ was denied by the Circuit Court. The Supreme Court of the State affirmed the judgment. 113 S. W. 2d 783. We granted certiorari, October 10, 1938.

Petitioner is a citizen of Missouri. In August, 1935, he was graduated with the degree of Bachelor of Arts at the Lincoln University, an institution maintained by the State of Missouri for the higher education of negroes. That University has no law school. Upon the filing of his application for admission to the law school of the University of Missouri, the registrar advised him to communicate with the president of Lincoln University and the latter directed petitioner's attention to § 9622 of the Revised Statutes of Missouri (1929), providing as follows:

"*Sec. 9622. May arrange for attendance at university of any adjacent state—Tuition fees.*—Pending the full development of the Lincoln university, the board of curators shall have the authority to arrange for the attendance of negro residents of the state of Missouri at the university of any adjacent state to take any course or to study any subjects provided for at the state university of Missouri, and which are not taught at the Lincoln university and to pay the reasonable tuition fees for such attendance; *provided* that whenever the board of curators deem it advisable they shall have the power to open any necessary school or department. (Laws 1921, p. 86, § 7.)''

Petitioner was advised to apply to the State Superintendent of Schools for aid under that statute. It was admitted on the trial that petitioner's "work and credits at the Lincoln University would qualify him for admission to the School of Law of the University of Missouri if he were found otherwise eligible.'' He was refused admission upon the ground that it was "contrary to the constitution, laws and public policy of the State to admit a negro as a student in the University of Missouri.'' It appears that there are schools of law in connection with the state universitites of four adjacent States, Kansas, Nebraska, Iowa and Illinois, where nonresident negroes are admitted.

The clear and definite conclusions of the state court in construing the pertinent state legislation narrow the issue. The action of the curators, who are representatives of the State in the management of the state university (R. S. Mo., § 9625), must be regarded as state action. The state constitution provides that separate free public schools shall be established for the education of children of African descent (Art.XI, § 3), and by statute separate high school facilities are supplied for colored students equal to those provided for white students (R. S. Mo., § § 9346-9349). While there is no express constitutional provision requiring that the white and negro races be separated for the purpose of higher education, the state court on a comprehensive review of the state statutes held that it was intended to separate the white and negro races for that purpose also. Referring in particular to Lincoln University, the court deemed it to be clear ''that the Legislature intended to bring the Lincoln University up to the standard of the University of Missouri, and give to the whites and negroes an equal opportunity for higher education—the whites at the University of Missouri, and the negroes at Lincoln University.'' Further, the court concluded that the provisions of § 9622 (above quoted) to the effect that negro residents ''may attend the university of any adjacent State with their tuition paid, pending the full development of Lincoln University,'' made it evident ''that the Legislature did not intend that negroes and whites should attend the same university in this State.'' In that view it necessarily followed that the curators of the University of Missouri acted in accordance with the policy of the State in denying petitioner admission to its School of Law upon the sole ground of his race.

In answering petitioner's contention that this discrimination constituted a denial of his constitutional right, the state court has fully recognized the obligation of the State to provide negroes with advantages for higher education substantially equal to the advantages afforded to white students. The State has sought to fulfill that obligation by furnishing equal facilities in separate schools, a method the validity of which has been sustained by our decisions. *Plessy v. Ferguson*, 163 U. S. 537, 544; *McCabe v. Atchison, T. & S. F. Ry. Co..*, 235 U. S. 151, 160; *Gong Lum v. Rice*, 275 U. S. 78, 85, 86. Compare *Cumming* v. *Board of Education*, 175 U. S. 528, 544, 545. Respondents' counsel have appropriately emphasized the special solicitude of the State for the higher education of negroes as shown in the establishment of Lincoln University, a state institution well conducted on a plane with the University of Missouri so far as the offered courses are concerned. It is said that Missouri is a pioneer in that field and is the only State in the Union which has established a separate university for negroes on the same basis as the state university for white students. But, commendable as is that action, the fact remains that instruction in law for negroes is not now afforded by the State, either at Lincoln University or elsewhere within the State, and that the State excludes negroes from the advantages of the law school it has established at the University of Missouri.

It is manifest that this discrimination, if not relieved by the provisions we shall presently discuss, would constitute a denial of equal protection. That was the conclusion of the Court of Appeals of Maryland in circumstances substantially similar in that aspect. *University of Maryland* v. *Murray*, 169 Md. 478; 182 A. 590. It there appeared that the State of Maryland had "undertaken the function of education in the law" but had "omitted students of one race from the only adequate provision made for it, and omitted them solely because of their color"; that if those students were to be offered "equal treatment in the performance of the function, they must at present, be admitted to the one school provided." *Id.*, p. 489. A provision for scholarships to enable negroes to attend colleges outside the State, mainly for the purpose of professional studies, was found to be inadequate (*Id.*, pp. 485, 486) and the question, "whether with aid in any amount it is sufficient to send the negroes outside the State for legal education," the Court of Appeals found it unnecessary to discuss. Accordingly, a writ of mandamus to admit the applicant was issued to the officers and regents of the University of Maryland as the agents of the State entrusted with the conduct of that institution.

The Supreme Court of Missouri in the instant case has distinguished the decision in Maryland upon the ground—(1) that in Missouri, but not in Maryland, there is "a legislative declaration of a purpose to establish a law school for negroes at Lincoln University whenever necessary or practical"; and (1) that, "pending the establishment of such a school, adequate provision has been made for the legal education of negro students in recognized schools outside of this State." 113 S. W. 2d. p. 791. . . .

In the light of its [the lower courts] ruling we must regard the question whether the provision for the legal education in other States of negroes resident in Missouri is sufficient to satisfy the constitutional requirement of equal protection, as the pivot upon which this case turns.

The state court stresses the advantages that are afforded by the law schools of the adjacent States,—Kansas, Nebraska, Iowa and Illinois,— which admit non-resident negroes. The court considered that these were schools of high standing where one desiring to practice law in Missouri can get "as sound, comprehensive, valuable legal education" as in the University of Missouri; that the system of education in the former is the same as that in the latter and is designed to give the students a basis for the practice of law in any State where the Anglo-American system of law obtains; that the law school of the University of Missouri does not specialize in Missouri law and that the course of study and the case books used in the five schools are substantially identical. Petitioner insists that for one intending to practice in Missouri there are special advantages in attending a law school there, both in relation to the opportunities for the particular study of Missouri law and for the observation of the local courts, and also in view of the prestige of the Missouri law school among the citizens of the State, his prospective clients. Proceeding with its examination of relative advantages, the state court found that the difference in distances to be traveled afforded no substantial ground of complaint and that there was an adequate appropriation to meet the full tuition fees which petitioner would have to pay.

We think that these matters are beside the point. The basic consideration is not as to what sort of opportunities other States provide, or whether they are as good as those in Missouri, but as to what opportunities Missouri itself furnishes to white students and denies to negroes solely upon the ground of color. The admissibility of laws separating the races in the enjoyment of privileges afforded by the State rests wholly upon the equality of the privileges which the laws give to the separated groups within the State. The question here is not of a duty of the State to supply legal training, or of the quality of the training which it does supply, but of its duty when it provides such training to furnish it to the residents of the State upon the basis of an equality of right. By the operation of the laws of Missouri a privilege has been created for white law students which is denied to negroes by reason of their race. The white resident is afforded legal education within the State; the negro resident having the same qualifications is refused it there and must go outside the State to obtain it. That is a denial of the equality of legal right to the enjoyment of the privilege which the State has set up, and the provision for the payment of tuition fees in another State does not remove the discrimination.

The equal protection of the laws is "a pledge of the protection of equal laws." *Yick Wo* v. *Hopkins*, 118 U. S. 356, 369. Manifestly, the obligation of the State to give the protection of equal laws can be performed only where its laws operate, that is, within its own jurisdiction. It is there that the equality of legal right must be maintained. That obligation is imposed by the Constitution upon the States severally as governmental entities,—each responsible for its own laws establishing the rights and duties of persons within its borders. It is an obligation the burden of which cannot be cast by one State upon another, and no State can be excused from performance by what another State may do or fail to do. That separate responsibility of each State within its own sphere is of the essence of statehood maintained under our dual system. It seems to be implicit in respondents' argument that if other States did not provide courses for legal education, it would nevertheless be the constitutional duty of Missouri when it supplied such courses for white students to make equivalent provision for negroes. But that plain duty would exist because it rested upon the State independently of the action of other States. We find it impossible to conclude that what otherwise would be an unconstitutional discrimination, with respect to the legal right to the enjoyment of opportunities within the State, can be justified by requiring resort to opportunities elsewhere. That resort may mitigate the inconvenience of the discrimination but cannot serve to validate it.

Nor can we regard the fact that there is but a limited demand in Missouri for the legal education of negroes as excusing the discrimination in favor of whites. We had occasion to consider a cognate question in the case of *McCabe* v. *Atchison, T. & S. F. Ry. Co., supra*. There the argument was advanced, in relation to the provision by a carrier of sleeping cars, dining and chair cars, that the limited demand by negroes justified the State in permitting the furnishing of such accommodations exclusively for white persons. We found that argument to be without merit. It made, we said, the constitutional right "depend upon the number of persons who may be discriminated against, whereas the essence of the constitutional right is that it is a personal one. Whether or not particular facilities shall be provided may doubtless be conditioned upon there being a reasonable demand therefor, but, if facilities are provided, substantial equality of treatment of persons traveling under like conditions cannot be refused. It is the individual who is entitled to the equal protection of the laws, and if he is denied by a common carrier, acting in the matter under the authority of a state law, a facility or convenience in the course of his journey which under substantially the same circumstances is furnished to another traveler, he may properly complain that his constitutional privilege has been invaded." *Id.*, pp. 161, 162.

Here, petitioner's right was a personal one. It was as an individual that he was entitled to the equal protection of the laws, and the State was bound to furnish him within its borders facilities for legal education substantially equal to those which the State there afforded for persons of the white race, whether or not other negroes sought the same opporunity.

It is urged, however, that the provision for tuition outside the State is a temporary one,—that it is intended to operate merely pending the establishment of a law department for negroes at Lincoln University. While in that sense the discrimination may be termed temporary, it may nevertheless continue for an indefinite period by reason of the discretion given to the curators of Lincoln University and the alternative of arranging for tuition in other States, as permitted by the state law as construed by the state court, so long as the curators find it unnecessary and impracticable to provide facilities for the legal instruction of negroes within the State. In that view, we cannot regard the discrimination as excused by what is called its temporary character.

We do not find that the decision of the state court turns on any procedural question. The action was for mandamus, but it does not appear that the remedy would have been deemed inappropriate if the asserted federal right had been sustained. In that situation the remedy by mandamus was found to be a proper one in *University of Maryland* v. *Murray, supra.* In the instant case, the state court did note that petitioner had not applied to the management of Lincoln University for legal training. But, as we have said, the state court did not rule that it would have been the duty of the curators to grant such an application, but on the contrary took the view, as we understand it, that the curators were entitled under the state law to refuse such an application and in its stead to provide for petitioner's tuition in an adjacent State. That conclusion presented the federal question as to the constitutional adequacy of such a provision while equal opportunity for legal training within the State was not furnished, and this federal question the state court entertained and passed upon. We must conclude that in so doing the court denied the federal right which petitioner set up and the question as to the correctness of that decision is before us. We are of the opinion that the ruling was in error, and that petitioner was entitled to be admitted to the law school of the State University in the absence of other and proper provision for his legal training within the State.

The judgment of the Supreme Court of Missouri is reversed and the cause is remanded for further proceedings not inconsistent with this opinion.

Reversed.

SWEATT v. PAINTER ET AL.

CERTIORARI TO THE SUPREME COURT OF TEXAS.

No. 44.   Argued April 4, 1950.—Decided June 5, 1950.

Mr. Chief Justice Vinson delivered the opinion of the Court. . . .

The University of Texas Law School, from which petitioner was excluded, was staffed by a faculty of sixteen full-time and three part-time professors, some of whom are nationally recognized authorities in their field. Its student body numbered 850. The library contained over 65,000 volumes. Among the other facilities available to the students were a law review, moot court facilities, scholarship funds, and Order of the Coif affiliation. The school's alumni occupy the most distinguished positions in the private practice of the law and in the public life of the State. It may properly be considered one of the nation's ranking law schools.

The law school for Negroes which was to have opened in February, 1947, would have had no independent faculty or library. The teaching was to be carried on by four members of the University of Texas Law School faculty, who were to maintain their offices at the University of Texas while teaching at both insitutions. Few of the 10,000 volumes ordered for the library had arrived; nor was there any full-time librarian. The school lacked accreditation.

Since the trial of this case, respondents report the opening of a law school at the Texas State University for Negroes. It is apparently on the road to full accreditation. It has a faculty of five full-time professors; a student body of 23; a library of some 16,500 volumes serviced by a full-time staff; a practice court and legal aid association; and one alumnus who has become a member of the Texas Bar.

Whether the University of Texas Law School is compared with the original or the new law school for Negroes, we cannot find substantial equality in the educational opportunities offered white and Negro law students by the State. In terms of number of the faculty, variety of courses and opportunity for specialization, size of the student body, scope of the library, availability of law review and similar activities, the University of Texas Law School is superior. What is more important, the

University of Texas Law School possesses to a far greater degree those qualities which are incapable of objective measurement but which make for greatness in a law school. Such qualities, to name but a few, include reputation of the faculty, experience of the administration, position and influence of the alumni, standing in the community, traditions and prestige. It is difficult to believe that one who had a free choice between these law schools would consider the question close.

Moreover, although the law is a highly learned profession, we are well aware that it is an intensely practical one. The law school, the proving ground for legal learning and practice, cannot be effective in isolation from the individuals and institutions with which the law interacts. Few students and no one who has practiced law would choose to study in an academic vacuum, removed from the interplay of ideas and the exchange of views with which the law is concerned. The law school to which Texas is willing to admit petitioner excludes from its student body members of the racial groups which number 85% of the population of the State and include most of the lawyers, witnesses, jurors, judges and other officials with whom petitioner will inevitably be dealing when he becomes a member of the Texas Bar. With such a substantial and significant segment of society excluded, we cannot conclude that the education offered petitioner is substantially equal to that which he would receive if admitted to the University of Texas Law School.

It may be argued that excluding petitioner from that school is no different from excluding white students from the new law school. This contention overlooks realities. It is unlikely that a member of a group so decisively in the majority, attending a school with rich traditions and prestige which only a history of consistently maintained excellence could command, would claim that the opportunities afforded him for legal education were unequal to those held open to petitioner. That such a claim, if made, would be dishonored by the State, is no answer. "Equal protection of the laws is not achieved through indiscriminate imposition of inequalities." *Shelley* v. *Kraemer*, 334 U. S. 1, 22 (1948).

It is fundamental that these cases concern rights which are personal and present. This Court has stated unanimously that "The State must provide [legal education] for [petitioner] in conformity with the equal protection clause of the Fourteenth Amendment and provide it as soon as it does for applicants of any other group." *Sipuel* v. *Board of Regents*, 332 U. S. 631, 633 (1948). That case "did not present the issue whether a state might not satisfy the equal protection clause of the Fourteenth Amendment by establishing a separate law school for Negroes.'' *Fisher* v. *Hurst*, 333 U. S. 147, 150 (1948). In *Missouri ex rel. Gaines* v. *Canada*, 305 U. S. 337, 351 (1938), the Court, speaking through Chief Justice Hughes, declared that ''petitioner's right was a personal one. It was as an individual that he was entitled to the equal protection of the laws, and the State was bound to furnish him within its borders facilities for legal education substantially equal to those which the State there afforded for persons of the white race, whether or not other negroes sought the same opportunity.'' These are the only cases in this Court which present the issue of the constitutional validity of race distinctions in state-supported graduate and professional education.

In accordance with these cases, petitioner may claim his full constitutional right: legal education equivalent to that offered by the State to students of other races. Such education is not available to him in a separate law school as offered by the State. We cannot, therefore, agree with respondents that the doctrine of *Plessy* v. *Ferguson*, 163 U. S. 537 (1896), requires affirmance of the judgment below. Nor need we reach petitioner's contention that *Plessy* v. *Ferguson* should be reexamined in the light of contemporary knowledge respecting the purposes of the Fourteenth Amendment and the effects of racial segregation. See *supra*, p. 631.

We hold that the Equal Protection Clause of the Fourteenth Amendment requires that petitioner be admitted to the University of Texas Law School. The judgment is reversed and the cause is remanded for proceedings not inconsistent with this opinion.

Reversed.

McLAURIN *v.* OKLAHOMA STATE REGENTS FOR HIGHER EDUCATION ET AL.

APPEAL FROM THE UNITED STATES DISTRICT COURT FOR THE WESTERN DISTRICT OF OKLAHOMA.

No. 34 Argued April 3-4, 1950.—Decided June 5, 1950.

Mr. Chief Justice Vinson delivered the opinion of the Court. . . . It is said that the separations imposed by the State in this case are in form merely nominal. McLaurin uses the same classroom, library and cafeteria as students of other races; there is no indication that the seats to which he is assigned in these rooms have any disadvantage of location. He may wait in line in the cafeteria and there stand and talk with his fellow students, but while he eats he must remain apart.

These restrictions were obviously imposed in order to comply, as nearly as could be, with the statutory requirements of Oklahoma. But they signify that the State, in administering the facilities it affords for professional and graduate study, sets McLaurin apart from the other students. The result is that appellant is handicapped in his pursuit of effective graduate instruction. Such restrictions impair and inhibit his ability to study, to engage in discussions and exhange views with other students, and, in general, to learn his profession.

Our society grows increasingly complex, and our need for trained leaders increases correspondingly. Appellant's case represents, perhaps, the epitome of that need, for he is attempting to obtain an advanced degree in education, to become, by definition, a leader and trainer of others. Those who will come under his guidance and influence must be directly affected by the education he receives. Their own education and development will necessarily suffer to the extent that his training is unequal to that of his classmates. State-imposed restrictions which produce such inequalities cannot be sustained.

It may be argued that appellant will be in no better position when these restrictions are removed, for he may still be set apart by his fellow students. This we think irrelevant. There is a vast difference—a Constitutional difference—between restrictions imposed by the state which prohibit the intellectual commingling of students, and the refusal of individuals to commingle where the state presents no such bar. *Shelley* v. *Kramer*, 334 U. S. 1, 13-14 (1948). The removal of the state restrictions will not necessarily abate individual and group predilections, prejudices and choices. But at the very least, the state will not be depriving appellant of the opportunity to secure acceptance by his fellow students on his own merits.

We conclude that the conditions under which this appellant is required to receive his education deprive him of his personal and present right to the equal protection of the laws. See *Sweatt* v. *Painter, ante,* p. 629. We hold that under these circumstances the Fourteenth Amendment precludes differences in treatment by the state based upon race. Appellant,

having been admitted to a state-supported graduate school, must receive
the same treatment at the hands of the state as students of other races. The
judgment is

Reversed.

BROWN ET AL. *v.* BOARD OF EDUCATION OF TOPEKA ET AL.

NO. 1. APPEAL FROM THE UNITED STATES DISTRICT COURT FOR THE DISTRICT
OF KANSAS.

Argued December 9, 1952.—Reargued December 8, 1953.—
Decided May 17, 1954.

Mr. Chief Justice Warren delivered the opinion of the Court. . . .

In the first cases in this Court construing the Fourteenth Amendment,
decided shortly after its adoption, the Court interpreted it as proscribing
all state-imposed discriminations against the Negro race. The doctrine of
"separate but equal" did not make its appearance in this Court until 1896
in the case of *Plessy* v. *Ferguson, supra,* involving not education but
transportation. American courts have since labored with the doctrine for
over half a century. In this Court, there have been six cases involving the
"separate but equal" doctrine in the field of public education. In *Cumming* v. *County Board of Education,* 175 U. S. 528, and *Gong Lum* v.
Rice, 275 U. S. 78, the validity of the doctrine itself was not challenged.
In more recent cases, all on the graduate school level, inequality was
found in that specific benefits enjoyed by white students were denied to
Negro students of the same educational qualifications. *Missouri ex rel.
Gaines* v. *Canada,* 305 U. S. 337; *Sipuel* v. *Oklahoma,* 332 U. S. 631;
Sweatt v. *Painter,* 339 U. S. 629; *McLaurin* v. *Oklahoma State Regents,*
339 W. S. 637. In none of these cases was it necessary to re-examine the
doctrine to grant relief to the Negro plaintiff. And in *Sweatt* v. *Painter,
supra,* the Court expressly reserved decision on the question whether
Plessy v. *Ferguson* should be held inapplicable to public education.

In the instant cases, that question is directly presented. Here, unlike
Sweatt v. *Painter,* there are findings below that the Negro and white
schools involved have been equalized, or are being equalized, with
respect to buildings, curricula, qualifications and salaries of teachers,
and other "tangible" factors. Our decision, therefore, cannot turn on

merely a comparison of these tangible factors in the Negro and white schools involved in each of the cases. We must look instead to the effect of segregation itself on public education.

In approaching this problem, we cannot turn the clock back to 1868 when the Amendment was adopted, or even to 1896 when *Plessy* v. *Ferguson* was written. We must consider public education in the light of its full development and its present place in American life throughout the Nation. Only in this way can it be determined if segregation in public schools deprives these plaintiffs of the equal protection of the laws.

Today, education is perhaps the most important function of state and local governments. Compulsory school attendance laws and the great expenditures for education both demonstrate our recognition of the importance of education to our democratic society. It is required in the performance of our most basic public responsibilities, even service in the armed forces. It is the very foundation of good citizenship. Today it is a principal instrument in awakening the child to cultural values, in preparing him for later professional training, and in helping him to adjust normally to his environment. In these days, it is doubtful that any child may reasonably be expected to succeed in life if he is denied the opportunity of an education. Such an opportunity, where the state has undertaken to provide it, is a right which must be made available to all on equal terms.

We come then to the question presented: Does segregation of children in public schools solely on the basis of race, even though the physical facilities and other "tangible" factors may be equal, deprive the children of the minority group of equal educational opportunities? We believe that it does.

In *Sweatt* v. *Painter, supra,* in finding that a segregated law school for Negroes could not provide them equal educational opportunities, this Court relied in large part on "those qualities which are incapable of objective measurement but which make for greatness in a law school." In *McLaurin* v. *Oklahoma State Regents, supra,* the Court, in requiring that a Negro admitted to a white graduate school be treated like all other students, again resorted to intangible considerations: ". . . his ability to study, to engage in discussions and exchange views with other students, and, in general, to learn his profession." Such considerations apply with added force to children in grade and high schools. To separate them from others of similar age and qualifications solely because of their race generates a feeling of inferiority as to their status in the community that may affect their hearts and minds in a way unlikely ever to be undone. The effect of this separation on their educational opportunities was well stated by a finding in the Kansas case by a court which nevertheless felt compelled to rule against the Negro plaintiffs:

> "Segregation of white and colored children in public schools has a detrimental effect upon the colored children. The impact is greater when it has the sanction of the law; for the policy of separating the races is usually interpreted as denoting the inferiority of the negro group. A sense of inferiority affects the motivation of a child to learn. Segregation with the sanction of law, therefore, has a tendency to [retard] the educational and mental development of negro children and to deprive them of some of the benefits they would receive in a racial [y] integrated school system."

Whatever may have been the extent of psychological knowledge at the time of *Plessy* v. *Ferguson*, this finding is amply supported by modern authority. Any language in *Plessy* v. *Ferguson* contrary to this finding is rejected.

We conclude that in the field of public education the doctrine of "separate but equal" has no place. Separate educational facilities are inherently unequal. Therefore, we hold that the plaintiffs and others similarly situated for whom the actions have been brought are, by reason of the segregation complained of, deprived of the equal protection of the laws guaranteed by the Fourteenth Amendment. This disposition makes unnecessary any discussion whether such segregation also violates the Due Process Clause of the Fourteenth Amendment.

Because these are class actions, because of the wide applicability of this decision, and because of the great variety of local conditions, the formulation of decrees in these cases presents problems of considerable complexity. On reargument, the consideration of appropriate relief was necessarily subordinated to the primary question—the constitutionality of segregation in public education. We have now announced that such segregation is a denial of the equal protection of the laws. In order that we may have the full assistance of the parties in formulating decrees, the cases will be restored to the docket, and the parties are requested to present further argument on Questions 4 and 5 previously propounded by the Court for the reargument this Term. The Attorney General of the

United States is again invited to participate. The Attorneys General of the states requiring or permitting segregation in public education will also be permitted to ppear as *amici curiae* upon request to do so by September 15, 1954, and submission of briefs by October 1, 1954.

It is so ordered.

BROWN ET AL. *v.* BOARD OF EDUCATION OF TOPEKA ET AL.

NO 1. APPEAL FROM THE UNITED STATES DISTRICT COURT FOR THE DISTRICT OF KANSAS.

Reargued on the question of relief April 11-14, 1955.—Opinion and judgments announced May 31, 1955.

Mr. Chief Justice Warren delivered the opinion of the Court.

These cases were decided on May 17, 1954. The opinions of that date, declaring the fundamental principle that racial discrimination in public education is unconstitutional, are incorporated herein by reference. All provisions of federal, state, or local law requiring or permitting such discrimination must yield to this principle. There remains for consideration the manner in which relief is to be accorded.

Because these cases arose under different local conditions and their disposition will involve a variety of local problems, we requested further argument on the question of relief. In view of the nationwide importance of the decision, we invited the Attorney General of the United States and the Attorneys General of all states requiring or permitting racial discrimination in public education to present their views on that question. The parties, the United States, and the States of Florida, North Carolina, Arkansas, Oklahoma, Maryland, and Texas filed briefs and participated in the oral argument.

These presentations were informative and helpful to the Court in its consideration of the complexities arising from the transition to a system of public education freed of racial discrimination. The presentations also demonstrated that substantial steps to eliminate racial discrimination in public schools have already been taken, not only in some of the communities in which these cases arose, but in some of the states appearing as *amici curiae,* and in other states as well. Substantial progress has been made in the District of Columbia and in the communities in Kansas and Delaware involved in this litigation. The defendants in the cases coming to us from South Carolina and Virginia are awaiting the decision of this Court concerning relief.

Full implementation of these constitutional principles may require solution of varied local school problems. School authorities have the primary responsibility for elucidating, assessing, and solving these problems; courts will have to consider whether the action of school authorities constitutes good faith implementation of the governing constitutional principles. Because of their proximity to local conditions and the possible need for further hearings, the courts which originally heard these cases can best perform this judicial appraisal. Accordingly, we believe it appropriate to remand the cases to those courts.

In fashioning and effectuating the decrees, the courts will be guided by equitable principles. Traditionally, equity has been characterized by a practical flexibility in shaping its remedies and by a facility for adjusting and reconciling public and private needs. These cases call for the exercise of these traditional attributes of equity power. At stake is the personal interest of the plaintiffs in admission to public schools as soon as practicable on a nondiscriminatory basis. To effectuate this interest may call for elimination of a variety of obstacles in making the transition to school systems operated in accordance with the constitutional principles set forth in our May 17, 1954, decision. Courts of equity may properly take into account the public interest in the elimination of such obstacles in a systematic and effective manner. But it should go without saying that the vitality of these constitutional principles cannot be allowed to yield simply because of disagreement with them.

While giving weight to these public and private considerations, the courts will require that the defendants make a prompt and reasonable start toward full compliance with our May 17, 1954, ruling. Once such a start has been made, the courts may find that additional time is necessary to carry out the ruling in an effective manner. The burden rests upon the defendants to establish that such time is necessary in the public interest and is consistent with good faith compliance at the earliest practicable date. To that end, the courts may consider problems related to administration, arising from the physical condition of the school plant, the school transportation system, personnel, revision of school districts and attendance areas into compact units to achieve a system of determining admission to the public schools on a nonracial basis, and revision of local laws and regulations which may be necessary in solving the foregoing problems. They will also consider the adequacy of any plans the defendants may propose to meet these problems and to effectuate a transition to a racially nondiscriminatory school system. During this period of transition, the courts will retain jurisdiction of these cases.

The judgments below, except that in the Delaware case, are accordingly reversed and the cases are remanded to the District Courts to take such proceedings and enter such orders and decrees consistent with this opinion as are necessary and proper to admit to public schools on a racially nondiscriminatory basis with all deliberate speed the parties to these cases. . . .

Document III-9: THE IMPORTANCE OF ORGANIZATION

James G. Birney was one of that small number of especially effective Southern crusaders against slavery. Freeing his own slaves, he moved north from Alabama, attempting to establish colonization efforts in the border states, then moving to Cincinnati, where he published the anti-slavery newspaper *The Philanthropist* after it had been squelched in Danville, Kentucky. "It, probably, would not be too much to say that the fate of slavery was sealed in the region about Danville and Cincinnati during the ensuing years [1833-37], with Birney and Theodore Weld conducting the prosecution," wrote Dwight L. Dumond with particular reference to Birney's press and to the Lane Seminary debate. (The quotation is from Dumond's introduction to *The Letters of James Gillespie Birney, 1831-1857.* New York, Appleton-Century, 1938, vol. I, p. xii.) Birney ran as the Liberty Party's presidential candidate in 1844.

The passage reproduced here is one of the four documents identified as exceptionally influential by Professor Dumond (the others coming from William Jay, Joshua Leavitt, and Lewis Tappan). It resulted from an effort by Birney to engage in debate slavery's leading proponent, John C. Calhoun. Instead of responding directly Calhoun passed on Birney's letter to Congressman Franklin H. Elmore of South Carolina, who sent Birney a polite cover letter along with the list of fourteen well-conceived questions about anti-slavery activities.

Birney's answer constitutes the most concise-yet-comprehensive, persuasive, and prophetic discussion of the slavery question. It includes a Southerner's view of the growth of slaveholding and of its justifications. It describes the nature and extent of the anti-slavery movement—down to the last paper and the last penny. It tells why the abolitionists found it necessary to "muckrake" on the evils of life among the slaves and to attack the "peculiar institution" with Biblical citations. It explains the dilemma of the churches. In a long passage not reproduced it foresees— as perhaps only a Southerner could—the lure of secession and argues against all of its principal appeals. As only a Southerner could, Birney also went straight for the jugular vein of sensitivity in attacking the Southern delusions concerning the civilizing force of slavery—a direct assault on Calhoun.

This document is submitted as a culmination of anti-slavery materials not only because of its comprehensiveness. It shows the full panoply of reform assumptions and arguments: the moral, the rational, the pragmatic. Furthermore, it helps point out how heavily the success or failure of a reform movement depends on the existence of sustained, organized effort. The movement must have geographical scope and ideological breadth; but above all, it must have the inexhaustible attention to detail of a Weld or a Birney. Reform may have its moments of high art and high drama; but its progress depends on such unglamorous daily activities as going to press, selling pamphlets, organizing chapters, raising money, and getting out the vote.

The National Association for the Advancement of Colored People did a great deal more than attack segregated schools through court action (see III-8) and make sure that department stores sometimes hired a black Santa Claus. Yet these two allusions suggest the range of its interests. It is, in its own words, "the new abolition society"; and there are indeed many resemblances between the American Anti-Slavery Society and the NAACP.

Both relied heavily on a national league of local and regional chapters. Both made heavy use of regular publications with skilled writers and editors. Both attempted to change feelings about racial questions through all the devices in the reformer's arsenal from children's savings banks through poems and stories to conventions and picnics. Both developed a kind of expertise appropriate to their aims: the AA-SS working more through the Congress and the NAACP working more through the courts.

In some ways the NAACP may now be viewed as a transitional organization, notably through the shift in civil rights leadership from white to black. The AA-SS was led by white people. Today, the Urban League, the Congress on Racial Equality, the Southern Christian Leadership Conference—and of course the militant and separatist groups—have exclusively or predominantly black leadership. In between came the NAACP, dominated by the figure of that black American who made the force of his mind and personality felt most widely: W. E. Burghardt Du Bois. Surrounding Du Bois was a group of white people, some of them as impressive as Du Bois, many of them lawyers. Steadily, with the rise to prominence of men like Thurgood Marshall (who was the principal counsel in all of the Supreme Court cases cited in III-8), the racial balance shifted.

The pages reproduced below represent the range of activities in the earlier years when the NAACP stood almost alone on the civil rights front and when *Crisis* was becoming the outstanding periodical devoted to the interests of the American Negro. These pages radiate the early-morning zest of that evangelism which awakened the nation from its long slumber on the race question. The names of Americans eminent on frontiers of social action (Jane Addams, Oswald G. Villard, Joel E. Spingarn, Archibald H. Grimké) appear with impressive regularity. The responses from the readership sometimes show quite clearly the length of the road up ahead. With Birney's description of the AA-SS, these pages from *Crisis* show the unchanging need for organized, ubiquitous patience at the heart of any successful reform movement.

SOURCES: A: *Correspondence between the Hon. F. H. Elmore and James G. Birney.* New York, American Anti-Slavery Society, 1838, pp. 7-8, 9-23, abridged. B: *The Crisis*, vol. VII (December, 1913), pp. 88-91; vol. VII (April, 1914), pp. 289-292.

A: BIRNEY ON THE AMERICAN ANTI-SLAVERY SOCIETY

ANTI-SLAVERY OFFICE, *New York, March 8, 1838*
Hon. F. H. ELMORE,
Member of Congress from S. Carolina:

SIR,—I take pleasure in furnishing the information you have so politely asked for, in your letter of the 16th ult., in relation to the American Anti-Slavery Society;—and trust, that this correspondence,

THE REFORM SPIRIT IN AMERICA

by presenting in a sober light, the objects and measures of the society, may contribute to dispel, not only from your own mind, but—if it be diffused throughout the South—from the minds of our fellow-citizens there generally, a great deal of undeserved prejudice and groundless alarm. I cannot hesitate to believe, that such as enter on the examination of its claims to public favour, without bias, will find that it aims intelligently, not only at the promotion of the interests of the slave, but of the master,—not only at the re-animation of the Republican principles of our Constitution, but at the establishment of the Union on an enduring basis.

I shall proceed to state the several questions submitted in your letter, and answer them, in the order in which they are proposed. You ask,—

"1. *How many societies, affiliated with that of which you are corresponding secretary, are there in the United States? And how many members belong to them* IN THE AGGREGATE?"

ANSWER.—Our anniversary is held on the Tuesday immediately preceding the second Thursday in May. Returns of societies are made only a short time before. In May, 1835, there were 225 auxiliaries reported. In May, 1836, 527. In May, 1837, 1006. Returns for the anniversary in May next have not come in yet. It may, however, be safely said, that the increase, since last May, is not less than 400. Of late, the multiplication of societies has not kept pace with the progress of our principles. Where these are well received, our agents are not so careful to organize societies as in former times, when our numbers were few; *societies, now,* being not deemed so necessary for the advancement of our cause. The auxiliaries average not less than 80 members each; making an aggregate of 112,480. Others estimate the auxiliaries at 1500, and the average of members at 100. I give you, what I believe to be the lowest numbers.

"2. *Are there any other societies similar to yours, and not affiliated with it in the United States? And how many, and what is the aggregate of their members?"*

ANSWER.—Several societies have been formed in the Methodist connection within the last two years,—although most of the Methodists who are abolitionists, are members of societies auxiliary to the American. These societies have been originated by Ministers, and others of weight

and influence, who think that their brethren can be more easily persuaded, as a religious body, to aid in the anti-slavery movement by this
twofold action. None of the large religious denominations bid fairer soon
to be on the side of emancipation than the Methodist. Of the number of
the Methodist societies that are not auxiliary, I am not informed.—The
ILLINOIS SOCIETY comes under the same class. The REV. ELIJAH P.
LOVEJOY, the corresponding secretary, was slain by a mob, a few days
after its organization. It has not held a meeting since; and I have no data
for stating the number of its members. It is supposed not to be large.—
Neither is the DELAWARE SOCIETY, organized a few weeks ago, at
Wilmington, auxiliary to the American. I have no information as to its
numbers.—The MANUMISSION SOCIETY in this city, formed in 1785,
with JOHN JAY its first, and ALEXANDER HAMILTON its second president,
might, from its name, be supposed to be affiliated with the American.
Originally, its object, so far as regarded the slaves, and those illegally
held in bondage *in this state*, was, in a great measure, similar. Slavery
being extinguished in New York in 1827, as a state system, the efforts of
the Manumission Society are limited now to the rescue, from kidnappers
and others, of such persons as are really free by the laws, but who have
been reduced to slavery. Of the old Abolition societies, organized in the
time, and under the influence of Franklin and Rush and Jay, and the most
active of their coadjutors, but few remain. Their declension may be
ascribed to this defect,—they did not inflexibly ask for *immediate* emancipation.—THE PENNSYLVANIA ABOLITION SOCIETY, formed in 1789,
with DR. FRANKLIN, president, and DR. RUSH, secretary, is still in
existence—but unconnected with the American Society. Some of the
most active and benevolent members of both the associations last named,
are members of the American Society. Besides the societies already
mentioned, there may be in the country a few others of antislavery name;
but they are of small note and efficiency, and are unconnected with
this. . . .

"5. *What do you estimate the number of those who co-operate in the*
matter at? What proportion do they bear in the population of the
northern states, and what in the middle non-slaveholding states? Are
they increasing, and at what rate?"

ANSWER.—Those who stand *ready to join* our societies on the first suitable occasion, may be set down as equal in number to those who are now *actually members.* Those who are ready *fully to co-operate with us* in supporting the freedom of speech and the press, the right of petition, &c, may be estimated at *double,* if not *treble,* the joint numbers of those who *already are members,* and those who are *ready to become members.* The Recording secretary of the MASSACHUSETTS SOCIETY stated, a few weeks ago, that the abolitionists in the various minor societies in that state were one in thirty of the whole population. The proportion of abolitionists to the whole population is greater in Massachusetts than in any other of the free states, except VERMONT,—where the spirit of liberty has almost entirely escaped the corruptions which slavery has infused into it in most of her sister states, by means of commercial and other intercourse with them.

In MAINE, not much of systematic effort has, as yet, been put forth to enlighten her population as to our principles and proceedings. I attended the anniversary of the State Society on the 31st of January, at Augusta, the seat of government. The Ministers of the large religious denominations were beginning, as I was told, to unite with us—and Politicians, to descry the ultimate prevalence of our principles. The impression I received was, that much could, and that much would, speedily be done.

In NEW HAMPSHIRE, more labor has been expended, and a greater effect produced. Public functionaries, who have been pleased to speak in contemptuous terms of the progress of abolitionism, both in Maine and New Hampshire, will, it is thought, soon be made to see, through a medium not at all deceptive, the grossness of their error.

In RHODE ISLAND, our principles are fast pervading the great body of the people. This, it is thought, is the only one of the free states, in which the subject of abolition has been fully introduced, which has not been disgraced by a mob, triumphant, for the time being, over the right of the people to discuss any, and every, matter in which they feel interested. A short time previous to the last election of members of Congress, questions, embodying our views as to certain political measures, were propounded to the several candidates. Respectful answers, and, in the main, conformable with our views, were returned. I shall transmit you a newspaper containing both the questions and the answers.

In CONNECTICUT, there has not been, as yet, a great expenditure of abolition effort. Although the moral tone of this state, so far as slavery is concerned, has been a good deal weakened by the influence of her multiform connexions with the south, yet the energies that have been put forth to reanimate her ancient and lofty feelings, so far from proving fruitless, have been followed by the most encouraging results. Evidence of this is found in the faithful administration of the laws by judges and juries. In May last, a slave, who had been brought from Georgia to Hartford, successfully asserted her freedom under the laws of Connecticut. The cause was elaborately argued before the Supreme court. The most eminent counsel were employed on both sides. And it is but a few days, since two anti-abolition rioters (the only ones on trial) were convicted before the Superior court in New Haven, and sentenced to pay a fine of twenty dollars each, and to be imprisoned six months, the longest term authorized by the law. A convention, for the organization of a State Society, was held in the City of Hartford on the last day of February. It was continued three days. The *call* for it (which I send you) was signed by nearly EIGHTEEN HUNDRED of the citizens of that state. SEVENTEEN HUNDRED, as I was informed, are legal voters. The proceedings of the convention were of the most harmonious and animating character.

In NEW YORK, our cause is evidently advancing. The state is rapidly coming up to the high ground of principle, so far as universal liberty is concerned, on which the abolitionists would place her. Several large Anti-Slavery conventions have lately been held in the western counties. Their reports are of the most encouraging character. Nor is the change more remarkable in the state than in this city. Less than five years ago, a few of the citizens advertised a meeting, to be held in Clinton Hall, to form a City Anti-Slavery Society. A mob prevented their assembling at the place appointed. They repaired, privately, to one of the churches. To this they were pursued by the mob, and routed from it, though not before they had completed, in a hasty manner, the form of organization. In the summer of 1834, some of the leading political and commercial journals of the city were enabled to stir up the mob against the persons and property of the abolitionists, and several of the most prominent were compelled to leave the city for safety; their houses were attacked, broken into, and in one instance, the furniture publicly burnt in the street. *Now*, things are much changed. Many of the merchants and mechanics are favorable to our cause; gentlemen of the bar, especially the younger and more growing ones, are directing their attention to it; twenty-one of our city ministers are professed abolitionists; the churches are beginning to be more accessible to us; our meetings are held in them openly, attract large numbers, are unmolested; and the abolitionists sometimes hear themselves commended in other assemblies, not only for their honest *intentions*, but for their *respectability* and *intelligence.*

NEW JERSEY has, as yet, no State Society, and the number of avowed abolitionists is small. In some of the most populous and influential parts of the state, great solicitude exists on the subject; and the call for lecturers is beginning to be earnest, if not importunate.

PENNSYLVANIA has advanced to our principles just in proportion to the labor that has been bestowed, by means of lectures and publications in enlightening her population as to our objects, and the evils and dangers impending over the whole country, from southern slavery. The act of her late Convention, in depriving a large number of their own constituents (the colored people) of the elective franchise, heretofore possessed by them without any allegation of its abuse on their part, would seem to prove an unpropitious state of public sentiment. We would neither deny, nor elude, the force of such evidence. But when this measure of the convention is brought out and unfolded in its true light—shown to be a party measure to bring succor from the south—a mere following in the wake of North Carolina and Tennessee, who led the way, in their *new* constitutions, to this violation of the rights of their colored citizens, that they might the more firmly compact the wrongs of the enslaved—a pernicious, a profitless violation of great principles—a vulgar defiance of the advancing spirit of humanity and justice—a relapse into the by-gone darkness of a barbarous age—we apprehend from it no serious detriment to our cause.

OHIO has been well advanced. In a short time, she will be found among the most prominent of the states on the right side in the contest now going on between the spirit of liberty embodied in the free institutions of the north, and the spirit of slavery pervading the south. Her Constitution publishes the most honorable reprobation of slavery of any other in the Union. In providing for its own revision or amendment, it declares, that *no alteration of it shall ever take place, so as to introduce slavery or involuntary servitude into the state.* Her Supreme court is intelligent and firm. It has lately decided, virtually, against the constitutionality of an act of the Legislature, made, in effect, to favor southern slavery by the persecution of the colored people within her bounds. She has, already, abolitionists enough to turn the scale in her elections, and an abundance of excellent material for augmenting the number.

In INDIANA but little has been done, except by the diffusion of our publications. But even with these appliances, several auxiliary societies have been organized.

In MICHIGAN, the leaven of abolitionism pervades the whole population. The cause is well sustained by a high order of talent; and we trust soon to see the influence of it in all her public acts.

In ILLINOIS, the murder of Mr. Lovejoy has multiplied and confirmed abolitionists, and led to the formation of many societies, which in all probability, would not have been formed so soon, had not that event taken place.

I am not possessed of sufficient data for stating, with precision, what proportion the abolitionists bear in the population of the Northern and Middle non-slaveholding states respectively. Within the last ten months, I have travelled extensively in both these geographical divisions. I have had whatever advantage this, assisted by a strong interest in the general cause, and abundant conversations with the best informed abolitionists, could give, for making a fair estimate of their numbers. In the Northern states I should say, they are *one in ten*—in New York, New Jersey, and Pennsylvania, *one in twenty*—of the whole adult population. That the abolitionists have multiplied, and that they are still multiplying rapidly, no one acquainted with the smallness of their numbers at their first organization a few years ago, and who has kept his eyes about him since, need ask. That they have not, thus far, been more successful, is owing to the vastness of the undertaking, and the difficulties with which they have had to contend, from comparatively limited means, for presenting their measures and objects, with the proper developments and explanations, to the great mass of the popular mind. The progress of their principles, under the same amount of intelligence in presenting them, and where no peculiar causes of prejudice exist in the minds of the hearers, is generally proportioned to the degree of religious and intellectual worth prevailing in the different sections of the country where the subject is introduced. I know no instance, in which any one notoriously profane or intemperate, or licentious, or of openly irreligious *practice*, has professed, cordially to have received our principles.

"6. What is the object your associations aim at? Does it extend to abolition of slavery only in the District of Columbia, or in the whole slave country?"

ANSWER.—This question is fully answered in the second Article of the Constitution of the American Anti-Slavery Society, which is in these words:—

"The object of this society is the entire abolition of slavery in the United States. While it admits that each state, in which slavery exists, has, by the Constitution of the United States, the exclusive right to *legislate* in regard to its abolition in said state, it shall aim to convince all our fellow-citizens, by arguments addressed to their understandings and consciences, that slaveholding is a heinous crime in the sight of God, and that the duty, safety, and best interests of all concerned require its immediate abandonment, without expatriation. The society will also endeavor, in a constitutional way, to influence Congress to put an end to the domestic slave-trade, and to abolish slavery in all those portions of our common country which come under its control, especially in the District of Columbia; and likewise to prevent the extension of it to any state that may hereafter be admitted to the Union."

Other objects, accompanied by a pledge of peace, are stated in the third article of the Constitution,—

"This Society shall aim to elevate the character and condition of the people of color, by encouraging their intellectual, moral, and religious improvement, and by removing public prejudice,—that thus they may, according to their intellectual and moral worth, share an equality with the whites of civil and religious privileges; but this Society will never in any way, countenance the oppressed in vindicating their rights by resorting to physical force."

"7. By what means and by what power do you propose to carry your views into effect?"

ANSWER.—Our "means" are the Truth,—the "Power" under whose guidance we propose to carry our views into effect, is, the Almighty. Confiding in these means, when directed by the spirit and wisdom of Him, who has so made them as to act on the hearts of men, and so constituted the hearts of men as to be affected by them, we expect, 1. To bring the CHURCH of this country to repentance for the sin of OPPRESSION.

Not only the Southern portion of it that has been the oppressor—but the Northern, that has stood by, consenting, for half a century, to the wrong. 2. To bring our countrymen to see, that for a nation to persist in injustice is, but to rush on its own ruin; that to do justice is the highest expediency—to love mercy its noblest ornament. In other countries, slavery has sometimes yielded to fortuitous circumstances, or been extinguished by physical force. *We* strive to win for truth the victory over error, and on the broken fragments of slavery to rear for her a temple, that shall reach to the heavens, and toward which all nations shall worship. It has been said, that the slaveholders of the South will not yield, nor hearken to the influence of the truth on this subject. We believe it not—nor give we entertainment to the slander that such an unworthy defence of them implies. We believe them *men,*—that they have understandings that arguments will convince—consciences to which the appeals of justice and mercy will not be made in vain. If our principles be true—our arguments right—if slaveholders be men—and God have not delivered over our guilty country to the retributions of the oppresssor, not only of the STRANGER but of the NATIVE—our success is certain.

"8. What has been for three years past, the annual income of your societies? And how has it been raised?"

ANSWER.—The annual income of the societies at large, it would be impossible to ascertain. The total receipts of this society, for the year ending 9th of May, 1835—leaving out odd numbers—was $10,000; for the year ending 9th of May, 1837, $25,000; and for the year ending 11th of May, 1838, $38,000. From the last date, up to this—not quite ten months—there has been paid into the treasury the sum of $36,000. These sums are independent of what is raised by state and auxiliary societies, for expenditure within their own particular bounds, and for their own particular exigencies. Also, of the sums paid in subscriptions for the support of newspapers, and for the printing (by auxiliaries,) of periodicals, pamphlets, and essays, either for sale at low prices, or for gratuitous distribution. The moneys contributed in these various modes would make an aggregate greater, perhaps, than is paid into the treasury of any one of the Benevolent societies of the country. Most of the wealthy contributors of former years suffered so severely in the money-pressure of this, that they have been unable to contribute much to our funds. This has made it necessary to call for aid on the great body of abolitionists—persons, generally, in moderate circumstances. They have well responded to the call, considering the hardness of the times. To show you the extremes that meet at our treasury,—General Sewall, of Maine, a revolutionary officer, eighty-five years old—William Philbrick, a little boy near Boston, not four years old—and a colored woman, who makes her subsistence by selling apples in the streets in this city, lately sent in their respective sums to assist in promoting the emancipation of the ''poor slave.''

All contributions of whatever kind are *voluntary.*

''9. In what way, and to what purposes do you apply these funds?''

ANSWER.—They are used in sustaining the society's office in this city—in paying lecturers and agents of various kinds—in upholding the press—in printing books, pamphlets, tracts, &c, containing expositions of our principles—accounts of our progress—refutations of objections—and disquisitions on points, scriptural, constitutional, political, legal, economical, as they chance to arise and become important. In this office three secretaries are employed in different departments of duty; one editor; one publishing agent, with an assistant, and two or three young men and boys, for folding, directing, and despatching papers, executing errands, &c. The business of the society has increased so much of late, as to make it necessary, in order to ensure the proper despatch of it, to employ additional clerks for the particular exigency. Last year, the society had in its service about sixty ''permanent agents.'' This year, the number is considerably diminished. The deficiency has been more than made up by creating a large number of ''Local'' agents—so called, from the fact, that being generally Professional men, lawyers or physicians in good practice, or ministers with congregations, they are confined, for the most part, to their respective neighborhoods. Some of the best minds in our country are thus engaged. Their labors have not only been eminently successful, but have been rendered at but small charge to the society; they receiving only their travelling expenses, whilst employed in lecturing and forming societies. In the case of a minister, there is the additional expense of supplying his pulpit while absent on the business of his agency. However, in many instances, these agents, being in easy circumstances, make no charge, even for their expenses.

In making appointments, the executive committee have no regard to party discrimination. This will be fully understood, when it is stated, that on a late occasion, two of our local agents were the candidates of their respective political parties for the office of Secretary of State for the state of Vermont.

It ought to be stated here, that two of the most effective advocates of the anti-slavery cause are females—the Misses Grimké—natives of South Carolina—brought up in the midst of the usages of slavery—most intelligently acquainted with the merits of the system, and qualified, in an eminent degree, to communicate their views to others in public addresses. They are not only the advocates of the slave at their own charge, but they actually contribute to the funds of the societies. So successfully have they recommended the cause of emancipation to the crowds that attended their lectures during the last year, that they were permitted on three several occasions publicly to address the joint committee (on slavery) of the Massachusetts Legislature, now in session, on the interesting matters that occupy their attention.

"10. *How many printing-presses and periodical publications have you?*"

ANSWER.—We own no press. Our publications are all printed by contract. The EMANCIPATOR and HUMAN RIGHTS are the organs of the Executive Committee. The first (which you have seen,) is a large sheet, is published weekly, and employs almost exclusively the time of the gentleman who edits it. Human Rights is a monthly sheet of smaller size, and is edited by one of the secretaries. The increasing interest that is fast manifesting itself in the cause of emancipation and its kindred subjects will, in all probability, before long, call for the more frequent publication of one or both of these papers.—THE ANTI-SLAVERY MAGAZINE, a quarterly, was commenced in October, 1835, and continued through two years. It has been intermitted, only to make the necessary arrangements for issuing it on a more extended scale.—It is proposed to give it size enough to admit the amplest discussions that we or our opponents may desire, and to give *them* a full share of its room—in fine, to make it, in form and merit, what the importance of the subject calls for. I send you a copy of the Prospectus for the new series.—THE ANTI-SLAVERY RECORD, published for three years as a monthly, has been discontinued *as such*, and it will be issued hereafter, only as occasion may require.— THE SLAVE'S FRIEND, a small monthly tract, of neat appearance, intended principally for children and young persons, has been issued for several years. It is replete with facts relating to slavery, and with accounts of the hair-breadth escapes of slaves from their masters and pursuers that rarely fail to impart the most thrilling interest to its little readers.—Besides these, there is the ANTI-SLAVERY EXAMINER, in which are published, as the times call for them, our larger essays partaking of a controversial character such as Smith's reply to the Rev. Mr. Smylie—Grimké's letter and "Wythe." By turning to page 32 of our Fourth Report (included in your order for books, &c,) you will find, that in the year ending 11th May, the issues from the press were—bound volumes, 7,877—Tracts and Pamphlets, 47,250—Circulars, &c, 4,100—Prints, 10,490—Anti-Slavery Magazine, 9,000—Slave's Friend, 131,050—Human Rights, 189,400—Emancipator, 217,000. These are the issues of the American Anti-Slavery Society, from their office in this city. Other publications of similar character are issued by State Societies or individuals—the LIBERATOR, in Boston; HERALD of FREEDOM, in Concord, N. H.; Zion's WATCHMAN and the COLORED AMERICAN in this city. The latter is conducted in the editorial, and other departments, by colored citizens. You can judge of its character, by a few numbers that I send to you. Then, there is the FRIEND OF MAN, in Utica, in this state. The NATIONAL ENQUIRER, in Philadelphia; the CHRISTIAN WITNESS, in Pittsburgh; the PHILANTHROPIST, in Cincinnati.—All these are sustained by the friends, and devoted almost exclusively to the cause, of emancipation. Many of the Religious journals that do not make emancipation their main object have adopted the sentiments of abolitionists, and aid in promoting them. The Alton Observer, edited by the late Mr. Lovejoy, was one of these.

From the data I have, I set down the newspapers, as classed above, at upwards of one hundred. Here it may also be stated, that the presses which print the abolition journals above named, throw off besides, a great variety of other anti-slavery matter, in the form of books, pamphlets, single sheets, &c, &c, and that, at many of the principal commercial points throughout the free states, DEPOSITORIES are established, at which our publications of every sort are kept for sale. A large and fast increasing number of the Political journals of the country have become, within the last two years, if not the avowed supporters of our cause, well inclined to it. Formerly, it was a common thing for most of the leading *party*-papers, especially in the large cities, to speak of the abolitionists in terms signally disrespectful and offensive. Except in rare instances, and these, it is thought, only where they are largely subsidized by southern patronage, it is not so now. The desertions that are taking place from their ranks will, in a short time, render their position undesirable for any, who aspire to gain, or influence, or reputation in the North.

"11. *To what class of persons do you address your publications— and are they addressed to the judgment, the imagination, or the feelings?*"

ANSWER.—They are intended for the great mass of intelligent mind, both in the free and in the slave states. They partake, of course, of the intellectual peculiarities of the different authors. Jay's "INQUIRY" and Mrs. Child's "APPEAL" abound in facts—are dispassionate, ingenious, argumentative. The "BIBLE AGAINST SLAVERY," by the most careful and laborious research, has struck from slavery the prop, which careless Annotators, (writing, unconscious of the influence, the prevailing system of slavery throughout the Christian world exercised on their own minds,) have admitted was furnished for it in the Scriptures. "Wythe" by a pains-taking and lucid adjustment of facts in the history of the Government, both before and after the adoption of the Constitution, and with a rigor of logic, that cannot, it is thought, be successfully encountered, has put to flight forever with unbiased minds, every doubt as to the "Power of Congress over the District of Columbia."

There are among the abolitionists, Poets, and by the acknowledgment of their opponents, poets of no mean name too—who, as the use of poets is, do address themselves often—as John G. Whittier does *always*— powerfully to the imagination and feelings of their readers.

Our publications cannot be classed according to any particular style or quality of composition. They may be characterized generally, as well suited to affect the public mind—to rouse into healthful activity the conscience of this nation, stupified, torpid, almost dead, in relation to HUMAN RIGHTS, the high theme of which they treat!

It has often been alleged, that our writings appeal to the worst passions of the slaves, and that they are placed in their hands with a view to stir them to revolt. Neither charge has any foundation in truth to rest upon. The first finds no support in the tenor of the writings themselves; the last ought forever to be abandoned, in the absence of any single well authenti-cated instance of their having been conveyed by abolitionists to slaves, or of their having been even found in their possession. To instigate the slaves to revolt, as the means of obtaining their liberty, would prove a lack of wisdom and honesty that none would impute to abolitionists, except such as are unacquainted with their character. Revolt would be followed by the sure destruction, not only of all the slaves who might be concerned in it, but of multitudes of the innocent. Moreover, the abolitionists, as a class, are religious—they favor peace, and stand pledged in their constitution, before the country and heaven, to abide in peace, so far as a forcible vindication of the right of the slaves to their freedom is concerned. Further still, no small number of them deny the right of defence, either to individuals or nations, even when forcibly and wrongfully attacked. This disagreement among ourselves on this single point—of which our adversaries are by no means ignorant, as they often throw it reproachfully in our teeth—would forever prevent concert in any scheme that looked to instigating servile revolt. If there be, in all our ranks, one, who—personal danger out of the question—would excite the slaves to insurrection and massacre, or who would not be swift to reveal the earliest attempt to concoct such an iniquity—I say, on my obligations as a man, he is unknown to me.

Yet it ought not to be matter of surprise to abolitionists, that the South should consider them "fanatics," "incendiaries," "cut-throats," and call them so too. The South has had their character reported to them by the North, by those who are their neighbors, who, it was supposed, knew, and would speak the truth, and the truth only, concerning them. It would, I apprehend, be unavailing for abolitionists now to enter on any formal vindication of their character from charges that can be so easily repeated after every refutation. False and fraudulent as they know them to be, they must be content to live under them till the consummation of the work of Freedom shall prove to the master that they have been *his* friends, as well as the friends of the slave. The mischief of these charges has fallen on the South—the malice is to be placed to the credit of the North.

"12. *Do you propagate your doctrines by any other means than oral and written discussions—for instance, by prints and pictures in manu-*

factures—say of pocket-handkerchiefs, calicoes, &c? Pray, state the various modes?"

ANSWER.—Two or three years ago, an abolitionist of this city procured to be manufactured, at his own charge, a small lot of children's pocket-handkerchiefs, impressed with anti-slavery pictures and mottoes. I have no recollection of having seen any of them but once. None such, I believe, are now to be found, or I would send you a sample. If any manufactures of the kinds mentioned, or others similar to them, are in existence, they have been produced independently of the agency of this society. It is thought that none such exist, unless the following should be supposed to fall within the terms of the inquiry. Female abolitionists often unite in sewing societies. They meet together, usually once a week or fortnight, and labor through the afternoon, with their own hands, to furnish means for advancing the cause of the slave. One of the company reads passages from the Bible, or some religious book, whilst the others are engaged at their work. The articles they prepare, especially if they be of the "fancy" kind, are often ornamented with handsomely executed emblems, underwritten with appropriate mottoes. The picture of a slave kneeling (such as you will see impressed on one of the sheets of this letter) and supplicating in the words, "AM I NOT A MAN AND A BROTHER," is an example. The mottoes or sentences are, however, most generally selected from the Scriptures; either appealing to human sympathy in behalf of human suffering, or breathing forth God's tender compassion for the oppressed, or proclaiming, in thunder tones, his avenging justice on the oppressor. A few quotations will show their general character:—

"Blessed is he that considereth the poor."
"Defend the poor and fatherless; do justice to the afflicted and needy. Deliver the poor and the needy; rid him out of the hand of the wicked."
"Open thy mouth for the dumb, plead the cause of the poor and needy."
"Blessed are the merciful, for they shall obtain mercy."
"First, be reconciled to thy brother, and then come and offer thy gift."

"Thou shalt love thy neighbor as thyself."
"All things whatsoever ye would that men should do to you, do ye even so to them."

Again:—

"For he shall deliver the needy when he crieth; the poor also, and him that hath no helper."
"The Lord looseth the prisoners; the Lord raiseth them that are bowed down; the Lord preserveth the strangers."
"He hath sent me to heal the broken-hearted, to preach deliverance to the captives, to set at liberty them that are bruised."
"For the oppression of the poor, for the sighing of the needy, now will I arise, saith the Lord; I will set him in safety from him that puffeth at him."

Again:—

"The Lord executeth righteousness and judgment for all that are oppressed."
"Rob not the poor because he is poor, neither oppress the afflicted in the gate; for the Lord will plead their cause, and spoil the soul of those that spoiled them."
"And I will come near to you to judgment, and I will be a swift witness against those that oppress the hireling in his wages, the widow and the fatherless, and that turn aside the stranger from his right, and fear not me, saith the Lord of hosts."
"Wo unto him that buildeth his house by unrighteousness, and his chambers by wrong; that useth his neighbor's service without wages, and giveth him not for his work."

B: FROM *THE CRISIS*

The National Association for the Advancement of Colored People is the new abolition society. It has twenty branches, ranging from New York to Washington and from Boston to San Francisco and Tacoma. It has the machinery to fight discrimination, and everywhere it is making that fight—against segregation in Baltimore and other cities, against segregation in work in the United States government departments, against "grandfather" laws and "Jim Crow" laws before the Supreme Court of the United States. Its branches are holding meetings of protest, its officers and directors are volunteering as speakers.

Its chairman, in spite of the fact that he has been for twenty years a friend of Mr. Wilson, and has warmly supported the present administration, personally and through his paper has taken a most aggressive stand in denunciation of the undemocratic policy of segregation which is being inaugurated in Washington. He has interviewed members of the Cabinet and the President himself. He has addressed large meetings of protest in Baltimore and Washington and is now preparing an article for one of the leading magazines.

The association sent an investigator to visit the departments in Washington where segregation was said to be in force. This report was released to the Associated Press and to other news services on November 17, when it was also sent to 500 newspapers, fifty religious papers, to magazine editors, to members of Congress, to ministers and to many others. Copies may be obtained free of charge by applying to the National Association.

Cases affecting the colored people now before the Supreme Court of the United States may decide the legal and political status of the Negro for years to come. The National Association is the only organization appearing for the colored people in these cases. It has filed a brief in the "grandfather" case now before the Supreme Court. This was prepared by the president, Mr. Moorfield Storey, one of the leaders of the American bar, who, with Mr. Harrison of Oklahoma, will argue the "Jim Crow" case set for this term.

The association has just engaged a lawyer to assist the legal committee in its work. The association has also engaged a man to watch every bill introduced into the House and Senate in Washington. Discriminating bills have been appearing with increasing frequency, and without the careful watching of an expert may be railroaded through at any moment. The association is now preparing to fight the "Jim Crow" car bill which it is generally understood will be introduced in Congress in February. "Jim Crow" cars in Washington mean "Jim Crow" cars in Cleveland, Cincinnati, Indianapolis, St. Louis and perhaps even in New York and Boston.

If you want to protest, enroll with us as a new abolitionist in the National Association, and do it now.

BRANCHES.
BALTIMORE.

Only a mention of the remarkable mass meetings recently held in Baltimore and Washington was included in the last number of THE CRISIS, since it went to press before the meetings had taken place. The Bethel African Methodist Episcopal Church, where the Baltimore meeting was held, was crowded to the doors. Mr. Warner T. McGuinn presided. Resolutions were adopted and wired to the President. The speakers were Dr. Spingarn, Miss Ovington and Mr. Villard. After comparing the un-American policy of race segregation to the example set by Russia, Mr. Villard said in part: "But the stupidity of raising this issue does not stop there. It differs but very little from the one which rent the Union. The great struggle which convulsed the United States was, in its simplest terms, nothing else than the atempt of an aristocracy of cotton and land to create two classes of human beings in this country—the slaves and the free. They were willing to sacrifice the Union and everything else to this end. Those who in this day and generation are seeking to establish two classes of citizens—the disfranchised and enfranchised—to say that there shall be two kinds of government employees—as does Mr. McAdoo's Cabinet associate—they are on the high road to convulsing anew this land of liberty, which will never know peace and quiet as long as there are discriminations among its citizens. Upon their heads will be the responsibility of forcing the issue and not upon ours."

BOSTON

A large and enthusiastic audience attended the mass meeting of protest against segregation which was held in the Park Street Church on October 20. Mr. Storey presided. The speakers included Senator Moses E. Clapp, Mr. Albert E. Pillsbury, formerly attorney-general of the State, the Rev. Samuel H. Crothers, the Rev. Mr. Auten, Mr. Rolfe Cobleigh, assistant editor of the *Congregationalist*, and Mr. Butler R. Wilson, secretary of the branch. Letters were received from Governor Foss, Congressman A. P. Gardner and Mr. C. S. Bird. Governor Foss wrote: "I have undertaken, as a citizen and as governor, to bring this matter to the attention of the President, and have asked him to take such action as may bring an end to race discrimination in any department of government. It is proper for me to say, however, that I can hardly believe that at this late day any national administration will reopen the question of race discrimination in the United States. I therefore cannot believe that the reported acts of discrimination are a part of a settled policy, and cannot doubt that President Wilson will speedily put an end to conditions which, as reported to me, are unworthy of any free people.''

TACOMA.

On October 17 a mass meeting of protest against segregation was held at Everett by the Tacoma branch. Delegates from Seattle and Tacoma were present and delivered addresses. Judge Bell, of the Superior Court of Everett, presided. Other speakers were Father Saindon, through whose courtesy the lecture room of the Catholic church was placed at the disposal of the meeting; Capt. K. K. Beecham, a veteran of the Civil War and captain of a Negro regiment: and Mrs. Nettie J. Asberry, secretary of the Tacoma branch, who explained the aims and objects of the National Association. Resolutions read by Mr. Joseph Griffin, secretary of the meeting, were forwarded to the President in care of Congressman Falconer.

TOPEKA.

An entire evening devoted to the work of the National Association was arranged by the branch at the recent fair held at Lane Chapel. Mrs. Roundtree, secretary of the branch, spoke on the origin of the association; Mr. N. Sawyer, on its object; Mr. Guy, on the progress it had made, and the Rev. Mr. Walker, on the outlook. The branch plans to publish a series of short articles in the Topeka *Daily Capital.* These will be by white and colored writers of prominence, and will aim to explain and further the work of the association.

WASHINGTON.

Within five blocks of the White House, in the Metropolitan African Methodist Episcopal Church, on October 27, the most remarkable and epoch-making meeting ever held in the District of Columbia protested against the segregation of colored employees in government departments. The crowd has been variously estimated at from 8,000 to 10,000 people. The meeting was advertised for 8 o'clock, but shortly after half-past seven the detachment of police, detailed to keep order, directed that the doors of the church be closed. Some idea of the throng can be inferred from the fact that when Dr. Holmes, one of the speakers, arrived, and finally pushed his way through to the iron fence surrounding the church, it was necessary to lift him bodily over the fence, so that he might reach a side entrance leading to the auditorium. Because of the size of the crowd the speakers were obliged to deliver their addresses first to the meeting within the church and afterward to an overflow meeting of over 4,000 outside.

Mr. Archibald H. Grimke, president of the branch, presided. Judge Wendell Phillips Stafford and ex-Senator Blair spoke briefly. The principal addresses were made by Dr. Walter H. Brooks, of Washington, Dr. John Haynes Holmes, the noted Unitarian minister of New York, and Mr. Villard. Musical selections were artistically given by the Howard University choir. Dr. Holmes made a stirring and powerful address. He said, among other things, that segregation, instead of allaying race prejudice, was really the cause of all the friction, and characterized it as the "new crucifixion."

When Mr. Villard arose he received a veritable ovation. He prefaced his address by reading a letter which he had just received from Mr. McAdoo, Secretary of the Treasury, and his personal friend, requesting him not to speak, because in criticising Mr. Wilson's administration "he would be doing injustice to a just man." Mr. Villard said that he had been urged by those in high authority to use his influence to keep the colored people in "cool and just equipoise." "It is beyond me to influence them much in this direction," he said, "but I would not if I could. On the contrary, I shall lose no opportunity to preach the doctrine of peaceful rebellion and revolution against discrimination of every kind." His speech has been given wide publicity in the press and much favorable editorial comment. A writer in the Chicago *Tribune*, in speaking of it and of the present administration's "officializing of race prejudice," said: "It would be more inspiring to read Mr. Wilson's declaration that we must prove ourselves the Latin-American's friends and champions upon terms of equality and honor if we were not reminded at the same moment by Mr. Villard that Mr. Wilson is countenancing race discrimination in his own country."

A collection of about $300 was taken for the work of the National Association. After the meeting the executive committee of the branch appointed a committee of fifty to raise funds, and already $1,200 has been subscribed, to be paid not later than January 1. This committee has expressed itself as favoring an endowment for the association.

Other noteworthy meetings against segregation were held by the Northern California branch, by the colored people of New Haven, where Mr. George W. Crawford, one of the directors of the association, made an inspiring speech; and also in Portland, Me., where Dr. Mason addressed a large audience.

LEGAL.

On November 1 the association engaged an attorney, Mr. Chapin Brinsmade, to assist the legal committee in carrying on its work. Up to this time this committee, comprising some of the most eminent lawyers in this country, without compensation have handled all legal cases referred to the association. The work has developed so rapidly and has increased so in volume and importance that it has become necessary to have a lawyer at national headquarters who can devote his entire time to this important department under the direction of the legal committee.

Mr. Brinsmade graduated from Harvard College with the class of 1907. During his senior year, 1906-1907, he was absent from the University, teaching at the Gunnery School in Washington, Conn., of which his father, John C. Brinsmade, is head master. In the fall of 1907 he returned to Cambridge to enter the law school from which he was graduated in 1910. Since that time he has been practising law in New York City. He was admitted to the New York bar in 1911. During the years 1911 and 1912 he has been associated with the law firm of Van Wyck & Mygatt, and later with their successors, Wherry & Mygatt, at 40 Wall Street.

The chairman of the board of directors wishes to express in this way his appreciation of the support and good work of those branches which contributed $100 each to enable the association to employ an attorney, and of Bishop John Hurst, of Baltimore, who personally gave $100 for this purpose. The branches which so generously came to the aid of the association are Indianapolis, Washington, Baltimore, Quincy, Tacoma, Topeka and Detroit. Two of our largest branches, Boston and Chicago, which have always been most generous in their contributions to head-quarters, were not asked to contribute, nor were the branches which had just been admitted. Especially appreciated was the co-operation of Quincy and Tacoma, which at the time they made their contributions were our smallest branches, numbering not more than twenty members each.

MR. VILLARD:

After your speech last night I and many others are convinced that you must have a strain of Negro blood, or you would not have come here and made the remarks you did to incite the Negro to worse crimes than have been committed, and the most terrible ones they commit against white women. We cannot walk on the streets of this city now after nightfall, as many of us are compelled to do in coming from our work, without fear that we may be the next victim.

Take them to New York and let them associate with your wives and daughters.

A crime committed in the North, against a white woman by a Negro, receives only a few lines notice by your Northern papers, but let the same crime be committed in the *South*—the *New York* papers *especially* have a *half column*.

If your blood is *tainted*, as many here believe, you, of course, will be excused only on that believe.

A WASHINGTON WOMAN.

Washington, October 28, 1913.

Children of the Sun
By FENTON JOHNSON

I.

We are children of the sun,
Rising sun!
Weaving Southern destiny,
Waiting for the mighty hour
When our Shiloh shall appear
With the flaming sword of right,
With the steel of brotherhood,
And emboss in crimson die
Liberty! Fraternity!

II.

We are the star-dust folk,
Striving folk!
Sorrow songs have lulled to rest;
Seething passions wrought through wrongs,
Led us where the moon rays dip
In the night of dull despair,
Showed us where the star gleams shine,
And the mystic symbols glow—
Liberty! Fraternity!

III.

We have come through cloud and mist,
Mighty men!
Dusk has kissed our sleep-born eyes,
Reared for us a mystic throne
In the splendor of the skies.
That shall always be for us.
Children of the Nazarene.
Children who shall ever sing
Liberty! Fraternity!

THE ANNUAL CONFERENCE OF THE NATIONAL ASSOCIATION FOR THE ADVANCEMENT OF COLORED PEOPLE.

The sixth annual conference of the National Association will be held in Baltimore May 3, 4 and 5, with a post-conference meeting in Washington May 6, and a meeting with the National Conference of Charities and Correction in Memphis, Tenn., during the week of May 8.

The opening session of the Baltimore conference will be Sunday afternoon, May 3, and there will be afternoon and evening sessions Monday and Tuesday. All the sessions will be public, with the exception of the executive sessions Monday and Tuesday mornings, which will be open only to members.

Various aspects of the following subjects will be considered at the conference: Education, segregation, "Jim Crow" cars and the political rights of the Negro. Among the speakers are Mr. Charles J. Bonaparte, ex-Attorney-General of the United States, a grandson of a brother of Napoleon Bonaparte; Dr. Katherine Bement Davis, commissioner of correction of New York City; Senator Wesley L. Jones, of Washington, who led the fight for the Jones amendment to the Smith-Lever bill; Mrs. La Follette, wife of Senator LaFollette; Mr. Oswald Garrison Villard; Mrs. Coralie F. Cook; Bishop John Hurst; the Rev. R. W. Bagnall; Mr. Archibald H. Grimké and others.

The local committee of arrangements in Baltimore consists of Dr. Harvey Johnson, chairman; Dr. F. N. Cardoza, vice-chairman; Dr. G. R. Waller; Mr. W. T. McGuinn; Dr. H. S. McCard; Mr. C. L. Davis; Mr. John Murphy, Sr., and Miss Lucy D. Slowe, secretary. Additional members of the various committees are Prof. Mason A. Hawkins, Messrs. James Hughes and Harry O. Wilson and Mrs. Jennie Ross. They have already begun their work. Clippings just received at national head-quarters announce a concert to be given under the auspices of the committee at Albaugh's Theatre, March 19, to raise the funds necessary to meet the expenses of the conference. The branch has engaged the Williams colored singers for the occasion.

Baltimore is the furthest South that the National Association has yet called a conference. We urge every reader of THE CRISIS and every member of the association to help us by advertising the conference and by being present, if possible, in person to encourage us in our work.

PHILADELPHIA.

The Philadelphia branch, which has had a most creditable increase in its members, announces a meeting to be held in the Friends' Meeting House. Dr. Edgar F. Smith, provost of the University of Pennsylvania, is to be the chief speaker. Mr. Henry Wilbur, secretary of the Friends' general conference, will make the welcoming address, and there will be other noted people on the program.

PROVIDENCE.

The recently elected officers of the Providence branch are: Dr. J. J. Robinson, president; Mr. J. C. Minkins, first vice-president and chair-man of the executive board; Rev. C. C. Alleyne, second vice-president; Mr. Frederic Carter, third vice-president; Miss Roberta J. Dunbar, secretary; Rev. Zechariah Harrison, treasurer; executive board: Mr. James Dixon, Mr. William A. Heathman, Dr. A. L. Jackson, Mr. William P. H. Freeman, Mr. Robert L. Smith.

SEATTLE.

The officers of the branch recently formed in Seattle are as follows: Mrs. Letitia A. Graves, president; Mr. G. W. Jones, vice-president; Mrs. Zoe Graves Young, recording secretary; Mrs. W. L. Presto, corresponding secretary; Mr. G. O. Allen, treasurer; executive board: Mr. G. W. Thompson, Mr. Lee A. Hankins, Mr. B. F. Tutt, Mrs. S. D. Stone, Mr. A. R. Black, Mr. S. H. Stone.

TALLADEGA.

The Talladega branch announces the following officers elected at their last meeting: Prof. William Pickens, president; Mr. E. E. Lightner, secretary; Mr. Hampton Taylor, treasurer; executive committee: Dr. E. H. Jones, Dr. J. P. Barton, Dr. F. W. Terry, Rev. W. L. Boyd, Mr. V. A. Brockman, Rev. A. T. Clark.

TRENTON.

The officers of the Trenton branch are as follows: Rev. J. A. White, president; Mr. Nathan Hovington, Vice-president; Mr. T. Edward Kinney, secretary; Mr. J. Williams, treasurer; Rev. R. M. Johnson, chaplain; executive committee: Dr. Solomon Porter Hood, chairman; Rev. L. O. Jones, Prof. George W. Clark, Mr. Philip Logan, Mr. D. J. Graham, Dr. Howard Bundy, Rev. L. C. Hurdle, Mr. John Lewis, Mr. William H. Salters, Mr. John M. Herbert.

SEGREGATION.

That segregation among civil service is still with us is indicated by the bills introduced by Congressman Edwards, of Georgia, and Aswell, of Louisiana, which propose the segregation of the races in various government departments and throughout the civil service in the United States. At a hearing before the House committee on reform in the civil service, held on March 6, Mr. Edwards frankly said that if he could have his way he would eliminate the colored government employee.

Mr. Archibald H. Grimké, president of the District of Columbia branch, represented the National Association. Mr. Grimké predicted that the colored race would be a part of the governing class of this country within fifty years. He declared that the South had handled the Negro problem in the wrong way and that this eventually would become apparent. Mr. Grimké made a deep impression.

OUR LEGAL BUREAU
By CHAPIN BRINSMADE
Attorney-in-charge

If the National Association for the Advancement of Colored People is to obtain the best possible results from its legal work we should keep constantly in mind the ultimate object which we hope to accomplish by it. This object we conceive to be the building up of a body of judicial decisions which shall comprehensively state the law on the subject of civil and political rights; which shall mold that law, so far as possible, along lines which admit of no distinctions whatever on grounds of race or color; and which, in so far as they fail to do this, shall point out the direction which legislation calculated to supplement these decisions should take.

Viewing the matter in this light, it is apparent at once that the work becomes a national and not a local problem. Of course, each locality has its peculiar needs. Discrimination manifests itself differently in different places, so that one locality necessarily devotes particular attention to civil-rights cases, another to educational matters and still another to residential segregation. All, however, should look at these problems from the same point of view. All should regard them as different manifestations of the one evil which we are fighting, namely, race discrimination. That is the principle under which all these seemingly different problems can be harmonized.

If then we are to regard this matter as a national problem it is apparent that close co-operation between the various branches of the National Association for the Advancement of Colored People and between each branch and the national attorney is essential. The national attorney must know at all times what cases are being handled by the different branches. He is in a position to view the problem as a whole, to see in what respects the law of race discrimination is lagging behind and in what directions it is keeping abreast of the times. If having this viewpoint he has also the benefit of cordial co-operation with the branches, he can not only more successfully conduct his own work, but also can the better advise the branches with respect to their cases.

In an attempt to put the legal work upon this desirable basis, all the branches have been asked to send a statement describing (1) the organi-

zation and personnel of their legal-redress committees; (2) the arrangements, financial and otherwise, which they have made with attorneys,
and (3) the legal work which they have recently done, are now doing or
have in prospect. The procuring of this information, it is hoped, will
inaugurate a system of cordial and helpful co-operation which should get
results.

The following are some of the matters on which the attorney is now
engaged:

CIVIL RIGHTS.

New York has proved a difficult place to win civil-rights actions. Of
the six or seven cases recently reported, all but one were such that, for
one reason or another, we did not feel justified in pressing them. As to the
one good case, we are moving slowly. Our object is not to bring as many
cases as possible, but to win one or two decisively. It is hoped that in the
next issue of THE CRISIS we shall have something of importance to report
in this connection.

CONGRESS

Smith-Lever Bill—Whatever the final outcome of our fight for justice
in the distribution of funds for agricultural extension work, much will
have been accomplished. The name of the association was brought
prominently before the Senate and through it before the people of the
country as a champion of equality and justice. The attorney, during his
stay in Washington, saw a great number of Senators, and in personal
interviews brought clearly to their attention the work of the association.
A large part of his time was also spent in seeing newspaper men and
getting them to give space to our side of the question. But, best of all, the
fact that it was our association which caused the two days' debate in the
Senate and forced the acceptance by the South of the Shafroth amendment was made plain to the Senate. Senator Gallinger read on the floor of
the Senate a letter of protest from this association, commenting on the
fact that such people as Mr. Storey, Miss Addams and Mr. Villard were
members of our board, and Senator Works read a telegram from the
California branch of the National Association for the Advancement of

Colored People. Our part in the fight was made clear to the people of the country through newspaper comments which stated that the Jones amendment was instigated by this association.

The bill is now in conference, the House having declined to concur in the Senate amendments. The personnel of the conference committee is as follows: For the Senate: Smith, of Georgia; Smith, of South Carolina, and Brady, of Idaho. For the House: Lever, of South Carolina; Lee, of Georgia, and Haugen, of Iowa. All the Democrats are Southern Democrats. Moreover, Brady was one of the two Republicans who opposed the Jones amendment throughout. We have therefore only one friend on the conference committee. In spite of this fact, we hope for a favorable conference report on the Shafroth amendment. We believe that the chairman of the committee and the man who will probably control it, Hoke Smith, of Georgia, will prevent the rejection of the amendment, not from any fondness for it—far from it—but from a disinclination which seems to be shared by a number of other Southern Senators for a further debate on the race question in the Senate.

Should the conference committee reject the amendment our friends are prepared to make a fight against the report. Should this fight fail our protest will be promptly made to the President, urging him to veto the bill.

JUDGE TERRELL.

Apprised by newspaper reports of Senator Vardaman's announced intention to defeat Judge Terrell's confirmation, we promptly sent to Senator Clapp an open letter protesting against such action. The letter has received wide publicity and will serve to call the attention of the country to the fact that Southern Senators are openly making color a reason for declining to confirm an appointment of the President. Judge Terrell's record on the bench has been such that the South was unable to find any pretext for this opposition. It was forced to come out into the open and oppose him on account of his color. Senator Clapp has stated that he will do all in his power to get the Senate to act favorably on the nomination.

PRIVATE ANDERSON.

The association has achieved another notable success in the legal-aid work. Some months ago Private Samuel Anderson, of the mounted detachment of the 25th Infantry, a soldier who had served one enlistment blamelessly in the 9th Cavalry and had never had a serious charge against him in the 25th Infantry, was sentenced by a court martial in Honolulu to a period of five years' imprisonment on the charge of having burglariously entered the quarters of a white woman, wife of a soldier, with intent to do wrong. The testimony was largely circumstantial and the character of the chief witness against him was not what it had first appeared. Fortunately, Anderson found a warm champion in Capt. Charles F. Bates, of the 25th Infantry. Captain Bates laid the matter before the then chairman of the association, Mr. Oswald Garrison Villard, in September last, and Mr. Villard personally interviewed the judge-advocate-general of the army. Captain Bates brought the details of the case to New York in December, when he arrived on leave of absence, most of which he has devoted in the most self-sacrificing way to this case. In addition, in connection with Captain Bates, Mr. Villard submitted to the judge-advocate-general three opinions on the case obtained from John Chipman Gray, of the Harvard law school, Moorfield Storey, our national president, and ex-judge William G. Choate, of New York, all of which strongly upheld the view that the conviction was an improper one. The case was duly passed upon by the judge-advocate-general, the Assistant Secretary of War and the Secretary of War, and as a result of the association's work Samuel Anderson has been released from confinement and given his liberty. This does not undo the wrong done, but at least it saves him from four and a half years' imprisonment.

Document III-10: GRIMKE ON FEMALE EQUALITY

In many respects the woman's rights movement elaborates the understanding of reform provided by the documents dealing with anti-slavery and civil rights for black Americans. In other respects the woman's movement is so exceptional that many historians of American reform have been inclined to hide or dismiss the subject—not out of hostility, necessarily, but out of bewilderment. In a collection that is meant to illustrate the *patterns* of American reform, the subject is peculiarly resistant to analysis. It does not, literally, illustrate any pattern. Yet it is far too important to be overlooked. The documents that follow will not solve the problem of immersing the woman's movement into the main currents of American reform. They will serve to illustrate some things that are importantly representative, some that are importantly unique.

An initial barrier is the distinction between ''women in reform'' and ''reform for women.'' Even without documents III 10-15 this collection would still indicate—however incompletely—the central importance of American women in such causes as civil rights, education, the labor movement, communitarianism, various kinds of muckraking, and the broadening of the franchise. These contributions are so impressive that, could they be treated separately, they might invite the generalization that they outweigh in importance the efforts on behalf of woman's rights itself.

Such a comparison would be fallacious. In all reform activity, including the woman's rights movement, women and men have worked so closely together that it would be impossible separately to weigh their respective achievements. This fact is less true of the woman's rights movement than of most others; but, particularly in the middle years of the nineteenth century, the woman's movement would have been much slower to progress without the help of certain key male figures. Secondly, there has been an inevitable interrelationship between many of these special crusades and the rights movement itself. Women have earned public attention through their advocacy of Negro emancipation, international peace, temperance; they have then used this platform to speak out on behalf of the liberation of their sex. Further, even when successful women reformers have pled no special case for women, their very example has been used as a case in the feminist argument.

Then there is the troublesome fact that women, unlike other special groups aided by reform movements, are not a minority. There is some question—not altogether facetious—as to whether women have in the large sense been exploited or deprived of natural and logical rights and desires. The nearly dead conventions of chivalry and gentlemanly deportment once allowed women to pass first through doors, accept seats on crowded conveyances, and have their coats held for them. The diminution of these signs of deference is equated with woman's liberation only by some. More basic to the reform scene is a question like special legislation to insure women from economic victimization through low wages and long hours. For many years this kind of measure was sought by reformers of both genders; now it is held as discriminatory.

Other special groups have had at least as an alternative aim the process of integration into the dominant culture. If the future does fulfill the promise of human birth in the laboratory, and if human physiology is as adaptable as some students think, then women may at some point have the reasonable right to work toward full integration if they so choose. But throughout history this movement has been uniquely caught on the dilemma that, however far the cause of women might be advanced, it still represented a group that had apparently been definitively differentiated by nature. Thus equal treatment, logically speaking, meant at best only parallel treatment. Fulfillment meant the achievement of the best in womanhood, not in manhood. That these assumptions may be susceptible to attack is one of the truly revolutionary possibilities of the future.

Many observers think they have already seen a revolution in the changing place of women during the last decade. Surely the partisans of liberation have the stage. Not to claim this example as representative, but the daily paper resting at my elbow contains a long discussion of the role of women in voluntary reform movements, a description of women laborers engaged in local subway construction, and even a sports-page feature about a woman basketball coach at a male college (Washington *Post*, July 19, 1973, pp. Cl, 7; El, Fl, 5-6). The latest issue of *Esquire* (once considered a magazine for men) is devoted to a seriously intended discussion of woman's liberation. This week the CBS radio network is devoting short features throughout the broadcast day to special aspects of the woman question. What woman's partisans will do with this attention remains to be seen. The liberated woman of the 1970s still resembles the "new woman," as she was called at the turn of the century, in many ways. Both were informed and aggressive. Both were willing to abandon the deference sometimes paid "ladies" in return for the freedom of being less circumscribed as women. Today's woman is willing to risk receiving even less in terms of special treatment in order to gain even more in terms of responsibility and its rewards.

Enfranchisement, to many women today, has become a disappointment. The sense of nobility and high morality that was to have come with the woman's vote has not appeared. It is true that the vote has not meant proportionate representation in elective office; but those women who have attained political prominence have not comported themselves in a manner that is dramatically better or worse than men. Because of unsolved problems in both nature and society, women in America—

educated better than any large group of women anywhere in history—represent the most grievously untapped source of labor supply at all levels. To generalize beyond these statements is only to invite controversy, albeit this task is performed exceptionally well by the author of the final document in this section (III-15).

To the student of reform, the most important aspect of the woman's movement is its omnipresence. Even when the climate for reform is most unfavorable—as will be suggested below—the cause of woman's rights is always visible. It has functioned, along with the temperance movement, as a kind of stabilizing force. It provides a continuum when all else fails. It gathers together the men and women of goodwill and keeps open the lines of humanitarian communication until the next crisis of opportunity presents itself. It may be useful—as Claire Nader first suggested to me and as others have stated in print—to consider the cause of women as the unfinished business of American reform. It is true that women not only use other causes to rise to visibility but that they are distracted from the cause of women by these very same issues. Thus only when the slave is freed, the amendment adopted, or the depression passed, do the advocates of woman's rights return to the fold. Thus, the movement acts as reservoir where is stored the personnel, the apparatus, the memories, the connections that were useful before and will be useful again not only for women but in other interests as well.

To study this movement is most rewarding; it is fraught, however, with perils at either extreme. On one hand there is more trivial, reactionary, small-minded, predictable superficiality wasted on the woman's movement than on any other; at the other extreme is the distraction of profundity. To know what one should about the woman question is to know the most important facts and the latest revelations about physiology, neurology, psychology, anthropology, history, and philosophy. In pursuing this curriculum one will learn a great deal that is important, albeit relatively little about American reform; for to study womankind is to raise all the basic questions about the meaning and experience of human existence.

The woman's movement got an early start in America. Several of its historians and compilers have gathered evidence of individual assertions and even of temporary group activity on the part of colonial and revolutionary women. (See the early chapters of: Elizabeth Cady Stanton, *et al.*, *History of Woman Suffrage*, vol. I. New York, Fowler &

Wells, 1881. Eleanor Flexner, *Century of Struggle*, 2nd edition. New York, Atheneum, 1973; Inez H. Irwin, *Angels and Amazons*. New York, Doubleday, Doran, 1933.) One thing required to forge these scattered people and episodes together was a unifying document that would state the discontents and objectives in ways that a large number of action-minded women could accept. Such a document has usually been taken to be Margaret Fuller's justly famous *Woman in the Nineteenth Century*, originally published as an article in *Dial* (July, 1843) and expanded into book form and separately published in New York, 1845. According to Flexner the earlier work of Sarah Grimké was widely taken in England as the first important work on woman's rights by an American and deserves much of the esteem usually accorded Fuller's work.

Sarah Grimké's work, a collection of letters, each signed "in the bonds of womanhood," helps make several points about the movement. By the late 1830s, it already had some focal issues and personages. It was from the beginning closely connected to other reform crusades as typified by the Grimké sisters' centrality in both the anti-slavery movement and to the cause of female emancipation. Indeed, they precipitated a storm over the priorities involved in these two movements only partly settled at the altar. The first woman to make a formal presentation before a legislative body was Sarah's sister, Angelina Grimké; the occasion was, fittingly, the Massachusetts state legislature's discussion of anti-slavery petitions in February, 1838. (See Flexner, p. 49; *Weld-Grimké Letters* II, 564.)

The woman's crusade changed its emphasis with the times; or, to put it another way, the movement consistently reflected the values and priorities of the day. In the substance and rhetoric of antebellum reform, morality and religion were preeminent. It was an era of evangelical conversion, of zionism in the wilderness, of the kind of perfection attainable through Christ's second coming or through spiritualistic contacts. Just as slavery had to be argued on Biblical grounds, so the woman's movement would never get started unless Eve could to some extent be relieved of blame for her contribution toward the fall from Eden and unless Saint Paul's strictures against womankind could in some way be mitigated.

Thus Sarah Grimké opens on a moral note and devotes most of her letter to these Biblical and generally Christian questions. Before she is through, as the second excerpt will show, she has not only saved women from a Biblical put-down, but has made some very wide-ranging statements about fundamental rights and some very subtle distinctions between rights and deference.

SOURCE: Sarah M. Grimké, *Letters on the Equality of the Sexes and the Condition of Woman addressed to Mary S. Parker, President of the Boston Female Anti-Slavery Society.* Boston, Knapp, 1838, pp. 3-8; 121-128.

THE ORIGINAL EQUALITY OF WOMAN.

Amesbury, 7th Mo. 11th, 1837.

MY DEAR FRIEND,—In attempting to comply with thy request to give my views on the Province of Woman, I feel that I am venturing on nearly untrodden ground, and that I shall advance arguments in opposition to a corrupt public opinion, and to the perverted interpretation of Holy Writ, which has so universally obtained. But I am in search of truth; and no obstacle shall prevent my prosecuting that search, because I believe the welfare of the world will be materially advanced by every new discovery we make of the designs of Jehovah in the creation of woman. It is impossible that we can answer the purpose of our being, unless we understand that purpose. It is impossible that we should fulfil our duties, unless we comprehend them; or live up to our privileges, unless we know what they are. In examining this important subject, I shall depend solely on the Bible to designate the sphere of woman, because I believe almost every thing that has been written on this subject, has been the result of a misconception of the simple truths revealed in the Scriptures, in consequence of the false translation of many passages of Holy Writ. My mind is entirely delivered from the superstitious reverence which is attached to the English version of the Bible. King James's translators certainly were not inspired. I therefore claim the original as my standard, *believing that to have been inspired,* and I also claim to judge for myself what is the meaning of the inspired writers, because I believe it to be the solemn duty of every individual to search the Scriptures for themselves, with the aid of the Holy Spirit, and not be governed by the views of any man, or set of men.

We must first view woman at the period of her creation. 'And God said, Let us make man in our own image, after our likeness; and let them have dominion over the fish of the sea, and over the fowl of the air, and over the cattle, and over all the earth, and over every creeping thing that creepeth upon the earth. So God created man in his own image, in the image of God created he him, male and female created he them.' In all this sublime description of the creation of man, (which is a generic term including man and woman,) there is not one particle of difference intimated as existing between them. They were both made in the image of God; dominion was given to both over every other creature, but not over each other. Created in perfect equality, they were expected to exercise the vicegerence intrusted to them by their Maker, in harmony and love.

Let us pass on now to the recapitulation of the creation of man:—'The Lord God formed man of the dust of the ground, and breathed into his nostrils the breath of life; and man became a living soul. And the Lord God said, it is not good that man should be alone, I will make him an help meet for him.' All creation swarmed with animated beings capable of natural affection, as we know they still are; it was not, therefore, merely to give man a creature susceptible of loving, obeying, and looking up to him, for all that the animals could do and did do. It was to give him a companion, *in all respects* his equal; one who was like himself *a free agent*, gifted with intellect and endowed with immortality; not a partaker merely of his animal gratifications, but able to enter into all his feelings as a moral and responsible being. If this had not been the case, how could she have been an help meet for him? I understand this as applying not only to the parties entering into the marriage contract, but to all men and women, because I believe God designed woman to be an help meet for man in every good and perfect work. She was a part of himself, as if Jehovah designed to make the oneness and identity of man and woman perfect and complete; and when the glorious work of their creation was finished, 'the morning stars sang together, and all the sons of God shouted for joy.'

This blissful condition was not long enjoyed by our first parents. Eve, it would seem from the history, was wandering alone amid the bowers of Paradise, when the serpent met with her. From her reply to Satan, it is evident that the command not to eat 'of the tree that is in the midst of the garden,' was given to both, although the term man was used when the prohibition was issued by God. 'And the woman said unto the serpent, we may eat of the fruit of the trees of the garden, but of the fruit of the tree which is in the midst of the garden, God hath said, YE shall not eat of it, neither shall YE touch it, lest YE die.' Here the woman was exposed to temptation from a being with whom she was unacquainted. She had been accustomed to associate with her beloved partner, and to hold communion with God and with angels; but of satanic intelligence, she was in all probability entirely ignorant. Through the subtelty of the serpent, she was beguiled. And 'when she saw that the tree was good for food, and that it was pleasant to the eyes, and a tree to be desired to make one wise, she took of the fruit thereof and did eat.'

We next find Adam involved in the same sin, not through the instrumentality of a supernatural agent, but through that of his equal, a being whom he must have known was liable to transgress the divine command, because he must have felt that he was himself a free agent, and that he was restrained from disobedience only by the exercise of faith and love towards his Creator. Had Adam tenderly reproved his wife, and endeavored to lead her to repentance instead of sharing in her guilt, I should be much more ready to accord to man that superiority which he claims; but as the facts stand disclosed by the sacred historian, it appears to me that to say the least, there was as much weakness exhibited by Adam as by Eve. They both fell from innocence, and consequently from happiness, *but not from equality.*

Let us next examine the conduct of this fallen pair, when Jehovah interrogated them respecting their fault. They both frankly confessed their guilt. 'The man said, the woman whom thou gavest to be with me, she gave me of the tree and I did eat. And the woman said, the serpent beguiled me and I did eat.' And the Lord God said unto the woman, 'Thou wilt be subject unto thy husband, and he will rule over thee.' That this did not allude to the subjection of woman to man is manifest, because the same mode of expression is used in speaking to Cain of Abel. The truth is that the curse, as it is termed, which was pronounced by Jehovah upon woman, is a simple prophecy. The Hebrew, like the French language, uses the same word to express shall and will. Our translators having been accustomed to exercise lordship over their wives, and seeing only through the medium of a perverted judgment, very naturally, though I think not very learnedly or very kindly, translated it *shall* instead of *will*, and thus converted a prediction to Eve into a command to Adam; for observe, it is addressed to the woman and not to the man. The consequence of the fall was an immediate struggle for dominion, and Jehovah foretold which would gain the ascendency; but as he created them in his image, as that image manifestly was not lost by the fall, because it is urged in Gen. 9:6, as an argument why the life of man should not be taken by his fellow man, there is no reason to suppose that sin produced any distinction between them as moral, intellectual and responsible beings. Man might just as well have endeavored by hard labor to fulfil the prophecy, thorns and thistles will the earth bring forth to thee, as to pretend to accomplish the other, 'he will rule over thee,' by asserting dominion over his wife.

> 'Authority usurped from God, not given.
> He gave him only over beast, flesh, fowl,
> Dominion absolute: that right he holds
> By God's donation: but man o'er woman
> He made not Lord, such title to himself
> Reserving, human left from human free.'

Here then I plant myself. God created us equal;—he created us free agents;—he is our Lawgiver, our King and our Judge, and to him alone is woman bound to be in subjection, and to him alone is she accountable for the use of those talents with which her Heavenly Father has entrusted her. One is her Master even Christ.

Thine for the oppressed in the bonds of womanhood,
—*Sarah M. Grimké.*

DUTIES OF WOMEN.

One of the duties which devolve upon women in the present interesting crisis, is to prepare themselves for more extensive usefulness, by making use of those religious and literary privileges and advantages that are within their reach, if they will only stretch out their hands and possess them. By doing this, they will become better acquainted with their rights as moral beings, and with their responsibilities growing out of those rights: they will regard themselves, as they really are, FREE AGENTS, immortal beings, amenable to no tribunal but that of Jehovah, and bound not to submit to any restriction imposed for selfish purposes, or to gratify that love of power which has reigned in the heart of man from Adam down to the present time. In contemplating the great moral reformations of the day, and the part which they are bound to take in them, instead of puzzling themselves with the harassing, because unnecessary inquiry, how far they may go without overstepping the bounds of propriety, which separate male and female duties, they will only inquire, 'Lord, what wilt thou have us to do?' They will be enabled to see the simple truth, that God has made no distinction between men and women as moral beings; that the distinction now so much insisted upon between male and female virtues is as absurd as it is unscriptural, and has been the fruitful source of much mischief—granting to man a license for the exhibition of brute force and conflict on the battle field; for sternness, selfishness, and the exercise of irresponsible power in the circle of home—and to woman a permit to rest on an arm of flesh, and to regard modesty and delicacy, and all the kindred virtues, as peculiarly appropriate to her. Now to me it is perfectly clear, that WHATSOEVER IT IS MORALLY RIGHT FOR A MAN TO DO, IT IS MORALLY RIGHT FOR A WOMAN TO DO; and that confusion must exist in the moral world, until woman takes her stand on the same platform with man, and feels that she is clothed by her Maker with the *same rights*, and, of course, that upon her devolve the *same duties*.

It is not my intention, nor indeed do I think it is in my power, to point out the precise duties of women. To him who still teacheth by his Holy Spirit as never man taught, I refer my beloved sisters. There is a vast field of usefulness before them. The signs of the times give portentous evidence, that a day of deep trial is approaching; and I urge them, by every consideration of a Savior's dying love, by the millions of heathen in our midst, by the sufferings of woman in almost every portion of the world, by the fearful ravages which slavery, intemperance, licentiousness and other iniquities are making of the happiness of our fellow creatures, to come to the rescue of a ruined world, and to be found co-workers with Jesus Christ.

> 'Ho! to the rescue, ho!
>   Up every one that feels—
> 'Tis a sad and fearful cry of woe
>   From a guilty world that steals.
> Hark! hark! how the horror rolls,
>   Whence can this anguish be?
> 'Tis the groan of a trammel'd people's souls,
>   *Now bursting* to be free.'

And here, with all due deference for the office of the ministry, which I believe was established by Jehovah himself, and designed by Him to be the means of spreading light and salvation through a crucified Savior to the ends of the earth, I would entreat my sisters not to *compel* the ministers of the present day to give their names to great moral reformations. The practice of making ministers life members, or officers of societies, when their hearts have not been touched with a live coal from the altar, and animated with love for the work we are engaged in, is highly injurious to them, as well as to the cause. They often satisfy their consciences in this way, without doing anything to promote the anti-slavery, or temperance, or other reformations; and we please ourselves with the idea, that we have done something to forward the cause of Christ, when, in effect, we have been sewing pillows like the false prophetesses of old under the arm-holes of our clerical brethren. Let us treat the ministers with all tenderness and respect, but let us be careful how we cherish in their hearts the idea that they are of more importance to a cause than other men. I rejoice when they take hold heartily. I love and honor some ministers with whom I have been associated in the anti-slavery ranks, but I do deeply deplore, for the sake of the cause, the prevalent notion, that the clergy must be had, either by persuasion or by bribery. They will not need persuasion or bribery, if their hearts are with us; if they are not, we are better without them. It is idle to suppose that the kingdom of heaven cannot come on earth, without their co-operation. It is the Lord's work, and it must go forward with or without their aid. As well might the converted Jews have despaired of the spread of Christianity, without the co-operation of Scribes and Pharisees.

Let us keep in mind, that no abolitionism is of any value, which is not accompanied with deep, heartfelt repentance; and that, whenever a minister sincerely repents of having, either by his apathy or his efforts, countenanced the fearful sin of slavery, he will need no inducement to come into our ranks; so far from it, he will abhor himself in dust and ashes, for his past blindness and indifference to the cause of God's poor and oppressed: and he will regard it as a privilege to be enabled to do something in the cause of human rights. I know the ministry exercise vast power; but I rejoice in the belief, that the spell is broken which encircled them, and rendered it all but blasphemy to expose their errors and their sins. We are beginning to understand that they are but men, and that their station should not shield them from merited reproof.

I have blushed for my sex when I have heard of their entreating ministers to attend their associations, and open them with prayer. The idea is inconceivable to me, that Christian women can be engaged in doing God's work, and yet cannot ask his blessing on their efforts, except through the lips of a man. I have known a whole town scoured to obtain a minister to open a female meeting, and their refusal to do so spoken of as quite a misfortune. Now, I am not glad that the ministers do wrong; but I am glad that my sisters have been sometimes compelled to act for themselves: it is exactly what they need to strengthen them, and prepare them to act independently. And to say the truth, there is something really ludicrous in seeing a minister enter the meeting, open it with prayer, and then take his departure. However, I only throw out these hints for the consideration of women. I believe there are solemn responsibilities resting upon us, and that in this day of light and knowledge, we cannot plead ignorance of duty. The great moral reformations now on the wheel are only practical Christianity; and if the ministry is not prepared to labor with us in these righteous causes, let us press forward, and they will follow on to know the Lord.

CONCLUSION.

I have now, my dear sister, completed my series of letters. I am aware, they contain some new views; but I believe they are based on the immutable truths of the Bible. All I ask for them is, the candid and prayerful consideration of Christians. If they strike at some of our bosom sins, our deep-rooted prejudices, our long cherished opinions, let us not condemn them on that account, but investigate them fearlessly and prayerfully, and not shrink from the examination; because, if they are true, they place heavy responsibilities upon women. In throwing them before the public, I have been actuated solely by the belief, that if they are acted upon, they will exalt the character and enlarge the usefulness of my own sex, and contribute greatly to the happiness and virtue of the other. That there is a root of bitterness continually springing up in families and troubling the repose of both men and women, must be manifest to even a superficial observer; and I believe it is the mistaken notion of the inequality of the sexes. As there is an assumption of superiority on the one part, which is not sanctioned by Jehovah, there is an incessant struggle on the other to rise to that degree of dignity, which God designed women to possess in common with men, and to maintain those rights and exercise those privileges which every woman's common sense, apart from the prejudices of education, tells her are inalienable; they are a part of her moral nature, and can only cease when her immortal mind is extinguished.

One word more. I feel that I am calling upon my sex to sacrifice what has been, what is still dear to their hearts, the adulation, the flattery, the attentions of trifling men. I am asking them to repel these insidious enemies whenever they approach them; to manifest by their conduct, that, although they value highly the society of pious and intelligent men, they have no taste for idle conversation, and for that silly preference which is manifested for their personal accommodation, often at the expense of great inconvenience to their male companions. As an illustration of what I mean, I will state a fact.

I was traveling lately in a stage coach. A gentleman, who was also a passenger, was made sick by riding with his back to the horses. I offered to exchange seats, assuring him it did not affect me at all unpleasantly; but he was too polite to permit a lady to run the risk of being discommoded. I am sure he meant to be very civil, but I really thought it was a foolish piece of civility. This kind of attention encourages selfishness in woman, and is only accorded as a sort of quietus, in exchange for those *rights* of which we are deprived. Men and women are equally bound to cultivate a spirit of accommodation; but I exceedingly deprecate her being treated like a spoiled child, and sacrifices made to her selfishness and vanity. In lieu of these flattering but injurious attentions, yielded to her as an inferior, as a mark of benevolence and courtesy, I want my sex to claim nothing from their brethren but what their brethren may justly claim from them, in their intercourse as Christians. I am persuaded woman can do much in this way to elevate her own character. And that we may become duly sensible of the dignity of our nature, only a little lower than the angels, and bring forth fruit to the glory and honor of Emanuel's name, is the fervent prayer of

Thine in the bonds of womanhood,

—Sarah M. Grimké.

Document III-11: WOMAN'S RIGHTS IN CONVENTION

By the end of the 1840s American women had identified a number of figures and documents around which to rally both their own movement and their contributions to anti-slavery and other crusades. But they lacked a central organization. The first step was taken in 1833 when a group of women assembled after the founding of the American Anti-Slavery Society to form the Philadelphia Female Anti-Slavery Society. Four years later in New York the first national association was convened through the attendance of delegates from twelve states.

The landmark gathering, however, was reserved till 1848 when five women called together a meeting in Seneca Falls, New York, "to discuss the social, civil and religious rights of women." The summoners were Elizabeth Cady Stanton, who had just moved to Seneca Falls; Lucretia Mott, whose husband presided; Jane Hunt, Martha Wright, and Mary Ann McClintock. A move to petition immediately for the ballot was stopped short, but the assembly did produce a statement of grievances and a loose plan of action.

The device of parodying the Declaration was employed here for neither the first nor the last time (See II-17). It is an appealing way to present oneself as the long-suffering victim of outrage and to claim association with the revered revolutionaries of 1776. Implied in the shape of this Enlightenment document is the idea that social justice is available through the application of reason and logic to a community in which all beings are at least potentially equal. Particularly from a feminist point of view, generalized "man" equates well with the distant and arbitrary King George III. The metaphor of slavery was the most common in woman's rights literature as "emancipation" was sought; this document shows the alternative imagery of depicting women as a colonized group, unrepresented in the councils of the governors, and justifiably seeking liberty. The means set forth in the closing paragraph astutely substitute the tactics of agitation for the threat of revolution.

SOURCE: "Declaration of Sentiments," Elizabeth Cady Stanton, *et al., History of Woman Suffrage.* New York, Fowler & Wells, 1881, vol. I, pp. 70-71.

"DECLARATION OF SENTIMENTS"

When, in the course of human events, it becomes necessary for one portion of the family of man to assume among the people of the earth a position different from that which they have hitherto occupied, but one to which the laws of nature and of nature's God entitle them, a decent respect to the opinions of mankind requires that they should declare the causes that impel them to such a course.

We hold these truths to be self-evident: that all men and women are created equal: that they are endowed by their Creator with certain inalienable rights; that among these are life, liberty, and the pursuit of happiness; that to secure these rights governments are instituted, deriving their just powers from the consent of the governed. Whenever any form of government becomes destructive of these ends, it is the right of those who suffer from it to refuse allegiance to it, and to insist upon the institution of a new government, laying its foundation on such principles, and organizing its powers in such form, as to them shall seem most likely to effect their safety and happiness. Prudence indeed, will dictate that governments long established should not be changed for light and transient causes: and accordingly all experience hath shown that mankind are more disposed to suffer, while evils are sufferable, than to right themselves by abolishing the forms to which they were accustomed. But when a long train of abuses and usurpations, pursuing invariably the same object evinces a design to reduce them under absolute depotism, it is their duty to throw off such government, and to provide new guards for their future security. Such has been the patient sufferance of the women under this government, and such is now the necessity which constrains them to demand the equal station to which they are entitled.

The history of mankind is a history of repeated injuries and usurpations on the part of man toward woman, having in direct object the establishment of an absolute tyranny over her. To prove this, let facts be submitted to a candid world.

He has never permitted her to exercise her inalienable right to the elective franchise.

He has compelled her to submit to laws, in the formation of which she had no voice.

He has withheld from her rights which are given to the most ignorant and degraded men—both natives and foreigners.

Having deprived her of this first right of a citizen, the elective franchise, thereby leaving her without representation in the halls of legislation, He has oppressed her on all sides.

He has made her, if married, in the eye of the law, civilly dead.

He has taken from her all right in property, even to the wages she earns.

He has made her, morally, an irresponsible being, as she can commit many crimes with impunity, provided they be done in the presence of her husband. In the covenant of marriage, she is compelled to promise obedience to her husband, he becoming, to all intents and purposes, her master—the law giving him power to deprive her of her liberty, and to administer chatisement.

He has so framed the laws of divorce, as to what shall be the proper causes, and in case of separation, to whom the guardianship of the children shall be given, as to be wholly regardless of the happiness of women—the law, in all cases, going upon a false supposition of the supremacy of man, and giving all power into his hands.

After depriving her of all rights as a married woman, if single, and the owner of property, he has taxed her to support a government which recognizes her only when her property can be made profitable to it.

He has monopolized nearly all the profitable employments, and from those she is permitted to follow, she receives but a scanty remuneration. He closes against her all the avenues to wealth and distinction which he considers most honorable to himself. As a teacher of theology, medicine, or law, she is not known.

He has denied her the facilities for obtaining a thorough education, all colleges being closed against her.

He allows her in Church, as well as State, but a subordinate position, claiming Apostolic authority for her exclusion from the ministry, and, with some exceptions, from any public participation in the affairs of the Church.

He has created a false public sentiment by giving to the world a different code of morals for men and women, by which moral delinquencies which exclude women from society, are not only tolerated, but deemed of little account in man.

He has usurped the prerogative of Jehovah himself, claiming it as his right to assign for her a sphere of action, when that belongs to her conscience and to her God.

He has endeavored, in every way that he could, to destroy her confidence in her own powers, to lessen her self-respect, and to make her willing to lead a dependent and abject life.

Now, in view of this entire disfranchisement of one-half the people of this country, their social and religious degradation—in view of the unjust laws above mentioned, and because women do feel themselves aggrieved, oppressed, and fraudulently deprived of their most sacred rights, we insist that they have immediate admission to all the rights and privileges which belong to them as citizens of the United States.

In entering upon the great work before us, we anticipate no small amount of misconception, misrepresentation, and ridicule; but we shall use every instrumentality within our power to effect our object. We shall employ agents, circulate tracts, petition the State and National legislatures, and endeavor to enlist the pulpit and the press in our behalf. We hope this Convention will be followed by a series of Conventions embracing every part of the country.

Document III-12: TRUTH IN CONVENTION

In the months after Mrs. Stanton's proposal was quashed at Seneca Falls, suffrage sympathy grew among the women's rights leaders to the extent that a special convention was called for Akron, Ohio, on May 28-29, 1851. Frances D. Gage was elected president; and the extract that follows relies heavily on her reminiscences.

In setting the stage for those recollections, the editors paused to comment on the role of men at these conventions—a comment that will be explored below—making particular reference to the unsympathetic attitude of the clergy. This judgment must be qualified, however, by the abundant evidence of ministerial participation in reform in general and of the sympathy of men of the cloth to woman's emancipation in particular. The idea of the moral superiority of women may have been a myth useful to men; but it did at least relate to the fact that the church was one institution in which women have participated rather fully in the United States. This seems to have been especially true of the Society of Friends and of other denominations whence emanated much of the momentum for social reform. Not only history but common sense would dictate that the ministry of these churches support the organizational impulse of their female parishioners.

The famous speech of Sojourner Truth echoes the continuing preoccupation with moral and Biblical arguments. It leaps ahead of its day in its graphic readiness to confront sexual distinction on a physical basis, and it recaptures the intense drama that made some of these gatherings so memorable as impromptu theater. Sojourner Truth's role also introduces the question of black women in a movement originally sparked by whites. Although Frederick Douglass was a frequent participant and was invariably invited at least to speak and occasionally to preside, black women were featured much more sparingly. Eleanor Flexner reproduced the account of a female anti-slavery meeting in Boston in 1835 attended by both black and white women. Threatened by mob violence, "each white lady present took a colored 'sister' by the hand, and two by two, they walked calmly down the stairs and out the building '. . . their eyes busily identifying the genteel leaders of the mob.' " (See Flexner, *Century of Struggle*, p. 43.) The episode in 1851 startlingly reversed that role.

The relationship between woman's liberation and civil rights today is no less complex. The woman's movement leadership is still predominantly white. Black women participate to some extent and often concur in principle. Yet, according to the testimony of some of the leadership, black women fear going too far with feminism lest they be dissociated from racial crusades which are, in the final analysis, more vital to them. The legacy of Sojourner Truth is multifold, however, and little of it is lost. The local newspaper this week featured photographs of three strapping women, two of them black, performing heavy labor in the construction of Washington D. C.'s subway (Washington *Post*, July 19, 1973, p. C1).

SOURCE: Stanton, *History*, vol. I, pp. 114-117.

THE AKRON CONVENTION

This Convention was remarkable for the large number of men who took an active part in the proceedings. And as we have now an opportunity to express our gratitude by handing their names down to posterity, and thus make them immortal, we here record Joseph Barker, Marius Robinson, Rev. D. L. Webster, Jacob Heaton, Dr. K. G. Thomas, L. A. Hine, Dr. A. Brooke, Rev. Mr. Howels, Rev. Geo. Schlosser, Mr. Pease, and Samuel Brooke. The reports of this Convention are so meagre that we can not tell who were in the opposition; but from Sojourner Truth's speech, we fear that the clergy, as usual, were averse to enlarging the boundaries of freedom.

In those early days the sons of Adam crowded our platform, and often made it the scene of varied pugilistic efforts, but of late years we invite those whose presence we desire. Finding it equally difficult to secure the services of those we deem worthy to advocate our cause, and to repress those whose best service would be silence, we ofttimes find ourselves quite deserted by the "stronger sex" when most needed.

Sojourner Truth, Mrs. Stowe's "Lybian Sibyl," was present at this Convention. Some of our younger readers may not know that Sojourner Truth was once a slave in the State of New York, and carried to-day as many marks of the diabolism of slavery, as ever scarred the back of a victim in Mississippi. Though she can neither read nor write, she is a woman of rare intelligence and common-sense on all subjects. She is still living, at Battle Creek, Michigan, though now 110 years old. Although the exalted character and personal appearance of this noble woman have been often portrayed, and her brave deeds and words many times rehearsed, yet we give the following graphic picture of Sojourner's appearance in one of the most stormy sessions of the Convention, from:

Reminiscences By Frances D. Gage

SOJOURNER TRUTH

The leaders of the movement trembled on seeing a tall, gaunt black woman in a gray dress and white turban, surmounted with an uncouth sun-bonnet, march deliberately into the church, walk with the air of a queen up the aisle, and take her seat upon the pulpit steps. A buzz of disapprobation was heard all over the house, and there fell on the listening ear, "An abolition affair!" "Woman's rights and niggers!" "I told you so!" "Go it, darkey!"

I chanced on that occasion to wear my first laurels in public life as president of the meeting. At my request order was restored, and the business of the Convention went on. Morning, afternoon, and evening exercises came and went. Through all these sessions old Sojourner, quiet and reticent as the "Lybian Statue," sat crouched against the wall on the corner of the pulpit stairs, her sun-bonnet shading her eyes, her elbows on her knees, her chin resting upon her broad, hard palms. At intermission she was busy selling the "Life of Sojourner Truth," a narrative of her own strange and adventurous life. Again and again, timorous and trembling ones came to me and said, with earnestness, "Don't let her speak, Mrs. Gage, it will ruin us. Every newspaper in the land will have our cause mixed up with abolition and niggers, and we shall be utterly denounced." My only answer was, "We shall see when the time comes."

The second day the work waxed warm. Methodist, Baptist, Episcopal, Presbyterian, and Universalist ministers came in to hear and discuss the resolutions presented. One claimed superior rights and privileges for man, on the ground of "superior intellect"; another, because of the "manhood of Christ; if God had desired the equality of woman, He would have given some token of His will through the birth, life, and death of the Saviour." Another gave us a theological view of the "sin of our firstmother."

There were very few women in those days who dared to "speak in meeting"; and the august teachers of the people were seemingly getting the better of us, while the boys in the galleries, and the sneerers among the pews, were hugely enjoying the discomfiture, as they supposed, of the "strong-minded." Some of the tender-skinned friends were on the point of losing dignity, and the atmosphere betokened a storm. When, slowly from her seat in the corner rose Sojourner Truth, who, till now, had scarcely lifted her head. "Don't let her speak!" gasped half a dozen in my ear. She moved slowly and solemnly to the front, laid her old bonnet at her feet, and turned her great speaking eyes to me. There was a hissing sound of disapprobation above and below. I rose and announced "Sojourner Truth," and begged the audience to keep silence for a few moments.

The tumult subsided at once, and every eye was fixed on this almost Amazon form, which stood nearly six feet high, head erect, and eyes piercing the upper air like one in a dream. At her first word there was a profound hush. She spoke in deep tones, which, though not loud, reached every ear in the house, and away through the throng at the doors and windows.

"Wall, chilern, whar dar is so much racket dar must be somethin' out o' kilter. I tink dat 'twixt de niggers of de Souf and de womin at de Norf, all talkin' 'bout rights, de white men will be in a fix pretty soon. But what's all dis here talkin' 'bout?

"Dat man ober dar say dat womin needs to be helped into carriages, and lifted ober ditches, and to hab de best place everywhar. Nobody eber helps me into carriages, or ober mudpuddles, or gibs me any best place!" And raising herself to her full height, and her voice to a pitch like rolling thunder, she asked, "And a'n't I a woman? Look at me! Look at my arm! (and she bared her right arm to the shoulder, showing her tremendous muscular power). I have ploughed, and planted, and gathered into barns, and no man could head me! And a'n't I a woman? I could work as much and eat as much as a man—when I could get it—and bear de lash as well! And a'n't I a woman? I have borne thirteen chilern and seen 'em mos' all sold off to slavery, and when I cried out with my mother's grief, none but Jesus heard me! And a'n't I a woman?

"Den dey talks 'bout dis ting in de head; what dis dey call it?" ("Intellect," whispered some one near.) "Dat's it, honey. What's dat got to do wid womin's rights or nigger's rights? If my cup won't hold but a pint, and yourn holds a quart, wouldn't ye be mean not to let me have my little half-measure full?" And she pointed her significant finger, and sent a keen glance at the minister who had made the argument. The cheering was long and loud.

"Den dat little man in black dar, he say women can't have as much rights as men, 'cause Christ wan't a woman! Whar did your Christ come from?" Rolling thunder couldn't have stilled that crowd, as did those deep, wonderful tones, as she stood there with outstretched arms and eyes of fire. Raising her voice still louder, she repeated, "Whar did your Christ come from? From God and a woman! Man had nothin' to do wid Him." Oh, what a rebuke that was to that little man.

Turning again to another objector, she took up the defense of Mother Eve. I can not follow her through it all. It was pointed, and witty, and solemn; eliciting at almost every sentence deafening applause; and she ended by asserting: "If de fust woman God ever made was strong enough to turn de world upside down all alone, dese women togedder (and she glanced her eye over the platform) ought to be able to turn it back, and get it right side up again! And now dey is asking to do it, de men better let 'em.'' Long-continued cheering greeted this, '' 'Bleeged to ye for hearin' on me, and now ole Sojourner han't got nothin' more to say.''

Amid roars of applause, she returned to her corner, leaving more than one of us with streaming eyes, and hearts beating with gratitude. She had taken us up in her strong arms and carried us safely over the slough of difficulty turning the whole tide in our favor. I have never in my life seen anything like the magical influence that subdued the mobbish spirit of the day, and turned the sneers and jeers of an excited crowd into notes of respect and admiration. Hundreds rushed up to shake hands with her, and congratulate the glorious old mother, and bid her God-speed on her mission of ''testifyin' agin concerning the wickedness of this 'ere people.''

Document III-13: FEMINISM AND CONSUMERISM

Between the era of Sojourner Truth and the ''new woman'' of the 1890s the movement expanded its horizons and acquired new methods. Temperance, a cause always closely related to the woman's movement, became even more important after the Emancipation Proclamation. Just as the anti-slavery campaign furnished women the first platforms whence they could address large, mixed audiences, so the war on drink consolidated and expanded women's reform techniques. The example of Frances Willard—her patience, her organizational skills, her wise reliance on education as the principal means for making long-term gains—created a model for such groups of lasting influence as the League of Women Voters. Similarly, the Anti-Saloon League learned lessons in militancy and lobbying which were quickly applied to the battle for woman suffrage on state, local, and national levels.

Temperance was by no means the only direction taken by women after the Civil War. In addition to working in the Freedmen's Bureaus and other agencies to educate black citizens, Northern women continued their pressure for property rights, the ten-hour day, and the right to vote at least in local school-board elections. Dress reform, begun in the 1840s, made little progress during these years but continued to catch the public eye. It is true that the Civil War overshadowed reform activity not directly connected with the sectional conflict; but it is also true that temperance and woman's rights made the quickest recovery of their antebellum momentum.

The more obvious importance of the following document is its illustration of the strengthening concern over economic issues, which interest can be traced at least to Frances Wright's involvement with the labor movement (see II-10). Woman's economic platform included the pursuit of property rights for married and divorced women. It paid special attention to wages and hours for children as well as women. It built on Belva Lockwood's work for female federal employees in Washington. It continues today in the insistence on equal pay for equal work and on the full opportunity for advancement in all fields of endeavor.

On a slightly more subtle level, Annie MacLean's testimony shows how the woman's movement reflected the modes and topics of the times: in this case, the beginnings of Progressivism. Prepared for an academic journal, it attempts to apply the new techniques of social science to a recognized social problem. While awaiting the franchise, it implies, women may make themselves effective economically through their power as consumers. At the conclusion, the researcher abandons her objectivity and pleads for action—in the true Progressive spirit—through a league of consumers.

With an extraordinarily sensitive reading, these pages can be made to represent those special characteristics which women tended to bring into the purview of reform. It may be noted that there was concern not just for the hard facts of hours and pay, but for cleanliness and nourishment. It took a woman, probably, to worry about the problems of getting to and from work in a chancy neighborhood. It took a person of more sensibility than most men to worry about physical exploitation by employers, about rudeness from customers, and about the indignity of explaining the need to leave work to a member of the opposite sex. This subtle level of observation not only reflects attitudes of the turn of the century but humanizes what might otherwise have been a completely dry documentary report. Together with the more patent evidence, it tells a lot about America, American women, and American reform in 1899.

SOURCE: Annie Marion MacLean, "Two Weeks in Department Stores," *American Journal of Sociology,* vol. IV (May, 1899), pp. 721-741, abridged.

"TWO WEEKS IN DEPARTMENT STORES" [1]

It is so common for those who purchase goods to think nothing at all about the clerk in attendance, or the conditions under which the goods were produced, that it seems timely just now, when the Consumers' League[2] has started upon a crusade of educating the public, to give a true picture of some conditions existing in Chicago.

The necessity for a thorough investigation of the work of women and children in the large department stores in the city was apparent, and the difficulties manifold. With a view to ascertaining some things which could be learned only from the inside, the investigation which is to form the subject-matter of this paper was undertaken. It seemed evident that valuable information could be obtained if someone were willing to endure the hardships of the saleswoman's life, and from personal experience be able to pass judgment upon observed conditions. The urgency of the need, coupled with an enthusiastic interest in the work for which the Consumers' League stands, led me to join the ranks of the retail clerks for two weeks during the rush of the holiday trade. It may be urged that just judgments could not be formed at a time when conditions must be abnormal. It is true that conditions were abnormal, but the importance of knowing to what extent cannot be overestimated. The consumer should know how far his Christmas shopping works hardship for the clerks. Moreover, he should concern himself with the question as to whether the abnormal conditions he has helped to create are in part mitigated by adequate payment for the work exacted. The law in Illinois[3] prohibits the employment of children under fourteen years, and limits the working day of those between the ages of fourteen and sixteen to ten hours in

1. It should be distinctly stated that the two department stores in which the material for this paper was collected are not the establishments which have the best reputations of their class in Chicago.

2. The Consumers' League of Illinois was organized by the collegiate alumnae of this city in February, 1897, when a standard was adopted and a provisional constitution drawn up. A permanent organization, with Mrs. Charles Henrotin as president, was effected at a meeting held in Hull-House, November 30, 1898. The league at the present time has about eight hundred members.

3. Child-labor law of Illinois, February, 1897.

manufacturing and mercantile establishments, and it should be a matter of concern to the purchaser if his persistence in late shopping leads the merchant to break, or at least evade the law. It is admittedly a menace to the social weal to have children and young girls working late at night, and thus exposed to the dangers of city streets at a time when physical and moral safety demand that they be at home. One of the objects of this investigation was to find the amount of overtime exacted, and the compensation, if any, that was given. Employers are always ready to tell the best conditions that exist; it remains to others to find the worst. And the Consumers' League utterly refuses to indorse stores that do not live up to its standard all the time.

And yet some will argue that any effort in behalf of the employés in the great stores is unnecessary. Many objections were urged against factory legislation in the early days of that reform. The champions of the movement in England met with strenuous opposition, but finally their frightful revelations of actual conditions overcame their opponents, and a wave of enthusiastic reform set in. The history in this country is similar. From 1830 to 1874 agitation for the protection of women and children in the factories was kept up, till finally, at the latter date, the Massachusetts act became a reality. Then other states followed the example set, until, at the present time, almost all the states having large manufacturing interests have very good factory laws. Illinois is a notable exception.[4] Such, in a word, has been the history of the factory laws. We are just on the eve of an agitation for the amelioration of the conditions under which a vast army of saleswomen and cash children work. Thoughtful people all over the country have already recognized the necessity for this; but the whole body of the people must be awakened. And to help, in a small way, the educative movement here my labor was undertaken.

The difficulty of finding employment was not so great as might be supposed. Owing to the holiday rush, and the consequent need of large reinforcements to the original help, the employers were not insistent on experience as a requisite for the successful applicant. However, it was not until several visits had been made that I was promised a position at three dollars a week. Work was to begin the following Monday, which would give me just two weeks of the Christmas trade. Employment being promised, it seemed desirous to engage board in some home for working

---

4. The supreme court declared the law of 1893 unconstitutional.

women; for the environment which such a place would provide gave promise of the best results. I was fortunate in finding a most satisfactory place not far from the heart of the city, and there I went as a working-woman. This home is deserving of more than passing mention. It provides board and lodging, together with the use of pleasant parlors and library, to working-women under thirty years of age for two dollars and a half a week, if they are content to occupy a single bed in a dormitory. These dormitories are thoughtfully planned, and accommodate from ten to fifteen each. A large proportion of the sixty-five residents were saleswomen, and they, in the course of conversation, gave me much useful information. All classes of girls were there, and most of them received very low wages. A few entries in the house register are here inserted to show the nature of the records kept, and the way in which the girls fill in the columns.

Name	Age	Nationality	Occupation	Wages per week
_____	18	American	Saleslady	$4.00
_____	27	Virginian	Stenographer	6.00
_____	24	American	Clerk	4.50
_____	23	American	Clerk	3.00
_____	29	German	Cashier	6.50
_____	23	Irish	Saleswoman	6.00
_____	28	American	Fur worker	5.00
_____	20	American	Saleslady	3.00

This, then, was the place from which I started out to work on the appointed Monday morning. The hurried breakfast, the rush out into the street thronged with a lunch-carrying humanity hastening to the downtown district, and the cars packed with pale-faced, sleepy-eyed men and women, made the working world seem very real. Hurrying workers filled the heart of the city; no one else was astir. I reached my destination promptly at eight, the time of opening. Then I had to stand in line at the manager's office awaiting my more definite appointment, which was received in due time. But the manager had changed his mind about wages, and said he would give me two dollars a week plus 5 per cent commission on sales, instead of the regular salary he had mentioned in our former interview. I was then given a number, and by "424" I was known during my stay there. I was sent to the toy department, where I found sixty-seven others who were to be my companions in toil. The place was a dazzling array of all kinds of toys, from a monkey beating a drum to a doll that said "mamma," and a horse whose motor force was to be a small boy. Our business was first to dust and condense[5] the stock, and then to stand ready for customers. We all served in the double capacity of floorwalkers and clerks, and our business was to see that no one escaped without making a purchase. The confusion can be readily imagined. As soon as the elevators emptied themselves on the floor, there was one mad rush of clerks with a quickly spoken, "What would you like, madam?" or, "Something in toys, sir?" And the responses to these questions were indicative of the characters of the people making them. The majority were rude, some amused, and a few alarmed at the urgency of the clerks. One young boy, on being assailed by half a dozen at once, threw up his hands in horror, and said: "For God's sake, let me get out of here!" and fled down the stairs, not even waiting for the elevator. The cause of such watchful activity on the part of so many employés was the 5 per cent. commission which was to eke out the two or three dollars a week salary. Those who were experienced received the latter sum. And the extra nickels earned meant so much to many of them. Most of the girls in that department lived at home or with relatives, but in many cases the necessity for money was most urgent.

One of the difficult things at first was keeping track of the prices, for they were frequently changed during the day, and the penalty for selling under price was immediate discharge, while selling above price met with no disapproval.

Every morning there were special sales. Sometimes articles that had sold for one dollar would be reduced to ninety-eight cents, with much blowing of trumpets, while, again, twenty-five cent articles would be offered at a bargain for *forty cents* "today only." But we soon learned what things were to be "leaders" from day to day, and the manager's brief instructions each morning were sufficient to keep us posted on the bargains. The charms of the bargain counter vanish when one has been behind the scenes and learned something of its history. The humor of it seemed to impress the clerks, for often knowing winks would be exchanged when some unwary customer was being victimized.

---

5. This meant to pile like things together in as small space as possible.

Oh, the weariness of that first morning! The hours seemed days. "Can I possibly stand up all day?" was the thought uppermost in my mind, for I soon learned from my companions that abusive language was the share of the one who was found sitting down. Later in the week I found this to be true. One of the girls who was well-nigh exhausted sat a moment on a little table that was for sale—there was not a seat of any kind in the room, and the only way one could get a moment's rest was to sit on the children's furniture that was for sale on one part of the floor. The manager came along and found the poor girl resting. The only sympathy he manifested was to call out in rough tones: "Get up out of that, you lazy huzzy, I don't pay you to sit around all day!" Under such circumstances it is small wonder that the stolen rests were few. By night the men as well as the women were limping wearily across the floor, and many sales were made under positive physical agony. . . .

My first day ended at half-past six. Through some oversight, a supper ticket was not given to me, and so I was allowed to go home. I went wearily to the cloak-room and more wearily to my boarding place. When I arrived there, I could only throw myself upon my little white cot in the dormitory and wildly wonder if it would be all right for a working girl to cry. Presently I was dreaming that blows from an iron mallet were falling fast upon me; and in a little while it was morning, and another day was begun. Hundreds of clerks in the city were starting out for work just as weary as I, but with them there was not the knowledge that labor could be ended at will.

It must be understood that "our house" was open every evening till about ten o'clock, and the only compensation given for the extra work was a supper, the market value of which was about fifteen cents. That, like the lunch, had to be eaten in great haste. The maximum time allowed, in either case, was thirty minutes, but our instructions were to "hurry back." That half an hour was wholly inadequate one can readily imagine. It sometimes took ten or fifteen minutes to get a simple order filled in the crowded restaurants near by. The lunch outside meant from ten to fifteen cents a day out of our small earnings, but the breath of even the smoky outdoor air was worth that to us. The air inside was always foul, and the continual noise was fairly maddening. We were obliged to eat our supper in the store, where it was provided. The second day I partook of what the management magnanimously called the "free supper.'' We were fed in droves and hurried away before the last mouthful was swallowed. The menu consisted of a meat dinner and an oyster stew, the latter of which I always elected with the lingering hope that it had not been made of scraps left from the regular café dinner earlier in the day. The said stew consisted of a bowl of hot milk, in the bottom of which lurked *three* oysters, except on that memorable day when I found *four*. . . .

A shop girl might die on the bare, hard floor, while easy chairs and couches in another room were unoccupied. Surely it would not be unreasonable to require that suitable rest-rooms be provided for the employés. Undue advantage could not well be taken of such a thing, for we could not leave the floor without asking the floorwalker—a man—for a pass, and his injunction always was, ''Don't stay long.'' The unpleasantness of asking for a pass was sometimes overcome by girls slipping away in the crowd without permission. We thought some woman might be commissioned to grant such requests. We had to endure so many unnecessary hardships.

The cloak-, toilet-, and lunch-rooms were the gloomiest and filthiest it was ever my misfortune to enter. The cobwebs and dirt-besmeared floors looked ''spooky'' under the flickering glare of insufficient gaslight. The only ventilation came through a foul basement, and there the little girl attendants stayed all day and late into the night. And that was where the girls who brought lunches had to eat them. A few rough board tables and chairs in a more or less advanced state of ruin were provided, and scores of hungry girls sat around and ate lunches from newspaper parcels and drank coffee from tin cans.[6] It was not a healthful atmosphere, either physically or morally, and yet it was typical of the poorer class of stores. The slang of the streets, interspersed with oaths, formed the staple medium of communication. A young and innocent newcomer could not fail to feel shocked at what she heard. But the surroundings were not conducive of elevated thoughts. Refinement of thought and speech would soon disappear in such an environment. I never saw a clean towel in the toilet-room. Several hundred pairs of hands were wiped on the coarse, filthy piece of crash each day, and there was no woman in attendance to see that things were kept in a sanitary condition. Two little

6. Coffee was supplied to employés at the rate of two cups for five cents.

girls were in the cloak-room, but they had nothing to do with the adjoining places. The rooms were merely narrow hallways. The wretchedness of all these appointments was forced upon me the day my fellow-worker was so ill. It was so hard to get our wraps at night, for then all the employés were there pushing their way to the front. One night a young girl in the line was rather restless, and one of the store officials charged her with crowding, and jerked her out of line so that she struck against a counter on the right. He then shoved her back with such force that she fell against another on the left. She was badly hurt, and the uproar which followed was mob-like in its intensity. The boys were going to shoot the offender, they said, but he only smiled, secure in the justness of his attack. The case was afterward reported to the managers, but no reparation was ever made. The girl was unable to work the next day on account of the soreness of her back. In addition to the physical discomfort she had to endure, she lost a day's wages. From that warlike atmosphere we went forth into the night, and many of us had to go alone. That night I felt timid; so I asked if anyone was going my way. A little cash girl of only thirteen years spoke up and said: "I'll go wid yez." She had eight blocks to walk after she left me. The only mitigating circumstance was her total lack of fear. She was used to sights and sounds to which I was a stranger. There were always men on the street corners ready to speak to a girl alone, and one hesitating step meant danger. Almost every morning the girls had some story to tell of encounters with men of that class; and that they were not exaggerating was proved satisfactorily to me by an experience of my own. I stepped from the car one night after midnight, and soon found that I was being followed. The chase continued for two blocks, when I staggered breathless into my doorway, with my pursuer not five feet away. My terror had given me power to outrun him. . . .

Sunday in the home was a quiet day. Everybody was tired and discouraged. There had been extra work, but no extra pay, and there were so many Christmas things to be bought. Sunday had to be the general mending day, and that day many were making little gifts for the friends at home. Most of the girls were sensible about dress, and they guarded their small earnings carefully. I guided my expenditure by theirs and kept an accurate account of my expenses for the week. The items are here presented:

Board for one week	$2.50
Car fare, 6 days[7] at 10c.	.60
Lunch, 5 days, at 15c.	.75
'' , 1 day, at 10c.	.10
For charity dinner[8]	.13
Paper, 3 nights	.06
Postal cards	.05
Candy[9]	.10
Stamps	.10
Oranges[9]	.09
Present for table girl	.05
'' '' matron	.10
Laundry	.16
Total expense	$4.79

What I earned for the week was as follows:

Wages	$2.00
Commission	3.25
	$5.25
Less fines[10]	.30
Total earnings	$4.95

[7]Many of the girls walked as far as two miles to save car fare.
[8]The matron asked for contributions from two cents up. Every girl in the home responded.
[9]These articles were for a "treat."
[10]A fine of ten cents was imposed for each tardiness, unless over half an hour; then twenty-five cents was charged.

Thus I had a balance of sixteen cents after my bills were paid, and that was as much as many had. At that rate it would take a long time to earn enough to buy a pair of boots. . . .

The organization that is attempting to mitigate the evils connected with life in mercantile establishments has most laudable aims and methods. The ameliorative movement on the part of consumers is a rational one. It is representative of the most enlightened forces in society, and rests on a sound basis. So long as the consumer will patronize bad stores, so long will they exist; so long as people will buy clothing produced under inhuman conditions, so long will they continue to be produced under just those conditions. Has the public no duty in the matter? Women and children are in the industrial world, and it is useless to wrangle over the expediency of their filling the places they do. They are there, and as the weaker members of society they need protection. Inhuman and demoralizing conditions must be removed. Some of the evils here could be speedily remedied by legislation and faithful inspection. Those who have not already considered the matter would do well to peruse carefully the Consumers' standard of a fair house, and ask themselves whether or not they can do something to lessen the hardships of the salespeoples' lives.

CONSUMERS' LEAGUE OF ILLINOIS

CONSUMERS' STANDARD

Children.—A standard house is one in which no child is allowed to work after six o'clock in the evening, and the requirements of the child-labor law are all complied with.

Wages.—A standard house is one in which equal pay is given for work of equal value, irrespective of sex. In the departments where women only are employed the minimum wages are $6 per week for adult workers of six months' experience, and fall in few instances below $8.

In which wages are paid weekly or fortnightly.

In which fines, if imposed, are paid into a fund for the benefit of the employés.

In which the minimum wages of cash girls and boys are $2.25 per week, with the same conditions regarding weekly payments and fines.

Hours.—A standard house is one in which the hours from 8 A. M. to 6 P.M. (with not less than three quarters of an hour for lunch) constitute the working day, and a general half holiday is given on one day of each week during the summer months.

In which a vacation of not less than one week is given, with pay, during the summer season to employés of six months' standing.

In which all overtime is compensated for.

Physical conditions.—A standard house is one in which work-, lunch-, and retiring rooms are apart from each other and are in good sanitary condition.

In which seats are provided for saleswomen and the use of seats permitted.

Other conditions.—A standard house is one in which humane and considerate behavior toward employés is the rule.

In which fidelity and length of service meet with the consideration which is their due.

It is a comparatively easy matter to enlist the sympathy of intelligent and educated people, and through them reform must be brought about. The great body of buyers who regularly patronize the cheap stores will take no interest in the matter. Some may feel that they have done their duty when they cease buying at stores where evils exist; but that is a dwarfed conception of social obligation. We should not rest until the bad stores improve or go out of business.

Document III-14: SYMBOLS OF FEMALE EMANCIPATION

The two following photographs suggest some of the difficulties involved in interpreting the woman's crusade. Both pictures seem to have been taken at about the same time. They both show demonstrations on behalf of women against the established order. Probably both of them focused on suffrage. It is further probable that the leaders of these demonstrations would have agreed on what they were opposing. Yet when one asks of these documents, "Emancipate women for what?" there comes a contradiction that has divided the woman's movement at least as seriously as "separation versus assimilation" has divided movements on behalf of minority groups.

The smiling suffragette marcher seems to be seeking emancipation into the man's world just as clearly as the tableau of "Greek maidens at play" was meant to be perceived as emancipation for the sake of a more complete and unrestrained feminity. Like so many other reform programs on behalf of special groups, the woman's movement faces a large and often irreverent hostility from many men and women who prefer the status quo. Furthermore, it faces a serious division within its ranks between those who want the special group to become more like its counterpart (more like men, in this case) and those who want it to become more importantly distinctive and more fully expressive of its own special potentiality.

A clever interpreter could compose an entire history of woman's rights through the symbolic use of dress and grooming. Oneida, one of the more interesting of the communitarian settlements, freed women from many traditional household chores while imposing simplified hairstyles and apparel. Just as female fashions reached their most ludicrous—in the "tie-back" and its varied distortions of the human shape—the famous alternative inaccurately named for Amelia Bloomer came on the scene. Two postbellum fads—croquet and cycling—demanded shorter skirts and split skirts or trousers. As women became more serious about active sports—swimming, basketball, tennis, golf—Victorian modesty had to be compromised. Surging rapidly toward the ultimate, dress reform led to the bikini and to topless swimsuits: eventualities that may cause some bewilderment as to whether they should be attributed to the physical liberation of women or to "sexploitation." The same may be said of "bralessness," a symbol of the revolt of the female in the late 1960s, coming as a kind of logical continuation of campaigns against the constraints of rigid and tightly laced undergarments which had menaced the health of fashionable women in many decades. To discard the brassiere was to reject the tyranny both of fashion and of "sex object" stereotypes.

Each step in dress reform has had its counterpoint in the high styles of grooming and vestment which continued to attract followers. Many women have accepted expense, discomfort, and inconvenience in order to make themselves modishly attractive. The length of skirts may not

Emancipation ballet

Suffrage marching costume

always, as superstition has it, presage conversely the level of stock prices; but the attention to simplified and functional dress usually parallels a renewed concentration on some aspect of woman's emancipation. Thus both the militaristic marching costume exposing a putteed leg, in what many women would have regarded as a brazen mannner, and the free-flowing robes suggestive of the overemancipated Isadora Duncan provided indices to the force and direction of the movement.

SOURCE: Both photographs from the Prints and Photographs Division, Library of Congress, c. 1910.

Document III-15: WOMAN'S LIBERATION TODAY

The foregoing documents have meant to suggest that action to change the role and status of women in American society began early and is still with us. Like other movements it has shifted with the times, reflected moods and helped shape them. Sojourner Truth did not *choose* to argue for women on Biblical grounds: the argument was thrust upon her. From Frances Wright through Shirley Chisholm women have added their vantage point to the economic debates of the day. Those who campaigned for suffrage and prohibition showed the results of hard study and experience in political activism rarely matched in this country. The socialization of the woman's cause through education has constantly picked up momentum, as has the enlightened use of the courts.

Thus it is not surprising to see a woman's strike in Washington, D. C., aimed at the passage of an Equal Rights Amendment guaranteeing women equal opportunity in employment, education, income, and the end of second-class citizenship. Even more representative of the 1970s is the increasing emphasis on liberation from those characteristics that had been long thought inseparable from being a woman. Birth control is not new, but it is new to have it so conveniently available as seems possible with oral contraceptives, and to have "the pill" accepted as a license for a new perception of physical sex. With the pill came evidence that women can and should enjoy the physical aspects of sexual acts at least as much and as freely as men. New too is the legalization of abortion and the free treatment of venereal disease which combine to remove some of the traditional hazards attendant on what used to be called promiscuity. For women who want children there is the demand for day-care centers; for women who want children without marriage there is the attempt to create new social attitudes toward bastardy.

Women have been rather specially affected by technology. The first factories gave a however arduous alternative to home and marriage. The telegraph and the telephone created jobs at desks and switchboards that were less physically demanding than factory labor. Inventions for the use of the housewife lightened physical burdens at home, helped her survive the end of low-paid servants, and freed her time. Thus technology, plus education, have combined to create the latest thrust by women who want to go further. Now the technology of the pill and of safe abortion techniques have freed her from unwanted children. On the horizon, some think, is an era when infants will be produced outside the human body; when—to put it in a dramatic way—technology will have replaced sex, or at least gender. Those who look toward the future advise that biology is adaptable and that the physiological reasons for distinguishing between male and female may effectively recede to the point where behavioral roles can be redesigned to suit individual and social goals. If this is true, the "assimilators" will certainly have had the last word over the "separatists."

The following essay was chosen primarily because it represents an effective digest of a great amount of complex contemporary material. The author writes in a nonpolitical setting and, with the other contributors to the volume in question, seeks as much objectivity as possible in order to focus in the spirit of scientific investigation on an identifiable problem. Nonetheless, she is a "sensitized" woman attuned to the rhetoric of polemics. Not all of her statements are impartial. To some extent, then, this excellent summary may itself be read as a reflection of concern with the further accommodation of society to the aims of female fulfillment.

SOURCE: Mordeca Jane Pollock, "Changing the Role of Women," in Helen Wortis and Clara Rabinowitz, eds. *The Women's Movement: Social and Psychological Perspectives.* New York, AMS Press, 1972, pp. 10-20.

CHANGING THE ROLE OF WOMEN

Women's liberation, or the New Feminism, is the second wave of an American social movement with intellectual roots reaching back at least to the eighteenth century, and political beginnings that may be traced to the nineteenth. While Mary Wollstonecroft's *Vindication of the Rights of Women* (1792) may be considered the first manifesto of conscious political feminism, the expression of feminism in literature and thought is clearly discernible from the troubadours through Virginia Woolf. In the nineteenth century, women in the temperance and abolition movements began to turn their eyes on their own status as women, as Eleanor Flexner has written in an impressively documented, if at times partisan, account of the first movement. To the temperance workers, it soon became obvious that without basic legal protections—in most states, woman had no legal recourse should her husband fail to support the family—their fight against social evil would never be won from the major opponent, the alcohol industry. The abolitionists began to compare their own legal servitude with the involuntary servitude of black slaves: Women's property was no longer their own once they married; women could not make contracts or engage in business on their own; any monies earned became their husbands'; and women did not have the franchise. Finally, the struggle to organize the American labor force included the struggle to end the exploitation of female labor in the mills and sweatshops of the industrial states.

The accomplishments of the "first movement," as it is called, are by no means inconsiderable. Starting with no political leverage, no money, and the overwhelming weight of conventional morality against them, the suffragists won those civil rights women now enjoy. Among their victories were the enactment of the Married Women's Property Acts in the latter half of the nineteenth century and, of course, the adoption of the Nineteenth Amendment to the Constitution in 1920. However, as historian Ann Firor Scott (3) notes:

> Until quite recently, American historians by and large have behaved as if women did not exist. In some major textbooks the whole history of American women takes up less space than a minor political party.

The period of prosperity and social change of the 1920s saw great advances in the social and economic status of women. But with the Depression and the war, gains women had made in many spheres were halted; indeed, a backward trend set in. After World War II, moveover, by dint of causes ranging from prosperity to prevailing psychiatric theory, American women fell under the influence of the *feminine mystique*. As redefined by Betty Friedan (4) and currently understood by American feminists, the term denotes the congruence of attitudes and values that defines a woman solely as a function of someone else (her husband and children) or some *thing* else (her homemaking activities). Consider the attributes valued most highly in American culture (individual striving, professional or political ambition, financial success) and those we have come increasingly to value (creativity, commitment to larger issues, self-realization). All were deemed abnormalities in women. Popular culture and accepted norms of "health" circumscribed women's activities and strivings; the image of the happy housewife shaped the lives and expectations of a whole generation of American women. As Friedan (4) wrote, there has grown up a whole generation of American women,

> who adjust to the feminine mystique, who expect to live through their husbands and children, who want only to be loved and secure, to be accepted by others, who never make a commitment of their own to society. . . . The adjusted or cured ones who live without conflict or anxiety in the confined world of the home have forfeited their own being. (p. 300)

But the mystique was bound to lose its grip over women—for some very concrete reasons. From 1948 to 1970, the number of women in the American work force grew from 17.3 million to 31.1 million, so that women now constitute about 40% of those gainfully employed (14). Roughly 60% of the women who work *must* work; they are widowed, divorced, single, or their husbands earn less than $5,000 a year. Today there are about 18 million married women in the work force, and more than half of these women have children under eighteen years of age. Finally, one out of ten American families is headed by a woman.

Prosperity and technological sophistication, as well as changing economic patterns, have worked a revolution in women's life-styles. The burden of domestic labor has been potentially halved in the past fifty years. The increasing mobility dictated by economic circumstance has meant the virtual end of the extended family as the prevailing basic unit of American society and the emergence of the nuclear family. Increasing numbers of middle-class Americans have chosen to live in the "bedroom communities" of suburbia. As a result, women are often isolated from their men for half of the day and have, moreover, to confront hitherto unknown problems of childrearing and social interaction.

Advances in medical science and technology along with advances in our standard of living have created three profoundly revolutionary changes in women's life patterns: 1) We may now regulate the number of children to whom we give birth; 2) for the first time in human history, we may bring a limited number of children into the world with the reasonable assurance that they will live to maturity; and 3) we are the first generation of women in history to have a life-expectancy of three-quarters of a century—thirty years beyond the childrearing age.

In these changing circumstances, at least two eloquent voices rose to reawaken the feminist consciousness. In 1949, Simone de Beauvoir (2) analysed the attitudes that have cast women into the role of "the other," not really the full person. "To pose woman is to pose the absolute Other," she wrote, "without reciprocity, denying against all experience that she is a subject, a fellow human being." And in 1963, Friedan (4) discerned the cultural attitudes that had created a surprising *malaise* among American women: feelings of isolation and depression, a dimly perceived sense of worthlessness, emptiness, and frustration. The problems de Beauvoir and Friedan underscored frightened many women, for the implications of these problems are far-reaching indeed. At the same time, many women began to understand that feelings and situations they had thought to be personal were symptoms of a deeper, cultural illness that they had been conditioned to perceive as inevitable and natural.

The New Feminism is also an outgrowth of the new trends in political attitudes and participation that are the mark of the 1960s in the United States. Here, the experience of modern American feminists parallels that of their great-grandmothers in the suffragist movement. Working for civil rights, working for peace, working to elect male political candidates to high office—raising the funds, addressing the envelopes, pouring the coffee, but rarely participating in making the decisions—women turned their eyes to their own status. This shift in consciousness held equally true for SDS "chicks" and Republican committeewomen in the '60s as the nation underwent a revolution of rising political expectations.

It was therefore inevitable that women begin to examine their own status, the roles into which they had been cast, and their self-perceptions. Scrutinizing the economic sphere, women found that, in 1968, the average full-time female worker earned fifty-eight cents for every dollar the average full-time male worker earned. The median annual income for full-time work in that year was as follows: white males, $7800; non-white males, $5500; white females, $4500; non-white females, $3500. A female with four years of college earned on the average the same amount as a male with an eighth-grade education. (12) In 1970, of the 5.4 million American families headed by women, one out of every four was living below what the United States government deems the poverty level, while of the non-white families headed by women, one out of every two lived below the imaginary cut-off point. (6)

An analysis of jobs revealed that women are not only the victims of salary discrimination, but of type-casting in employment. Women are clerical, domestic, and sales "help," rather than industrial workers, crafts*men*, or managers. (12) Non-professional female workers do the housekeeping of business and industry and provide a supply of cheap labor. Women in the professions are conspicuous by their rarity, accounting for 1% of the nation's engineers, 7% of its physicians (the same proportion as in Spain), 9% of its scientists, 19% of its college and university professors. There are not even token numbers of women in the top jobs of business and industry.

Public and private educational institutions perpetuate women's economic disabilities. Members of the Boston Commission on the Status of Women recently found that vocational training programs in the high schools channel women into lower-paying jobs, while offering numerous courses for men in lucrative trades or skills. Three of the four college preparatory high schools in Boston do not admit women. In some states, women need higher grades than men to enter public colleges and universities. For example, "21,000 women were turned down for college entrance in the State of Virginia; during the same period not one application of a male was rejected." (16) Women have been virtually locked out of postgraduate education for the liberal professions. Harvard University, a quarter of whose undergraduates are female, did not admit women in its law school until after World War II; in March 1970, there were only 122 women in a total enrollment of 1,550 at Harvard Law School, according to the Registrar of the University. Education in the United States is far from coeducational; schools and universities reinforce women's vocational roles and allow the potential talents of half the population to remain untapped.

Despite the impressive achievements of the first movement, women are still inferior to men in the eyes of the law. (8) Social Security regulations actually penalize families with working wives. (11) While businessmen and professionals may deduct the most lavish expenses, working mothers usually may not deduct child care fees from their taxable income. The 1964 Civil Rights Act, which prohibits sex discrimination in employment, does not guarantee women's right to equity in education or public accommodations. In many states, a married woman does not have the right to choose her domicile, the address from which she votes, runs for office, attends the public schools or universities, or receives welfare assistance. Progress in upgrading women's legal status has been piecemeal because there is no clear constitutional guarantee of legal equality for women. And until very recently, the Federal courts, presided over almost exclusively by male judges, have not been willing to overturn discriminatory precedents. See Kanowitz,(8) pp. 149-196.

New Feminists examining the social legislation affecting women found that in areas such as paid maternity leave and job security for pregnant women, the United States lags dramatically behind other industrial countries. The nation is also remarkably retrograde in the area of child care facilities. In April 1970, it was reported to the President that 700,000 migrant children and 1,373,000 economically deprived children were in need of day care, a need singled out as "the most serious barrier to job training and employment for low income mothers." (11) These findings did not extend to all working mothers, yet we know that about nine million women in the work force have children under eighteen. Adequate parent-controlled facilities where children learn and grow are exceptional and, generally speaking, open only to the very affluent and some of the very poor. Most working women must be satisfied with inadequate child care facilities, or none at all.

Laws governing the termination of pregnancy through abortion have drawn both critical scrutiny and profound concern from feminists. In most states, it is virtually impossible—unless one is affluent, infirm, or mentally ill—to obtain an abortion under therapeutic conditions. Nonetheless, it has been estimated (the statistics are conservative) that at least a million American women undergo abortions every year. (9) Since the overwhelming majority of these operations are performed extra-legally, often under dangerous conditions, it comes as no surprise that at least a thousand women die each year at the hands of charlatans or due to their own efforts to induce abortion, and that eight out of ten of these women are non-white. (9)

Feminists believe that the criminal abortion statutes enforce involuntary servitude on women by determining how they are to use their bodies and spend their lives. It is cruel and unusual punishment to force a person to choose between breaking the law and risking sterilization or death on the one hand, and bearing an unwanted child on the other. But the issue of abortion has still other implications. The laws enforce a double standard of morality, punishing the woman for her sexual behavior while absolving the man involved. Beyond the issue of patriarchal sexual attitudes is the no less-important issue of self-determination for women. To seek new life-styles and to make new life choices, women must exercise the basic right to control their own reproductive processes.

Examining women's political status, feminists have concluded that—the franchise notwithstanding—women's political power is non-existent. Although women constitute more than half of the nation's electorate, there are no women in high executive offices and not even token numbers in the legislative and judicial branches. Women are also absent from the powerful positions in business, industry, the military, and the universities, all of which influence, indeed may shape, political decision. Many feminists point to this lack of representation as dangerous, feeling that men's current conditioning tends to separate them from a full grasp of the worth of human life. Men have been trained to equate power with power *over* others, to view aggression as a valid means of problem-solving, and have thus become capable of dealing with the complicated mathematics of overkill while unable to confront the simple arithmetic of underfeed.

But these observable signs of women's status give only a partial picture of the limited life-style open to women who wish, or are conditioned, to follow the conventional path. A woman is expected to enter into a monogamous marriage, live in a nuclear—often emotionally isolated—family, and limit her activities to domestic concerns, volunteer work, and social interests that are, in the final analysis, severely circumscribed. A woman who chooses or is compelled to work is nonetheless expected to run the household and bear the major responsibility for child-rearing; she must make adjustments to marriage never asked of a man. The woman who chooses not to marry moves outside the mainstream of currently acceptable life-styles, and her penalty is often high. While men are also limited in their life patterns—monogamy and the nuclear family being the norm—they nonetheless enjoy a much wider choice of careers and social activities, and a greater potential influence on their community. Thus, women have been forced to make what have been called "half-choices." This applies as well to the type of interaction and self-perceptions expected of women. The taboos attendant upon types of interaction with men and, to a certain extent, with other women, are very restrictive. Women are conditioned to behave passively, whatever their emotions. Consider the meaning of the word "assertive" as applied to women and as applied to men.

All these aspects of women's role in society—her economic and legal disabilities, and restricted life-style—are signs of a psychologically enforced cultural myth, a set of assumptions and values concerning women that has been transmitted consciously and unconsciously for millennia.

Our very habits of speech reveal and perpetuate these values. Roget's Thesaurus lists the word "masculine" under the heading, "Strength," in a list of adjectives that includes, "strong, mightly, vigorous, stout, robust, irresistible, invincible, all-powerful." The adjective "womanish" is listed under the general heading of "Weakness," while synonyms for "effeminate"—often an insult in our language—are to be found under the headings, "Weak, womanlike, timorous, sensual." It is obvious that women are assumed to be less strong, less upright, less brave than men, for "manliness" is taken to denote desirable moral attributes.

Our religions consecrate and transmit the mythology revealed in our language. The young child who is taken to church hears the male minister speak of God as "He," "Our Father," "Lord our God, King of the Universe." Further, the puritanism characteristic of Western religions has projected onto women the feelings of guilt and sin erroneously and doggedly attached to sexuality. Indeed, the patristic writings are redolent with pathological anti-feminism.

Psychiatrists and psychologists—to whom we have looked increasingly for moral guidance—have also perpetuated the mythology; many have transmuted women's situation into her nature or essence. Thus, even the great Freud (5) could write that "women soon come into opposition to civilization and display their retarding influence. . . . The work of civilization has become increasingly the business of men, it confronts them with ever more difficult instinctual sublimations of which women are little capable." Following uncritically the lead of Freud, practitioners have been all too eager to qualify as "abnormal" females who do not wish to cast their identity in terms of their "primal instincts of sex and reproduction." Puritanism, and its placement of women in a lesser status, has entered through the back door. Hopelessly fudged accounts of women's psychological development and of female sexuality—mainly the result of implicit Victorianism and male fantasy—have also contributed to perpetuating the myths.

Consider the concept of "penis envy," which describes a political rather than a psychological reality. Here is Ernest Jones (7) on that topic: "What in the meantime has been the attitude toward the penis? It is likely enough that the initial one is purely positive, manifested by the desire to suck it. But penis envy soon sets in and apparently always." Pre-Masters and Johnson accounts of female sexuality are no less exaggerated in their error: "What man and woman, driven by obscure primitive urges, wish to feel in the sexual act, is the essential force of *maleness*, which expresses itself in a sort of violent and absolute *possession* of the woman." The same author (15) fared no better—and showed remarkable lack of neurological knowledge—when he wrote of female orgasm, "The final reflex in the woman may receive its signal from her realization of the muscular contractions of the man's orgasm; or from the impact of the vital fluid."

These linguistic habits and normative views rest on the assumption that females are by nature radically different from and, more important, inferior to men. The degree to which this sexism shapes the viewpoint even of counseling professionals, male and female, was suggested by a recent study (1) that found "behavioral attributes which are regarded as healthy for an adult, sex unspecified, and thus presumably viewed from an ideal, absolute standpoint, will more often be considered by clinicians as more healthy or appropriate for men than for women." While the authors impute this "double standard of health" to the adjustment viewpoint that they believe dominates counseling, I believe that the underlying "negative assessment of women" demonstrates the degree to which sexism molds even the most rationally based disciplines. It is a powerful mythology indeed that impels clinicians of both sexes to expect women *not* to react, think, and behave as adult persons.

The fantasy purveyors in advertising understand the potential of the myth, and manipulate it in its least rational manifestations. In their work, our norms of health, our God-given truths are metamorphised into a stream of injunctions. Women are told repeatedly that they will be valueless, lonely, unhappy unless they emulate the slim, glamourous, young model in the ads; they are told that, like the dumb housewife of another kind of ad, they will find security, fulfillment, even ecstasy in sinks and sheets that are whiter than white. Advertisements geared to men, tacitly or overtly promise adoring and available women as the reward for purchase.

If sexism is unjust and unrelated to reality, we must face the question, *Why the mythology?* Why are women defined as less than fully human, inferior in social interaction or civilization, capable only of circumscribed feeling and thinking, closer by nature to those functions and emotions we have cloaked in taboos—and, therefore, sinful?

The sexist mythology exists because the relationship between male and female is a political one, a relationship of superordinate to subordinate—and a relationship that obtains in the most intimate and personal as well as the most massive and public of our activities. This is, *grosso modo*, Kate Millet's (10) thesis in *Sexual Politics*. Once we deny any "natural" social and political inequality between men and women, the purpose of sexist propaganda becomes clear: to sanctify a situation that is by definition unfair, and that requires *ipso facto* the introjection by both parties of the values and conceptions necessary to maintain it. Feminism, then, is a radical insight, intellectual and intuitive in its scope, that alone accounts for numerous phenomena—psychological, political, behavioral, and social. (6)

By the close of the last decade, many women who had become aware of the intellectual itinerary—and reached the conclusions—just outlined, set about to complete the unfinished business of their suffragist great-grandmothers.

Moderate feminists, who tend to construe women's liberation as a civil rights issue, see the unfinished business as that of equality. Groups such as the National Organization for Women have taken the initiative in pressing for long overdue equality of opportunity for women in employment and education. They are working for the enactment of social legislation to meet the needs of the 30 million women in the work force, for the funding and establishment of adequate child-care facilities, and for the winning of women's basic right to control what happens to and within their own bodies. Participation in current political life is central to the program of the moderates, who feel that only when women have substantial political power can their goals be achieved. For many moderates, women's participation in government would mean a massive realignment of national and international priorities. They believe that patriarchy has brought us to the doors of total war, eco-catastrophe, and overpopulation, and that it is time for women to wield the instrumentalities of power.

For radical feminists (a grouping that must be loosely defined, since varying ideologies interlock with radical feminism), the unfinished business of the first movement is the dissolution of patriarchy—its social and political forms, and the psychological attitudes and modes of thought it generates. To gain power within existing economic or political structures, they argue, is in itself a meaningless goal, since it is the institutions of patriarchy—from the "child-owning" nuclear family to the capitalist organizations that profit from sexism—that must be replaced. They see patriarchy, with its built-in forms of unjust dominance of others, at the root of most unwarranted uses and conceptions of power; since patriarchy is the prototype for existing forms of social organization and psychological conditioning, the programs of feminism must be revolutionary in character and shape. It is on this basis that radical feminists view women's liberation as "the ultimate revolution."

My own belief is that patriarchy has left us with no choice but to dissolve it; it is unjust and dangerous. We must replace it with more humane means of classifying human beings, and with more humane forms of social organization. The necessary first step is to render the sexist mythology inoperative by changing women's status now, and by altering women's ways of viewing themselves. It is this process that will engage the coming generation of women's liberationists; it is out of this process that the new conceptions of women, the new forms of human organization and interaction will develop.

References

(1) BROVERMAN ET AL. 1970. Sex role stereotypes and clinical judgments of mental health. J. Cons. Clin. Psychol. 34(1).

(2) DE BEAUVOIR, S. 1953. The Second Sex. Knopf, New York.

(3) FLEXNER, E. 1968. Century of Struggle. Atheneum, New York.

(4) FRIEDAN, B. 1964. The Feminine Mystique. Dell, New York.

(5) FREUD, S. 1961. Civilization and Its Discontents. Norton, New York.

(6) GORNICK, V. 1970. The light of liberation can be blinding. Village Voice (Dec. 10).

(7) JONES, E. 1966. The early development of female sexuality. *In* Psychoanalysis and Female Sexuality, H. Ruitenbeek, ed. College and University Press, New Haven.

(8) KANOWITZ, L. 1969. Women and the Law: The unfinished Revolution. University of New Mexico Press, Albuquerque.

(9) LADER, L. 1966. Abortion, Beacon Press, Boston.

(10) MILLET, K. 1970. Sexual Politics. Doubleday, New York.

(11) PRESIDENT'S TASK FORCE ON WOMEN'S RIGHTS AND RESPONSIBILITIES. 1970. A Matter of Simple Justice: Message to Congress Proposing Legislation, April 1970, pp. 4-13.

(12) Rebelling women: the reason. U. S. News and World Report, April 13, 1970.

(13) SCOTT, A. 1970. Where we have been and where we are going. In What is Happening to American Women, A. Scott, ed. Southern Newspaper Publishers Association, Atlanta.

(14) U.S. DEPT. OF LABOR, WAGE AND LABOR STANDARDS ADMINISTRATION, 1970. Background Facts on Women Workers in the United States. U.S. Government Printing Office, Washington, D.C.

(15) VAN DE VELDE, T. 1959. Ideal Marriage: Its Physiology and Technique, Random House, New York.

(16) VIRGINIA COMMISSION FOR THE STUDY OF EDUCATIONAL FACILITIES IN THE STATE OF VIRGINIA, 1964.

Part IV

MODEL BUILDERS

THE typical reformer is a repairman. He observes an aspect of society that is not functioning as he thinks it should, and he sets out to improve it. Observing poverty, he works for unemployment relief. Noting a lack of political representation, he works to extend the franchise. Confronted with evidence of prejudicial treatment, he works for equal rights. Since repair responds to malfunction, most reform is negatively generated.

Yet there are reformers who behave more like architects than repairmen. They plan and sometimes execute a model toward which society as a whole may strive. If their drawings are attractive and the estimates reasonable, they invite large numbers of clients.

As early as colonial days both kinds of reform were evident. Colonists began as British subjects with rather common political grievances. As these complaints continued unattended, however, the colonists began to imagine a society more nearly ideal than any in Europe. This vision, based on freedom, abundant land, and the chance to avoid institutionalized error, expressed itself in essays, declarations, and constitutions. Albeit most revolutionaries of 1776 simply opposed British rule, some clearly held in their minds the idea of a model society.

This section is designed to show the flow of these ideas through the nineteenth and twentieth centuries. It opens with those who took the whole nation as a model, counting on freely owned land, on neoclassical order, or on a second coming of the Lord to bring the ideal state to pass. Then came the communitarians building model settlements in the wilderness as examples to the nation at large, invoking social planning, shared

503

property, or divine inspiration. Although these settlements had almost disappeared from the American landscape by the opening of the Civil War, the impetus that had produced them continued strong.

Urban and regional planning is, in one important sense, a direct consequence of communitarianism. Communes had provided an experience in controlling the environment in a way that showed respect for nature and at the same time enhanced the efficiency and compatibility of man. This thread can be traced from Olmsted to Wright, from Greenbelt to Columbia.

Socialism and utopianism also continued beyond the first wave of communitarianism. Whether religious or sectarian, most communes had practiced some degree of shared property and authority. Those settlements that followed the ideas of Fourier, Brisbane or Owen were of course explicitly socialistic. In Bellamy and the other utopian romancers one can see a kind of complex, fictitious, urban community which was offered to the America of the 1880s in much the same way that the small, rural commune was put forth as a model to a more bucolic society.

The building of models is brought up to date with the recognition of the supranational model, inheritor not only of the planning but also of the pacifism inherent in the early communes. Science fiction, social engineering, and the grand designs of Buckminster Fuller all comment on the quest for the social ideal. In a fullness of cycle rarely enjoyed by the historian this section recognizes the second, recent, and increasingly widespread new wave of communes offering their own set of social alternatives.

This section represents far fewer individuals and movements in the history of reform than were selectively identified in the two foregoing sections. Yet these reformers with their more complete and more positive visions have their own special value—particularly in revealing the goals, motivations, and ideas of order that have underlain the quest for social amelioration. Some visions rest on God, some await the end of economic competition. Some rely heavily on education or on an adjustment in the environment that will drastically change human behavior. Some, like weary medieval Europeans hailing a bright new world to the west, call for a new start on a new planet. Others need but a plot of ground, a few ripe seeds, and love.

Document IV-1: LAND, HOME, AND SOCIAL ORDER

Early Americans from Penn to Oglethorpe, from Jefferson to Winthrop, envisioned varying models. The most pervasive dream for the newborn nation was made up of numerous parts which fit together only roughly at times.

The dream began with the concept of a nation where—in contrast to Europe—working men lived on their own land and owned their own homes. Thus and only thus would they be freed from the tyranny of landlords, banks, and usurers. Thus and only thus would be provided the basic economic security essential for the unconstrained expression of individual political views. Thus and only thus would the system acquire guarantees against extremes of wealth that invites manipulation and poverty that attracts exploitation.

In the first document reproduced below T. Thomas describes and argues for the kind of worker's house that would fit this utopia. Since even a humble structure might be beyond the means of a young laborer, Thomas couples to his pamphlet a formula for establishing an association for lending money to homeowners without incurring the stigmata and potentially real problems associated with banks.

But a home must be more than an economic warranty; its design must be efficient and uplifting, a mark of both civilization and democracy. Here, as James Fenimore Cooper wittily observed in *Home as Found* (1838), the fashion was Greek. The first widespread model for America, the classical world showed its symbolic influence in the naming of the senate, in the selection of a site for a capitol hill, in the popularity of Athens and Rome as names for New World towns along with Troy and Sparta, Ithaca and Utica. The intellectual character of eighteenth-century Europe, sometimes known as the Augustan Age, was drawn in part from a rediscovery of the ancient wisdom. Platonic rationalism was well suited to an age of Newton, Locke, and Franklin. The flight from Europe was seen as an escape from the evil that inevitably attaches itself to institutions over time. Freed from this handicap, the New World might approach the true classical spirit. Furthermore, since Greek democracy tolerated slavery, and since the example of Rome rested on patrician responsibility, the incipient aristocracy of both South and North could accept the classical models where the more recent egalitarian uprising in France left many of them shaken and appalled.

The classical symbols in America were offered as a way of cloaking this recent wilderness in the dignity that could not otherwise be imparted. There were limits to the value of this symbolism, as Horatio Greenough discovered when he sculpted Washington in a toga; but public sentiment was predominantly Grecian. "We build little besides [Greek] temples," continued Cooper's commentary, "for our churches, our banks, our taverns, our courthouses, and our dwellings. A friend of mine has just built a brewery on the model of the Temple of the Winds" (p. 15).

Cooper found this slavery to classical architectural models ludicrous, as have others when confronted with the Capitol's corinthian columns adapted to ears of corn and tobacco leaves. But at best, as in the homes of Samuel McIntire, classical design became an attractive and useful setting. Lacking the advantages of study in London and Rome, which steered to the top his colleague Charles Bulfinch, McIntire worked in a similar mode on more humble subject matter. He rendered fences, gateposts, moldings, staircases, and entire houses with a dignity and sense of proportion that have continually charmed and inspired those who have felt their influence. The entranceway here shown is built on Grecian lines and proportions but in a very human scale, somewhat reminiscent of the English Adam brothers, softened by the rosettes along the porch beam and the heart-shaped leadings in the lights alongside the doorway. Thus domesticated, American classical architecture may be better symbolized in the McIntire house than in the grandiose halls and rotundas of the Capitol with their corn-cob columns. In domesticating the classical, McIntire came closer to the idea of elevating the common man of America to classical stature than did those who tried to cloak public institutions in a grandeur that was never Rome.

Like McIntire, Thomas also favored a simplified classical model. A better known and slightly later treatise extends the subject into the more eclectic "cottage style" and applies the architecture more to rural needs. The author, Andrew Downing, goes beyond Thomas in insisting that civilization rests on taste and that taste begins in the home. (See *Architecture of Country Houses.* New York, Appleton, 1852.)

SOURCE: A. T. Thomas, *Working-Man's Cottage Architecture*. New York, R. Martin, 1848, pp. 3-5, 16-17, 46-47, abridged. B: Main portico of "Oak Hill," one of the houses done by Samuel McIntire for the Derby family. This one was built in Peabody, Massachusetts, in 1800-01. Much of the original woodwork is now in the Boston Museum of Fine Arts. This photograph was made before the 1878 alterations and is reproduced through the courtesy of the Henry Francis du Pont Winterthur Museum.

A: *WORKING-MAN'S COTTAGE ARCHITECTURE*

Although many excellent treatises already exist on the subject of domestic architecture, they have been mainly intended for the illustration and improvement of the private residences of merchants, or other possessors of wealth and taste. The industrious and frugal mechanic, with limited means at his disposal, can rarely find any information in such productions that is adapted to his circumstances. To impart sufficient information to be immediately useful to that numerous body of the people whose wants and tastes must necessarily be regulated by rigid economy, is the intended design of this little work.

Much instructive reading might be given, perhaps, in endeavoring to trace the reasons why the domestic comfort of our mechanics, farmers, laborers, and other useful members of society, has been so singularly overlooked. In a book like the present, however, confessedly utilitarian and solely practical, we have no place to discuss such matters, but must leave them to the hopeful guidance of sound principles. Among such principles, none are of more permanent importance to the political and social welfare of a nation than those which show how harmoniously good taste and practical economy may be combined.

One remarkable characteristic seems to prevail throughout nearly all the modern projects of social reform. It may be seen in their constant reference to some probably impracticable, possibly unattainable, but always far-distant result. This work, with its facts, figures, and results, *proves* the practicability and importance of beginning *immediately* to secure a comfortable home; and subsequently to attain independence by such gradual degrees as would always be consoled with the consciousness of possessing such an indispensable foundation for true happiness.

With the plans and specifications herein annexed, the possessor of small means will perceive how readily he may improve his own social condition at once. It will be seen that roomy cottages, in delightful situations, can be built and owned for $250—a sum no greater than that which the humblest class of tenants must necessarily pay every two or three years for rent, in places which are surrounded by all the unhealthy and immoral influences of city life, when combined with vulgar associations. How different must be the feelings of a working-man who pays his hardly-earned money totally away, *away for ever*, in the shape of rent—as compared with those which inspire the bosom of one who judiciously exchanges his savings for a house to live in, and then steps into it, knowing that it is his own!

In the descriptions accompanying each of the cottage plans in this work, it may be seen how much tasteful comfort and positive independence are within the reach of all who desire to occupy or own such residences. The insular position of the city of New York, renders such information particularly valuable in that neighborhood, for the eligible sites and delightful scenery with which the lovely bay and harbor are surrounded, seem to form a pleasing compensation for the necessity which all classes are under of seeking a residence as contiguous as possible to the place whence they derive their subsistence. The facilities of ferriage, and the opportunities for healthful exercise, (if desired,) are all favorable to suburban residents; while a family residence within the city is (at best) but a poor reward to citizens in active life, who might almost as well be doomed to perpetual confinement at their place of business.

With one other remark, we shall now proceed to describe the distinctive merits of each of the subjoined plans. Throughout all the specifications, our prevailing principle has been to pay equal attention to the accommodation of occupants and to the interest of such proprietors of land as may hereafter be induced to observe, that all social prosperity is infallibly enhanced by encouraging the working classes to be steady and persevering, and ultimately to enjoy A HOME OF THEIR OWN—sacred to all the pure and noble affections, and cherishing a moral influence which will be as a strong castle to their children's children.

It may be necessary to observe, with reference to the estimates of the several designs, that the cost of a building cannot be accurately determined without knowing the value of labor and materials in the locality where it is to be erected. Much also will depend upon the style of finish. However, the estimates, as approximations, will, we hope, be a guide both to the employer and the builder. . . .

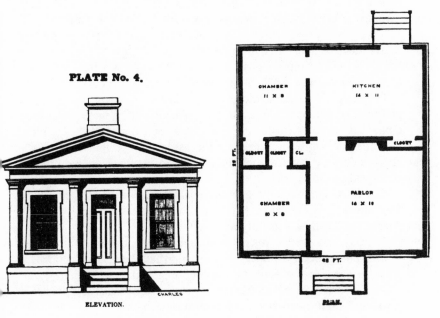

PLATE No. 4.

ELEVATION.

PLATE NO. 4

GIVES a design for a one-story cottage, 23 feet front and 25 feet deep. The principal entrance opens into a parlor 14 feet by 13 feet, having a closet. The parlor communicates in the rear with a kitchen 14 feet by 11 feet, which is also provided with a closet. There is a chamber attached to each of these apartments, one of 11 feet by 8, and one of 10 feet by 8, each having a convenient closet. The floor is intended to rise four steps above the ground level, and the apartments to be 10 feet high to ceiling.

This building would be a very neat and desirable dwelling for a small family. The cost, exclusive of cellar or foundation, would be about 305 dollars. . . .

Building and Loan Associations

The preceding pages of this little work having furnished such plans and specifications as would be useful to those who are about erecting cottages on economical principles, we will now proceed to show the manner in which persons desirous of having "one's own house" may make their earnings or other income immediately available for that purpose.

It is generally conceded that Mrs. Glass's directions for cooking a hare derive much of their value from the leading sentence—"First catch your hare." So also, to raise a house, we must either possess better means than a vague hope, or else call in the aid of our neighbors.

The principle of association, when rightly understood, is capable of producing every desirable social improvement. Unfortunately, this principle has been occasionally perverted by misdirected agitation. Nevertheless, unity of action, by the association of individuals for a specific purpose, agreed upon by mutual consent, must always produce beneficial results.

Benefit societies and life-assurance companies are usually praiseworthy; and their utility, in cases of illness or death, has been abundantly proved, and is now generally admitted.

There is, however, a much more encouraging and remunerative form in which the general principles of association have been lately applied, as may be seen in the formation of building and loan societies; for, wherever such an association exists, it exercises a persuasive influence in favor of sobriety, economy, and industrious ambition.

To illustrate their operation, let us suppose one of these building and loan societies to be composed of five hundred members, each paying into their general fund one dollar a week. The collective proceeds of each week ($500) should form a result of ownership to some individual member, either in the shape of a loan or by a building worth that amount. As the members are generally men to whom time is valuable, once in four weeks might be often enough to meet and decide (by appointed method) who are the four successful members. Those who take the loan then commence paying in such a rate of interest as the by-laws require,— suppose 5 per cent. Those desiring a house are entitled to one of the value of their respective shares at the time, subject to the mortgage and interest required in the by-laws. The accumulations in the interest fund become not only a compensation for those who may be delayed in their choice of privilege, but render the society a safe and sound investment for all classes, whether seeking a profit on capital or aiming at an economical independence of rent paying.

The list of members should be closed when the required number of subscribers has been obtained. The by-laws might allow one member to hold several shares, if desired; but we think the number of shares held by any one member should in no case exceed ten. Each new association will always profit by the experience and example of those already existing. They have heretofore operated with great success under different forms of constitutional government, and they are especially favorable to the development of individual comfort and national prosperity under American institutions.

Thus it may be seen that *immediate* good follows the formation of these associations,—without any new agitations, new laws, new revolutions, or new martyrdoms of any description.

The spreading circles of contentment and morality which these societies originate are incalculable in number and in benefit. It is impossible to estimate the social blessings they *immediately* commence by their exemplary influence; and, without wishing to speak disparagingly of other societies professing to seek the amelioration of the working classes, we must be allowed to express our conviction that building and loan societies will induce more rational and permanent improvement in the welfare of the country than all the other societies combined.

For a practical proof of the advantages derived from a judicious appropriation of the united funds contributed by individuals for that purpose, we may point out (from among English and American cases) the example exhibited by "The Brooklyn Accumulating Fund Association." As a suggestive guide in such matters, we have subjoined their "articles of association." By their "first annual report" (always the best commentary on any new project) it appears that 184 members who paid in $2.50 per month for 12 months, being $30 in the year, found their shares to be worth $62.78, showing an advance above the money paid in of $32.78 for each member! It is evident, therefore, that these societies present the most pleasing inducements for persons of limited income to unite and form such or similar associations throughout the country.

The beneficial results of these building and loan associations are neither imaginary nor distant—they are immediate and positive. They are neither selfish nor exclusive—they are eminently harmonious and diffusive,—extending the cheering influences of wealth and comfort throughout the land by a brotherly union of labor and capital.

B: McIntire's "Oak Hill"

Document IV-2: SHAKERS AND COMMUNITY

Although some reformers have continued to hope that the whole nation might become a model society, many others felt from the outset that America was too large and varied to respond at once to a unifying order. The appearance of a large number of communitarian experiments early in the nineteenth century represents an approach to reform that differed from the mainstream in that it was neither individualistic, gradualistic, nor revolutionary. (See Arthur Bestor, *Backwoods Utopias.* Philadelphia, University of Pennsylvania, 1950, p. 4.) As voluntaristic groups living apart, the communards were in a position to initiate drastic changes without delay or violence. Their isolation from the institutional fallibility that surrounded them allowed them to serve as examples to America in very much the same way that the New World hoped to serve as an example to the Old.

These communities showed extreme variety. Some were insistently and narrowly religious; others were secular and permissive. Some were made up entirely of recent immigrants. Some were extremely democratic, some were extremely autocratic. Some were peopled by visionaries who did not know one end of a saw from the other; others distinguished themselves through their artisanship. A few had wealthy members or sponsors; most had as their principal resource the sweat of their brows.

Consistently the communitarians offered alternatives to conventional institutions. Most of them honored the concept of shared property and of celibacy, but few of them completely outlawed family life and private possessions. Notable was a stress on equality of the sexes, experimental education, communal decision making, improved conditions of labor, and more equitable access to material goods. In one sense these communes may be seen as a network of social outposts where new modes could be tested. At best, however, they achieved an integrated way of life that offered a total alternative form of social organization.

One kind of integrity can be inferred from so limited an exhibit as the Shaker room here reproduced. It effectively symbolizes a way of life that was both functional and plain. The stove is well designed both for heating the room and warming the kettle. The chairs and bed are comfortable as well as graceful. The built-in closets keep the room uncluttered; the row of pegs holds all furnishings while the floor is cleaned or while the room is used for other purposes, such as the famous Shaker spiritual dances.

Of many widely sold and imitated products, Shaker furniture represented a primary virtue among this cult, "the gift to be simple." Its lack of adornment reflected a determination to let nothing frivolous or inessential stand between the believer and his God. That the furniture fell into but a very few standard types represents a shift in emphasis from private to common property. The firm, narrow cot indicates a disdain for fleshly indulgence including conjugal love. Thus the United Society of Believers, as they were officially titled, revealed in their habitations and furnishings a fully integrated way of life. (See Edward D. and Faith Andrews, *Religion in Wood*. Bloomington, Indiana University, 1966, Chapter Two.)

Begun in France, this faith came to America in the person of an Englishwoman, Ann Lee Stanley, who, as Mother Ann, became centrally responsible for its rapid spread until dozens of colonies from New England to Kentucky housed an estimated six thousand believers. The rigorously primitive Christian views, the severe austerity of the lifestyle, coupled with the sense of imminent perfection through spiritualism and the fast-approaching second coming of Christ, combined to epitomize the religious communism of this era. Among the first and at one time the largest of these communal sects, the Shakers in 1973 were reduced to two eldresses and eight communal sisters. They have decided to admit no more converts and will therefore expire as a living religion in America. Although they have dwindled steadily in numbers and visibility, their artifacts have continued to represent one model for social reform. In parting, at least, they will earn the respect of their more materialistic contemporaries. The avidly nonmercenary Shakers will leave behind them a trust fund of more than two million dollars. (See the Washington *Post* of August 10, 1973, p. B-18.)

SOURCE: Photograph of a room at the Henry Francis du Pont Winterthur Museum, reproduced through the museum's courtesy.

Shaker room

Document IV-3: RAPPITES AND COMMUNITY

Just as a Shaker chair can speak volumes in testimony to the austere life of spiritual devotion of which it formed a part, so the total shape of a community can attest to its integrated way of life. No group expressed itself as effectively in this vein as the Harmony Society under the leadership of George Rapp, who, between his arrival from Germany in 1803 and 1824, planted three successive villages in the wilderness. Each time a combination of agricultural and manufacturing skills brought abundance to the Harmonists.

Sites were chosen with an eye toward transportation and commerce as well as soil and climate. As a clearing was made, temporary shelters were built on the margin while permanent structures of sturdy construction were begun according to a preconceived plan. As structural timbers were cut and milled, they were marked with numbers and prepared for use in a manner anticipating modern prefabrication techniques. In the rendering of reconstructed Economy, the last Rappite village, can be seen the large Feast Hall which contained a magnificent open chamber for both religious and secular convocations. The spired church rose above all other structures, expressing central religious purpose. But the large open common with its Gothic grotto bespoke the rejection by this group of the dry rationalism which provoked their exodus from the German Lutheran church.

The mixture of large and small residences reflects a middle position between the ideal of celibacy and the willingness to accept family units. Houses were placed on their lots with care to preserve easy access and garden space. Workers lived as close as possible to their place of work, except that sources of pollution—the foul-smelling tannery—were perched carefully on the edge of town. The "Great House," elegantly furnished, was meant to impress the visitor and to serve certain communal functions. It was also a physical representation of the spiritual superiority of the leader, George Rapp.

The Rappites were typical in their dependence on a strong "father" whose death they did not long outlast. Although many experiments failed for economic reasons, the Rappites showed that a backwoods utopia could prosper if it were efficiently managed and if it could produce salable products in a commercially accessible location. Like many sects, the Rappites had trouble with a schismatic group; even the center of their disagreement—celibacy—is representative of the obstacles encountered in an effort to blend ascetic idealism with human nature. The sale of the second Harmonist village in Indiana to the Owenites can be taken as a concrete representation of the many ways in which religiously inspired communities experientially paved the way for the socialism of Fourierists and other secular groups.

While they flourished the Rappites provided a strong example for the many communities—utopian and otherwise—struggling for survival in the unsettled interior. Their skills at planning, building, and shaping their environment combined with loyalty and devotion to produce a sense of harmony much admired by their visitors. Had they been able to avoid some troubling questions of doctrine, and had they developed a competent succession of leadership, they—like so many other communities which they resemble—might have proved an even more usable model for a nation which then as now continues its search for that elusive quality called "a sense of community."

(Note: My feeling for the Rappites has been notably sharpened by Dr. Paul Douglas's dissertation, which I have had the pleasure of guiding, on the material culture of this community.)

SOURCE: Drawing by Charles Stotz, architect for the restoration of Economy, Pennsylvania. This central core of the village was surrounded by additional homes, shops, farms, and farm buildings. Photograph courtesy of the Pennsylvania Museum and Historical Commission.

Document IV-4: THE PHALANX SEEN BY OLMSTED

As the nineteenth century passed its first quarter communitarianism shifted its center from the religious to the secular. Famous experiments like Brook Farm and Oneida were influenced rather than dominated by religious movements; they were succeeded by settlements that reflected the nonreligious social views of men like Robert Dale Owen and Charles Fourier. These models depended not so much on inspiration and messianic leadership as on the power of an organizing philosophy. Like the

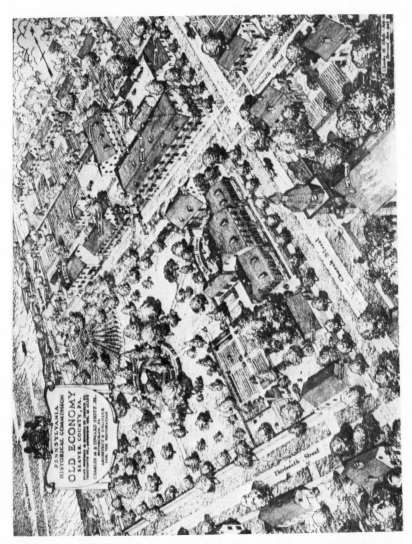

religious communities, they departed from private ownership and internal competition. Lacking an arbitrary leader they developed schemes for the division of labor that rested on special incentives for the least desirable chores. Cooperation was to minimize selfishness and lead eventually to a high culture in the creative arts and the life of the mind.

The ideas of Charles Fourier, especially as interpreted in America by

THE REFORM SPIRIT IN AMERICA

Albert Brisbane, became the most attractive framework for socialistic communitarianism. The most celebrated example was the North American Phalanx near Red Bank, New Jersey, which lasted from 1843 to 1854. In 1852 it was visited by Frederick Law Olmsted, who candidly described his impressions in a letter to his friend Charles Loring Brace, then revised this letter for newspaper publication.

The framing of the article makes it clear that the Phalanx was a topic of considerable contemporary interest. Olmsted regarded it, as he assumed his readers would, as a serious alternative to the existing social order. The letter begins with the comic picture of a "female Horace Greeley in bloomers," which was deleted from the article along with Olmsted's frank objections to menial labor. He assesses the "associationists" as not *very* intelligent and complains that, although cheerful and hard-working, they may have sacrificed too many of the social and intellectual amenities simply in order to make the cooperative enterprise pay. These reservations come through the newspaper version but in a more guarded way and accompanied by an attempt to explain the author's disappointment. In the end, however, he had to admire these Phalansterists because they had found a way of life not only more workable than the one they had left, but also more Christian.

Like Robert Frost and William Faulkner—albeit with much more reason—Olmsted liked to refer to himself as a farmer. This unaccountably neglected figure has come to light only in the last very few years with centennial exhibits of his work and with some much needed biographical and editorial attention. No one more than Olmsted saw America's needs for planning the growth of its cities and suburbs, for preserving of its parks, and public lands, for adapting the natural environment to the physical and aesthetic advantage of man. His comments on Red Bank, although qualified, amount to high praise from this incipient giant in the business of creating alternative social settings. His appearance toward the end of the antebellum communitarian movement foreshadows its dissolution into directions where Olmsted himself would lead.

(Note: I am indebted to my colleague, Charles C. McLaughlin, editor of the Olmsted papers, for allowing me to consult the annotated Brace letter and for furnishing me a typescript of the newspaper version.)

SOURCE: New York *Daily Tribune*, July 29, 1852, p. 6.

ASSOCIATION
The Phalanstery and the Phalansterians
by an Outsider
To the Editors of The N.Y. Tribune:

I have just made a visit to the "North American Phalanx," Monmouth County, N.J. Many of the readers of *The Tribune*, however unwilling they may be to accept the views of its Editors on the subject of Association, must have a curiosity to know how such ideas work in practice. It was such a motive induced me to accept an invitation from a member whose acquaintance I lately made, to visit this community, and I feel bound to give a candid relation of my observations. I confess to have paid but little attention to the subject previously and to have had no more knowledge or definite thoughts about it than any one must who has been in the habit of perusing *The Tribune* with much respect for the good intention and good sense of its editors, for several years.

There are six hundred acres of land in the domain of the Association, most of it of the ordinary quality of "Jersey land." About two hundred acres are under cultivation, much improved within a few years by dressing with marl, two beds of which, of superior quality, are on the property. A stream of water running through it, gives a small milling power. The nearest tide-water is five miles distant, where steamboat communication may be had daily, but at irregular hours, with New York, a poor sandy road to be traveled over between. The land cost twenty-five dollars an acre, and I believe I have stated all the material advantages of the location. The Association have a grist and a saw-mill driven with the aid of a steam-engine that they have added to the small water-power. No other branch of mechanical or manufacturing industry is carried on, and the labor of the members is mainly given to farming and market-gardening; and it is from the sale of agricultural products almost entirely that they must get their living and their profit.

The *Phalanstery* is much like the large hotel of a watering place, or a sea-shore house, made to accommodate 150 persons. There are chambers for single persons, and *suites* of rooms for families. There are also tenements detached from the main building, but having a covered way, that the members may reach it dry-shod in rainy weather. —These are each occupied by a family. There are certain common apartments also in the phalanstery, such as a reception room for visitors, a reading room, a dining hall; the kitchen, dairy and other domestic offices. A small steam-engine is employed for washing, mangling, churning, &c., and the arrangements of the domestic departments are all admirably contrived for saving labor. I should guess roughly that one woman could do the work of ten, with the ordinary farm-house kitchen conveniences—in other words, as far this goes, farmers would save their wives and *women folk* all but about one-tenth of their now necessary drudgery by living on the associated plan.

There is some pretty natural wood and a picturesque ravine near the house, but no garden or pleasure ground; indeed the *grounds* about the house are wholly neglected and have a shabby and uninviting appearance. It is evident that the Association have neglected everything else in their endeavor to make the experiment successful, financially. They have worked hard and constantly for this, and though, from entire inexperience at the business of market-gardening, to which their attention was chiefly directed, they at first made numerous mistakes, similar to those playfully alluded to by Hawthorne at Bythedale, and though they had a great many peculiar difficulties they have been rewarded in finding it *pay.* Last year, after paying the members at the rate of wages for labor higher than that ordinarily given by farmers in this vicinity, the Association divided five per cent on the capital invested in the undertaking among the shareholders. When we consider how hard it is for farmers in general to make a decent living, we must acknowledge that they have proved a great advantage in the coöperative principle, as applied to agriculture.

That the financial success of the community is the legitimate result of the association of labor and capital, I am satisfied, and I should judge the peculiar description of husbandry to which its attention has been directed, was that in which it was least likely to have been profitably employed, because it is that in which labor-saving implements and machinery can be employed with the least advantage. In addition to the profits divided last year, it should be mentioned that extensive orchards, as yet making scarcely any returns, are growing.

The Refectory is a fine, spacious hall, with perhaps twenty tables, each long enough for a dozen persons to dine off. There are bills of fare changed every day, in which the dishes provided for each meal are mentioned, with their cost—as at an eating-house. By buying at wholesale, and using all possible contrivances to lessen labor in preparing and cooking food, of course the cost of living is very low; but every little item counts. Thus: bread 1 cent, butter 1/2 cent, as well as roast-beef 3 cents, and ice-cream (a large ration of the richest "Philadelphia") 2 cents. During drouth and short pasture the buttercakes are graduated by the stamp a trifle smaller, which I mention as an indication of the systematic exactness to which the domestic economy of the establishment is brought. There are several summer or transient boarders at the establishment, and these are charged, in addition to the cost of the food they choose and a small rent for their bed-chamber, $2 a week for the profit of the Association. The waiters are mainly from among the most refined and pleasing young ladies of the Association. On taking a seat you are introduced to the lady who attends your table, and you feel yourself to be in the relation of guest, not of superior, to her. She takes part in the general conversation of the table, but comes, and goes as there is need—is a very good waiter indeed, doing her duty with tact, sweetness and grace. "Why do so many of the best of your young people choose to be waiters and so deprive themselves in a great measure of the social enjoyment of dining with their friends?" "They all dine together afterward; and as they are among the best of us, it is a privilege to dine with them—of course to *wait* with them."

One great point they have succeeded in perfectly; in making labor honorable. Mere physical labor they have too much elevated I think, but any rate the *lowest* and most menial and disagreeable duties of a civilized community are made really reputable and honorable, as well as generally easy and agreeable. A man who spent a large part of his time in smoking and reading newspapers, and chatting it away, or in merely recreative employments, would feel ashamed of himself here, would feel *small* and consider it a privilege to be allowed to black boots or sweep, or milk, a part of the time.

As to the people of the community, in general I have a strong respect for them as earnest, unselfish, hard-working livers in the faith of a higher life for man here below as well as hereafter "above." I think they are living devoutly and more in accordance with the principles of Christ *among themselves*, than any neighborhood of an equal number that I know of. There are fewer *odd* characters among them than I expected to see; generally there was much simplicity and self-containedness: they seem to care very little—too little—"for appearance" or what the world outside thought of them, and greatly to love one another. They are so far as I could learn, strongly attached to the *Phalanx*, feel confident it is the right way to live, have *enjoyed* it and thus far fully realized their hopes in joining it: "I wouldn't leave for worlds"—"couldn't live, it seems to me, in any other way;" "It is like the opening of heaven compared to what life was before I came here," I heard from different individuals. One Episcopal clergyman who was formerly much respected and beloved, and paid $1,000 a year for his services as Rector of a country church, and who, after a great struggle with the conviction that the morality and religion he was educated to preach were not the morality and faith preached by Christ and designed by him for the conversion of the world from its ancient state of sin and misery, declares that he is satisfied that here is the true church of Christ's gospel, and in this way it must be that the Kingdom must come. There is also a Unitarian clergyman who came hither by much the same road.

I cannot tell what sort of people the majority were when they came here, and thus find a difficulty in judging what the effect of the associative life has been upon them. Mostly New-Englanders, I should think, and working people; few or none independently wealthy. (The *stock* of the Phalanx is mostly held by New-York capitalists.) Whether any considerable number were actually day laborers, living from hand to mouth, uneducated and uncouth, I could not be satisfied. Some of the later additions plainly are so, many of the older ones might have been, and if so they have been a good deal refined and civilized by this life. If we compare their situation with an average of the agricultural class, laborers and all, even in the best of New-England, it is a most *blessed* advance. They are better in nearly all respects, and I don't see why, if such associations were common, and our lowest class— (I mean poorest and least comfortable and least in the way of improvement moral and mental,) of laborers, could be drawn of their own will into them, why they should not be similarly advanced in every way. Put a *common-place* man, of our poorest agricultural or manufacturing class into *such circumstances*, and it looks to me every way probable that he would be greatly elevated, be made a *new man* of in a few years. On the other hand, take the average of our people of *all* classes, and on the whole, it seems as if the influence of the system, if they would keep to it a little while, would be favorable. They would be likely to live more sensibly, happier, healthier and better. If you take our most religious and cultivated sensible people, then I think it would depend much on individual tastes and character. For most of these, particularly of English blood, it would require a change, a good deal of a struggle to come handsomely and profitably into it.

The long and short of it is, I am more of a *Fourierite* than before I visited the experiment. The united household (and semi-conglomeration) of families even, works better than I was willing to believe possible. Nevertheless, I don't think I shall be a Fourierite for myself, but for many, for a large part of an American community (people,) I think I may be. It wouldn't suit me, but many, I think, it would; and if I was obliged to live mainly by *manual* labor I am not sure but I should go in for it myself.

An *Associationist* I very decidedly am, more than I was before I went to the Phalanx. The advantages of coöperation are manifestly great, the saving of labor immense; the cheapening of food, rent, &c., enough to make starvation abundance. The advantages by making knowledge, intellectual and moral culture and esthetic culture more easy—popular, that is, the advantages by *democratizing* religion, science, art, mental cultivation and social refinement, I am induced to think *might be* almost equally great among the *associated.* They *are not* at the N.A. Phalanx— and yet are to some degree. Those who came there refined, religious and highly intelligent, may have suffered. I saw no evidence that they had, but should have expected it, because they have given themselves up to too narrow ranges of thought, have worked too hard to make the Association succeed; sacrificed themselves, if so, for the benefit of the world's progress over them. It is not by any means yet a well organized and arranged establishment. They are constantly improving—seeing errors, and returning to do up matters which, in the haste of a struggle to get started, were overlooked. There is yet an immense deal, as they are aware, to be attended to and better arranged when they get time. They are in great need of mechanics, but I suspect it is an error of their theory that they are. What they need for improvement as a *community of moral creatures* is more attention to the intellectual. They want an *"Educational Series"* very much. A Frenchman acts as teacher to the fry, but there is no proper nursing department, and the children, and not the children alone, are growing without proper discipline of mind: A rough lot one would expect them to make, but I must confess those who are breaking into manhood, and especially into womanhood, tell well for the system. They are young *ladies* and young *gentlemen* naturally, and

524 THE REFORM SPIRIT IN AMERICA

without effort or disagreeable selfconsciousness. If I had a boy to educate, who at sixteen had acquired at home habits of continued perserving application of mind in study, and who was tolerably stocked with facts and formulas, I would a good deal prefer that he should spend the next few years of his life as a working member of the North American Phalanx than at Yale or Harvard.

I have neglected to notice a number of points at the Phalanx that would be interesting, a good deal to praise, a good deal to reprove; but they do not bear upon the important questions which it is the purpose of the members to do something by their association to solve. If there are any slight errors in my statements, observations and conjectures, they will be excused as not materially affecting these. I have endeavored to notice what I thought most desirable for the public to know and reflect upon, and I can not conclude without, as one of the public, expressing my gratitude to the members for the generous earnesses with which, for the public good, they are making their experiment. I pray for their success; but whether it comes as they anticipate or not, they will have their reward.

July 24, 1852 —*An American Farmer*

Document IV-5: AN OLMSTED COMMUNITY: RIVERSIDE

The visit of Frederick Law Olmsted to Red Bank may not have been the most important event in his early life, but when he turned from observing communities to planning them he produced certain echoes of his earlier criteria. The proposal to build a suburb outside Chicago, Illinois, is a highly functional piece of prose, designed to convince investors that they should pledge their resources in a certain way. Much of it is very specific, referring to demography, transportation, and roadbeds. Thence the author shows those qualities that made him so much in advance of his time: the care for preserving hills, streams, and vegetation; the hope that arrangements in the physical setting could make men more healthy, sociable, and efficient. Warming toward his peroration, seven paragraphs from the end, he writes that the anticipated suburbanites should be conceived of as "Christians, loving one another" and that this fact should "be everywhere manifest in the completeness, and choiceness, and beauty of the means they possess of coming together, of being together, and especially of recreating and enjoying them together on common ground. . . ."

Olmsted never said that a single model community of any size could be planned and executed in a way that would solve man's eternal social problems. In this sense he was not a communitarian. But, as the communitarian movement ended, its force was transmitted in part to those few practical idealists like Olmsted who could see that—models or no—the face of America needed planning. One of his principal arguments for Central Park in New York City was the European urban example of how parks assured peaceful congregation and contentment among the workers. His plan for the Bronx was more than modern in its realization that public transportation must be effective and convenient yet somehow unobtrusive. From Asheville to Washington he showed that great buildings would fail to carry their message were they not arranged against the appropriate natural setting. To some extent his campuses and parks were ideal communities. Riverside, as an early planned "bedroom" suburb, was in no way meant to be self-sufficient. Its meaning was as an extension of Chicago; in fact, argued Olmsted, only with places like Riverside in which to reside, could the city be accepted as a constructive force in the life of the individual. (Riverside today still reflects to a surprising degree the Olmsted intentions.)

SOURCE: Both the plan and the report are in the papers of Frederick Law Olmsted, Sr., Manuscripts Division, Library of Congress. They have been reproduced together with related materials (including the record of Olmsted's efforts to keep his plan intact) by Theodora Kimball in "Riverside, Illinois: A Residential Neighborhood Designed over Sixty Years Ago," *Landscape Architecture* Vol. XXI (July, 1931), pp. 257-291.

PRELIMINARY REPORT UPON THE PROPOSED SUBURBAN VILLAGE AT RIVERSIDE, NEAR CHICAGO BY OLMSTED, VAUX & CO.

LANDSCAPE ARCHITECTS

TO THE RIVERSIDE IMPROVEMENT COMPANY.

Gentlemen:

You have requested a report from us, upon an enterprise which you desire to bring before the public, and which appears to rest on the following grounds:

First.—Owing partly to the low, flat, miry, and forlorn character of the greater part of the country immediately about Chicago, and the bleak surface, arid soil, and exposure of the remainder to occasional harsh and frigid gusts of wind off the lake, and partly to the fact that the rapidity with which the town is being enlarged, causes all the available environs to be laid out with a view to a future demand solely for town purposes, and with no regard to the satisfaction of rural tastes, the city, as yet, has no true suburbs or quarters in which urban and rural advantages are agreeably combined with any prospect of long continuance.

Second.—If, under these circumstances, sites offering any very decided and permanent advantages for suburban residences could be put in the market, there would at once be a demand for them, which would continue and increase with the enlargement and progress in wealth and taste of the population of the city.

Third.—You have secured a large body of land, which, much beyond any other, has natural advantages for this purpose.

Fourth.—If, by a large outlay, these advantages could be developed to the utmost, and could be supplemented by abundant artificial conveniences of a high order, and the locality could thus be rendered not only very greatly superior to any other near Chicago, but could be made to compare satisfactorily, on the whole, with the most favored suburbs to be found anywhere else, a good return for such outlay might reasonably be expected.

We propose to review these grounds so far as they are not matters of fact easily put to the test of observation by those interested.

To understand the character of the probable demand for semi-rural residences near Chicago, it must be considered that the most prominent characteristic of the present period of civilization has been the strong tendency of people to flock together in great towns. This tendency unquestionably is concurrent, and probably identical, with an equally unprecedented movement of invention, energy, and skill, toward the production of certain classes of conveniences and luxuries, which, even yet, can generally be fully enjoyed by great numbers of people only in large towns. Arrangements for the easy gratification of certain tastes, which, until recently, were possessed by but a very few, even of the most wealthy class of any country, have consequently, of late, become common to thousands in every civilized land, while numerous luxuries, that the largest fortunes in the old world could not have commanded even half a century since, are enjoyed by families of comparatively moderate means, in towns which have sprung up from the wilderness, within the memory of some still living in them.

Progress in this way was never more rapid than at the present moment, yet in respect to the corresponding movement of populations there are symptoms of a change; a counter-tide of migration, especially affecting the more intelligent and more fortunate classes, although as yet of but moderate strength, is clearly perceptible, and almost equally so, in Paris, London, Vienna, Berlin, New York, Boston and Philadelphia. The most substantial manifestation of it perhaps, is to be found in the vast increase in value of eligible sites for dwellings near public parks, and in all localities of much natural beauty within several hours' journey of every great town. Another evidence of the same tendency, not less conclusive because it indicates an impulse as yet undecided and incomplete, is found in the constant modification which has occurred in the manner of laying out all growing towns, and which is invariably in the direction of a separation of business and dwelling streets, and toward rural spaciousness in the latter. The broader the streets are made, provided they are well prepared in respect to what are significantly designated ''the modern conveniences,'' and especially if some slight rural element is connected with them, as by rows of trees or little enclosures of turf and foliage, the greater is the demand for dwelling-places upon them.

There is no evidence that the large class of conveniences, comforts and luxuries, which have been heretofore gained by close congregation, is beginning to have less positive attractiveness or commercial value, but it is very clear that the conviction is becoming established in the minds of great numbers of people that the advance in this respect, which has occurred in towns, has been made at too great a sacrifice of certain advantages which can at present be only enjoyed by going out of them. That this is a sound conviction, and not a mere whim, caprice, or reaction of fancy, temporarily affecting the rich, fashionable and frivolous, appears from the fact that it is universally held as the result of careful study by philanthropists, physicians and men of science. It is an established conclusion, for instance, as explained by Dr. Ramsay, in his recent annual address before the British Association for the Advancement of Social Science, that the mere proximity of dwellings which characterizes all strictly urban neighborhoods, is a prolific source of morbid conditions of the body and mind, manifesting themselves chiefly in nervous feebleness or irritability and various functional derangements, relief or exemption from which can be obtained in no way without great sacrifices of convenience and social advantages, except by removal to suburban districts.

It thus becomes evident that the present outward tendency of town populations is not so much an ebb as a higher rise of the same flood, the end of which must be, not a sacrifice of urban conveniences, but their combination with the special charms and substantial advantages of rural conditions of life. Hence a series of neighborhoods of a peculiar character is already growing up in close relation with all large towns, and though many of these are as yet little better than rude over-dressed villages, or fragmentary half-made towns, it can hardly be questioned that, already, there are to be found among them the most attractive, the most refined and the most soundly wholesome forms of domestic life, and the best application of the arts of civilization to which mankind has yet attained.

It would appear then, that the demands of suburban life, with reference to civilized refinement, are not to be retrogression from, but an advance upon, those which are characteristic of town life, and that no great town can long exist without great suburbs. It would also appear that whatever element of convenient residence is demanded in a town will soon be demanded in a suburb, so far as is possible for it to be associated with the conditions which are the peculiar advantage of the country, such as purity of air, umbrageousness, facilities for quiet out-of-door recreation and distance from the jar, noise, confusion, and bustle of commercial thoroughfares.

There need then be no fear that a happy combination of these conditions would ever fail to be exceedingly attractive to the people of Chicago, or that a demand for residences where it is found, would be liable to decline; on the contrary, it would be as sure to increase, as the city is sure to increase in population and in wealth, and for the same reason.

We proceed to consider the intrinsic value of your property for the purpose in view.

The question of access first demands attention. The centre of the proposed suburb is nine miles from the business centre of Chicago, the nearer points being about six miles apart. There is a double-track railroad from Chicago of remarkably good construction, with its first out-of-town station, at which every train is required to stop in the midst of your property. The advantages of the locality, in this respect, are already superior to those of many thriving suburbs.

A railroad, however, at the best affords a very inadequate and unsatisfactory means of communication between a rural habitation and a town, either for a family or for a man of business: as, moreover, one of the chief advantages of a suburban home, is the opportunity which it gives of taking air and exercise in driving, riding, and walking, it is a great desideratum, especially where time is so valuable as it is generally in Chicago, that a business man should be able to enjoy such an opportunity incidentally to his necessary communication with his store or office. . . .

We should advise you, in the first place, to obtain possession, if possible, of a strip of ground from two hundred to six hundred feet wide, extending from the city to the nearest border of your property, to secure its thorough drainage, to plant it with trees, and to carry through it a series of separate, but adjoining ways, especially adapted in construction—first for walking, second for riding, third for pleasure-driving, and fourth to give convenient access to houses to be built on the route and accommodate heavy freighting, without inconvenience to the through pleasure travel.

The main drive should be constructed in a very thorough and finished manner, so that, without perfect rigidity of surface, it will be storm- and frost-proof.

The ride should adjoin the drive, so that equestrians can at pleasure turn from it to converse with friends in carriages; it should have a soft and slightly yielding surface, that the great jar and danger of slipping, which occurs in a paved road, may be avoided.

The grateful influences of the grove extending through the prairie, with the amelioration of climate and soil which would result from thorough drainage and wind-breaks, and the advantages which would be found in the several proposed means of communication at all seasons of the year, would be such that continuous lines of villas and gardens would undoubtedly soon be established adjoining it, and the hour's drive through it, necessary to reach your property, would be neither tedious nor fatiguing.

At certain intervals upon the route, it would be desirable to provide openings with some special decorations, and here should be sheltered seats and watering places.

We see no reason why, if this suggestion is carried out liberally, it should not provide, or, at least, begin to provide, another pressing desideratum of the city of Chicago, namely, a general promenade ground. The promenade is a social custom of great importance in all the large towns of Europe. It is an open-air gathering for the purpose of easy, friendly, unceremonious greetings, for the enjoyment of change of scene, of cheerful and exhilarating sights and sounds, and of various good cheer, to which the people of a town, of all classes, harmoniously resort on equal terms, as to a common property. There is probably no custom which so manifestly displays the advantages of a Christian, civilized and democratic community, in contra-distinction from an aggregation of families, clans, sects, or castes. There is none more favorable to a healthy civic pride, civic virtue, and civic prosperity. As yet, the promenade has hardly begun to be recognised as an institution in Chicago, but there is no doubt that it soon must be, and it is evident from the present habits and manners of the people, that when once established, the custom will nowhere else be more popular or beneficent in its influence. Even now, with no tolerable accommodations for a general out-of-door pleasure gathering, nor any drives adapted for pleasure vehicles, which are not crowded when a few hundred carriages come together, there are probably more horses, in proportion to the population, kept for pleasure use, than in any city of the old, if not of the new world. There is understood to be no ground about the city possessing natural advantages for the formation of a public pleasure-ground of the character of the great parks in which the promenades of other metropolitan cities are generally held. By making the accommodations of your approach sufficiently large and sufficiently attractive, by associating with it several turning-points and resting-places in the midst of pleasure-grounds of moderate extent, your enterprise would, therefore, not merely supply Chicago, as you propose that it shall do, with a suburb, as well adapted as any of the suburbs of other cities, both for permanent habitations and country seats, and for occasional rural fetes and holiday recreations of families living in the town, but, in all probability, would provide it also with a permanent promenade-ground, having a character peculiar to itself, and not without special advantages. This result would be greatly enhanced if, as would probably be the case, certain entirely practicable improvements of the plan of the city should be made in connection with the construction of your approach.

The benefit which would result from this to your original enterprise is evident. Having means of communication with the city through the midst of such a ground, made gay and interesting by the movement of fine horses and carriages, and of numbers of well-dressed people, mainly cheerful with the enjoyment of recreation and the common entertainment, the distance would not be too great for the interchange of friendly visits, for the exercise of hospitality to a large circle of acquaintance, or for the enjoyment of the essential, intellectual, artistic, and social privileges which specially pertain to a metropolitan condition of society; and yet it would be sufficient to justify a neglect, on the part of a suburban resident, of most of those ceremonial social duties which custom seems to require, and in which so much time is necessarily spent in all great towns. . . .

The misfortune of most existing suburbs is, that in such parts of them as have been built up little by little, without any general plan, the highways are usually adapted only to serve the bare irresistible requirements of agriculture, and that in such other parts as have been laid out more methodically, no intelligent design has been pursued to secure any distinctly rural attractiveness, the only aim apparently being to have a plan, which, seen on paper, shall suggest the possibility of an extension of the town-streets over the suburb, and of thus giving a town value to the lots upon them.

Exactly the opposite of this should be aimed at in your case, and, in regard to those special features whereby the town is distinguished from the country, there should be the greatest possible contrast which is compatible with the convenient communication and pleasant abode of a community; economy of room, and facilities for business, being minor considerations.

In the highways, celerity will be of less importance than comfort and convenience of movement, and as the ordinary directness of line in town-streets, with its resultant regularity of plan would suggest eagerness to press forward, without looking to the right hand or the left, we should recommend the general adoption, in the design of your roads, of gracefully-curved lines, generous spaces, and the absence of sharp corners, the idea being to suggest and imply leisure, contemplativeness and happy tranquility.

Without turf, and foliage, and birds, the character of the highways, whatever their ground plan, would differ from those of the town chiefly in the quality of desolation and dreariness. Turf and trees should abound then, and this implies much space in the highways, besides that which is requisite for the passage of vehicles and people on foot. . . .

We cannot judiciously attempt to control the form of the houses which men shall build, we can only, at most, take care that if they build very ugly and inappropriate houses, they shall not be allowed to force them disagreeably upon our attention when we desire to pass along the road upon which they stand. We can require that no house shall be built within a certain number of feet of the highway, and we can insist that each house-holder shall maintain one or two living trees between his house and his highway-line.

A few simple precautions of this kind, added to a tasteful and convenient disposition of shade trees, and other planting along the roadsides and public places, will, in a few years, cause the whole locality, no matter how far the plan may be extended, to possess, not only the attraction of neatness and convenience, and the charm of refined sylvan beauty and grateful umbrageousness, but an aspect of secluded peacefulness and tranquility more general and pervading than can possibly be found in suburbs which have grown up in a desultory hap-hazard way. If the general plan of such a suburb is properly designed on the principles which have been suggested, its character will inevitably also, notwithstanding its tidiness, be not only informal, but, in a moderate way, positively picturesque, and when contrasted with the constantly repeated right angles, straight lines, and flat surfaces which characterize our large modern towns, thoroughly refreshing. . . .

There are two aspects of suburban habitation that need to be considered to ensure success; first, that of the domiciliation of men by families, each family being well provided for in regard to its domestic in-door and out-door private life; second, that of the harmonious association and co-operation of men in a community, and the intimate relationship and constant intercourse, and inter-dependence between families. Each has its charm, and the charm of both should be aided and acknowledged by all means in the general plan of every suburb.

As, however, it can be no part of a general plan to provide for the interior arrangements of ground which is to be private, the domestic advantages which a suburb will possess can be little more than suggested through the arrangement of the means of division, and of passage between private and public ground. It is especially desirable, therefore, that these means of division and of passage should be carefully studied. They should be enjoyable in themselves; they should on no account be imaginary lines, nor should they be obscured or concealed, as it would be better that they should be if such divisions or means of restraint were unfortunately required for any reason in a park.

On the public side of all such dividing lines, the fact that the families dwelling within a suburb enjoy much in common, and all the more enjoy it because it is in common, the grand fact, in short, that they are Christians, loving one another, and not Pagans, fearing one another, should be everywhere manifest in the completeness, and choiceness, and beauty of the means they possess of coming together, of being together, and especially of recreating and enjoying them together on common ground, and under common shades.

We should recommend the appropriation of some of the best of your property for public grounds, and that most of these should have the character of informal village-greens, commons and play-grounds, rather than of enclosed and defended parks or gardens. We would have, indeed, at frequent intervals in every road, an opening large enough for a natural group of trees, and often provide at such points croquet or ball grounds, sheltered seats and drinking fountains, or some other objects which would be of general interest or convenience to passers-by.

It will probably be best to increase the height of the mill-dam so as to enlarge the area of the public water suitable for boating and skating, and so as to completely cover some low, flat ground now exposed in low stages of the river. At the same time, a larger outlet should be provided to prevent floods above the dam from injuring the shore. A public drive and walk should be carried near the edge of the bank in such a way as to avoid destroying the more valuable trees growing upon it, and there should be pretty boat-landings, terraces, balconies overhanging the water, and pavilions at points desirable for observing regattas, mainly of rustic character, and to be half overgrown with vines.

All desirable improvements of this character, more and better than can be found in any existing suburb in the United States, can be easily supplied at comparatively small cost. That which it is of far more consequence to secure at the outset, and which cannot be obtained at small cost, unfortunately, is a system of public ways of thoroughly good construction.

As we have already shown, in speaking upon the question of approach, your property is not without special advantages for this purpose, and, on the whole, we feel warranted in expressing the opinion that your scheme, though it will necessarily require a large outlay of capital, is a perfectly practicable one, and if carried out would give Chicago a suburb of highly attractive and substantially excellent character.

It should be well understood that this is a preliminary report, and that our observations have been necessarily of a somewhat superficial character. A complete topographical survey, and a much more deliberate study of the conditions to be dealt with, must precede the preparation of a definite plan, if it is to have any assured value.

Respectfully,

OLMSTED, VAUX & CO.,
Landscape Architects.

110 Broadway, New York, Sept 1, 1868.

Document IV-6: WRIGHT'S BROADACRE CITY

In an article that makes helpful connections between several items in this section, Martin Meyerson found Frank Lloyd Wright to be distinctive as a planner because of his effort to combine the best of city and country as they now exist. (See "Utopian Traditions and the Planning of

B: Wright's Broadacre City

Cities," *Daedalus*, Vol. XC [Winter, 1961], p. 189.) For all his eminence as an architect, Wright never got the chance to function fully as a
planner. He was easily capable of setting forth the physical specifications
for his ideal community in realizable terms. To accommodate the kind of
life he envisioned, however, some degree of political and economic
transformation would have been mandatory.

His prose reads like a kind of practical Transcendentalism, especially
in its attribution of almost mystical power to the quality of individualism
and to the principle of organic relationships. Although he called his
Usonia, or Broadacre City, a capitalist experiment, he believed in severe
restraints on the entrepreneurial class. Inventions and credit, he thought,
should belong to the people. In his feeling for land ownership and
taxation he reminds one of both Thomas Jefferson and Henry George (see
II-21). Airspace, the common carrier of the future, would also belong to
the people as decentralization attacked the feudalistic attitudes symbolized by the large cities with their thick walls and locked doors.

A plan of Broadacre City would show an Olmsted-like respect for the
preservation of varied topography and vegetation. Decentralization of

population into communities of modest size provided an example to the planners of Columbia (see IV-8). To regard as implausibly visionary the physical aspects of this dream is to forget the many architectural innovations and prophecies attributable to this influential American.

SOURCE: A: Baker Brownell and Frank Lloyd Wright, *Architecture and Modern Life.* New York, Harper, 1937, pp. 308-328, abridged. (For the interesting and related view of Mr. Wright's interviewer, see Baker Brownell, *The Human Community: Its Philosophy and Practice for a Time of Crisis.* New York, Harper, 1950.) B: A view of the community discussed in IV-6A, Broadacre City as drawn by F. L. Wright. Arthur Drexler, *The Drawings of Frank Lloyd Wright.* New York, Museum of Modern Art, 1962, plate 266.

A: BROADACRE CITY DISCUSSED

Wright: Before we proceed with the details of Broadacre City, let us get a little clearer the basis upon which it was conceived. Broadacre City is no city at all in the sense that you are using the word. Broadacre City is everywhere or nowhere. It is the country itself come alive as a truly great city. It is out of the ground into the light by way of man's sense of himself in his work. With his feet on his own ground each man is not only a potential but an actual capitalist. So you see, while the present condition under which he lives is money-bound first and is everything else afterward, in Broadacre City a man's own capabilities in his work become his wealth and by means of that wealth he obtains, more directly than is possible now, those things of which he dreams and that he desires. He is not and never can be unemployed or a slave in any sense. The true wealth of our nation would be increased enormously instead of funneled down to the little drip that we are in the habit of calling our financial resources.

Brownell: Does that mean that he lives in a comparatively self-sustaining system?

Wright: Not comparatively self-sustaining. Absolutely self-sustaining, if he is a true self. A true self still lives in most men notwithstanding the ravages of such libertine individualism as the once famous Liberty League called upon in the name of freedom.

Brownell: Still he must buy tools, automobiles, power, with money, must he not?

Wright: Not with money as a speculative commodity, but by some simple social medium of exchange which enables the fruits of his labor in connection with natural resources to be exchanged for the fruits of another man's labor in that connection. . . .

We are now in a society built like some badly planned factory, run like a factory, systematically turning out herd-struck humans as machinery turns out shoes. Our society is a cultural weed of a dangerous kind: dangerous to ourselves and to others. When life itself becomes a restless tenant, as it has become on our farms no less than in big cities, the citizen must lose sight of the true aims of human existence and voluntarily accept substitutes. His life, now unnaturally gregarious, tends towards the blind adventure of a crafty animal. To live, or "get by," is some form of graft, coupled with some febrile pursuit of sex. Only in these does he find or see relief from the factual routine in this mechanical uproar of mechanical conflicts of this mechanical life of his—conflicts that seem to hypnotize him while they crucify him. . . .

Brownell: What would the average citizen do in Broadacre City? What would be his pattern of work and enjoyment?

Wright: As a matter of fact there would be no "average citizen" in Broadacre City. Broadacre City aims to eliminate the "average citizen."

Brownell: What would the "unaverage citizen" do?

Wright: Let us understand, first, that we are concerned here with a future for individuality in organic sense. I believe individuality to be the prime integrity of the human being as integer of the race. Without such integrity I believe there can be no real culture whatsoever, no matter what we may choose to call civilization. I have called this city Broadacre City because it is a broad freedom for the individual, honestly democratic, based upon the ground—the minimum of one acre to the person. To date our capitalism has miscalled personality individuality. Our eclecticism, which must be called mere personality instead of true individuality, has, by way of what we call taste—we have used taste as a substitute for culture—obstructed where it has not obscured the integrity of individuality. And we, on account of that vicious, fundamental misunderstanding, have become the prey of our captains turned playboys, our kept universities, our high-powered culture-mongers and we—the people, yes—stand in danger of losing our chance at this free life. Nevertheless, our charter of liberty originally held it out to us. And now I see a pattern for that free life in Broadacre City. It is a life that reckons with the law of change as a desirable circumstance, not as fatality.

Brownell: That is a good statement of the ideal of life in Broadacre City. But is there anything in your plan that explains how it will come into existence?

Wright: Ask me rather, first, "What is the nature of this plan?" And I will say it is a free pattern. It is of the ground and with the ground. Wherever this free pattern is applied it varies with the ground and as the conditions of climate and life vary. The ground may happen to lie suited to one kind of life or to many kinds. The common spirit of the people involved is disciplined automatically from within by means and methods and materials which are all organic.

It is a great unity in diversity I have sought.

The changes that Broadacre sees and accepts as natural and desirable have already made the big city no longer efficient or endurable. But the city struggles, as it must, against the change. For example, let's say that the present city spacing was based fairly enough on the human being on his feet or sitting in some trap behind a horse or two. So all now is too small, too mean for the automobile. And originally the city was a group life of powerful individualities true to life, conveniently enough spaced. But by way of instantaneous communications and easy mobilization this better life has already left the modern city. Not only such genius as the city has known for many a day is recruited from the country, but success in the city means life in the country. What, then, is the overgrown city for? Almost all necessities that once chained the individual to city life are dying away and the present citizens must die there as these needs die. It is only as life has been taken from him and he has meekly accepted substitutes offered to placate or fleece him that any citizen voluntarily remains in the city. The fundamental unit of space-measurement has so radically changed that the man now bulks ten to one in space, and a thousand to one in speed, when seated in his motor car. Mobilization is rapidly become universal. This circumstance alone would render the present form of our cities obsolete. Like some dead dwelling the city is inhabited only because we have it. We feel that we must use it and cannot afford to throw it away to build the new one we now know we need. But compulsion is here. I imagine we'll soon be willing to give all we have, to get this new freedom that might so easily be ours. We will give what we have left to get it for our posterity, even if we may not have it ourselves. Devouring human individuality invariably ends in desolation, some kind of desertion such as is under way. Invariably, as history records, greed ends in destruction of the devourer. The city is in this case the devourer, and the impulses that exaggerated the mechanical forces that built it are senile in nearly every phase.

Brownell: Now what of the new Broadacre City?

Wright: The principles underlying the free pattern called Broadacre City are simply those of an organic architecture. Organic architecture now comes with a demand for finer integrity in order to unite modern improvements with natural resources in the service of men. Integration is here, as set dead against centralization. By the natural working of organic forces and ideas man is now to be brought forward to his inheritance, the ground, that he may become a whole man again. There is no longer much excuse for him to remain the parasite that spasmodic centralization has succeeded, almost, in making of him. The practical solution is this matter of social structure or free pattern. And definitely it is a matter of what we call organic architecture. So we must begin to learn to see life as organic architecture and begin to learn to see organic architecture as life. Broadacre City is not only the only democratic city; it is the only possible city looking towards any future for these United States. . . .

Let us first take the problem of the poor. That means the housing problem receiving so much philanthropic attention from higher up at the moment. Beneficent though it is, it can only result in putting off by mitigation the day of regeneration for the poor. The majority of the poor are those damaged most by this growth of unearned increment as it piles up into vast fortunes by way of some kind of rent. Where is the place of the poor in this city now built by triple rent, that is to say rent within rent upon rent for rent? A vicious circle. There is always some dignity in freedom, even though one's own way may sink to license or filth. But what dignity can there be in the cell of a soulless economic repetition? What dignity is there in spiritual poverty, even though some posy be stuck in a flower box, like a gratuity, for each poor man by those who, having bested him, would now better him?

Why not make more free to the poor the land they were born to inherit as they were born to inherit air to breathe and daylight to see by and water to drink? Else why are they born? I am aware of the academic economist's reaction to any land question. Nevertheless, Henry George clearly enough showed us the basis of poverty in human society. Some organic solution of this land problem is not only needed, it is imperative. Broadacre City proposes one and it is not the Single Tax.

What hope is there for a great or even a good architecture while land holds the improvements instead of the improvements made by the man holding the land? For any organic economic structure this is the wrong end about. Our architecture in the circumstances can only be for some landlord. But by some form of exemption and subsequent sharing of the increase in land values, we can now make his acre available to each so-called poor man, or rather make more than an acre available according to his ability to use the land. And let us begin to call his "education" that training which makes him competent in respect to this birthright of his—the ground. He has been industrialized to the limit. Now agrarianize him. . . .

See the plans. They are truly ground plans. And where? Well, you will see in the models that mobilization is already his by way of a mobilized traffic lane that used to be the railroad, or some bus or perhaps a second-hand Ford, or perhaps a new one of his own, as the prices for Fords and other cars are going now. Emancipated from the rent that he must now pay in the city in order to work at all (everything he earns he must spend to keep him on the job), the machine worker goes back by way of this machine to his birthright in the ground. Ten miles or twenty is now easy for him. So where? Anywhere almost. He may go to work, perhaps, for some manufacturing employer in some decentralized factory unit near by. Fifteen miles is near by now by any modern standard of space or of time.

Now as to "how." Let us say that the poor man—the man at the machine is usually the poor man—buys the modern, civilized, standardized privy (it is a duplicate or even triplicate bathroom) manufactured and delivered complete in a single unit, even as his car or bathtub is manufactured and ready to use when connected to a standard tile septic tank or a cesspool. These costly civic improvements that cost so much are growing less necessary every day. Pass the hat, please, for Mr. Insull! The free man plants this first unit on his free ground as a focal point to which a standardized complete kitchen unit appropriate to the general plan of Broadacres may be added. As the months go by, the rent saved may buy other standardized units, harmonizing with the first. He earns them by work he has been trained to do on his own ground or trained also to do in the factory units scattered about within, say, fifteen to thirty miles. Near by. The units would be suited in general scheme of design to assembly either on flat land or on hillside and be so designed as to make a well planned whole when put together. These various organic units cheaply become the machine worker's by way of his labor either in the factory unit near by or on his own ground or the ground of others. The benefits of standardization thus become his, just as the automobile has become his by the cheapening power of a mass production that serves him. Serves him now as a man and not as a machine. Such is the pre-fabricated house in Broadacres. . . .

Brownell: But I am wondering if there is here an adequate instrumentation of the ideal. What will make it actual? And for that matter, how can you save people from their own bad taste?

Wright: Two questions at once. I will answer the latter. Save people from bad taste? By allowing them to grow up more naturally, cultured as well as "educated" (perhaps instead)—providing meantime designs for manufacture that are organic designs. They may be had even now. Where then would be bad things that a man could buy to outrage the sensibilities of others? Where could he get inferior designs? You may ask where he would get superior designs. In the changed circumstances, he would probably make them himself. Or, if not, he would have a wide range of choice in designs made by those who could. He would himself, however, determine various relationships that would still give individuality to the whole arrangement. In any case, bad units he could not find. Nor could he assemble those he could find in any way to do violence to the unity of the whole. Because the scheme, I would remind you, is organic in character

Document IV-7: THE FEDERAL GOVERNMENT AS PLANNER

Although the federal government does not like to think of itself as a creator of utopias, it has played its part in developing and extending certain models. Early in this section there was identified a not unusual hope that the whole nation might become a harmonious society of homeowners standing foursquare on their own modest acreage. Land reform and homesteading involved the federal government in this dream for most of the nineteenth century (see II-12). When in the 1930s, the federal government guaranteed low-interest loans to homeowners and home builders it was reviving a dream expressed long ago by men like T.

Thomas. The immediate impetus for the Federal Housing Authority and the Home Owners' Loan Corporation was the collective need of the unemployed and dislocated; the response was well within established reform tradition.

The Depression also propelled the government more directly into community planning; the exigencies of World War II kept it there. Some planning was narrowly functional: homes for defense workers near newly built plants; but even in this setting techniques like assembly-line prefabricating created capabilities that were to be of use in more complex projects. In some cases the planning itself was more ambitious. Radburn, New Jersey, for example, was the first moderate-income residential community based on the assumption that every family would own an automobile. Thus efforts were made to separate vehicular from pedestrian traffic. Educational and cultural activities were encouraged through planned village autonomy. As Radburn went up, however, it presented the spectacle only of a number of small, undistinguished homes crammed close together with no visually redeeming features.

More interesting visually was Greenbelt, Maryland, represented below with a photograph taken during construction. The dwellings were not for single families, nor did they offer any particularly distinguished design. Yet the plan as a whole positively reflected the influence of planners like Olmsted and Wright in its respect for the topography and vegetation, in its surrender to curved lines and nonsymmetrical patterns, and in its recognition that planned areas of "green" were needed to separate residential suburbs from one another as well as from the urban, industrial areas.

By far the most ambitious effort at planning by the federal government is the Tennessee Valley Authority. Included below are some sections from the act which are intended to suggest how complicated a task was the establishment of this agency. Any number of fears and suspicions had to be allayed, any number of negative provisions had to be included, and the concept of social planning was tactfully buried in the few vague references which have been reproduced. (See sections 22 and 23.) The very passage of this act, with all its departures from historic sovereignty, was a political miracle. Without the argument that the anticipated power was needed for national defense, passage would have been most unlikely.

Technologically, the project succeeded. The dams were built. The floods that had regularly ravaged the Tennessee and its tributary rivers came under control. Power plants and improved water transportation brought new industries into this seven-state watershed. The federal government has shown that it is possible to cross political borders to recognize geographical and social unities. The TVA has become America's most widely imitated regional planning device.

Forty years after its birth, the TVA is still highly controversial. Did its authority indeed compete with state and local government? Did its power challenge privately owned utilities? Did it properly assume that industrialization should be the goal of a traditionally agricultural region like this? Has it substituted any new sense of community for the impoverished yet homogeneous and recognizable culture it invaded? Did it anticipate and successfully react to the ecological impact? Did it achieve the delicate balance it sought between regionally autonomous voluntarism and the long arm of the federal government?

Volumes have been devoted to answering these complex questions. The interested reader is referred to David Lilienthal's predictably enthusiastic *TVA: Democracy on the March*, New York, Harper, 1953; to Philip Selznick's dissertation, researched in 1942-43, which found a main social direction to be resistance: *TVA and the Grass Roots*, Berkeley, University of California, 1949; and to Leonard W. Doob, who offered a more balanced evaluation against the background of social planning in *Plans of Men*, New Haven, Yale, 1940. To all who thought to notice, however, the TVA was responsible for at least one model community made from diverse components yet welded into a cohesive unit with a great sense of cooperation and loyalty: the employees of the Authority imported into the region to execute the project.

SOURCE: A: Aerial view of Greenbelt, Maryland, taken in November, 1937; from the files of the Farm Security Administration, Office of War Information, Prints and Photographs Division, Library of Congress. B: *U.S. Code* 1970 Edition. Washington, D.C., Government Printing Office, 1971. Title 16, Sect. 831 (vol. IV), abridged.

B: TVA: AN ACT

To improve the navigability and to provide for the flood control of the Tennessee River; to provide for reforestation and the proper use of marginal lands in the Tennessee Valley; to provide for the agricultural and industrial development of said valley; to provide for the national defense by the creation of a corporation for the operation of Government properties at and near Muscle Shoals in the State of Alabama, and for other purposes

Be it enacted by the Senate and House of Representatives of the United States of America in Congress assembled. That for the purpose of maintaining and operating the properties now owned by the United States in the vicinity of Muscle Shoals, Alabama, in the interest of the national defense and for agricultural and industrial development, and to improve navigation in the Tennessee River and to control the destructive flood waters in the Tennessee River and Mississippi River Basins, there is hereby created a body corporate by the name of the "Tennessee Valley Authority" (hereinafter referred to as the "Corporation"). The board of directors first appointed shall be deemed the incorporators, and the incorporation shall be held to have been effected from the date of the first meeting of the board. This Act may be cited as the "Tennessee Valley Authority Act of 1933."

SEC.2.(a) The board of directors of the Corporation (hereinafter referred to as the "board") shall be composed of three members, to be appointed by the President, by and with the advice and consent of the Senate. In appointing the members of the board, the President shall designate the chairman. All other officials, agents, and employees shall be designated and selected by the board. . . .

(f) No director shall have financial interest in any public-utility corporation engaged in the business of distributing and selling power to the public nor in any corporation engaged in the manufacture, selling, or distribution of fixed nitrogen or fertilizer, or any ingredients thereof, nor shall any member have any interest in any business that may be adversely affected by the success of the Corporation as a producer of concentrated fertilizers or as a producer of electric power.

(g) The board shall direct the exercise of all the powers of the Corporation.

(h) All members of the board shall be persons who profess a belief in the feasibility and wisdom of this Act.

SEC. 3. The board shall without regard to the provisions of Civil Service laws applicable to officers and employees of the United States, appoint such managers, assistant managers, officers, employees, attorneys, and agents, as are necessary for the transaction of its business, fix their compensation, define their duties, require bonds of such of them as the board may designate, and provide a system of organization to fix responsibility and promote efficiency. Any appointee of the board may be removed in the discretion of the board. No regular officer or employee of the Corporation shall receive a salary in excess of that received by the members of the board.

All contracts to which the Corporation is a party and which require the employment of laborers and mechanics in the construction, alteration, maintenance, or repair of buildings, dams, locks, or other projects shall contain a provision that not less than the prevailing rate of wages for work of a similar nature prevailing in the vicinity shall be paid to such laborers or mechanics.

In the event any dispute arises as to what are the prevailing rates of wages, the question shall be referred to the Secretary of Labor for determination, and his decision shall be final. In the determination of such prevailing rate or rates, due regard shall be given to those rates which have been secured through collective agreement by representatives of employers and employees.

SEC. 4. Except as otherwise specifically provided in this Act, the Corporation—. . . .

(k) Shall have power in the name of the United States—

(a) to convey by deed, lease, or otherwise, any real property in the possession of or under the control of the Corporation to any person or persons, for the purpose of recreation or use as a summer residence, or for the operation on such premises of pleasure resorts for boating, fishing, bathing, or any similar purpose;

(b) to convey by deed, lease, or otherwise, the possession and control of any such real property to any corporation, partnership, person, or persons for the purpose of erecting thereon docks and buildings for shipping purposes or the manufacture or storage thereon of products for the purpose of trading or shipping in transportation: *Provided,* That no transfer authorized herein in (b) shall be made without the approval of Congress: *And provided further,* That said Corporation, without further action of Congress, shall have power to convey by deed, lease, or otherwise, to the Ingalls Shipbuilding Corporation, a tract or tracts of land at or near Decatur, Alabama, and to the Commercial Barge Lines, Inc., a tract or tracts of land at or near Guntersville, Alabama;

(*c*) to transfer any part of the possession and control of the real estate now in possession of and under the control of said Corporation to any other department, agency, or instrumentality of the United States: *Provided, however,* That no land shall be conveyed, leased, or transferred, upon which there is located any permanent dam, hydroelectric power plant, or munitions plant heretofore or hereafter built by or for the United States or for the Authority, except that this prohibition shall not apply to the transfer of Nitrate Plant Numbered 1, at Muscle Shoals, Alabama, or to Waco Quarry: *And provided further,* That no transfer authorized herein in (a) or (c), except leases for terms of less than twenty years, shall be made without the approval of the President of the United States, if the property to be conveyed exceeds $500 in value; and

(*d*) to convey by warranty deed, or otherwise, lands, easements, and rights of way to States, counties, municipalities, school districts, railroad companies, telephone, telegraph, water and power companies, where any such conveyance is necessary in order to replace any such lands, easements, or rights-of-way to be flooded or destroyed as the result of the construction of any dam or reservoir now under construction by the Corporation, or subsequently authorized by Congress, and easements and rights of way upon which are located transmission or distribution lines. The Corporation shall also have power to convey or lease Nitrate Plant Numbered 1, at Muscle Shoals, Alabama, and Waco Quarry, with the approval of the War Department and the President.

(l) Shall have power to advise and cooperate in the readjustment of the population displaced by the construction of dams, the acquisition of reservoir areas, the protection of watersheds, the acquisition of rights of way, and other necessary acquisitions of land, in order to effectuate the purposes of the Act; and may cooperate with Federal, State, and local agencies to that end. . . .

SEC. 6. In the appointment of officials and the selection of employees for said Corporation, and in the promotion of any such employees or officials, no political test or qualification shall be permitted or given consideration, but all such appointments and promotions shall be given and made on the basis of merit and efficiency. Any member of said board who is found by the President of the United States to be guilty of a violation of this section shall be removed from office by the President of the United States, and any appointee of said board who is found by the board to be guilty of a violation of this section shall be removed from office by said board. . . .

SEC. 11. It is hereby declared to be the policy of the Government so far as practical to distribute and sell the surplus power generated at Muscle Shoals equitably among the States, counties, and municipalities within transmission distance. This policy is further declared to be that the projects herein provided for shall be considered primarily as for the benefit of the people of the section as a whole and particularly the domestic and rural consumers to whom the power can economically be made available, and accordingly that sale to and use by industry shall be a secondary purpose, to be utilized principally to secure a sufficiently high load factor and revenue returns which will permit domestic and rural use at the lowest possible rates and in such manner as to encourage increased domestic and rural use of electricity. It is further hereby declared to be the policy of the Government to utilize the Muscle Shoals properties so far as may be necessary to improve, increase, and cheapen the production of fertilizer and fertilizer ingredients by carrying out the provisions of this Act. . . .

SEC. 12a. In order (1) to facilitate the disposition of the surplus power of the Corporation according to the policies set forth in this Act; (2) to give effect to the priority herein accorded to States, counties, municipalities, and nonprofit organizations in the purchase of such power by enabling them to acquire facilities for the distribution of such power; and (3) at the same time to preserve existing distribution facilities as going concerns and avoid duplication of such facilities, the board is authorized to advise and cooperate with and assist, by extending credit for a period of not exceeding five years to, States, counties, municipalities and nonprofit organizations situated within transmission distance from any dam where such power is generated by the Corporation in acquiring, improving, and operating (a) existing distribution facilities and incidental works, including generating plants; and (b) interconnecting transmission lines; or in acquiring any interest in such facilities, incidental works, and lines. . . .

Sec. 19. The Corporation, as an instrumentality and agency of the Government of the United States for the purpose of executing its constitutional powers, shall have access to the Patent Office of the United States for the purpose of studying, ascertaining, and copying all methods, formulae, and scientific information (not including access to pending applications for patents) necessary to enable the Corporation to use and employ the most efficacious and economical process for the production of fixed nitrogen, or any essential ingredient of fertilizer, or any method of improving and cheapening the production of hydroelectric power, and any owner of a patent whose patent rights may have been thus in any way copied, used, infringed, or employed by the exercise of this authority by the Corporation shall have as the exclusive remedy a cause of action against the Corporation to be instituted and prosecuted on the equity side of the appropriate district court of the United States, for the recovery of reasonable compensation for such infringement. The Commissioner of Patents shall furnish to the Corporation, at its request and without payment of fees, copies of documents on file in his office: *Provided,* That the benefits of this section shall not apply to any art, machine, method of manufacture, or composition of matter, discovered or invented by such employee during the time of his employment or service with the Corporation or with the Government of the United States.

Sec. 20. The Government of the United States hereby reserves the right, in case of war or national emergency declared by Congress, to take possession of all or any part of the property described or referred to in this Act for the purpose of manufacturing explosives or for other war purposes; but, if this right is exercised by the Government, it shall pay the reasonable and fair damages that may be suffered by any party whose contract for the purchase of electric power or fixed nitrogen or fertilizer ingredients is hereby violated, after the amount of the damage has been fixed by the United States Court of Claims in proceedings instituted and conducted for that purpose under rules prescribed by the court. . . .

Sec. 22. To aid further the proper use, conservation, and development of the natural resources of the Tennessee River drainage basin and of such adjoining territory as may be related to or materially affected by the development consequent to this Act, and to provide for the general welfare of the citizens of said areas, the President is hereby authorized, by such means or methods as he may deem proper within the limits of appropriations made therefor by Congress, to make such surveys of and general plans for said Tennessee basin and adjoining territory as may be useful to the Congress and to the several States in guiding and controlling the extent, sequence, and nature of development that may be equitably and economically advanced through the expenditure of public funds, or through the guidance or control of public authority, all for the general purpose of fostering an orderly and proper physical, economic, and social development of said areas; and the President is further authorized in making said surveys and plans to cooperate with the States affected thereby, or subdivisions or agencies of such States, or with cooperative or other organizations, and to make such studies, experiments, or demonstrations as may be necessary and suitable to that end.

SEC. 23. The President shall, from time to time, as the work provided for in the preceding section progresses, recommend to Congress such legislation as he deems proper to carry out the general purposes stated in said section, and for the especial purpose of bringing about in said Tennessee drainage basin and adjoining territory in conformity with said general purposes (1) the maximum amount of flood control; (2) the maximum development of said Tennessee River for navigation purposes; (3) the maximum generation of electric power consistent with flood control and navigation; (4) the proper use of marginal lands; (5) the proper method of reforestation of all lands in said drainage basin suitable for reforestation; and (6) the economic and social well-being of the people living in said river basin. . . .

Document IV-8: COLUMBIA, A NEW TOWN

Frank Lloyd Wright's Broadacre City was never built. Edward Bellamy's utopian Nationalism never came to pass. (See IV-9.) Nor did federal planning from Greenbelt to the TVA ever become a model worthy of full imitation; the "model cities program" begun in President Kennedy's administration amounted to a gross misuse of the word "model." Yet from these and other sources came concepts that could be drawn upon: Olmsted's particular way of working from nature; Wright's feeling for organically related clusters of human-scale communities; Radburn's efforts at segregated traffic; Greenbelt's use of natural buffer areas; TVA's demonstration that some degree of successful planning could be achieved for an extensive area. Although underused, planners had achieved professional status in the late nineteenth century and had made considerable headway. The Garden City Movement was but one reflection.

Drawing on all of this experience came the New Town movement in the 1950s, first visible in England and Brazil. In America an interesting example is unfolding in Columbia, Maryland, under the leadership of James W. Rouse, a mortgage banker with a sense of mission. Rouse got his start building shopping centers. He learned to make these centers glamorous with malls and galleries; he learned to provide free meeting rooms and activity centers. By so doing he raised occupancy rates, rents, and profits. By so doing, he changed the life patterns of the community he served.

With this experience behind him Rouse acquired 15,000 acres between Baltimore and Washington, D.C., and asked Howard County, Maryland, for zoning changes that would allow for the eventual construction of a "city" of 110,000 people. It was to be a special kind of city; to plan it Rouse assembled not only the usual committee of engineers and architects, but consultants in family life, golf, charities, community structure, libraries, education, class structure, psychology, church planning, and ecology. They asked each other where a community began; before they completed their answer they had also brought in professors of philosophy, music, and art.

The answer most consistently stated was that neighborhoods began with schools. Thus the villages, or "petals" of the flowerlike plan, represent enough families to populate a primary school; the whole flower has at its center a high school. The city as a whole will house a county junior college, a branch of Antioch College, and a university named after Dag Hammarskjold. Furthermore, extraordinary stress was placed on education outside the schools. Even before the population had passed its first five thousand, there were scheduled extension classes in ballet, bridge, politics, painting, reading, karate, sewing, drama, and "charm."

Like many planned communities it has built artificial lakes and preserved wooded areas. Streets are named with the poetic evocation of nature in mind. Promotional literature quotes Thoreau and reads like Emerson. But there are some differences. Enough industry was attracted early in the planning stage to ensure the city a reasonable tax base as well as a self-contained source of jobs. Religion has been advertised as varied and cooperative. Real efforts have been made to attract low-middle-income families and members of minority groups. Social services tend toward the paternalistic with an unusually comprehensive medical plan. A whole, brightly colored issue of the promotional publication was devoted to convincing youth that it could "swing" in Columbia.

If Columbia is to distinguish itself in important ways, however, it will depend on how well Rouse has defined the job of starting his plans with "people." That he regards his city as a laboratory for ameliorating America's most pervasive problems comes clearly through the address reproduced below. Rouse's confidence is reflected in the name he most often used to describe Columbia: "the next America." (For a recent appraisal of the New Town movement with special emphasis on Columbia, see the Washington *Post*, January 12-17, 1975, a six-part series by Thomas W. Lippman and Bill Richards with related articles.)

SOURCE: A: "It Can Happen Here," a paper delivered by James W. Rouse at the Conference on the Metropolitan Future, University of California, Berkeley, September 26, 1963, abridged. B: A view of the model of the Columbia Town center. Photograph by Ezra Stoller Associates. Both items courtesy of the Rouse Company.

A: *"IT CAN HAPPEN HERE"*

One-half the houses in California in 1980 will have been built between now and then, says the conference background paper. The population gained by 1980 "will be sufficient to duplicate the entire existing metropolitan system—core cities—suburbs and all—with some left over."

Thus, in California we see, in exaggerated form, the problem and the opportunity which our nation faces over the next twenty years. The country's population growth is projected at roughly 70,000,000, with all of this increase expected to occur in our metropolitan areas. My sleepy old home town of Baltimore has added almost 700,000 people to its population (a city larger than San Diego) since 1940 and is scheduled to add another 800,000 people (a city larger than Denver) by 1980. At the same time Washington, only thirty-five miles away, will be adding another 1,200,000 population (a city larger than Houston).

How will we as a country handle this growth? In what kinds of communities will our people live in 1980? How timely that the University of California should focus our sights on this task.

What are the current prospects for "The Good Environment" in 1980? Not very good. There is evidence at every hand that our cities are already oppressively out of scale with people. It would be very difficult indeed to claim that our urban society, as we know it today in America, is a healthy soil for the growth of our civilization. Slums, blight, disorder, congestion, ugliness, grimness, juvenile gangs, declining self-reliance, slipping morality, increasing neurosis, loneliness, bewilderment, lack of high purpose and principle—with increasing force and frequency, these are becoming the hallmarks of the American city. . . .

Isn't it time we began to ask what we are planning for? What is the purpose of the community? What kind of community would constitute a successful community? What would be an unsuccessful community? What are the tests or guide posts or comparisons by which we would measure the success of one community against another? . . .

I believe that the ultimate test of civilization is whether or not it contributes to the growth—improvement of mankind. Does it uplift, inspire, stimulate, and develop the best in man? There really can be no other right purpose of community except to provide an environment and an opportunity to develop better people. The most successful community would be that which contributed the most by its physical form, its institutions, and its operation to the growth of people.

And then we have to ask: What constitutes "growth" in people? Is it increase in physical capacity?—improvement of the intellect?—strengthening emotional balance, security, personal effectiveness? Perhaps it's all of these things, but in searching for ultimate purpose in the development of a community, I find no test so embracing and so satisfactory as the Biblical injunction, "Thou shalt love the Lord thy God with all thy heart and with all thy soul and with all thy mind. Thou shalt love thy neighbor as thyself." If that were the target and the test of community planning; if we were really trying to create inspired, concerned, and loving people, might not this begin to influence the kind of plans we would unfold; and might it not point the way to answers we are not now perceiving?

An inspired and concerned society will dignify man; will find ways to develop his talents; will put the fruits of his labor and intellect to effective use; will struggle for brotherhood and for the elimination of bigotry and intolerance; will care for the indigent, the delinquent, the sick, the aged; will seek the truth and communicate it; will respect differences among men. The raising of such a target would provide direction and purpose and basic testing for the pieces of planning which ultimately make the whole community. To shoot at it all would require questions and answers that aren't flowing today among the people planning and developing our communities. . . .

Personally, I hold some very unscientific conclusions to the effect that people grow best in small communities where the institutions which are the dominant forces in their lives are within the scale of their comprehension and within reach of their sense of responsibility and capacity to manage. I believe that a broader range of friendships and relationships occurs in a village or small town than in a city; that there is a greater sense of responsibility for one's neighbor and also a greater sense of support by one's fellow man in a small town than in a city; that self-reliance is promoted; that relationship to nature—to the out of doors—to the freer forms of recreation and human activity is encouraged in a smaller community.

I believe there should be a strong infusion of nature—natural nature—not sterilized and contrived nature—throughout a network of towns; that people should be able to fish and watch birds; find solitude; study nature in a natural environment; feel the spaces of nature—all as a part of their everyday life.

I believe that many of the most serious problems of our society flow from the fact that the city is out of scale with people; that it is too big for people to comprehend; to feel a part of; to feel responsible for; to feel important in. I believe this out-of-scaleness promotes loneliness, irresponsibility, superficial values.

My ideas, if correct, would lead to a different kind of plan than Ed Bacon's big concentrated city plan. I would visualize a series of small communities separated by topography, highways, public institutions, or greenbelts and united by a center that provided cultural, educational, recreational facilities for many (say, ten to twenty) small towns around it.

But am I right? What experiences are there in the United States to indicate that one environment or another contributes to healthy growth or to the erosion of human personality? What has happened to the personality, character, creativity of people in Ed Bacon's Philadelphia when studied in comparison with the small towns and cities of Pennsylvania? What could we learn from experience about "The Good Environment" if we looked for answers and guidelines?

How can we plan for "The Good Environment" until we have first determined what we believe a good environment to be? By this I do not mean that we can find one right answer—that there would be one conclusion as to the good environment. But, rather, if we thoughtfully asked and answered the right questions, we would produce a variety of conclusions and a variety of plans directed at fulfilling those conclusions, and each plan would be purposeful and vital in shooting at its target.

To get the Urban Design Bus on the road toward "The Good Environment" three important changes in attitude must occur:

1. *The architect, the planner, and the schools in which they are educated must change their attitudes toward urban design. They must become people-centered.* Whatever freedom and personal delight self-expression may afford in the design of an individual building, it must take a back seat in the design of a community. The urban design process must be rooted first in a sense of community service. The architect and planner developing a community plan must find their excitement in discovering what works for people. Lacking training or experience themselves in the social sciences, they must seek help from others who are trained to give it. This "seeking" in itself could stimulate a revolution in Architecture and Planning.

   The universities, seeing the community development task for what it really is, must feed into their students (and hopefully into their alumni) a new understanding of the task and of the responsibility of the designer in the urban design process. There has been too much emphasis on the role of the architect as an artist, measuring his success by the aesthetic quality of his creation—and not enough on his role as a social servant.

I have many good friends in the design professions. I know their hearts to be good and their purpose noble, but they have been trained and they have worked in an environment which has placed high premium on sophisticated considerations of beauty, taste, "integrity" and little or no premium on the social purposes and implications of architecture and planning. And if you will forgive me for saying so, this environment has generated attitudes of arrogance and self-righteousness in matters of design among men who are humble, liberal, big-minded in their attitudes toward political or social problems not seemingly related to design. Our talented designers need to be hauled away from their myopic view of buildings as man-made works of art and lifted up to the bigger view of communities as gardens in which we are growing people and a civilization.

2.   *We must have more thoughtful research as to what works well and what works badly for people in American communities.* We must comprehensively examine the problems we face in our urban society and study how those problems may be solved or relieved in the planning, development, and operation of our communities. Such research as has been conducted in the past, along these lines, has proceeded in a vacuum with little awareness that it might be relevant to future physical planning. The social scientist and urban designer must be linked together in a way we have not yet seen in America. The designer must be looking to the social scientists for knowledge and experience; but, perhaps more important, the social scientist must be conducting his work in an atmosphere of hard-headed reality, aware of the fact that his efforts will be put to work with direct influence on families who will live in the environment he has helped to create. This new sense of humility on the part of the architect and of imminent responsibility on the part of the social scientist would introduce creative new disciplines for each.

3.   *We need a new attitude among public officials*—a conviction that we can make our new communities into whatever we really want them to be; that we are not helpless victims before a flood of growth, but part of a living, growing, dynamic society which has the resources, if it only had the will, to control its destiny.

B: Model of Columbia

There is a bewildering attitude that prevails among us all—
professionals, citizens, public officials—that we really can't handle the
problem of the city and its growth. It's as if no one really expected to
see a well-organized, efficient, livable, beautiful city. We talk about it,
but the talk isn't real. We subconsciously discount in advance the
do-ability of the plans we agree are essential. Where in the United
States is any community saying: "We see our problems—of the past
and the future. We are making plans to deal with them—full, complete,
comprehensive, detailed plans. When they are completed eighteen
months from now (and not eighteen years) we will lay out a program
and a financial plan to execute our plans, and we will propose such new
powers as may be necessary in local government to see the job
through." . . .

Document IV-9: UTOPIA AS SEEN BY BELLAMY

Olmsted's transfer of the communitarian urge to the art of planning
represented a deep change of mode in nineteenth-century reform. The
communitarians, for all their craftsmanship and clever management,
were really moving in the opposite direction from the larger part of
society that was rapidly making itself urban and industrial. Utopia for an
urban industrial society cannot be constructed on one hundred acres with
a low, handcrafted profile. To create a model relevant to the nation's
dominant direction would be to work in terms of the technological city;
and to articulate the terms of this model, there sprung up a new vogue: the
utopian romance. The genre traced its lineage to Plato and Thomas More.
It rose in America in the 1880s as a clear, almost universally critical
response to the exploitative nature of monopolistic industry and finance
in league with a compliant, passive political structure.

Most utopian novels were futuristic. This viewpoint allowed for a
comparison between the shortcomings of the day and the panaceas of
tomorrow. A nonmilitant socialism colored many of these novels which,
in the main, were happy, technological fantasies, where everyone
enjoyed a life of abundance and ease supported by efficient machines,
and a sense of duty easily discharged in a few hours a day. This literary
fashion arrived, suddenly, in the 1880s and, just as suddenly, diminished
drastically after the first few years of the new century. The movement

took its central character from the one memorable work which influenced most of the others, Edward Bellamy's *Looking Backward.* (The most complete discussion of the utopian genre and its contemporary meaning is in an unpublished doctoral dissertation submitted at George Washington University, 1968, by Charles J. Rooney, "Utopian Literature as a Reflection of Social Forces in America, 1865-1917.")

What Bellamy was advocating was as completely socialistic as anything proposed by Marxists, Fourierists, or Fabians. It appealed to Americans because it was homegrown, because it avoided stress on class warfare, and because it allowed for detailed appreciation of technological gadgetry. Not only did it spawn dozens of imitative novels but it led to the formation of Nationalist Clubs whose target for social change Bellamy had identified in his novel. Along with Henry George (see II-21) Edward Bellamy offered a widely accepted alternative to the existing politico-economic system. Between the communitarian socialism of Robert Dale Owen and John Humphrey Noyes, and the candidacy of Eugene V. Debs (see II-30), his was the most popular socialistic vision of America.

The passage below only hints at the fascinating intricacy of Bellamy's social and technical imagination. It does reveal the deeper concerns that moved him. Julian West, the protagonist, falls asleep in the Boston of 1887, apparently awakening in the year 2000. The sermon he hears during the first Sunday of his dream life makes use of his presence to reflect on the moral failings of the late nineteenth century. Typical of the book as a whole is the centrality of competition as the major villain.

SOURCE: Edward Bellamy, *Looking Backward, 2000-1887.* Boston, Houghton, Mifflin, 1888, pp. 271-292, abridged.

From *LOOKING BACKWARD*

I think if a person were ever excusable for losing track of the days of the week, the circumstances excused me. Indeed, if I had been told that the method of reckoning time had been wholly changed and the days were now counted in lots of five, ten, or fifteen instead of seven, I should have been in no way surprised after what I had already heard and seen of the twentieth century. The first time that any inquiry as to the days of the week occurred to me was the morning following the conversation related in the last chapter. At the breakfast table Dr. Leete asked me if I would care to hear a sermon.

"Is it Sunday, then?" I exclaimed.

"Yes," he replied. "It was on Friday, you see, when we made the lucky discovery of the buried chamber to which we owe your society this morning. It was on Saturday morning, soon after midnight, that you first awoke, and Sunday afternoon when you awoke the second time with faculties fully regained."

"So you still have Sundays and sermons," I said. "We had prophets who foretold that long before this time the world would have dispensed with both. I am very curious to know how the ecclesiastical systems fit in with the rest of your social arrangements. I suppose you have a sort of national church with official clergymen."

Dr. Leete laughed, and Mrs. Leete and Edith seemed greatly amused.

"Why, Mr. West," Edith said, "what odd people you must think us. You were quite done with national religious establishments in the nineteenth century, and did you fancy we had gone back to them?"

"But how can voluntary churches and an unofficial clerical profession be reconciled with national ownership of all buildings, and the industrial service required of all men?" I answered.

"The religious practices of the people have naturally changed considerably in a century," replied Dr. Leete; "but supposing them to have remained unchanged, our social system would accommodate them perfectly. The nation supplies any person or number of persons with buildings on guarantee of the rent, and they remain tenants while they pay it. As for the clergymen, if a number of persons wish the services of an individual for any particular end of their own, apart from the general service of the nation, they can always secure it, with that individual's own consent, of course, just as we secure the service of our editors, by contributing from their credit-cards an indemnity to the nation for the loss of his services in general industry. This indemnity paid the nation for the individual answers to the salary in your day paid to the individual himself; and the various applications of this principle leave private initiative full play in all details to which national control is not applicable. Now, as to hearing a sermon to-day, if you wish to do so, you can either go to a church to hear it or stay at home."

"How am I to hear it if I stay at home?"

"Simply by accompanying us to the music room at the proper hour and selecting an easy chair. There are some who still prefer to hear sermons in church, but most of our preaching, like our musical performances, is not in public, but delivered in acoustically prepared chambers, connected by wire with subscribers' houses. If you prefer to go to a church I shall be glad to accompany you, but I really don't believe you are likely to hear anywhere a better discourse than you will at home. I see by the paper that Mr. Barton is to preach this morning, and he preaches only by telephone, and to audiences often reaching 150,000.''

''The novelty of the experience of hearing a sermon under such circumstances would incline me to be one of Mr. Barton's hearers, if for no other reason,'' I said.

An hour or two later, as I sat reading in the library, Edith came for me, and I followed her to the music room, where Dr. and Mrs. Leete were waiting. We had not more than seated ourselves comfortably when the tinkle of a bell was heard, and a few moments after the voice of a man, at the pitch of ordinary conversation, addressed us, with an effect of proceeding from an invisible person in the room. This was what the voice said:—

MR. BARTON'S SERMON.

''We have had among us, during the past week, a critic from the nineteenth century, a living representative of the epoch of our great-grandparents. It would be strange if a fact so extraordinary had not somewhat strongly affected our imaginations. Perhaps most of us have been stimulated to some effort to realize the society of a century ago, and figure to ourselves what it must have been like to live then. In inviting you now to consider certain reflections upon this subject which have occurred to me, I presume that I shall rather follow than divert the course of your own thoughts. . . .

''I venture to assume that one effect has been common with us as a result of this effort at retrospection, and that it has been to leave us more than ever amazed at the stupendous change which one brief century has made in the material and moral conditions of humanity.

''Still, as regards the contrast between the poverty of the nation and the world in the nineteenth century and their wealth now, it is not greater, possibly, than had been before seen in human history, perhaps not greater, for example, than that between the poverty of this country during the earliest colonial period of the seventeenth century and the relatively great wealth it had attained at the close of the nineteenth, or between the England of William the Conqueror and that of Victoria. Although the aggregate riches of a nation did not then, as now, afford any accurate criterion of the masses of its people, yet instances like these afford partial parallels for the merely material side of the contrast between the nineteenth and the twentieth centuries. It is when we contemplate the moral aspect of that contrast that we find ourselves in the presence of a phenomenon for which history offers no precedent, however far back we may cast our eye. One might almost be excused who should exclaim, 'Here, surely, is something like a miracle!' Nevertheless, when we give our idle wonder, and begin to examine the seeming prodigy critically, we find it no prodigy at all, much less a miracle. It is not necessary to suppose a moral new birth of humanity, or a wholesale destruction of the wicked and survival of the good, to account for the fact before us. It finds its simple and obvious explanation in the reaction of a changed environment upon human nature. It means merely that a form of society which was founded on the pseudo self-interest of selfishness, and appealed solely to the anti-social and brutal side of human nature, has been replaced by institutions based on the true self-interest of a rational unselfishness, and appealing to the self-interest of a rational unselfishness, and appealing to the social and generous instincts of men.

"My friends, if you would see men again the beasts of prey they seemed in the nineteenth century, all you have to do is to restore the old social and industrial system, which taught them to view their natural prey in their fellow-men, and find their gain in the loss of others. No doubt it seems to you that no necessity, however dire, would have tempted you to subsist on what superior skill or strength enabled you to wrest from others equally needy. But suppose it were not merely your own life that you were responsible for. I know well that there must have been many a man among our ancestors who, if it had been merely a question of his own life, would sooner have given it up than nourished it by bread snatched from others. But this he was not permitted to do. He had dear lives dependent on him. Men loved women in those days, as now. God knows how they dared be fathers, but they had babies as sweet, no doubt, to them as ours to us, whom they must feed, clothe, educate. The gentlest creatures are fierce when they have young to provide for, and in that wolfish society the struggle for bread borrowed a peculiar desperation from the tenderest sentiments. For the sake of those dependent on him, a man might not choose, but must plunge into the foul fight,—cheat, overreach, supplant, defraud, buy below worth and sell above, break down the business by which his neighbor fed his young ones, tempt men to buy what they ought not and to sell what they should not, grind his laborers, sweat his debtors, cozen his creditors. Though a man sought it carefully with tears, it was hard to find a way in which he could earn a living and provide for his family except by pressing in before some weaker rival and taking the food from his mouth. Even the ministers of religion were not exempt from this cruel necessity. While they warned their flocks against the love of money, regard for their families compelled them to keep an outlook for the pecuniary prizes of their calling. Poor fellows, theirs was indeed a trying business, preaching to men a generosity and unselfishness which they and everybody knew would, in the existing state of the world, reduce to poverty those who should practice them, laying down laws of conduct which the law of self-preservation compelled men to break. Looking on the inhuman spectacle of society, these worthy men bitterly bemoaned the depravity of human nature; as if angelic nature would not have been debauched in such a devil's school! Ah, my friends, believe me, it is not now in this happy age that humanity is proving the divinity within it. It was rather in those evil days when not even the fight for life with one another, the struggle for mere existence, in which mercy was folly, could wholly banish generosity and kindness from the earth.

"It is not hard to understand the desperation with which men and women, who under other conditions would have been full of gentleness and ruth, fought and tore each other in the scramble for gold, when we realize what it meant to miss it, what poverty was in that day. For the body it was hunger and thirst, torment by heat and frost, in sickness neglect, in health unremitting toil; for the moral nature it meant oppression, contempt, and the patient endurance of indignity, brutish associations from infancy, the loss of all the innocence of childhood, the grace of womanhood, the dignity of manhood; for the mind it meant the death of ignorance, the torpor of all those faculties which distinguish us from brutes, the reduction of life to a round of bodily functions.

"Ah, my friends, if such a fate as this were offered you and your children as the only alternative of success in the accumulation of wealth, how long do you fancy would you be in sinking to the moral level of your ancestors? . . .

"Although the idea of the vital unity of the family of mankind, the reality of human brotherhood, was very far from being apprehended by them as the moral axiom it seems to us, yet it is a mistake to suppose that there was no feeling at all corresponding to it. I could read you passages of great beauty from some of their writers which show that the conception was clearly attained by a few, and no doubt vaguely by many more. Moreover, it must not be forgotten that the nineteenth century was in name Christian, and the fact that the entire commercial and industrial frame of society was the embodiment of the anti-Christian spirit must have had some weight, though I admit it was strangely little, with the nominal followers of Jesus Christ.

"When we inquire why it did not have more, why, in general, long after a vast majority of men had agreed as to the crying abuses of the existing social arrangement, they still tolerated it, or contented themselves with talking of petty reforms in it, we come upon an extraordinary fact. It was the sincere belief of even the best of men at that epoch that the only stable elements in human nature, on which a social system could be safely founded, were its worst propensities. They had been taught and believed that greed and self-seeking were all that held mankind together, and that all human associations would fall to pieces if anything were done to blunt the edge of these motives or curb their operation. In a word, they believed—even those who longed to believe otherwise—the exact reverse of what seems to us self-evident; they believed, that is, that the anti-social qualities of men, and not their social qualities, were what furnished the cohesive force of society. It seemed reasonable to them that men lived together solely for the purpose of overreaching and oppressing one another, and of being overreached and oppressed, and that while a society that gave full scope to these propensities could stand, there would be little chance for one based on the idea of coöperation for the benefit of all. It seems absurd to expect any one to believe that convictions like these were ever seriously entertained by men; but that they were not only entertained by our great-grandfathers, but were responsible for the long delay in doing away with the ancient order, after a conviction of its intolerable abuses had become general, is as well established as any fact in history can be. Just here you will find the explanation of the profound pessimism of the literature of the last quarter of the nineteenth century, the note of melancholy in its poetry, and the cynicism of its humor.

"Feeling that the condition of the race was unendurable, they had no clear hope of anything better. They believed that the evolution of humanity had resulted in leading it into a *cul de sac*, and that there was no way of getting forward. The frame of men's minds at this time is strikingly illustrated by treatises which have come down to us, and may even now be consulted in our libraries by the curious, in which laborious arguments are pursued to prove that despite the evil plight of men, life was still, by some slight preponderance of considerations, probably better worth living than leaving. Despising themselves, they despised their Creator. There was a general decay of religious belief. Pale and watery gleams, from skies thickly veiled by doubt and dread, alone lighted up the chaos of earth. That men should doubt Him whose breath is in their nostrils, or dread the hands that moulded them, seems to us indeed a pitiable insanity; but we must remember that children who are brave by day have sometimes foolish fears at night. The dawn has come since then. It is very easy to believe in the fatherhood of God in the twentieth century.

"Briefly, as must needs be in a discourse of this character, I have adverted to some of the causes which had prepared men's minds for the change from the old to the new order, as well as some causes of the conservatism of despair which for a while held it back after the time was ripe. To wonder at the rapidity with which the change was completed after its possibility was first entertained is to forget the intoxicating effect of hope upon minds long accustomed to despair. The sunburst, after so long and dark a night, must needs have had a dazzling effect. From the moment men allowed themselves to believe that humanity after all had not been meant for a dwarf, that its squat stature was not the measure of its possible growth, but that it stood upon the verge of an avatar of limitless development, the reaction must needs have been overwhelming. It is evident that nothing was able to stand against the enthusiasm which the new faith inspired. . . .

"You know the story of that last, greatest, and most bloodless of revolutions. In the time of one generation men laid aside the social traditions and practices of barbarians, and assumed a social order worthy of rational and human beings. Ceasing to be predatory in their habits, they became co-workers, and found in fraternity, at once, the science of wealth and happiness. 'What shall I eat and drink, and wherewithal shall I be clothed?' stated as a problem beginning and ending in self; had been an anxious and an endless one. But when once it was conceived, not from the individual, but the fraternal standpoint, 'What shall we eat and drink, and wherewithal shall we be clothed?—its difficulties vanished.

"Poverty with servitude had been the result, for the mass of humanity, of attempting to solve the problem of maintenance from the individual standpoint, but no sooner had the nation become the sole capitalist and employer than not alone did plenty replace poverty, but the last vestige of the serfdom of man to man disappeared from earth. Human slavery, so often vainly scotched, at last was killed. The means of subsistence no longer doled out by men to women, by employer to employed, by rich to poor, was distributed from a common stock as among children at the father's table. It was impossible for a man any longer to use his fellow-men as tools for his own profit. His esteem was the only sort of gain he could thenceforth make out of him. There was no more either arrogance or servility in the relations of human beings to one another. For the first time since the creation every man stood up straight before God. The fear of want and the lust of gain became extinct motives when abundance was assured to all and immoderate possessions made impossible of attainment. There were no more beggars nor almoners. Equity left charity without an occupation. The ten commandments became well-nigh obsolete in a world where there was no temptation to theft, no occasion to lie either for fear or favor, no room for envy where all were equal, and little provocation to violence where men were disarmed of power to injure one another. Humanity's ancient dream of liberty, equality, fraternity, mocked by so many ages, at last was realized.

"As in the old society the generous, the just, the tender-hearted had been placed at a disadvantage by the possession of those qualities, so in the new society the cold-hearted, the greedy, and self-seeking found themselves out of joint with the world. Now that the conditions of life for the first time ceased to operate as a forcing process to develop the brutal qualities of human nature, and the premium which had heretofore encouraged selfishness was not only removed, but placed upon unselfishness, it was for the first time possible to see what unperverted human nature really was like. The depraved tendencies, which had previously overgrown and obscured the better to so large an extent, now withered like cellar fungi in the open air, and the nobler qualities showed a sudden luxuriance which turned cynics into panegyrists and for the first time in human history tempted mankind to fall in love with itself. Soon was fully revealed, what the divines and philosophers of the old world never would have believed, that human nature in its essential qualities is good, not bad, that men by their natural intention and structure are generous, not selfish, pitiful, not cruel, sympathetic, nor arrogant, godlike in aspirations, instinct with divinest impulses of tenderness and self-sacrifice, images of God indeed, not the travesties upon Him they had seemed. The constant pressure, through numberless generations, of conditions of life which might have perverted angels, had not been able to essentially alter the natural nobility of the stock, and these conditions once removed, like a bent tree, it had sprung back to its normal uprightness. . . .

"But how is it with us who stand on this height which they gazed up to? Already we have well-nigh forgotten, except when it is especially called to our minds by some occasion like the present, that it was not always with men as it is now. It is a strain on our imaginations to conceive the social arrangements of our immediate ancestors. We find them grotesque. The solution of the problem of physical maintenance so as to banish care and crime, so far from seeming to us an ultimate attainment, appears but as a preliminary to anything like real human progress. We have but relieved ourselves of an impertinent and needless harassment which hindered our ancestors from undertaking the real ends of existence. We are merely stripped for the race; no more. We are like a child which has just learned to stand upright and to walk. It is a great event, from the child's point of view, when he first walks. Perhaps he fancies that there can be little beyond that achievement, but a year later he has forgotten that he could not always walk. His horizon did but widen when he rose, and enlarge as he moved. A great event indeed, in one sense, was his first step, but only as a beginning, not as the end. His true career was but then first entered on. The enfranchisement of humanity in the last century, from mental and physical absorption in working and scheming for the mere bodily necessities, may be regarded as a species of second birth of the race, without which its first birth to an existence that was but a burden would forever have remained unjustified, but whereby it is now abundantly vindicated. Since then, humanity has entered on a new phase of spiritual development, an evolution of higher faculties, the very existence of which in human nature our ancestors scarcely suspected. In place of the dreary hopelessness of the nineteenth century, its profound pessimism as to the future of humanity, the animating idea of the present age is an enthusiastic conception of the opportunities of our earthly existence, and the unbounded possibilities of human nature. The betterment of mankind from generation to generation, physically, mentally, morally, is recognized as the one great object supremely worthy of effort and of sacrifice. We believe the race for the first time to have entered on the realization of God's ideal of it, and each generation must now be a step upward.

"Do you ask what we look for when unnumbered generations shall have passed away? I answer, the way stretches far before us, but the end is lost in light. For twofold is the return of man to God 'who is our home,' the return of the individual by the way of death, and the return of the race by the fulfilment of the evolution, when the divine secret hidden in the germ shall be perfectly unfolded. With a tear for the dark past, turn we then to the dazzling future, and, veiling our eyes, press forward. The long and weary winter of the race is ended. Its summer has begun. Humanity has burst the chrysalis. The heavens are before it.''

Document IV-10: UTOPIA AS SEEN BY STRONG

Bellamy, like many utopians and planners, assumed the basic benignity of man; thence argued that a superior environment would produce a superior society. Other visionaries assumed, contrariwise, that human nature was fundamentally sinful and could be corrected only by spiritual conversion. Thus social melioration rested on religious awakening. By dramatizing the millennium this viewpoint relegated social change through collective, secular means to a distinctly secondary status. The believer confidently turned his back on politics and poverty and awaited a day of divine judgment.

The "social gospel," which Josiah Strong helped develop, tended to reconcile the believer with the social reformer. The leaders of this movement—Francis Peabody, Washington Gladden, Walter Rauschenbusch—pushed the church beyond its traditional concern with piety, theology, and conversion. The church, they said, must respond to social needs. If, in so doing, the church becomes politicized, so be it. The social gospel was not a utopian dream; it led to settlement houses, welfare programs, and adult education.

If a utopian wing of the social gospel can be found, it would be located in figures like the Reverend Charles M. Sheldon, whose famous novel sold copies beyond counting. *In His Steps; "What Would Jesus Do?"*, first appearing in 1897, showed how the members of a particular congregation applied the teaching of Jesus. In rejecting selfish materialism and learning to turn the other cheek, this small community moved toward a kind of model society, based on Christian principles, which Sheldon believed could survive and grow, even in the midst of a modern city.

Josiah Strong, also a Congregational minister, stood somewhere between the simplistic utopia of Sheldon and the more fragmented, pragmatic program of his fellow proponents of the social gospel. His most popular work, *Our Country* (1885), written originally as a missionary handbook, made patriotism a central value. Yet he was no reactionary. He recognized danger in disproportionate accumulations of capital and he sympathized with the plight of labor. His *Twentieth Century City*, from which the following quotation is taken, represents as well as any other single document the Christian model which the more progressive Protestant church leaders would hold up to society. It also serves as an interesting link between Edward Bellamy and Frank Lloyd Wright.

Strong recognized that the city was to be the inevitable form of social organization; but, he wrote, the modern city shows an overdeveloped sense of materialism and stands in need of mental and moral achievement. He placed a heavy value on secular education, yet at the heart of his model was the applicability of the teachings of Jesus to modern problems. In the manner of his Puritan forebears, he felt that an American nation, guided by Christian principles, could become that shining city on a hill, exemplar to the world.

SOURCE: Josiah Strong, *The Twentieth Century City*. New York, Baker and Taylor, 1898, pp. 116-130.

THE TWENTIETH CENTURY CITY

John Robinson told the Pilgrim Fathers that more light would yet break forth from the Word of God. This prophecy might be safely made in every age, because that Word reveals Him who is the light of the world, the light of every century.

The new civilization, with its new social problems, has led us to search for the social teachings of Jesus, which had been long neglected; and we find that those teachings fit modern conditions as a key fits its lock.

During all these Christian centuries this light has been beating upon blind eyes, seeking to fill them with day. Now that new social conditions have opened our eyes to new needs, we see the light; and the prophecy of the Pilgrims' pastor is fulfilled in our own generation.

It is proposed to show in this chapter how beautifully the social teachings of Christianity are calculated to solve the social problems of the new century.

Modern social conditions have been produced by modern industrial conditions. As industry becomes more highly organized and the division of labor more complete, the interdependence of men becomes more entire, and the oneness of the life of society grows more real and more obvious. Society is beginning to arrive at self-consciousness; that is, it is beginning to recognize itself as an organism whose life is one and whose interests are one.

With the dawn of social self-consciousness there are appearing a social conscience, a new social spirit, and a new social ideal. Let us glance at each.

Conscience has more to say of duties than of rights, but the world has for centuries been familiar with the *"rights* of conscience," while the *duties* of conscience has a new, strange sound. The individualistic age, now closing, was one of self-assertion; hence, with the increasing self-consciousness of the individual came great reforms, characterized by the perception and assertion of rights. In the social age, upon which we are now entering, as social self-consciousness becomes more distinct, the awakening social conscience will perceive more and more social obligations; hence, there will be another long list of noble reforms which will demand the recognition and acceptance of duties. The watchword of the old era was "Rights"; that of the new will be "Duties." The spirit of the old was, "I am as good as you;" that of the new will be, "You are as good as I."

This leads us to the new social spirit. We are beginning to see that the material well-being and the moral and physical health of different classes are strangely bound up in one bundle. Neither individuals, nor classes, nor nations can remain indifferent to one another. Increasing common interests are creating more of mutual sympathy. The spirit of competition is still dominant and fierce, but the spirit of coöperation is growing. The new social spirit is fraternal, and if it is not yet widely prevalent, men are at least beginning to see that the new civilization profoundly needs it.

The new social ideal springs from new possibilities. When muscles did the world's work one man could little more than provide the necessaries of life for those dependent on him. The working-power of the world could be increased only slowly; and to double the number of muscles meant to double the number of mouths. Under such conditions the world could never be rich; a few might be, and were, but generally at the expense of the many. Mechanical power, on the other hand, can be indefinitely increased without any increase of population. With its advent, therefore, came the possibility of general comfort and the ultimate possibility of universal wealth.

This possibility has awakened hope, and men begin to believe that no class has been doomed to perpetual want and ignorance. Suffering is no longer deemed necessary, but rather abnormal, and social reformers feel bound to find and remove its causes. Thus, with the growth of the philanthropic spirit, the progress of science, the increase of intelligence, and the creation of wealth, men have transferred the golden age of the world from the past to the future, and the common man has begun to dream of a perfected civilization in the far future, which has been seen in prophetic vision and sung by poets in every age.

But this new social ideal is little more than a millennium of creature comfort. It needs to be elevated, illuminated, and glorified by Christ's social ideal. It is quite possible for society to be at the same time well housed, well fed, well clothed, well educated, and *well rotted*. The world can never be saved from misery until it is saved from sin, and never ought to be. The ideal of Christianity is that of a society in which God's will is done as perfectly as it is in heaven; one in which absolute obedience is rendered to every law of our being, physical, mental, spiritual, social; and this is nothing more nor less than the kingdom of God fully come in the earth. The new social ideal, dim and imperfect, when fully focussed, is seen to be the kingdom of heaven for which our Lord taught us daily to pray, and which he bade us first to seek.

In like manner Christianity meets the conscious need of a new social spirit. So far as the spirit of fraternity grows out of common interests and mutual dependence, it is only mildly unselfish and largely passive. When the social spirit has been Christianized we shall have, not a fraternity of convenience but a genuine brotherhood of love sprung from a common fatherhood. Such a social spirit will be a vital and active principle, powerful to hasten the blessed consummation of peace on earth.

Again, the awakening social conscience needs to be educated, and the teachings of Jesus contain precisely the fundamental principles necessary for its instruction. The multiplied and complex relations of the new civilization have greatly increased and complicated our social obligations. Men are raising new questions of duty, which can be answered only by Christian ethics.

This new social conscience, this new social spirit, and this new social ideal all belong to the great social organism which is now becoming conscious of itself as a result of the new civilization. This organism is as yet extremely imperfect; how can it be perfected and the new social ideal realized?

There are two laws, fundamental to every living organism, which must be perfectly obeyed before society can be perfected; one is the law of service, the other that of sacrifice.

Every organism possesses different organs, having different functions, each of which exists, not for itself but to serve all the others. The eye sees for hand and foot and brain; the hand toils for the whole body; the brain thinks for every member; the heart beats for every fibre of the organism. If any organ refuses to perform its proper function, there is disease, perhaps death.

Again, every organism is composed of numberless living cells, each of which, we are told, possesses the power of sensation, of nutrition, of locomotion, and of reproduction. These cells freely give their lives for the good of the organism. Work, play, thought, feeling, all cost the sacrifice of living cells. If these cells were capable of selfishness, and should adopt the motto, "Every cell for itself," it would mean the dissolution of the organism. When living cells which disregard the laws of the organism enter it, and there multiply, there results typhoid fever, small-pox, diphtheria, or some other zymotic disease. If these intruders become numerous enough to overcome the law-abiding cells of the body, the result is anarchy, which is death. Individuals may be said to constitute the cells of the social organism, and, in addition to the powers which belong to the cells described above, they are endowed with self-consciousness and will. They are therefore capable of introducing selfishness and disorder into the social organism. The great social laws of service and of sacrifice are, accordingly, very imperfectly obeyed; hence the many diseases which afflict society, and which can be cured only by bringing all men under these two laws. But how can this be done? How can selfish men be made unselfish? How can a whirlpool be transformed into a fountain?

Let us turn for an answer to the teachings of Jesus. They contain three social laws which are fundamental to Christianity; they are the three great laws of the kingdom of God—laws which were reiterated in the Master's teachings, and exemplified in his life and death. These laws when announced seemed nothing less than absurd to the world, so utterly counter did they run to the convictions and habits of men.

The first is the law of service: "Whosoever will be chief among you, let him be your servant." In the Roman world slavery degraded labor; to serve was menial, and yet the Master took a towel, girded himself and washed the feet of his disciples. This he did for an example that they might do as he had done. "The servant is not greater than his lord." He declared that he had come, "Not to be ministered unto but to minister;" and "As the Father sent me into the world, so send I you." The law of service was made binding on everyone who would become his disciple.

No less binding is the second great law, that of sacrifice. He came "to give his life a ransom for many"; and he not only accepted the cross himself, but made its acceptance the condition of discipleship. "If any man will come after me, let him deny himself, and take up his cross and follow me"—follow him to the place of crucifixion whither he bore his cross. We talk of our "crosses;" he spoke of *the cross*. The word meant then what the gallows means to-day, namely, *death*. The law of sacrifice, even to dying unto self, is laid upon all who would follow Christ.

The third great law—that of love—is the most fundamental of all. It is this which vitalizes the other two. To him who loves, service is its own reward, and sacrifice is privilege. Love is the fulfilling of all law, and is the root from which service and sacrifice spring. Love can transform the heart from a maelstrom into a fountain, whose rivers shall make glad the desert of life.

Two of these laws, as we have seen, are fundamental to every organism; and the third, the law of love, must become the law of the social organism before the laws of service and of sacrifice can be energized and made regnant. Selfishness is disintegrative and anti-social. Love is the antidote for selfishness; and as love is the most fundamental law of

Christianity, the Christianity of Christ is, and is to be, the great social or organizing power in this new era. Thus it appears that the religion of Jesus is profoundly social, and as perfectly adapted to the saving of society as if that were its only object.

It is not strange that in an individualistic age the interpretation of Christianity should have been individualistic and narrow. The new needs of a new civilization open our eyes to the opulence of Christ's teachings and the sufficiency of Christianity for every age.

The teachings of Jesus contain the fundamental principles necessary both for the individual and for society. Exclusively they are neither individualistic nor social; inclusively they are both.

Twentieth century Christianity will instruct the social conscience, will teach that the kingdom of God fully come in the earth is the true social ideal; that the brotherhood of the kingdom creates the true social spirit, and that the three fundamental laws of the kingdom—those of service, sacrifice, and love—are the only laws by obedience to which society can be perfected.

In a word, twentieth century Christianity will be the Christianity of Christ, and will teach that he is the only Saviour of society as well as the only Saviour of the individual.

Document IV-11: UTOPIA AS SEEN BY THE IWW

Models for society come from all directions. From the right, for example, came Bradford Peck, a successful merchant, who described a utopia characterized by efficient organization of social functions placed in an architectural setting that was meant to inspire automatic respect (*The World a Department Store*. Lewiston, Me., Peck, 1900). Unlike most conservative dreams of the perfect society, Peck eschewed the "good old days" in favor of a kind of administrative genius. A rather similar end product, couched in diametrically opposite rhetoric, may be found in what Samuel Gompers called "Father Hagerty's Wheel of Fortune." Thomas J. Hagerty, looking ahead from a labor viewpoint to the day when the means of production would be the property of the public, solved the problem of efficient social organization by placing administration at the hub of a wheel whence emanated departments for dealing with manufacture, instruction, transportation, and so forth. (See Joyce L. Kornbluh, *Rebel Voices*. Ann Arbor, University of Michigan, 1964, pp. 10-11; the plan was first published in 1905.)

Father Hagerty, one of the voices associated with the Industrial Workers of the World, helps introduce the role of radicalism and the labor movement in proposing models toward which society should work. To some extent labor views have been represented in Part II (see 7, 30, 36, 38). Radicalism included the political socialism of Eugene Debs; it also included the anarchism of Alexander Berkman and Emma Goldman. Its popular forms were in the antebellum communes, in the technological utopias like Bellamy's, and—at one extreme—in the Industrial Workers of the World.

Where to present the IWW in a discussion of American reform is not easy. To be sure, the "Wobblies" were part of the labor movement, but their impatience with the gradual spread of democracy to provide economic equity placed them essentially outside the tradition documented in Part II. Some of their most notorious activity—on behalf of migrant workers then unrepresented in conventional unions—made them appropriate subjects for Part III, efforts on behalf of special groups. In spite of foreign influences, they were distinctively American. They dressed in the clothes of American workers. They took their powerful songs from the American folk and popular traditions. They used the weapon of the political cartoon in an abundantly American way. They affected American institutions from the forests of the Northwest to the social forums of Greenwich Village.

Seen in their grandest perspective, they were the would-be creators of a model society. Although the membership varied greatly in its acceptance of violence and its expectation of revolution, they would all have welcomed an opportunity for Father Hagerty to put into motion his famous wheel. Their password eventually crystallized into the phrase "one big union," or its initial letters. Just as Peck would have reordered the nation on the model of his store, so the Wobblies would have started with the model of a nondiscriminatory national union, open to all and pledged to justice for all. Utopia would be assured if everyone could be enrolled; so the legendary Joe Hill signed his letters "Yours for the OBU." Much of this spirit can be seen in the words of the Manifesto reproduced below. Its hoped-for amalgamation of the American workers' dream can also be adduced from the names appearing as signers.

SOURCE: *Proceedings of the First Convention of the Industrial Workers of the World.* New York, *Labor News*, 1905, pp. 3-7.

MANIFESTO.

Social relations and groupings only reflect mechanical and industrial conditions. The *great facts* of present industry are the displacement of human skill by machines and the increase of capitalist power through concentration in the possession of the tools with which wealth is produced and distributed.

Because of these facts trade divisions among laborers and competition among capitalists are alike disappearing. Class divisions grow ever more fixed and class antagonisms more sharp. Trade lines have been swallowed up in a common servitude of all workers to the machines which they tend. New machines, ever replacing less productive ones, wipe out whole trades and plunge new bodies of workers into the ever-growing army of tradeless, hopeless unemployed. As human beings and human skill are displaced by mechanical progress, the capitalists need use the workers only during that brief period when muscles and nerves respond most intensely. The moment the laborer no longer yields the maximum of profits, he is thrown upon the scrap pile, to starve alongside the discarded machine. A *dead line* has been drawn, and an age-limit established, to cross which, in this world of monopolized opportunities, means condemnation to industrial death.

The worker, wholly separated from the land and the tools, with his skill of craftsmenship rendered useless, is sunk in the uniform mass of wage slaves. He sees his power of resistance broken by craft divisions, perpetuated from out-grown industrial stages. His wages constantly grow less as his hours grow longer and monopolized prices grow higher. Shifted hither and thither by the demands of profit-takers the laborer's home no longer exists. In this helpless condition he is forced to accept whatever humiliating conditions his master may impose. He is submitted to a physical and intellectual examination more searching than was the chattel slave when sold from the auction block. Laborers are no longer classified by differences in trade skill, but the employer assigns them according to the machines to which they are attached. These divisions, far from representing differences in skill or interests among the laborers, are imposed by the employers that workers may be pitted against one another and spurred to greater exertion in the shop, and that all resistance to capitalist tyranny may be weakened by artificial distinctions.

While encouraging these outgrown divisions among the workers the capitalists carefully adjust themselves to the new conditions. They wipe out all differences among themselves and present a united front in their war upon labor. Through employers' associations, they seek to crush, with brutal force, by the injunctions of the judiciary, and the use of military power, all efforts at resistance. Or when the other policy seems more profitable, they conceal their daggers beneath the Civic Federation and hoodwink and betray those whom they would rule and exploit. Both methods depend for success upon the blindness and internal dissensions of the working class. The employers' line of battle and methods of warfare correspond to the solidarity of the mechanical and industrial concentration, while laborers still form their fighting organizations on lines of long-gone trade divisions. The battles of the past emphasize this lesson. The *textile* workers of Lowell, Philadelphia and Fall River; the *butchers* of Chicago, weakened by the disintegrating effects of trade divisions; the *machinists* on the Santa Fe, unsupported by their fellow-workers subject to the same masters; the long-struggling *miners* of Colorado, hampered by lack of unity and solidarity upon the industrial battle-field, all bear witness to the helplessness and impotency of labor as at present organized. . . .

Universal economic evils afflicting the working class can be eradicated only by a universal working class movement. Such a movement of the working class is impossible while separate craft and wage agreements are made favoring the employer against other crafts in the same industry, and while energies are wasted in fruitless jurisdiction struggles which serve only to further the personal aggrandizement of union officials.

A movement to fulfill these conditions must consist of one great industrial union embracing all industries,—providing for craft autonomy locally, industrial autonomy internationally, and working class unity generally.

It must be founded on the class struggle, and its general administration must be conducted in harmony with the recognition of the irrepressible conflict between the capitalist class and the working class.

It should be established as the economic organization of the working class, without affiliation with any political party.

All power should rest in a collective membership.

Local, national and general administration, including union labels, buttons, badges, transfer cards, initiation fees, and per capita tax should be uniform throughout.

All members must hold membership in the local, national or international union covering the industry in which they are employed, but transfers of membership between unions, local, national or international, should be universal.

Workingmen bringing union cards from industrial unions in foreign countries should be freely admitted into the organization.

The general administration should issue a publication representing the entire union and its principles which should reach all members in every industry at regular intervals.

A *central defense fund,* to which all members contribute equally, should be established and maintained.

All workers, therefore, who agree with the principles herein set forth, will meet in convention at Chicago the 27th day of June, 1905, for the purpose of forming an economic organization of the working class along the lines marked out in this Manifesto.

Representation in the convention shall be based upon the number of workers whom the delegate represents. No delegate, however, shall be given representation in the convention on the numerical basis of an organization unless he has credentials—bearing the seal of his union, local, national or international, and the signatures of the officers thereof—authorizing him to install his union as a working part of the proposed economic organization in the industrial department in which it logically belongs in the general plan of organization. Lacking this authority, the delegate shall represent himself as an individual.

Adopted at Chicago, January 2, 3 and 4, 1905.

A. G. SWING,
A. M. SIMONS,
W. SHURTLEFF,
FRANK M. McCABE,
JOHN M. O'NEIL,

GEO. ESTES,
WM. D. HAYWOOD,
MOTHER JONES,
ERNEST UNTERMANN,
W. L. HALL,
CHAS. H. MOYER,
CLARENCE SMITH,
WILLIAM ERNEST TRAUTMANN,
JOS. SCHMIDT,
JOHN GUILD,
DANIEL McDONALD,
EUGENE V. DEBS,
THOS. J. De YOUNG,
THOS. J. HAGERTY,
FRED D. HENION,
W. J. BRADLEY,
CHAS. O. SHERMAN,
M. E. WHITE,
WM. J. PINKERTON,
FRANK KRAFFS,
J. E. FITZGERALD,
FRANK BOHN.

Document IV-12: STREIT AND WORLD GOVERNMENT

The peace movement has a long and interesting history in the annals of American reform. Merle Curti has traced it from 1636. Its ideals have attracted William Lloyd Garrison, Jane Addams, Clarence S. Darrow, and many others. Although peace movements must originate somewhere, their progress depends on transcending political boundaries and becoming international. In that sense, a study of the peace movement may reveal less that is distinctive of national behavior. Nonetheless, there have been special aspects to this movement in America: the long history of the Friends, who opposed all wars from colonial times to the present yet managed to avoid a universal stigma of disloyalty; the wonderfully naive episode surrounding Henry Ford's Peace Ship with its benign self-confidence possible only in a man who combined Ford's genius with his provinciality; the establishment in 1960 by Robert Gilmore and David Riesman of a Council for Correspondence on the American colonial model to agitate against nuclear war; the Peace Corps with its large aim of avoiding war through international understanding and its peculiarly American style of learning through working.

Ideal communities invariably advocate peace. Many of the antebellum communitarians were explicitly pacifistic and some of them came to the American wilderness to avoid European armies. Modern communes had a parallel relationship to the Vietnam War. Utopian romances like Bellamy's were predicated on peace, usually through the substitution of service, efficiency, and productive technology for nation-based competition. There were dystopian renderings of holocaust and disaster both in the Bellamy mode and in the style of science fiction; but most futuristic works included a formula for ending man's destruction of man.

If it were possible to represent the American approach to world peace in a single document—which it is not—that document might well be Clarence Streit's *Union Now.* A reporter assigned to cover the League of Nations after World War I, Streit saw its limitations while he inhaled its hopes. His vision and experience made him into that kind of reformer that may be distinctively American: the practical idealist. The sections of his book reproduced below are designed to show both sides of Streit's character: the hard journalistic prose directed at self-interest and arguing from necessity; and, with this, the faith that man and his capabilities are invariably greater than man could imagine. The book includes an illustrative Constitution for an international federal union explicitly adapted from the Constitution of the United States with innovations drawn from the Swiss and Canadian experiences.

Streit's original proposal was for a federal union of fifteen nations most of which bordered the North Atlantic. (See item 7 in the document quoted for a list; the Union of South Africa was dropped on its adoption of *apartheid.*) As Hitler's power spread, Streit urged an immediate provisional federation with Britain and the self-governing Dominions in order to "shorten the war and win the peace." The post-war establishment of a North Atlantic Treaty Organization and of a United Nations quartered in New York has doubtless made Streit's message seem less urgent to many, but he has continued devoting his full energies to the cause of a Federal Union of the Free both as President of Federal Union, Inc., and as editor of the magazine *Freedom & Union.*

Since 1949 resolutions have been introduced into each U. S. Congress calling for the authorization of an American delegation to attend an international conference dedicated to exploring the feasibility of an Atlantic union. In 1960 Congress passed a version of this resolution which, although it avoided the vocabulary of World Federalism, urged the same purposes and eventuated in a Paris conference attended in 1962 by delegations from all the Atlantic allies but Portugal. The convention resolved in favor of working toward ''a true Atlantic Community'': a resolution with no tangible consequences. Clarence Streit, who attended as an observer, nonetheless viewed the conference as a successful laboratory for solving procedural problems such as proportional representation and voting order.

Failing to attract State Department support, the Atlantic Unionists went back to the Congressional strategy and, beginning again in 1965, have encouraged the submission of resolutions to move the Atlantic alliance toward a federal union. Practical prospects shift with Congressional majorities as well as with White House tenancy; meanwhile the dream persists of a worldwide model community in the American federal style. Its antithetical ideology is not so much the Nationalism of Bellamy (IV-9) as the patriotism of Strong (IV-10).

[Editor's note: Clarence Streit has been kind enough to read the foregoing headnote and to improve its accuracy. Some of the phrasing is his. In using his work to represent aspects of American reform, I have not been totally fair to Clarence Streit and the movement he heads. He would urge interested readers to pay special heed to Chapters I, X, and XIII of *Union Now*; to consult *Freedom's Frontier—Atlantic Union Now* (New York: Harper, 1961) and to make use of the magazine *Freedom & Union* now in its thirtieth year. I am most grateful for Clarence Streit's help, patience and generosity.]

SOURCE: Clarence K. Streit, *Union Now: a Proposal for a Federal Union of the Democracies of the North Atlantic.* New York, Harper, 1939, pp. 57-61, 206-208, 243-251, abridged.

From *UNION NOW*

We in the Americas are no longer a far-away continent to which the eddies of controversies beyond the seas could bring no interest or no harm. Instead we in the Americas have become a consideration to every propaganda office and to every general staff beyond the seas. The vast amount of our resources, the vigor of our commerce, and the strength of our men have made us vital factors in world peace whether we choose or not.—President Roosevelt, Aug. 18, 1938.

The problem of world government is of peculiar urgency for us partly because it does not seem to be. We are less exposed than others to some of the dangers besetting mankind, but that exposes us most of all to one of the worst of dangers,—to the delusion that we shall be spared in any general calamity our species suffers. We suffer from that delusion to the point where our approach to the common problems of mankind has become habitually one of self-sacrifice rather than self-interest, of doing the world a favor rather than recognizing that we have anything to gain from the world, of donating rather than trading. We can not be safe while our thinking is wrong, and no thinking can be right that starts with the assumption that the United States is not a part of the world but a world apart.

The problem of world government is most urgent for us because the factors that expose us less than other nations—such as the ocean—belong to the past and are rapidly losing force, while the factors that expose us more than others belong to the present and future, and are rapidly gaining force. No other nation is so advanced as we are in world-needing and world-making machines. No other has so much to lose economically, politically, and morally as we by failure to solve in time the problem of world government.

We have already seen why the development of world machines makes increasingly urgent the need of world government, especially for the more advanced peoples. There seems no need to prove that we lead the world in developing these machines, and that therefore our position is particularly exposed and that we less than any other people can expect or afford to live in our world today on yesterday's political basis. But we can hardly recall too often that the depression struck no people so swiftly and savagely as it struck the people who believed what Irving T. Bush expressed in 1927: "The future destiny of America is in our hands, and is not dependent upon other nations." . . .

We have a phrase that covers our position now as then: "The higher you are, the harder you fall." Whether or not we can gamble on being able to keep out of European or Asiatic war, we can not even gamble on keeping clear of the economic and financial effects of the world ungovernment to which we contribute so prodigally. Just as the war side of the catastrophe that ungovernment is bringing is more liable to strike first again in Europe or Asia and spread to us from there, its economic side is more liable to begin again with us and spread to Europe and Asia.

We have more than money to lose in depression. The Germans and Italians lost their individual freedom to no foreign aggressor but to dictators who rose from inside with hard times and unemployment brought on by world ungovernment. We can be the next great people to lose inside our state what we made it for. If we lose our freedom that way while the British and the French lose theirs to foreign autocrats, shall we be the better off? If we must risk it I would rather risk losing it to an autocrat from without than from within. . . .

Our Rome need not fall. To live and grow to greater marvels it needs but the faith that made it, the faith in Man. Man's worst weakness is that he is always under-estimating Man. He has never seen too large, he has always seen too small, too small. He has never had too much faith in what Man could do; he has always had too little.

Since time began, the western world lay there across the sea, but even when Columbus came he saw himself as the discoverer not of a new world but of a new route. The kettle steamed through thousands of years of human slavery; then came Watt—and which would amaze him most today: The automobile or the negro owning one? Once a man believed that Man could make a ship go without sails against a river. Other men called his ship *Fulton's Folly*. But he kept faith in Man, in one man,—himself,—and *Fulton's Folly* went paddling up the Hudson. Fulton saw far for his time, but doubtless he himself would have called it folly to believe the oil he used to cure a cold in the head could ever drive gigantic ships across the Atlantic in a hundred hours.

The fathers of the American Republic, the leaders of the French Revolution, the authors of the Bill of Rights, the political liberators of men everywhere had faith in Man—but they had no idea of all the forces they were freeing. They had no idea of all the rapid growth in civilization, all the transformation of the world, all the victories of men over autocracy and Nature that would come from freeing those then called *la canaille.* Washington, Jefferson, Hamilton, all voiced despair of the American Union even after its establishment, but they are not remembered for their doubts. They are known for what faith they showed in Man.

Man has still to find the limit of what he can do if only he has faith in himself. And yet each generation has seen wonders done by men who believed in Man. Man's greatest achievements have been the work of some obscure man or handful of men with faith in themselves, helping mankind against mankind's stubborn opposition. These inventors, discoverers, artists, statesmen, poets,—each of our benefactors has always had to overcome not only Nature but his own species. And always these lone men with faith have worked this wonder. As Andrew Jackson said, one man with courage makes a majority.

We have seen a village unknown through all the ancient Roman era become in a century Mecca to a world greater than Rome ever ruled, because there lived there then one man with faith in himself. We know what marvels one single simple individual with faith in Man can work— one Mohammed, one Joan of Arc, one Gutenberg, one Paine, Pasteur, Edison. What we do not know is what marvels could be done if the fifteen elected leaders of the 300,000,000 free men and women once worked together with the faith of one Columbus. We know that, working together,—which means depending on each other,—the Wright brothers did one of the many things that Man had always dreamed and failed of doing. But the Wright brothers were two simple citizens; they were not fifteen leaders in whom millions of men already trusted.

"As I stand aloof and watch [Walt Whitman wrote] there is something profoundly moving in great masses of men following the leadership of men who do not believe in man."

Yet the leaders who have believed in Man and have appealed not to his lowest but to his highest instincts have always in the end been not only followed but alone remembered by all mankind. There is nowhere a monument to those who burned Bruno at the stake; there is in Rome a monument raised, in 1889, which says: "To Bruno, the century he foresaw, here where he burned."

As the dust are all those of our species who said that Man could never bring the lightning down against his other natural foes. Green still is the name of Franklin. Who were those twenty-seven men who, preferring the freedom of New York to the freedom of New Yorkers, came so near to preventing the American Union? It is their opponent, Alexander Hamilton, whose name still evokes eloquence in Europe as in America.

The difficulties that now seem so certain to keep us apart,—will men remember them a generation hence more than they now remember those that seemed to make the Union of Americans impossible in 1787? Will our own children be the first to honor those who kept Man divided against himself, at war with himself and a prey to ignorance, poverty, disease, premature death? . . .

The draft constitution that follows is meant to make the proposed Union clearer by illustrating how the democracies might unite. I would stress what I have already pointed out in Chapter X. This draft is not intended to be a hard and fast plan. Practically all of its provisions, however, are time-tested.

The draft is drawn entirely from the Constitution of the American Union, except for (1) a few provisions that, although not drawn from it, are based on American practice (notably Art. II, sections 1, 2, 4, 5), and (2) a few innovations: These latter are given in italics so that they may be seen at once. Most of the draft taken from the American Constitution has been taken textually, though its provisions have sometimes been re-arranged with a view to greater clarity and condensation, and once or twice they have been made more explicit and somewhat expanded. The Preamble is the only serious example of this last. In the American Constitution the Preamble reads:

We the People of the United States, in order to form a more perfect Union, establish Justice, insure domestic Tranquility, provide for the common defence, promote the general Welfare, and secure the Blessings of Liberty to ourselves and our Posterity, do ordain and establish this Constitution for the United States of America.

No important element in the American Constitution has been omitted. The draft follows:

ILLUSTRATIVE CONSTITUTION

We the people of the Union of the Free, in order to secure freedom equally to every man and woman now and to come, to lessen ignorance, poverty, and disease, to insure our defense, to promote justice and the general welfare, to provide government of ourselves, by ourselves, and for ourselves on the principle of the equality of men, and to bring peace on earth and union to mankind, do establish this as our Constitution.

PART I
THE RIGHTS OF MAN

ARTICLE I.—In the individual freedom this Constitution is made to secure we include:

1. Freedom of speech and of the press and of conscience.

2. Freedom to organize ourselves for any purpose except to change by violence this Constitution and the laws made under it; freedom to assemble peaceably and to ask redress of grievances and make proposals.

3. Freedom of our persons, dwellings, communications, papers and effects from unreasonable searches and seizures, and from warrants unless issued upon probable cause, supported by oath or affirmation, and particularly describing the place to be searched and the persons or things to be seized.

4. Freedom from ex post facto law and from bills of attainder.

5. Freedom from suspension of the writ of habeas corpus except when public safety may temporarily require it in case of rebellion or invasion.

6. Freedom from being held to answer for a capital or infamous crime except on indictment of a grand jury—save in the armed forces in time of war or public danger—and from being twice put in jeopardy of life or limb or liberty for the same offence, and from being deprived of life, liberty, or property without due process of law, and from having property taken for public use without just compensation.

7. The right when accused of any crime to have a speedy public trial by an impartial jury of the country and district wherein the crime shall have been committed, as previously ascertained by law, and to be informed in good time of the nature and cause of the accusation, to be

confronted with the witnesses against one, to have compulsory process for obtaining witnesses in one's favor, to be under no compulsion to be a witness against oneself, and to have the assistance of counsel for one's defense.

8. Freedom from excessive bail or excessive fines or cruel and unusual punishments.

9. Freedom from slavery, and from involuntary servitude and forced labor except in legal punishment for crime.

10. The right to equality before the law and to the equal protection of the laws.

11. The preceding enumeration is not exhaustive nor shall it be construed to deny or disparage other rights which we retain.

PART II
THE GOVERNMENT OF THE UNION

ARTICLE II.—THE PEOPLE OF THE UNION.

1. All persons born or naturalized in the self-governing states of the Union are citizens of the Union and of the state wherein they reside. All citizens above the age of 21, except those in institutions for the feebleminded or mentally deranged or in prison, are entitled to vote in all Union elections, and to hold any Union office for which their age qualifies them.

2. All other persons in the territory of the Union shall enjoy all rights of citizens except the right to vote in Union elections. The Union shall seek to extend this right to them at the earliest time practicable by helping prepare their country to enter the Union as a self-governing state.

3. *The self-governing states of the Union at its foundation are Australia, Belgium, Canada, Denmark, Finland, France, Ireland, the Netherlands, New Zealand, Norway, Sweden, Switzerland, the Union of South Africa, the United Kingdom, and the United States of America.*

4. The non-self-governing territory of these states and of all states admitted later to the Union is transferred to the Union to govern while preparing it for self-government and admission to the Union.

5. *Before casting his or her first vote each citizen of the Union shall*

take this oath in conditions to be prescribed by law: "I do solemnly swear (or affirm) that I will preserve, protect and defend the Constitution of the Union of the Free against all enemies, foreign and domestic."

6. Treason can be committed only by citizens against the Union and can consist only in levying war against it or in adhering to its enemies, aiding and comforting them. No one shall be convicted of treason unless on the testimony of two witnesses to the same overt act or on confession in open court. . . .

ARTICLE IV.—THE LEGISLATIVE POWER.

1. The legislative power of the Union is vested in the Congress, which shall consist of a House of Deputies and a Senate. Each shall choose its own officers, judge the elections, returns, and qualifications of its own members, determine its rules of procedure, have the power to punish its members for disorderly behavior, to compel their attendance, and to expel them by two-thirds majority; keep and publish a record of its proceedings, meet and vote in public except when two-thirds shall ask for a private meeting on a particular question, vote by roll call when one-fifth of the members ask this, form with a majority a quorum to do business though fewer may adjourn from day to day, act by majority except where otherwise stipulated in this Constitution.

2. The Congress shall meet at least once a year at a regular date it shall fix. During a session neither branch shall adjourn more than three days or to any other place without the other's consent.

3. Members of Congress shall not be questioned outside their branch of it for anything they said in it, nor shall they be arrested on any charge except treason, felony, or breach of the peace, during attendance at a session of Congress or while going to and from it.

4. No member of Congress shall hold other public office in the Union or in a state during his term, *except in the Cabinet.*

5. The Deputies shall be at least 25 years old, and shall be elected directly by the citizens every *third* year.

The number of Deputies from each state shall be determined according to population, a census being taken at least every ten years, and shall not exceed one for every *1,000,000* inhabitants or major fraction thereof, though each state shall have at least one.

6. Senators shall be at least 30 years old, shall have resided since at

least 10 years in the State by which elected, and shall be elected at large from each state directly by the citizens every *eight* years, except that in the first election half the Senators of each state shall be elected for only four years. There shall be two Senators from each state *of less than 25,000,000 population, and two more for each additional 25,000,000 population or major fraction thereof.*

7. To begin with the apportionment of Deputies and Senators shall be:

Australia	7	2
Belgium	8	2
Canada	11	2
Denmark	4	2
Finland	4	2
France	42	4
Ireland	3	2
Netherlands	8	2
New Zealand	2	2
Norway	3	2
Sweden	6	2
Switzerland	4	2
Union of South Africa	4	2
United Kingdom	47	4
United States	126	10
Totals	287	42

. . . ARTICLE V.—THE EXECUTIVE POWER.

1. The executive power of the Union is vested in the *Board. It shall be composed of five citizens at least 35 years old. Three shall be elected directly by the citizens of the Union and one by the House and one by the Senate. One shall be elected each year for a five-year term, except that in the first election the citizens shall elect three, and the House shall then elect one for two years and the Senate shall then elect one for four years, and the Board shall then by lot assign terms of one, three, and five years respectively to the three Members elected by the citizens.*

2. *A majority of the Board shall form a quorum, and it shall act by majority thereof unless otherwise provided herein.*

3. The *Board* shall be commander-in-chief of all the armed forces of the Union, shall commission all officers of the Union and appoint ambassadors, ministers and consuls, may grant reprieves and pardons for offences against the Union, shall have the power to make treaties by and with the advice and consent of the *Premier and Congress* and to appoint with the advice and consent of the Senate the justices of the Supreme Court and of all lower Union Courts, and to make any other appointments required of it by law.

4. The *Board* shall from time to time report to the people and Congress on the state of the Union, *its progress toward its objectives, and the effects and need of change,* and shall recommend to their consideration such policies and measures as it shall judge necessary and expedient; it may require the opinion of any one in the service of the Union on any subject relating to the duties of his office.

The *Board* may convene extraordinarily Congress, adjourn it when its two houses cannot agree on adjournment, *or dissolve it or either branch of it for the purpose of having it elected anew as shall be prescribed by law.*

The *Board* shall receive ambassadors and other public ministers.

5. *The Board shall delegate all executive power not expressly retained by it herein to a Premier, who shall exercise it with the help of a Cabinet of his choice until he loses the confidence of House or Senate, whereupon the Board shall delegate this power to another Premier. . . .*

ARTICLE IX.—RATIFICATION

1. The ratification of this Constitution by *ten* states, *or by France, the United Kingdom, and the United States,* shall suffice to establish it among them.

An endeavor to conciliate mankind, to render their condition happy, to unite nations that have hitherto been enemies, and to extirpate the horrid practice of war, and break the chains of slavery and oppression.—Paine's description of his *Rights of Man.*

They are two to one against us. . . . Tell them that the Convention shall never rise until the Constitution is adopted.—Hamilton when asked by a friend what to tell New York City about the prospects of the New York State Convention ratifying the American Constitution. In six weeks he changed a hostile majority of two-thirds into a favorable majority of three.

Document IV-13: SCIENCE FICTION UTOPIAS: CLOUGH

Science fiction is both a close relative and a continuation of the utopian romance; yet distinctions must be made. The classics of science fiction—unlike nearly all utopias—contain very little social commentary. Rather, they emphasize a future in which science and technology give birth to amazing problems and solutions.

When these works are not purely escapist, they perform a serious mission in preparing for change. Whereas the 1920s saw science fiction as a diversion, the 1930s witnessed in this literature some of the early, dramatic warnings against overpopulation, ecological imbalance, over-specialization, and other forms of extremism. Should a social message become too strident, however, the cultist is likely to sneer at a deviant genre he sometimes calls "social science fiction." (For a knowledgeable attempt to be arbitrary about boundaries, see Isaac Asimov's contribution to *Modern Science Fiction*, Reginald Bretnor, ed. New York, Coward-McCann, 1953, pp. 158-196.)

The work excerpted below is made up of almost equal parts of utopian romance and science fiction. It comes as close as any work to illustrating Isaac Asimov's definition of social science fiction. In it a young man is put to sleep for one thousand years and awakes to a "golden age" of humanistic triumph made possible by advanced technology and social evolution. The model society has a definite Deistic cast: social progress having been most seriously inhibited by the three great enemies of man—religion, war, and government. In the golden age, world government presides in the form of a benign commission. Every citizen (see IV-1) owns his own luxurious home on a plot of ground which—though small—is sufficient to all his needs. The excerpts reflect what Fred Clough saw as the major points of contrast between 1923 and 2923. Also present in this world of air coupes and immediate communication is a

Martian visitor who reveals that a "diamond age" has been achieved on Mars where less error, superstition, and brutality stood in the way.

Clough excoriates the wealthy of his own day for their conscienceless use of power. To improve distribution of wealth he calls on Henry George (II-21); to replace nationalism he envisages continental federations. Although he depicts a world of equality and social responsibility, he reflects the bias of his own times by locating initiative in the acceptance of the "white man's burden."

SOURCE: Fred M. Clough, *The Golden Age, or, the Depth of Time.* Boston, Roxburgh, 1923, pp. 138-174, abridged.

THE GOLDEN AGE

"Fellow Citizens: I deem myself the most fortunate of mortals, after resting one thousand years in the shade of the trees that are waving so gentle a welcome just over the river on that voiceless shore, and during that time being under the watchful care of the world's most skillful scientists, by science then revivified and called back from the long sleep to pulsating life, to a regenerated world where truth is the pole star and service its hand maid. In this golden age there is no latitude or longitude of segregated humanity, no menials, slaves or bondsmen; but citizens of the world, co-workers and beneficiaries in the abundance of this earth, enjoying the blessings of an enlightened civilization, social and governmental order, genuine liberty and equality and a true democracy, that is not a dream but the priceless heritage of all. At the beginning of my long sleep beneath the veneer of twenty or more centuries, man was still an ungarmented creature of snarl, teeth and fangs. . . . The dark clouds of barbarism, human selfishness, extreme greed and war, petty political jealousies and strife, inefficient and burdensome governments, religious bigotry and superstition have been overcome. The sun of higher intellectuality floods the world with its benign light, and has led man to a higher civilization.

"Life in the Golden Age is not one continual struggle for existence; a few hours' work a day provides abundant comforts for each individual; science and inventions have brought innumerable benefits to the human family and are used for the benefits of all instead of the few. By the social and governmental reforms, it has made money no longer the god of man,

man and woman are no longer sized up in the scale of importance by the amount of money or property that they possess, State ownership of land has banished land monopoly and the serfdom of tenantry, has provided homes for the millions with peace and plenty, and has proven the sovereign balm for nearly all the social ills of the past.

"The great world war cost over 350 billions of dollars or over 60 percent of all the earnings of the world since man began to crawl out of the dents and caves to 1918, when the war came to an end. Forty-three million lives had been lost as a direct result of such war. . . .

In this Golden Age we have, happily, removed all these and allied burdens, which were so enormous and destructive to the higher social and intellectual and ennobling attributes of mankind. We have wrought into full fruitage that principle, that truth, so long ago enunciated by Henry George of the innate right of all mankind to a piece of mother earth. There is no monetary consideration confronting the individual that wants a piece of land; it is as free as the air we breathe or the water that we drink. The only consideration is that the soil must be properly cared for. . . . The tax is very small to support local governmental needs. The system gives to generations unborn the same privilege as those of today, and has banished forever tenantry, or landed serfs from the earth. The government controls all the natural utilities, nature's gifts to the human race, under wise and beneficial management for all the people, cutting out waste and exhaustive methods. . . . Money is no longer the god of the human race. Doing away with the extremes of wealth, the idle rich, and the constantly toiling poor has done away with the cause of so much criminality. We have long since woke [sic] up to the white man's burden and are not content to see vast blocks of humanity grow up in ignorance and with such environments that were the breeding places of criminality. This service of enlightenment and philanthropy and scientific morality has brought happiness, peace, joy and plenty to the world. We no longer tolerate vast navies; great standing armies; poison gas factories. These belong to a barbarous past and are not within the province of an enlightened civilization to maintain such destructive and burdensome agencies.

"We have now the United States of Europe; the confederation of the South American Republics; the United States of South America, and the tendency in all parts of the world to come together; to co-operate with one another, for the general good has taken vast burdens from productive toil.

The commission form of government in national, state, and municipal has done away with legions of costly officials and with the opportunity of free land, they all, or nearly so, are producers of their own food. In fact the human race has got back to mother earth, it has come into its own, they [sic] live close to the soil in comfort, peace, and happiness, leaving off the frills and frivolities of those ancient days and cultivating the higher and nobler attributes of the mind.

"In this Golden Age we have gotten away from the barbarous and cruel customs of the Christian Age of vast slaughter-houses, where hundreds of thousands of animals were slaughtered and people everywhere, eating and feasting on their flesh. This alone is an index of the brutality of the times. We now grow nut-bearing trees, shrubs and plants, that furnish the necessary fat that the human system requires, and it is nature's true food for the human system. And as a result we have gotten away from many dangerous and destructive diseases that during the meat-eating ages infested the human family. Then millions of acres were used for the pasturing and feeding of stock, necessitating incalculable labor and much of it unremunerating. . . . Man's intense selfishness, greed, egotism and without care or thought for the condition under which his fellow man was laboring, had been the great burdening and destructive moral and social force of the world, but happily they do not prevail in this Golden Age.

"The great stumbling block to human progress down the centuries was the disposition to cling tenaciously to precedent and old methods, so aloof to strike out along new lines. The educator, the explorer, the inventor, the scientist, the discoveries made in research, made imperative a new adjustment of the social and governmental order, and are sweeping away old precedents and customs, and abortive and unnecessary laws and have brought forcibly to the front the relation of man to man. The social problem was a difficult and complicated one, and always caused a titanic struggle to throw off the precedents and customs of an old world, for the realities of a new.

"The world has been drawn very close together by invention and science, by the cable and the ocean liners and freighters, but is infinitely more closely drawn by the wireless and airship. This has done away with the isolation of nations. These instruments of intercommunication and transportation, the social and industrial methods of one nation materially affects all other nations. This requires the yielding of certain of their individualistic rights and prerogatives, in order to benefit the world at large. The nation or state that assumes as its prerogative to act as it pleases without regard to other nations or states, is tyrannical and autocratic.

"It has been a toilsome and hard fought journey to establish the principle of the greatest good to the greatest numbers, for the welfare of communities takes precedence to that of individuals. The liberty of individuals must be circumscribed for the benefit of the community as a whole. Not so very far back in human history, the attitude of capital to labor was that might made right, and the relationship between capital and labor was that of owner and slave. Then a liberation when he became master and man, then emerging from this to employer and employe, then entering the period of copartnership where the employe shared more equable *[sic]* in the profits of the business. Then the idea of nationalization of all means of production and distribution; the suppression of the capitalistic system by an industrial and social order based on public ownership and control of instruments of production and distribution, the government control of all public utilities. The evolution in the industrial world must of necessity have reformation in the system of government. In the golden age we have garnered in all these social and government reforms."

Document IV-14: SOCIAL ENGINEERING AND MODERN COMMUNES

The first wave of communitarianism began about 1800, waxed through the 1830s and forties, and had pretty well died out by the Civil War. There was no screeching halt to the movement. Communities like Oneida and Amana lived on through the products they learned to make with competitive skill. The Mormons, first notable as communitarians with a strong zionist flavor, have continued to grow into a highly successful worldwide Church of Jesus Christ of the Latter Day Saints. Shaker authority has continued for nearly two hundred years, however shrunk in numbers (see IV-2). New communities—religious and secular —came and some endured. But for the hundred years between 1860 and 1960 communitarianism went almost unnoticed and involved a decreasing percentage of the population.

Now, in the last ten years, the process has reversed itself and communitarian experiments are attracting more and more people. In 1972, several periodicals emanating from these new groups merged to form one: *Communities*. Its purpose, briefly stated, was to form a network of communitarians so that each could learn from the other; so that prospective members could choose the one best suited to them; and so that the nation, observing the communal example, could make its conventional communities more communelike in their habits and values. The first issue provided a directory of about two hundred communes in Canada and the United States, ranging from the Alternate Society Collective to the Zen Mountain Center. A separate guide to "spiritual groups" was cited.

The literature of the new movement shows itself to be quite conscious of the antebellum experience. The general preference for an isolated, agricultural setting, coupled with the goals expressed in the following documents, are indeed strongly reminiscent of Ephrata and Economy. So too is the notion that these outposts should form a self-conscious network through which they not only will learn survival but will rescue the "straight culture" from its sins "too numerous to mention." These generalizations would seem to apply, however, only to a certain kind of group. Many are still simply retreating, protesting, or "dropping out." When our neighbor tells us, "Grace has left home and is living in a commune," we may be right to picture a downtown rowhouse which has very little to do with Brook Farm. The list of desirable communal characteristics presented below is a result, quite obviously, of experiences which David Hackett found as vividly negative as positive.

A number of new books have grown out of individual communes; there are even some brave attempts to make generalizations (Rosabeth Kanter, *Commitment and Community*. Cambridge, Harvard University Press, 1972; and Robert Houriet, *Getting Back Together*. New York, Coward, McCann & Geoghegan, 1971). With the help of these analyses it is possible to identify the origins of this new communitarianism in the group achievements of the civil rights and anti-war protestors, in a mixed experience like Haight-Ashbury, and in positive models like Israel's *kibbutzim*. (See "The Commune Way: Israeli Version," *Intellectual Digest*. February, 1973, pp. 19-22.) Although communes share a great many antipathies they show nothing so much as variety when it comes to their positive objectives.

One positive influence comes from behaviorism and relates to a vision of society which has excited many individuals, reform-minded or not. The most powerful and widely read statement of this vision came from psychologist B. F. Skinner in the form of a utopian novel titled *Walden Two* (New York, Macmillan, 1948). In it Skinner depicted an ideal community immediately accessible through a radical transformation of values and a drastic application of social controls. Alluding to a Transcendental ideal in his title, Skinner also echoed such reformers as Thomas Jefferson, Edward Bellamy, and John Dewey. His most revolutionary principle he attributed to Jesus of Nazareth. In spite of these revered associations, Skinner's ideas sounded to many humanists more like the dystopia of Aldous Huxley's *Brave New World* wherein human beings were "engineered" into predetermined roles without their conscious assent. (For a quick initiation into *Walden Two*, see pp. 100-115 of the paperback edition. For the most impressive attack on Skinner, see Joseph Wood Krutch, *Measure of Man.* Indianapolis, Bobbs-Merrill, 1954.)

The second document usefully combines insights into communitarianism with a test case in the precepts of Skinner. Twin Oaks was founded explicitly to apply the ideas set forth in *Walden Two*. The description below was probably written by Kathleen "Kat" Kinkade, the only founding member still in residence and author of *A Walden Two Experiment: the First Five Years of Twin Oaks Community* (New York, Morrow, 1973). This brief account includes an exemplary definition of commune. Intended for an audience of fellow communards, it stresses practical problems and essential methods. It is remarkably candid as to achievements, failures, and reasons therefore. A reporter who visited Twin Oaks after reading Skinner concluded his piece by judging that Skinner would be seriously disappointed if he ever visited the "laboratory." (Richard Todd, " 'Walden Two': Three? Many More?" *New York Times Magazine*, March 15, 1970, pp. 24-25, 114-125.) Nevertheless, Skinner represents that variety of reform vision which will become more accessible as biological technology produces more ways of controlling heredity and conditioning behavior. With these developments will come a crucial intensification of the Skinner-Krutch debate: Is Walden Two a dream or a nightmare?

(Two recent interpretive works, germane to these questions are: Kenneth Rexroth, *Communalism: From its Origins to the Twentieth Century.*

New York: Continuum/Seabury, 1975; and James Sellers, *Warming Fires: the Quest for Community in America.* New York: Crossroad/Seabury, 1975.)

SOURCE: A: David G. Hackett, "Guiding Principles for Communes," *Alternatives Journal.* Vol. II (December 1-15, 1972), pp. 1-2. B: "Twin Oaks," anonymous article in *Communities.* Number 1 (December, 1972), pp. 24-28, abridged.

A: GUIDING PRINCIPLES FOR COMMUNES

After living in a community for eight months, I have been traveling around the country looking for fundamental similarities among a variety of communal gatherings. These experiences have obliged me to rely on eight guiding principles that to me seem to form the foundation for a prospering settlement.

#1 A SHARED PURPOSE

Whether it is selling leather goods, guarding a shrine, or feeding transient hippies, I have found that all viable communities have a conscious intent and meaningful function. This conscious sense of purpose is the actualizing force if a community intends to be something more than a particularization of the social malaise it seeks to answer. A group becomes a community only when each member's aim is shared by every other member and is aware that its highest fulfillment can only be expressed through a collective aim which justifies and governs the existence of that community.

#2 REGULAR GROUP INTERACTIONS

This collective aim can best be realized through regular group interactions that foster an understanding of the efforts taken toward that shared purpose. Meetings, meals, religious services and similar gatherings both serve to strengthen unity and minimize misunderstandings. Through these scheduled group activities each individual can identify with the larger objectives of the group and at the same time play a part in shaping the means toward those objectives.

#3 A LEADER

A third element that I have repeatedly seen to be essential, stresses the need for each community to have one or more respected individuals who have the understanding, commitment, and capacity to guide the group through its early stages toward the collective purpose. This community leader should have the clearest vision of the group's future, be able to judge what matters in relation to that vision, and the selflessness to relinquish his leadership when others come to share his viewpoint.

#4 LIVE AND WORK ON THE SAME GROUNDS

Living and working on the same grounds seems to be a necessary catalyst in a community's pursuit of its shared purpose. Almost all successful gatherings believe that community members should live and work on the same grounds. They feel that the chances of realizing their collective aim are increased if everyone tries to live and work together. Although the fundamental needs of food, clothing, and shelter may at times force them to be apart, I have seen that once self-sufficiency is achieved community members try to remain together.

#5 DRUGS

Widespread drug use is symptomatic of a community's instability. This is particularly true in the early stages of a group settlement when the uncertainties and experimentation involved in developing a community are accompanied by their pervasive use. Only when a collective aim, organization, and leadership begin to evolve do drug regulations become increasingly important. Once this cohesive communalism develops, drugs should be judged in relation to the community's shared purpose.

#6 HOUSING

A community should provide at least enough housing for each person to have a place to go where he or she can be alone.

#7 DIVERSE AGES

Though it may not be as pressing as the previous six criteria, I have found that the communities that number a diverse assortment of ages among their membership afford a far fuller community life. Whether they are grandmothers, fathers, younger brothers or babes, all of the classic social roles should be present in a community. Brought together to pursue a collective aim, each offers the other a different chronological view of their community effort. This fuller experience makes community life seem more like an enduring process than a momentary happening.

#8 COMMUNITY SIZE

This last principle is more rooted in my own thoughts than gathered from the communities I have visited. It concerns a direct relationship I have found between a community's population and the efforts needed to accomplish its collective aim. A community that is too large prevents each member from getting well acquainted with every other member. This inhibited intimacy deprives the members of a keenly sought warmth and enhances the formation of factions whose differences affect the pursuit of the community's shared purpose. My feeling is that a community should never become so large that it interferes with these efforts toward its collective aim.

B: TWIN OAKS

To Twin Oaks, a 50-member commune in its sixth year, B. F. Skinner's novel *Walden Two* is an inspiration and a pain in the neck. It is an important point of reference and source of radical ideas that has helped shape this community into a vital and viable social alternative. But because many people see *Walden Two* as an anti-utopia or hear "B. F. Skinner" as an epithet, Twin Oaks has been the victim of undue criticism. I'd like to clarify for friends and critics the sense in which I see Twin Oaks as a "behaviorist" community, like and unlike Walden Two. And while I'm at it I'd like to clarify the sense in which I see other groups functioning as "behavioral" experiments.

A capsule sketch of Twin Oaks and its history: A Walden Two planning conference was convened in Ann Arbor in 1966. Though a $5,000,000, five-year plan was conceived, a few impatient people went ahead in 1967 and through luck obtained the use of a 123-acre farm in central Virginia. Starting with eight members and an old farmhouse, the community has so far built three buildings and grown to fifty adult members. (Some little ones are on the way!) We raise our own beef, pork, and organic produce; supply our own dairy products; do our own repairs on cars, trucks, and farm machinery; are architects, carpenters, plumbers, and electricians; and produce income mainly through the manufacture and sale of handmade rope hammocks, but also through the sale of our own publications, typing services, miscellaneous crafts, and through some short-term work in nearby cities. There is no one leader. A planner-manager government is responsible for formalizing decisions reached by group input and consensus. A labor credit system helps us organize and share equally a constantly changing flow of work. All income and most property are held in common. Each individual's needs for food, clothing, shelter, and medical services are met by the community as a whole. Over time, Twin Oaks has evolved a unique culture that continues to grow. Cooperation instead of competition; sharing rather than possessiveness; equality in place of exploitation; gentleness, not aggression; reason instead of authority; an end to sexism, racism, and consumerism: these are some of the ideals around which our culture has developed. It is this culture, contrived by common consent, that occasions and maintains our behavior and which is the essence of our "behavioralness".

Twin Oaks has been labeled a "behaviorist" community because it is based on *Walden Two*. I'm not sure what this label conjures up in people's minds, but there is a sense in which the Twin Oaks experiment in alternative culture-building is more "behaviorist" than other groups are. The differences between Twin Oaks and other groups on this score have been blown out of proportion. There is a sense in which *all* communal experiments are "behaviorist", and this similarity among groups is also important. We *all* are affected by our alternative culture experiments in that our cultural environments affect the ways we act, think, and feel.

In a behavioristic view, our behavior is said to be controlled, or determined, or influenced by our total environment. People say this for the sake of convenience. Unfortunately the words "controlled", "determined", and "influenced" can have bad connotations. These words are misleading. They imply that a person is an object that is pushed or pulled around by some external force. They imply that a person is separate from his environment. Not so. People are *part of* the environment; this is what the science of ecology is all about. The interrelationships of our behaviors with the rest of our environment (external and internal, cosmic and mundane, particular and gestalt) can be thought of as the ecology of behavior. Our actions are so inextricably bound up with our total set of circumstances—who our friends are, what work we do, where we reside, what season it is—that we cannot define ourselves as something distinct from these conditions. We are complex expressions of a rich ecological pattern. Behaviorism is the study of the inseparability of person and environment. Person and environment are two sides of the same coin, and behaviorism is concerned with the coin. In Zen terms, we are fully human only when we cease making ourselves distinct from the "flow of life". B. F. Skinner, meet Alan Watts.

As a member of the communal movement, Twin Oaks is one of many experiments in the design of new cultural environments. All communes are an attempt to create conditions of harmony, happiness, meaningfulness, and fulfillment in counter-distinction to the general American culture that is exploitative, inhumane, aggressive, and profane in too many ways to list. Communities do this by trying to create environments that consist of like-minded people, living in a specific setting (on a farm, in a large house), engaged in some common activities centered around shared goals. Such conditions will more easily bring out human warmth or energetic work or childlike curiosity or meditative calm or whatever behaviors are valued by the particular group. In establishing counter-culture or alternative lifestyles, many groups develop intuitively and spontaneously. At the other end of the spectrum are groups that develop rationally and systematically. Most communal groups are a blend of planning and happening. Twin Oaks is a blend. . . .

At some levels we, as individuals and as Twin Oaks Community, *are* self-conscious about changing ourselves. Though we do not approach the task as behavioral technicians, we do approach the design of our cultural environment deliberately. We do things like establish ways of sharing work that encourages non-exploitative behavior, create community policies that ensure equalitarian behavior, and build community norms that facilitate interpersonal honesty. Here are some commonplace examples of how such lofty goals are actually achieved: If I consistently do my share of the work, then I am likely to be told by various people that they appreciate my hardworking attitude. If I become a planner and contribute all my outstanding financial assets to the community, then I will gain the continued approval and trust of the group, which can be assured that none of my decisions will be influenced by vested monetary interests. If I refrain from taking over the power saw from an inexperienced worker in order to "get the job done right", then I may earn that person's warmth instead of avoidance. If I come to a weekly "feedback" meeting and express feelings of anger that grew out of hearing habitual complaining, then I will probably receive the group's close attention and approval for being open and honest.

There are many ways in which being "behaviorist" has paid off for us, but self-consciousness has not prevented failures. Conditions exist at

Twin Oaks that produce undesirable behaviors. Sometimes we can change these conditions and sometimes we can't. We failed at first to institutionalize a form of government that does not reward the Strong-voice. Twin Oaks tried consensus decision making and found that a few people dominated meetings by talking loudest, longest, and sharpest. Other people tended to get tired or bored or fed-up—which left the actual decision in the hands of the more stubborn meeting-goers, thus reinforcing their poor meeting behaviors. Now decisions are made with group input through a board of planners that serves to moderate and distribute participation at meetings.

Some behaviors have proved difficult to change. Cigarette smoking is one. Though some people have quit, most smokers have found the rewards of quitting less powerful than the cigarette itself. Laziness is another behavior that has inherently reinforcing qualities. Both smoking and inactivity have unpleasant consequences as well as pleasant ones, but the pleasant ones are more immediate. Another behavior that is a problem is group carelessness with tools. This stems directly from the contingency that if *I* lose a tool *we* pay for it. This contingency hardly punished carelessness; and because our group is loath to employ punishment as a technique for changing behavior, we have paid for more than one new hammer. No doubt many groups share these and similiar failings.

Though Twin Oaks has, for the time being, solved some cultural problems that continue to beset other groups, there are reasons why the community's culture is not yet ideal. First, people come to the community with well-established patterns of un-ideal behavior. We have been taught to be jealous, self-deprecating, or insensitive to group needs, etc. Diverse histories of experiences add up to weak community norms. Weak norms retard behavior change. Second, we do not always agree on what behaviors are ideal; hence conflicting behaviors may both pay off. Third, even when we agree on an ideal and agree that we are short of it, we sometimes have no strong desire to change or we have no desire to change deliberately. Another way of saying this is that the contingencies that could help shape new behavior are too weak—for instance, the admiration of others is not enough to maintain non-jealous behavior. Fourth, where behavioral engineering involves the expense of money or labor, the community has been reluctant to pay. Even though building an ideal culture will pay off, it has not been as immediately rewarding as surviving, growing, and increasing our standards of living. Fifth, and finally, it takes skill and subtlety to understand principles of behavioral ecology. And it takes creativity and the consent of the group to accomplish cultural change. Ignorance and misunderstanding of a behavioral approach result in resistance to change or in slow or accidental change.

Failures and problems notwithstanding, we have successfully evolved new social institutions. In an old newsletter of ours, Rudy wrote about one effective use of behavioral engineering.

The one interesting aspect of cooperation is that reinforcement for the individual must be contingent on the joint efforts of the people who are to cooperate. Thus in community if you want cooperation in the everyday tasks, you make the reinforcements of food, shelter, clothing, recreation, health, etc., for each individual contingent on the joint efforts of the members of the community. To accomplish this, an economic system is necessary which makes the betterment of the individual contingent on the betterment of the community. At Twin Oaks there are no individual salaries; and the level of food, shelter, clothing, etc., is contingent for all members on the prosperity of the overall community. Thus . . . each member of the community must cooperate with the others in order to raise his standard of living.

Some people think that if a society doesn't have a competitive system where each person determines his own reinforcement, then "initiative" will be lost and no one will work. This is obviously not the case. We have not removed the reinforcers: we have merely made them contingent on cooperation rather than on competition. This contingency, teamed with an accounting system that maintains equality of labor (the labor credit system) makes for a society in which the cut-throat tactics of competition and the "every man for himself" attitude are no longer reinforced and thus become extinguished. At Twin Oaks the only way to be selfish is to do something that will make the community better and thus your own private life better.

Though most of us are not into behavioral psychology, we are in general aware of behavioristic ways of looking at things. Twin Oaks does not require its members to understand behavioral principles. But because of the culture that has evolved here, people do tend to have at least an intuitive understanding of the principle of positive reinforcement, for example. (This is not unique to Twin Oaks, of course.) When we pay greater attention (through praise, affection, and other ordinary social conventions) to desirable behavior than to undesirable behavior, we are functioning as "behaviorists" whether we know it or not. Much of the time we do know it and this, I suppose, makes Twin Oaks more a "behaviorist" community than other groups are.

The ways in which Twin Oaks is commonly thought of as "behaviorist" are the obvious ways, which are also sometimes the less important ways. Casual visitors hear members speak about "reinforcement" or "aversive" work or situational "contingencies". Visitors see bulletin board notes that read "Orange juice fund is low—pick up a dish today." and "Don't forget you can take two extra labor credits for handing in your completed labor credit sheet on time." and "Chocolate chip cookies are available again in the hammock shop." By themselves, these things are trivial uses of the principle of positive reinforcement. There is a level, however, at which these things are important.

Take cookies in the hammock shop, for example. One day Bruce, who is the hammock making manager, decided to reward people working in the hammock shop by giving them chocolate chip cookies. A couple of times a day, but at no particular time, he would sing out "Cookie time!" and each person actually working in the shop at that moment would be offered a cookie. This is an instance of the use of variable-interval positive reinforcement. People with only a superficial understanding of Twin Oaks and behaviorism mock such "bribery". A more sensitive look at us shows that we at Twin Oaks treat this use of "positive reinforcement" as a game, mocking it ourselves for its blatantly manipulative connotations. But this turns it into joking with the hammock manager, or counter-controlling just when the cookies will be passed around, or having fun in the kitchen baking the cookies, and so on. And it is *these* things that make the hammock shop a happy place to be and make the community fun to be a part of. Now I'm not sure how many people still feel that cookies in the hammock shop is an insidious attempt to manipulate innocent humans. Anyone who does feel so might consider this: (1) no one is forced to stay in the hammock shop, (2) anyone can go to the kitchen and bake an unlimited quantity of chocolate chip cookies, and (3) there is no profit for the "manipulator"; the other people benefit from their work exactly as much as the cookie-man.

So what do I mean when I say Twin Oaks is a "behaviorist" community? I mean we're deliberately trying to build an alternative cultural lifestyle. We are evolving a total environment that has the potential to radically alter the behavior of people who live in it. Other experimental communes are "engineering behavior" in this same sense. I also mean we are somewhat aware of "behaviorism" and are not unwilling to try out self-conscious means of changing ourselves. We try to grow and change as individuals, sometimes with the help of "behavioral self-management techniques", mostly with the help of our friends. We try to grow and change as a community, too. If you come visit and live with us for a couple of weeks you may feel something in the quality of our life that is our reinforcement for being a behaviorist community based on *Walden Two*.

Document IV-15: FULLER AND THE WORLD PLAN

The meaning of Buckminster Fuller to a student of American reform is too broad to be represented in any one section of this collection (see V-6). Some of his ideas and creations are, however, particularly useful in pulling together the several strains of thought identifiable in the presentation of an ideal community.

Like McIntire and the Shakers he believes that democratic man needs a simple, functional, dignified environment; toward this end he has contributed the simplest of all structures—the dome. Like Thomas, he believes in efficient, reasonably priced single-family dwellings as a pillar for economic equity; toward this end he has contributed the mass-produced, readily assembled dymaxion house. Like Olmsted, he believes in planning for man in such a way that nature becomes a model instead of an object of pillage. Like Bellamy, he stresses cooperation in place of competition as the necessary mood for an ideal social order. Like Streit, he believes it essential to consider "the world as one town," with the corollary that town planning must now be seen as world planning. Like the authors of science fiction, he believes that today's fantasy is tomorrow's reality; he urges the use of experience accumulated in space travel in order to confront environmental questions on earth.

Among all the individuals represented in this section, however, Fuller has the most in common with Frank Lloyd Wright. As was Wright, he is by profession an architect and designer; as did Wright, he emphasizes the most economic and efficient use of modern materials and technological processes; as with Wright he sees the hope of the future in a planned community which will free man of his inequities and disabilities and will make possible his transcendent self-realization. Yet between the two there is a significant difference of degree most directly attributable to the fact that Fuller has lived and written in a world where the production of nuclear energy and travel by jet are accomplished facts. Broadacre City must have a worldwide scope.

An essential duality in Fuller's thought is the simultaneous stress on both the microcosm and macrocosm. Science, with its powerful microscopes and space probes, is leading both ways. Thus man has the opportunity to advance his knowledge and solve his problems with increasing appropriateness on both a large and small scale. Symbolic of this thought are the two objects here reproduced.

The first is the bathroom for a dymaxion house, first developed in 1927. Made of metal alloys and prefabricated with pipes and wiring molded in, the parts for an entire house can be stacked in nested parts, loaded on a single flatbed truck, and assembled on a level site in a matter of hours. In Bucky Fuller's ideal world, a traveler merely telephones; a helicopter arrives; the nuclear human environment is assembled.

The macrocosmic approach is visualized here by the superimposition of a large, clear dome over midtown Manhattan. In some ways this concept may be better remembered by visitors to Montreal's Expo '67 where Fuller's twenty-story dome of steel pipes and plastic cover housed the United States exhibit. Within this controlled environment Fuller depicts the planner's dream where man can be provided with precisely that background against which he functions best—freed from excessive noise, dirt, and extremes of temperature; erecting partitions from desire and not from need. In such a setting, Fuller projects, human nature will improve to match the ideal environment.

SOURCE: Pictures courtesy of R. Buckminster Fuller: A: Schematic drawing of dymaxion house bathroom. B: Photograph of New York City with two-mile-diameter dome superimposed over midtown Manhattan.

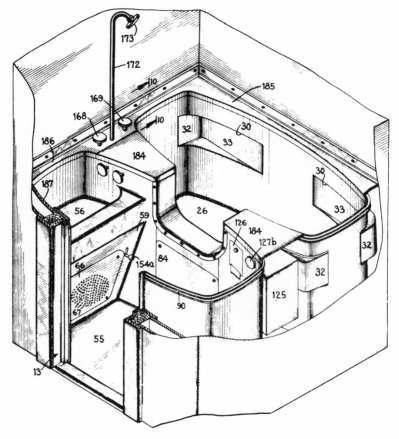

A: Dymaxion bathroom

B: Manhattan dome

Part V

REFORM IN AMERICA

RED Smith says that the day reformers will remember is April 8, 1971, when legalized off-track betting in Grand Central Terminal signaled the decline of organized crime in Manhattan. The "Chicago 7" feel they can change the world by throwing obscene fits in the path of courtroom proceedings. Tom Wolfe points out that the Black Panthers, proclaimed violent enemies of the white power structure, have been embraced by the fashionable creative-intellectual wing of that very structure. A Catholic priest and his followers destroy draft records and plan to hold high federal officials hostage for the end of the Southeast Asian hostilities. A singer and an actress take their crusades to jail and to Hanoi. The citizens of Fogo Island find they can precipitate needed social change by having one group make movies for the others. *What the hell is going on here!*

Or, to put it more calmly, how does one separate ephemera from important change? Have the 1960s and 1970s revealed new modes and issues or merely new packaging on old concerns and old techniques? How does one avoid the historian's mistake of seeing nothing as new without making the tabloid writer's mistake of seeing everything as new?

Were space unlimited it would be useful to bring together a group of documents focused on this question. It might open with Lyndon B. Johnson's final State of the Union message, which comprises a true compendium of the historic reform agenda. If the classic causes have, then, come under the federal umbrella, what has happened to social ferment? For new topics one might look toward the stress on ecology or

toward the homosexual community, whose situation has begun to attract
serious attention. For new methods one might look toward the guerrilla
theater, toward new techniques for promoting group participation, and
particularly toward the efforts of Ralph Nader and John Gardner as they
have attempted to institutionalize an active conscience for the nation at
large.

Obviously, there *are* new topics and new techniques. It is probably
true, however, that the foregoing sections have provided the appropriate
background for discerning the more important links between past and
present. Part II shows that much contemporary effort is still being
devoted to the extension of participatory democracy for the sake of
eliminating special privilege and improving the distribution of wealth.
Part III, dealing with anti-slavery and civil rights for black Americans,
was deliberately arranged so as to show how the essential attitudes and
techniques of the antebellum reformers have been expressed and asserted
once again in the 1950s and 1960s. The same is true for the woman's
movement with the strong exceptions noted in the concluding document
(III-15). Part IV shows more of an evolution in the reformer's vision of
an ideal community as this vision has yielded to technology, behavioral
psychology, urban, regional, and global planning.

It is clear that reform today exhibits considerable continuity with its
past. There is strong current interest in world peace and in prison reform,
issues that have emerged many times in the past. Yet the Strategic Arms
Limitations Talks represent a quantitative difference in subject matter
that may properly suggest a whole new qualitative dimension. Likewise,
the war on drug abuse could be construed as a ramification of the
temperance movement, looking from a reform perspective; but are the
social consequences of heroin addiction of a different order than those of
alcohol? Concern for new minorities may be a logical extension of the
movement on behalf of blacks, but is the new concern with ecology more
than an extension of earlier conservation crusades?

During the 1960s the Old Left reached a kind of culmination in the
domestic programs of Presidents Kennedy and Johnson. Simultaneously
the New Left was defining itself in campus-centered revolts against the
war and in civil rights demonstrations, mainly in the South. With the
approach of the 1970s a new agenda emerged. On the surface were the
programs for Indians, women, Americans with Spanish-American
ancestry; the new communitarianism; and an incipient anti-trust move-

ment particularizing agribusiness and the multinational corporation. The counter-culture defined itself most strongly as opposing technology and consumer orientation. These concerns were not confined to a small, disaffiliated group, however, but emerged in the congressional rejection of support for a supersonic transport as well as continuing attacks on consumer goods.

Sometimes it is hard to separate style from substance. Did electronic amplification make possible a new order of street demonstration? Did the rise of sensitivity groups make it possible for social agitators to reach out to their audience in a more telling fashion? Is the principal legacy of the Watergate affair to be a new reform frontier against the invasion of privacy through electronic surveillance? Is the rise of advocacy law and the activism of the Warren Court an indication of a new institutional dynamic for social change? Does the emergence of groups like Common Cause and Public Citizen, Inc., indicate that the individualized, spontaneous public conscience is a thing of the past? Such questions will arise as each calendar page turns over. The answers are not only in the perspective built into compilations such as this but in the daily awareness of the living citizen. The evidence is everywhere.

Implied in this collection is an effort not only to make distinctions by topic and era but also to identify a national pattern which may not be entirely shared by other nations. Is there anything American about American reform?

Broadly speaking, the whole book is an answer. Part I proposes that a few strong concepts combined and alternated to account for most of the rationale and motivation behind reform in this country. Part II—by its very length—states that the principal occupation of the American reformer has been with the improvement of a political means toward an economic objective. In Part III there is a deliberate implication that the reform experience in America has been importantly and distinctively shaped by questions revolving around Negro slaves and black citizens and—only slightly less—by considerations of the role of women in American democracy. This section also self-consciously focuses on modes and methods of reform that have appeared to dominate in this national context. Part IV is devoted to dreams that are to some extent shared with men and women from other nations but which have peculiar American aspects.

How American are these values, these subjects, these methods, and these goals? The only really logical way to answer this question is to interpose another: as compared to what other nation or culture? In fact, even before debating this composite picture as nationally representative one would want to ask some very tough additional questions about variations between a dominant mode and a number of subcultural differences clearly observable within the continental boundaries. Because of these necessary qualifications, this section makes no claim to representing anything definitively or logically. The documents collected here depict values, attitudes, and methods which occur with enough frequency and insistence to seem especially important for understanding the American scene. They do not claim individual uniqueness; in combination, however, they surely make up a set of reform attributes that would not be found in any other place or time.

Document V-1: THE CONCEPT OF MUCKRAKING

Alexis de Tocqueville noted it; James Bryce made a major point of it: the distinctiveness of the American press as an agent for social change. In fact, the reform impulse often arises in a way that makes it almost impossible to distinguish the formative power of the public mind from the influence of those who would work upon it. To many observers, however, it has been clear that movements for social change have been born from those exchanges of sentiment between the media and the public which—when they focused on social evils—came to be called muckraking. The reporter and the cartoonist, by dramatizing abuses, deliberately aroused a storehouse of popular feeling which then became available for the organizers, the agitators, and the lawmakers.

The use of cartoons to stimulate this process dates from the earliest days of the republic. It flowered in the days of Jackson and "Tippecanoe." It reached a full statement in the person of Thomas Nast, who hounded Boss Tweed to the far corners of the earth and placed a damning design of "dollar marks" on the expansive vest of Marcus Hanna. When newspaper publishers struggled for large circulations to go with their whirring presses they made full use of Homer Davenport, George Y. Coffin, and Frederick B. Opper to attack the trusts, the politicos, and the

PUCK.

THEY HATE THE LIGHT, BUT THEY CAN'T ESCAPE IT

"Exposure"

makers of foreign policy (see II-28). More contemporary examples would include Ollie Harrington, Bill Mauldin, and Herbert Block. Alongside these penmen the media have ranged agitators whose prose has been no less vivid than the imaginations of the cartoonists. Thomas Paine will serve as a starting point for a tradition that has included a great roster of reform luminaries such as William Lloyd Garrison, Frances Wright, George Evans (see II-12), Henry George (see II-21), Ida Tarbell, Lincoln Steffens (see II-31), and many spiritual ancestors of those two determined young reporters—Bob Woodward and Carl Bernstein—who gnawed at the bone of an act of political sabotage until "Watergate" was added to the language. Jacob Riis, a powerful user of words, augmented his prose with pictures made from photographs, a transitional technique that soon gave way to photojournalism, another important weapon in the hands of muckrakers against such visually oppressive evils as slums and wars (see III-1).

To the cartoonist, the investigative reporter, the columnist, and the photojournalist must be added the novelist, the poet, the playwright, and the painter. The patterns of reform in America reveal a special role for the media in the process of muckraking; they also reveal an unusual commitment on the part of the creative artist from Stowe through John Steinbeck (see the introduction to III; also III-3). The fact that many of the painters of the "ashcan school" were also radical cartoonists is more representative of reform in America than it is unusual (see II-38). Thus the document reproduced below represents the importance of the process of exposure, and the engagement of public opinion by the media and the creative arts.

SOURCE: Lithograph after a cartoon by J. Keppler in *Puck*, 1890.

Document V-2: RELIGION AND VOLUNTARISM

The prominence of public opinion in America is but one oft-noted aspect of national behavior which has special importance in the reform process. Another is the urge toward affiliation often called "voluntarism" or "associationalism." It has been said of Greeks abroad that if two of them meet they will open a restaurant. Of Americans at home it has similarly been said that any two will soon become an organization. Much of this associational impulse has been directed toward reform, building on sentiment aroused by the muckrakers typified above.

In its reform sense, voluntarism describes a coordinated movement on behalf of social change. Usually, but not always, this term identifies groups that operate outside of immediate self-interest and thus excludes unions and leagues of workers and entrepreneurs. Typically, the organization is devoted to a specific cause and, like the American Anti-Slavery Society, will live only as long as its crusade is active. Some idea of the process and pattern of organization has been offered in documents III-5 and 9 as they relate to the cause of black Americans.

It is not surprising, however, that with all this associative experience there should have been some multipurpose reform organizations foreshadowing Common Cause and Public Interest, Inc. A number of these earlier prototypes resemble the National Christian Citizenship League and the Evangelical Alliance described in the following document. Others were the National Bureau of Reforms, Josiah Strong's American Institute of Social Service, and its predecessor, the League for Social Service. These groups reflect an interesting blend of religious zeal, social science detachment, and organizational efficiency. (An important inside commentary on this phenomenon is in Wilbur F. Crafts, *Practical Christian Sociology.* New York, Funk & Wagnalls, 1895; a good scholarly history is in Charles H. Hopkins, *The Rise of the Social Gospel in American Protestantism, 1865-1915.* New Haven, Yale, 1940.) Carlos Martyn, another socially committed protestant minister, explains the need for organization in the following document in a metaphor that blends old-time religious values with modern problems.

Martyn's prose reflects the era of "the white man's burden" and the American Protective Association and reveals some stereotypical thinking that seems shocking in the arguments of a reformer. His work is interesting not only for its stress on carefully organized voluntaristic energy, but also for its use of the Christian frame of reference. Most scholars accept as a fact the importance of Christian ethics in social change. There has been considerable debate, however, as to whether evangelical Protestantism, by focusing on converting the individual, has in effect stood in the way of collective reforms. Martyn hardly stumbled over this contradiction as he translated God's interest in the salvation of the individual into a Christian duty to promote the welfare of the group. (See also III-6, 7.)

In guaranteeing freedom of religion in a pragmatic context, Martyn wrote, America provides a peculiar test for Christianity as an effective social force. Thus, although his theology differed widely from that of Cotton Mather, he shared a common feeling that American society must serve as an earthly exemplar in the socio-religious sense. In addition to echoing the "city on a hill" concept, this document also stresses the special importance of organized voluntarism. Although this particular blend of sociology and religion offers a special turn-of-the-century flavor, it also serves to record the continuing impact of religion on American reform. The progressive agenda which Martyn compiled toward the end of these pages relates closely to the point of view represented earlier in II-21, 31, 32, and heralds the emergence of a more scientific approach to reform.

, *CHRISTIAN CITIZENSHIP*
ORGANIZATION—BASIS, OBJECTS, AND METHODS.

In every age Christianity demands a special application to meet characteristic conditions. The Apostolic Church was occupied in laying Christian foundations. At the period of the Reformation the doctrines of religion needed a Biblical statement as against prevailing heresies, which masqueraded in the garb of orthodoxy. Under Wesley and Whitefield a new demonstration was given of the power of the Holy Ghost to revivify dead forms of faith. In our day, the mission of the church is largely sociological.

The first and great, commandment, love to God, has not been over-emphasized, but the second, love to our neighbor, has been under-emphasized. They go together. Either alone is a half-part. The first results in pietism; the second produces humanitarianism. When they are combined we have Christianity. An oarsman using but one oar, rows in a circle, with both oars, he pulls straight and forges ahead. Those churches which are based too largely on the love of God, and those other churches which are founded exclusively on the love of man, must marry and beget good works towards God and man.

Dean Hurlbert, of the Chicago Theological Seminary, in a passage of
rare power, remarks that "the evangelical church, numbering
13,500,000 communicants, stoutly denies that unaided human power
can save this country, and as stoutly affirms that Divine power present in
Christianity can perpetuate it. In her criticism and rejection of other
agencies, she provokes a challenge of her own. The enemy of the church,
appealing to Christian history, seeks to discredit her claims by showing
that she is weakest to-day in her original strongholds, and strongest in
lands which were then unknown; that in the Roman Empire she was
herself submerged in a baptized heathenism; and that, after a trial of two
thousand years, church formality and spiritual deadness are the blight of
modern France, Italy, Spain, and Germany. What assurance is there that
history is not to repeat itself in the Western world? The Americans are
inclined to 'prove all things,' Christianity included. She does not go
unchallenged. Certainly, never was there a fairer chance to show her
power and prove her claims. No obnoxious restrictions are put upon her.
She labors under no arbitrary and unnatural disadvantages. The State
suffers no interference with her faith or worship. The Constitution
provides that 'no religious test shall ever be required as a qualification to
any office or public trust under the United States,' and that 'Congress
shall make no law respecting an establishment of religion, or prohibiting
the free exercise thereof.' A code of ethics whose truth and worth are
manifest to enlightened reason constitutes that 'general Christianity,'
which the courts have held to be the common law of the land. Milton
said: 'Though all the winds of doctrine were let loose upon the earth, so
truth be among them we need not fear. Let her and falsehood grapple.
Who ever knew her to be put to the worst in a free and open encounter?'
In free and open America Christianity is thrust into this 'free and open
encounter.' Satanic forces are seeking the nation's ruin; Christian forces
are set for her defense. Force faces force. The issues are joined. The
conflict is on, and is irresistible—it is a life-and-death struggle. Christianity herself can not escape. She has no option—she must fight. Retreat
means defeat. This momentous encounter will decide whether Christianity is stronger than the opposition. Christianity is on trial—she will never
have a fair chance. Numbers, wealth, intelligence, social standing,
manifold resources are on her side. She is trying to win the most
unprejudiced, open-hearted, clean-skinned, clear-brained people on the
face of the earth. Now is the time, and here is the place, to vindicate her

august, transcendent claims. If she can not triumph here, where on earth can she triumph? 'If she has run with the footmen and they have wearied her, then how can she contend with horses?' If she can not rule her own house, and have her own children in subjection, how can she take care of the rest of the world? The challenger of our faith meets us with the inquiry: How is it that Christianity, decrying all other remedies, is failing to apply her own? What means this degeneracy in modern times which Christianity seems incapable of arresting? Why is it that vices and corruption are spreading with terrific rapidity—to which Christianity is offering only a feeble barrier? All sorts of direful evils are on the increase—the political powers of the saloon increasing; discontent among wageworkers increasing; the misuse of ill-gotten wealth increasing; the breach between the classes and the masses increasing; the estrangement between capital and labor increasing; the suspicion and hatred of the churches increasing; pauperism and crime, the social vice and gambling, skepticism and materialism increasing; the membership in the evangelical churches increasing; Christian intelligence and respectability increasing. Why in the world is not the political salvation of this nation increasing? What is the matter with Christianity that it stands impotent in the face of these corrupting and destroying forces?''

The answer to these thunder-clap questions is, that hitherto Christianity has lacked organization. It has wrought in a sporadic way, through individual churches, fighting

> ''A battle, whose great aim and scope
>   They little care to know;
> Content, like men-at-arms, to cope
>   Each with his fronting foe.''

It has lacked the power which comes from the synthesis of church-life and activity. The generalship has been on the other side. The evils which assail the nation are organized and allied. So are all the great factors of civilization—war, commerce, business, politics, education, everything, except religion. Is it any wonder that increase of numbers, and wealth, and culture have not insured to Christianity a victory when it has never federated for great common offensive and defensive purposes? Discipline is mightier than numbers. Have we not seen in our generation little

Japan, with a small, but disciplined army, skilfully led, put to rout the innumerable, but unorganized forces of colossal China? The vital need of the hour is church union, not a union of outward forms, but of spirit and endeavor. Whether we shall ever have, or had better have a common formula to express our faith, or one liturgy to embody our worship, is a question. But if Christianity is to dominate this continent, nay, if it is to survive at all, it must bind its adherents together in triumphant cooperation, and swing them into line to fulfil the aspiration of the Lord's Prayer, "Thy kingdom come."

In searching for an acceptable basis of union, we find it in the fact, of common acknowledgement, that Jesus Christ is the Savior not alone of the individual, but of society through the individual. Every saved man, and every group of saved men in every church, is to be a savior—each for all and all for each. Christians agree in believing that all efforts at social amelioration should be made tributary to the bringing all men under the law of Christ, and into vital relations with Him. For, while it is important that men be well housed, well-fed, well-clothed, well-employed, and well-governed, it is essential that they be bound through brotherhood to the heart and service of the all-Father. Therefore, Christian citizenship is not the end, but only a means to the end.

As to the objects of this union, the first is the regeneration of America—because this means the regeneration of the earth. It begins to be evident that the Anglo-Saxon character and language are destined to rule the world. A century ago as keen an observer as Franklin thought the French people and tongue would dominate. Then 42,000,000 spoke French, and only 18,000,000 spoke English. To-day 120,000,000 speak English, and 150,000,000 understand it, and the foremost of philologists, Prof. Max Müller, contends that within two centuries English will become the universal language.

Already, according to Dr. Clark, "the English language, saturated with Christian ideas, is the great agent of Christian civilization throughout the world, and is molding the character of half the human race." By common consent, America is the coming custodian of the Anglo-Saxon character and language. Listen to a few authoritative voices on both sides of the Atlantic. Alexander Hamilton has said: "It is ours to be either the grave in which the hopes of the world shall be entombed, or the pillar of cloud that shall pilot the race onward to millenial glory." Matthew Arnold has said: "America holds the future." Herbert Spencer has said:

"The Americans are producing a more powerful type of man than has hitherto existed," and "may reasonably look forward to a time when they will have produced a civilization grander than any the world has yet known." John Fisk has said: "The world's center of gravity has shifted from the Mediterranean and the Rhine to the Atlantic and the Mississippi, from the men who spoke Latin to the men who speak English." Emerson has said: "America is another name for opportunity. Our whole history appears like a last effort of Divine providence in behalf of the human race." Ought we not, therefore, to push Christianizing agencies with overwhelming urgency?

The second object of Christian union is the bringing conscience to bear on the civic life of the nation. "A quickened and enlightened conscience," observes Dr. Josiah Strong, "is the great need of the times in the relation of employer and employe in all private business, in all public trusts, in politics, and in legislation, municipal, State, and national. In whatever sphere men *ought*, there it is the right and duty of the Church to urge the dictates of the Christian conscience. But in the unorganized condition of the churches there is no medium through which the Christian conscience of the city, the State, the nation can utter itself. For lack of this saving salt, municipal government has rotted, and legislatures have become corrupt. Every year needed reform legislation fails and laws are enacted which do violence to the Christian conscience of the State, because there is no medium through which that conscience can be brought to bear. By such an organization, as is proposed, a legislature could be flooded with hundreds of thousands of names in petition or protest in a single week."

On the basis of this general recognition of Jesus Christ as the Savior of the social order, and with the two-fold object of regenerating America, and of bringing the Christian conscience to bear on civic life as the means of regeneration, what are the proper methods of organization?

Happily, the political framework of the country supplies us with a suggestive model. The national Union is composed of forty-five States. Each of these is distinct and independent in local affairs, while in matters of common concern each is reinforced by all the rest. Thus their individual autonomy is jealously guarded, and at the same time the overwhelming power of national unity is secured. Just so the churches exist in various denominational relations. The individual churches are like the towns or counties of the State. The denominations are like the States themselves. Both churches and denominations are proud of their independence, and set upon the maintenance of self-government. Without parting with these prerogatives of sovereignty, they might come into some form of federal union, which should enable them quickly to converge their separate influence into a unit of power for defense or attack. It is not the province of this chapter to sketch in the details of such a compact. These can be easily manipulated and all discordant interests adjusted, when once the desire for inter-denominational federation takes possession of the Christian heart.

Meantime, we call attention to the fact that some good beginnings have been already made. "The National Christian Citizenship League" was incorporated some time since, and has auxiliaries in a number of States. It is locally an unsectarian, non-partizan league of individuals; nationally, a league of leagues. Since neither the churches nor the young people's societies can, as such, take political action, the members are under obligation to enter some outside related body through which they can make their Christian influence and votes tell for civic righteousness. "Christian citizenship," remarks Mr. Edwin D. Wheelock, the founder and first president of the League, "maintains the supreme right of Jesus Christ to rule municipal, State, and national life, as well as private life. These should be governed on the principles laid down by him. Upon the application of these principles depends the final solution of every present-day problem. It believes our government to be appointed of God, and therefore sacred—too sacred to be left in the hands of corrupt men, whatever their party name. It believes that the dangers which threaten our country arise less from the strength and activity of bad men, than from the apathy and cowardice of good men. It believes that Christian citizens are called to put their loyalty to Jesus Christ into their politics, to serve Him at the primaries, and to vote as He would have them vote. It believes the Bible to teach obedience to law, and that the office of a law-maker or administrator is so sacred that to put a bad man into it is sacrilege. The presence of a corrupt governor, legislator, mayor, alderman, or judge ought to fill every Christian citizen with such an intensity of grief that he will 'cry aloud and spare not' until the evil be corrected."

The platform of the League is as follows:

1. "To prevent by personal effort the nomination and election of corrupt candidates, and the enactment of corrupt laws in city, State and nation.

2. "To secure fidelity on the part of officers entrusted with the execution of the laws.

3. "To exterminate the saloon as the greatest enemy of Christ and humanity.

4. "To preserve the Sabbath.

5. "To purify and elevate the elective franchise.

6. "To promote the study of social wrongs and the application of the remedies.

7 "In general, to seek the reign of whatsoever things are true, honest, just, pure, lovely, and of good report."

A suggestive constitution for local leagues may be found in the Appendix.

"The Evangelical Alliance," an older and stronger organization, has recently symmetrized itself, by adding to its original spiritual purpose, which was the cultivation of Christian fellowship and the forwarding of evangelization, a correlative social department, covering the whole field of civics. It is thus the most complete agency in existence for all kinds of Christian work, and a possible nucleus of continental Christian citizenship phase of the Alliance. A copy of its constitution may also be seen in the Appendix."

We turn now from these methods of organization to consider some related matters. The experience of a hundred years has revealed certain characteristic defects in our political system. We boast of "government of the people, by the people, and for the people." In reality we have government of the majority, by the majority, and for the majority. And no matter how small the majority may be, it is dominant. Nay, what is yet more unfair, we are not unfrequently governed by a minority. Suppose, for example, a State to be divided between three or four parties, and suppose one of them to have a preponderance of votes over each of the others, although in a minority as against the combined ballots of the opposition. As things now stand, the first party would control legislation. This is government not by majority but by plurality. Not only so, but the actual majority, because of its divisions, is misrepresented; public policies, hateful to it, are adopted and administered. Small parties have no representation in legislative bodies, and therefore no voice in the discussion of pending measures. Size, if it be small, operates as perpetual disfranchisement.

To remedy these defects, *Proportional Representation* has been advocated by eminent writers on government on both sides of the water—by John Stuart Mill, in Europe; and by Prof. John R. Commons, in America. To illustrate the working of this scheme, Mr. W. D. McCracken supposes that "an imaginary State is to elect ten representatives by means of 1,000 votes. Then every party which can muster one-tenth of the total, or 100 votes, ought to be entitled to one representative. If this imaginary State contains 400 Republicans, 300 Democrats, 200 Populists, and 100 Prohibitionists, its legislature should be composed of 4 Republicans, 3 Democrats, 2 Populists, and 1 Prohibitionist. Under present conditions, the Populists and Prohibitionists could not elect their candidates at all, while the slight plurality of Republicans would probably allow them to sweep the State."

Proportional representation has been introduced into certain Swiss cantons, and here it is in use in Illinois, in the election of members to the lower house of the State legislature; in Boston, in the election of aldermen to the city council; and it was employed in New York, in 1867, in the election of delegates to a State constitutional convention.

The practical difficulty in this country has been to find an electoral substitute for the existing division into electoral districts, based upon territorial apportionment—an arrangement which has led to, and encouraged, continental "gerrymandering." Several feasible methods have been elaborated—Hare's plan, the limited vote, the cumulative vote, etc. One or another of these is in actual use: the limited vote, in Boston; the cumulative vote, in Illinois. We lack space to describe these methods—those interested are referred to books on the general subject.

Another undemocratic feature of our government is the alienation from the people of a direct voice in legislation, and of the power authoritatively to propose it. We have, indeed, the right of petition. But the powers that be are under no obligation to do anything with a petition beyond receiving it, and, practically, this is all that is ever done. There is hardly an instance on record of legislation introduced by petition.

With a view to democratic government, two methods of direct popular legislation have been recently suggested, viz., the *Initiative* and the *Referendum*. The first may be defined as an institution by which a certain percentage of voters may initiate laws; and the second, as an institution by which the whole body of voters may vote "yes" or "no" upon the proposition introduced by the initiative. In the last analysis, the process is simply this. So many voters—in Switzerland, where these institutions

are in vogue, 50,000—are authorized to propose such and such legislation, through the medium of the government; which is then obliged to
submit the matter thus initiated to a direct popular vote.

The special advantage claimed for these measures is that they make it
possible for any considerable number of voters to secure the verdict of the
people upon any measure which the legislature might not be willing to act
upon, or might act upon adversely to the wishes of its proposers. It is
difficult, for instance, to get from any legislature a favorable response to
a petition for a prohibitory law. The initiative and the referendum would
enable a given number of the friends of temperance to demand an
expression from the people at large, independently of the legislature. On
the other hand, in prohibitory States, like Maine or North Dakota, the
saloons could pursue the same course for the purpose of overturning
temperance legislation. The larger number of the Swiss cantons have
adopted the initiative and the referendum. Their experiment is being
watched with eager interest. Meantime it must be acknowledged that
there is not a consensus of opinion among political economists regarding
the real value of these measures. Perhaps it is too early to decide.

An ingenious theory, which is held by its friends to be a panacea, is the
Single Tax, elaborated by Mr. Henry George. By this expedient, it is
proposed, at one stroke, to obviate all existing evils by destroying the
vicious principle which, it is claimed, begets them—land monopoly; and
to abate the nuisance of multiform taxes, by empowering each community to collect rent upon the lands within its limits, in lieu therefor, thus
securing a fund warranted to be more than sufficient to pay all communal
expenses.

We quote a few characteristic sentences on this subject from an
eminent exponent of the single tax:

"The most glaring sign of our national corruption is the rapid growth
of economic inequality.

"Magnates manipulate all the unparalleled natural opportunities of the
country, independent workingmen are losing their individuality in the
great army of the employed. Of course, this wretched and unnatural state
of things is not confined to America; it is characteristic of this latter end
of the nineteenth century, and is found to a greater or lesser degree all the
world over. But as Americans are of all people the most sensitive to the
spirit of the age, its tendencies are necessarily exaggerated with us. Our
millionaires at one end of the scale, and our tramps at the other, are more

pronounced specimens of their kind than can be found in Europe. The former seem more extravagantly luxurious, the latter more abjectly miserable, because our State is founded upon the assumption of equality.

"Economic inequality reacts upon legislation. The magnates control the markets, and, therefore, make the laws. Special interests require special bills. Bribery becomes the ordinary, every-day method of lawmaking. Every corrupting cause is followed by its natural effect in a vicious and infallible sequence.

"But there is one principal injustice which lies at the base of this decay of democracy,—the monopoly of land with everything that that term implies. The great unearned fortunes of this country are based on the increment of land values. Real estate magnates, oil, mining, lumber, and railroad magnates are primarily monopolizers of land. They deal in some form of the crust of the earth. It is upon this part of their business interests that they make the most successful speculations and accumulate fortunes. Improvements, such as houses, mining, and railroad plants deteriorate with use; land alone increases in value, because its supply is a fixed quantity.

"Mere land owners do not perform any proper economic function. They are simply preemptors of rights, collectors of toll or rent. It is only in so far as they improve their land that they become useful members of society. Private property in improvements is, therefore, just and logical, but private property in mere land bears in its train a long series of abuses and tyrannies.

"Every succeeding generation requires the use of the crust of the earth for all its material needs, as it also requires air and water. Food, clothing, tools, etc., must all be wrought from land by labor. But if some inhabitants arrogate to themselves exclusive rights to the earth's surface, it is evident that the rest must make terms with them before they can satisfy their simplest wants. Private property in land, therefore, tends inevitably to divide men into masters and slaves, no matter how carefully political equality may be guarded." The single tax seeks to vest the ownership of the land in the people, and to award merely the use of it to individuals—to make it unprofitable to hold without improvement, and subject to a tax for revenue graduated by the degree of such improvement.

Yet another *fin de Siècle* method of reform is *Arbitration*—national, for domestic controversies; inter-national, for differences arising between foreign states. This, if generally adopted, would supersede war, unburden nations by disarmament, and put an end to strikes on one hand, and lockouts on the other, by compelling both capital and labor to appeal to a Board of Arbitration for a friendly settlement of disagreements.

A question increasingly mooted, nowadays, is the public ownership of public franchises—light, water, railroads, wharfs, etc. In a previous chapter we have spoken of the prominence of cities in our day. The trend of civilization is urban. Hence, whatever increases the comfort, promotes the health, and widens the horizon of life in cities, is of foremost importance. Two-thirds of the Scotch people, and three-fourths of the English, are now townsfolk. Forty per cent. of the French, forty per cent. of the Germans, and nearly as large a proportion of the Hollanders, Belgians, and Italians are grouped in cities; while the urban tendency is as marked in the valley of the Danube as it is in the valley of the Mississippi. The dawn of the industrial era has caused this state of things, and made the science of the modern town the most vital of any in the encyclopedia.

Singularly enough, the most radical of people must go to the most conservative, the United States must go to Great Britain for instruction on the subject of municipal collectivism. Manchester and Birmingham in England, and Glasgow, in Scotland, are easily the model municipalities of the world. They have housed their populations in the best tenements, municipalized the gas supply, and reduced the cost to 50 or 60 cents per 1,000 cubic feet; provided municipal lodgings for men and women; purchased the water-works and doubled the per capita supply; absorbed the street railways—called tramways there—reduced the hours of the employes, and of the cost of fares; transformed the problem of sewage from a menace to the public health into a source of revenue, by a system of filtration which makes garbage a fertilizer; and increased the happiness while decreasing the burdens of their denizens. Glasgow has deepened the Clyde from a fordable stream into a river capable of floating vessels of heaviest draught; lined its banks with the greatest shipyards in the world, and municipalized the whole harbor—wharfs, ferries, and all, thus securing a princely revenue.

Before we could go safely into such business here, we would need to reform our civil service. The putting of millions of positions into politics, and filling them at the will of party bosses as a reward for party service, would plunge this nation into chaos.

We catalogue these various projects of reform without indorsing them.

Since they are urged by reputable men, they are entitled to a respectful hearing. Christian citizens need large heads, and should carry generous hearts hospitable towards anything, everything which promises to advance the public welfare. St. Paul's dictum applies to this whole subject of methods of reform: "Prove all things, hold fast that which is good."

Document V-3: PUBLIC DEBATE

The overlapping history of politics and reform in America is marked with great public debates. The Federalist Papers document a revolutionary debate which was soon followed by a running verbal war between the Jeffersonians and the Hamiltonians. Jackson's war on the Bank of the United States became a public debate, as did the eloquent exchanges between Webster and Calhoun, Lincoln and Douglas. Some grew out of courtroom battles: the Dred Scott case, the Granger cases, the trial of Sacco and Vanzetti. Many began on the floor of some legislative body or its committees: nullification, the disputed election of 1876, the investigation of communism in government, the Watergate hearings. Although these controversies all had a direct political meaning, none is irrelevant to the central history of reform. Exemplification of this point includes II-4, 18, 26, 33, 34, 36; III-6, 12. Some debates may have amounted to conscious distractions for the public while crucial issues were settled behind the scenes; but the reformer likes to expose the issues as much as the politician sometimes likes to obscure them.

The debate in American reform has been more than the inevitable clash of opposing points of view, as in the famous Lane debate which split in two the organization that engendered it. To a considerable degree public debate was an art form. It mixed the virtually lost art of oratory with techniques of theater and evangelism. It might be interesting to compare the confrontation by Garrison of the Rynders Mob, as depicted in III-6, with some of the contemporary protest scenes as seen through the dramatist's eyes. Since confrontation is supposed to lead to change, social agitators relish debates. Public discussions have characterized many American rituals from the Fourth of July to the quadrennial elections. Until recently their impact has been limited or delayed by the range of the human voice or the speed of the mails. Whereas the slavery

NEW YORK.—THE SUMMER ENCAMPMENT AT CHAUTAUQUA LAKE—THE "CHAUTAUQUA SALUTE" DURING THE REUNION OF THE
YOUNG MEN'S CHRISTIAN ASSOCIATIONS, AUGUST 8TH.—FROM A SKETCH BY JOSEPH BECKER.—SEE PAGE 135.

Chautaqua

debaters had to take their show on the road, radio and television have importantly altered the situation.

One of the ways in which national television was anticipated was in such institutions as the lyceum and the chautauqua. Here, on a recurring basis or in special summer meetings, Americans listened to the notable speakers of their day discuss the pressing social issues from temperance through labor reform. Although the level of decorum was high, the issues were often powerfully drawn. The actual scene depicted below was doubtless noncontroversial; but it helps to visualize the setting for many intense reform debates with a large, rapt audience responding vigorously to the great orator, distant to the eye but insistently present to the ear and the mind.

SOURCE: Wood engraving after a sketch by Joseph Baker of a summer encampment at Lake Chautauqua, New York. *Frank Leslie's Illustrated Newspaper*, August 28, 1880.

Document V-4: REFORM WITH PROFIT AND EFFICIENCY

Perhaps the shortest route to understanding the uniqueness of Eli Thayer is by way of the following quotation:

> Sir, it is a great mistake to suppose that a good cause can only be sustained by the lifeblood of its friends. But when a man can do a magnanimous act, when he can do a decidedly good thing, and at the same time make money by it, all his faculties are in harmony. (*Six Speeches with a Sketch of the Life of Hon. Eli Thayer.* Boston, Brown & Taggard, 1860, p. 12.)

To this many listeners must have muttered to themselves that reformers cannot be all bad. Unfortunately for those who would mix profit with reform, men like Eli Thayer are rare indeed. In his totality he typifies nothing; rather, he represents a combination of attitudes, motivations, and devices that could have converged only in nineteenth-century America.

Thayer's place in history rests with the New England (first named Massachusetts) Emigrant Aid Company. Its conception, purpose, original charter, promotion, and (enthusiastic) evaluation are all included in the following document. Although Thayer exaggerated the importance of his efforts, modern historians assign him a noteworthy role in promoting free-soil emigration from New England to Kansas. Thayer himself thought enough of the results to propose his methods as the best way of settling the rest of the American West and, in the process, converting the border states to free soil and ending polygamy in Utah. As the quoted pages below end with his depiction of a Southern slave empire looking toward Latin America, he later came to see his concept of organized emigration as an alternative to filibustering in Nicaragua and as a way of "Americanizing" all undersettled parts of the globe. (See Chapter XXIII of unpublished account of Thayer's life, Manuscript Division, Library of Congress.)

The characteristics that identify Thayer as an "only in America" reformer include:

his appeal to the profit motive;
his conviction that America might solve its problems by moving and in particular, by moving westward;
his reliance on such business concepts as land development and speculation; heavy-equipment leasing; mail-order supply; reduced-fare group travel; the use of the corporate form and the vertical integration of all enterprise in the founding, development, and sale of an entire community;
his appeal to Christian virtues by name and to the missionary spirit;
his stress on efficiency and technology;
his conclusion that America could develop a method for social change that would not only save the nation but would become a model whose imitation would save the world.

This fascinating combination of American traits could be extended; but it must be remembered that—in spite of the passionate hatred he held for Garrison and his followers—Thayer was first, last, and always a New England foe of slavery and secession.

As a modern reader looks at Thayer's plan and contemplates its extension overseas, he may well be reminded of the Peace Corps. A particular invitation to enlistment has been reproduced with the deliberate intent of inviting comparison with the Emigrant Aid Company. Was the Peace Corps a Cold War equivalent to the EAC? Was it meant to Americanize the technologically underdeveloped nations of the world? Or was it to internationalize the volunteer? Was it an opportunity for idealists to commit a portion of their lives or was it a chance for free travel and new experiences while savings grew at home? In spite of what has been written and legislated about the Peace Corps, these questions—as staff and volunteers will readily admit—are still very much open for debate.

SOURCE: A: Eli Thayer, *The New England Emigrant Aid Company.* Worcester, Mass., Rice, 1887, pp. 13-30, 46-48, abridged. B. This advertisement was prepared and published as a public service by the Advertising Council along with several newspapers and periodicals. It appeared widely in the spring of 1965. See, for example, the Washington *Post*, April 5, 1965, p. A14.

A: *THE NEW ENGLAND EMIGRANT AID COMPANY*

During the winter of 1854 I was, for the second time, a Representative from Worcester in the Legislature of Massachusetts. I had felt to some degree the general alarm in anticipation of the repeal of the Missouri Compromise, but not the depression and despondency that so affected others who regarded the cause of liberty as hopelessly lost. As the winter wore away, I began to have a conviction which came to be ever present, that something *must* be done to end the domination of Slavery. I felt a personal responsibility, and though I long struggled to evade the question, I found it to be impossible. I pondered upon it by day, and dreamed of it by night. By what plan could this great problem be solved? What force could be effectively opposed to the power that seemed about to spread itself over the continent? Suddenly, it came upon me like a revelation. It was ORGANIZED AND ASSISTED EMIGRATION. Then came the question, was it possible to create such an agency to save Kansas? I believed the time for such a noble and heroic development had come; but could hope be inspired, and the pulsations of life be started beneath the ribs of death? The projected plan would call upon men to risk life and property in establishing freedom in Kansas. They would be called to pass over millions of acres of better land than any in the disputed territory was supposed to be, and where peace and plenty were assured, to meet the revolver and the bowie knife defending Slavery and assailing Freedom. Could such men be found, they would certainly prove themselves to be the very highest type of Christian manhood, as much above all other emigrants, as angels are above men. *Could* such men be found?

It happened, that on the evening of the 11th of March, 1854, there was a large meeting in the City Hall in Worcester, to protest against the passage of the Kansas-Nebraska Bill, and the repeal of the Missouri Compromise. I attended the meeting, and not having yet taken counsel of anyone, determined to see how the plan would be received by an intelligent New England audience without any preparation for the announcement. Accordingly, making the last speech of the evening I for the first time disclosed the plan. The Worcester *Spy* of March 13th, has the conclusion of my speech as follows:

> "It is time now to think of what is to be done in the event of the passage of the Kansas-Nebraska Bill. Now is the time to organize an opposition, that will utterly defeat the schemes of the selfish men who misrepresent the nation at Washington. Let every effort be made and every appliance be brought to bear, to fill up that vast and fertile territory, with free men—with men who hate slavery, and who will drive the hideous thing from the broad and beautiful plains where they go to raise their free homes. [Loud cheers.]
> "I for one am willing to be taxed one fourth of my time or of my earnings, until this be done—until a barrier of free hearts and strong hands shall be built around the land our fathers consecrated to freedom, to be her heritage forever. [Loud cheers.]"

If instead of this impetuous, spontaneous and enthusiastic response there had been only a moderate approbation of the plan, you would never have heard of the Emigrant Aid Company. The citizens of Worcester were sponsors at its baptism, and upon their judgment I implicitly relied, and I was not deceived. I did not expect that all who applauded would go to Kansas, or even that any of them would go, but I knew that whatever a Worcester audience would applaud in that manner I could find men to perform. There was no more doubt in my mind from that time.

Without further delay I drew up the charter of the "Massachusetts Emigrant Aid Company," and by personal solicitation secured the corporators. I introduced the matter in the Legislature and had it referred to the committee on the judiciary, of which James D. Colt, afterwards a justice of the State Supreme Court, was chairman. At the hearing I appeared before the committee and said in behalf of the petition:

> "This is a plan to prevent the forming of any more slave states. If you will give us the charter there shall never be another slave

state admitted into the Union. In the halls of Congress we have been invariably beaten for more than thirty years, and it is now time to change the battle-ground from Congress to the prairies, where we shall invariably triumph."

Mr. Colt replied:

"We are willing to gratify you, by reporting favorably your charter; but we all believe it to be impracticable and utterly futile. Here you are fifteen hundred miles from the battle ground, while the most thickly settled portion of Missouri lies on the eastern border of Kansas, and can in one day blot out all you can do in a year. Neither can you get men who now have peaceful and happy homes in the East to risk the loss of everything by going to Kansas."

But Mr. Colt reported in favor of the charter, and it passed, though it cost its author much labor, for not one member either of the Senate or House had any faith in the measure.

The following is the first section of the charter:

"SEC. 1. Benjamin C. Clark, Isaac Livermore, Charles Allen, Isaac Davis, William G. Bates, Stephen C. Phillips, Charles C. Hazewell. Alexander H. Bullock, Henry Wilson, James B. Whitney, Samuel E. Sewall, Samuel G. Howe, James Holland, Moses Kimball, James D. Green, Francis W. Bird, Otis Clapp, Anson Burlingame, Eli Thayer and Otis Rich, their associates, successors and assigns, are hereby made a corporation, by the name of the Massachusetts Emigrant Aid Company, for the purpose of assisting emigrants to settle in the West; and for this purpose, they have all the powers and privileges, and be subject to all the duties, restrictions and liabilities, set forth in the thirty-eighth and forty-fourth chapters of the Revised Statutes.

The charter was signed by the Governor on the 26th day of April. On the 4th of May a meeting was held at the State House, by the corporators and others, and a committee chosen to report a plan of organization and work. This committee consisted of Eli Thayer, Alexander H. Bullock and Edward E. Hale of Worcester, Richard Hildreth and Otis Clapp of Boston. They made a report at an adjourned meeting showing the proposed operation of the enterprise, of which the following is an extract:

> "The Emigrant Aid Company has been incorporated to protect emigrants, as far as may be, from the inconveniences we have enumerated. Its duty is to organize emigration to the West and bring it into a system. This duty, which should have been attempted long ago, is particularly essential now in the critical position of the Western Territories.
>
> "The Legislature has granted a charter, with a capital sufficient for these purposes. This capital is not to exceed $5,000,000. In no single year are assessments to a larger amount than ten per cent. to be called for. The corporators believe that if the company be organized at once, as soon as the subscriptions to the stock amounts to $1,000,000, the annual income to be derived from that amount, and the subsequent subscriptions, may be so appropriated as to render most essential service to the emigrants; to plant a free state in Kansas, to the lasting advantage of the country; and to return a handsome profit to the stockholders upon their investment.
>
> ....
>
> "To accomplish the object in view, it is recommended, 1st, that the Directors contract immediately with some one of the competing lines of travel for the conveyance of twenty thousand persons from the northern and middle states, to that place in the West which the Directors shall select for their first settlement.
>
> "It is believed that passage may be obtained, in so large a contract, at half the price paid by individuals. We recommend that emigrants receive the full advantage of this diminution in price, and that they be forwarded in companies of two hundred, as they apply, at these reduced rates of travel.
>
> "2d. It is recommended that at such points as the Directors select for places of settlement, they shall at once construct a boarding-house or receiving-house, in which three hundred persons may receive temporary accommodation on their arrival—and that the number of such houses be enlarged as necessity may dictate. The new comers or their families may thus be provided for in the necessary interval which elapses while they are making their selection of a location.
>
> "3d. It is recommended that the Directors procure and send forward steam saw-mills, and such other machines as shall be of

constant service in a new settlement, which cannot, however, be purchased or carried out conveniently by individual settlers. These machines may be leased or run by the company's agents. At the same time it is desirable that a printing press be sent out, and a weekly newspaper established. This would be the organ of the company's agents; would extend information regarding its settlement; and be from the very first an index of that love of freedom and of good morals which it is to be hoped may characterize the State now to be formed.

"4th. It is recommended that the company's agents locate and take up for the company's benefit the sections of land in which the boarding-houses and mills are located, and no others. And further, that whenever the Territory shall be organized as a Free State, the Directors shall dispose of all its interests, then replace, by the sales, the money laid out, declare a dividend to the stockholders, and

"5th. That they then select a new field, and make similar arrangements for the settlement and organization of another Free State of this Union.

....

"Under the plan proposed, it will be but two or three years before the Company can dispose of its property in the territory first occupied—and reimburse itself for its first expenses. At that time, in a State of 70,000 inhabitants, it will possess several reservations of 640 acres each, on which are boarding houses and mills, and the churches and schools which it has rendered necessary. From these centers will the settlements of the State have radiated. In other words, these points will then be the large commercial positions of the new State. If there were only one such, its value, after the region should be so far peopled, would make a very large dividend to the company which sold it, besides restoring the original capital with which to enable it to attempt the same adventure elsewhere.

....

"It is recommended that a meeting of the stockholders be called on the first Wednesday in June, to organize the company for one year, and that the corporators at this time, make a temporary organization, with power to obtain subscriptions to the stock and make any necessary preliminary arrangements.

"ELI THAYER,
For the Committee."

It will be seen by the above that the enterprise was intended to be a money-making affair as well as a philanthropic undertaking. The fact that we intended to make it pay the investors pecuniarily brought upon us the reproaches and condemnation of some of the Abolitionists, at least one of whom declared in my hearing that he had rather give over the territory to Slavery than to make a cent out of the operation of saving it to Freedom. In all my emigration schemes I intended to make the results return a profitable dividend in cash.

In pursuance of the last recommendation of the above report, the corporators made a temporary organization by the choice of Eli Thayer as President *pro tem.*, and Dr. Thomas H. Webb, of Boston, as Secretary; and opened books of subscription in Boston, Worcester and New York.

The capital stock of the Massachusetts Company was originally fixed at $5,000,000, from which it was proposed to collect an assessment of four per cent. for the operations of 1854, as soon as $1,000,000 had been subscribed. Books for stock subscriptions were opened and the undertaking was fairly started. I felt confident that even a few colonies from the North would make the freedom of Kansas a necessity; for the whole power of the free states would be ready to protect their sons in that territory.

I at once hired Chapman Hall in Boston, and began to speak day and evening in favor of the enterprise. I also addressed meetings elsewhere, and labored in every possible way to make converts to my theory.

Not only was a new plan proposed but it was advocated by new arguments, some points of which were as follows:

The present crisis was to decide whether Freedom or Slavery should rule our country for centuries to come. That Slavery was a great national curse; that it practically ruined one half of the nation and greatly impeded the progress of the other half. That it was a curse to the negro, but a much greater curse to white men. It made the slaveholders petty tyrants who had no correct idea of themselves or of anybody else. It made the poor white of the South more abject and degraded than the slaves themselves. That it was an insurmountable obstacle in the way of the nation's progress and prosperity. That it must be overcome and extirpated. That the way to do this was to go to the prairies of Kansas and show the superiority of free labor civilization; to go with all our free labor trophies: churches and schools, printing presses, steam engines and mills; and in a peaceful contest convince every poor man from the South of the superiority of free labor. That it was much better to *go* and *do* something for free labor than to stay at home and talk of manacles and auction-blocks and blood-hounds, while deploring the never-ending aggressions of slavery. That in this contest the South had not one element of success. We had much greater numbers, much greater wealth, greater readiness of organization and better facilities of migration. That we should put a cordon of Free States from Minnesota to the Gulf of Mexico, and stop the forming of Slave States. After that we should colonize the northern border Slave States and exterminate Slavery. That our work was not to make women and children cry in anti-slavery conventions, by sentimental appeals, BUT TO GO AND PUT AN END TO SLAVERY. . . .

I again entered upon the work with renewed courage, and spoke nightly, and sometimes oftener, to large and enthusiastic audiences. The effort now was to form a colony as soon as possible and start them on their way to carry freedom to Kansas. But few volunteered to join the first colony. After making a great number of speeches, after great efforts to influence by the strongest appeals the young men to join our colony, we had gathered a party numbering twenty-four; and on the 17th of July, 1854, I started with them towards Kansas. The colony was put on board a boat at Buffalo, having received an addition of two at Rochester. To one of the emigrants—Mr. Mallory of Worcester—I gave a letter directed to Charles H. Branscomb (who with Charles Robinson had been sent on in advance to receive the emigrants at St. Louis) saying: "Take this colony through the Shawnee reservation and locate them on the south bank of the Kansas, on the first good town site you find west of the reservation." Mr. Branscomb followed literally the instructions of the letter and founded the city of Lawrence.

Leaving the colony at Buffalo, I returned to the East, and two weeks later the Company sent another colony several times larger than the first; and then the entire North and West began to be aroused, and to prepare to go if needed or to help others to go, and from this time the emigration continued to move on with increased activity. I was sent to raise colonies and to organize Kansas leagues, and I travelled all over New England, some parts of it more than once, and also spoke in all the principal places in New York State.

The effect of the influx of free state settlers into Kansas soon began to be manifested. What had at first been viewed by the Missourians with contempt and derision, and by many at the East with indifference, now became to the friends of the South a matter of serious alarm, and aroused the most malignant passions of the Missouri border ruffians. It created a feeling that spread through the entire slave-holding community, and excited an intense opposition towards a scheme which it was plain to them, was to establish an effectual barrier to the extension of slavery, and in time exterminate the institution. The South saw that it was impotent in a struggle of this kind with the North; that the latter with its resources of wealth and population and its spirit of enterprise, would inevitably overwhelm them in this contest. All the powers of press and rostrum were brought to bear against the new scheme, and bluster and threats were resorted to in the endeavor to stem the current that was to engulf them. More extreme methods were applied on the scene of action, but it is not my purpose in this paper, to give any narration of what took place in Kansas; that has already become a part of national history.

Soon the greatest enthusiasm was excited in the North. Immense crowds gathered along the route of our emigrant companies, and the journeys through New England, and as far west as Chicago, were continued ovations. This spirit was shown even in the domestic circle. "I know people," said R. W. Emerson, "who are making haste to reduce their expenses and pay their debts, not with a view to new accumulations, but in preparation to save and earn for the benefit of Kansas emigrants." . . .

The work of saving Kansas, was done before the eyes of the whole world. We said we would do it, and stop the making of Slave States. We also laid down our methods; we went on just as we had promised and used the methods proposed, and accomplished the results aimed at, without the help of politicians, and in spite of the active hostility of the abolitionists.

No man, unless he is ignorant of the facts in the Kansas struggle, or is completely blinded by malice or envy, will ever attempt to defraud the Emigrant Aid Company of the glory of having saved Kansas, by defeating the Slave Power, in a great and decisive contest.

The results of the Kansas contest may be briefly summarized:

1. It stopped the making of Slave States.
2. It made the Republican Party.
3. It nearly elected Fremont and *did* elect Lincoln.

4. It united and solidified the Northern states against slavery, and was a necessary training, to enable them to subdue the Rebellion.
5. It drove the slave-holders, through desperation, into secession.
6. It has given us a harmonious and enduring Union.
7. It has emancipated the white race of the South, as well as the negroes, from the evils of Slavery.
8. It is even now regenerating the South.

In 1854, there floated, in careless security, the staunch old battle-ship SLAVERY. She was then undisputed mistress of all American waters. For more than thirty years, she had been victorious in every contest. She had seen the power of her enemies constantly diminishing, while her own had been constantly increasing. At this time, from the top of her tallest mast, was displayed the broad pennant of the Commodore—from the other masts floated other pennants and streamers bearing the legends of her many victories. On one was the inscription "THE ADMISSION OF TEXAS;" on another, "THE FUGITIVE SLAVE BILL:" there "THE DRED SCOTT DECISION;" while here was haughtily displayed, the record of her latest triumph "THE REPEAL OF THE MISSOURI COMPROMISE." Her officers, in complacent mood, were proudly pacing her decks, recounting the unvarying success of the past, and laying plans for new triumphs in the future:—Cuba to be acquired; Central America and Mexico to be secured; and all to be devoted to the building up of a colossal slave empire.

While in this blissful security, in this paradise of memory and hope, a billow from Boston harbor struck her side. It was not a heavy wave, but it made the old ship tremble and aroused the attention of officers and crew. All hands on board soon had enough to do. Billow after billow came.

For three whole years these bounding billows came with increasing strength and most destructive force, while the brave old ship pitched and groaned and quivered more and more with each successive shock. Her joints were loosened and the waters rushed in. Her officers were utterly disheartened and ran her for safety upon the shoals of Secession. At length the dark waves of the Rebellion swept her fragments away, and not one vestige was left in 1865, of the famous craft, which was queen of all American waters in 1854.

That staunch old battle-ship was the hideous "BLACK POWER" which had ruled the United States with despotic sway, for more than thirty years. The billows which struck her, were the self-sacrificing organized colonies of sturdy Northern Yeomen, who had determined that Slavery should be no more. These were the billows that destroyed the old ship.

But some say it was not the billows at all, but the foam on their crests that made the wreck. Some say it was not the thousands upon thousands of brave patriotic Union-loving citizens, organized for this very work, and risking their all for Freedom, that brought this speedy end to Slavery, but that it was three or four adventurers and sensationalists—all haters of the Union and, friends of anarchy—that achieved this great victory. Let the country judge upon the evidence of the facts.

Document V-5: PRACTICAL IDEALISM

John Jay Chapman is useful in a number of ways to a chronicler of reform. His study of Garrison (see III-6) has already helped make a point about some forms of public agitation. One biographer called him a latter-day abolitionist (M. A. DeWolfe Howe in the *Dictionary of American Biography*, supplement one); he is surely a link between the humanitarian reform spirit of antebellum days and the world of the end-of-the-century political bosses. His essay on "The Doctrine of Non-Resistance" places him between Henry David Thoreau and Martin Luther King. His decision to accept and work within a business-dominated society marks him as a distinctively pragmatic reformer. His perception of politics and economics as functionally inseparable relates him importantly to those patterns recorded in Part II.

Chapman is cited in this section so as to identify a reform type that may be more indigenous to this culture than to some others: the practical idealist. From Thomas Jefferson (see also IV-1) through Buckminster Fuller we have seemingly produced more than our share. Even against this setting Chapman is an extreme case. He was expelled from his preparatory school for his excess of religiosity. In college he struck a classmate in a fight over a girl; then, outraged by the unseemliness of his own act, stuck his offending fist into the fire until it was burned so badly that it had eventually to be amputated. As a grown man he hired a hall in Coatesville, Pennsylvania, on the anniversary of the lynching of a black man there, and delivered an impassioned address to an audience of three. Before he was forty he had retired from political life, grown an unfash-

The Peace Corps brings idealists down to earth.

You could join.
Fill out this coupon.

The Peace Corps.
Washington, D. C. 20525.

☐ Please send me information
☐ Please send me an application.

NAME_____

ADDRESS_____

CITY_____

STATE _____ ZIP CODE_____

B: Peace Corps ad

ionable beard, and committed himself to religious causes. Clearly, this was a man in whom the fires of moral and ethical passion burned bright and high.

In between Coatesville and his retirement from politics he became adept at reform. Edmund Wilson called him a great essayist and placed him in "the first battalion of political reformers" whose observations were so astute that they now seem commonplace (in *New Republic*, Vol. LIX [May 22, 1929], p. 29). It may be that Chapman did not understand practical politics well enough to bring victories to his reform candidates in New York; but he does represent a visible stripe in the ranks of American reformers who mix—almost as intensely and inextricably as in the following passages—the quality of idealism with the concern for effective practical action.

SOURCE: John Jay Chapman, *Causes and Consequences.* New York, Scribner, 1898, pp. 3-17, 39-44; and *Practical Agitation.* New York, Scribner, 1900, pp. 1-32, abridged.

CAUSES AND CONSEQUENCES

Misgovernment in the United States is an incident in the history of commerce. It is part of the triumph of industrial progress. Its details are easier to understand if studied as a part of the commercial development of the country than if studied as a part of government, because many of the wheels and cranks in the complex machinery of government are now performing functions so perverted as to be unmeaning from the point of view of political theory, but which become perfectly plain if looked at from the point of view of trade.

The growth and concentration of capital which the railroad and the telegraph made possible is the salient fact in the history of the last quarter-century. That fact is at the bottom of our political troubles. It was inevitable that the enormous masses of wealth, springing out of new conditions and requiring new laws, should strive to control the legislation and the administration which touched them at every point. At the present time, we cannot say just what changes were or were not required by enlightened theory. It is enough to see that such changes as came were inevitable; and nothing can blind us to the fact that the methods by which they were obtained were subversive of free government.

Whatever form of government had been in force in America during this era would have run the risk of being controlled by capital, of being bought and run for revenue. It happened that the beginning of the period found the machinery of our government in a particularly purchasable state. The war had left the people divided into two parties which were fanatically hostile to each other. The people were party mad. Party name and party symbols were of an almost religious importance.

At the very moment when the enthusiasm of the nation had been exhausted in a heroic war which left the Republican party-managers in possession of the ark of the covenant, the best intellect of the country was withdrawn from public affairs and devoted to trade. During the period of expansion which followed, the industrial forces called in the ablest men of the nation to aid them in getting control of the machinery of government. The name of king was never freighted with more power than the name of party in the United States; whatever was done in that name was right. It is the old story: there has never been a despotism which did not rest upon superstition. The same spirit that made the Republican name all powerful in the nation at large made the Democratic name valuable in Democratic districts.

The situation as it existed was made to the hand of trade. Political power had by the war been condensed and packed for delivery; and in the natural course of things the political trademarks began to find their way into the coffers of the capitalist. The change of motive power behind the party organizations—from principles, to money—was silently effected during the thirty years which followed the war. Like all organic change, it was unconscious. It was understood by no one. It is recorded only in a few names and phrases; as, for instance, that part of the organization which was purchased was called the "machine," and the general manager of it became known as the "boss." The external political history of the country continued as before. It is true that a steady degradation was to be seen in public life, a steady failure of character, a steady decline of decency. But questions continued to be discussed, and in form decided, on their merits, because it was in the interest of commerce that they should in form be so decided. Only quite recently has the control of money become complete; and there are reasons for believing that the climax is past.

Let us take a look at the change on a small scale. A railroad is to be run through a country town or small city, in New York or Pennsylvania. The railroad employs a local attorney, naturally the ablest attorney in the place. As time goes on, various permits for street uses are needed; and instead of relying solely upon popular demand, the attorney finds it easier to bribe the proper officials. All goes well: the railroad thrives, the town grows. But in the course of a year new permits of various kinds are needed. The town ordinances interfere with the road and require amendment. There is to be a town election; and it occurs to the railroad's attorney that he might be in alliance with the town officers before they are elected. He goes to the managers of the party which is likely to win; for instance, the Republican party. Everything that the railroad wants is really called for by the economic needs of the town. The railroad wants only fair play and no factious obstruction. The attorney talks to the Republican leader, and has a chance to look over the list of candidates, and perhaps even to select some of them. The railroad makes the largest campaign subscription ever made in that part of the country. The Republican leader can now employ more workers to man the polls, and, if necessary, he can buy votes. He must also retain some fraction of the contribution for his own support, and distribute the rest in such manner as will best keep his "organization" together.

The party wins, and the rights of the railroad are secured for a year. It is true that the brother of the Republican leader is employed on the road as a brakeman; but he is a competent man.

During the year, a very nice point of law arises as to the rights of the railroad to certain valuable land claimed by the town. The city attorney is an able man, and reasonable. In spite of his ability, he manages somehow to state the city's case on an untenable ground. A decision follows in favor of the railroad. At the following election, the city attorney has become the Republican candidate for judge, and the railroad's campaign subscription is trebled. In the conduct of railroads, even under the best management, accidents are common; and while it is true that important decisions are appealable, a trial judge has enormous powers which are practically discretionary. Meanwhile, there have arisen questions of local taxation of the railroad's property, questions as to grade crossings, as to the lighting of cars, as to time schedules, and the like. The court calendars are becoming crowded with railroad business; and that business is now more than one attorney can attend to. In fact, the half dozen local lawyers of prominence are railroad men; the rest of the lawyers would like to be. Every one of the railroad lawyers receives deferential treatment, and, when possible, legal advantage in all of the public offices. The community is now in the control of a ring, held together by just one thing, the railroad company's subscription to the campaign fund.

By this time a serious scandal has occurred in the town,—nothing less than the rumor of a deficit in the town treasurer's accounts, and the citizens are concerned about it. One of the railroad's lawyers, a strong party man, happens to be occupying the post of district attorney; for the yearly campaign subscriptions continue. This district attorney is, in fact, one of the committee on nominations who put the town treasurer into office; and the Republican party is responsible for both. No prosecution follows. The district attorney stands for re-election.

An outsider comes to live in the town. He wants to reform things, and proceeds to talk politics. He is not so inexperienced as to seek aid from the rich and respectable classes. He knows that the men who subscribed to the railroad's stock are the same men who own the local bank, and that the manufacturers and other business men of the place rely on the bank for carrying on their business. He knows that all trades which are specially touched by the law, such as the liquor-dealers' and hotel-keepers', must "stand in" with the administration; so also must the small shopkeepers, and those who have to do with sidewalk privileges and town ordinances generally. The newcomer talks to the leading hardware merchant, a man of stainless reputation, who admits that the district attorney has been remiss; but the merchant is a Republican, and says that so long as he lives he will vote for the party that saved the country. To vote for a Democrat is a crime. The reformer next approaches the druggist (whose father-in-law is in the employ of the railroad), and receives the same reply. He goes to the florist. But the florist owns a piece of real estate, and has a theory that it is assessed too high. The time for revising the assessment rolls is coming near, and he has to see the authorities about that. The florist agrees that the town is a den of thieves; but he must live; he has no time to go into theoretical politics. The stranger next interviews a retired grocer. But the grocer has lent money to his nephew, who is in the coal business, and is getting special rates from the railroad, and is paying off the debt rapidly. The grocer would be willing to help, but his name must not be used.

It is needless to multiply instances of what every one knows. After canvassing the whole community, the stranger finds five persons who are willing to work to defeat the district attorney: a young doctor of good education and small practice, a young lawyer who thinks he can make use of the movement by betraying it, a retired anti-slavery preacher, a maiden lady, and a piano-tuner. The district attorney is re-elected by an overwhelming vote.

All this time the railroad desires only a quiet life. It takes no interest in politics. It is making money, and does not want values disturbed. It is conservative.

In the following year worse things happen. The town treasurer steals more money, and the district attorney is openly accused of sharing the profits. The Democrats are shouting for reform, and declare that they will run the strongest man in town for district attorney. He is a Democrat, but one who fought for the Union. He is no longer in active practice, and is, on the whole, the most distinguished citizen of the place. This suggestion is popular. The hardware merchant declares that he will vote the Democratic ticket, and there is a sensation. It appears that during all these years there has been a Democratic organization in the town, and that the notorious corruption of the Republicans makes a Democratic victory possible. The railroad company therefore goes to the manager of the Democratic party, and explains that it wants only to be let alone. It explains that it takes no interest in politics, but that, if a change is to come, it desires only that So-and-So shall be retained, and it leaves a subscription with the Democratic manager. In short, it makes the best terms it can. The Democratic leader, if he thinks that he can make a clean sweep, may nominate the distinguished citizen, together with a group of his own organization comrades. It obviously would be of no use to him to name a full citizens' ticket. That would be treason to his party. If he takes this course and wins, we shall have ring rule of a slightly milder type. The course begins anew, under a Democratic name; and it may be several years before another malfeasance occurs.

But the Republican leader and the railroad company do not want war; they want peace. They may agree to make it worth while for the Democrats not to run the distinguished citizen. A few Democrats are let into the Republican ring. They are promised certain minor appointive offices, and some contracts and emoluments. Accordingly, the Democrats do not nominate the distinguished citizen. The hardware man sees little choice between the two nominees for district attorney; at any rate, he will not vote for a machine Democrat, and he again votes for his party nominee.

All the reform talk simmers down to silence. The Republicans are returned to power.

The town is now ruled by a Happy Family. Stable equilibrium has been reached at last. Commercialism is in control. Henceforth, the railroad company pays the bills for keeping up both party organizations, and it receives care and protection from whichever side is nominally in power. . . .

Moreover, time fights for reform. The old voters die off, and the young men care little about party shibboleths. Hence these non-partisan movements. Every election, local or national, which causes a body of men to desert their party is a blow at the boss system. These movements multiply annually. They are emancipating the small towns throughout the Union, even as commerce was once disfranchising them. As party feeling dies out in a man's mind, it leaves him with a clearer vision. His conscience begins to affect his conduct very seriously, when he sees that a certain course is indefensible. It is from this source that the reform will come.

The voter will see that it is wrong to support the subsidized boss, just as the capitalist has already begun to recoil from the monster which he created. He sees that it is wrong at the very moment when he is beginning to find it unprofitable. The old trademark has lost its value.

The citizens' movement is, then, a purge to take the money out of politics. The stronger the doses, the quicker the cure. If the citizens maintain absolute standards, the old parties can regain their popular support only by adopting those standards. All citizens' movements are destined to be temporary; they will vanish, to leave our politics purified. But the work they do is as broad as the nation. . . .

PRACTICAL AGITATION

. . . Campaign platforms are merely creeds. "I believe in Civil Service Reform" is a way of saying "I do not believe in theft," and the phrase was a fragmentary and incomplete formulation of the greater truth. It was the sign that a movement was beginning among the people due to reawakening instinct, reawakening sensibility. It was the forerunner of all those changes for the better that have been spreading over our administrative government during the last thirty years. A quiet revolution has been going forward under our eyes, recorded step by step. It is only because our standards have been going up faster than the reforms came in that we believe the evils are growing worse. Such changes go on all the time all over the world, but the value and rarity of this one come from its unity and coherence. Such a thing might happen in Germany or in England, but you could not disentangle the forces. . . .

That subtle change of attitude in the citizen towards his public duty which is now in progress, has in it something of the religious. The whole matter becomes comprehensible the moment we cease to think of it as politics, and see in it a widespread and perfectly natural reaction against an era of wickedness. Had our framework of government afforded no outlet to the force, had our ills been irremediably crystallized into formal tyranny, we should perhaps have witnessed great revivalist upheavals, sacraments, saints, prophets, prostrations, and adoration. As it is, we have seen deadly pamphlets, schedules, enactments, documents which it required our whole attention and our whole time to understand; and behind each of them a remorseless interrogator with a white cravat and a face of iron. What motive drives them on? What oil fills their lamps? Who feeds them? These horrid things they bring, these instruments forged by unremitting toil, technical, insufferable,—they are the cure. With such levers, and with them only, can the stones be lifted off the hearts of men. They are the alternatives of revolution. . . .

The battle of the standards goes forward ceaselessly; but all standards are going up. What the half-way reformer calls "politics," the idealist calls chicanery; what the idealist calls politics, the half-way reformer calls Utopia. But in 1871 they are discussing whether or not the reformers shall falsify the returns; in 1894 they are discussing whether or not they shall expose fraud in their own camp.

The men engaged in all these struggles are in perfect ignorance that they are really leading a religious reaction. They think that since they are in politics the doctrines of compromise apply. They are drawn into politics by conscience, but once there, they have only their business training to guide them,—a training in the art of subserving material interests. Now if a piece of your land has an uncertain boundary, you have a right to compromise on any theory you like, because you own the land. But if you start out with the sole and avowed purpose of upholding honesty in politics, and you uphold anything else or subserve any other interest whatever, you are a deceiver. When you began you did not say "I stand for a readjustment of political interests. There will be a continuation of many abuses under my administration, to be sure; but I hope they will not be quite so bad as heretofore. I shall not insist on the absolutely unselfish conduct of my office. It is not practical.'' If you had said this, you might have got the friendly support of a few doctrinaires. But you would never have got the support and approval of the great public. You would not have been elected. And therefore you did not say it. On the contrary, what our reformers do is this: They begin, before election, by promising an absolutely pure administration. They make proclamations of a new era, and after they have secured a certain following they proceed to chaffer over how much honesty they will demand and how much take, as if they were rescuing property.

These men are, then, in their desires a part of the future, and in their practices of the past. Their desires move society forward, their practices set it back; and so we have moved forward by jolts, until, like a people emerging from the deep sea, the water looks clearer above our heads and we can almost see the sky.

Every advance has cost great effort. It took as much courage for a Mugwump to renounce his party allegiance in 1884 as it does now for a man to denounce both national parties as dens of thieves. It took as much hard thinking some years ago for the leaders of the Reform Democrats to cut loose from Tammany Hall as it does now for the Independent to see that there is in all our politics only one machine, held together by all the bosses and their heelers, and that the whole thing must be attacked at once.

How gradual has been the process of emancipation from intellectual bondage! How inevitably people are limited by the terms in which they think! A generation of men has been consumed by the shibboleth "reform within the party,''—a generation of educated and right-minded men, who accomplished in their day much good, and left the country better than they found it, but are floating to-day like hulks in the trough of the sea of politics, because all their mind and all their energy were exhausted in discovering certain superficial evils and in fighting them. Their analysis of political elements left the deeper causes mysterious. They did not see mere human nature. They still treated Republicanism and Democracy—empty superstitions—as ideas, and they handled with reverence the bones of bogus saints, and the whole apparatus of clap-trap by which they had been governed.

And yet it is owing to the activity of these men that the deeper political conditions became visible. Men cannot transcend their own analysis and see themselves under the microscope. The work we do transforms us into social factors. We are a part of the changes we bring in. Before we know it, we ourselves are the problem. . . .

The short lesson that comes out of long experience in political agitation is something like this: *all* the motive power in all of these movements is the instinct of religious feeling. All the obstruction comes from attempting to rely on anything else. Conciliation is the enemy. It is just as impossible to help reform by conciliating prejudice as it is by buying votes. Prejudice is the enemy. Whoever is not for you is against you. . . .

Consider what you are trying to do. A party under control of a machine is held together by an appeal to self-interest. Its caucuses, affiliations, resources, methods are constructed on that principle. Your body, whose aim is to increase the unselfishness and intellect of your fellow-citizens, must be held together at every point by self-sacrifice.

If the reform body shall blindly do just the opposite of what a party does, it will pursue practical politics. The regular party is in theory representative of enrolled voters. You represent the sentiment of undiscovered people. The party appeals to old forces and extant conditions. You appeal to new feelings and new voters. The party offers a gift to every adherent. You must offer him nothing but labor. That is your protection against traitors. The party accords every man the weight of his vote in its counsels. You must give him nothing but the influence of his mind.

"But," you shout, "this is not politics. You can never hold men together without bonds." The fact is otherwise. There is some force at work in this town which, year after year, brings forward groups of men who proclaim a new dispensation. They are, in so far as they have any cohesion, held together without bonds now. All formal bonds will chain them to the past. For electrical force you must adopt electrical machinery; for moral force, moral bonds. All this political system is the harness for the wrong passion. Every scrap of it imprisons your power. The average American citizen is slow to see that you can exercise political influence without the current machinery. This is a part of The Machine in his brain. He cannot see the operation of law by which virtue always tells. But his ignorance does not affect the operation of that law, even upon himself.

This elaborate analysis of just how the force of feeling in yourself can best be used politically, is, after all, only an instance of a general law. The shortest path between two points always turns out to be a straight line. People who believe in the complexity of life, and have theories about crooked lines, want something else beside moral influence. They want influence through office, or influence toward special ends, or influence with particular persons. "Can't you see you are destroying your influence?" they cry, while every stroke is telling. "A thinks you are a lunatic." Praise God. "B has withdrawn his subscription." I had not hoped for this so soon. "But he has joined Platt." You misstate the case. He was always with Platt, but now he has revealed it. These refractory molecules are breaking up. See the lines of force begin to show a clean cleavage. Ten thousand intelligences now see the man for what he is. . . .

There is always great difficulty in this world as to who shall bell the cat; but conventions of mice do not further the matter. The way to do it is for a parcel of mice to take their political lives in their hands and proceed to do it.

Document V-6: REFORM TRAITS PERSONIFIED: FULLER

From the only work that attempts to generalize about American reformers on the basis of extensive biographical information there emerges no single stereotype. A man like Carlos Martyn (see V-2) might come as close as any to representing late-nineteenth-century figures since he was well educated, had religious training, argued for some form of socialism, and worked for more than one cause. (See Henry J. Silverman, "American Social Reformers in the Late Nineteenth and Early Twentieth Century," unpublished dissertation at the University of Pennsylvania, 1963.) More than 60 percent of the subjects of this study could be recorded as multiple-cause advocates: a fact that supports a mild generalization.

It may be more helpful to recognize several stereotypes. One type—like many of the anti-slavery crusaders—was wedded to a single cause and would use any appropriate method to achieve it. A counterpart is the reformer who has grasped a particular method and is willing to apply this cure-all to any number of situations: e.g., land reform (see II-21), emigrant aid (see V-4A) single tax (see II-21), labor organization (see IV-11), or international federations (see IV-12). Less rigid stereotypes would include both the religious reformer who applies Christian principles to a broad front of social problems (like Martyn), and the "scientific" reformer who uses a careful, academic knowledge of society in order to effect changes in several areas. The latter case is well exemplified by a man like H. C. Adams (see the *Journal of Political Economy*, Vol. XXX [1922], pp. 201-211). At the extremes are men like Garrison, with one main cause and one central method, and—at the opposite end—a man like Stephen Pearl Andrews who slid blithely and enthusiastically from abolitionism to anarchism, from phonography to free love. (See Madeline B. Stern, *The Pantarch, a Biography of Stephen Pearl Andrews*. Austin, University of Texas, 1968.)

In some ways Richard Buckminster Fuller mirrors all of these stereotypes. His work has been placed here, as the final word in this collection, because he is a kind of universal reformer and—more especially—because he summarizes in a single human expression all of the basic philosophies introduced in Part I as well as many of the forms through which these attitudes have expressed themselves. Fuller's closest intellectual kinship is doubtless with Franklin and Jefferson; he can be seen here most usefully as a man who has sought to extend the Enlightenment through a pragmatic application of technology. But he stresses technology only when it brings man closer to natural law. Its ultimate use will be to free man from the errors of overcompetitiveness and to release his innate goodness. (See *Nine Chains to the Moon*. Carbondale, Southern Illinois University, 1963, pp. v-viii.)

But there is not only an intellectual kinship with Jefferson and Franklin; there is an actual kinship to another pillar of American reform: his great-aunt, Margaret Fuller. Like her he is something of a visionary. As she did he uses the word "transcendental" frequently and in order to express the potentiality and necessity for human development beyond what is merely physical and material. In the selection below Buckminster Fuller allies himself with the moral reformers like Cotton Mather, asking God's help in setting a stage for what is humanly possible. Also like Mather and so many others, he sees America as having an exemplary role in leading the world toward its higher calling.

Fuller has often pointed to that overburdened model for participatory democracy, the New England town meeting. His feeling for this institution is not merely nostalgic, however. With computers and telephones, he argues, all voters could vote daily on all issues: thus could direct democracy be effected in the modern age. These convictions could have allowed for his inclusion at the end of Part II, just as his efforts to plan the one-town world were placed as a culmination of Part IV.

To end this collection with some further references to Fuller is not to insist that all his work is of an even quality. This is not so; and perhaps the theory and philosophy are less impressive than the objects and designs he has created. For a long time the world seemed to be wondering whether Bucky Fuller must be taken as a mad idealist or a practical engineer. Time has added impressively to those who support him. Although he will never cease to cause debate, he should never be considered as either a visionary or an inventor without a recognition of how the two sides of Fuller affect each other. In a history of American reform, Fuller has more than two sides: enough to allow for a discussion of American reform's most important patterns.

SOURCE: R. Buckminster Fuller, *No More Secondhand God.* Carbondale, Southern Illinois University, 1963, pp. 12-17, 24-28, 30-31.

Democracy has potential within it
the satisfaction of every individual's need.

But Democracy must be structurally modernized
must be mechanically implemented
to give it a one-individual-to-another
speed and spontaneity of reaction
commensurate with the speed and scope
of broadcast news
now world-wide in seconds.

Through mechanical developments
of the industrial age
the cumulative production of human events
within the span of a four-year administration
is now the quantitative equivalent
of the events of a four-hundred-year
pre-industrial dynasty.

But it is the producer salesman
who has been super instrumented
and merged into a tinker colossus,
a Pan-Continental
blacksmith, baker, and light maker.

Democracy must, as consumer and worker,
as soldier and mother,
as scientist, or simple enjoyer,
be made adequate cathode
to the mighty merged anode.

Devise a mechanical means
for nation-wide voting
daily and secretly
by each adult citizen
of Uncle Sam's family:
Then—I assure you
will Democracy "be saved,"
indeed exist,
for the first time in history.

This is a simple mechanical problem
involving but fractional effort
of that involved in distributing
the daily mails to the nation.

Telephone talks in the U.S. each day
are three times the number
of votes which were cast
for President
in the record election year.

Electrified voting as bride
to our most prodigal
wildcat broadcasting
and beloved son—journalism,
promises a household efficiency

superior to any government of record
because it incorporates
not only the speed of decision
which is the greatest strength of the dictator,
(a boon if he's godly,
a death-ray if he is not)
but additional advantages which can never be his.

Additional advantages of electrified voting
first coming to mind:

1. Provides an instantaneous contour map of the
   workable frontier of the people's wisdom,
   for purposes of legislation.
   administration, future exploration, and debate,
   so that neither over nor under
   estimate may occur,
   of their will and ability.

2. Certifies spontaneous popular co-operation
   in the carrying out of each decision.

3. Allows for continuous correction of the course,
   or even complete reaction,
   should (and as) experience indicate desirability,
   without political scapegoating.

4. No foreign power in the world
   can stand up against
   the unified might thus invoked
   through the thrilling mystical awareness
   of multimillions of individuals
   that they personally
   have taken responsibility for the course,
   and that their own inward secret moral decision
   coincides with the majority
   in the application of their mutual strength,
   (vast now in U.S.A.

by the will of God
beyond any in history)
in the righteous salvation
of the peoples of the earth.

5. The credit and imagination
   of all outside peoples of the world
   will be so stimulated that nothing will stop them
   short of attaining a line to that voice.
   But so to do
   they must join up with Democracy.

6. The possibility mathematically
   of effective abuse through cheating
   is nil.
   I venture to say that the self-policing
   by the honor system
   spontaneously invoked
   would make the fate of horse thieves
   or snatchers of absent-newsvendors' pennies
   frivolous by comparison.
   No block or pressure group
   that is not a constitutional enemy
   could consider running the risk of "stuffing."
   The direct votes of any subversive enemy to
       Democracy within
   the U.S. would be inconsequential in number—
   would eventually disappear in such a system.

7. It cuts right across
   all red-tape of legal precedent
   and any question of constitutionality, and
   may be started extra-mural to the constitution
   while getting out the bugs,
   for instance by Charlie McCarthy, and Clifton Fadiman,
   script by "Time Questions," sponsored by Coca-Cola.
   Someday to be constitutionally adopted when tuned up.

8. The economic credit base is self-contained.

9. As direct evolution it cancels
   the possibility of revolution.

   Accomplishment of this VOICE
   must be a deed of organized responsibility
   of the U.S. press in its broadest sense.

   If having tried it,
   a modernized, electrified, direct Democracy
   proves inferior as a survival means
   against all-comers,
   then may the people turn with contentment
   to the superior means.
   But if direct Democracy is not tried now,
   future generations will again champion it,
   and there will be world civil wars
   until it receives adequate trial.

   I believe America has now
   won the right to be
   first to try Democracy
   that it is both sufficiently experienced
   and intellectually developed
   to provide a safety factor margin
   which can insure success after
   all deductions:
   for bitter hardship
   of mental and physical stress;
   for surprise, and panic;
   and most importantly for gross error.
   But whatever America's
   choice—I go with it
   with heart and soul for
   its sagacity and time sense
   I believe infallible.

   . . . .

People of the United States,
(I believe the vast majority of them)
who are at present especially staked out
to be fooled in a big way,
which is vitally and mortally,
by all the warring or plotting factions
foreign and domestic,
are precisely those who alone remain unmoved.

It is these silent propagandees
who unerringly appraise
the pro- or anti-social values
of each world event;
of each communiqué;
and even of each personal happening
at other times trivial:
as these too may shade the outcome values
of man's transition
from dominant self-deceit
to preponderant self-mastery;
from stomach rule to dictate of reason;
from politicians tricking
to scientific guidance;
from a fear to a happy comprehension motivation.

And because he is innately
aware of these things,
does man evade past snares—
steel himself against artful pathos;
welcome the speedy destruction
of those former barriers to world happiness
which have been humanly insuperable
without fracture
by any individual member of the old order,
from annihilist to deacon,
from clerk to Prime Minister,
no matter how distinguished
by courage and integrity.

But now common man has
implicit faith in common man;
can safely negotiate a roadway
with any unknown other man—
even passing each other
at one hundred and forty miles an hour
in opposite directions—
has only been prevented
from intercommunicating that faith directly,
but now is willing to wager all
on mutual effective comprehension
at the crucial moment—
will not be shamed out of his faith
by attempts to falsely identify him—
has weighed his distress
over concentrate frightfulness
of an exquisite moment
against unending elusive
and unmitigated greater suffering.

The revolution has come—
set on fire from the top.
Let it burn swiftly.
Neither the branches, trunk, nor roots will be
    endangered.
Only last year's leaves and
the parasite-bearded moss and orchids
will not be there
when the next spring brings fresh growth
and free standing flowers.

Man now vastly instrumented
and attendant upon universal laws
in his "blind" flying through life
will give ever less heed
to the seat-of-the-pants opinions
of personal equation aces
for he knows it was those detonations

which formerly misguided him
into his betrayal by selfish scheming.

Here is true world democracy in the swift making;
a democracy which socializes all plenty
as that plenty is wrested from scarcity
by world-widening co-operative industry;
a democracy which, scientifically
seeking categorical validity for all the motivations,
taxes only inertia
and awards copiously its individuals
who radiantly expand the commonwealth;
awarding them out of the newly integrated wealth
captured from the unseen fresh fruits
of the limitless environment—
and not by the slightest impoverishment
of commonwealth,
either by mortgage
or individual indebtedness.

Here is God's purpose—
for God, to me, it seems,
is a verb
not a noun,
proper or improper;
is the articulation
not the art, objective or subjective;
is loving,
not the abstraction "love" commanded or entreated;
is knowledge dynamic,
not legislative code,
not proclamation law,
not academic dogma, nor ecclesiastic canon.
Yes, God is a verb,
the most active,
connoting the vast harmonic
reordering of the universe
from unleashed chaos of energy.

And there is born unheralded
a great natural peace,
not out of exclusive
pseudo-static security
but out of including, refining, dynamic balancing.
Naught is lost.
Only the false and nonexistent are dispelled.

....

"Let us not subscribe to remedy by amputation—
first of all of our heads."
Let us say to the East and West and the North and the
    South
to its now reality spokesmen,
"Here is our helping hand
forget your fighting.

Let's put things to rights.
We'll take care of the inconsequential accounting
when mankind has been salvaged if you insist on
    accounting;
for we won't!"

That is the active, realistic loving
of this one moment in all time.

No one in America will say that its leader
is overstepping his authorized bounds
if he takes sincere, forthright, and
adequately big steps
to accomplish world healing.

God will be handling the radio-telegraph
for such a mandated dictatorship; and
Democracy is not challenged by such a dictator
whose very first move must and will be
tidal-waved with Demos authority.

Stop "calling names"
names that are meaningless;
you can't suppress God
by killing off people
which are, physically, only trans-ceiver mechanisms
through which God is broadcasting.

But his requirement is dynamic and if man-mechanism proves too
inefficient as an invention
he will immediately devise a cataclysmic improvement.

INDEX

665